CHAMBERS

MINI

THESAURUS

CHAMBERS

CHAMBERS
An imprint of Chambers Harrap Publishers Ltd
7 Hopetoun Crescent, Edinburgh, EH7 4AY

First published by Chambers Harrap Publishers Ltd 2005

We have made every effort to mark as such all words which we believe to be trademarks. We should also like to make it clear that the presence of a word in the thesaurus, whether marked or unmarked, in no way affects its legal status as a trademark.

A CIP catalogue record for this book is available from the British Library.

ISBN 0550 10162 4

Project Manager: Ian Brookes
Editorial Assistance: Alice Grandison, Elaine O'Donoghue, Emma Redfern
Publishing Manager: Patrick White
Prepress Manager: Sharon McTeir
Prepress Controller: David Reid

Designed and typeset by Chambers Harrap Publishers Ltd, Edinburgh
Printed in China by Toppan

Contents

Preface

A thesaurus is a book that contains lists of synonyms – that is, words that have a similar meaning to another word. A thesaurus allows you to look up a common word and find a range of words that have the same or nearly the same meaning. This can help you to find a more exact word when the one that comes to mind is not quite right for the occasion, or it can help you to find an alternative word when you don't want to repeat a word you have already used.

While the main purpose of a thesaurus is to provide the user with similar words and phrases, this thesaurus also contains two other useful features. Many entries also contain opposites (antonyms) of the word, and lists of these are clearly indicated by the symbol ⇄. In addition, there are over 80 distinctive lists of words scattered through the book answering the question, 'What kinds of ... are there?'. These lists cover subjects as different as 'Types of building', 'Human bones' and 'Breeds of dog'.

Chambers Mini School Thesaurus has been specially designed for use by students aged 9-14 and is an ideal companion to the *Chambers Mini School Dictionary.* In addition to the main thesaurus, we have also included a supplement containing a **word workshop** discussing alternatives to some overused words, such as *nice*, *very* and *great*, and also some **word games**.

Whether for seeking out alternative or opposite words, or simply browsing for pleasure, we hope students will enjoy using this handy wordfinder.

WWW

To help make best use of Chambers School titles, teachers can download photocopiable versions of the workshop material, along with games and exercises, from our website at **www.chambers.co.uk**

How to use the thesaurus

Headwords appear in bold at the beginning of each entry.

accommodate *verb* **1** *accommodate someone in a hotel*: lodge, board, put up, house, shelter. **2** *we try to accommodate all our customers*: oblige, help, assist, aid, serve, provide, supply, comply, conform.

accommodation

Many lists of word families are included.

Types of accommodation include: apartment, barracks, bedsit, bedsitter, digs (*infml*), dwelling, flat, halls of residence, hostel, lodgings, pad (*infml*), residence, rooms, shelter, squat (*infml*); bed and breakfast, boarding-house, guest-house, hotel, inn, motel, timeshare, villa, youth hostel. *See also* **building**; **house**; **room**.

Example sentences show the meaning of each different sense of a word.

accompany *verb* **1** *accompany someone on holiday*: escort, attend, convoy, chaperon(e), usher, conduct, follow. **2** *a book accompanied by a study guide*: coexist, coincide, belong to, go with, complement, supplement.

Where the entry is not split into separate meanings, synonyms are simply listed after the headword.

accomplice *noun* assistant, helper, abettor, mate, henchman, conspirator, collaborator, ally, confederate, partner, associate, colleague, participator, accessory.

accomplish *verb* achieve, attain, do, perform, carry out, execute, fulfil, discharge, finish, complete, conclude, consummate, realize, effect, bring about, engineer, produce, obtain.

deal *noun* **1** *cause a great deal of trouble*: quantity, amount, extent, degree, portion, share. **2** *a better deal*: agreement, contract, understanding, pact, transaction, bargain, buy. **3** *it's your deal*: round, hand, distribution.
▪ *verb* **1** *deal the cards/deal out punishment*: apportion, distribute, share, dole out, divide, allot, dispense, assign, mete out, give, bestow. **2** *dealing in antiques*: trade, negotiate, traffic, bargain, treat.
dealer *noun* trader, merchant, wholesaler, marketer, merchandiser.
dear *adjective* **1** *my dear friend*: loved, beloved, treasured, valued, cherished, precious, favourite, esteemed, intimate, close, darling, familiar. **2** *a car was too dear so I bought a bike*: expensive, high-priced, costly, overpriced, pricey (*infml*).
F3 **1** disliked, hated. **2** cheap.
▪ *noun* beloved, loved one, precious, darling, treasure.
death *noun* **1** *cause many deaths/death by hanging*: decease, end, finish, loss, demise, departure, fatality, cessation, passing, expiration, dissolution. **2** *the death of communism*: destruction, ruin, undoing, downfall, annihilation, extermination, extinction, obliteration, eradication.

Parts of speech or word classes, eg *noun*, *verb* and *adjective*, are spelled out in full. A new part of speech within an entry appears on a new line.

The sign **F3** indicates antonyms – words that mean the opposite of the headword.

Pronunciation guide

This thesaurus provides help in cases where a word can be pronounced in more than one way depending on its meaning. The system used is designed to make pronunciations immediately understandable. The syllables are separated by hyphens, and the stressed syllable (the syllable pronounced with most emphasis) is shown in thick black type. Any vowel or group of vowels which is pronounced as a neutral 'uh' sound is shown in italic type. Pronunciations are given directly after the part of speech, for example:

abuse *verb* /*a*-**byooz**/ …
▪ *noun* /*a*-**byoos**/

A few sounds are difficult to show in normal English letters. Here is a guide to the letter combinations that are used to show these sounds:

Consonants

'ng' shows the sound as in ri**ng**
'ngg' shows the sound as in fi**ng**er
'th' shows the sound as in **th**in
'dh' shows the sound as in **th**is
'sz' shows the sound as in deci**s**ion, mea**s**ure
'kh' shows the sound as in lo**ch**

Vowels

'uw' shows the sound as in b**oo**k, p**u**t
'oo' shows the sound as in m**oo**n, l**o**se
'ah' shows the sound as in **ar**m, d**a**nce
'aw' shows the sound as in s**aw**, ign**ore**
'er' shows the sound as in f**er**n, b**ir**d, h**ear**d
'ei' shows the sound as in d**ay**, s**a**me
'ai' shows the sound as in m**y**, p**i**ne
'oi' shows the sound as in b**oy**, s**oi**l
'oh' shows the sound as in b**o**ne, n**o**, th**ough**
'ow' shows the sound as in n**ow**, b**ough**

Sound combinations

'eer' shows the sound as in n**ear**, b**eer**, t**ier**
'eir' shows the sound as in h**air**, c**are**, th**ere**
'oor' shows the sound as in p**oor**, s**ure**
'air' shows the sound as in f**ire**, h**igher**

Abbreviations used in the thesaurus

fml formal
infml informal
US United States

Aa

abandon *verb* **1** *abandon one's loved ones*: desert, leave, forsake, ditch (*infml*), leave in the lurch (*infml*), maroon, strand, leave behind. **2** *abandon ship*: vacate, evacuate, quit. **3** *abandon an activity*: renounce, resign, give up, forgo, relinquish, surrender, yield, waive, drop.
F∃ **1** support, maintain, keep. **3** continue.

abbreviate *verb* shorten, cut, trim, clip, truncate, curtail, abridge, summarize, précis, abstract, digest, condense, compress, reduce, lessen, shrink, contract.
F∃ extend, lengthen, expand, amplify.

abbreviation *noun* shortening, clipping, curtailment, abridgement, summarization, summary, synopsis, résumé, précis, abstract, digest, compression, reduction, contraction.
F∃ extension, expansion, amplification.

ability *noun* **1** *the ability to teach*: capability, capacity, faculty, facility, potentiality, power. **2** *someone of great ability*: skill, dexterity, deftness, adeptness, competence, proficiency, qualification, aptitude, talent, gift, endowment, knack, flair, touch, expertise, know-how (*infml*), genius, forte, strength.
F∃ **1** inability. **2** incompetence, weakness.

able *adjective* **1** *are you able to tell us what he said?*: allowed, permitted, free, willing. **2** *a very able candidate*: capable, fit, dexterous, adroit, deft, adept, competent, proficient, qualified, practised, experienced, skilled, accomplished, clever, expert, masterly, skilful, ingenious, talented, gifted, strong, powerful, effective, efficient.
F∃ **1** unable. **2** incapable, incompetent, ineffective.

abnormal *adjective* odd, strange, singular, peculiar, curious, queer, weird, eccentric, paranormal, unnatural, uncanny, extraordinary, exceptional, unusual, uncommon, unexpected, irregular, anomalous, aberrant (*fml*), erratic, wayward, deviant, divergent, different.
F∃ normal, regular, typical.

abnormality *noun* oddity,

peculiarity, singularity, eccentricity, strangeness, bizarreness, unnaturalness, unusualness, irregularity, exception, anomaly, deformity, flaw, aberration, deviation, divergence, difference.
F3 normality, regularity.

abolish *verb* do away with, annul, nullify, invalidate, quash, repeal, rescind, revoke, cancel, obliterate, blot out, suppress, destroy, eliminate, eradicate, get rid of (*infml*), stamp out, end, put an end to, terminate, subvert, overthrow, overturn.
F3 create, retain, authorize, continue.

abominable *adjective* loathsome, detestable, hateful, horrid, horrible, abhorrent (*fml*), odious, repugnant, repulsive, repellent, disgusting, revolting, obnoxious, nauseating, foul, vile, heinous (*fml*), atrocious, appalling, terrible, reprehensible, contemptible, despicable, wretched.
F3 delightful, pleasant, desirable.

about *preposition* **1** *write about a subject*: regarding, concerning, relating to, referring to, connected with, concerned with, as regards, with regard to, with respect to, with reference to. **2** *somewhere about the house*: close to, near, nearby, beside, adjacent to. **3** *walk about the town*: round, around, surrounding, encircling, encompassing, throughout, all over.
▪ *adverb* **1** *about twenty*: around, approximately, roughly, in the region of, more or less, almost, nearly, approaching, nearing. **2** *run about*: to and fro, here and there, from place to place.

above *preposition* over, higher than, on top of, superior to, in excess of, exceeding, surpassing, beyond, before, prior to.
F3 below, under.
▪ *adverb* overhead, aloft, on high, earlier.
F3 below, underneath.
▪ *adjective* above-mentioned, above-stated, foregoing, preceding, previous, earlier, prior.

abreast *adverb* **1** *walk abreast*: side by side, level, next to each other. **2** *keep abreast of the news*: in touch, up to date, informed, acquainted, knowledgeable, in the picture (*infml*), au fait, conversant (*fml*), familiar.
F3 **2** unaware, out of touch.

abroad *adverb* overseas, in foreign parts, out of the country, far and wide, widely, extensively.
F3 at home.

abrupt *adjective* **1** *abrupt departure*: sudden, unexpected, unforeseen, surprising, quick, rapid, swift, hasty, hurried, precipitate (*fml*). **2** *an abrupt drop*: sheer, precipitous, steep, sharp. **3** *an abrupt reply/manner*: brusque, curt, terse, short, brisk, snappy, gruff, rude, uncivil, impolite, blunt, direct.
F3 **1** gradual, slow, leisurely.

3 expansive, ceremonious, polite.

absence *noun* **1** *absence from school*: truancy, non-attendance, non-appearance, absenteeism, non-existence. **2** *absence of colour*: lack, need, want, deficiency, dearth, scarcity, unavailability, default, omission, vacancy.
F3 1 presence, attendance, appearance. **2** existence.

absent *adjective* **1** *absent from school/the meeting*: missing, not present, away, out, unavailable, gone, lacking, truant. **2** *an absent smile*: inattentive, daydreaming, dreamy, faraway, elsewhere, absent-minded, vacant, vague, distracted, preoccupied, unaware, oblivious, unheeding.
F3 1 present. **2** alert, aware.

absent-minded *adjective* forgetful, scatterbrained, absent, abstracted, withdrawn, faraway, distracted, preoccupied, absorbed, engrossed, pensive, musing, dreaming, dreamy, inattentive, unaware, oblivious, unconscious, heedless, unheeding, unthinking, impractical.
F3 attentive, practical, matter-of-fact.

absolute *adjective* **1** *in absolute confidence/silence*: utter, total, complete, entire, full, thorough, exhaustive, supreme, definitive, conclusive, final, categorical, definite, unequivocal, unquestionable, decided, decisive, positive, sure, certain, genuine, pure, perfect, sheer, unmixed, unqualified, downright, out-and-out, outright. **2** *absolute power/ruler*: omnipotent, totalitarian, autocratic, tyrannical, despotic, dictatorial, sovereign, unlimited, unrestricted.

absolutely *adverb* utterly, totally, dead, completely, entirely, fully, wholly, thoroughly, exhaustively, perfectly, supremely, unconditionally, conclusively, finally, categorically, definitely, positively, unequivocally, unambiguously, unquestionably, decidedly, decisively, surely, certainly, infallibly, genuinely, truly, purely, exactly, precisely.

absorb *verb* **1** *absorb liquid/facts*: take in, ingest, drink in, imbibe, suck up, soak up, consume, devour, engulf, digest, assimilate, understand, receive, hold, retain. **2** *absorb your attention*: engross, involve, fascinate, enthral, monopolize, preoccupy, occupy, fill (up).
F3 1 exude.

absorbing *adjective* interesting, amusing, entertaining, diverting, engrossing, preoccupying, intriguing, fascinating, captivating, enthralling, spellbinding, gripping, riveting, compulsive, unputdownable (*infml*).
F3 boring, off-putting.

abstain *verb* refrain, decline, refuse, reject, resist, forbear (*fml*), shun, avoid, keep from, stop,

cease, desist, give up, renounce, forgo, go without, deny oneself.
F3 indulge.

abstract *adjective* non-concrete, conceptual, intellectual, hypothetical, theoretical, unpractical, unrealistic, general, generalized, indefinite, metaphysical, philosophical, academic, complex, abstruse (*fml*), deep, profound, subtle.
F3 concrete, real, actual.

absurd *adjective* ridiculous, ludicrous, preposterous, fantastic, incongruous, illogical, paradoxical, implausible, untenable, unreasonable, irrational, nonsensical, meaningless, senseless, foolish, silly, stupid, idiotic, crazy, daft (*infml*), farcical, comical, funny, humorous, laughable, risible, derisory.
F3 logical, rational, sensible.

abundant *adjective* plentiful, in plenty, full, filled, well-supplied, ample, generous, bountiful, rich, copious, profuse, lavish, exuberant, teeming, overflowing.
F3 scarce, sparse.

abuse *verb* /a-**byooz**/ **1** *abuse authority*: misuse, misapply, exploit, take advantage of. **2** *abuse children*: oppress, wrong, ill-treat, maltreat, hurt, injure, molest, damage, spoil, harm. **3** *abuse immigrants*: insult, swear at, defame (*fml*), libel, slander, smear, disparage (*fml*), malign, revile, scold, upbraid (*fml*).
F3 **2** cherish, care for. **3** compliment, praise.
▪ *noun* /a-**byoos**/ **1** *the abuse of privilege/drugs*: misuse, misapplication, exploitation, imposition. **2** *child/physical abuse*: oppression, wrong, mistreatment, maltreatment, ill-treatment, cruelty, hurt, injury, molestation, assault, damage. **3** *shout abuse*: insults, obscenities, invective, defamation (*fml*), libel, slander, disparagement (*fml*), reproach, scolding, upbraiding (*fml*), tirade.
F3 **2** care, attention. **3** compliment, praise.

abusive *adjective* insulting, offensive, rude, scathing, hurtful, injurious, cruel, destructive, defamatory (*fml*), libellous, slanderous, derogatory, disparaging (*fml*), pejorative, vilifying, maligning, reviling, censorious, reproachful, scolding, upbraiding (*fml*).
F3 complimentary, polite.

abyss *noun* gulf, chasm, crevasse, fissure, gorge, canyon, crater, pit, depth, void.

academic *adjective* **1** *she's very academic*: scholarly, erudite, learned, well-read, studious, bookish, scholastic, pedagogical, educational, instructional, literary, highbrow. **2** *an academic, not practical, approach*: theoretical, hypothetical, conjectural, speculative, notional, abstract, impractical.
▪ *noun* professor, don, master,

fellow, lecturer, tutor, student, scholar, man of letters.

accelerate *verb* **1** *the car/driver accelerated*: quicken, speed, speed up, go faster, pick up/gather speed, step on it (*infml*). **2** *accelerate a process*: speed up, hasten, hurry, step up, expedite, precipitate (*fml*), stimulate, facilitate, advance, further, promote.
F3 **1**, **2** decelerate, slow down.

accent *noun* pronunciation, enunciation, articulation, brogue, twang (*infml*).

accentuate *verb* accent, stress, emphasize, underline, highlight, intensify, strengthen, deepen.
F3 play down, weaken.

accept *verb* **1** *accept a gift*: take, receive, obtain, acquire, gain, secure. **2** *accept a decision*: acknowledge, recognize, admit, allow, approve, agree to, consent to, take on, adopt. **3** *accept ill-treatment*: tolerate, put up with, stand, bear, abide, face up to, yield to.
F3 **1** refuse, turn down. **2** reject.

acceptable *adjective* satisfactory, tolerable, moderate, passable, adequate, all right, OK (*infml*), so-so (*infml*), unexceptionable, admissible, suitable, conventional, correct, desirable, pleasant, gratifying, welcome.
F3 unacceptable, unsatisfactory, unwelcome.

accepted *adjective* authorized, approved, ratified, sanctioned, agreed, acknowledged, recognized, admitted, confirmed, acceptable, correct, conventional, orthodox, traditional, customary, time-honoured, established, received, universal, regular, standard, normal, usual, common.
F3 unconventional, unorthodox, controversial.

access *noun* admission, admittance, entry, entering, entrance, gateway, door, key, approach, passage, road, path, course.
F3 exit, outlet.

accessible *adjective* **1** *accessible from the motorway*: reachable, get-at-able (*infml*), attainable, handy. **2** *facilities made accessible to everyone*: possible, obtainable, available, on hand, ready, achievable, convenient, near, nearby. **3** *an accessible book*: user-friendly, understandable, intelligible, easy to understand.
F3 **1** inaccessible, remote. **3** incomprehensible, unintelligible.

accessory *noun* **1** *computer accessories*: extra, supplement, addition, appendage, attachment, extension, component, fitting, accompaniment. **2** *accessories to match an outfit*: decoration, adornment, frill, trimming. **3** *an accessory to a crime*: accomplice, partner, associate, colleague, confederate, assistant, helper, help, aid.

accident *noun* **1** *happen by accident*: chance, hazard, fortuity (*fml*), luck, fortune, fate, serendipity, contingency, fluke (*infml*). **2** *an accident with boiling water*: misfortune, mischance, misadventure, mishap, casualty, blow, calamity, disaster. **3** *a road accident*: collision, crash, shunt (*infml*), prang (*slang*), pile-up (*infml*), smash.

accidental *adjective* unintentional, unintended, inadvertent, unplanned, uncalculated, unexpected, unforeseen, unlooked-for, chance, fortuitous (*fml*), flukey (*infml*), uncertain, haphazard, random, casual, incidental.
F intentional, deliberate, calculated, premeditated.

acclaim *verb* praise, commend, extol (*fml*), exalt, honour, hail, salute, welcome, applaud, clap, cheer, celebrate.
▪ *noun* acclamation, praise, commendation, homage, tribute, eulogy, exaltation, honour, welcome, approbation (*fml*), approval, applause, ovation, clapping, cheers, cheering, shouting, celebration.
F criticism, disapproval.

accommodate *verb* **1** *accommodate someone in a hotel*: lodge, board, put up, house, shelter. **2** *we try to accommodate all our customers*: oblige, help, assist, aid, serve, provide, supply, comply, conform.

---

accommodation

Types of accommodation include:
apartment, barracks, bedsit, bedsitter, digs (*infml*), dwelling, flat, halls of residence, hostel, lodgings, pad (*infml*), residence, rooms, shelter, squat (*infml*); bed and breakfast, boarding-house, guest-house, hotel, inn, motel, timeshare, villa, youth hostel. *See also* **building**; **house**; **room**.

---

accompany *verb* **1** *accompany someone on holiday*: escort, attend, convoy, chaperon(e), usher, conduct, follow. **2** *a book accompanied by a study guide*: coexist, coincide, belong to, go with, complement, supplement.

accomplice *noun* assistant, helper, abettor, mate, henchman, conspirator, collaborator, ally, confederate, partner, associate, colleague, participator, accessory.

accomplish *verb* achieve, attain, do, perform, carry out, execute, fulfil, discharge, finish, complete, conclude, consummate, realize, effect, bring about, engineer, produce, obtain.

according to *preposition* in accordance with, in keeping with, obedient to, in conformity with, in line with, consistent with, commensurate with, in proportion to, in relation to, after, in the light of, in the manner of, after the manner of.

account *noun* **1** *an account of what happened*: narrative, story, tale, chronicle, history, memoir, record, statement, report, communiqué, write-up, version, portrayal, sketch, description, presentation, explanation. **2** *the accounts of a business*: ledger, book, books, register, inventory. **3** *pay an account*: statement, invoice, bill, tab, charge, reckoning, computation, tally, score, balance.

accountable *adjective* answerable, responsible, liable, amenable, obliged, bound.

accumulate *verb* gather, assemble, collect, amass, aggregate, cumulate, accrue, grow, increase, multiply, build up, pile up, hoard, stockpile, stash (*infml*), store.
F3 disseminate.

accurate *adjective* correct, right, unerring, precise, exact, well-directed, spot-on (*infml*), faultless, perfect, word-perfect, sound, authentic, factual, true, truthful, just, proper, close, faithful, well-judged, careful, rigorous, scrupulous, meticulous, strict, minute.
F3 inaccurate, wrong, imprecise, inexact.

accuse *verb* charge, indict, impugn (*fml*), denounce, arraign, impeach, cite, allege, attribute, impute (*fml*), blame, censure, recriminate, incriminate, criminate, inform against.
F3 defend.

accustomed *adjective* used, in the habit of, given to, confirmed, seasoned, hardened, inured, disciplined, trained, adapted, acclimatized, acquainted, familiar, wonted, habitual, routine, regular, normal, usual, ordinary, everyday, conventional, customary, traditional, established, fixed, prevailing, general.
F3 unaccustomed, unusual.

ache *verb* **1** *my neck aches*: hurt, be sore, suffer, agonize, throb, pound, twinge, smart, sting. **2** *aching to tell her*: yearn, long, pine, hanker, desire, crave, hunger, thirst, itch.
▪ *noun* pain, hurt, soreness, suffering, anguish, agony, throb, throbbing, pounding, pang, twinge, smarting, stinging.

achieve *verb* accomplish, attain, reach, get, obtain, acquire, procure, gain, earn, win, succeed, manage, do, perform, carry out, execute, fulfil, finish, complete, consummate, effect, bring about, realize, produce.
F3 miss, fail.

achievement *noun* **1** *the achievement of our aims*: accomplishment, attainment, acquirement, performance, execution, fulfilment, completion, success, realization, fruition. **2** *great achievements*: act, deed, exploit, feat, effort.

acid *adjective* **1** *tastes acid*: sour, bitter, tart, vinegary, sharp, pungent, acidic, acerbic, caustic, corrosive. **2** *an acid remark*:

stinging, biting, mordant (*fml*), cutting, incisive, trenchant (*fml*), harsh, hurtful.

acknowledge *verb* **1** *acknowledge an error*: admit, confess, own up to, declare, recognize, accept, grant, allow, concede. **2** *acknowledged us with a nod*: greet, address, notice, salute, recognize. **3** *acknowledge a letter*: answer, reply to, respond to, confirm.
F3 **1** deny. **2** ignore.

act *noun* **1** *acts of bravery*: deed, action, undertaking, enterprise, operation, manoeuvre, move, step, doing, execution, accomplishment, achievement, exploit, feat, stroke. **2** *put on an act*: pretence, make-believe, sham, fake, feigning, dissimulation, affectation, show, front. **3** *an act of parliament*: law, statute, ordinance, edict, decree, resolution, measure, bill. **4** *a juggler's act*: turn, item, routine, sketch, performance, gig (*slang*).
▪ *verb* **1** *act in a certain way*: behave, be, move, do, conduct, exert, work. **2** *the drug will act soon*: take effect, have an effect, work, operate, function. **3** *the gear acts as a brake*: work, function, serve, operate, do, do the job of. **4** *act upset*: pretend, feign, put on, assume, simulate. **5** *act in a play*: mimic, imitate, impersonate, portray, represent, mime, play, perform, enact.

acting *adjective* temporary, provisional, interim, stopgap, supply, stand-by, substitute, reserve.

action *noun* **1** *his prompt action*: act, move, deed, exploit, feat, accomplishment, achievement, performance, effort, endeavour, enterprise, undertaking, proceeding, process, activity. **2** *people of action*: liveliness, spirit, energy, vigour, power, force. **3** *put an idea into action*: exercise, exertion, work, functioning, operation, mechanism, movement, motion. **4** *killed in action*: warfare, battle, conflict, combat, fight, fray, engagement, skirmish, clash. **5** *a legal action*: litigation, lawsuit, suit, case, prosecution.

activate *verb* start, initiate, trigger, set off, fire, switch on, set in motion, mobilize, propel, move, stir, rouse, arouse, stimulate, motivate, prompt, animate, energize, impel, excite, galvanize.
F3 deactivate, stop, arrest.

active *adjective* **1** *an active person*: busy, occupied, on the go (*infml*), industrious, diligent, hardworking, forceful, spirited, vital, forward, dynamic. **2** *active members*: enterprising, enthusiastic, devoted, engaged, involved, committed, militant, activist. **3** *active for his age*: agile, nimble, sprightly, light-footed, quick, alert, animated, lively, energetic, vigorous. **4** *the system is active*: in

operation, functioning, working, running.
F3 2 passive. 3 inactive. 4 inert, dormant.

activity *noun* **1** *there is always a lot of activity around the town centre*: liveliness, life, activeness, action, motion, movement, commotion, bustle, hustle, industry, labour, exertion, exercise. **2** *holiday activities*: occupation, job, work, act, deed, project, scheme, task, venture, enterprise, endeavour, undertaking, pursuit, hobby, pastime, interest.
F3 1 inactivity.

actor *noun* actress, play-actor, comedian, tragedian, ham, thespian (*fml*), player, performer, artist, impersonator, mime.

actual *adjective* real, existent, substantial, tangible, material, physical, concrete, positive, definite, absolute, certain, unquestionable, indisputable, confirmed, verified, factual, truthful, true, genuine, legitimate, bona fide, authentic, realistic.
F3 theoretical, apparent, imaginary.

actually *adverb* in fact, as a matter of fact, as it happens, in truth, in reality, really, truly, indeed, absolutely.

acute *adjective* **1** *an acute shortage*: severe, intense, extreme, violent, dangerous, serious, grave, urgent, crucial, vital, decisive, sharp, cutting, poignant, distressing. **2** *an acute mind*: sharp, keen, incisive, penetrating, astute, shrewd, judicious (*fml*), discerning, observant, perceptive.
F3 1 mild, slight.

adapt *verb* alter, change, qualify, modify, adjust, convert, remodel, customize, fit, tailor, fashion, shape, harmonize, match, suit, conform, comply, prepare, familiarize, acclimatize.

adaptable *adjective* alterable, changeable, variable, modifiable, adjustable, convertible, conformable, versatile, plastic, malleable, flexible, compliant, amenable, easy-going.
F3 inflexible, refractory.

adaptation *noun* alteration, change, shift, transformation, modification, adjustment, accommodation, conversion, remodelling, reworking, reshaping, refitting, revision, variation, version.

add *verb* append, annex, affix, attach, tack on, join, combine, supplement, augment.
F3 take away, remove.

addict *noun* **1** *a chess addict*: enthusiast, fan, buff (*infml*), fiend, freak (*infml*), devotee, follower, adherent. **2** *a drug addict*: drug taker, drug user, user (*infml*), dope-fiend, junkie (*infml*).

addiction *noun* dependence, craving, compulsion, habit, obsession.

addition *noun* **1** *the addition of a conservatory*: adding, annexation, accession, extension,

enlargement, increasing, increase, gain. **2** *an addition to the report*: adjunct, supplement, additive, addendum, appendix, appendage, accessory, attachment, extra, increment. **3** *addition of numbers*: summing-up, totting-up, totalling, counting, reckoning, inclusion.
F3 1 removal. **3** subtraction.

additional *adjective* added, extra, supplementary, spare, further, increased, other, new, fresh.

address *noun* **1** *one's home/business address*: residence, dwelling, abode (*fml*), house, home, lodging, direction, whereabouts, location, situation, place. **2** *the president's address to the nation*: speech, talk, lecture, sermon, oration (*fml*), discourse, dissertation.
▪ *verb* **1** *addressing me in his normal tone of voice*: speak to, talk to, greet, salute, hail. **2** *addressed his remarks to me*: direct, convey, communicate.

adept *adjective* skilled, accomplished, expert, masterly, experienced, versed, practised, polished, proficient, able, adroit, deft, nimble.

adequate *adjective* enough, sufficient, commensurate, requisite, suitable, fit, able, competent, capable, serviceable, acceptable, satisfactory, passable, tolerable, fair, respectable, presentable.
F3 inadequate, insufficient.

adjacent *adjective* adjoining, abutting, touching, contiguous, bordering, alongside, beside, juxtaposed, next-door, neighbouring, next, closest, nearest, close, near.
F3 remote, distant.

adjoining *adjective* adjacent to, abutting, touching, meeting, bordering, neighbouring, alongside, next to.

adjust *verb* **1** *adjust one's plans/the volume*: modify, change, adapt, alter, convert, dispose, shape, remodel, fit, suit, accommodate, measure, rectify, regulate, balance, temper, tune, fine-tune, fix, set, arrange, compose, settle, square. **2** *adjust to new conditions*: accustom, habituate, acclimatize, reconcile, harmonize, conform.
F3 1 disarrange, upset.

ad-lib *verb* improvise, make up, invent, extemporize (*fml*).
▪ *adverb* impromptu, spontaneously, extemporaneously (*fml*), off the cuff (*infml*), off the top of one's head (*infml*).

administer *verb* **1** *the body that administers golf*: govern, rule, lead, head, preside over, officiate, manage, run, organize, direct, conduct, control, regulate, superintend, supervise, oversee. **2** *administer the medicine*: give, provide, supply, distribute, dole out, dispense, measure out, mete out, execute, impose, apply.

administrative *adjective* governmental, legislative,

authoritative, directorial, managerial, executive, organizational, regulatory, supervisory.

admirable *adjective* praiseworthy, commendable, laudable, creditable, deserving, worthy, respected, fine, excellent, superior, wonderful, exquisite, choice, rare, valuable.

F3 contemptible, despicable, deplorable.

admiration *noun* esteem, regard, respect, reverence, veneration, worship, adoration, affection, approval, praise, appreciation, pleasure, delight, wonder, astonishment, amazement, surprise.

F3 contempt.

admire *verb* esteem, respect, revere, venerate, worship, idolize, adore, approve, praise, laud (*fml*), applaud, appreciate, value.

F3 despise, censure.

admirer *noun* follower, disciple, adherent, supporter, fan, enthusiast, devotee, worshipper, suitor, boyfriend, girlfriend, sweetheart, lover.

F3 critic, opponent.

admission *noun* confession, acknowledgement, granting, recognition, acceptance, allowance, concession, affirmation, declaration, profession, disclosure, divulgence, revelation, exposé.

F3 denial.

admit *verb* **1** *admit I was wrong*: confess, own (up), grant, acknowledge, recognize, accept, allow, concede, agree, affirm, declare, profess, disclose, divulge, reveal. **2** *be admitted to the palace*: let in, allow to enter, give access, accept, receive, take in, introduce, initiate.

F3 **1** deny. **2** shut out, exclude.

adolescence *noun* teens, puberty, youth, minority, boyhood, girlhood, development, immaturity, youthfulness, boyishness, girlishness.

adolescent *adjective* teenage, young, youthful, juvenile, boyish, girlish, growing, developing, pubescent.

▪ *noun* teenager, young person, young adult, youth, juvenile, minor.

adopt *verb* take on, accept, assume, take up, appropriate, embrace, follow, choose, select, take in, foster, support, maintain, back, endorse, ratify, approve.

F3 repudiate, disown.

adorable *adjective* lovable, dear, darling, precious, appealing, sweet, winsome, charming, enchanting, captivating, winning, delightful, pleasing, attractive, fetching.

F3 hateful, abominable.

adore *verb* love, cherish, dote on, admire, esteem, honour, revere, venerate, worship, idolize, exalt, glorify.

F3 hate, abhor.

adorn *verb* decorate, deck,

bedeck, ornament, crown, trim, garnish, gild, enhance, embellish, doll up (*infml*), enrich, grace.

adult *adjective* grown-up, of age, full-grown, fully grown, developed, mature, ripe, ripened.
immature.

advance *verb* **1** *advance to the next stage*: proceed, go forward, move on, move forward, go ahead, progress, push on (*infml*). **2** *advance his career considerably*: accelerate, speed, further, promote, improve, boost, upgrade, foster, support, assist, benefit, facilitate. **3** *technology advanced very rapidly*: improve, develop, prosper, thrive. **4** *advance an idea*: present, submit, suggest, allege, cite, put/bring forward, offer, provide, supply. **5** *advance a sum of money*: lend, loan, pay beforehand, pay, give.
1 retreat. **2** retard, impede.
▪ *noun* **1** *an important technological advance*: progress, forward movement, onward movement, headway, step, advancement, breakthrough, development, growth, increase, improvement. **2** *an advance on his salary*: deposit, down payment, prepayment, credit, loan.
1 retreat, recession.

advanced *adjective* leading, foremost, ahead, forward, precocious, progressive, forward-looking, avant-garde, ultra-modern, sophisticated, complex, higher.
backward, retarded, elementary.

advantage *noun* **1** *the advantages of electric light*: asset, blessing, benefit, good, welfare, interest, service, help, aid, assistance, use, avail, convenience, usefulness, utility, profit, gain, start. **2** *an advantage over other candidates*: lead, edge (*infml*), upper hand, superiority, precedence, pre-eminence, sway.
1 disadvantage, drawback, hindrance.

advantageous *adjective* beneficial, favourable, opportune, convenient, helpful, useful, worthwhile, valuable, profitable, gainful, remunerative, rewarding.
disadvantageous, adverse, damaging.

adventure *noun* exploit, venture, undertaking, enterprise, risk, hazard, escapade, chance, speculation, experience, incident, occurrence.

adventurous *adjective* daring, intrepid, bold, audacious, headstrong, impetuous, reckless, rash, risky, venturesome, enterprising.
cautious, wary, prudent.

adverse *adjective* hostile, antagonistic, opposing, opposite, counter, contrary, conflicting, counter-productive, negative, disadvantageous, unfavourable, inauspicious, unfortunate, unlucky, inopportune, detrimental, harmful, noxious,

injurious, hurtful, unfriendly, uncongenial.
F3 advantageous, favourable.

advertise *verb* publicize, promote, push, plug (*infml*), praise, hype (*infml*), trumpet, blazon, herald, announce, declare, proclaim, broadcast, publish, display, make known, inform, notify.

advertisement *noun* advert (*infml*), ad (*infml*), commercial, publicity, promotion, plug (*infml*), hype (*infml*), display, blurb, announcement, notice, poster, bill, placard, leaflet, circular, handout, propaganda.

advice *noun* warning, caution, do's and don'ts, injunction, instruction, counsel, help, guidance, direction, suggestion, recommendation, opinion, view.

advisable *adjective* recommended, sensible, wise, prudent, judicious (*fml*), sound, profitable, beneficial, desirable, suitable, fitting, appropriate, apt, fit, proper, correct.
F3 inadvisable, foolish.

advise *verb* **1** *advised him to say nothing*: counsel, guide, warn, forewarn, caution, instruct, teach, tutor, suggest, recommend, commend, urge. **2** *advised us of his arrival*: notify, inform, tell, acquaint, make known, report.

adviser *noun* counsellor, consultant, authority, guide, teacher, tutor, instructor, coach, helper, aide, right-hand man, mentor, confidant(e), counsel, lawyer.

advocate *verb* defend, champion, campaign for, press for, argue for, plead for, justify, urge, encourage, advise, recommend, propose, promote, endorse, support, uphold, patronize, adopt, subscribe to, favour, countenance.
F3 impugn (*fml*), disparage (*fml*), deprecate (*fml*).

affable *adjective* friendly, amiable, approachable, open, expansive, genial, good-humoured, good-natured, mild, benevolent, kindly, gracious, obliging, courteous, amicable, congenial, cordial, warm, sociable, pleasant, agreeable.
F3 unfriendly, reserved, reticent, cool.

affair *noun* **1** *a curious affair*: business, transaction, operation, proceeding, undertaking, activity, project, responsibility, interest, concern, matter, question, issue, subject, topic, circumstance, happening, occurrence, incident, episode, event. **2** *have an affair*: relationship, liaison, intrigue, love affair, romance, amour.

affect *verb* **1** *affecting the climate/ doesn't affect us*: concern, regard, involve, relate to, apply to, bear upon, impinge upon, act on, change, transform, alter, modify, influence, sway, prevail over, attack, strike, impress, interest, stir, move, touch, upset, disturb, perturb, trouble, overcome.

2 *affect an air of indifference*: adopt, assume, put on, feign, simulate, imitate, fake, counterfeit, sham, pretend, profess, aspire to.

affectation *noun* airs, pretentiousness, mannerism, pose, act, show, appearance, façade, pretence, sham, simulation, imitation, artificiality, insincerity.
≠ artlessness, ingenuousness.

affected *adjective* assumed, put-on, feigned, simulated, artificial, fake, counterfeit, sham, phoney (*infml*), contrived, studied, precious, mannered, pretentious, pompous, stiff, unnatural, insincere.
≠ genuine, natural.

affection *noun* fondness, attachment, devotion, love, tenderness, care, warmth, feeling, kindness, friendliness, goodwill, favour, liking, partiality, inclination, penchant, passion, desire.
≠ dislike, antipathy.

affectionate *adjective* fond, attached, devoted, doting, loving, tender, caring, warm, warm-hearted, kind, friendly, amiable, cordial.
≠ cold, undemonstrative.

affirm *verb* confirm, corroborate, endorse, ratify, certify, witness, testify, swear, maintain, state, assert, declare, pronounce.
≠ refute, deny.

affirmative *adjective* agreeing, concurring, approving, assenting, positive, confirming, corroborative, emphatic.
≠ negative, dissenting.

afflict *verb* strike, visit, trouble, burden, oppress, distress, grieve, pain, hurt, wound, harm, try, harass, beset, plague, torment, torture.
≠ comfort, solace.

affliction *noun* distress, grief, sorrow, misery, depression, suffering, pain, torment, disease, illness, sickness, plague, curse, cross, ordeal, trial, tribulation, trouble, hardship, adversity, misfortune, calamity, disaster.
≠ comfort, consolation, solace, blessing.

afford *verb* 1 *can't afford a holiday*: have enough for, be able to pay, spare, allow, manage. 2 *afford some relief*: provide, supply, furnish, give, grant, offer, impart, produce, yield, generate.

affront *noun* offence, insult, slur, rudeness, discourtesy, disrespect, indignity, snub, slight, wrong, injury, abuse, provocation, vexation, outrage.
≠ compliment.

afraid *adjective* frightened, scared, alarmed, terrified, fearful, timorous, daunted, intimidated, faint-hearted, cowardly, reluctant, apprehensive, anxious, nervous, timid, distrustful, suspicious.
≠ unafraid, brave, bold, confident.

after *preposition* following, subsequent to, as a result of, in

consequence of, behind, below.
F3 before.

again *adverb* once more, once again, another time, over again, afresh, anew, encore.

against *preposition* **1** *against the wall*: abutting, adjacent to, close up to, touching, in contact with, on. **2** *against the proposal/against our wishes*: opposite to, facing, fronting, in the face of, confronting, opposing, versus, opposed to, in opposition to, hostile to, resisting, in defiance of, in contrast to.
F3 2 for, pro.

age *noun* **1** *the age of steam*: era, epoch, day, days, generation, date, time, period, duration, span, years, aeon. **2** *age was creeping up on him*: old age, maturity, elderliness, seniority, dotage, senility, decline.
F3 2 youth.
▪ *verb* grow old, decline, deteriorate, degenerate.

agent *noun* **1** *a travel/estate/government agent*: representative, rep (*infml*), broker, middleman, go-between, intermediary, negotiator, mover, doer, performer, operator, operative, functionary, worker. **2** *the agent of change*: instrument, vehicle, channel, means, agency, cause, force.

aggravate *verb* **1** *aggravate the problem*: exacerbate, worsen, inflame, increase, intensify, heighten, magnify, exaggerate. **2** (*infml*) *don't aggravate him!*: annoy, irritate, vex, needle (*infml*), get on someone's nerves (*infml*), exasperate, incense, provoke, tease, pester, harass.
F3 1 improve, alleviate. **2** appease, mollify.

aggressive *adjective* argumentative, quarrelsome, contentious, belligerent, warlike, pugnacious (*fml*), hostile, offensive, provocative, intrusive, invasive, bold, assertive, pushy (*infml*), go-ahead, forceful, vigorous, zealous, ruthless, destructive.
F3 peaceable, friendly, submissive, timid.

aggrieved *adjective* wronged, offended, hurt, injured, insulted, maltreated, ill-used, resentful, pained, distressed, saddened, unhappy, upset, annoyed.
F3 pleased.

aghast *adjective* shocked, appalled, horrified, horror-struck, thunderstruck, stunned, stupefied, amazed, astonished, astounded, startled, confounded, dismayed.

agile *adjective* active, lively, nimble, spry, sprightly, mobile, flexible, limber, lithe, fleet, quick, swift, brisk, prompt, sharp, acute, alert, quick-witted, clever, adroit, deft.
F3 clumsy, stiff.

agitate *verb* **1** *the noise and bustle agitated them*: rouse, arouse, stir up, excite, stimulate, incite, inflame, ferment, work up, worry, trouble, upset, alarm, disturb, unsettle, disquiet, discompose,

fluster, ruffle, flurry, unnerve, confuse, distract, disconcert. **2** *agitating the leaves/the water*: shake, rattle, rock, stir, beat, churn, toss, convulse.
⇔ **1** calm, tranquillize.

agony *noun* anguish, torment, torture, pain, spasm, throes, suffering, affliction, tribulation, distress, woe, misery, wretchedness.

agree *verb* **1** *agree with each other*: concur, see eye to eye, get on, settle, accord, match, suit, fit, tally, correspond, conform. **2** *agree to his offer*: consent, allow, permit, assent, accede, grant, admit, concede, yield, comply.
⇔ **1** disagree, differ, conflict. **2** refuse.

agreement *noun* **1** *the final agreement*: settlement, compact, covenant, treaty, pact, contract, deal, bargain, arrangement, understanding. **2** *be in agreement*: concurrence, accord, concord, unanimity, union, harmony, sympathy, affinity, compatibility, similarity, correspondence, consistency, conformity, compliance, adherence, acceptance.
⇔ **2** disagreement.

ahead *adverb* forward, onward, leading, at the head, in front, in the lead, winning, at an advantage, advanced, superior, to the fore, in the forefront, in advance, before, earlier on.

aid *noun* help, assistance, prop, support, relief, benefit, subsidy, donation, contribution, funding, grant, sponsorship, patronage, favour, encouragement, service.
⇔ hindrance, impediment, obstruction.
▪ *verb* help, assist, support, subsidize, sustain, promote, boost, encourage, expedite, facilitate, ease.
⇔ hinder, impede, obstruct.

aim *verb* **1** *aim their guns at*: point, direct, take aim, level, train, sight, zero in on (*infml*), target. **2** *aiming to get into Oxford or Cambridge*: aspire, want, wish, seek, resolve, purpose, intend, propose, mean, plan, design, strive, try, attempt, endeavour.
▪ *noun* aspiration, ambition, hope, dream, desire, wish, plan, design, scheme, purpose, motive, end, intention, object, objective, target, mark, goal, direction, course.

aimless *adjective* pointless, purposeless, unmotivated, irresolute, directionless, rambling, undirected, unguided, stray, chance, random, haphazard, erratic, unpredictable, wayward.
⇔ purposeful, positive, determined.

air *noun* **1** *open the window to get a little air*: oxygen, breath, puff, waft, draught, breeze, wind. **2** *birds flying in the air*: sky, heavens, atmosphere. **3** *an air of indifference*: appearance, look, aspect, aura, bearing, demeanour, manner, character, effect,

impression, feeling, quality.
▪ *verb* **1** *air a room*: ventilate, aerate, freshen. **2** *air an opinion*: utter, voice, express, give vent to, make known, declare, communicate, tell, reveal, disclose, divulge, expose, make public, broadcast, publish, circulate, disseminate, exhibit, display, parade, publicize.

airy *adjective* **1** *a bright and airy office*: roomy, spacious, open, well-ventilated. **2** *his manner was airy*: cheerful, happy, light-hearted, high-spirited, lively, nonchalant, offhand.
F3 **1** airless, stuffy, close, heavy, oppressive.

alarm *noun* **1** *jumped back in alarm*: fright, scare, fear, terror, panic, horror, shock, consternation, dismay, distress, anxiety, nervousness, apprehension, trepidation, uneasiness. **2** *sound the alarm*: danger signal, alert, warning, distress signal, siren, bell, alarm-bell, fire alarm, tocsin (*fml*).
F3 **1** calmness, composure.
▪ *verb* frighten, scare, startle, put the wind up (*infml*), terrify, panic, unnerve, daunt, dismay, distress, agitate.
F3 reassure, calm, soothe.

alarming *adjective* frightening, scary, startling, terrifying, unnerving, daunting, ominous, threatening, dismaying, disturbing, distressing, shocking, dreadful.
F3 reassuring.

alert *adjective* attentive, wide-awake, watchful, vigilant, on the lookout, sharp-eyed, observant, perceptive, sharp-witted, on the ball (*infml*), on your toes (*infml*), quick, nimble, ready, prepared, careful, heedful, circumspect (*fml*), wary.
F3 slow, listless, unprepared.
▪ *verb* warn, forewarn, notify, inform, tip off, signal, make aware.

alias *noun* pseudonym, false name, assumed name, nom de guerre, nom de plume, pen name, stage name, nickname, sobriquet (*fml*).
▪ *preposition* also known as, a.k.a. (*infml*), also called, otherwise.

alibi *noun* defence, justification, story, explanation, excuse, pretext, reason.

alien *adjective* strange, unfamiliar, outlandish, incongruous, foreign, exotic, extraterrestrial, extraneous, remote, estranged, separated, opposed, contrary, conflicting, antagonistic, incompatible.
F3 akin.
▪ *noun* foreigner, immigrant, newcomer, stranger, outsider.
F3 native.

alight *adjective* lighted, lit, ignited, on fire, burning, blazing, ablaze, flaming, fiery, lit up, illuminated, bright, radiant, shining, brilliant.
F3 dark.

align *verb* **1** *aligned the two edges of the fabric*: straighten, range, line up, make parallel, even (up), adjust. **2** *aligned themselves with Labour*: ally, side, sympathize, associate, affiliate, join, co-operate, agree.

alike *adjective* similar, resembling, comparable, akin, analogous, corresponding, equivalent, equal, the same, identical, duplicate, parallel, even, uniform.
F3 dissimilar, unlike, different.
▪ *adverb* similarly, analogously, correspondingly, equally, in common.

alive *adjective* **1** *didn't know if he was alive or dead*: living, having life, live, animate, breathing, existent, in existence, real. **2** *alive with insects*: full of, overflowing with, crawling with (*infml*), teeming with, abounding in.
F3 **1** dead, extinct.

all *adjective* **1** *all people are equal/ all Europe was at war*: each, every, each and every, every single, every one of, the whole of, every bit of. **2** *go with all speed*: complete, entire, full, total, utter, outright, perfect, greatest.
F3 **1** no, none.
▪ *noun* everything, sum, total, aggregate, total amount, whole amount, whole, entirety, the lot (*infml*), comprehensiveness, utmost, universality.
F3 nothing, none.
▪ *adverb* completely, entirely, wholly, fully, totally, utterly, altogether.

allegation *noun* accusation, charge, claim, profession, assertion, affirmation, declaration, statement, testimony, plea.

allege *verb* assert, affirm, declare, state, attest (*fml*), maintain, insist, hold, contend, claim, profess, plead.

alleged *adjective* supposed, reputed, inferred, so-called, professed, declared, stated, claimed, described, designated, doubtful, dubious, suspect, suspicious.

allegiance *noun* loyalty, fidelity, faithfulness, constancy, duty, obligation, obedience, devotion, support, adherence, friendship.
F3 disloyalty, enmity.

allergic *adjective* sensitive, hypersensitive, susceptible, affected, incompatible, averse, disinclined, opposed, hostile, antagonistic.
F3 tolerant.

alliance *noun* confederation, federation, association, affiliation, coalition, league, bloc, cartel, conglomerate, consortium, syndicate, guild, union, partnership, marriage, agreement, compact, bond, pact, treaty, combination, connection.
F3 separation, divorce, estrangement, enmity, hostility.

allocate *verb* assign, designate, budget, allow, earmark, set aside, allot, apportion, share out, distribute, dispense, mete.

allot *verb* divide, ration,

apportion, share out, distribute, dispense, mete, dole out (*infml*), allocate, assign, designate, budget, allow, grant, earmark, set aside.

allow *verb* **1** *allow the children to stay up late*: permit, let, enable, authorize, sanction, approve, tolerate, put up with (*infml*), endure, suffer. **2** *allow two hours for the journey*: allot, allocate, assign, apportion, afford, give, provide. **3** *allow that he had a point*: admit, confess, own, acknowledge, concede, grant.
≠ **1** forbid, prevent. **3** deny.

allowance *noun* **1** *their weekly allowance of milk and eggs*: allotment, lot, amount, allocation, portion, share, ration, quota. **2** *give him an allowance of £200 a month*: payment, remittance, pocket money, grant, maintenance, stipend, pension, annuity.

alloy *noun* blend, compound, composite, amalgam, combination, mixture, fusion, coalescence.

all right *adjective* **1** *it was all right, I suppose*: satisfactory, passable, unobjectionable, acceptable, allowable, adequate, fair, average, OK (*infml*). **2** *are you all right?*: well, healthy, unhurt, uninjured, unharmed, unimpaired, whole, sound, safe, secure.
≠ **1** unacceptable, inadequate.

allude *verb* mention, refer to, speak of, hint at, imply, insinuate, touch on/upon, suggest.

ally *noun* confederate, associate, consort, partner, sidekick, colleague, co-worker, collaborator, helper, helpmate, accomplice, accessory, friend.
≠ antagonist, enemy.
▪ *verb* confederate, affiliate, league, associate, collaborate, join forces, band together, team up, fraternize, side, join, connect, link, marry, unite, unify, amalgamate, combine.
≠ estrange, separate.

almighty *adjective* **1** *the almighty Caesar*: omnipotent, all-powerful, supreme, absolute, great, invincible. **2** *an almighty bang*: enormous, severe, intense, overwhelming, overpowering, terrible, awful, desperate.
≠ **1** impotent, weak.

almost *adverb* nearly, well-nigh, practically, virtually, just about, as good as, all but, close to, not far from, approaching, nearing, not quite, about, approximately.

alone *adjective* only, sole, single, unique, solitary, separate, detached, unconnected, isolated, apart, by oneself, by itself, on one's own, lonely, lonesome, deserted, abandoned, forsaken, forlorn, desolate, unaccompanied, unescorted, unattended, solo, single-handed, unaided, unassisted, mere.
≠ together, accompanied, escorted.

aloof *adjective* distant, remote,

offish, standoffish, haughty, supercilious, unapproachable, inaccessible, detached, forbidding, cool, chilly, cold, unsympathetic, unresponsive, indifferent, uninterested, reserved, unforthcoming, unfriendly, unsociable, formal.
F3 sociable, friendly, concerned.

aloud *adverb* out loud, audibly, intelligibly, clearly, plainly, distinctly, loudly, resoundingly, sonorously, noisily, vociferously.
F3 silently.

also *adverb* too, as well, and, plus, along with, including, as well as, additionally, in addition, besides, further, furthermore, moreover.

alter *verb* change, vary, diversify, modify, qualify, shift, transpose, adjust, adapt, convert, turn, transmute, transform, reform, reshape, remodel, recast, revise, amend, emend, tweak (*infml*).
F3 fix.

alteration *noun* change, variation, variance, difference, diversification, shift, transposition, modification, adjustment, adaptation, conversion, transformation, transfiguration, metamorphosis, reformation, reshaping, remodelling, revision, amendment.
F3 fixity.

alternate *verb* /**ol**-*te*-neit/ interchange, reciprocate, rotate, take turns, follow one another, replace each other, substitute, change, alter, vary, oscillate, fluctuate, intersperse.
▪ *adjective* /ol-**tern**-*a*t/ alternating, every other, every second, interchanging, reciprocal, rotating, alternative.

alternative *noun* option, choice, selection, preference, other, recourse, substitute, back-up.
▪ *adjective* substitute, second, another, other, different, unorthodox, unconventional, fringe, alternate.

altogether *adverb* totally, completely, entirely, wholly, fully, utterly, absolutely, quite, perfectly, thoroughly, in all, all told, in toto, all in all, as a whole, on the whole, generally, in general.

always *adverb* every time, consistently, invariably, without exception, unfailingly, regularly, repeatedly, continually, constantly, perpetually, unceasingly, eternally, endlessly, evermore, forever, ever, twenty-four-seven (*infml*).
F3 never.

amalgamate *verb* merge, blend, mingle, commingle, intermix, homogenize, incorporate, alloy, integrate, compound, fuse, coalesce, synthesize, combine, unite, unify, ally.
F3 separate.

amateur *noun* non-professional, layman, ham (*infml*), dilettante, dabbler, enthusiast, fancier, buff (*infml*).
F3 professional.
▪ *adjective* non-professional, lay,

unpaid, unqualified, untrained, amateurish, inexpert, unprofessional.
F3 professional.

amaze *verb* surprise, startle, astonish, astound, stun, stupefy, daze, floor (*infml*), stagger, dumbfound, flabbergast (*infml*), shock, dismay, disconcert, confound, bewilder.

amazement *noun* surprise, astonishment, shock, dismay, confusion, perplexity, bewilderment, admiration, wonderment, wonder, marvel.

ambassador *noun* emissary, envoy, legate, diplomat, consul, plenipotentiary, deputy, representative, agent, minister, apostle.

ambiguity *noun* double meaning, double entendre, equivocality, equivocation, enigma, puzzle, confusion, obscurity, unclearness, vagueness, woolliness, dubiousness, doubt, doubtfulness, uncertainty.
F3 clarity.

ambiguous *adjective* double-meaning, equivocal, multivocal, double-edged, back-handed, cryptic, enigmatic, puzzling, confusing, obscure, unclear, vague, indefinite, woolly, confused, dubious, doubtful, uncertain, inconclusive, indeterminate.
F3 clear, definite.

ambition *noun* **1** *his ambition to be a jockey*: aspiration, aim, goal, target, objective, intent, purpose, design, object, ideal, dream, hope, wish, desire, yearning, longing, hankering, craving, hunger. **2** *a woman of ambition*: enterprise, drive, push, thrust, striving, eagerness, commitment, zeal.
F3 2 apathy, diffidence.

ambitious *adjective* **1** *an ambitious politician who wants to get to the top*: aspiring, hopeful, desirous, intent, purposeful, pushy (*infml*), bold, assertive, go-ahead, enterprising, driving, energetic, enthusiastic, eager, keen, striving, industrious, zealous. **2** *isn't this plan a trifle ambitious?*: formidable, hard, difficult, arduous, strenuous, demanding, challenging, exacting, impressive, grandiose, elaborate.
F3 1 lazy, unassuming. **2** modest, uninspiring.

amble *verb* walk, saunter, toddle (*infml*), stroll, promenade, wander, drift, meander, ramble.
F3 stride, march.

ambush *verb* lie in wait, waylay, surprise, trap, ensnare.

amend *verb* revise, correct, rectify, emend, fix, repair, mend, remedy, redress, reform, change, alter, adjust, modify, qualify, enhance, improve, ameliorate (*fml*), better.
F3 impair, worsen.

amends *noun* atonement, expiation, requital, satisfaction, recompense, compensation, indemnification, indemnity, reparation, redress, restoration, restitution.

amid *preposition* amidst, midst, in the midst of, in the thick of, among, amongst, in the middle of, surrounded by.

among *preposition* amongst, between, in the middle of, surrounded by, amid, amidst, midst, in the midst of, in the thick of, with, together with.

amount *noun* quantity, number, sum, total, sum total, whole, entirety, aggregate, lot, quota, supply, volume, mass, bulk, measure, magnitude, extent, expanse.

amphibian

Amphibians include:

axolotl, bullfrog, eft, frog, horned toad, midwife toad, mud puppy, natterjack, newt, salamander, toad, tree frog.

---

ample *adjective* **1** *a room of ample proportions*: large, big, extensive, expansive, broad, wide, full, voluminous, roomy, spacious, commodious, great. **2** *there were ample supplies/opportunities*: considerable, substantial, handsome, generous, bountiful, munificent, liberal, lavish, copious, abundant, plentiful, plenty, unrestricted, profuse, rich.

F3 2 insufficient, inadequate, meagre.

amplify *verb* enlarge, magnify, expand, dilate, fill out, bulk out, add to, supplement, augment, increase, extend, lengthen, widen, broaden, develop, elaborate, enhance, boost, intensify, strengthen, deepen, heighten, raise.

F3 reduce, decrease, abridge.

amputate *verb* cut off, remove, sever, dissever, separate, dock, lop, curtail, truncate.

amuse *verb* entertain, divert, regale, make laugh, tickle (*infml*), crease (*infml*), slay (*infml*), cheer (up), gladden, enliven, please, charm, delight, enthral, engross, absorb, interest, occupy, recreate, relax.

F3 bore, displease.

amusement *noun* entertainment, diversion, distraction, fun, enjoyment, pleasure, delight, merriment, mirth, hilarity, laughter, joke, prank, game, sport, recreation, hobby, pastime, interest.

F3 boredom, monotony.

amusing *adjective* funny, humorous, hilarious, comical, laughable, ludicrous, droll, witty, facetious, jocular, jolly, enjoyable, pleasant, charming, delightful, entertaining, interesting.

F3 dull, boring.

anaesthetize *verb* desensitize, numb, deaden, dull, drug, dope, stupefy.

analogy *noun* comparison, simile, metaphor, likeness, resemblance, similarity, parallel, correspondence, equivalence, relation, correlation, agreement.

analyse *verb* break down, separate, divide, take apart, dissect, anatomize, reduce, resolve, sift, investigate, study, examine, scrutinize, review, interpret, test, judge, evaluate, estimate, consider.

analysis *noun* breakdown, separation, division, dissection, reduction, resolution, sifting, investigation, enquiry, study, examination, scrutiny, review, exposition, explication, explanation, interpretation, test, judgement, opinion, evaluation, estimation, reasoning.
F3 synthesis.

anarchic *adjective* lawless, ungoverned, anarchistic, libertarian, nihilist, revolutionary, rebellious, mutinous, riotous, chaotic, disordered, confused, disorganized.
F3 submissive, orderly.

anarchy *noun* lawlessness, unrule, misrule, anarchism, revolution, rebellion, insurrection, mutiny, riot, pandemonium, chaos, disorder, confusion.
F3 rule, control, order.

anatomical terms

Anatomical terms include:
aural, biceps, bone, cardiac, cartilage, cerebral, dental, diaphragm, dorsal, duodenal, elbow, epidermis, epiglottis, Fallopian tubes, funny bone (*infml*), gastric, gingival, gristle, groin, gullet, hamstring, helix, hepatic, hock, intercostal, jugular, lachrymal, ligament, lumbar, mammary, membral, muscle, nasal, neural, ocular, oesophagus, optical, pectoral, pedal, pulmonary, renal, spine, tendon, triceps, umbilicus, uterus, uvula, voice box, windpipe, wisdom tooth, womb. *See also* **bone**.

---

ancestor *noun* forebear, forefather, progenitor (*fml*), predecessor, forerunner, precursor, antecedent.
F3 descendant.

ancestry *noun* ancestors, forebears, forefathers, progenitors (*fml*), parentage, family, lineage, line, descent, blood, race, stock, roots, pedigree, genealogy, extraction, derivation, origin, heritage, heredity.

anchor *verb* moor, berth, tie up, make fast, fasten, attach, affix, fix.

ancient *adjective* **1** *ancient manuscripts*: old, aged, time-worn, age-old, antique, antediluvian, prehistoric, fossilized, primeval, immemorial. **2** *an ancient record-player*: old-fashioned, out-of-date, antiquated, archaic, obsolete, bygone, early, original.
F3 **1** recent, contemporary. **2** modern, up-to-date.

anecdote *noun* story, tale, yarn, sketch, reminiscence.

angelic *adjective* cherubic, seraphic, celestial, heavenly, divine, holy, pious, saintly, pure, innocent, unworldly, virtuous,

lovely, beautiful, adorable.
☒ devilish, fiendish.

anger *noun* annoyance, irritation, antagonism, displeasure, irritability, temper, pique, vexation, ire, rage, fury, wrath, exasperation, outrage, indignation, gall, bitterness, rancour, resentment.
☒ forgiveness, forbearance.
▪ *verb* annoy, irritate, aggravate (*infml*), wind up (*infml*), vex, irk, rile, miff (*infml*), needle (*infml*), nettle, bother, ruffle, provoke, antagonize, offend, affront, gall, madden, enrage, incense, infuriate, exasperate, outrage.
☒ please, appease, calm.

angle *noun* **1** *form an angle*: corner, nook, bend, flexure, hook, crook, elbow, knee, edge, point. **2** *look at something from a different angle*: aspect, outlook, facet, side, approach, direction, position, standpoint, viewpoint, point of view, slant, perspective.

angry *adjective* annoyed, cross, irritated, aggravated (*infml*), displeased, uptight (*infml*), irate, mad (*infml*), enraged, incensed, infuriated, furious, raging, passionate, heated, hot, exasperated, outraged, indignant, bitter, resentful.
☒ content, happy, calm.

animal *noun* creature, mammal, beast, brute, barbarian, savage, monster, cur, pig, swine.

Animals include:
aardvark, antelope, ape, armadillo, baboon, badger, bear, beaver, bison, buffalo, bull, camel, caribou, cat, cheetah, chimpanzee, cougar, cow, deer, dog, dolphin, eland, elephant, elk, ermine, ferret, fox, gazelle, gerbil, giant panda, gibbon, giraffe, gnu, goat, gorilla, grizzly bear, hamster, hare, hedgehog, hippopotamus, horse, hyena, impala, jaguar, kangaroo, koala, lemur, leopard, lion, llama, mink, mole, mongoose, monkey, moose, mouse, ocelot, orang-utan, otter, panda, panther, pig, platypus, polar bear, polecat, possum, puma, rabbit, racoon, rat, reindeer, rhinoceros, seal, sea lion, sheep, skunk, squirrel, tiger, wallaby, walrus, weasel, whale, wolf, wolverine, wombat, yak, zebra. *See also* **amphibian**; **bird**; **cat**; **dog**; **fish**; **insect**; **mammal**; **marsupial**; **reptile**; **rodent**.

---

animated *adjective* lively, spirited, buoyant, vibrant, ebullient, vivacious, alive, vital, quick, brisk, vigorous, energetic, active, passionate, impassioned, vehement, ardent, fervent, glowing, radiant, excited, enthusiastic, eager.
☒ lethargic, sluggish, inert.

annex *verb* **1** *annexing part of northern France*: acquire, appropriate, seize, usurp, occupy, conquer, take over. **2** *annexed to the main report*: add, append, affix, attach, fasten, adjoin, join, connect, unite, incorporate.

annexe *noun* wing, extension, attachment, addition, supplement, expansion.

annihilate *verb* eliminate, eradicate, obliterate, erase, wipe out, liquidate (*infml*), murder, assassinate, exterminate, extinguish, raze, destroy, abolish.

announce *verb* declare, proclaim, report, state, reveal, disclose, divulge, make known, notify, intimate, promulgate, propound, publish, broadcast, advertise, publicize, blazon.
F3 suppress.

announcement *noun* declaration, proclamation, report, statement, communiqué, dispatch, bulletin, notification, intimation, revelation, disclosure, divulgence, publication, broadcast, advertisement.

announcer *noun* broadcaster, newscaster, newsreader, commentator, compère, master of ceremonies, MC, town crier, herald, messenger.

annoy *verb* irritate, rile, needle (*infml*), aggravate (*infml*), displease, anger, vex, irk, madden, exasperate, tease, provoke, ruffle, trouble, disturb, bother, pester, plague, harass, molest.
F3 please, gratify, comfort.

annoyance *noun* **1** *just a minor annoyance*: nuisance, pest, disturbance, bother, trouble, bore, irritant, bind (*infml*), pain (*infml*), headache (*infml*), tease, provocation. **2** *express one's annoyance*: irritation, aggravation (*infml*), displeasure, anger, vexation, exasperation, harassment.
F3 **2** pleasure.

annoyed *adjective* irritated, cross, displeased, angry, vexed, piqued, exasperated, provoked, harassed.
F3 pleased.

annoying *adjective* irritating, aggravating (*infml*), vexatious, irksome, troublesome, bothersome, tiresome, trying, maddening, exasperating, galling, offensive, teasing, provoking, harassing.
F3 pleasing, welcome.

anonymous *adjective* unnamed, nameless, unsigned, unacknowledged, unspecified, unidentified, unknown, incognito, faceless, impersonal, nondescript, unexceptional.
F3 named, signed, identifiable, distinctive.

answer *noun* **1** *gave them his answer*: reply, acknowledgement, response, reaction, rejoinder, retort, riposte, comeback, retaliation, rebuttal, vindication, defence, plea. **2** *the answer to the riddle*: solution, explanation.
▪ *verb* **1** *answer a letter/query*: reply, acknowledge, respond, react, retort, retaliate, refute, solve. **2** *answer a need*: fulfil, fill, meet, satisfy, match up to, correspond, correlate, conform, agree, fit, suit, serve, pass.

answerable *adjective* liable, responsible, accountable, chargeable, blameworthy, to blame.

antagonize *verb* alienate, estrange, disaffect, repel, embitter, offend, insult, provoke, annoy, irritate, anger, incense.
F3 disarm.

anthology *noun* selection, collection, compilation, compendium, digest, treasury, miscellany.

anticipate *verb* **1** *trying to anticipate any problems*: forestall, pre-empt, intercept, prevent, obviate, preclude. **2** *eagerly anticipate his arrival*: expect, foresee, predict, forecast, look for, await, look forward to, hope for, bank on, count upon.

anticlimax *noun* comedown, let-down, disappointment, fiasco, bathos (*fml*).

antics *noun* foolery, tomfoolery, silliness, buffoonery, clowning, frolics, capers, skylarking, playfulness, mischief, tricks, monkey-tricks, pranks, stunts, doings.

antidote *noun* remedy, cure, counter-agent, antitoxin, neutralizer, countermeasure, corrective.

antique *adjective* antiquarian, ancient, old, veteran, vintage, quaint, antiquated, old-fashioned, outdated, archaic, obsolete.
▪ *noun* antiquity, relic, bygone, period piece, heirloom, curio, museum piece, curiosity, rarity.

antiseptic *adjective* disinfectant, medicated, aseptic, germ-free, clean, pure, unpolluted, uncontaminated, sterile, sterilized, sanitized, sanitary, hygienic.
▪ *noun* disinfectant, germicide, bactericide, purifier, cleanser.

antisocial *adjective* asocial, unacceptable, disruptive, disorderly, rebellious, belligerent, antagonistic, hostile, unfriendly, unsociable, uncommunicative, reserved, retiring, withdrawn, alienated, unapproachable.
F3 sociable, gregarious.

anxiety *noun* worry, concern, care, distress, nervousness, apprehension, dread, foreboding, misgiving, uneasiness, restlessness, fretfulness, impatience, suspense, tension, stress.
F3 calm, composure, serenity.

anxious *adjective* worried, concerned, nervous, apprehensive, afraid, fearful, uneasy, restless, fretful, impatient, in suspense, on tenterhooks, tense, taut, distressed, disturbed, troubled, tormented, tortured.
F3 calm, composed.

apart *adverb* **1** *live apart/stand apart*: separately, independently, individually, singly, alone, on one's own, by oneself, privately, aside, to one side, away, afar, distant, aloof, excluded, isolated, cut off, separated, divorced, separate, distinct. **2** *fall/tear apart*: to pieces, to bits, into parts, in pieces, in bits.

ape *verb* copy, imitate, echo, mirror, parrot, mimic, take off, caricature, parody, mock, counterfeit, affect.

apologetic *adjective* sorry, repentant, penitent, contrite, remorseful, conscience-stricken, regretful, rueful.
F3 unrepentant, impenitent, defiant.

apology *noun* acknowledgement, confession, excuse, explanation, justification, vindication, defence, plea.
F3 defiance.

appal *verb* horrify, shock, outrage, disgust, dismay, disconcert, daunt, intimidate, unnerve, alarm, scare, frighten, terrify.
F3 reassure, encourage.

appalling *adjective* horrifying, horrific, harrowing, shocking, outrageous, atrocious, disgusting, awful, dreadful, frightful, terrible, dire, grim, hideous, ghastly, horrible, horrid, loathsome, daunting, intimidating, unnerving, alarming, frightening, terrifying.
F3 reassuring, encouraging.

apparatus *noun* machine, appliance, gadget, device, contraption, equipment, gear, tackle, outfit, tools, implements, utensils, materials, machinery, system, mechanism, means.

apparent *adjective* seeming, outward, visible, evident, noticeable, perceptible, plain, clear, distinct, marked, unmistakable, obvious, manifest, patent, open, declared.
F3 hidden, obscure.

apparently *adverb* seemingly, ostensibly, outwardly, superficially, plainly, clearly, obviously, manifestly, patently.

appeal *noun* **1** *an appeal for calm/ mercy*: request, application, petition, suit, solicitation, plea, entreaty, supplication, prayer, invocation. **2** *have great appeal*: attraction, allure, interest, fascination, enchantment, charm, attractiveness, winsomeness, beauty, charisma, magnetism.
▪ *verb* **1** *appeal for help*: ask, request, call, apply, address, petition, sue, solicit, plead, beg, beseech, implore, entreat, supplicate, pray, invoke, call upon. **2** *appeals to the young*: attract, draw, allure, lure, tempt, entice, invite, interest, engage, fascinate, charm, please.

appear *verb* **1** *appear out of nowhere*: arrive, enter, turn up, attend, materialize, develop, show (up), come into sight, come into view, loom, rise, surface, arise, occur, crop up, come to light, come out, emerge, issue, be published. **2** *appeared to be dead*: seem, look, turn out. **3** *appear in a show*: act, perform, play, take part.
F3 **1** disappear, vanish.

appearance *noun* **1** *the appearance of a new political party*: appearing, arrival, advent,

coming, rise, emergence, début, introduction. **2** *have a strange appearance*: look, expression, face, aspect, air, bearing, demeanour, manner, looks, figure, form, semblance, show, front, guise, illusion, impression, image.
F3 **1** disappearance.

appendix *noun* addition, appendage, adjunct, addendum, supplement, epilogue, codicil, postscript, rider.

appetite *noun* hunger, stomach, relish, zest, taste, propensity, inclination, liking, desire, longing, yearning, craving, eagerness, passion, zeal.
F3 distaste.

appetizing *adjective* mouthwatering, tempting, inviting, appealing, palatable, tasty, delicious, scrumptious (*infml*), succulent, piquant, savoury.
F3 disgusting, distasteful.

applaud *verb* clap, cheer, acclaim, compliment, congratulate, approve, commend, praise, laud (*fml*), eulogize (*fml*), extol (*fml*).
F3 criticize, censure.

applause *noun* ovation, clapping, cheering, cheers, acclaim, acclamation, accolade, congratulation, approval, commendation, praise.
F3 criticism, censure.

applicable *adjective* relevant, pertinent, apposite, apt, appropriate, fitting, suited, useful, suitable, fit, proper, valid, legitimate.
F3 inapplicable, inappropriate.

applicant *noun* candidate, interviewee, contestant, competitor, aspirant, suitor, petitioner, inquirer.

application *noun* **1** *an application for a driving licence*: request, appeal, petition, suit, claim, inquiry. **2** *has many applications*: relevance, pertinence (*fml*), function, purpose, use, value. **3** *he shows great application*: diligence, industry, effort, commitment, dedication, perseverance, keenness, attentiveness.

apply *verb* **1** *apply for a job*: request, ask for, requisition, put in for, appeal, petition, solicit, sue, claim, inquire. **2** *apply oneself to a task*: address, buckle down, settle down, commit, devote, dedicate, give, direct, concentrate, study, persevere. **3** *apply new methods*: use, exercise, utilize, employ, bring into play, engage, harness, ply, wield, administer, execute, implement, assign, direct, bring to bear, practise, resort to. **4** *applies to us all*: refer, relate, be relevant, pertain, fit, suit. **5** *apply ointment*: put on, spread on, lay on, cover with, paint, anoint, smear, rub.

appoint *verb* **1** *appoint a new minister*: name, nominate, elect, install, choose, select, engage, employ, take on, commission, delegate, assign, allot, designate, command, direct, charge, detail.

2 *appointing a time for the meeting*: decide, determine, arrange, settle, fix, set, establish, ordain, decree, destine.

F3 **1** reject, dismiss, discharge.

appointment *noun* **1** *an appointment with the doctor*: arrangement, engagement, date, meeting, rendezvous, interview, consultation. **2** *take up his new appointment*: job, position, situation, post, office, place. **3** *the appointment of a new archbishop*: naming, nomination, election, choosing, choice, selection, commissioning.

appraisal *noun* valuation, rating, survey, inspection, review, examination, once-over (*infml*), evaluation, assessment, estimate, estimation, judgement, reckoning, opinion, appreciation.

appreciate *verb* **1** *appreciate art*: enjoy, relish, savour, prize, treasure, value, cherish, admire, respect, regard, esteem, like, welcome, take kindly to. **2** *appreciate in value*: grow, increase, rise, mount, inflate, gain, strengthen, improve, enhance. **3** *appreciate that you have had difficulties*: understand, comprehend, perceive, realize, recognize, acknowledge, sympathize with, know.

F3 **1** despise. **2** depreciate.

apprehensive *adjective* nervous, anxious, worried, concerned, uneasy, doubtful, suspicious, mistrustful, distrustful, alarmed, afraid.

F3 assured, confident.

apprentice *noun* trainee, probationer, student, pupil, learner, novice, beginner, starter, recruit, newcomer, tiro.

F3 expert.

approach *verb* **1** *approaching the border*: advance, move towards, draw near, near, gain on, catch up, reach, meet. **2** *approached me for help*: apply to, appeal to, sound out. **3** *approached the job with a positive attitude*: begin, commence, set about, undertake, introduce, mention. **4** *approaching perfection*: resemble, be like, compare with, approximate, come close.

▪ *noun* **1** *the approach of winter*: advance, coming, advent, arrival. **2** *the approach to his estate*: access, road, avenue, way, passage, entrance, doorway, threshold. **3** *an approach from a rival company*: application, appeal, overture, proposition, proposal. **4** *take another approach*: attitude, manner, style, technique, procedure, method, means.

appropriate *adjective* applicable, relevant, pertinent, to the point, well-chosen, apt, fitting, right, suitable, fit, befitting, becoming, proper, correct, spot-on (*infml*), well-timed, timely, seasonable, opportune.

F3 inappropriate, irrelevant, unsuitable.

approval *noun* **1** *win their approval*: admiration, esteem, regard, respect, good opinion, liking, appreciation, approbation (*fml*), favour, recommendation, praise, commendation, acclaim, acclamation, honour, applause. **2** *gain approval for the scheme*: agreement, concurrence, assent, consent, permission, leave, sanction, authorization, licence, mandate, go-ahead, green light (*infml*), blessing, OK (*infml*), certification, ratification, validation, confirmation, support.
F3 **1** disapproval, condemnation.

approve *verb* **1** *approve of their methods*: admire, esteem, regard, like, appreciate, favour, recommend, praise, commend, acclaim, applaud. **2** *approve a proposal*: agree to, assent to, consent to, accede to, allow, permit, pass, sanction, authorize, mandate, bless, countenance, OK (*infml*), ratify, rubber-stamp (*infml*), validate, endorse, support, uphold, second, back, accept, adopt, confirm.
F3 **1** disapprove, condemn.

approximate *adjective* /*a*p-**rok**-sim-*a*t/ estimated, guessed, rough, inexact, loose, close, near, like, similar, relative.
F3 exact.
▪ *verb* /*a*p-**rok**-sim-eit/ approach, border on, verge on, be tantamount to, resemble.

approximately *adverb* roughly, around, about, circa, more or less, loosely, approaching, close to, nearly, just about.

apt *adjective* **1** *an apt comment*: relevant, applicable, apposite, appropriate, fitting, suitable, fit, seemly, proper, correct, accurate, spot-on (*infml*), timely, seasonable. **2** *an apt pupil*: clever, gifted, talented, skilful, expert, intelligent, quick, sharp. **3** *apt to be noisy*: liable, prone, given, disposed, likely, ready.
F3 **1** inapt. **2** stupid.

aptitude *noun* ability, capability, capacity, faculty, gift, talent, flair, facility, proficiency, cleverness, intelligence, quickness, bent, inclination, leaning, disposition, tendency.
F3 inaptitude.

arbitrary *adjective* random, chance, capricious, inconsistent, discretionary, subjective, instinctive, unreasoned, illogical, irrational, unreasonable.
F3 reasoned, rational, circumspect (*fml*).

arbitration *noun* judgement, adjudication, intervention, mediation, negotiation, settlement, decision, determination.

arch *noun* archway, bridge, span, dome, vault, concave, bend, curve, curvature, bow, arc, semicircle.
▪ *verb* bend, curve, bow, arc, vault, camber.

archaic *adjective* antiquated, old-fashioned, outmoded, old hat

(*infml*), passé, outdated, out-of-date, obsolete, old, ancient, antique, quaint, primitive.
F3 modern, recent.

archetype *noun* pattern, model, standard, form, type, prototype, original, precursor, classic, paradigm, ideal.

architect *noun* designer, planner, master builder, prime mover, originator, founder, instigator, creator, author, inventor, engineer, maker, constructor, shaper.

archives *noun* records, annals, chronicles, memorials, papers, documents, deeds, ledgers, registers, roll.

arduous *adjective* hard, difficult, tough, rigorous, severe, harsh, formidable, strenuous, tiring, taxing, fatiguing, exhausting, backbreaking, punishing, gruelling, uphill, laborious, onerous.
F3 easy.

area *noun* **1** *a run-down area of the city*: neighbourhood, environment, environs, locality, quarter, sector, department, precinct, enclave, terrain, district, region, zone. **2** *an area of desert/ ocean*: expanse, stretch, section, sector, tract, patch, breadth, width, portion. **3** *an area of study/ knowledge*: field, sphere, branch, subject.

argue *verb* **1** *arguing over every little detail*: quarrel, squabble, bicker, row, wrangle, haggle, remonstrate, join, take issue, fight, feud, fall out, disagree, dispute. **2** *argue the point*: question, debate, discuss. **3** *argued that it couldn't be so*: reason, assert, contend, hold (*fml*), maintain, claim, plead, exhibit, display, show, manifest, demonstrate, indicate, denote, prove, evidence, suggest, imply.

argument *noun* **1** *a heated argument*: quarrel, squabble, row, wrangle, controversy, debate, discussion, dispute, disagreement, clash, conflict, fight, feud. **2** *putting forward his argument*: reasoning, reason, logic, assertion, contention, claim, demonstration, defence, case, synopsis, summary, theme.

argumentative *adjective* quarrelsome, contentious, polemical, opinionated, belligerent, perverse, contrary.
F3 complaisant.

arise *verb* **1** *main point arising from the discussion*: originate, begin, start, commence, derive, stem, spring, proceed, flow, emerge, issue, appear, come to light, crop up, occur, happen, result, ensue, follow. **2** (*fml*) *arose from his bed/ chair*: rise, get up, stand up.

aristocracy *noun* upper class, gentry, nobility, peerage, ruling class, gentility, élite.
F3 common people.

aristocrat *noun* noble, patrician, nobleman, noblewoman, peer, peeress, lord, lady.
F3 commoner.

aristocratic *adjective* upper-

class, highborn, well-born, noble, patrician, blue-blooded (*infml*), titled, lordly, courtly, gentle, thoroughbred, élite.
F3 plebeian, vulgar.

arm[1] *noun* **1** *with folded arms*: limb, upper limb, appendage. **2** *the air arm of the fighting forces*: branch, projection, extension, offshoot, section, division, detachment, department.

arm[2] *verb* provide, supply, furnish, issue, equip, rig, outfit, ammunition, prime, prepare, forearm, gird, steel, brace, reinforce, strengthen, fortify, protect.

arms *noun* **1** *arms race*: weapons, weaponry, firearms, guns, artillery, instruments of war, armaments, ordnance, munitions, ammunition. **2** *the family arms*: coat-of-arms, armorial bearings, insignia, heraldic device, escutcheon, shield, crest, heraldry, blazonry.

army *noun* armed force, military, militia, land forces, soldiers, troops, legions, cohorts, multitude, throng, host, horde.

aroma *noun* smell, odour, scent, perfume, fragrance, bouquet, savour.

around *preposition* **1** *all around*: surrounding, round, encircling, encompassing, enclosing, on all sides of, on every side of. **2** *around a dozen*: approximately, roughly, about, circa, more or less.
▪ *adverb* **1** *jump around*: everywhere, all over, in all directions, on all sides, about, here and there, to and fro. **2** *stay around*: close, close by, near, nearby, at hand.

arouse *verb* rouse, startle, wake up, waken, awaken, instigate, summon up, call forth, spark, kindle, inflame, whet, sharpen, quicken, animate, excite, prompt, provoke, stimulate, galvanize, goad, spur, incite, agitate, stir up, whip up.
F3 calm, lull, quieten.

arrange *verb* **1** *arranging the cards in his hand*: order, tidy, range, array, marshal, set out, dispose, distribute, position, lay out, align, group, class, classify, sift, categorize, sort (out), file, systematize, methodize, regulate, adjust. **2** *arrange a meeting*: organize, co-ordinate, prepare, fix, plan, project, design, devise, contrive, determine, settle. **3** *arrange music*: adapt, set, score, orchestrate, instrument, harmonize.
F3 1 untidy, disorganize, muddle.

arrangement *noun* **1** *change the arrangement of the furniture*: order, array, display, disposition, layout, line-up, grouping, classification, structure, system, method, set-up, organization, preparation, planning, plan, scheme, design, schedule. **2** *come to an arrangement with someone*: agreement, settlement, contract, terms, compromise. **3** *a musical* *arrangement*: adaptation, version, interpretation, setting, score, orchestration, instrumentation, harmonization.

array *noun* arrangement, display, show, exhibition, exposition, assortment, collection, assemblage, muster, order, formation, line-up, parade.

arrest *verb* **1** *arrest a criminal*: capture, catch, seize, nick (*infml*), run in, apprehend, detain. **2** *arrest its development*: stop, stem, check, restrain, inhibit, halt, interrupt, stall, delay, slow, retard, block, obstruct, impede, hinder.

arrival *noun* appearance, entrance, advent, coming, approach, occurrence.
F3 departure.

arrive *verb* reach, get to, appear, materialize, turn up, show up (*infml*), roll up (*infml*), enter, come, occur, happen.
F3 depart, leave.

arrogant *adjective* haughty, supercilious, disdainful, scornful, contemptuous, superior, condescending, patronizing, high and mighty, lordly, overbearing, high-handed, imperious, self-important, presumptuous, assuming, insolent, proud, conceited, boastful.
F3 humble, unassuming, bashful.

art *noun* **1** *study art*: fine art, painting, sculpture, drawing, artwork, craft, artistry, draughtsmanship, craftsmanship. **2** *the art of public speaking*: skill, knack, technique, method, aptitude, facility, dexterity, finesse, ingenuity, mastery, expertise, profession, trade. **3** *with the art of a conjurer*: artfulness, cunning, craftiness, slyness, guile, deceit, trickery, astuteness, shrewdness.

Arts and crafts include:
fresco, oil painting, painting, portrait painting, watercolours; architecture, caricature, drawing, illustration, sketching; calligraphy, engraving, etching, lithography; film, graphics, photography, video; marquetry, modelling, origami, sculpture, woodcarving, woodcraft; ceramics, collage, jewellery, metalwork, pottery, stained glass; batik, crochet, embroidery, knitting, needlework, patchwork, silk-screen printing, spinning, tapestry, weaving.

---

artful *adjective* cunning, crafty, sly, foxy, wily, tricky, scheming, designing, deceitful, devious, subtle, sharp, shrewd, smart, clever, masterly, ingenious, resourceful, skilful, dexterous.
F3 artless, naive, ingenuous.

article *noun* **1** *article in a magazine*: feature, report, story, account, piece, review, essay, commentary, composition, paper. **2** *a few articles of jewellery*: item, thing, object, commodity, unit, part, constituent, piece, portion, division.

articulate *adjective* distinct, well-spoken, clear, lucid, intelligible,

comprehensible, vocal, understandable, coherent, fluent, expressive, meaningful.
inarticulate, incoherent.

artificial *adjective* **1** *an artificial smile*: false, fake, bogus, counterfeit, spurious, phoney (*infml*), pseudo, specious, sham, insincere, assumed, affected, mannered, forced, contrived, made-up, feigned, pretended, simulated. **2** *artificial flowers*: synthetic, plastic, man-made, manufactured, imitation, mock, non-natural, unnatural.
1 genuine, true. **2** real, natural.

artisan *noun* craftsman, craftswoman, artificer, journeyman, expert, skilled worker, mechanic, technician.

artist

Types of artist and artisan include:

architect, blacksmith, carpenter, cartoonist, designer, draughtsman, draughtswoman, engraver, goldsmith, graphic designer, illustrator, installation artist, painter, photographer, potter, printer, sculptor, silversmith, weaver, video artist.

---

artistic *adjective* aesthetic, ornamental, decorative, beautiful, exquisite, elegant, stylish, graceful, harmonious, sensitive, tasteful, refined, cultured, cultivated, skilled, talented, creative, imaginative.
inelegant, tasteless.

artistry *noun* craftsmanship, workmanship, skill, craft, talent, flair, brilliance, genius, finesse, style, mastery, expertise, proficiency, accomplishment, deftness, touch, sensitivity, creativity.
ineptitude.

as *conjunction, preposition* **1** *he waved as the train drew out*: while, when. **2** *as her mother was before her*: such as, for example, for instance, like, in the manner of. **3** *as he was working late, I asked him to lock up*: because, since, seeing that, considering that, inasmuch as, being.

ascend *verb* rise, take off, lift off, go up, move up, slope upwards, climb, scale, mount, tower, float up, fly up, soar.
descend, go down.

ascent *noun* **1** *their ascent of Everest*: ascending, ascension, climb, climbing, scaling, escalation, rise, rising, mounting. **2** *a steep ascent*: slope, gradient, incline, ramp, hill, elevation.
1 descent.

ascribe *verb* attribute, credit, accredit (*fml*), put down, assign, impute (*fml*), charge, chalk up to (*infml*).

ashamed *adjective* sorry, apologetic, remorseful, contrite, guilty, conscience-stricken, sheepish, embarrassed, blushing, red-faced, mortified, humiliated, abashed, humbled, crestfallen, distressed, confused, reluctant,

hesitant, shy, self-conscious, bashful, modest, prudish.
F3 shameless, unashamed, proud, defiant.

aside *adverb* apart, on one side, in reserve, away, out of the way, separately, in isolation, alone, privately, secretly.
▪ *noun* digression, parenthesis, departure, soliloquy, stage whisper, whisper.

ask *verb* **1** *ask for help/advice*: request, appeal, petition, sue, plead, beg, entreat, implore, clamour, beseech, pray, supplicate, crave, demand, order, bid, require, seek, solicit, invite, summon. **2** *ask awkward questions*: inquire, query, question, interrogate, quiz, press. **3** *ask him out/round*: invite, have round, entertain.

asleep *adjective* sleeping, napping, snoozing, fast asleep, sound asleep, dozing, slumbering, dormant (*fml*), resting, inactive, inert, unconscious, numb.

aspect *noun* **1** *view the problem from a different aspect/an aspect of his life*: angle, direction, detail, side, facet, feature, dimension, standpoint, point of view, view. **2** *take on a more promising aspect*: appearance, look, air, manner, bearing, demeanour, mien (*fml*), face, expression, countenance. **3** *a house with a northern aspect*: direction, outlook, view, situation, position, prospect.

aspire *verb* aim, intend, purpose, seek, pursue, hope, dream, wish, desire, yearn, long, crave, hanker.

aspiring *adjective* would-be, aspirant, striving, endeavouring, ambitious, enterprising, keen, eager, hopeful, optimistic, wishful, longing.

assault *noun* **1** *an assault on the nerves*: attack, offensive, onslaught, blitz, strike, raid, invasion, incursion, storm, storming, charge. **2** *charged with assault*: battery, grievous bodily harm, GBH (*infml*), mugging (*infml*), rape, abuse.
▪ *verb* attack, charge, invade, strike, hit, assail, set upon, fall on, beat up (*infml*), mug (*infml*), rape, molest, abuse.

assemble *verb* **1** *assemble in the playground*: gather, congregate, muster, rally, convene, meet, join up, flock, group, collect, accumulate, amass, bring together, round up, marshal, mobilize. **2** *assemble a model aeroplane*: construct, build, put together, piece together, compose, make, fabricate, manufacture.
F3 **1** scatter, disperse. **2** dismantle.

assembly *noun* **1** *an assembly of bishops*: gathering, rally, meeting, convention, conference, convocation (*fml*), congress, council, group, body, company, congregation, flock, crowd, multitude, throng, collection, assemblage. **2** *assembly of the components*: construction, building, fabrication, manufacture.

assert *verb* affirm, attest (*fml*), swear, testify to, allege, claim, contend, maintain, insist, stress, protest, defend, vindicate, uphold, promote, declare, profess, state, pronounce, lay down, advance.
F3 deny, refute.

assertive *adjective* bold, confident, self-assured, forward, pushy (*infml*), insistent, emphatic, forceful, firm, decided, strong-willed, dogmatic, opinionated, presumptuous, assuming, overbearing, domineering, aggressive.
F3 timid, diffident.

assess *verb* gauge, estimate, evaluate, appraise, review, judge, consider, weigh, size up, compute, determine, fix, value, rate, tax, levy, impose, demand.

assessment *noun* gauging, estimation, estimate, evaluation, appraisal, review, judgement, opinion, consideration, calculation, determination, valuation, rating, taxation.

asset *noun* strength, resource, virtue, plus (*infml*), benefit, advantage, blessing, boon, help, aid.
F3 liability.

assets *noun* estate, property, possessions, goods, holdings, securities, money, wealth, capital, funds, reserves, resources, means.

assign *verb* **1** *assigned them various tasks*: allocate, apportion, grant, give, dispense, distribute, allot, consign, delegate, name, nominate, designate, appoint, choose, select, determine, set, fix, specify, stipulate. **2** *to what do you assign your popularity?*: attribute, accredit (*fml*), ascribe, put down.

assignment *noun* commission, errand, task, project, job, position, post, duty, responsibility, charge, appointment, delegation, designation, nomination, selection, allocation, consignment, grant, distribution.

assist *verb* help, aid, abet, rally round, co-operate, collaborate, back, second, support, reinforce, sustain, relieve, benefit, serve, enable, facilitate, expedite, boost, further, advance.
F3 hinder, thwart.

assistance *noun* help, aid, succour, co-operation, collaboration, backing, support, reinforcement, relief, benefit, service, boost, furtherance.
F3 hindrance, resistance.

assistant *noun* helper, helpmate, aide, right-hand man, auxiliary, ancillary, subordinate, backer, second, supporter, accomplice, accessory, abettor, collaborator, colleague, partner, ally, confederate, associate.

associate *verb* **1** *don't associate the one with the other*: connect, link, couple, correlate, identify, put together. **2** *associate with bad company*: socialize, mingle, mix, fraternize, consort, hang around (*infml*).

association *noun* **1** *an association of women's groups*: organization, corporation, company, partnership, league, alliance, coalition, confederation, confederacy, federation, affiliation, consortium, cartel, union, syndicate, society, club, fraternity, fellowship, clique, group, band. **2** *a close association*: bond, tie, connection, correlation, relation, relationship, involvement, intimacy, friendship, companionship, familiarity.

assorted *adjective* miscellaneous, mixed, varied, different, differing, heterogeneous (*fml*), diverse, sundry, various, several, manifold (*fml*).

assortment *noun* miscellany, medley, pot-pourri, jumble, mixture, variety, diversity, collection, selection, choice, arrangement, grouping.

assume *verb* **1** *assumed that it was correct*: presume, surmise, accept, take for granted, expect, understand, deduce, infer, guess, postulate, suppose, think, believe, imagine, fancy. **2** *assume a disguise*: affect, take on, feign, counterfeit, simulate, put on, pretend. **3** *assume command*: undertake, adopt, embrace, seize, commandeer, appropriate, usurp, take over.

assumed *adjective* false, bogus, counterfeit, fake, phoney (*infml*), sham, affected, feigned, simulated, pretended, made-up, fictitious, hypothetical.
F3 true, real, actual.

assumption *noun* presumption, surmise, inference, supposition, guess, conjecture, theory, hypothesis, premise, postulate, idea, notion, belief, fancy.

assure *verb* affirm, guarantee, warrant, pledge, promise, vow, swear, tell, convince, persuade, encourage, hearten, reassure, soothe, comfort, boost, strengthen, secure, ensure, confirm.

assured *adjective* **1** *his future was assured*: sure, certain, indisputable, irrefutable, confirmed, positive, definite, settled, fixed, guaranteed, secure. **2** *an assured young woman*: self-assured, confident, self-confident, self-possessed, bold, audacious, assertive.
F3 **1** uncertain. **2** shy.

astonish *verb* surprise, startle, amaze, astound, stun, stupefy, daze, stagger, floor (*infml*), dumbfound, flabbergast (*infml*), shock, confound, bewilder.

astounding *adjective* surprising, startling, amazing, astonishing, stunning, breathtaking, stupefying, overwhelming, staggering, shocking, bewildering.

astray *adverb* adrift, off course, lost, amiss, wrong, off the rails (*infml*), awry, off the mark.

astute *adjective* shrewd, prudent, sagacious (*fml*), wise, canny, knowing, intelligent, sharp,

penetrating, keen, perceptive, perspicacious (*fml*), discerning, subtle, clever, crafty, cunning, sly, wily.
stupid, slow.

asylum *noun* haven, sanctuary, refuge, shelter, retreat, safety.

asymmetrical *adjective* unsymmetrical, unbalanced, uneven, crooked, awry, unequal, disproportionate, irregular.
symmetrical.

atheist *noun* unbeliever, non-believer, disbeliever, sceptic, infidel, pagan, heathen, free-thinker.

athletic *adjective* fit, energetic, vigorous, active, sporty, muscular, sinewy, brawny, strapping, robust, sturdy, strong, powerful, well-knit, well-proportioned, wiry.
puny.

atmosphere *noun* **1** *pollution in the atmosphere*: air, sky, aerospace, heavens, ether. **2** *a hotel with a pleasant atmosphere*: ambience, environment, surroundings, aura, feel, feeling, mood, spirit, tone, tenor, character, quality, flavour.

atom *noun* molecule, particle, bit (*infml*), morsel, crumb, grain, spot, speck, mite, shred, scrap, hint, trace, scintilla, jot, iota, whit.

atrocious *adjective* shocking, appalling, abominable, dreadful, terrible, horrible, hideous, ghastly, heinous (*fml*), grievous, savage, vicious, monstrous, fiendish, ruthless.
admirable, fine.

attach *verb* **1** *attach a label*: affix, stick, adhere, fasten, fix, secure, tie, bind, weld, join, unite, connect, link, couple, add, annex. **2** *attach too much significance to*: ascribe, attribute, impute (*fml*), assign, put, place, associate, relate to, belong.
1 detach, unfasten.

attachment *noun* **1** *an attachment for the drill/to the will*: accessory, fitting, fixture, extension, appendage, extra, supplement, addition, adjunct, codicil. **2** *form an attachment*: fondness, affection, tenderness, love, liking, partiality, loyalty, devotion, friendship, affinity, attraction, bond, tie, link.

attack *noun* **1** *a military/verbal attack*: offensive, blitz, bombardment, invasion, incursion, foray, raid, strike, charge, rush, onslaught, assault, battery, aggression, criticism, censure, abuse. **2** *have an attack*: seizure, fit, convulsion, paroxysm, spasm, stroke.
▪ *verb* **1** *attacked by Vikings/a gang*: invade, raid, strike, storm, charge, assail, assault, set about, set upon, fall on, lay into, do over (*slang*). **2** *attacked in the press*: criticize, censure, blame, denounce, revile, malign, abuse.
1 defend, protect.

attacker *noun* assailant, mugger (*infml*), aggressor, invader, raider, critic, detractor, reviler, abuser, persecutor.
defender, supporter.

attempt *noun* try, endeavour, shot (*infml*), go (*infml*), effort, struggle, bid, undertaking, venture, trial, experiment.
▪ *verb* try, endeavour, aspire, seek, strive, undertake, tackle, venture, experiment.

attend *verb* **1** *attend school/a meeting*: be present, go to, frequent, visit. **2** *wasn't attending to what was being said*: pay attention, listen, hear, heed, mind, mark, note, notice, observe. **3** *attended by her lady-in-waiting*: escort, chaperon(e), accompany, usher, follow, guard, look after, take care of, care for, nurse, tend, minister to, help, serve, wait on.

attendant *noun* aide, helper, assistant, auxiliary, steward, waiter, servant, page, retainer, guide, marshal, usher, escort, companion, follower, guard, custodian.

attention *noun* alertness, vigilance, concentration, heed, notice, observation, regard, mindfulness, awareness, recognition, thought, contemplation, consideration, concern, care, treatment, service.
inattention, disregard, carelessness.

attentive *adjective* **1** *an attentive audience*: alert, awake, vigilant, watchful, observant, concentrating, heedful, mindful, careful, conscientious. **2** *an attentive husband*: considerate, thoughtful, kind, obliging, accommodating, polite, courteous, devoted.
1 inattentive, heedless. **2** inconsiderate.

attitude *noun* feeling, disposition, mood, aspect, manner, bearing, pose, posture, stance, position, point of view, opinion, view, outlook, perspective, approach.

attract *verb* pull, draw, lure, allure, entice, seduce, tempt, invite, induce, incline, appeal to, interest, engage, fascinate, enchant, charm, bewitch, captivate, excite.
repel, disgust.

attraction *noun* pull, draw, magnetism, lure, allure, bait, enticement, inducement, seduction, temptation, invitation, appeal, interest, fascination, enchantment, charm, captivation.
repulsion.

attractive *adjective* pretty, fair, fetching, good-looking, handsome, beautiful, gorgeous, stunning (*infml*), glamorous, lovely, pleasant, pleasing, agreeable, appealing, winning, enticing, seductive, tempting, inviting, interesting, engaging, fascinating, charming, captivating, magnetic.
unattractive, repellent.

attribute *verb* /*a*-**trib**-yoot/ ascribe, accredit (*fml*), credit, impute (*fml*), assign, put down, blame, charge, refer, apply.
▪ *noun* /**a**-trib-yoot/ property,

quality, virtue, point, aspect, facet, feature, trait, characteristic, idiosyncrasy, peculiarity, quirk, note, mark, sign, symbol.

audible *adjective* clear, distinct, recognizable, perceptible, discernible, detectable, appreciable.
F inaudible, silent, unclear.

audience *noun* spectators, onlookers, house, auditorium, listeners, viewers, crowd, turnout, gathering, assembly, congregation, fans, devotees, regulars, following, public.

auspicious *adjective* favourable, propitious, encouraging, cheerful, bright, rosy, promising, hopeful, optimistic, fortunate, lucky, opportune, happy, prosperous.
F inauspicious, ominous.

austere *adjective* **1** *an austere building*: stark, bleak, plain, simple, unadorned, grim, forbidding. **2** *life at the monastery was austere*: severe, stern, strict, cold, formal, rigid, rigorous, exacting, hard, harsh, spartan, grave, serious, solemn, sober, abstemious, self-denying, restrained, economical, frugal, ascetic, self-disciplined, puritanical, chaste.
F **1** ornate, elaborate.

authentic *adjective* genuine, true, real, actual, certain, bona fide, legitimate, honest, valid, original, pure, factual, accurate, true-to-life, faithful, reliable, trustworthy.
F false, fake, counterfeit, spurious.

authenticate *verb* guarantee, warrant, vouch for, attest (*fml*), authorize, accredit (*fml*), validate, certify, endorse, confirm, verify, corroborate.

author *noun* **1** *a famous author*: writer, novelist, dramatist, playwright, composer, pen, penman, penwoman. **2** *the principal author of the reforms*: creator, founder, originator, initiator, parent, prime mover, mover, inventor, designer, architect, planner, maker, producer.

authoritative *adjective* scholarly, learned, official, authorized, legitimate, valid, approved, sanctioned, accepted, definitive, decisive, authentic, factual, true, truthful, accurate, faithful, convincing, sound, reliable, dependable, trustworthy.
F unofficial, unreliable.

authority *noun* **1** *assert one's authority over others*: sovereignty, supremacy, rule, sway, control, dominion, influence, power, force, government, administration, officialdom. **2** *have no legal authority to enter the premises*: authorization, permission, sanction, permit, warrant, licence, credentials, right, prerogative, mandate. **3** *an authority on antiques*: expert, pundit, connoisseur, specialist, professional, master, scholar.

authorize *verb* legalize, validate, ratify, confirm, license, entitle, accredit (*fml*), empower, enable, commission, warrant, permit, allow, consent to, sanction, approve, give the go-ahead.

automatic *adjective* **1** *an automatic washing machine*: automated, self-activating, mechanical, mechanized, programmed, self-regulating, computerized, push-button, robotic, self-propelling, unmanned. **2** *an automatic response*: spontaneous, reflex, involuntary, unwilled, unconscious, unthinking, natural, instinctive, routine, necessary, certain, inevitable, unavoidable, inescapable.

available *adjective* free, vacant, to hand, within reach, at hand, accessible, handy, convenient, on hand, ready, on tap, obtainable.
⇌ unavailable.

avenge *verb* take revenge for, take vengeance for, punish, requite, repay, retaliate.

average *adjective* mean, medial, median, middle, intermediate, medium, moderate, satisfactory, fair, mediocre, middling, indifferent, so-so (*infml*), passable, tolerable, undistinguished, run-of-the-mill, ordinary, everyday, common, usual, normal, regular, standard, typical, unexceptional.
⇌ extreme, exceptional, remarkable.
▪ *noun* mean, mid-point, norm, standard, rule, par, medium.
⇌ extreme, exception.
▪ *verb* find the mean, equalize, standardize, normalize.

aversion *noun* dislike, hate, hatred, loathing, abhorrence (*fml*), abomination, horror, phobia, reluctance, unwillingness, distaste, disgust, revulsion, hostility, opposition, antagonism.
⇌ liking, sympathy, desire.

avert *verb* turn away, deflect, turn aside, parry, fend off, ward off, stave off, forestall, frustrate, prevent, obviate, avoid, evade.

avid *adjective* eager, earnest, keen, enthusiastic, fanatical, devoted, dedicated, zealous, ardent, fervent, intense, passionate, insatiable, ravenous, hungry, thirsty, greedy, grasping, covetous.
⇌ indifferent.

avoid *verb* evade, elude, sidestep, dodge, shirk, duck (*infml*), escape, get out of, bypass, circumvent, balk, prevent, avert, shun, abstain from, refrain from, steer clear of.

awake *adjective* wakeful, wide-awake, aroused, alert, vigilant, watchful, observant, attentive, conscious, aware, sensitive, alive.

award *verb* give, present, distribute, dispense, bestow, confer, accord, endow, gift, grant, allot, apportion, assign, allow, determine.
▪ *noun* prize, trophy, decoration, medal, presentation,

dispensation, bestowal, conferral, endowment, gift, grant, allotment, allowance, adjudication, judgement, decision, order.

aware *adjective* conscious, alive to, sensitive, appreciative, sentient, familiar, conversant (*fml*), acquainted, informed, enlightened, au courant, knowing, knowledgeable, cognizant, mindful, heedful, attentive, observant, sharp, alert, on the ball (*infml*), shrewd, sensible.
unaware, oblivious, insensitive.

awe *noun* wonder, veneration, reverence, respect, admiration, amazement, astonishment, fear, terror, dread, apprehension.
contempt.

awful *adjective* terrible, dreadful, fearful, frightful, ghastly, unpleasant, nasty, horrible, hideous, ugly, gruesome, dire, abysmal, atrocious, horrific, shocking, appalling, alarming, spine-chilling.
wonderful, excellent.

awkward *adjective* **1** *too awkward to be a good dancer*: clumsy, unco-ordinated, ungainly, gauche, inept, inexpert, unskilful, bungling, ham-fisted, graceless, ungraceful, inelegant. **2** *feeling awkward in their presence*: uncomfortable, ill at ease, embarrassed. **3** *he's just being awkward*: obstinate, stubborn, unco-operative, irritable, touchy, prickly, rude, unpleasant. **4** *an awkward problem/size*: cumbersome, unwieldy, inconvenient, difficult, fiddly, delicate, troublesome, perplexing.
1 graceful, elegant.
2 comfortable, relaxed.
3 amenable, pleasant.
4 convenient, handy.

axe *noun* hatchet, chopper, cleaver, tomahawk, battle-axe.
▪ *verb* cancel, terminate, discontinue, remove, withdraw, eliminate, get rid of, throw out, dismiss, discharge, sack (*infml*), fire (*infml*).

B

babble *verb* chatter, gabble, jabber, cackle, mutter, mumble, murmur.

baby *noun* infant, babe (*fml*), new-born, child, toddler.

babyish *adjective* childish, juvenile, puerile (*fml*), infantile, silly, foolish, soft (*infml*), baby, young, immature, naive.
mature, precocious.

back *noun* rear, stern, end, tail, tail end, hind part, hindquarters, posterior, reverse.
F3 front, face.
▪ *adjective* rear, end, tail, posterior, hind, hindmost, reverse.
F3 front.
▪ *verb* **1** *back into the garage/out of the room*: go backwards, reverse, recede, regress, backtrack, retreat, retire, withdraw, back away, recoil. **2** *back the Labour candidate/a new business venture*: support, sustain, assist, side with, champion, advocate, encourage, promote, boost, favour, sanction, countenance, endorse, second, sponsor, finance, subsidize, underwrite.
F3 **1** advance, approach. **2** oppose.

backbone *noun* **1** *a chair that supports the backbone*: spine, spinal column, vertebrae, vertebral column. **2** *the backbone of the company*: mainstay, support, core, foundation. **3** *a coward with no backbone*: courage, mettle, pluck, nerve, grit, determination, resolve, tenacity, steadfastness, toughness, stamina, strength, character, power.
F3 **3** spinelessness, weakness.

backfire *verb* recoil, rebound, ricochet, boomerang, miscarry, fail, flop.

background *noun* **1** *the background of the story*: setting, surroundings, environment, context, circumstances. **2** *with a science background/from a different background*: record, history, credentials, experience, grounding, preparation, education, upbringing, breeding, culture, tradition.

backing *noun* support, accompaniment, aid, assistance, helpers, championing, advocacy, encouragement, moral support, favour, sanction, promotion, endorsement, seconding, patronage, sponsorship, finance, funds, grant, subsidy.

backlash *noun* reaction, response, repercussion, reprisal, retaliation, recoil, backfire.

backward *adjective* **1** *a backward step*: retrograde, retrogressive, regressive. **2** *a backward child/region*: slow, dull, immature, retarded, subnormal, stupid, behind, behindhand, underdeveloped.
F3 **1** forward. **2** precocious.

bacteria *noun* germs, bugs (*infml*), microbes, micro-organisms, bacilli.

bad *adjective* **1** *a bad smell/habit/experience/accident*: unpleasant, disagreeable, nasty, undesirable, unfortunate, distressing, adverse, detrimental, harmful, damaging, injurious, serious, grave, severe, harsh. **2** *a bad person*: evil, wicked, sinful, criminal, corrupt, immoral, vile. **3** *bad workmanship/service/eyesight*: poor, inferior, substandard, imperfect, faulty, defective, deficient, unsatisfactory, useless. **4** *this meat/milk/butter is bad*: rotten, mouldy, decayed, spoilt, putrid, rancid, sour, off, tainted, contaminated. **5** *a bad child*: naughty, mischievous, ill-behaved, disobedient. **6** *a bad time to call*: inconvenient, unfortunate, unsuitable, inappropriate.

F3 1 good, pleasant, mild, slight. **2** good, virtuous. **3** excellent, skilled. **4** fresh. **5** well-behaved. **6** good.

badge *noun* identification, emblem, device, insignia, sign, mark, token, stamp, brand, trademark, logo.

badly *adverb* **1** *badly injured/damaged*: greatly, extremely, exceedingly, intensely, deeply, acutely, bitterly, painfully, seriously, desperately, severely, critically, crucially. **2** *behave badly*: wickedly, criminally, immorally, shamefully, unfairly. **3** *go/spell/drive badly*: wrong, wrongly, incorrectly, improperly, defectively, faultily, imperfectly, inadequately, unsatisfactorily, poorly, incompetently, negligently, carelessly. **4** *turn out badly*: unfavourably, adversely, unfortunately, unsuccessfully.

F3 1 slightly. **2** well, virtuously. **3** well, correctly, competently. **4** successfully.

bad-tempered *adjective* irritable, cross, crotchety, crabbed, crabby, snappy, grumpy, querulous (*fml*), petulant, cantankerous, fractious, stroppy (*infml*).

F3 good-tempered, genial, agreeable.

baffle *verb* puzzle, perplex, mystify, bemuse, bewilder, confuse, confound, bamboozle (*infml*), flummox (*infml*), daze, upset, disconcert, foil, thwart, frustrate, hinder, check, defeat, stump (*infml*).

F3 enlighten, help.

bag *noun* container, sack, case, suitcase, grip, carrier, hold-all, handbag, shoulder-bag, satchel, rucksack, haversack, backpack.
▪ *verb* **1** (*infml*) *bag the front seat*: obtain, acquire, get, gain, corner, take, grab, appropriate, commandeer, reserve. **2** *bag a couple of rabbits*: catch, capture, trap, land, kill, shoot.

baggage *noun* luggage, suitcases, bags, belongings, things, equipment, gear (*infml*), paraphernalia, impedimenta (*fml*).

baggy *adjective* loose, slack, roomy, ill-fitting, billowing, bulging, floppy, sagging, droopy.

F3 tight, firm.

bail *noun* security, surety, pledge, bond, guarantee, warranty.

bait *noun* lure, incentive, inducement, bribe, temptation, enticement, allurement, attraction.

F3 disincentive.

balance *verb* **1** *balance a ball on its nose*: steady, poise, stabilize. **2** *balance the two sides of the scales/ledger*: level, square, equalize,

equate, match, counterbalance, adjust. **3** *balanced the lower mark with the higher one*: offset, counteract, neutralize. **4** *balancing the risks and benefits*: compare, consider, weigh (up), estimate.
F3 1 unbalance, overbalance.
▪ *noun* equilibrium, steadiness, stability, evenness, symmetry, equality, parity, equity, equivalence, correspondence.
F3 imbalance, instability.

balcony *noun* terrace, veranda, gallery, upper circle, gods.

bald *adjective* **1** *a completely bald head/a bald patch*: bald-headed, hairless, smooth, uncovered. **2** *bald of all vegetation*: bare, naked, bleak, stark, barren, treeless. **3** *a bald statement*: forthright, direct, straight, plain, simple, unadorned, outright, downright, straightforward.
F3 1 hairy, hirsute. **3** adorned.

ball *noun* sphere, globe, orb, globule, drop, conglomeration, pellet, pill, shot, bullet, slug (*infml*).

ballot *noun* poll, polling, vote, voting, election, referendum, plebiscite.

ban *verb* forbid, prohibit, disallow, proscribe, bar, exclude, ostracize, outlaw, banish, suppress, restrict.
F3 allow, permit, authorize.

banal *adjective* trite, commonplace, ordinary, everyday, humdrum, boring, unimaginative, hackneyed, clichéd, stock, stereotyped, corny (*infml*), stale, threadbare, tired, empty.
F3 original, fresh, imaginative.

band[1] *noun* strip, belt, ribbon, tape, bandage, binding, tie, ligature, bond, strap, cord, chain.

band[2] *noun* **1** *a band of disciples*: troop, gang, crew, group, herd, flock, party, body, association, company, society, club, clique. **2** *a rock/jazz/dance band*: group, orchestra, ensemble.

bandit *noun* robber, thief, brigand, marauder, outlaw, highwayman, pirate, buccaneer, hijacker, cowboy, gunman, desperado, gangster.

bang *noun* **1** *a bang on the head*: blow, hit, knock, bump, crash, collision, smack, punch, thump, wallop (*infml*), stroke, whack (*infml*). **2** *a loud bang*: explosion, detonation, pop, boom, clap, peal, clang, clash, thud, thump, slam, noise, report, shot.
▪ *verb* **1** *bang one's head/a nail in*: strike, hit, bash, knock, bump, rap, drum, hammer, pound, thump. **2** *fireworks banging*: explode, burst, detonate, boom, echo, resound, crash, slam, clatter, clang, peal, thunder.

banish *verb* expel, eject, evict, deport, transport, exile, outlaw, ban, bar, debar, exclude, shut out, ostracize, excommunicate, dismiss, oust, dislodge, remove, get rid of, discard, dispel, eliminate, eradicate.
F3 recall, welcome.

bank[1] *noun* accumulation, fund, pool, reservoir, depository, repository, treasury, savings, reserve, store, stock, stockpile, hoard, cache.

bank[2] *noun* heap, pile, mass, edge, mound, earthwork, ridge, rampart, slope, embankment, side, tilt, shore.

bankrupt *adjective* insolvent, in liquidation, ruined, failed, beggared, destitute, impoverished, broke (*infml*), gone bust (*infml*).
F3 solvent, wealthy.

banter *noun* joking, jesting, pleasantry, badinage, repartee, word play, chaff, chaffing, kidding (*infml*), ribbing, derision, mockery, ridicule.

baptize *verb* christen, name, call, term, style, title, introduce, initiate, enrol, recruit, immerse, sprinkle, purify, cleanse.

bar *noun* **1** *a resort with good bars and restaurants*: public house, pub (*infml*), inn, tavern, saloon, lounge, counter. **2** *a gold/chocolate bar*: slab, block, lump, chunk, wedge, ingot, nugget. **3** *an iron bar/a five-bar gate*: rod, stick, shaft, pole, stake, stanchion, batten, cross-piece, rail, railing, paling, barricade. **4** *a bar to progress*: obstacle, impediment, hindrance, obstruction, barrier, stop, check, deterrent.
▪ *verb* **1** *barred from entering*: exclude, debar, ban, forbid, prohibit, prevent, preclude, hinder, obstruct, restrain. **2** *bar the door*: barricade, lock, bolt, latch, fasten, secure.

barbaric *adjective* barbarous, primitive, wild, savage, fierce, ferocious, cruel, inhuman, brutal, brutish, uncivilized, uncouth, vulgar, coarse, crude, rude.
F3 humane, civilized, gracious.

bare *adjective* **1** *bare legs/a bare hillside*: naked, nude, unclothed, undressed, stripped, denuded, uncovered, exposed. **2** *the bare truth/essentials*: plain, simple, unadorned, unfurnished, bald, stark, basic, essential.
F3 **1** clothed. **2** decorated, detailed.

barely *adverb* hardly, scarcely, only just, just, almost.

bargain *noun* **1** *make a bargain*: deal, transaction, contract, treaty, pact, pledge, promise, agreement, understanding, arrangement, negotiation. **2** *the best place to find bargains*: discount, reduction, snip, giveaway, special offer.
▪ *verb* negotiate, haggle, deal, trade, traffic, barter, buy, sell, transact, contract, covenant, promise, agree.

barge *verb* bump, hit, collide, impinge, shove, elbow, push (in), muscle in, butt in, interrupt, gatecrash, intrude, interfere.

bark *noun, verb* yap, woof, yelp, snap, snarl, growl, bay, howl.

barrage *noun* bombardment, shelling, gunfire, cannonade, broadside, volley, salvo, burst, assault, attack, onset, onslaught, deluge, torrent, stream, storm, hail, rain, shower, mass, profusion.

barren *adjective* arid, dry, desert, desolate, empty, flat, treeless, waste, infertile, unproductive, useless.
F3 fertile, productive, useful.

barricade *noun* blockade, obstruction, barrier, fence, stockade, bulwark, rampart, protection.
▪ *verb* block, obstruct, bar, fortify, defend, protect.

barrier *noun* **1** *build a barrier across the road*: wall, fence, railing, barricade, blockade, boom, rampart, fortification, ditch, frontier, boundary, bar, check. **2** *a barrier to success*: obstacle, hurdle, stumbling block, impediment, obstruction, hindrance, handicap, limitation, restriction, drawback, difficulty.

barter *verb* exchange, swap, trade, traffic, deal, negotiate, bargain, haggle.

base *noun* **1** *the base of the statue*: bottom, foot, pedestal, plinth, stand, rest, support, foundation, bed, groundwork. **2** *the element that forms the base*: basis, fundamental, essential, principle, key, heart, core, essence, root, origin, source. **3** *a naval base/the base for operations*: headquarters, centre, post, station, camp, settlement, home, starting point.
▪ *verb* **1** *base oneself somewhere*: establish, locate, station. **2** *a theory based on observation*: found, ground, build, construct, derive, depend, hinge.

basic *adjective* fundamental, elementary, primary, root, underlying, key, central, inherent, intrinsic, essential, indispensable, vital, necessary, important.
F3 inessential, minor, peripheral.

basically *adverb* fundamentally, at bottom, at heart, inherently, intrinsically, essentially, principally, primarily.

basin *noun* bowl, dish, sink, crater, cavity, hollow, depression, dip.

basis *noun* base, bottom, footing, support, foundation, ground, groundwork, fundamental, premise, principle, essential, heart, core, thrust.

bask *verb* sunbathe, lie, lounge, relax, laze, wallow, revel, delight in, enjoy, relish, savour.

basket *noun* hamper, creel, pannier, punnet, trug, bassinet.

bass *adjective* /beis/ deep, low, low-toned, resonant.

batch *noun* lot, consignment, parcel, pack, bunch, set, assortment, collection, assemblage, group, contingent, amount, quantity.

bath *noun* wash, scrub, soak (*infml*), shower, douche, tub, sauna, Jacuzzi®.
▪ *verb* bathe, wash, clean, soak, shower.

bathe *verb* **1** *bathe the wound*: wash, clean, cleanse, rinse, immerse, soak. **2** *bathe in the Mediterranean*: swim, go swimming, paddle.

batter *verb* beat, pound, pummel, buffet, smash, dash, pelt, lash, thrash, wallop (*infml*), abuse, maltreat, ill-treat, manhandle, maul, assault, hurt, injure, bruise, disfigure, mangle, distress, crush, demolish, destroy, ruin, shatter.

battered *adjective* beaten, abused, ill-treated, injured, bruised, weather-beaten, dilapidated, tumbledown, ramshackle, crumbling, damaged, crushed.

battle *noun* war, warfare, hostilities, action, conflict, strife, combat, fight, engagement, encounter, attack, fray, skirmish, clash, struggle, contest, campaign, crusade, row, disagreement, dispute, debate, controversy.
▪ *verb* fight, combat, war, feud, contend, struggle, strive, campaign, crusade, agitate, clamour, contest, argue, dispute.

bay *noun* gulf, bight, inlet, sound, cove, estuary.

be *verb* **1** *to be or not to be?*: exist, breathe, live, be alive. **2** *will be for centuries to come*: stay, remain, abide (*fml*), last, endure, persist, continue, survive, stand, prevail. **3** *how can that be?*: happen, occur, arise, come about, take place, come to pass, befall, develop.

beach *noun* sand, sands, shingle, shore, strand, seashore, seaside, water's edge, coast, seaboard.

bead *noun* drop, droplet, drip, globule, glob (*infml*), blob, dot, bubble, pearl, jewel, pellet.

beam *noun* **1** *a beam of light*: ray, shaft, gleam, glint, glimmer, glow. **2** *oak/steel beam*: plank, board, timber, rafter, joist, girder, spar, boom, bar, support.
▪ *verb* **1** *sunlight beaming down/ sun beaming all day*: emit, radiate, shine, glare, glitter, glow, glimmer. **2** *pictures beamed around the world*: broadcast, transmit. **3** *beam with pleasure*: smile, grin.

bear *verb* **1** *bear pain/ inconvenience*: tolerate, stand, put up with, cope with, endure, abide, suffer, take (*infml*). **2** *bear something's weight*: hold, carry, support, take. **3** *bear a grudge*: sustain, maintain, harbour, cherish. **4** *bear a child/fruit*: give birth to, breed, propagate, beget (*fml*), engender, produce, generate, develop, yield, bring forth. **5** *bearing the names of the fallen*: display, exhibit, show, have. **6** *bearing the coffin*: carry, convey, transport, transfer, move, take, bring.

bearable *adjective* tolerable, endurable, sufferable, supportable, sustainable, acceptable, manageable.
F3 unbearable, intolerable.

bearer *noun* carrier, conveyor, porter, courier, messenger, runner, holder, possessor.

bearing *noun* **1** *have no bearing on the matter*: relevance, significance, connection, relation, reference. **2** *of military bearing*: demeanour, manner, mien (*fml*), air, aspect, attitude, behaviour, comportment (*fml*), poise, deportment, carriage, posture.

beast *noun* animal, creature, brute, monster, savage, barbarian, pig, swine, devil, fiend.

beat *noun* **1** *feel the rapid beat of its heart*: pulsation, pulse, stroke, throb, thump, palpitation, flutter. **2** *two beats to the bar*: rhythm, time, tempo, metre, measure, rhyme, stress, accent. **3** *a policeman on his beat*: round, rounds, territory, circuit, course, journey, way, path, route.

▪ *verb* **1** *beat the child/beaten by his father*: whip, flog, lash, tan (*infml*), cane, strap, thrash, lay into, hit, punch, strike, swipe, knock, bang, wham, bash, pound, hammer (*infml*), batter, buffet, pelt, bruise. **2** *beating faintly*: pulsate, pulse, throb, thump, race, palpitate, flutter, vibrate, quiver, tremble, shake, quake. **3** *beat the enemy/all comers*: defeat, trounce, hammer (*infml*), slaughter (*infml*), conquer, overcome, overwhelm, vanquish (*fml*), subdue, surpass, excel, outdo, outstrip, outrun.

beautiful *adjective* attractive, fair, pretty, lovely, good-looking, handsome, gorgeous, radiant, ravishing, stunning (*infml*), pleasing, appealing, alluring, charming, delightful, fine, exquisite.

≠ ugly, plain, hideous.

beautify *verb* embellish, enhance, improve, grace, gild, garnish, decorate, ornament, deck, bedeck, adorn, array, glamorize.

≠ disfigure, spoil.

beauty *noun* attractiveness, fairness, prettiness, loveliness, (good) looks, glamour, handsomeness, appeal, allure, charm, grace, elegance, symmetry, excellence.

≠ ugliness, repulsiveness.

because *conjunction* as, for, since, owing to, in that, on account of, by reason of, thanks to.

beckon *verb* summon, motion, gesture, signal, nod, wave, gesticulate, call, invite, attract, pull, draw, lure, allure, entice, tempt, coax.

become *verb* **1** *become a handsome young man*: turn, grow, get, change into, develop into. **2** *green becomes you*: suit, befit, flatter, enhance, grace, embellish, ornament, set off, harmonize.

bed *noun* **1** *sleeping on a bed*: divan, couch, bunk, berth, cot, mattress, pallet, sack (*infml*). **2** *riverbed/seabed*: watercourse, channel, bottom. **3** *bed of flowers*: garden, border, patch, plot.

bedraggled *adjective* untidy, unkempt, dishevelled, disordered, scruffy, slovenly, messy, dirty, muddy, muddied, soiled, wet, sodden, drenched.

≠ neat, tidy, clean.

before *adverb* ahead, in front, in advance, sooner, earlier, formerly, previously.
F3 after, later.

beforehand *adverb* in advance, preliminarily, already, before, previously, earlier, sooner.

beg *verb* request, require, desire, crave, beseech, plead, entreat, implore, pray, supplicate, petition, solicit, cadge, scrounge, sponge.

begin *verb* start, commence, set about, embark on, set in motion, activate, originate, initiate, introduce, found, institute, instigate.
F3 end, finish, cease.

beginner *noun* novice, tiro, starter, learner, trainee, apprentice, student, freshman, fresher, recruit, cub, tenderfoot (*US*), fledgling.
F3 veteran, old hand, expert.

beginning *noun* **1** *the beginning of the story/race/process*: start, commencement, onset, outset, opening, preface, prelude, introduction, initiation, establishment, inauguration, inception, starting point. **2** *the beginning of time/life/democracy*: birth, dawn, origin, source, fountainhead, root, seed, emergence, rise.
F3 **1** end, finish.

behalf *noun* sake, account, good, interest, benefit, advantage, profit, name, authority, side, support.

behave *verb* act, react, respond, work, function, run, operate, perform, conduct oneself, acquit oneself, comport oneself (*fml*).

behaviour *noun* conduct, manner, manners, actions, doings, dealings, ways, habits, action, reaction, response, functioning, operation, performance, comportment (*fml*).

behead *verb* decapitate, execute, guillotine.

behind *adverb* after, following, next, subsequently, behindhand, late, overdue, in arrears, in debt.
▪ *preposition* **1** *who's behind all this?*: causing, responsible for, instigating, initiating. **2** *behind you all the way*: supporting, backing, for.

beige *adjective* buff, fawn, mushroom, camel, sandy, khaki, coffee, ecru, neutral.

being *noun* **1** *put her whole being into the performance*: existence, actuality, reality, life, animation, essence, substance, nature, soul, spirit. **2** *a living being/a being from another planet*: creature, animal, beast, human being, mortal, person, individual, thing, entity.

belief *noun* **1** *demonstrate their belief in the project*: conviction, persuasion, credit, trust, reliance, confidence, assurance, certainty, sureness. **2** *it's my belief that it will end soon*: presumption, expectation, feeling, intuition, impression, notion, theory, view, opinion, judgement. **3** *religious beliefs*: ideology, faith, creed,

doctrine, dogma, tenet, principle.
F3 1 disbelief.

believable *adjective* credible, imaginable, conceivable, acceptable, plausible, possible, likely, probable, authoritative, reliable, trustworthy.
F3 unbelievable, incredible, unconvincing.

believe *verb* **1** *can't believe anything they say*: accept, wear (*infml*), swallow (*infml*), credit, trust, count on, depend on, rely on. **2** *believed that it cured baldness*: swear by, hold (*fml*), maintain. **3** *he believes that it may work*: assume, postulate, presume, gather, speculate, conjecture, guess, imagine, think, consider, reckon, suppose, deem, judge.
F3 1 disbelieve, doubt.

belittle *verb* demean, minimize, play down, trivialize, dismiss, underrate, undervalue, underestimate, lessen, diminish, detract from, deprecate (*fml*), decry, disparage (*fml*), run down, deride, scorn, ridicule.
F3 exaggerate, praise.

belong *verb* fit, go with, be part of, attach to, link up with, tie up with, be connected with, relate to.

belongings *noun* possessions, property, chattels (*fml*), goods, effects, things, stuff (*infml*), gear (*infml*), paraphernalia.

below *adverb* beneath, under, underneath, down, lower, lower down.
F3 above.
▪ *preposition* **1** *below the table*: under, underneath, beneath. **2** *below him in rank*: inferior to, lesser than, subordinate to, subject to.
F3 above.

belt *noun* sash, girdle, waistband, girth, strap.

bench *noun* seat, form, settle, pew, ledge, counter, table, stall, workbench, worktable.

bend *verb* curve, turn, deflect, swerve, veer, diverge, twist, contort, flex, shape, mould, buckle, bow, incline, lean, stoop, crouch.
F3 straighten.
▪ *noun* curvature, curve, arc, bow, loop, hook, crook, elbow, angle, corner, turn, twist, zigzag.

beneath *adverb* below, under, underneath, lower, lower down.
▪ *preposition* **1** *the floor beneath the table*: under, underneath, below, lower than. **2** *thought being a waiter was beneath him*: unworthy of, unbefitting.

beneficial *adjective* advantageous, favourable, useful, helpful, profitable, rewarding, valuable, improving, edifying, wholesome.
F3 harmful, detrimental, useless.

benefit *noun* advantage, good, welfare, interest, favour, help, aid, assistance, service, use, avail, gain, profit, asset, blessing, plus (*infml*).
F3 disadvantage, harm, damage.
▪ *verb* help, aid, assist, serve, avail,

advantage, profit, improve, enhance, better, further, advance, promote.

F3 hinder, harm, undermine.

benign *adjective* **1** *a benign expression on his face*: benevolent, good, gracious, gentle, kind, obliging, friendly, amiable, genial, sympathetic. **2** *a benign tumour*: curable, harmless.

F3 **1** hostile. **2** malignant.

bent *noun* tendency, inclination, leaning, preference, ability, capacity, faculty, aptitude, facility, gift, talent, knack, flair, forte.

▪ *adjective* angled, curved, bowed, arched, folded, doubled, twisted, hunched, stooped.

F3 straight, upright.

berserk *adjective* mad, crazy, demented, insane, amok, maniacal, deranged, frantic, frenzied, wild, raging, furious, violent, rabid, raving.

F3 sane, calm.

beside *preposition* alongside, abreast of, next to, adjacent, abutting, bordering, neighbouring, next door to, close to, near, overlooking.

besides *preposition* apart from, other than, in addition to, over and above.

▪ *adverb* also, as well, too, in addition, further, additionally, furthermore, moreover.

besiege *verb* **1** *besieging the city*: lay siege to, blockade, surround, encircle, confine. **2** *besieged by biting flies*: trouble, bother, importune, assail, beset, beleaguer, harass, pester, badger, nag, hound, plague.

besotted *adjective* infatuated, doting, obsessed, smitten, bewitched, hypnotized, spellbound, intoxicated.

F3 indifferent, disenchanted.

best *adjective* optimum, optimal, first, foremost, leading, unequalled, unsurpassed, matchless, incomparable, supreme, crème de la crème, greatest, highest, largest, finest, excellent, outstanding, superlative, first-rate, first-class, perfect.

F3 worst.

▪ *adverb* greatly, extremely, exceptionally, excellently, superlatively.

F3 worst.

bet *noun* wager, flutter (*infml*), gamble, speculation, risk, venture, stake, ante, bid, pledge.

▪ *verb* wager, gamble, punt, speculate, risk, hazard, chance, venture, lay, stake, bid, pledge.

betray *verb* **1** *betray a friend*: inform on, dupe, shop (*slang*), sell (out), double-cross, desert, abandon, grass (*slang*), forsake. **2** *betray one's emotions*: disclose, give away, tell, divulge, expose, reveal, show, manifest.

F3 **1** defend, protect. **2** conceal, hide.

betrayal *noun* treachery, treason, sell-out, disloyalty, unfaithfulness, double-dealing, duplicity (*fml*),

deception, trickery, falseness.
⇔ loyalty, protection.

better *adjective* **1** *a better deal/example*: superior, bigger, larger, longer, greater, worthier, finer, surpassing, preferable. **2** *getting better*: improving, progressing, on the mend (*infml*), recovering, fitter, healthier, stronger, recovered, restored.
⇔ **1** inferior. **2** worse.

between *preposition* mid, amid, amidst, among, amongst.

beware *verb* watch out, look out, mind, take heed, steer clear of, avoid, shun, guard against.

bewildered *adjective* confused, muddled, uncertain, disoriented, nonplussed, bamboozled (*infml*), baffled, puzzled, perplexed, flummoxed (*infml*), mystified, bemused, surprised, stunned.
⇔ unperturbed, collected.

beyond *preposition* past, further than, apart from, away from, remote from, out of range of, out of reach of, above, over, superior to.

biased *adjective* slanted, angled, distorted, warped, twisted, loaded, weighted, influenced, swayed, partial, predisposed, prejudiced, one-sided, unfair, bigoted, blinkered, jaundiced.
⇔ impartial, fair.

bicker *verb* squabble, row, quarrel, wrangle, argue, scrap, spar, fight, clash, disagree, dispute.
⇔ agree.

bid *verb* **1** *he bid more than the painting was worth*: offer, proffer, tender, submit, propose. **2** (*fml*) *bid me go/enter*: ask, request, desire, instruct, direct, command, enjoin, require, charge, call, summon, invite, solicit.
▪ *noun* **1** *a higher bid*: offer, tender, sum, amount, price, advance, submission, proposal. **2** *his latest bid to climb the mountain*: attempt, effort, try, go (*infml*), endeavour, venture.

big *adjective* **1** *big ears/big muscles/a big house*: large, great, sizable, considerable, substantial, huge, enormous, immense, massive, colossal, gigantic, mammoth, burly, bulky, extensive, spacious, vast. **2** *a big occasion/a big step*: important, significant, momentous, serious, main, principal, eminent, prominent, influential.
⇔ **1** small, little. **2** insignificant, unknown.

bigoted *adjective* prejudiced, biased, intolerant, illiberal, narrow-minded, narrow, blinkered, closed, dogmatic, opinionated, obstinate.
⇔ tolerant, liberal, broad-minded, enlightened.

bigotry *noun* prejudice, discrimination, bias, injustice, unfairness, intolerance, narrow-mindedness, chauvinism, jingoism, sectarianism, racism, racialism, sexism, dogmatism, fanaticism.
⇔ tolerance.

bill *noun* **1** *pay the telephone bill*: invoice, statement, account, charges, reckoning, tally, score. **2** *a parliamentary bill*: proposal, measure, legislation.

bind *verb* **1** *bind the two pieces together with tape/bind their wounds*: attach, fasten, secure, clamp, tie, lash, truss, strap, bandage, cover, wrap. **2** *bound by a solemn oath*: oblige, force, compel, constrain, necessitate, restrict, require, confine, restrain.

biography *noun* life story, life, history, autobiography, memoirs, recollections, curriculum vitae, account, record.

biology

Terms used in biology include:
amino acid, anatomy, bacillus, bacteria, biochemistry, botany, cell, chromosome, class, corpuscle, cytoplasm, deoxyribonucleic acid (DNA), diffusion, ecology, ecosystem, ectoplasm, embryo, endocrinology, enzyme, evolution, excretion, extinction, flora and fauna, food chain, fossil, gene, genetic engineering, genetic fingerprinting, genetics, germ, meiosis, membrane, metabolism, microbe, micro-organism, mitosis, molecule, mutation, natural selection, nucleus, nutrition, organism, osmosis, photosynthesis, pollution, protein, protoplasm, reproduction, respiration, ribonucleic acid (RNA), secretion, symbiosis, virus, zoology.

---

bird

Birds include:
blackbird, bluetit, bullfinch, chaffinch, crow, cuckoo, dove, dunnock, goldfinch, greenfinch, jackdaw, jay, linnet, magpie, martin, nightingale, pigeon, raven, robin, rook, shrike, skylark, sparrow, starling, swallow, swift, thrush, tit, wagtail, warbler, woodpecker, wren, yellowhammer; albatross, auk, avocet, bittern, coot, cormorant, crane, curlew, dipper, duck, eider, flamingo, gannet, goose, guillemot, heron, kingfisher, lapwing, mallard, moorhen, peewit, petrel, pelican, plover, puffin, seagull, snipe, stork, swan, teal, tern; buzzard, condor, eagle, falcon, hawk, kestrel, kite, osprey, owl, sparrowhawk, vulture; emu, kiwi, ostrich, peacock, penguin; chicken, grouse, partridge, pheasant, quail, turkey; bird of paradise, budgerigar, budgie (*infml*), canary, cockatiel, cockatoo, kookaburra, macaw, mockingbird, myna bird, parakeet, parrot, toucan.

---

birth *noun* **1** *the birth of their son/a difficult birth*: childbirth, parturition (*fml*), confinement, delivery, nativity. **2** *of noble birth*: ancestry, family, parentage, descent, line, lineage, genealogy, pedigree, blood, stock, race, extraction, background, breeding. **3** *the birth of the nation*: beginning, rise, emergence, origin, source, derivation.

bisect *verb* halve, divide, separate, split, intersect, cross, fork, bifurcate.

bit *noun* fragment, part, segment, piece, slice, crumb, morsel, scrap, atom, mite, whit, jot, iota, grain, speck.

bite *verb* **1** *bite the apple/one's lip*: chew, masticate (*fml*), munch, gnaw, nibble, champ, crunch, crush. **2** *the dog bit her hand*: nip, pierce, wound, tear, rend.
▪ *noun* nip, wound, sting, smarting, pinch.

bitter *adjective* **1** *bitter taste/fruit*: sour, tart, sharp, acid, vinegary, unsweetened. **2** *became old and bitter*: resentful, embittered, jaundiced, cynical, rancorous, acrimonious, acerbic, hostile. **3** *a bitter wind/dispute*: intense, severe, harsh, fierce, cruel, savage, merciless, painful, stinging, biting, freezing, raw.
F3 **1** sweet. **2** contented. **3** mild.

bizarre *adjective* strange, odd, queer, curious, weird, peculiar, eccentric, way-out (*infml*), outlandish, ludicrous, ridiculous, fantastic, extravagant, grotesque, freakish, abnormal, deviant, unusual, extraordinary.
F3 normal, ordinary.

black *adjective* **1** *black hair*: jet-black, coal-black, jet, ebony, sable, inky, sooty. **2** *the sky became black*: dark, unlit, moonless, starless, overcast, dingy, gloomy, sombre, funereal. **3** *black with soot*: filthy, dirty, soiled, grimy, grubby.
F3 **2** bright. **3** clean.

blacken *verb* **1** *faces blackened by coal-dust*: darken, dirty, soil, smudge, cloud. **2** *blackening someone's character*: defame (*fml*), malign, slander, libel, vilify (*fml*), revile, denigrate, detract, smear, sully (*fml*), stain, tarnish, taint, defile (*fml*), discredit, dishonour.
F3 **2** praise, enhance.

blackmail *noun* extortion, chantage, hush money (*infml*), intimidation, protection, pay-off, ransom.
▪ *verb* extort, bleed, milk, squeeze, hold to ransom, threaten, lean on (*infml*), force, compel, coerce, demand.

black out *verb* faint, pass out, collapse, flake out (*infml*).

blackout *noun* **1** *suffer from headaches and blackouts*: faint, coma, unconsciousness, oblivion. **2** *used candles and torches during the blackout*: power failure, power cut.

blade *noun* edge, knife, dagger, sword, scalpel, razor, vane.

blame *noun* censure, criticism, stick (*infml*), reprimand, reproof, reproach, recrimination, condemnation, accusation, charge, rap (*infml*), incrimination, guilt, culpability, fault, responsibility, accountability, liability, onus.
▪ *verb* accuse, charge, tax, reprimand, chide, reprove,

upbraid (*fml*), reprehend (*fml*), admonish, rebuke, reproach, censure, criticize, find fault with, disapprove, condemn.
F3 exonerate, vindicate.

blameless *adjective* innocent, guiltless, clear, faultless, perfect, unblemished, stainless, virtuous, sinless, upright, above reproach, irreproachable, unblamable, unimpeachable.
F3 guilty, blameworthy.

bland *adjective* **1** *a bland design/ appearance*: boring, monotonous, humdrum, tedious, dull, uninspiring, uninteresting, unexciting, nondescript. **2** *a bland tasting mixture/a bland smile*: characterless, flat, insipid, tasteless, weak, mild, smooth, soft, gentle, non-irritant.
F3 **1** lively, stimulating.

blank *adjective* **1** *a blank page*: empty, unfilled, void, clear, bare, unmarked, plain, clean, white. **2** *a blank stare*: expressionless, deadpan, poker-faced, impassive, apathetic, glazed, vacant, uncomprehending.
▪ *noun* space, gap, break, void, emptiness, vacancy, vacuity, nothingness, vacuum.

blanket *noun* covering, coating, coat, layer, film, carpet, rug, cloak, mantle, cover, sheet, envelope, wrapper, wrapping.

blare *verb* trumpet, clamour, roar, blast, boom, resound, ring, peal, clang, hoot, toot, honk.

blasé *adjective* nonchalant, offhand, unimpressed, unmoved, unexcited, jaded, weary, bored, uninterested, uninspired, apathetic, indifferent, cool, unconcerned.
F3 excited, enthusiastic.

blasphemous *adjective* profane, impious, sacrilegious, godless, ungodly, irreligious, irreverent.

blasphemy *noun* profanity, curse, expletive, cursing, swearing, execration (*fml*), impiety, irreverence, sacrilege, desecration, violation, outrage.

blast *noun* **1** *destroyed in the blast*: explosion, detonation, bang, crash, clap, crack, volley, burst, outburst, discharge. **2** *a blast of cold air*: draught, gust, gale, squall, storm, tempest. **3** *the blast of trumpets*: sound, blow, blare, roar, boom, peal, hoot, wail, scream, shriek.
▪ *verb* **1** *blasting the rocks in the quarry*: explode, blow up, burst, shatter, destroy, demolish, ruin, assail, attack. **2** *music blasting from the loudspeakers*: sound, blare, roar, boom, peal, hoot, wail, scream, shriek.

blatant *adjective* flagrant, brazen, barefaced, arrant, open, overt, undisguised, ostentatious, glaring, conspicuous, obtrusive, prominent, pronounced, obvious, sheer, outright, unmitigated.

blaze *noun* fire, flames, conflagration, bonfire, flare-up, explosion, blast, burst, outburst, radiance, brilliance, glare, flash, gleam, glitter, glow, light, flame. ▪ *verb* burn, flame, flare (up), erupt, explode, burst, fire, flash, gleam, glare, beam, shine, glow.

bleach *verb* whiten, decolorize, fade, pale, lighten.

bleak *adjective* **1** *a bleak prospect*: gloomy, sombre, leaden, grim, dreary, dismal, wintry, depressing, joyless, cheerless, comfortless, hopeless, discouraging, disheartening. **2** *a bleak hillside/landscape*: cold, chilly, raw, weather-beaten, unsheltered, windy, windswept, exposed, open, barren, bare, empty, desolate, gaunt.

1 bright, cheerful.

bleed *verb* haemorrhage, gush, spurt, flow, run, exude, weep, ooze, seep, trickle.

blemish *noun* **1** *a facial blemish*: flaw, imperfection, defect, fault, deformity, disfigurement, birthmark, naevus, spot, mark, speck, smudge, blotch. **2** *a long service record without blemish*: blot, stain, taint, disgrace, dishonour. ▪ *verb* flaw, deface, disfigure, spoil, mar, damage, impair, spot, mark, blot, blotch, stain, sully (*fml*), taint, tarnish.

blend *verb* **1** *blend the ingredients*: merge, amalgamate, coalesce, compound, synthesize, fuse, unite, combine, mix, mingle. **2** *flavours/colours that blend well*: harmonize, complement, fit, match.

1 separate.

bless *verb* **1** *bless the wine/the little children*: anoint, sanctify, consecrate, hallow, dedicate, ordain. **2** *bless his name*: praise, extol (*fml*), magnify, glorify, exalt, thank. **3** *blessed the undertaking/blessed with children*: approve, countenance, favour, grace, bestow, endow, provide.

1 curse. **2** condemn.

blessed *adjective* **1** *Christ's blessed name*: holy, sacred, hallowed, sanctified, revered, adored, divine. **2** *a blessed relief*: happy, contented, glad, joyful, joyous. **3** *live a blessed existence*: lucky, fortunate, prosperous, favoured, endowed.

1 cursed.

blessing *noun* **1** *the blessing of the bread*: consecration, dedication, benediction, grace, thanksgiving, invocation. **2** *a real blessing in disguise*: benefit, advantage, favour, godsend, windfall, gift, gain, profit, help, service. **3** *give a proposal one's blessing*: approval, concurrence, backing, support, authority, sanction, consent, permission, leave.

2 curse, blight. **3** condemnation.

blind *adjective* **1** *a blind person*: sightless, unsighted, unseeing, eyeless, purblind, partially sighted. **2** *blind faith/panic*: impetuous, impulsive, hasty, rash, reckless, wild, mad, indiscriminate, careless, heedless, mindless, unthinking, unreasoning, irrational. **3** *blind to*

their distress: ignorant, oblivious, unaware, unconscious, unobservant, inattentive, neglectful, indifferent, insensitive, thoughtless, inconsiderate. **4** *a blind alley*: closed, obstructed, hidden, concealed, obscured.
⇄ **1** sighted. **2** careful, cautious. **3** aware, sensitive.

bliss *noun* blissfulness, ecstasy, euphoria, rapture, joy, happiness, gladness, blessedness, paradise, heaven.
⇄ misery, hell, damnation.

blister *noun* sore, swelling, cyst, boil, abscess, ulcer, pustule, pimple, carbuncle.

bloated *adjective* swollen, puffy, blown up, inflated, distended, dilated, expanded, enlarged, turgid, bombastic.
⇄ thin, shrunken, shrivelled.

blob *noun* drop, droplet, globule, glob (*infml*), bead, pearl, bubble, dab, spot, lump, mass, ball, pellet, pill.

block *noun* **1** *a block of stone*: piece, lump, ingot, mass, chunk, hunk, square, cube, brick, bar. **2** *a mental block/writer's block*: obstacle, barrier, bar, jam, blockage, stoppage, resistance, obstruction, impediment, hindrance, let, delay.
▪ *verb* choke, clog, plug, stop up, dam up, close, bar, obstruct, impede, hinder, stonewall, stop, check, arrest, halt, thwart, scotch, deter, veto.

blockage *noun* blocking, obstruction, stoppage, occlusion, block, clot, jam, log-jam, congestion, hindrance, impediment.

blood *noun* extraction, birth, descent, lineage, family, kindred, relations, ancestry, descendants, kinship, relationship.

bloodcurdling *adjective* horrifying, chilling, spine-chilling, hair-raising, terrifying, frightening, scary, dreadful, fearful, horrible, horrid, horrendous.

bloodshed *noun* killing, murder, slaughter, massacre, blood-bath, butchery, carnage, gore, bloodletting.

bloodthirsty *adjective* murderous, homicidal, warlike, savage, barbaric, barbarous, brutal, ferocious, vicious, cruel, inhuman, ruthless.

bloom *noun* blossom, flower, bud.
▪ *verb* bud, sprout, grow, wax, develop, mature, blossom, flower, blow, open.
⇄ fade, wither.

blossom *noun* bloom, flower, bud.
▪ *verb* develop, mature, bloom, flower, blow, flourish, thrive, prosper, succeed.
⇄ fade, wither.

blot *noun* spot, stain, smudge, blotch, smear, mark, speck, blemish, flaw, fault, defect, taint, disgrace.
▪ *verb* spot, mark, stain, smudge, blur, sully (*fml*), taint, tarnish,

spoil, mar, disfigure, disgrace.

blotch *noun* patch, splodge, splotch, splash, smudge, blot, spot, mark, stain, blemish.

blotchy *adjective* spotty, spotted, patchy, uneven, smeary, blemished, reddened, inflamed.

blow[1] *verb* **1** *blow on the hot soup/ wind blowing the dry leaves around*: breathe, exhale, pant, puff, waft, fan, flutter, float, flow, stream, rush, whirl, whisk, sweep, fling, buffet, drive, blast. **2** *blow a horn*: play, sound, pipe, trumpet, toot, blare.

blow[2] *noun* **1** *blow to the head*: concussion, box, cuff, clip, clout, swipe, biff (*infml*), bash, slap, smack, whack (*infml*), wallop (*infml*), belt (*infml*), buffet, bang, clap, knock, rap, stroke, thump, punch. **2** *a blow to hopes of lasting peace*: misfortune, affliction, reverse, setback, comedown, disappointment, upset, jolt, shock, bombshell, calamity, catastrophe, disaster.

blue *adjective* **1** *blue sky/shades of blue*: azure, sapphire, cobalt, ultramarine, navy, indigo, aquamarine, turquoise, cyan. **2** *feeling blue*: depressed, low, down in the dumps (*infml*), dejected, downcast, dispirited, downhearted, despondent, gloomy, glum, dismal, sad, unhappy, miserable, melancholy, morose, fed up (*infml*).

E3 **2** cheerful, happy.

blueprint *noun* archetype, prototype, model, pattern, design, outline, draft, sketch, pilot, guide, plan, scheme, project.

bluff *verb* lie, pretend, feign, sham, fake, deceive, delude, mislead, hoodwink, blind, bamboozle (*infml*), fool.

▪ *noun* lie, idle boast, bravado, humbug, pretence, show, sham, fake, fraud, trick, subterfuge, deceit, deception.

blunder *noun* mistake, error, solecism (*fml*), howler (*infml*), bloomer (*infml*), clanger (*infml*), inaccuracy, slip, boob (*infml*), indiscretion, gaffe, faux pas, slip-up (*infml*), oversight, fault.

▪ *verb* stumble, flounder, bumble, err, slip up (*infml*), miscalculate, misjudge, bungle, botch, fluff (*infml*), mismanage.

blunt *adjective* **1** *a blunt knife/ pencil*: unsharpened, dull, worn, pointless, rounded, stubbed. **2** *a blunt approach*: frank, candid, direct, forthright, unceremonious, explicit, plain-spoken, honest, downright, outspoken, tactless, insensitive, rude, impolite, uncivil, brusque, curt, abrupt.

E3 **1** sharp, pointed. **2** subtle, tactful.

▪ *verb* dull, take the edge off, dampen, soften, deaden, numb, anaesthetize, alleviate, allay, abate, weaken.

E3 sharpen, intensify.

blur *noun* smear, smudge, blotch, haze, mist, fog, cloudiness, fuzziness, indistinctness, muddle, confusion, dimness, obscurity.

blurred *adjective* out of focus, fuzzy, unclear, indistinct, vague, ill-defined, faint, hazy, misty, foggy, cloudy, bleary, dim, obscure, confused.

F3 clear, distinct.

blurt out *verb* exclaim, cry, gush, spout, utter, tell, reveal, disclose, divulge, blab (*infml*), let out, leak, let slip, spill the beans (*infml*).

F3 bottle up, hush up.

blush *verb* flush, redden, colour, glow.

blushing *adjective* flushed, red, rosy, glowing, confused, embarrassed, ashamed, modest.

F3 pale, white, composed.

bluster *noun* boasting, crowing, bravado, bluff, swagger.

board *noun* **1** *a wooden board*: sheet, panel, slab, plank, beam, timber, slat. **2** *the board of directors*: committee, council, panel, jury, commission, directorate, directors, trustees, advisers. **3** *bed and board*: meals, food, provisions, rations.

▪ *verb* get on, embark, mount, enter, catch.

boast *verb* brag, crow, claim, exaggerate, talk big (*infml*), bluster, trumpet, vaunt, strut, swagger, show off, exhibit.

F3 belittle, deprecate (*fml*).

boastful *adjective* proud, conceited, vain, swollen-headed, big-headed (*infml*), puffed up, bragging, crowing, swanky (*infml*), cocky, swaggering.

F3 modest, self-effacing, humble.

bob *verb* bounce, hop, skip, spring, jump, leap, twitch, jerk, jolt, shake, quiver, wobble, oscillate, nod, bow, curtsy.

bodily *adjective* physical, corporeal, carnal, fleshly, real, actual, tangible, substantial, concrete, material.

F3 spiritual.

body *noun* **1** *the human body/scars on his head and body*: anatomy, physique, build, figure, trunk, torso. **2** *a dead body*: corpse, cadaver, carcase, stiff (*slang*). **3** *a large body of men*: company, association, society, corporation, confederation, bloc, cartel, syndicate, congress, collection, group, band, crowd, throng, multitude, mob, mass.

bog *noun* marsh, swamp, fen, mire, quagmire, quag, slough, morass, quicksands, marshland, swampland, wetlands.

bogus *adjective* false, fake, counterfeit, forged, dummy, fraudulent, phoney (*infml*), spurious, sham, pseudo, artificial, imitation.

F3 genuine, true, real, valid.

boil[1] *verb* **1** *boil water/potatoes*: simmer, stew, brew, gurgle, bubble, steam. **2** *boil with rage*: erupt, explode, fizz, rage, seethe, rave, storm, effervesce, froth, foam, fulminate (*fml*), fume.

boil[2] *noun* pustule, abscess, gumboil, ulcer, tumour, pimple, carbuncle, blister, inflammation.

boiling *adjective* **1** *a boiling cauldron*: turbulent, gurgling, bubbling, steaming. **2** *it's boiling outside*: hot, baking, roasting, scorching, blistering. **3** *boiling with rage*: angry, indignant, incensed, infuriated, enraged, furious, fuming, flaming.

boisterous *adjective* exuberant, rumbustious (*infml*), rollicking, bouncy, turbulent, tumultuous, loud, noisy, clamorous, rowdy, rough, disorderly, riotous, wild, unrestrained, unruly, obstreperous.
F3 quiet, calm, restrained.

bold *adjective* **1** *a bold fighter*: fearless, dauntless, daring, audacious, brave, courageous, valiant, heroic, gallant, intrepid, adventurous, venturesome, enterprising, plucky, spirited, confident, outgoing. **2** *a bold pattern*: eye-catching, striking, conspicuous, prominent, strong, pronounced, bright, vivid, colourful, loud, flashy, showy, flamboyant. **3** *bold behaviour*: brazen, brash, forward, shameless, unabashed, cheeky (*infml*), impudent, insolent.
F3 **1** cautious, timid, shy. **2** faint, restrained.

bolt *noun* bar, rod, shaft, pin, peg, rivet, fastener, latch, catch, lock.
▪ *verb* **1** *bolt the door*: fasten, secure, bar, latch, lock. **2** *bolt at the first sign of trouble*: abscond, escape, flee, fly, run, sprint, rush, dash, hurtle. **3** *bolt one's food*: gulp, wolf, gobble, gorge, devour, cram, stuff (*infml*).

bomb *verb* bombard, shell, torpedo, attack, blow up, destroy.

bombard *verb* attack, assault, assail, pelt, pound, strafe, blast, bomb, shell, blitz, besiege, hound, harass, pester.

bond *noun* connection, relation, link, tie, union, affiliation, attachment, affinity.
▪ *verb* connect, fasten, bind, unite, fuse, glue, gum, paste, stick, seal.

bone

Human bones include:

carpal, clavicle, coccyx, collarbone, femur, fibula, hip-bone, humerus, ilium, ischium, mandible, maxilla, metacarpal, metatarsal, patella, pelvic girdle, pelvis, pubis, radius, rib, sacrum, scapula, shoulderblade, skull, sternum, stirrup bone, temporal, thigh-bone, tibia, ulna, vertebra.

---

bonus *noun* advantage, benefit, plus (*infml*), extra, perk (*infml*), commission, dividend, premium, prize, reward, honorarium, tip, gratuity, gift, handout.
F3 disadvantage, disincentive.

bony *adjective* thin, lean, angular, lanky, gawky, gangling, skinny, scrawny, emaciated, rawboned, gaunt, drawn.
F3 fat, plump.

book[1] *noun* volume, tome, publication, work, booklet, tract.

Types of book include:

audio book, bestseller, e-book,

hardback, paperback; fiction, novel, thriller; annual, children's book, picture-book, primer; almanac, anthology, atlas, A to Z, catalogue, concordance, cookbook, dictionary, directory, encyclopedia, gazetteer, guidebook, handbook, lexicon, manual, omnibus, reference book, thesaurus, yearbook; album, diary, exercise book, jotter, journal, ledger, notebook, pad, scrapbook, sketchbook, textbook; hymnal, hymn-book, libretto, manuscript, missal, prayer book, psalter. *See also* **literature**; **story**.

---

book[2] *verb* reserve, bag (*infml*), engage, charter, procure, order, arrange, organize, schedule, programme.
F cancel.

boom *noun* **1** *an economic boom*: increase, growth, expansion, gain, upsurge, jump, spurt, boost, upturn, improvement, advance, escalation, explosion. **2** *the boom of the big guns*: bang, clap, crash, roar, thunder, rumble, reverberation, blast, explosion, burst.
F **1** failure, collapse, slump, recession, depression.

boost *noun* improvement, enhancement, expansion, increase, rise, jump, increment, addition, supplement, booster, lift, hoist, heave, push, thrust, help, advancement, promotion, praise, encouragement, fillip.
F setback, blow.
▪ *verb* raise, elevate, improve, enhance, develop, enlarge, expand, amplify, increase, augment, heighten, lift, hoist, jack up, heave, push, thrust, help, aid, assist, advance, further, promote, advertise, plug (*infml*), praise, inspire, encourage, foster, support, sustain, bolster, supplement.
F hinder, undermine.

booth *noun* kiosk, stall, stand, hut, box, compartment, cubicle, carrel.

booty *noun* loot, plunder, pillage, spoils, swag (*slang*), haul, gains, takings, pickings, winnings.

border *noun* **1** *the border between two countries/across national borders*: boundary, frontier, bound, bounds, confine, confines, limit, demarcation, borderline, margin, fringe, periphery, surround, perimeter, circumference, edge, rim, brim, verge, brink. **2** *a lace border*: trimming, frill, valance, skirt, hem, frieze.

border on *verb* **1** *bordering on our land*: adjoin, abut, touch, impinge, join, connect, communicate with. **2** *bordering on lunacy*: resemble, approximate, approach, verge on.

bore[1] *verb* drill, mine, pierce, perforate, penetrate, sink, burrow, tunnel, undermine.

bore[2] *verb* tire, weary, fatigue, jade, trouble, bother, worry, irritate, annoy, vex, irk.
F interest, excite.

▪ *noun* nuisance, bother, bind (*infml*), drag (*infml*), pain (*infml*), headache (*infml*).
☒ pleasure, delight.

boring *adjective* tedious, monotonous, routine, repetitious, uninteresting, unexciting, uneventful, dull, dreary, humdrum, commonplace, trite, unimaginative, uninspired, dry, stale, flat, insipid, tiresome.
☒ interesting, exciting, stimulating, original.

borrow *verb* steal, pilfer, filch, lift, plagiarize, crib, copy, imitate, mimic, echo, take, draw, derive, obtain, adopt, use, scrounge, cadge, sponge, appropriate, usurp.
☒ lend.

boss *noun* employer, governor, master, owner, captain, head, chief, leader, supremo, administrator, executive, director, manager, foreman, gaffer, superintendent, overseer, supervisor.

bossy *adjective* authoritarian, autocratic, tyrannical, despotic, dictatorial, domineering, overbearing, oppressive, lordly, high-handed, imperious, insistent, assertive, demanding, exacting.
☒ unassertive.

bother *verb* disturb, inconvenience, harass, hassle (*infml*), pester, plague, nag, annoy, irritate, irk, molest, trouble, worry, concern, alarm, dismay, distress, upset, vex.

▪ *noun* inconvenience, trouble, problem, difficulty, hassle (*infml*), fuss, bustle, flurry, nuisance, pest, annoyance, irritation, aggravation (*infml*), vexation, worry, strain.

bottle *noun* phial, flask, carafe, decanter, flagon, demijohn.

bottom *noun* underside, underneath, sole, base, foot, plinth, pedestal, support, foundation, substructure, ground, floor, bed, depths, nadir.
☒ top.

bounce *verb* spring, jump, leap, bound, bob, ricochet, rebound, recoil.

▪ *noun* **1** *give one's hair bounce*: spring, bound, springiness, elasticity, give, resilience, rebound, recoil. **2** *he's full of bounce*: ebullience, exuberance, vitality, vivacity, energy, vigour, go (*infml*), zip (*infml*), dynamism, animation, liveliness.

bound[1] *adjective* **1** *bound hand and foot*: fastened, secured, fixed, tied (up), chained, held, restricted, bandaged. **2** *bound by the agreement*: liable, committed, duty-bound, obliged, required, forced, compelled, constrained, destined, fated, doomed, sure, certain.

bound[2] *verb* jump, leap, vault, hurdle, spring, bounce, bob, hop, skip, frisk, gambol, frolic, caper, prance.

▪ *noun* jump, leap, vault, spring, bounce, bob, hop, skip, gambol, frolic, caper, dance, prance.

boundary *noun* border, frontier, barrier, line, borderline, demarcation, bounds, confines, limits, margin, fringe, verge, brink, edge, perimeter, extremity, termination.

boundless *adjective* unbounded, limitless, unlimited, unconfined, countless, untold, incalculable, vast, immense, measureless, immeasurable, infinite, endless, unending, interminable, inexhaustible, unflagging, indefatigable.
F3 limited, restricted.

bounds *noun* confines, limits, borders, marches, margins, fringes, periphery, circumference, edges, extremities.

bounty *noun* **1** *benefit from the king's bounty*: generosity, liberality, munificence, largesse, almsgiving, charity, philanthropy, beneficence (*fml*), kindness. **2** *earn a bounty*: reward, recompense, premium, bonus, gratuity, gift, present, donation, grant, allowance.

bouquet *noun* bunch, posy, nosegay, spray, corsage, buttonhole, wreath, garland.

bout *noun* **1** *a boxing bout*: fight, battle, engagement, encounter, struggle, set-to, match, contest, competition, round, heat. **2** *a bout of illness*: period, spell, time, stint, turn, go (*infml*), term, stretch, run, course, session, spree, attack, fit.

bow *noun* /bow/ bob, curtsy, genuflection, inclination, bending, nod, kowtow, salaam, salutation, acknowledgement.
■ *verb* **1** *bow one's head*: incline, bend, nod, bob, curtsy, genuflect, kowtow, salaam, stoop. **2** *bow to pressure*: yield, give in, consent, surrender, capitulate, submit, acquiesce, concede, accept, comply, defer.

bowl[1] *noun* receptacle, container, vessel, dish, basin, sink.

bowl[2] *verb* throw, hurl, fling, pitch, roll, spin, whirl, rotate, revolve.

box[1] *noun* container, receptacle, case, crate, carton, packet, pack, package, present, chest, coffer, trunk, coffin.

box[2] *verb* fight, spar, punch, hit, strike, slap, buffet, cuff, clout, sock (*infml*), wallop (*infml*), whack (*infml*).

boxer *noun* pugilist, fighter, prizefighter, sparring partner, flyweight, featherweight, lightweight, welterweight, middleweight, heavyweight.

boy *noun* son, lad, youngster, kid (*infml*), nipper (*infml*), stripling, youth, fellow.

boycott *verb* refuse, reject, embargo, ban, prohibit, disallow, bar, exclude, blacklist, outlaw, ostracize, cold-shoulder, ignore, spurn.
F3 encourage, support.

bracing *adjective* fresh, crisp, refreshing, reviving, strengthening, fortifying, tonic, rousing, stimulating, exhilarating, invigorating, enlivening,

energizing, brisk, energetic, vigorous.
F3 weakening, debilitating.

brag *verb* boast, show off, crow, bluster.
F3 be modest, deprecate (*fml*).

braid *verb* plait, interweave, interlace, intertwine, weave, lace, twine, entwine, ravel, twist, wind.
F3 undo, unravel.

brain *noun* **1** *use your brain*: cerebrum, grey matter, head, mind, intellect, nous, brains (*infml*), intelligence, wit, reason, sense, common sense, shrewdness, understanding. **2** *one of the brains of the operation*: mastermind, intellectual, highbrow, egghead (*infml*), scholar, expert, boffin, genius, prodigy.

brainy *adjective* (*infml*) intellectual, intelligent, clever, smart, bright, brilliant.
F3 dull, stupid.

brake *noun* check, curb, rein, restraint, control, restriction, constraint, drag.
▪ *verb* slow, decelerate, retard, drag, slacken, moderate, check, halt, stop, pull up.
F3 accelerate.

branch *noun* **1** *the branch of a tree*: bough, limb, sprig, shoot, offshoot. **2** *a different branch of the company*: department, office, part, section, arm, wing, division, subsection, subdivision.

brand *noun* make, brand-name, tradename, trademark, logo, mark, symbol, sign, emblem, label, stamp, hallmark, grade, quality, class, kind, type, sort, line, variety, species.
▪ *verb* mark, stamp, label, type, stigmatize, burn, scar, stain, taint, disgrace, discredit, denounce, censure.

brandish *verb* wave, flourish, shake, raise, swing, wield, flash, flaunt, exhibit, display, parade.

brave *adjective* courageous, plucky, unafraid, fearless, dauntless, undaunted, bold, audacious, daring, intrepid, stalwart, hardy, stoical, resolute, stout-hearted, valiant, gallant, heroic, indomitable.
F3 cowardly, afraid, timid.
▪ *verb* face, confront, defy, challenge, dare, stand up to, face up to, suffer, endure, bear, withstand.
F3 capitulate.

bravery *noun* courage, pluck, guts (*infml*), fearlessness, dauntlessness, boldness, audacity, daring, intrepidity, stalwartness, hardiness, fortitude, resolution, stout-heartedness, valiance, valour, gallantry, heroism, indomitability, grit, mettle, spirit.
F3 cowardice, faint-heartedness, timidity.

brawl *noun* fight, punch-up (*infml*), scrap, scuffle, dust-up (*infml*), mêlée, free-for-all, fray, affray, broil, fracas, rumpus, disorder, row, argument, quarrel, squabble, altercation (*fml*), dispute, clash.

breach *noun* **1** *a breach of the rules*: violation, contravention, infringement, trespass (*fml*), disobedience, offence, transgression, lapse, disruption. **2** *heal the breach between them*: quarrel, disagreement, dissension, difference, variance, schism, rift, rupture, split, division, separation, parting, estrangement, alienation, disaffection, dissociation. **3** *a breach in the hull*: break, crack, rift, rupture, fissure, cleft, crevice, opening, aperture, gap, space, hole, chasm.

bread *noun* loaf, roll, food, provisions, diet, fare, nourishment, nutriment, sustenance, subsistence, necessities.

breadth *noun* width, broadness, wideness, latitude, thickness, size, magnitude, measure, scale, range, reach, scope, compass, span, sweep, extent, expanse, spread, comprehensiveness, extensiveness, vastness.

break *verb* **1** *broke a bone/window*: fracture, crack, snap, split, sever, separate, divide, rend, smash, disintegrate, splinter, shiver, shatter, ruin, destroy, demolish. **2** *break the law*: violate, contravene, infringe, breach, disobey, flout. **3** *break for lunch*: pause, halt, stop, discontinue, interrupt, suspend, rest. **4** *break a wild horse/break someone's spirit*: subdue, tame, weaken, enfeeble, impair, undermine, demoralize. **5** *break the news*: tell, inform, impart, divulge, disclose, reveal, announce. **6** *break a record*: exceed, beat, better, excel, surpass, outdo, outstrip.

☒ **1** mend. **2** keep, observe, abide by.

▪ *noun* **1** *a break in the pipe*: fracture, crack, split, rift, rupture, schism, separation, tear, gash, fissure, cleft, crevice, rent, opening, gap, hole, breach. **2** *have a break for coffee*: interval, intermission, interlude, interruption, pause, halt, lull, let-up (*infml*), respite, rest, breather (*infml*), time out, holiday. **3** *give/get a break*: opportunity, chance, advantage, fortune, luck.

breakable *adjective* brittle, fragile, delicate, flimsy, insubstantial, frail.

☒ unbreakable, durable, sturdy.

breakdown *noun* **1** *a mechanical/mental breakdown*: failure, collapse, disintegration, malfunction, interruption, stoppage. **2** *a breakdown of the figures*: analysis, dissection, itemization, classification, categorization.

break-in *noun* burglary, house-breaking, robbery, raid, invasion, intrusion, trespass.

breakthrough *noun* discovery, find, finding, invention, innovation, advance, progress, headway, step, leap, development, improvement.

breath *noun* **1** *lose one's breath/ take a deep breath*: air, breathing, respiration, inhalation, exhalation, sigh, gasp, pant, gulp. **2** *not a breath of wind*: breeze, puff, waft, gust. **3** *not a breath of scandal*: hint, suggestion, suspicion, whiff, undertone, whisper, murmur.

breathe *verb* respire, inhale, exhale, expire, sigh, gasp, pant, puff.

breathless *adjective* **1** *feel breathless*: short-winded, out of breath, panting, puffing, puffed (out), exhausted, winded, gasping, wheezing, choking. **2** *breathless anticipation*: expectant, impatient, eager, agog, excited, feverish, anxious.

breathtaking *adjective* awe-inspiring, impressive, magnificent, overwhelming, amazing, astonishing, stunning, exciting, thrilling, stirring, moving.

breed *verb* **1** *breed rapidly/ successfully*: reproduce, procreate, multiply, propagate, hatch, bear, bring forth, rear, raise, bring up, educate, train, instruct. **2** *breed discontent*: produce, create, originate, arouse, cause, occasion, engender, generate, make, foster, nurture, nourish, cultivate, develop.

▪ *noun* species, strain, variety, family, ilk, sort, kind, type, stamp, stock, race, progeny (*fml*), line, lineage, pedigree.

breeding *noun* **1** *the breeding of domestic animals*: reproduction, procreation, nurture, development, rearing, raising, upbringing, education, training, background, ancestry, lineage, stock. **2** *have good breeding*: manners, politeness, civility, gentility, urbanity, refinement, culture, polish.

F3 **2** vulgarity.

breeze *noun* wind, gust, flurry, waft, puff, breath, draught, air.

brew *verb* **1** *let the tea brew/brew beer*: infuse, stew, boil, seethe, ferment, prepare, soak, steep, mix, cook. **2** *some devilment brewing*: plot, scheme, plan, project, devise, contrive, concoct, hatch, excite, foment, build up, gather, develop.

bribe *noun* incentive, inducement, allurement, enticement, back-hander (*infml*), kickback, payola, refresher (*infml*), sweetener (*infml*), hush money (*infml*), protection money.

▪ *verb* corrupt, suborn, buy off, reward.

bridal *adjective* wedding, nuptial (*fml*), marriage, matrimonial, marital, conjugal.

bridge *noun* arch, span, causeway, link, connection, bond, tie.

▪ *verb* span, cross, traverse, fill, link, connect, couple, join, unite, bind.

brief *adjective* **1** *a brief description*: short, terse, succinct, concise, pithy, crisp, compressed, thumbnail, laconic, abrupt, sharp, brusque, blunt, curt, surly. **2** *a brief interruption/stay*: short-lived, momentary, ephemeral, transient, fleeting, passing, transitory, temporary, limited, cursory, hasty, quick, swift, fast.

OPP 1 long. **2** lengthy.

▪ *noun* **1** *a brief for the task in hand*: orders, instructions, directions, remit, mandate, directive, advice, briefing, data, information. **2** *a lawyer's brief*: outline, summary, précis, dossier, case, defence, argument.

▪ *verb* instruct, direct, explain, guide, advise, prepare, prime, inform, fill in (*infml*), gen up (*infml*).

briefing *noun* meeting, conference, preparation, priming, filling-in (*infml*), gen (*infml*), low-down (*infml*), information, advice, guidance, directions, instructions, orders.

bright *adjective* **1** *bright lights/sunshine*: luminous, illuminated, radiant, shining, beaming, flashing, gleaming, glistening, glittering, sparkling, twinkling, shimmering, glowing, brilliant, resplendent, glorious, splendid, dazzling, glaring, blazing, intense, vivid. **2** *merry and bright/a bright smile*: happy, cheerful, glad, joyful, merry, jolly, lively, vivacious. **3** *the future looks bright*: promising, propitious, auspicious, favourable, rosy, optimistic, hopeful, encouraging. **4** *a very bright child*: clever, brainy (*infml*), smart, intelligent, quick-witted, quick, sharp, acute, keen, astute, perceptive. **5** *a bright colour*: clear, transparent, translucent, lucid. **6** *a bright day*: fine, sunny, cloudless, unclouded.

OPP 1 dull. **2** sad. **3** depressing. **4** stupid. **5** muddy. **6** dark.

brighten *verb* **1** *brighten a dark corner/the weather brightened up*: light up, illuminate, lighten, clear up. **2** *brightening the tarnished metal*: polish, burnish, rub up, shine, gleam, glow. **3** *she brightened a little when she got the news*: cheer up, gladden, hearten, encourage, enliven, perk up.

OPP 1 darken. **2** dull, tarnish.

brilliance *noun* **1** *his brilliance with figures*: talent, virtuosity, genius, greatness, distinction, excellence, aptitude, cleverness. **2** *a gem's brilliance/the brilliance of the emperor's court*: radiance, brightness, sparkle, dazzle, intensity, vividness, gloss, lustre, sheen, glamour, glory, magnificence, splendour.

brilliant *adjective* **1** *a brilliant pianist*: gifted, talented, accomplished, expert, skilful, masterly, exceptional, outstanding, superb, illustrious, famous, celebrated. **2** *a brilliant star*: sparkling, glittering, scintillating, dazzling, glaring, blazing, intense, vivid, bright, shining, glossy, showy, glorious, magnificent, splendid. **3** *a brilliant idea/analysis*: clever, brainy

(*infml*), intelligent, quick, astute.
F3 1 undistinguished. **2** dull. **3** stupid.

brim *noun* rim, perimeter, circumference, lip, edge, margin, border, brink, verge, top, limit.

bring *verb* **1** *bring the children/an umbrella*: carry, bear, convey, transport, fetch, take, deliver, escort, accompany, usher, guide, conduct, lead. **2** *bring disease/ despair/hope*: cause, produce, engender, create, prompt, provoke, force, attract, draw.

brink *noun* verge, threshold, edge, margin, fringe, border, boundary, limit, extremity, lip, rim, brim, bank.

brisk *adjective* **1** *her manner was brisk and efficient*: energetic, vigorous, quick, snappy, lively, spirited, active, busy, bustling, agile, nimble, alert. **2** *a brisk walk*: invigorating, exhilarating, stimulating, bracing, refreshing, fresh.
F3 1 lazy, sluggish.

bristle *noun* hair, whisker, stubble, spine, prickle, barb, thorn.

brittle *adjective* breakable, fragile, delicate, frail, crisp, crumbly, crumbling, friable, shattery, shivery.
F3 durable, resilient.

broad *adjective* **1** *a broad avenue/ river*: wide, large, vast, roomy, spacious, capacious, ample, extensive, widespread. **2** *a broad category*: wide-ranging, far-reaching, encyclopedic, catholic, eclectic, all-embracing, inclusive, comprehensive, general, sweeping, universal, unlimited.
F3 1 narrow. **2** restricted.

broadcast *verb* air, show, transmit, beam, relay, televise, report, announce, publicize, advertise, publish, circulate, promulgate, disseminate, spread.
▪ *noun* transmission, programme, show.

broaden *verb* widen, thicken, swell, spread, enlarge, expand, extend, stretch, increase, augment, develop, open up, branch out, diversify.

broad-minded *adjective* liberal, tolerant, permissive, enlightened, free-thinking, open-minded, receptive, unbiased, unprejudiced.
F3 narrow-minded, intolerant, biased.

brochure *noun* leaflet, booklet, pamphlet, prospectus, broadsheet, handbill, circular, handout, folder.

broke *adjective* (*infml*) insolvent, penniless, bankrupt, bust, ruined, skint (*infml*), impoverished, destitute.
F3 solvent, rich, affluent.

broken *adjective* **1** *a broken leg/ toy/pipe*: fractured, burst, ruptured, severed, separated, dud (*slang*), faulty, defective, out of order, shattered, destroyed, demolished, kaput (*slang*). **2** *a broken line/voice*: disjointed, disconnected, fragmentary,

discontinuous, interrupted, intermittent, spasmodic, erratic, hesitating, stammering, halting, imperfect. **3** *a broken man*: beaten, defeated, crushed, demoralized, down, weak, feeble, exhausted, tamed, subdued, oppressed.
≠ **1** mended. **2** continuous, fluent.

broken-down *adjective* dilapidated, worn-out, ruined, kaput (*slang*), collapsed, decayed, inoperative, out of order.

brood *verb* ponder, ruminate, meditate, muse, mull over, go over, rehearse, dwell on, agonize, fret, mope.
▪ *noun* clutch, chicks, hatch, litter, young, offspring, issue, progeny (*fml*), children, family.

brother *noun* sibling, relation, relative, comrade, friend, mate, partner, colleague, associate, fellow, companion, monk, friar.

brotherhood *noun* fraternity, association, society, league, confederation, confederacy, alliance, union, guild, fellowship, community, clique.

brown *adjective* mahogany, chocolate, coffee, hazel, bay, chestnut, umber, sepia, tan, tawny, russet, rust, rusty, brunette, dark, dusky, sunburnt, tanned, bronzed, browned, toasted.

browse *verb* **1** *browsing through the dictionary*: leaf through, flick through, dip into, skim, survey, scan, peruse. **2** *animals browsing on the vegetation*: graze, pasture, feed, eat, nibble.

bruise *noun* contusion, discoloration, black eye, shiner (*infml*), mark, blemish, injury.
▪ *verb* discolour, blacken, mark, blemish, pound, pulverize, crush, hurt, injure, insult, offend, grieve.

brush[1] *verb* **1** *brush the floor*: clean, sweep, flick, burnish, polish, shine. **2** *brushing against her cheek*: touch, contact, graze, kiss, stroke, rub, scrape.

brush[2] *noun* scrub, thicket, bushes, shrubs, brushwood, undergrowth, ground cover.

brutal *adjective* animal, bestial, beastly, brutish, inhuman, savage, bloodthirsty, vicious, ferocious, cruel, inhumane, remorseless, pitiless, merciless, ruthless, callous, insensitive, unfeeling, heartless, harsh, gruff, rough, coarse, crude, rude, uncivilized, barbarous.
≠ kindly, humane, civilized.

brutality *noun* savagery, bloodthirstiness, viciousness, ferocity, cruelty, inhumanity, violence, atrocity, ruthlessness, callousness, roughness, coarseness, barbarism, barbarity.
≠ gentleness, kindness.

brute *noun* animal, beast, swine, creature, monster, ogre, devil, fiend, savage, sadist, bully, lout.

bubble *noun* blister, vesicle, globule, ball, drop, droplet, bead.
▪ *verb* effervesce, fizz, sparkle, froth, foam, seethe, boil, burble, gurgle.

bubbly *adjective* **1** *bubbly champagne*: effervescent, fizzy, sparkling, carbonated, frothy, foaming, sudsy. **2** *a bubbly personality*: lively, bouncy, happy, merry, elated, excited, irrepressible.
⇄ **1** flat, still. **2** dull, lethargic.

bucket *noun* pail, can, bail, scuttle, vessel.

buckle *noun* clasp, clip, catch, fastener.
▪ *verb* fasten, clasp, catch, hook, hitch, connect, close, secure.

bud *noun* shoot, sprout, germ, embryo.

budding *adjective* potential, promising, embryonic, burgeoning, developing, growing, flowering.

budge *verb* move, stir, shift, remove, dislodge, push, roll, slide, propel, sway, influence, persuade, convince, change, bend, yield, give (way).

budget *noun* finances, funds, resources, means, allowance, allotment, allocation, estimate.
▪ *verb* plan, estimate, allow, allot, allocate, apportion, ration.

buff[1] *verb* polish, burnish, shine, smooth, rub, brush.

buff[2] *noun* expert, connoisseur, enthusiast, fan, admirer, devotee, addict, fiend, freak.

buffet[1] *noun* /**buwf**-ei/ snack-bar, counter, café, cafeteria.

buffet[2] *verb* /**buf**-it/ batter, hit, strike, knock, bang, bump, push, shove, pound, pummel, beat, thump, box, cuff, clout, slap.
▪ *noun* blow, knock, bang, bump, jar, jolt, push, shove, thump, box, cuff, clout, slap, smack.

bug *noun* **1** *a tummy bug*: virus, bacterium, germ, microbe, micro-organism, infection, disease. **2** *bugs in the computer program*: fault, defect, blemish, imperfection, flaw, failing, error, gremlin (*infml*).
▪ *verb* **1** *bug their offices*: tap, spy on, listen in. **2** (*infml*) *don't bug me with questions!*: annoy, irritate, vex, irk, needle (*infml*), bother, disturb, harass, badger.

build *noun* physique, figure, body, form, shape, size, frame, structure.
▪ *verb* **1** *build a house/a wall/a lasting peace*: erect, raise, construct, fabricate, make, form, constitute, assemble, knock together, develop, enlarge, extend, increase, augment, escalate, intensify. **2** *build an organization*: base, found, establish, institute, inaugurate, initiate, begin.
⇄ **1** destroy, demolish, knock down, lessen.

building *noun* edifice, dwelling, construction, fabrication, structure, architecture.

Types of building include:
block of flats, bungalow, cabin, castle, château, cottage, farmhouse, house, mansion, palace, villa; abbey, cathedral, chapel, church, monastery, mosque, pagoda, synagogue, temple; café, cinema, college,

factory, garage, gymnasium, hospital, hotel, inn, library, multiplex, museum, observatory, office block, power station, prison, pub (*infml*), public house, restaurant, school, shop, silo, skyscraper, sports hall, store, theatre, tower block, warehouse; barracks, fort, fortress, mausoleum, monument; barn, beach hut, boat-house, dovecote, gazebo, lighthouse, mill, outhouse, pavilion, pier, shed, stable, summerhouse, windmill. *See also* **house**; **shop**.

---

bulge *verb* swell, puff out, bulb, hump, dilate, expand, enlarge, distend, protrude, project, sag. ▪ *noun* swelling, bump, lump, hump, distension (*fml*), protuberance (*fml*), projection.

bulk *noun* size, magnitude, dimensions, extent, amplitude, bigness, largeness, immensity, volume, mass, weight, substance, body, preponderance, majority, most.

bulky *adjective* substantial, big, large, huge, enormous, immense, mammoth, massive, colossal, hulking, hefty, heavy, weighty, unmanageable, unwieldy, awkward, cumbersome.
F3 insubstantial, small, handy.

bullet *noun* shot, pellet, ball, slug (*infml*), missile, projectile.

bulletin *noun* report, newsflash, dispatch, communiqué, statement, announcement, notification, communication, message.

bully *noun* persecutor, tormentor, browbeater, intimidator, bully-boy, heavy (*infml*), ruffian, tough, thug. ▪ *verb* persecute, torment, terrorize, bulldoze, coerce, browbeat, bullyrag, intimidate, cow, tyrannize, domineer, overbear, oppress, push around.

bump *verb* **1** *bump one's head against the door*: hit, strike, knock, bang, crash, collide (with). **2** *bumping along on the uneven surface*: jolt, jerk, jar, jostle, rattle, shake, bounce.
▪ *noun* **1** *hit the other car with a bump*: blow, hit, knock, bang, thump, thud, smash, crash, collision, impact, jolt, jar, shock. **2** *a bump on the head*: lump, swelling, bulge, hump, protuberance (*fml*).

bumpy *adjective* jerky, jolting, bouncy, choppy, rough, lumpy, knobbly, uneven, irregular.
F3 smooth, even.

bunch *noun* **1** *a bunch of keys*: bundle, sheaf, tuft, clump, cluster, batch, lot, heap, pile, stack, mass, number, quantity, collection, assortment. **2** *a bunch of flowers*: bouquet, posy, spray. **3** *a bunch of thugs*: gang, band, troop, crew, team, party, gathering, flock, swarm, crowd, mob, multitude.

bundle *noun* bunch, sheaf, roll, bale, truss, parcel, package, packet, carton, box, bag, pack, batch, consignment, group, set, collection, assortment, quantity, mass, accumulation, pile, stack, heap.

bungle *verb* mismanage, foul up (*infml*), mess up (*infml*), ruin, spoil, mar, botch, fudge, blunder.

buoy *noun* float, marker, signal, beacon.

buoyant *adjective* **1** *in buoyant mood*: light-hearted, carefree, bright, cheerful, happy, joyful, lively, animated, bouncy. **2** *a buoyant container*: floatable, floating, afloat, light, weightless.
F3 1 depressed, despairing. **2** heavy.

burden *noun* cargo, load, weight, dead-weight, encumbrance, millstone, onus, responsibility, obligation, duty, inconvenience, imposition, strain, stress, worry, anxiety, care, trouble, trial, affliction, sorrow.

bureau *noun* service, agency, office, branch, department, division, counter, desk.

bureaucracy *noun* administration, government, ministry, civil service, the authorities, the system, officialdom, red tape, regulations.

burglar *noun* housebreaker, robber, thief, pilferer, trespasser.

burglary *noun* housebreaking, break-in, robbery, theft, stealing, trespass.

burly *adjective* big, well-built, hulking, hefty, heavy, stocky, sturdy, brawny, beefy, muscular, athletic, strapping, strong, powerful.
F3 small, puny, thin, slim.

burn *verb* **1** *fire burning/burn the rubbish*: flame, blaze, flare, flash, glow, flicker, smoulder, smoke, ignite, light, kindle, incinerate, cremate. **2** *burn one's finger/burn the food*: scald, scorch, singe, char, toast, sear. **3** *burn with indignation*: smart, sting, hurt, tingle, fume, simmer, seethe.

burning *adjective* **1** *a burning lamp*: ablaze, aflame, afire, fiery, flaming, blazing, flashing, gleaming, glowing, smouldering, alight, lit, illuminated. **2** *a burning sensation*: hot, scalding, scorching, searing, piercing, acute, smarting, stinging, prickling, tingling, biting, caustic, pungent. **3** *burning desire*: ardent, fervent, eager, earnest, intense, vehement, passionate, impassioned, frantic, frenzied, consuming. **4** *burning issue*: urgent, pressing, important, significant, crucial, essential, vital.
F3 2 cold. **3** apathetic. **4** unimportant.

burrow *noun* warren, hole, earth, set, den, lair, retreat, shelter, tunnel.
▪ *verb* tunnel, dig, delve, excavate, mine, undermine.

burst *verb* puncture, rupture, tear, split, crack, break, fragment, shatter, shiver, disintegrate, explode, blow up, erupt, gush, spout, rush, run.

bury *verb* **1** *bury the dead*: inter, entomb, lay to rest, shroud. **2** *buried under snow*: sink, submerge, immerse, plant,

implant, embed, conceal, hide, cover, enshroud, engulf, enclose.
F3 **1** disinter, exhume. **2** uncover.

bushy *adjective* hairy, thick, dense, luxuriant, shaggy.

business *noun* **1** *the business sector*: trade, commerce, industry, manufacturing, dealings, transactions, bargaining, trading, buying, selling. **2** *a successful business*: company, firm, corporation, establishment, venture, organization, concern, enterprise. **3** *went about his business quietly*: job, occupation, work, employment, trade, profession, line, calling, career, vocation, duty, task, responsibility. **4** *that's not our business*: affair, matter, issue, subject, topic, question, problem, point.

businesslike *adjective* professional, efficient, thorough, systematic, methodical, organized, orderly, well-ordered, well-organized, practical, matter-of-fact, precise, correct, formal, impersonal.
F3 inefficient, disorganized.

bustle *verb* dash, rush, scamper, scurry, hurry, hasten, scramble, fuss.
▪ *noun* activity, stir, commotion, tumult, agitation, excitement, fuss, ado, flurry, hurry, haste.

busy *adjective* **1** *busy at the office*: occupied, engaged, tied up (*infml*), employed, working, slaving. **2** *keep oneself busy*: active, lively, energetic. **3** *a busy street*: crowded, swarming, teeming, bustling. **4** *had a busy day*: hectic, eventful, strenuous, tiring. **5** *her busy fingers*: restless, tireless, diligent, industrious.
F3 **1** idle. **2** idle, lazy. **3** quiet. **4** quiet, restful. **5** idle.

busybody *noun* meddler, nosey parker (*infml*), intruder, pry, gossip, eavesdropper, snoop, snooper, troublemaker.

butt[1] *noun* stub, end, tip, tail, base, foot, shaft, stock, handle, haft.

butt[2] *noun* target, mark, object, subject, victim, laughing-stock, dupe.

butt[3] *verb* hit, bump, knock, buffet, push, shove, ram, thrust, punch, jab, prod, poke.

buy *verb* purchase, invest in (*infml*), pay for, procure, acquire, obtain, get.
F3 sell.
▪ *noun* purchase, acquisition, bargain, deal.

buyer *noun* purchaser, shopper, consumer, customer, vendee, emptor.
F3 seller, vendor.

buzz *verb* **1** *bees buzzing*: hum, drone, murmur, whirr, susurrate (*fml*). **2** *buzz with excitement*: hum, throb, pulse, bustle.

by *preposition* near, next to, beside, along, over, through, via, past.
▪ *adverb* near, close, handy, at hand, past, beyond, away, aside.

bypass *verb* avoid, dodge, sidestep, skirt, circumvent, ignore, neglect, omit.
by-product *noun* consequence, result, side-effect, fallout (*infml*), repercussion, after-effect.
bystander *noun* spectator, onlooker, looker-on, watcher, observer, witness, eye-witness, passer-by.

C

cabin *noun* **1** *the captain's cabin*: berth, quarters, compartment, room. **2** *log cabin*: hut, shack, lodge, chalet, cottage, shed, shelter.
cable *noun* line, rope, cord, chain, hawser, wire, flex, lead.
cadge *verb* scrounge, sponge, beg, hitch.
café *noun* coffee shop, tea shop, tea room, coffee bar, cafeteria, snack bar, bistro, brasserie, restaurant.
caged *adjective* shut up, locked up, cooped up, confined, fenced in, imprisoned, incarcerated.
F3 free.
cajole *verb* coax, persuade, wheedle, flatter, sweet-talk (*infml*), butter up (*infml*), tempt, lure, seduce, entice, beguile, inveigle (*fml*), mislead, dupe.
F3 bully, force, compel.
cake *noun* **1** *tea and cakes*: gâteau, fancy, madeleine, bun, pie, flan, pastry, sponge, tart. **2** *cake of soap*: lump, mass, bar, slab, block.
▪ *verb* coat, cover, encrust, dry, harden, solidify, consolidate, coagulate, congeal, thicken.
calamity *noun* disaster, catastrophe, mishap, trial, misadventure, mischance, misfortune, adversity, reverse, tribulation, ruin, affliction, distress, tragedy, downfall.
F3 blessing, godsend.
calculate *verb* compute, work out, count, enumerate, reckon, figure, determine, weigh, rate, value, estimate, gauge, judge, consider, plan, intend, aim.
calculated *adjective* considered, deliberate, purposeful, intended, intentional, planned, premeditated.
calculating *adjective* crafty, cunning, sly, devious, scheming, designing, contriving, sharp, shrewd.
F3 artless, naive.
calibre *noun* **1** *guns of different calibres*: diameter, bore, gauge, size, measure. **2** *candidates of the*

right calibre: talent, gifts, strength, worth, merit, quality, character, ability, capacity, faculty, stature, distinction.

call *noun* **1** *a call for assistance*: cry, exclamation, shout, yell, scream. **2** *a telephone call/doctor has several calls to make*: ring, visit, summons, invitation. **3** *calls for his resignation*: appeal, request, plea, order, command, claim, announcement, signal.
▪ *verb* **1** *they call him Bob*: name, christen, baptize, title, entitle, dub, style, term, label, designate. **2** *he called her name*: shout, yell, exclaim, cry. **3** *she called us all in for a meeting*: summon, invite, bid, send for, order, convene, assemble. **4** *I'll call you later*: telephone, phone, ring (up), contact.

calling *noun* mission, vocation, career, profession, occupation, job, trade, business, line, work, employment, field, province, pursuit.

callous *adjective* heartless, hard-hearted, cold, indifferent, uncaring, unsympathetic, unfeeling, insensitive, hardened, thick-skinned.
F3 kind, caring, sympathetic, sensitive.

calm *adjective* **1** *told us to remain calm*: composed, self-possessed, collected, cool, dispassionate, unemotional, impassive, unmoved, placid, sedate, unflappable, imperturbable, unexcitable, laid-back (*infml*), relaxed, unexcited, unruffled, unflustered, unperturbed, undisturbed, untroubled, unapprehensive. **2** *calm waters*: smooth, still, windless, unclouded, mild, tranquil, serene, peaceful, quiet, uneventful, restful.
F3 **1** excitable, worried, anxious. **2** rough, wild, stormy.
▪ *verb* compose, soothe, relax, sedate, tranquillize, hush, quieten, placate, pacify.
F3 excite, worry.
▪ *noun* calmness, stillness, tranquillity, serenity, peacefulness, peace, quiet, hush, repose.
F3 storminess, restlessness.

camouflage *noun* disguise, guise, masquerade, mask, cloak, screen, blind, front, cover, concealment, deception.
▪ *verb* disguise, mask, cloak, veil, screen, cover, conceal, hide, obscure.
F3 uncover, reveal.

campaign *noun* crusade, movement, promotion, drive, push, offensive, attack, battle, expedition, operation.
▪ *verb* crusade, promote, push, advocate, fight, battle.

cancel *verb* call off, abort, abandon, drop, abolish, annul, quash, rescind, revoke, repeal, countermand, delete, erase, obliterate, eliminate.

candidate *noun* applicant, aspirant, contender, contestant, competitor, entrant, runner, possibility, nominee, claimant, pretender, suitor.

canopy *noun* awning, covering, shade, shelter, sunshade, umbrella.

canvass *verb* electioneer, agitate, campaign, solicit, ask for, seek, poll.

canyon *noun* gorge, ravine, gully, valley, chasm, abyss, defile (*fml*).

capability *noun* ability, capacity, faculty, power, potential, means, facility, competence, qualification, skill, proficiency, talent.
F3 inability, incompetence.

capable *adjective* able, competent, efficient, qualified, experienced, accomplished, skilful, proficient, gifted, talented, masterly, clever, intelligent, fitted, suited, apt, liable, disposed.
F3 incapable, incompetent, useless.

capacity *noun* **1** *the capacity of the jug*: volume, space, room, size, dimensions, magnitude, extent, compass, range, scope. **2** *have the capacity to make people laugh*: capability, ability, faculty, power, potential, competence, efficiency, skill, gift, talent, genius, cleverness, intelligence, aptitude, readiness. **3** *in her capacity as president*: role, function, position, office, post, job, appointment.

cape[1] *noun* cloak, shawl, wrap, robe, poncho, mantle, cope, coat.

cape[2] *noun* headland, head, promontory, point, ness, peninsula.

capital *noun* **1** *the capital of Brazil*: most important city, administrative centre, centre of government. **2** *write in capitals*: block letter, block capital, capital letter, upper-case letter. **3** *the capital to start a business*: funds, finance, principal, money, cash, savings, investment(s), wealth, means, wherewithal, resources, assets, property, stock.
▪ *adjective* **1** *capital cities*: principal, important, leading, prime, main, major, chief, foremost. **2** *a capital crime*: serious, punishable by death.

capitalize *verb* profit, take advantage, exploit, cash in (*infml*).

capsize *verb* overturn, turn over, turn turtle, invert, keel over, upset.

capsule *noun* **1** *take the medicine in capsule form*: pill, tablet, lozenge. **2** *a seed capsule/space capsule*: receptacle, shell, sheath, pod, module.

captivate *verb* charm, enchant, bewitch, beguile, fascinate, enthral, hypnotize, mesmerize, lure, allure, seduce, win, attract, enamour, infatuate, enrapture, dazzle.
F3 repel, disgust, appal.

captive *noun* prisoner, hostage, slave, detainee, internee, convict.
▪ *adjective* imprisoned, caged, confined, restricted, secure, locked up, enchained, enslaved, ensnared.
F3 free.

captivity *noun* custody,

detention, imprisonment, incarceration, internment, confinement, restraint, bondage, duress, slavery, servitude.
F freedom.

capture *verb* catch, trap, snare, take, seize, nab (*infml*), arrest, apprehend, imprison, secure.

car *noun* automobile, motor car, motor, vehicle.

care *noun* **1** *full of care*: worry, anxiety, stress, strain, pressure, concern, trouble, distress, affliction, tribulation, vexation. **2** *drive without due care*: carefulness, caution, prudence, forethought, vigilance, watchfulness, pains, meticulousness, attention, heed, regard, consideration, interest. **3** *in their care*: keeping, custody, guardianship, protection, ward, charge, responsibility, control, supervision.
F **2** carelessness, thoughtlessness, inattention, neglect.
▪ *verb* worry, mind, bother.

career *noun* vocation, calling, life-work, occupation, pursuit, profession, trade, job, employment, livelihood.

carefree *adjective* unworried, untroubled, unconcerned, blithe, breezy, happy-go-lucky, cheery, light-hearted, cheerful, happy, easy-going (*infml*), laid-back (*infml*).
F worried, anxious, despondent.

careful *adjective* **1** *be careful*: cautious, prudent, circumspect (*fml*), judicious (*fml*), wary, chary, vigilant, watchful, alert, attentive, mindful. **2** *a careful study*: meticulous, painstaking, conscientious, scrupulous, thorough, detailed, punctilious, particular, accurate, precise, thoughtful.
F **1** careless, inattentive, thoughtless, reckless. **2** careless.

careless *adjective* **1** *a careless remark*: unthinking, thoughtless, inconsiderate, uncaring, unconcerned, heedless, unmindful, forgetful, remiss, negligent, irresponsible, unguarded. **2** *careless work*: inaccurate, messy, untidy, disorderly, sloppy, neglectful, slipshod, slapdash, hasty, cursory, offhand, casual.
F **1** thoughtful, prudent. **2** careful, accurate, meticulous.

caress *verb* stroke, pet, fondle, cuddle, hug, embrace, kiss, touch, rub.

cargo *noun* freight, load, pay-load, lading, tonnage, shipment, consignment, contents, goods, merchandise, baggage.

caricature *noun* cartoon, parody, lampoon, burlesque, satire, send-up, take-off, imitation, representation, distortion, travesty.

carnival *noun* festival, fiesta, gala, jamboree, fête, fair, holiday, jubilee, celebration, merrymaking, revelry.

carriage *noun* coach, wagon, car, vehicle.

carry *verb* **1** *carrying goods/ electricity*: bring, convey, transport, haul, move, transfer, relay, release, conduct, take, fetch. **2** *carried the entire weight*: bear, shoulder, support, underpin, maintain, uphold, sustain, suffer, stand.

cartoon *noun* comic strip, animation, sketch, drawing, caricature, parody.

cartridge *noun* cassette, canister, cylinder, tube, container, case, capsule, shell, magazine, round, charge.

carve *verb* cut, slice, hack, hew, chisel, chip, sculpt, sculpture, shape, form, fashion, mould, etch, engrave, incise, indent.

case[1] *noun* **1** *let me carry your case*: receptacle, holder, suitcase, trunk. **2** *a case of champagne*: container, crate, box, carton, casket, chest. **3** *a display case*: cabinet, showcase. **4** *a waterproof/metal case*: casing, cartridge, shell, capsule, sheath, cover, jacket, wrapper.

case[2] *noun* **1** *in this case*: circumstances, context, state, condition, position, situation, contingency, occurrence, occasion, event. **2** *a medical case/ a clear case of too much too soon*: specimen, example, instance, illustration, point. **3** *a legal case*: lawsuit, suit, trial, proceedings, action, process, cause, argument, dispute.

cash *noun* money, hard money, ready money, bank-notes, notes, coins, change, legal tender, currency, hard currency, dough (*infml*), bullion, funds, resources, wherewithal.

■ *verb* encash, exchange, realize, liquidate.

cast *verb* **1** *casting the seed on the earth*: throw, hurl, lob, pitch, fling, toss, sling, shy, launch, impel, drive, direct, project, shed, emit, diffuse, spread, scatter. **2** *cast in bronze*: mould, shape, form, model, found.

■ *noun* **1** *a cast of thousands*: company, troupe, actors, players, performers, entertainers, characters, dramatis personae. **2** *make a cast of the footprint*: casting, mould, shape, form.

castle *noun* stronghold, fortress, citadel, keep, tower, château, palace.

casual *adjective* **1** *a casual meeting/remark*: chance, fortuitous (*fml*), accidental, unintentional, unpremeditated, unexpected, unforeseen, irregular, random, occasional, incidental, superficial, cursory. **2** *a casual attitude*: nonchalant, blasé, lackadaisical, negligent, couldn't-care-less (*infml*), apathetic, indifferent, unconcerned, informal, offhand, relaxed, laid-back (*infml*). **3** *casual work*: temporary, irregular, occasional, part-time, short-term. **4** *casual clothes*: informal, comfortable, relaxed, leisure.

F3 **1** deliberate, planned. **2** formal. **3** permanent. **4** formal.

casualty *noun* injury, loss, death, fatality, victim, sufferer, injured person, wounded, dead person.

cat

Breeds of cat include:

Abyssinian, American shorthair, Balinese, Birman, Bombay, British longhair, British shorthair, Burmese, Carthusian, chinchilla, Cornish rex, Cymric, Devon rex, domestic tabby, Egyptian Mau, Exotic shorthair, Foreign Blue, Foreign spotted shorthair, Foreign White, Havana, Himalayan, Japanese Bobtail, Korat, Maine Coon, Manx, Norwegian Forest, Persian, rag-doll, rex, Russian Blue, Scottish Fold, Siamese, silver tabby, Singapura, Somali, Tiffany, Tonkinese, Tortoiseshell, Turkish Angora, Turkish Van.

---

catalogue *noun* list, inventory, roll, register, roster, schedule, record, table, index, directory, gazetteer, brochure, prospectus.

catastrophe *noun* disaster, calamity, cataclysm, debacle, fiasco, failure, ruin, devastation, tragedy, blow, reverse, mischance, misfortune, adversity, affliction, trouble, upheaval.

catch *noun* **1** *the catch on the bracelet*: fastener, clip, hook, clasp, hasp, latch, bolt. **2** *what's the catch?*: disadvantage, drawback, snag, hitch, obstacle, problem.
▪ *verb* **1** *catch a ball*: seize, grab, take, hold, grasp, grip, clutch. **2** *catch a thief*: capture, trap, entrap, snare, ensnare, hook, net, arrest, apprehend. **3** *try to catch them red-handed*: surprise, expose, unmask, find (out), discover, detect, discern. **4** *catch a cold*: contract, get, develop, go down with.
E3 **1** drop. **2** release, free.

catching *adjective* infectious, contagious, communicable, transmittable.

catchy *adjective* memorable, haunting, popular, melodic, tuneful, attractive, captivating.
E3 dull, boring.

categorical *adjective* absolute, total, utter, unqualified, unreserved, unconditional, downright, positive, definite, emphatic, direct, unequivocal, clear, explicit, express.
E3 tentative, qualified, vague.

category *noun* class, classification, group, grouping, sort, type, section, division, department, chapter, head, heading, grade, rank, order, list.

cater *verb* cook, provide, supply, furnish, serve.

catholic *adjective* broad, wide, wide-ranging, universal, global, general, comprehensive, inclusive, all-inclusive, all-embracing, liberal, tolerant, broad-minded.
E3 narrow, limited, narrow-minded.

cattle *noun* cows, bulls, oxen, livestock, stock, beasts.

cause *noun* **1** *what was the cause of the argument?*: source, origin,

beginning, root, basis, spring, originator, creator, producer, maker, agent, agency. **2** *the causes of war*: reason, motive, grounds, motivation, stimulus, incentive, inducement, impulse. **3** *a worthy cause*: object, purpose, end, ideal, belief, conviction, movement, undertaking, enterprise.
F3 **1** effect, result, consequence.
▪ *verb* begin, give rise to, lead to, result in, occasion, bring about, effect, produce, generate, create, precipitate (*fml*), motivate, stimulate, provoke, incite, induce, force, compel.
F3 stop, prevent.

caution *noun* **1** *show a little more caution*: care, carefulness, prudence, vigilance, watchfulness, alertness, heed, discretion, forethought, deliberation, wariness. **2** *a police caution*: warning, caveat, injunction, admonition, advice, counsel.
F3 **1** carelessness, recklessness.
▪ *verb* warn, alert, advise, counsel, forewarn.

cautious *adjective* careful, prudent, circumspect (*fml*), judicious (*fml*), vigilant, watchful, alert, heedful, discreet, tactful, chary, wary, cagey (*infml*), guarded, tentative, softly-softly, unadventurous.
F3 incautious, imprudent, heedless, reckless.

cave *noun* cavern, grotto, hole, pothole, hollow, cavity.

cease *verb* stop, desist, refrain, pack in (*infml*), halt, call a halt, break off, discontinue, finish, end, conclude, terminate, fail, die.
F3 begin, start, commence.

celebrate *verb* commemorate, remember, observe, keep, rejoice, toast, drink to, honour, exalt, glorify, praise, extol (*fml*), eulogize (*fml*), commend, bless, solemnize.

celebrated *adjective* famous, well-known, famed, renowned, illustrious, glorious, eminent, distinguished, notable, prominent, outstanding, popular, acclaimed, exalted, revered.
F3 unknown, obscure, forgotten.

celebration *noun* commemoration, remembrance, observance, anniversary, jubilee, festival, gala, merrymaking, jollification, revelry, festivity, party, rave-up (*infml*).

Celebrations include:

anniversary, banquet, baptism, bar mitzvah, birthday, centenary, christening, coming-of-age, fête, gala, harvest festival, homecoming, Independence Day, jubilee, marriage, May Day, party, reception, retirement, reunion, saint's day, thanksgiving, tribute, wedding. *See also* **party**.

---

celebrity *noun* personage, dignitary, VIP (*infml*), luminary, worthy, personality, name, big name, star, superstar.
F3 nobody, nonentity.

cemetery *noun* burial-ground,

graveyard, churchyard.

censor *verb* cut, edit, blue-pencil, bowdlerize, expurgate.

censure *noun* condemnation, blame, disapproval, criticism, admonishment, admonition, reproof, reproach, rebuke, reprimand, telling-off (*infml*).
F≠ praise, compliments, approval.
▪ *verb* condemn, denounce, blame, criticize, castigate (*fml*), admonish, reprehend (*fml*), reprove, upbraid (*fml*), reproach, rebuke, reprimand, scold, tell off (*infml*).
F≠ praise, compliment, approve.

central *adjective* middle, mid, inner, interior, focal, main, chief, key, principal, primary, fundamental, vital, essential, important.
F≠ peripheral, minor, secondary.

centre *noun* middle, mid-point, bull's-eye, heart, core, nucleus, pivot, hub, focus, crux.
F≠ edge, periphery, outskirts.

ceremonial *adjective* formal, official, stately, solemn, ritual, ritualistic.
F≠ informal, casual.

ceremony *noun* **1** *wedding ceremony*: service, rite, commemoration, observance, celebration, function, parade. **2** *without ceremony*: etiquette, protocol, decorum, propriety, formality, form, niceties, ceremonial, ritual, pomp, show.

certain *adjective* **1** *I'm certain he's telling the truth/it's now certain that they will win*: sure, positive, assured, confident, convinced, undoubted, indubitable, convincing, unquestionable, incontrovertible, undeniable, irrefutable, plain, conclusive, absolute, true. **2** *it was certain to happen sometime*: inevitable, unavoidable, bound, fated, destined. **3** *a certain person we both know/below a certain point*: specific, special, particular, individual, precise, express, fixed, established, settled, decided, definite. **4** *one of the few certain things in life*: dependable, reliable, trustworthy, constant, steady, stable.
F≠ **1** uncertain, unsure, hesitant, doubtful. **2** unlikely. **4** unreliable.

certainly *adverb* of course, naturally, definitely, for sure, undoubtedly, doubtlessly.

certainty *noun* sureness, positiveness, assurance, confidence, conviction, faith, trust, truth, validity, fact, reality, inevitability.
F≠ uncertainty, doubt, hesitation.

certificate *noun* document, award, diploma, qualification, credentials, testimonial, guarantee, endorsement, warrant, licence, authorization, pass, voucher.

certify *verb* declare, attest (*fml*), aver (*fml*), assure, guarantee, endorse, corroborate, confirm, vouch, testify, witness, verify, authenticate, validate, authorize, license.

chain *noun* **1** *prisoners in chains*: fetter, manacle, restraint, bond, link, coupling, union. **2** *chain of events*: sequence, succession, progression, string, train, series, set.
▪ *verb* tether, fasten, secure, bind, restrain, confine, fetter, shackle, manacle, handcuff, enslave.
F3 release, free.

challenge *noun* dare, defiance, confrontation, provocation, test, trial, hurdle, obstacle, question, ultimatum.
▪ *verb* **1** *challenge him to fight*: dare, defy, throw down the gauntlet, confront, brave, accost, provoke, test, tax, try. **2** *challenge the decision*: dispute, question, query, protest, object to.

champion *noun* winner, victor, conqueror, hero, guardian, protector, defender, vindicator, patron, backer, supporter, upholder, advocate.

chance *noun* **1** *come across it by chance/take a chance*: accident, fortuity (*fml*), coincidence, fluke (*infml*), luck, fortune, providence, fate, destiny, risk, gamble, speculation. **2** *a chance of winning millions*: possibility, prospect, probability, likelihood, odds. **3** *a second chance*: opportunity, opening, occasion, time.
F3 1 certainty.
▪ *adjective* fortuitous (*fml*), casual, accidental, inadvertent, unintentional, unintended, unforeseen, unlooked-for, random, haphazard, incidental.
F3 deliberate, intentional, foreseen, certain.

change *verb* **1** *changing into a butterfly/prices keep changing*: alter, modify, convert, reorganize, reform, remodel, restyle, transform, transfigure, metamorphose, mutate, vary, fluctuate, vacillate, shift. **2** *change one thing for another*: swap, exchange, trade, switch, transpose, substitute, replace, alternate, interchange.
▪ *noun* alteration, modification, conversion, transformation, metamorphosis, mutation, variation, fluctuation, shift, exchange, transposition, substitution, interchange, difference, diversion, novelty, innovation, variety, transition, revolution, upheaval.

changeable *adjective* variable, mutable, fluid, kaleidoscopic, shifting, mobile, unsettled, uncertain, unpredictable, unreliable, erratic, irregular, inconstant, fickle, capricious, volatile, unstable, unsteady, wavering, vacillating.
F3 constant, reliable.

channel *noun* duct, conduit, main, groove, furrow, trough, gutter, canal, flume, watercourse, waterway, strait, sound.
▪ *verb* direct, guide, conduct, convey, send, transmit, force.

chaos *noun* disorder, confusion, disorganization, anarchy,

lawlessness, tumult, pandemonium, bedlam.
F order.

chaotic *adjective* disordered, confused, disorganized, topsy-turvy, deranged, anarchic, lawless, riotous, tumultuous, unruly, uncontrolled.
F ordered, organized.

chapter *noun* part, section, division, clause, topic, episode, period, phase, stage.

character *noun* **1** *the place has a character all its own*: personality, nature, disposition, temperament, temper, constitution, make-up, individuality, peculiarity, feature, attributes, quality, type, stamp, calibre, reputation, status, position, trait. **2** *a bit of a character*: eccentric, oddball (*infml*), case (*infml*). **3** *characters in a play*: individual, person, sort, type, role, part.

characteristic *noun* peculiarity, idiosyncrasy, mannerism, feature, trait, attribute, property, quality, hallmark, mark, symptom.
▪ *adjective* distinctive, distinguishing, individual, idiosyncratic, peculiar, specific, special, typical, representative, symbolic, symptomatic.
F uncharacteristic, untypical.

charge *verb* **1** *charge a high price*: ask, demand, levy, exact, debit. **2** *charge him with theft*: accuse, indict, impeach, incriminate, blame. **3** *charged forward*: attack, assail, storm, rush.
▪ *noun* **1** *high charges*: price, cost, fee, rate, amount, expense, expenditure, outlay, payment. **2** *a charge of murder*: accusation, indictment, allegation, imputation. **3** *the charge of the Light Brigade*: attack, assault, onslaught, sortie, rush. **4** *in your charge*: custody, keeping, care, safekeeping, guardianship, ward, trust, responsibility, duty.

charitable *adjective* philanthropic, humanitarian, kind, benevolent, benign, compassionate, sympathetic, understanding, considerate, generous, magnanimous, liberal, tolerant, broad-minded, lenient, forgiving, indulgent, gracious.
F uncharitable, inconsiderate, unforgiving.

charity *noun* **1** *show a bit of charity*: generosity, bountifulness, alms-giving, beneficence (*fml*), philanthropy, unselfishness, altruism, benevolence, kindness, goodness, humanity, compassion, tender-heartedness, love, affection, clemency, indulgence. **2** *dispense/live on charity*: alms, gift, handout, aid, relief, assistance.
F **1** selfishness, malice.

charm *noun* **1** *have a lot of charm*: attraction, allure, magnetism, appeal, desirability, fascination, enchantment, spell, sorcery, magic. **2** *lucky charm*: trinket, talisman, amulet, fetish, idol.
▪ *verb* please, delight, enrapture, captivate, fascinate, beguile,

enchant, bewitch, mesmerize, attract, allure, cajole, win, enamour.
F3 repel.

charming *adjective* pleasing, delightful, pleasant, lovely, captivating, enchanting, attractive, fetching, appealing, sweet, winsome, seductive, winning, irresistible.
F3 ugly, unattractive, repulsive.

chart *noun* diagram, table, graph, map, plan, blueprint.
▪ *verb* map, map out, sketch, draw, draft, outline, delineate, mark, plot, place.

charter *noun* right, privilege, prerogative, authorization, permit, licence, franchise, concession, contract, indenture (*fml*), deed, bond, document.
▪ *verb* hire, rent, lease, commission, engage, employ, authorize, sanction, license.

chase *verb* pursue, follow, hunt, track, drive, expel, rush, hurry.

chasm *noun* gap, opening, gulf, abyss, void, hollow, cavity, crater, breach, rift, split, cleft, fissure, crevasse, canyon, gorge, ravine.

chat *noun* talk, conversation, natter (*infml*), gossip, chinwag (*infml*), tête-à-tête, heart-to-heart, rap (*infml*).
▪ *verb* talk, crack, natter (*infml*), gossip, chatter, rabbit (on) (*infml*).

chatty *adjective* talkative, gossipy, newsy, friendly, informal, colloquial, familiar.
F3 quiet.

cheap *adjective* **1** *a cheap hotel*: inexpensive, reasonable, dirt-cheap, bargain, reduced, cut-price, knock-down, budget, economy, economical. **2** *a cheap trick/made of cheap materials*: tawdry, tatty, cheapo (*infml*), shoddy, inferior, second-rate, worthless, vulgar, common, poor, paltry, mean, contemptible, despicable, low.
F3 **1** expensive, costly. **2** superior, noble, admirable.

cheat *verb* defraud, swindle, diddle, short-change, do (*infml*), rip off (*infml*), fleece, con (*infml*), double-cross, mislead, deceive, dupe, fool, trick, hoodwink, bamboozle (*infml*), beguile.
▪ *noun* cheater, dodger, fraud, swindler, shark (*infml*), con man (*infml*), extortioner, double-crosser, impostor, charlatan, deceiver, trickster, rogue.

check *verb* **1** *check the brakes/his work/the figures*: examine, inspect, scrutinize, give the once-over (*infml*), investigate, probe, test, monitor, study, research, compare, cross-check, confirm, verify. **2** *checked its progress*: curb, bridle, restrain, control, limit, repress, inhibit, damp, thwart, hinder, impede, obstruct, bar, retard, delay, stop, arrest, halt.
▪ *noun* **1** *a health check*: examination, inspection, scrutiny, once-over (*infml*), check-up, investigation, audit, test, research. **2** *a check on growth*: curb,

restraint, control, limitation, constraint, inhibition, damper, blow, disappointment, reverse, setback, frustration, hindrance, impediment, obstruction, stoppage.

cheeky *adjective* impertinent, impudent, insolent, disrespectful, forward, brazen, pert, saucy (*infml*), audacious.
F3 respectful, polite.

cheer *verb* **1** *cheering their team*: acclaim, hail, clap, applaud. **2** *cheered by the news*: comfort, console, brighten, gladden, warm, uplift, elate, exhilarate, encourage, hearten.
F3 **1** boo, jeer. **2** dishearten.
▪ *noun* acclamation, hurrah, bravo, applause, ovation.

cheerful *adjective* happy, glad, contented, joyful, joyous, blithe, carefree, light-hearted, cheery, good-humoured, sunny, optimistic, enthusiastic, hearty, genial, jovial, jolly, merry, lively, animated, bright, chirpy, breezy, jaunty, buoyant, sparkling, upbeat (*infml*).
F3 sad, dejected, depressed.

chemistry

Terms used in chemistry include:
acid, alkali, analytical chemistry, atom, atomic number, atomic structure, base, biochemistry, bond, catalyst, chain reaction, combustion, compound, corrosion, covalent bond, crystal, decomposition, diffusion, distillation, electrode, electrolysis, electron, element, emulsion, equation, fermentation, formula, free radical, gas, halogen, hydrolysis, inert gas, inorganic chemistry, ion, ionic bond, isomer, isotope, lipid, liquid, litmus paper, litmus test, mass, matter, metal, mixture, mole, molecule, neutron, noble gas, nucleus, organic chemistry, oxidation, periodic table, pH, physical chemistry, polymer, proton, radioactivity, reaction, reduction, salt, solution, solvent, substance, suspension, synthesis, valency.

chew *verb* masticate (*fml*), gnaw, munch, champ, crunch, grind.

chief *adjective* leading, foremost, uppermost, highest, supreme, grand, arch, premier, principal, main, key, central, prime, prevailing, predominant, pre-eminent, outstanding, vital, essential, primary, major.
F3 minor, unimportant.
▪ *noun* ruler, chieftain, lord, master, supremo, head, principal, leader, commander, captain, governor, boss, director, manager, superintendent, superior, ringleader.

chiefly *adverb* mainly, mostly, for the most part, predominantly, principally, primarily, essentially, especially, generally, usually.

child *noun* youngster, kid (*infml*), nipper (*infml*), brat (*infml*), baby, infant, toddler, tot (*infml*), minor, juvenile, offspring, issue, progeny (*fml*), descendant.

childhood *noun* babyhood, infancy, boyhood, girlhood, schooldays, youth, adolescence, minority, immaturity.

childish *adjective* babyish, boyish, girlish, infantile, puerile (*fml*), juvenile, immature, silly, foolish, frivolous.

F≡ mature, sensible.

childlike *adjective* innocent, naive, ingenuous, artless, guileless, credulous, trusting, trustful, simple, natural.

chill *verb* cool, refrigerate, freeze, ice.

F≡ warm, heat.

chilly *adjective* cold, fresh, brisk, crisp, nippy (*infml*), wintry.

F≡ warm.

chip *noun* **1** *chips on the paintwork*: notch, nick, scratch, dent, flaw. **2** *wood chips*: fragment, scrap, wafer, sliver, flake, shaving, paring.

choice *noun* option, alternative, selection, variety, pick, preference, say, decision, dilemma, election, discrimination, choosing, opting.

▪ *adjective* best, superior, prime, plum, excellent, fine, exquisite, exclusive, select, hand-picked, special, prize, valuable, precious.

F≡ inferior, poor.

choke *verb* **1** *tried to choke her*: throttle, strangle, asphyxiate, suffocate, stifle, smother, suppress. **2** *leaves choking the gutters*: obstruct, constrict, congest, clog, block, dam, bar, close, stop. **3** *smoke made him choke*: cough, gag, retch.

choose *verb* pick, select, single out, designate, predestine, opt for, plump for, vote for, settle on, fix on, adopt, elect, prefer, wish, desire, see fit.

chop *verb* cut, hack, hew, lop, sever, truncate, cleave, divide, split, slash.

christen *verb* baptize, name, call, dub, title, style, term, designate, inaugurate, use.

chronic *adjective* **1** *a chronic illness/shortage/liar*: incurable, deep-seated, recurring, incessant, persistent, inveterate, confirmed, habitual, ingrained, deep-rooted. **2** (*infml*) *his singing was chronic*: awful, terrible, dreadful, appalling, atrocious.

F≡ **1** acute, temporary.

chubby *adjective* plump, podgy, fleshy, flabby, stout, portly, rotund, round, tubby, paunchy.

F≡ slim, skinny.

chuckle *verb* laugh, giggle, titter, snigger, chortle, snort, crow.

chunk *noun* lump, hunk, mass, wodge (*infml*), wedge, block, slab, piece, portion.

church *noun* chapel, house of God, cathedral, minster, abbey, temple.

Names of church services include:

baptism, christening, Christingle, communion, confirmation, dedication, Eucharist, evening service, evensong, funeral, High Mass, Holy Communion, Holy Matrimony, Lord's Supper, marriage, Mass, matins, memorial service, Midnight Mass, morning service, nuptial Mass, Requiem Mass, Vigil Mass.

---

cinema *noun* **1** *interested in cinema*: films, pictures, movies (*infml*), big screen. **2** *go to the local cinema*: picture-house, multiplex, fleapit (*infml*), flicks (*slang*).

circle *noun* **1** *draw a circle/move in circles*: ring, hoop, loop, round, disc, sphere, globe, orb, cycle, turn, revolution, circuit, orbit, circumference, perimeter, coil, spiral. **2** *circle of friends*: group, band, company, crowd, set, clique, coterie, club, society, fellowship, fraternity.

▪ *verb* **1** *belt circling her waist/circle the globe*: ring, loop, encircle, surround, gird, encompass, enclose, hem in, circumscribe, circumnavigate. **2** *circling faster and faster*: rotate, revolve, pivot, gyrate, whirl, turn, coil, wind.

circuit *noun* lap, orbit, revolution, tour, journey, course, route, track, round, beat, district, area, region, circumference, boundary, bounds, limit, range, compass, ambit.

circular *adjective* round, annular, ring-shaped, hoop-shaped, disc-shaped.

▪ *noun* handbill, leaflet, pamphlet, notice, announcement, advertisement, letter.

circulate *verb* spread, diffuse, broadcast, publicize, publish, issue, propagate, pass round, distribute.

circumference *noun* circuit, perimeter, rim, edge, outline, boundary, border, bounds, limits, extremity, margin, verge, fringe, periphery.

circumstances *noun* details, particulars, facts, items, elements, factors, conditions, state, state of affairs, situation, position, status, lifestyle, means, resources.

cite *verb* quote, name, specify, enumerate, mention, refer to, advance, bring up.

citizen *noun* city-dweller, townsman, townswoman, inhabitant, denizen, resident, householder, taxpayer, subject.

city *noun* metropolis, town, municipality, conurbation.

civic *adjective* city, urban, municipal, borough, community, local, public, communal.

civil *adjective* **1** *he was very civil to me*: polite, courteous, well-mannered, well-bred, courtly, refined, civilized, polished, urbane, affable, complaisant, obliging, accommodating. **2** *civil affairs*: domestic, home, national, internal, interior, state, municipal, civic.

F3 **1** uncivil, discourteous, rude. **2** international, military.

civilization *noun* progress, advancement, development, education, enlightenment, cultivation, culture, refinement, sophistication, urbanity.

F3 barbarity, primitiveness.

civilize *verb* tame, humanize,

educate, enlighten, cultivate, refine, polish, sophisticate, improve, perfect.

civilized *adjective* advanced, developed, educated, enlightened, cultured, refined, sophisticated, urbane, polite, sociable.
F uncivilized, barbarous, primitive.

claim *verb* **1** *claimed he had been cheating*: allege, pretend, profess, state, affirm, assert, maintain, contend, hold (*fml*), insist. **2** *claim a refund*: ask, request, require, need, demand, exact, take, collect.

clamp *noun* vice, grip, press, brace, bracket, fastener.
▪ *verb* fasten, secure, fix, clinch, grip, brace.

clan *noun* tribe, family, house, race, society, brotherhood, fraternity, sect, faction, group, band, set, clique.

clap *verb* **1** *clapped as he took a bow*: applaud, acclaim, cheer. **2** *clapping him on the back*: slap, smack, pat, wallop (*infml*), whack (*infml*), bang.

clarify *verb* explain, throw light on, illuminate, elucidate, gloss, define, simplify, resolve, clear up.
F obscure, confuse.

clarity *noun* clearness, transparency, lucidity, simplicity, intelligibility, comprehensibility, explicitness, unambiguousness, obviousness, definition, precision.
F obscurity, vagueness, imprecision.

clash *noun* **1** *the clash of the cymbals*: crash, bang, jangle, clatter, noise. **2** *a clash with the police*: conflict, confrontation, showdown, fight, disagreement, brush.

clasp *noun* fastener, buckle, clip, pin, hasp, hook, catch.
▪ *verb* hold, grip, grasp, clutch, embrace, enfold, hug, squeeze, press.

class *noun* **1** *a class of people/animals/plants*: category, classification, group, set, section, division, department, sphere, grouping, order, league, rank, status, caste, quality, grade, type, genre, sort, kind, species, genus, style. **2** *a geography class*: lesson, lecture, seminar, tutorial, course.
▪ *verb* categorize, classify, group, sort, rank, grade, rate, designate, brand.

classic *adjective* typical, characteristic, standard, regular, usual, traditional, time-honoured, established, archetypal, model, exemplary, ideal, best, finest, first-rate, definitive, masterly, excellent, ageless, immortal, undying, lasting, enduring, abiding.
F unrepresentative, second-rate.

classical *adjective* elegant, refined, pure, traditional, excellent, well-proportioned, symmetrical, harmonious, restrained.
F modern, inferior.

classify *verb* categorize, class, group, pigeonhole, sort, grade, rank, arrange, dispose, distribute, systematize, codify, tabulate, file, catalogue.

clean *adjective* **1** *clean laundry/a clean record*: washed, laundered, sterile, aseptic, antiseptic, hygienic, sanitary, sterilized, decontaminated, purified, pure, unadulterated, fresh, unpolluted, uncontaminated, immaculate, spotless, unstained, unsoiled, unsullied, perfect, faultless, flawless, unblemished. **2** *a clean life*: innocent, guiltless, virtuous, upright, moral, honest, honourable, respectable, decent, chaste. **3** *clean lines*: smooth, regular, straight, neat, tidy.
1 dirty, polluted. **2** dishonourable, indecent. **3** rough.
▪ *verb* wash, bath, launder, rinse, wipe, sponge, scrub, scour, mop, swab, sweep, vacuum, dust, freshen, deodorize, cleanse, purge, purify, decontaminate, disinfect, sanitize, sterilize, clear, filter.
dirty, defile (*fml*).

clear *adjective* **1** *is that clear?*: plain, distinct, patent, comprehensible, intelligible, coherent, lucid, explicit, precise, unambiguous, well-defined, apparent, evident, obvious, manifest, conspicuous, unmistakable, unquestionable. **2** *clear about his instructions*: sure, certain, positive, definite, convinced. **3** *clear water/clear glass*: transparent, limpid, crystalline, glassy, see-through, clean, unclouded, colourless. **4** *a clear day*: cloudless, unclouded, fine, bright, sunny, light. **5** *the road was clear*: unobstructed, unblocked, open, free, empty, unhindered, unimpeded. **6** *his voice was clear*: audible, perceptible, pronounced, distinct, recognizable.
1 unclear, vague, ambiguous, confusing. **2** unsure, muddled. **3** opaque, cloudy. **4** dull. **5** blocked. **6** inaudible, indistinct.
▪ *verb* **1** *clear the drain/a path*: unblock, unclog, decongest, free, rid, extricate, disentangle, loosen. **2** *clear the windscreen/decks*: clean, wipe, erase, cleanse, refine, tidy, empty. **3** *cleared of all charges*: acquit, exculpate (*fml*), exonerate, absolve, vindicate, excuse, justify, free, liberate, release, let go.
1 block. **2** dirty, defile (*fml*). **3** condemn.

clergyman *noun* churchman, cleric, ecclesiastic (*fml*), divine, man of God, minister, priest, reverend, father, vicar, pastor, padre, parson, rector, canon, dean, deacon, chaplain, curate, presbyter, rabbi.

clerical *adjective* office, secretarial, white-collar, administrative.

clever *adjective* intelligent, brainy (*infml*), bright, smart, witty, gifted, expert, knowledgeable, adroit, apt, able, capable, quick, quick-witted, sharp, keen, shrewd,

knowing, discerning, cunning, ingenious, inventive, resourceful, sensible, rational.
F3 foolish, stupid, senseless, ignorant.
cliché *noun* platitude, commonplace, banality, truism, chestnut, stereotype.
client *noun* customer, patron, regular, buyer, shopper, consumer, user, patient, applicant.
cliff *noun* bluff, face, rock-face, scar, scarp, escarpment, crag, overhang, precipice.
climate *noun* weather, temperature, setting, milieu, environment, ambience, atmosphere, feeling, mood, temper, disposition, tendency, trend.
climax *noun* culmination, height, high point, highlight, acme, zenith, peak, summit, top, head.
F3 nadir, low point.
climb *verb* ascend, scale, shin up, clamber, mount, rise, soar, top.
cling *verb* clasp, clutch, grasp, grip, stick, adhere, cleave, fasten, embrace, hug.
clip *verb* trim, snip, cut, prune, pare, shear, crop, dock, poll, truncate, curtail, shorten, abbreviate.
clique *noun* circle, set, coterie, group, bunch, pack, gang, crowd, faction, clan.
cloak *noun* cape, mantle, robe, wrap, coat, cover, shield, mask, front, pretext.
clog *verb* block, choke, stop up, bung up, dam, congest, jam, obstruct, impede, hinder, hamper, burden.
F3 unblock.
close[1] *verb* /klohz/ **1** *close the gate*: shut, fasten, secure, lock, bar, obstruct, block, clog, plug, cork, stop up. **2** *closing the meeting*: end, finish, complete, conclude, terminate, wind up, stop, cease.
F3 1 open, separate. **2** start.
▪ *noun* end, finish, completion, conclusion, culmination, ending, finale, dénouement, termination, cessation, stop, pause.
close[2] *adjective* /klohs/ **1** *a close neighbour*: near, nearby, at hand, neighbouring, adjacent, adjoining. **2** *Christmas is very close*: impending, imminent. **3** *a close friend/we're very close*: intimate, dear, familiar, attached, devoted, loving. **4** *it's close in here*: oppressive, heavy, muggy, humid, sultry, sweltering, airless, stifling, suffocating, stuffy, unventilated.
F3 1, **2** far, distant. **3** cool, unfriendly. **4** fresh, airy.
clot *verb* coalesce, curdle, coagulate, congeal, thicken, solidify, set, gel.
clothes *noun* clothing, garments, wear, attire, garb, gear (*infml*), togs (*infml*), outfit, get-up (*infml*), dress, costume, wardrobe, vestments.

Clothes include:
caftan, dinner-gown, evening dress, frock, kimono, sari, shirtwaister; culottes, dirndl,

divided skirt, kilt, mini skirt, pencil skirt, pinafore skirt, sarong; blouse, boiled shirt, cardigan, dress shirt, fleece, guernsey, jersey, jumper, polo neck, polo shirt, pullover, shirt, smock, sweater, sweat-shirt, tabard, tank top, T-shirt, tunic, turtleneck, twinset, waistcoat; bell-bottoms, Bermuda shorts, breeches, Capri pants, cargo pants, combat trousers, cords, denims, drainpipes, dungarees, flannels, hipsters, hot pants, jeans, jodhpurs, leggings, palazzo pants, pedal-pushers, plus-fours, shorts, slacks; boiler suit, catsuit, coveralls, dress suit, jumpsuit, leisure suit, lounge suit, morning suit, overall, shell suit, three-piece suit, trouser suit, tracksuit, wet suit; basque, body stocking, bra, brassière, briefs, camiknickers, camisole, corset, girdle, garter, G-string, hosiery, liberty bodice, lingerie, panties, pantihose, pants, petticoat, shift, slip, stockings, suspender belt, suspenders, teddy, thong, tights; boxer-shorts, singlet, string vest, underpants, vest, Y-fronts; bathing costume, bikini, leotard, salopette, swimming costume, swimming trunks, swimsuit; bed-jacket, bedsocks, dressing-gown, housecoat, negligee, nightdress, nightie (*infml*), nightshirt, pyjamas; anorak, biker jacket, blazer, bomber jacket, cagoule, duffel coat, jacket, overcoat, mac (*infml*), parka, raincoat; belt, bow tie, braces, cravat, cummerbund, earmuffs, glove, leg warmers, mitten, muffler, necktie, pashmina, scarf, shahtoosh, shawl, shrug, sock, stole, tie; burka, veil, yashmak.

---

cloud *noun* vapour, haze, mist, fog, gloom, darkness, obscurity.
▪ *verb* mist, fog, blur, dull, dim, darken, shade, shadow, overshadow, eclipse, veil, shroud, obscure, muddle, confuse, obfuscate (*fml*).
E3 clear.

Types of cloud include:
altocumulus, altostratus, cirrocumulus, cirrostratus, cirrus, cumulonimbus, cumulus, fractocumulus, fractostratus, nimbostratus, nimbus, stratocumulus, stratus.

---

cloudy *adjective* nebulous, hazy, misty, foggy, blurred, blurry, opaque, milky, muddy, dim, indistinct, obscure, dark, murky, sombre, leaden, lowering, overcast, dull, sunless.
E3 clear, bright, sunny, cloudless.

club *noun* **1** *be a member of a club*: association, society, company, league, guild, order, union, fraternity, group, set, circle, clique. **2** *carrying a heavy club*: bat, stick, mace, bludgeon, truncheon, cosh (*infml*), cudgel.

clue *noun* hint, tip, suggestion, idea, notion, lead, tip-off, pointer, sign, indication, evidence, trace, suspicion, inkling, intimation.

clump *noun* cluster, bundle, bunch, mass, tuft, thicket.

clumsy *adjective* bungling, ham-fisted, unhandy, unskilful, inept, bumbling, blundering, lumbering, gauche, ungainly, gawky (*infml*), unco-ordinated, awkward, ungraceful, uncouth, rough, crude, ill-made, shapeless, unwieldy, heavy, bulky, cumbersome.
F3 careful, graceful, elegant.

cluster *noun* bunch, clump, batch, group, knot, mass, crowd, gathering, collection, assembly.
▪ *verb* bunch, group, gather, collect, assemble, flock.

clutch *verb* hold, clasp, grip, hang on to, grasp, seize, snatch, grab, catch, grapple, embrace.

clutter *noun* litter, mess, jumble, untidiness, disorder, disarray, muddle, confusion.
▪ *verb* litter, encumber, fill, cover, strew, scatter.

coach *noun* trainer, instructor, tutor, teacher.
▪ *verb* train, drill, instruct, teach, tutor, cram, prepare.

coalition *noun* merger, amalgamation, combination, integration, fusion, alliance, league, bloc, compact, federation, confederation, confederacy, association, affiliation, union.

coarse *adjective* **1** *coarse cloth*: rough, unpolished, unfinished, uneven, lumpy, unpurified, unrefined, unprocessed. **2** *coarse humour*: bawdy, ribald, earthy, smutty, vulgar, crude, offensive, foul-mouthed, boorish, loutish, rude, impolite, indelicate, improper, indecent, immodest.
F3 **1** smooth, fine. **2** refined, sophisticated, polite.

coast *noun* coastline, seaboard, shore, beach, seaside.
▪ *verb* free-wheel, glide, slide, sail, cruise, drift.

coat *noun* **1** *the fox's coat turns white*: fur, hair, fleece, pelt, hide, skin. **2** *a coat of paint*: layer, coating, covering.
▪ *verb* cover, paint, spread, smear, plaster.

coax *verb* persuade, cajole, wheedle, sweet-talk (*infml*), soft-soap, flatter, beguile, allure, entice, tempt.

code *noun* **1** *a code of conduct*: ethics, rules, regulations, principles, system, custom, convention, etiquette, manners. **2** *written in code*: cipher, secret language.

coil *verb* wind, spiral, convolute, curl, loop, twist, writhe, snake, wreathe, twine, entwine.
▪ *noun* roll, curl, loop, ring, convolution, spiral, corkscrew, helix, twist.

coin *verb* invent, make up, think up, conceive, devise, formulate, originate, create, fabricate, produce.
▪ *noun* piece, bit, money, cash, change, small change, loose change, silver, copper.

coincide *verb* coexist, synchronize, agree, concur, correspond, square, tally, accord, harmonize, match.

coincidence *noun* chance, accident, eventuality, fluke (*infml*), luck, fortuity (*fml*).

coincidental *adjective* chance, accidental, casual, unintentional, unplanned, flukey (*infml*), lucky, fortuitous (*fml*).
F deliberate, planned.

cold *adjective* **1** *a cold bedroom/ cold outside*: unheated, cool, chilled, chilly, chill, shivery, nippy (*infml*), parky (*infml*), raw, biting, bitter, wintry, frosty, icy, glacial, freezing, frozen, arctic, polar. **2** *cold and distant*: unsympathetic, unmoved, unfeeling, stony, frigid, unfriendly, distant, aloof, standoffish, reserved, undemonstrative, unresponsive, indifferent, lukewarm.
F **1** hot, warm. **2** friendly, responsive.
▪ *noun* coldness, chill, chilliness, coolness, frigidity, iciness.
F warmth.

collaborate *verb* conspire, collude, work together, co-operate, join forces, team up, participate.

collapse *verb* **1** *collapse with exhaustion*: faint, pass out, crumple. **2** *collapse in ruins*: fall, sink, founder, fail, fold (*infml*), fall apart, disintegrate, crumble, subside, cave in.
▪ *noun* failure, breakdown, flop, debacle, downfall, ruin, disintegration, subsidence, cave-in, faint, exhaustion.

colleague *noun* workmate, co-worker, team-mate, partner, collaborator, ally, associate, confederate, confrère, comrade, companion, aide, helper, assistant, auxiliary.

collect *verb* gather, assemble, congregate, convene, muster, rally, converge, cluster, aggregate, accumulate, amass, heap, hoard, stockpile, save, acquire, obtain, secure.
F disperse, scatter.

collected *adjective* composed, self-possessed, placid, serene, calm, unruffled, unperturbed, imperturbable, cool.
F anxious, worried, agitated.

collection *noun* **1** *a strange collection of people*: gathering, assembly, convocation (*fml*), congregation, crowd, group, cluster. **2** *a museum collection/a collection of small objects*: accumulation, hoard, conglomeration, mass, heap, pile, stockpile, store. **3** *a collection of poems*: set, assemblage, assortment, anthology, compilation.

collective *adjective* united, combined, concerted, co-operative, joint, common, shared, corporate, democratic, composite, aggregate, cumulative.
F individual.

collective nouns

Collective nouns (by animal) include:

shrewdness of *apes*, cete of *badgers*, sloth of *bears*, swarm of *bees*, obstinacy of *buffaloes*, clowder of *cats*, drove of *cattle*, brood of *chickens*, bask of *crocodiles*, murder of *crows*, herd of *deer*, pack of *dogs*, school of *dolphins*, dole of *doves*, team of *ducks*, parade of *elephants*, busyness of *ferrets*, charm of *finches*, shoal of *fish*, skulk of *foxes*, army of *frogs*, gaggle/skein of *geese*, tribe of *goats*, husk of *hares*, cast of *hawks*, brood of *hens*, bloat of *hippopotamuses*, string of *horses*, pack of *hounds*, troop of *kangaroos*, kindle of *kittens*, exaltation of *larks*, leap of *leopards*, pride of *lions*, swarm of *locusts*, tittering of *magpies*, troop of *monkeys*, watch of *nightingales*, family of *otters*, parliament of *owls*, pandemonium of *parrots*, covey of *partridges*, muster of *peacocks*, rookery of *penguins*, nye of *pheasants*, litter of *pigs*, school of *porpoises*, bury of *rabbits*, colony of *rats*, unkindness of *ravens*, crash of *rhinoceroses*, building of *rooks*, pod of *seals*, flock of *sheep*, murmuration of *starlings*, ambush of *tigers*, rafter of *turkeys*, turn of *turtles*, gam of *whales*, rout of *wolves*, descent of *woodpeckers*, zeal of *zebras*.

collectors and enthusiasts

Names of collectors and enthusiasts include:

zoophile (*animals*), antiquary (*antiques*), campanologist (*bell-ringing*), ornithologist (*birds*), bibliophile (*books*), audiophile (*broadcast and recorded sound*), lepidopterist (*butterflies*), cartophilist (*cigarette cards*), numismatist (*coins/medals*), conservationist (*countryside*), environmentalist (*the environment*), xenophile (*foreigners*), gourmet (*good food*), gastronome (*good living*), discophile (*gramophone records*), chirographist (*handwriting*), hippophile (*horses*), phillumenist (*matches/matchboxes*), monarchist (*the monarchy*), deltiologist (*postcards*), arachnologist (*spiders/arachnids*), philatelist (*stamps*), arctophile (*teddy bears*).

collide *verb* crash, bump, smash, clash, conflict, confront, meet.

collision *noun* impact, crash, bump, smash, accident, pile-up, clash, conflict, confrontation, opposition.

colloquial *adjective* conversational, informal, familiar, everyday, vernacular, idiomatic.
F3 formal.

colony *noun* settlement, outpost, dependency, dominion, possession, territory, province.

colossal *adjective* huge,

enormous, immense, vast, massive, gigantic, mammoth, monstrous, monumental.
E3 tiny, minute.

colour *noun* **1** *all the colours of the rainbow/lose its colour*: hue, shade, tinge, tone, tincture, tint, dye, paint, wash, pigment, pigmentation, coloration, complexion. **2** *put colour in her cheeks*: rosiness, ruddiness, glow.
▪ *verb* **1** *colouring her drawing*: paint, crayon, dye, tint, stain, tinge. **2** *colour one's judgement*: affect, bias, prejudice, distort, pervert, exaggerate, falsify.

The range of colours includes:
red, crimson, scarlet, vermilion, cherry, cerise, magenta, maroon, burgundy, ruby, orange, tangerine, apricot, coral, salmon, peach, amber, brown, chestnut, mahogany, bronze, auburn, rust, copper, cinnamon, chocolate, tan, sepia, taupe, beige, fawn, yellow, lemon, canary, ochre, saffron, topaz, gold, chartreuse, green, eau de nil, emerald, jade, bottle, avocado, sage, khaki, turquoise, aquamarine, cobalt, blue, sapphire, gentian, indigo, navy, violet, purple, mauve, plum, lavender, lilac, pink, rose, magnolia, cream, ecru, milky, white, grey, silver, charcoal, ebony, jet, black.

---

colourful *adjective* **1** *colourful robes*: multicoloured, kaleidoscopic, variegated, vivid, bright, brilliant, rich, intense. **2** *a colourful description*: vivid, graphic, picturesque, lively, stimulating, exciting, interesting.
E3 **1** colourless, drab.

colourless *adjective* **1** *colourless liquid/complexion*: transparent, clear, neutral, bleached, washed out, faded, pale, pallid, ashen, sickly, anaemic. **2** *a colourless performance*: insipid, lacklustre, dull, dreary, drab, plain, characterless, unmemorable, uninteresting, tame.
E3 **1** colourful. **2** bright, exciting.

column *noun* **1** *a column of marble*: pillar, post, shaft, upright, support, obelisk. **2** *a column of figures/tanks*: list, line, row, rank, file, procession, queue, string.

comb *verb* **1** *comb one's hair*: groom, neaten, tidy, untangle. **2** *combing the countryside*: search, hunt, scour, sweep, sift, screen, rake, rummage, ransack.

combat *noun* war, warfare, hostilities, action, battle, fight, skirmish, struggle, conflict, clash, encounter, engagement, contest, bout, duel.
▪ *verb* fight, battle, strive, struggle, contend, contest, oppose, resist, withstand, defy.

combine *verb* merge, amalgamate, unify, blend, mix, integrate, incorporate, synthesize, compound, fuse, bond, bind, join, connect, link, marry, unite, pool, associate, co-operate.
E3 divide, separate, detach.

come *verb* advance, move towards, approach, near, draw near, reach, attain, arrive, enter, appear, materialize, happen, occur.
F3 go, depart, leave.

comedy *noun* farce, slapstick, clowning, hilarity, drollery, humour, wit, joking, jesting, facetiousness.

comfort *verb* ease, soothe, relieve, alleviate, assuage (*fml*), console, cheer, gladden, reassure, hearten, encourage, invigorate, strengthen, enliven, refresh.
▪ *noun* **1** *no comfort to him/you've been a great comfort*: consolation, compensation, cheer, reassurance, encouragement, alleviation, relief, help, aid, support. **2** *live in comfort/all the comforts of home*: ease, relaxation, luxury, snugness, cosiness, well-being, satisfaction, contentment, enjoyment.
F3 1 distress. **2** discomfort.

comfortable *adjective* **1** *a comfortable bed/pair of shoes*: snug, cosy, comfy (*infml*), relaxing, restful, easy, convenient, pleasant, agreeable, enjoyable, delightful. **2** *comfortable with the decision*: at ease, relaxed, contented, happy. **3** *a comfortable living*: affluent, well-off, well-to-do, prosperous.
F3 1 uncomfortable, unpleasant. **2** uneasy, nervous. **3** poor.

comic *adjective* funny, hilarious, side-splitting, comical, droll, humorous, witty, amusing, entertaining, diverting, joking, facetious, light, farcical, ridiculous, ludicrous, absurd, laughable, priceless (*infml*), rich (*infml*).
F3 tragic, serious.

command *noun* **1** *give the command*: commandment, decree, edict, precept (*fml*), mandate, order, bidding, charge, injunction, directive, direction, instruction, requirement. **2** *be in command*: power, authority, leadership, control, domination, dominion, rule, sway, government, management.
▪ *verb* **1** *commanded that they stop*: order, bid, charge, enjoin, direct, instruct, require, demand, compel. **2** *commanding the army*: lead, head, rule, reign, govern, control, dominate, manage, supervise.

commemorate *verb* celebrate, solemnize, remember, memorialize, mark, honour, salute, immortalize, observe, keep.

commend *verb* praise, compliment, acclaim, extol (*fml*), applaud, approve, recommend.
F3 criticize, censure.

comment *noun* statement, remark, observation, note, annotation, footnote, explanation, elucidation, illustration, exposition, commentary, criticism.
▪ *verb* say, mention, interpose, interject, remark, observe, note.

commentary *noun* narration, voice-over, analysis, description, review, critique, explanation, notes, treatise.

commentator *noun* sportscaster, broadcaster, reporter, narrator, critic, annotator, interpreter.

commercial *adjective* trade, trading, business, sales, profit-making, profitable, sellable, saleable, popular, monetary, financial, mercenary, venal.

commission *noun* **1** *undertake a commission*: assignment, mission, errand, task, job, duty, function, appointment, employment, mandate, warrant, authority, charge, trust. **2** *the commission investigating war crimes*: committee, board, delegation, deputation, representative. **3** *commission on a sale*: percentage, cut (*infml*), rake-off (*infml*), allowance, fee.

▪ *verb* nominate, select, appoint, engage, employ, authorize, empower, delegate, depute, send, order, request, ask for.

commit *verb* **1** *commit a crime*: do, perform, execute, enact, perpetrate. **2** *commit his soul to God*: entrust, confide, commend, consign, deliver, hand over, give, deposit.

commitment *noun* undertaking, guarantee, assurance, promise, word, pledge, vow, engagement, involvement, dedication, devotion, adherence, loyalty, tie, obligation, duty, responsibility, liability.

F vacillation, wavering.

committee *noun* council, board, panel, jury, commission, advisory group, think-tank, working party, task force.

common *adjective* **1** *a common problem*: familiar, customary, habitual, usual, daily, everyday, routine, regular, frequent, widespread, prevalent, general, universal, standard, average, ordinary, plain, simple, workaday, run-of-the-mill, undistinguished, unexceptional, conventional, accepted, popular, commonplace. **2** *don't be so common!*: vulgar, coarse, unrefined, crude, inferior, low, ill-bred, loutish, plebeian. **3** *a common stairway/purpose*: communal, public, shared, mutual, joint, collective.

F **1** uncommon, unusual, rare, noteworthy. **2** tasteful, refined.

commonplace *adjective* ordinary, everyday, common, humdrum, pedestrian, banal, trite, widespread, frequent, hackneyed, stock, stale, obvious, worn out, boring, uninteresting, threadbare.

F memorable, exceptional.

commotion *noun* agitation, hurly-burly, turmoil, tumult, excitement, ferment, fuss, bustle, ado, to-do (*infml*), uproar, furore, ballyhoo (*infml*), hullabaloo (*infml*), racket, hubbub, rumpus, fracas, disturbance, bust-up (*infml*), disorder, riot.

communicate *verb* **1** *communicate information*:

announce, declare, proclaim, report, reveal, disclose, divulge, impart, inform, acquaint, intimate, notify, publish, disseminate, spread, diffuse, transmit, convey. **2** *communicate with each other*: talk, converse, commune, correspond, write, phone, telephone, contact.

communication *noun* information, intelligence, intimation, disclosure, contact, connection, transmission, dissemination.

Forms of communication include:

media, mass media, broadcasting, radio, wireless, television, TV, cable TV, digital TV, satellite, subscription TV, pay-per-view, pay TV, video, video-on-demand, teletext; telecommunications, data communication, information technology (IT); the Internet, the net, World Wide Web; newspaper, press, news, newsflash, magazine, journal, poster, leaflet, pamphlet, brochure, catalogue; post, dispatch, correspondence, letter, postcard, aerogram, e-mail, telegram, Telemessage®, cable, wire (*infml*), chain letter, junk mail, mailshot; conversation, word, message, dialogue, speech, gossip, grapevine (*infml*); notice, bulletin, announcement, communiqué, circular, memo, note, report; telephone, mobile phone, cell phone, MMS (multimedia messaging service), SMS (short message service), text message, intercom, answering machine, walkie-talkie, bleeper, tannoy, teleprinter, facsimile, fax, computer, word processor, typewriter, dictaphone, megaphone, loud-hailer; radar, Morse code, semaphore, Braille, sign language.

---

community *noun* district, locality, population, people, populace, public, residents, nation, state, colony, commune, kibbutz, settlement, society, association, fellowship, brotherhood, fraternity.

compact *adjective* small, short, brief, terse, succinct, concise, condensed, compressed, close, dense, impenetrable, solid, firm. **E3** large, rambling, diffuse.

companion *noun* fellow, comrade, friend, buddy (*infml*), crony (*infml*), chum (*infml*), pal (*infml*), intimate, confidant(e), ally, aide, confederate, colleague, associate, partner, mate, consort, escort, chaperon(e), attendant, assistant, accomplice, follower.

company *noun* **1** *a manufacturing company*: firm, business, concern, association, corporation, establishment, house, partnership, syndicate, cartel, consortium. **2** *a company of soldiers*: troupe, group, band, ensemble, set, circle, crowd, throng, body, troop, crew, party, assembly, gathering, community, society. **3** *have company*: guests, visitors, callers. **4** *good company/ look forward to your company*:

society, companionship, fellowship, support, attendance, presence.

comparable *adjective* similar, alike, related, akin, cognate, corresponding, analogous, equivalent, tantamount, proportionate, commensurate, parallel, equal.
dissimilar, unlike, unequal.

compare *verb* liken, equate, contrast, juxtapose, balance, weigh, correlate, resemble, match, equal, parallel.

comparison *noun* juxtaposition, analogy, parallel, correlation, relationship, likeness, resemblance, similarity, comparability, contrast, distinction.

compartment *noun* section, division, subdivision, category, pigeonhole, cubbyhole, niche, alcove, bay, area, stall, booth, cubicle, locker, carrel, cell, chamber, berth, carriage.

compassionate *adjective* kind-hearted, kindly, tender-hearted, tender, caring, warm-hearted, benevolent, humanitarian, humane, merciful, clement, lenient, pitying, sympathetic, understanding, supportive.
cruel, indifferent.

compatible *adjective* harmonious, consistent, congruous, matching, consonant, accordant, suitable, reconcilable, adaptable, conformable, sympathetic, like-minded, well-matched, similar.
incompatible, antagonistic, contradictory.

compel *verb* force, make, constrain, oblige, necessitate, drive, urge, impel, coerce, pressurize, hustle, browbeat, bully, strong-arm, bulldoze, press-gang, dragoon.

compelling *adjective* forceful, coercive, imperative, urgent, pressing, irresistible, overriding, powerful, cogent, persuasive, convincing, conclusive, compulsive, incontrovertible, irrefutable, gripping, enthralling, spellbinding, mesmeric.
weak, unconvincing, boring.

compensate *verb* balance, counterbalance, cancel, neutralize, counteract, offset, redress, satisfy, requite, repay, refund, reimburse, indemnify, recompense, reward, remunerate, atone, redeem, make good, restore.

compensation *noun* amends, redress, satisfaction, requital, repayment, refund, reimbursement, indemnification, indemnity, damages, reparation, recompense, reward, payment, remuneration, return, restoration, restitution, consolation, comfort.

compete *verb* vie, contest, fight, battle, struggle, strive, oppose, challenge, rival, emulate, contend, participate, take part.

competent *adjective* capable, able, adept, efficient, trained,

qualified, well-qualified, skilled, experienced, proficient, expert, masterly, equal, fit, suitable, appropriate, satisfactory, adequate, sufficient.
incompetent, incapable, unable, inefficient.

competition *noun* **1** *a swimming competition*: contest, championship, tournament, cup, event, race, match, game, quiz. **2** *competition between the brothers*: rivalry, opposition, challenge, contention, conflict, struggle, strife, competitiveness, combativeness.

competitive *adjective* combative, contentious, antagonistic, aggressive, pushy (*infml*), ambitious, keen, cut-throat.

competitor *noun* contestant, contender, entrant, candidate, challenger, opponent, adversary, antagonist, rival, emulator, competition, opposition.

complacent *adjective* smug, self-satisfied, gloating, triumphant, self-righteous, unconcerned.
diffident, concerned, discontented.

complain *verb* protest, grumble, grouse, gripe, beef, carp, fuss, lament, bemoan, bewail, moan, whine, groan, growl.

complaint *noun* **1** *received several complaints about his behaviour*: protest, objection, grumble, grouse, gripe, beef, moan, grievance, dissatisfaction, annoyance, fault-finding, criticism, censure, accusation, charge. **2** *a chest complaint*: ailment, illness, sickness, disease, malady, malaise, indisposition, affliction, disorder, trouble, upset.

complementary *adjective* reciprocal, interdependent, correlative, interrelated, corresponding, matching, twin, fellow, companion.
contradictory, incompatible.

complete *adjective* **1** *feel a complete fool/complete nonsense*: utter, total, absolute, downright, out-and-out, thorough, perfect. **2** *the job isn't complete yet*: finished, ended, concluded, over, done, accomplished, achieved. **3** *a complete version of the report/have our complete attention*: unabridged, unabbreviated, unedited, unexpurgated, integral, whole, entire, full, undivided, intact.
1 partial. **2** incomplete. **3** abridged.
▪ *verb* finish, end, close, conclude, wind up, terminate, finalize, settle, clinch, perform, discharge, execute, fulfil, realize, accomplish, achieve, consummate, crown, perfect.

complex *adjective* complicated, intricate, elaborate, involved, convoluted, circuitous, tortuous, devious, mixed, varied, diverse, multiple, composite, compound, ramified.
simple, easy.

▪ *noun* **1** *a shopping complex*: structure, system, scheme, organization, establishment, institute, development. **2** *has a bit of a complex about his weight*: fixation, obsession, preoccupation, hang-up (*infml*), phobia.

complexion *noun* skin, colour, colouring, pigmentation.

complicated *adjective* complex, intricate, elaborate, involved, convoluted, tortuous, difficult, problematic, puzzling, perplexing.
F3 simple, easy.

complication *noun* difficulty, drawback, snag, obstacle, problem, ramification, repercussion, complexity, intricacy, elaboration, convolution, tangle, web, confusion, mixture.

compliment *noun* flattery, admiration, favour, approval, congratulations, tribute, honour, accolade, bouquet, commendation, praise, eulogy.
F3 insult, criticism.

complimentary *adjective* **1** *she was very complimentary about my work*: flattering, admiring, favourable, approving, appreciative, congratulatory, commendatory, eulogistic. **2** *complimentary ticket*: free, gratis, honorary, courtesy.
F3 **1** insulting, unflattering, critical.

comply *verb* agree, consent, assent, accede, yield, submit, defer, respect, observe, obey, fall in, conform, follow, perform, discharge, fulfil, satisfy, meet, oblige, accommodate.
F3 defy, disobey.

component *noun* part, constituent, ingredient, element, factor, item, unit, piece, bit, spare part.

compose *verb* **1** *what is this material composed of?*: constitute, make up, form. **2** *compose a song/letter*: create, invent, devise, write, arrange, produce, make, form, fashion, build, construct, frame.

composition *noun* **1** *composition of a letter*: making, production, formation, creation, invention, design, formulation, writing, compilation. **2** *the composition of the soil/of the painting*: constitution, make-up, combination, mixture, form, structure, configuration, layout, arrangement, organization, harmony, consonance, balance, symmetry. **3** *a musical composition*: work, opus, piece, study, exercise.

compound *noun* alloy, blend, mixture, medley, composite, amalgam, synthesis, fusion, composition, amalgamation, combination.

comprehensive *adjective* thorough, exhaustive, full, complete, encyclopedic, compendious, broad, wide, extensive, sweeping, general, blanket, inclusive, all-inclusive,

all-embracing, across-the-board.
F3 partial, incomplete, selective.

compress *verb* press, squeeze, crush, squash, flatten, jam, wedge, cram, stuff, compact, concentrate, condense, contract, telescope, shorten, abbreviate, summarize.
F3 expand, diffuse.

comprise *verb* consist of, include, contain, incorporate, embody, involve, encompass, embrace, cover.

compromise *noun* bargain, trade-off, settlement, agreement, concession, give and take, co-operation, accommodation, adjustment.
F3 disagreement, intransigence.

compulsive *adjective* **1** *makes for compulsive viewing*: irresistible, overwhelming, overpowering, uncontrollable, compelling, driving, urgent. **2** *a compulsive liar*: obsessive, hardened, incorrigible, irredeemable, incurable, hopeless.

compulsory *adjective* obligatory, mandatory, imperative, forced, required, requisite, set, stipulated, binding, contractual.
F3 optional, voluntary, discretionary.

computer *noun* personal computer, PC, mainframe, processor, word-processor, data processor.

Computer terms include:
types of computer: mainframe, microcomputer, minicomputer, PC (personal computer), Apple Mac®, Mac (*infml*), iMac®, desktop, laptop, notebook, palmtop, handheld; *hardware*: chip, silicon chip, circuit board, motherboard, CPU (central processing unit), card, graphics card, sound card, video card, disk drive, floppy drive, hard drive, joystick, joypad, keyboard, light pen, microprocessor, modem, cable modem, monitor, mouse, pointer, printer, bubblejet printer, dot-matrix printer, inkjet printer, laser printer, screen, scanner, terminal, touchpad, trackball, VDU (visual display unit); *software*: program, application, abandonware, freeware, shareware; *memory*: backing storage, external memory, immediate access memory, internal memory, magnetic tape, RAM (Random Access Memory), ROM (Read Only Memory), CD-R (Compact Disc Recordable), CD-ROM (Compact Disc Read Only Memory), DVD-ROM (Digital Versatile Disc Read Only Memory); *disks*: Compact Disc (CD), Digital Versatile Disc (DVD), magnetic disk, floppy disk, hard disk, optical disk, zip disk; *programming languages*: BASIC, C, C++, COBOL, Delphi, FORTRAN, Java®, Pascal; *web*: e-mail or email, hit, hyperlink, Internet, international services digital network (ISDN), intranet, uniform resource locator (URL), World Wide Web (WWW); *miscellaneous*: access, ASCII, autosave, backup, binary, BIOS (Basic Input/Output System),

bitmap, boot, cold boot, reboot, warm boot, buffer, bug, bus, byte, gigabyte, kilobyte, megabyte, terabyte, cache, character, character code, client-server, compression, cracking, cursor, data, databank, database, Data Protection Act, debugging, default, desktop publishing (DTP), digitizer, directory, dots per inch (dpi), DOS (disk operating system), editor, file, format, FTP (File Transfer Protocol), function, grammar checker, graphics, GUI (graphical user interface), hacking, icon, installation, interface, Linux, login, log off, log on, Mac OS (Macintosh® operating system), macro, menu, message box, metafile, MS-DOS (Microsoft® disk operating system), mouse mat, multimedia, network, output, P2P (peer-to-peer), package, password, peripheral, pixel, platform, port, parallel port, serial port, protocol, script, scripting language, scroll bar, scrolling, shell, shellscript, spellchecker, spreadsheet, sprite, subdirectory, template, toggle, toolbar, Unicode, Unix®, upgrade, utilities, virtual reality (VR), virus, virus checker, wide area network (WAN), window, Windows®, word processing, workstation, worm, WYSIWYG (what you see is what you get).

---

con *verb* (*infml*) trick, hoax, dupe, deceive, mislead, inveigle (*fml*), hoodwink, bamboozle (*infml*), cheat, double-cross, swindle, defraud, rip off (*infml*), rook.

conceal *verb* hide, obscure, disguise, camouflage, mask, screen, veil, cloak, cover, bury, submerge, smother, suppress, keep dark, keep quiet, hush up (*infml*).
F3 reveal, disclose, uncover.

concede *verb* **1** *have to concede that she was right*: admit, confess, acknowledge, allow, recognize, own, grant, accept. **2** *conceding two goals in the first ten minutes*: yield, give up, surrender, relinquish, forfeit, sacrifice.
F3 **1** deny.

conceited *adjective* vain, boastful, swollen-headed, bigheaded (*infml*), egotistical, self-important, cocky, self-satisfied, complacent, smug, proud, arrogant, stuck-up (*infml*), toffee-nosed (*infml*).
F3 modest, self-effacing, diffident, humble.

concentrate *verb* **1** *can't concentrate on work*: apply oneself, think, pay attention, attend. **2** *concentrating around the centre*: focus, converge, centre, cluster, crowd, congregate, gather, collect, accumulate. **3** *concentrated the solution*: condense, evaporate, reduce, thicken, intensify.
F3 **2** disperse. **3** dilute.

concept *noun* idea, notion, plan, theory, hypothesis, thought, abstraction, conception, conceptualization, visualization, image, picture, impression.

concern *verb* **1** *concerned about their safety*: upset, distress, trouble, disturb, bother, worry. **2** *concerns your daughter*: relate to, refer to, regard, involve, interest, affect, touch.

▪ *noun* **1** *a cause for concern*: anxiety, worry, unease, disquiet, care, sorrow, distress. **2** *grateful for your concern*: regard, consideration, attention, heed, thought. **3** *it's not my concern*: responsibility, duty, charge, job, task, field, business, affair, matter, problem, interest, involvement. **4** *a new concern*: company, firm, business, corporation, establishment, enterprise, organization.

F3 **1** joy. **2** indifference.

concerned *adjective* **1** *concerned parents*: anxious, worried, uneasy, apprehensive, upset, unhappy, distressed, troubled, disturbed, bothered, attentive, caring. **2** *the people concerned*: connected, related, involved, implicated, interested, affected.

F3 **1** unconcerned, indifferent, apathetic.

concerning *preposition* about, regarding, with regard to, as regards, respecting, with reference to, relating to, in the matter of.

concise *adjective* short, brief, terse, succinct, pithy, compendious, compact, compressed, condensed, abridged, abbreviated, summary, synoptic.

F3 diffuse, wordy.

conclude *verb* **1** *conclude that they were innocent*: infer, deduce, assume, surmise, suppose, reckon, judge. **2** *conclude their discussions*: end, close, finish, complete, consummate, cease, terminate, culminate. **3** *conclude a deal*: settle, resolve, decide, establish, determine, clinch.

F3 **2** start, commence.

conclusive *adjective* final, ultimate, definitive, decisive, clear, convincing, definite, undeniable, irrefutable, indisputable, incontrovertible, unarguable, unanswerable, clinching.

F3 inconclusive, questionable.

concrete *adjective* real, actual, factual, solid, physical, material, substantial, tangible, touchable, perceptible, visible, firm, definite, specific, explicit.

F3 abstract, vague.

condemn *verb* disapprove, upbraid (*fml*), reproach, castigate (*fml*), blame, disparage (*fml*), revile, denounce, censure, slam (*infml*), slate (*infml*), convict.

F3 praise, approve.

condense *verb* **1** *condensing the novel*: shorten, curtail, abbreviate, abridge, précis, summarize, encapsulate, contract, compress, compact. **2** *condenses on the cold glass*: distil, precipitate (*fml*), concentrate, reduce, thicken, solidify, coagulate.

F⇄ 1 expand. 2 dilute.

condescend *verb* deign, see fit, stoop, bend, lower oneself, patronize, talk down.

condition *noun* **1** *the condition of the country*: state, circumstances, case, position, situation, predicament, plight. **2** *a condition of the contract*: requirement, obligation, prerequisite, terms, stipulation, proviso, qualification, limitation, restriction, rule. **3** *out of condition*: fitness, health, state, shape, form, fettle, nick (*infml*).

conditions *noun* surroundings, environment, milieu, setting, atmosphere, background, context, circumstances, situation, state.

condone *verb* forgive, pardon, excuse, overlook, ignore, disregard, tolerate, brook, allow.
F⇄ condemn, censure.

conduct *noun* **1** *good conduct*: behaviour, comportment (*fml*), actions, ways, manners, bearing, attitude. **2** *the conduct of their affairs*: administration, management, direction, running, organization, operation, control, supervision, leadership, guidance.
▪ *verb* **1** *conducting the meeting*: administer, manage, run, organize, orchestrate, chair, control, handle, regulate. **2** *conduct oneself in a dignified manner*: behave, acquit, comport oneself (*fml*), act. **3** *conducts heat*: convey, carry, bear, transmit. **4** *conducted me to my seat*: lead, accompany, escort, usher, guide, direct, pilot, steer.

confer *verb* discuss, debate, deliberate, consult, talk, converse.

conference *noun* meeting, convention, congress, convocation (*fml*), symposium, forum, discussion, debate, consultation.

confess *verb* admit, confide, own (up), come clean (*infml*), grant, concede, acknowledge, recognize, affirm, assert, profess, declare, disclose, divulge, expose.
F⇄ deny, conceal.

confide *verb* confess, admit, reveal, disclose, divulge, whisper, breathe, tell, impart, unburden.
F⇄ hide, suppress.

confidence *noun* certainty, faith, credence, trust, reliance, dependence, assurance, composure, calmness, self-possession, self-confidence, self-reliance, self-assurance, boldness, courage.
F⇄ distrust, diffidence.

confident *adjective* sure, certain, positive, convinced, assured, composed, self-possessed, cool, self-confident, self-reliant, self-assured, unselfconscious, bold, fearless, dauntless, unabashed.
F⇄ doubtful, diffident.

confidential *adjective* secret, top secret, classified, restricted, hush-hush (*infml*), off-the-record, private, personal, intimate, privy.

confine *verb* enclose, circumscribe, bound, limit,

restrict, cramp, constrain, imprison, incarcerate, intern, cage, shut up, immure, bind, shackle, trammel, restrain, repress, inhibit.
E3 free.

confirm *verb* **1** *confirm her version of events*: endorse, back, support, reinforce, strengthen, fortify, validate, prove, authenticate, corroborate, substantiate, verify, evidence. **2** *confirmed his position in the company*: establish, fix, settle, clinch, ratify, sanction, approve. **3** *confirm that he will go*: affirm, assert, assure, pledge, promise, guarantee.
E3 1 refute, deny.

confirmed *adjective* inveterate, entrenched, dyed-in-the-wool, rooted, established, long-established, long-standing, habitual, chronic, seasoned, hardened, incorrigible, incurable.

confiscate *verb* seize, appropriate, expropriate (*fml*), remove, take away, impound, sequester, commandeer.
E3 return, restore.

conflict *noun* **1** *a conflict of interest*: difference, variance, discord, contention, disagreement, dissension, dispute, opposition, antagonism, hostility, friction, strife, unrest, confrontation. **2** *the conflict in the Balkans*: battle, war, warfare, combat, fight, contest, engagement, skirmish, set-to, fracas, brawl, quarrel, feud, encounter, clash.
E3 1 agreement, harmony, concord.
▪ *verb* differ, clash, collide, disagree, contradict, oppose, contest, fight, combat, battle, war, strive, struggle, contend.
E3 agree, harmonize.

conform *verb* agree, accord, harmonize, match, correspond, tally, square, adapt, adjust, accommodate, comply, obey, follow.
E3 differ, conflict, rebel.

confront *verb* face, meet, encounter, accost, address, oppose, challenge, defy, brave, beard.
E3 evade.

confrontation *noun* encounter, clash, collision, showdown, conflict, disagreement, fight, battle, quarrel, set-to, engagement, contest.

confuse *verb* **1** *confusing her further*: puzzle, baffle, perplex, mystify, confound, bewilder, disorient, disconcert, fluster, upset, embarrass, mortify. **2** *don't confuse the blue and the brown wires*: muddle, mix up, mistake, jumble, disarrange, disorder, tangle, entangle, involve, mingle.
E3 1 enlighten, clarify.

confused *adjective* **1** *looked confused/a confused old lady*: puzzled, baffled, perplexed, flummoxed (*infml*), nonplussed, bewildered, disorientated. **2** *a confused mess of dirty plates and cutlery*: muddled, jumbled,

disarranged, disordered, untidy, disorderly, higgledy-piggledy (*infml*), chaotic, disorganized.
2 orderly.

congested *adjective* clogged, blocked, jammed, packed, stuffed, crammed, full, crowded, overcrowded, overflowing, teeming.
clear.

congratulate *verb* praise, felicitate (*fml*), compliment, wish well.
commiserate.

conical *adjective* cone-shaped, pyramidal, tapering, tapered, pointed.

connect *verb* join, link, unite, couple, combine, fasten, affix, attach, relate, associate, ally.
disconnect, cut off, detach.

connected *adjective* joined, linked, united, coupled, combined, related, akin, associated, affiliated, allied.
disconnected, unconnected.

connection *noun* junction, coupling, fastening, attachment, bond, tie, link, association, alliance, relation, relationship, interrelation, contact, communication, correlation, correspondence, relevance.
disconnection.

conquer *verb* **1** *conquering the Aztecs*: defeat, beat, overthrow, vanquish (*fml*), rout, overrun, best, worst, get the better of, overcome, surmount, win, succeed, triumph, prevail, overpower, master, crush, subdue, quell, subjugate, humble. **2** *conquer Everest/the market*: seize, take, annex, occupy, possess, acquire, obtain.
1 surrender, yield, give in.

conscience *noun* principles, standards, morals, ethics, scruples, qualms.

conscientious *adjective* diligent, hardworking, scrupulous, painstaking, thorough, meticulous, punctilious, particular, careful, attentive, responsible, upright, honest, faithful, dutiful.
careless, irresponsible, unreliable.

conscious *adjective* **1** *remained conscious during the operation*: awake, alive, responsive, sentient, sensible, rational, reasoning, alert. **2** *conscious of his failings/a conscious decision*: aware, self-conscious, heedful, mindful, knowing, deliberate, intentional, calculated, premeditated, studied, wilful, voluntary.
1 unconscious. **2** unaware, involuntary.

consciousness *noun* awareness, sentience, sensibility, knowledge, intuition, realization, recognition.
unconsciousness.

consecutive *adjective* sequential, successive, continuous, unbroken, uninterrupted, following, succeeding, running.
discontinuous.

consent *verb* agree, concur, accede, assent, approve, permit, allow, grant, admit, concede, acquiesce, yield, comply.
F3 refuse, decline, oppose.
▪ *noun* agreement, concurrence, assent, approval, permission, go-ahead, green light (*infml*), sanction, concession, acquiescence, compliance.
F3 disagreement, refusal, opposition.

consequence *noun* result, outcome, issue, end, upshot, effect, side effect, repercussion.
F3 cause.

conservation *noun* keeping, safekeeping, custody, saving, economy, husbandry, maintenance, upkeep, preservation, protection, safeguarding, ecology, environmentalism.
F3 destruction.

conservative *adjective* Tory, right-wing, hidebound, diehard, reactionary, establishmentarian, unprogressive, conventional, traditional, moderate, middle-of-the-road, cautious, guarded, sober.
F3 left-wing, radical, innovative.
▪ *noun* Tory, right-winger, diehard, stick-in-the-mud, reactionary, traditionalist, moderate.
F3 left-winger, radical.

conserve *verb* keep, save, store up, hoard, maintain, preserve, protect, guard, safeguard.
F3 use, waste, squander.

consider *verb* **1** *consider your options*: ponder, deliberate, reflect, contemplate, meditate, muse, mull over, chew over, examine, study, weigh, respect, remember, take into account. **2** *consider it an honour*: regard, deem, think, believe, judge, rate, count.

considerable *adjective* great, large, big, sizable, substantial, tidy (*infml*), ample, plentiful, abundant, lavish, marked, noticeable, perceptible, appreciable, reasonable, tolerable, respectable, important, significant, noteworthy, distinguished, influential.
F3 small, slight, insignificant, unremarkable.

considerate *adjective* kind, thoughtful, caring, attentive, obliging, helpful, charitable, unselfish, altruistic, gracious, solicitous, sensitive, tactful, discreet.
F3 inconsiderate, thoughtless, selfish.

consistency *noun* **1** *of the consistency of porridge*: viscosity, thickness, density, firmness. **2** *the consistency of her playing is impressive*: steadiness, regularity, evenness, uniformity, sameness, identity, constancy, steadfastness. **3** *ensure that there is consistency in our dealings with each other*: agreement, accordance, coherence, correspondence, congruity, compatibility, harmony.
F3 **3** inconsistency.

consistent *adjective* **1** *a consistent winner*: steady, stable, regular, uniform, unchanging, undeviating, constant, persistent, unfailing, dependable. **2** *consistent with the facts*: agreeing, accordant, consonant, congruous, coherent, compatible, harmonious, logical.
⇄ **1** irregular, erratic. **2** inconsistent.

consist of *verb* comprise, be composed of, contain, include, incorporate, embody, embrace, involve, amount to.

console *verb* comfort, cheer, hearten, encourage, relieve, soothe, calm.
⇄ upset, agitate.

consolidate *verb* reinforce, strengthen, secure, stabilize, unify, unite, join, combine, affiliate, amalgamate, fuse, cement, compact, condense, thicken, harden, solidify.

conspicuous *adjective* apparent, visible, noticeable, marked, clear, obvious, evident, patent, manifest, prominent, striking, blatant, flagrant, glaring, ostentatious, showy, flashy, garish.
⇄ inconspicuous, concealed, hidden.

conspire *verb* plot, scheme, intrigue, manoeuvre, connive, collude, hatch, devise.

constant *adjective* **1** *constant noise/interruptions*: continuous, unbroken, never-ending, non-stop, endless, interminable, ceaseless, incessant, eternal, everlasting, perpetual, continual, unremitting, relentless, persistent. **2** *a constant temperature/needs constant attention*: resolute, persevering, unflagging, unwavering, stable, steady, unchanging, unvarying, changeless, immutable, invariable, unalterable, fixed, permanent, firm, even, regular, uniform.
⇄ **1** variable, irregular, fitful, occasional.

constituent *adjective* component, integral, essential, basic, intrinsic, inherent.
▪ *noun* ingredient, element, factor, principle, component, part, bit, section, unit.
⇄ whole.

constitute *verb* represent, make up, compose, form, comprise, create, establish, set up, found.

constraint *noun* **1** *the constraint of legislation*: force, duress, compulsion, coercion, pressure, necessity, deterrent. **2** *the constraint of a large and expensive family*: restriction, limitation, hindrance, restraint, check, curb, damper.

constrict *verb* squeeze, compress, pinch, cramp, narrow, tighten, contract, shrink, choke, strangle, inhibit, limit, restrict.
⇄ expand.

construct *verb* build, erect, raise, elevate, make, manufacture, fabricate, assemble, put together, compose, form, shape, fashion,

model, design, engineer, create, found, establish, formulate.
demolish, destroy.

constructive *adjective* practical, productive, positive, helpful, useful, valuable, beneficial, advantageous.
destructive, negative, unhelpful.

consult *verb* refer to, ask, question, interrogate, confer, discuss, debate, deliberate.

consultant *noun* adviser, expert, authority, specialist.

consultation *noun* discussion, deliberation, dialogue, conference, meeting, hearing, interview, examination, appointment, session.

consume *verb* **1** *consuming large quantities of food*: eat, drink, swallow, devour, gobble, polish off (*infml*), ingest. **2** *consume energy*: use, absorb, spend, expend, deplete, drain, exhaust, use up, dissipate, squander, waste. **3** *consumed in the flames*: destroy, demolish, annihilate, devastate, ravage.

consumer *noun* user, end-user, customer, buyer, purchaser, shopper.

contact *noun* touch, impact, juxtaposition, contiguity, communication, meeting, junction, union, connection, association.
▪ *verb* approach, apply to, reach, get hold of, get in touch with, telephone, phone, ring, call, notify.

contagious *adjective* infectious, catching, communicable, transmissible, spreading, epidemic.

contain *verb* **1** *contains additives/ containing the major organs*: include, comprise, incorporate, embody, involve, embrace, enclose, hold, accommodate. **2** *contain one's anger*: repress, stifle, restrain, control, check, curb, limit.
1 exclude.

container *noun* receptacle, vessel, holder.

contaminate *verb* infect, pollute, adulterate, taint, soil, sully (*fml*), defile (*fml*), corrupt, deprave, debase, stain, tarnish.
purify.

contemplate *verb* **1** *contemplating the meaning of life*: meditate, reflect on, ponder, mull over, deliberate, consider, regard, view, survey, observe, study, examine, inspect, scrutinize. **2** *couldn't contemplate losing*: expect, foresee, envisage, plan, design, propose, intend, mean.

contemporary *adjective* **1** *contemporary architecture*: modern, current, present, present-day, recent, latest, up-to-date, fashionable, up-to-the-minute, ultra-modern. **2** *contemporary with the Surrealists*: contemporaneous, coexistent, concurrent, synchronous, simultaneous.
1 out-of-date, old-fashioned.

contempt *noun* scorn, disdain,

condescension, derision, ridicule, mockery, disrespect, dishonour, disregard, neglect, dislike, loathing, detestation.
F3 admiration, regard.

content *noun* /**kon**-tent/ substance, matter, essence, gist, meaning, significance, text, subject matter, ideas, contents, load, burden.
▪ *adjective* /kon-**tent**/ satisfied, fulfilled, contented, untroubled, pleased, happy, willing.
F3 dissatisfied, troubled.

contented *adjective* happy, glad, pleased, cheerful, comfortable, relaxed, content, satisfied.
F3 discontented, unhappy, annoyed.

contents *noun* **1** *the contents of the package*: constituents, parts, elements, ingredients, content, load, items. **2** *the contents of the book*: chapters, divisions, subjects, topics, themes.

contest *noun* competition, game, match, tournament, encounter, fight, battle, set-to, combat, conflict, struggle, dispute, debate, controversy.
▪ *verb* **1** *contest the decision*: dispute, debate, question, doubt, challenge, oppose, argue against, litigate, deny, refute. **2** *contesting one with the other*: compete, vie, contend, strive, fight.
F3 **1** accept.

contestant *noun* competitor, contender, player, participant, entrant, candidate, aspirant, rival, opponent.

context *noun* background, setting, surroundings, framework, frame of reference, situation, position, circumstances, conditions.

continual *adjective* constant, perpetual, incessant, interminable, eternal, everlasting, regular, frequent, recurrent, repeated.
F3 occasional, intermittent, temporary.

continue *verb* resume, recommence, carry on, go on, proceed, persevere, stick at, persist, last, endure, survive, remain, abide (*fml*), stay, rest, pursue, sustain, maintain, lengthen, prolong, extend, project.
F3 discontinue, stop.

continuity *noun* flow, progression, succession, sequence, linkage, interrelationship, connection, cohesion.
F3 discontinuity.

continuous *adjective* unbroken, uninterrupted, consecutive, non-stop, endless, ceaseless, unending, unceasing, constant, unremitting, prolonged, extended, continued, lasting.
F3 discontinuous, broken, sporadic.

contour *noun* outline, silhouette, shape, form, figure, curve, relief, profile, character, aspect.

contract *verb* /kon-**trakt**/ **1** *wood contracts when it gets cold*: shrink, lessen, diminish, reduce, shorten, curtail, abbreviate, abridge, condense, compress, constrict, narrow, tighten, tense, shrivel, wrinkle. **2** *contracted to build two warships*: pledge, promise, undertake, agree, stipulate, arrange, negotiate, bargain.
F3 **1** expand, enlarge, lengthen.
▪ *noun* /**kon**-trakt/ bond, commitment, engagement, covenant, treaty, convention, pact, compact, agreement, transaction, deal, bargain, settlement, arrangement, understanding.

contradict *verb* deny, disaffirm, confute, challenge, oppose, impugn (*fml*), dispute, counter, negate, gainsay.
F3 agree, confirm, corroborate.

contradictory *adjective* contrary, opposite, paradoxical, conflicting, discrepant, inconsistent, incompatible, antagonistic, irreconcilable, opposed, repugnant.
F3 consistent.

contraption *noun* contrivance, device, gadget, apparatus, rig, machine, mechanism.

contrary *adjective* opposite, counter, reverse, conflicting, antagonistic, opposed, adverse, hostile.
F3 like, similar.
▪ *noun* opposite, converse, reverse.

contrast *noun* /**kon**-trast/ difference, dissimilarity, disparity, divergence, distinction, differentiation, comparison, foil, antithesis, opposition.
F3 similarity.
▪ *verb* /kon-**trast**/ compare, differentiate, distinguish, discriminate, differ, oppose, clash, conflict.

contribute *verb* donate, subscribe, chip in (*infml*), add, give, bestow, provide, supply, furnish, help, lead, conduce.
F3 withhold.

contrived *adjective* unnatural, artificial, false, forced, strained, laboured, mannered, elaborate, overdone.
F3 natural, genuine.

control *verb* **1** *the policeman controlled the traffic*: lead, govern, rule, command, direct, manage, oversee, supervise, superintend, run, operate. **2** *control the temperature*: regulate, adjust, monitor, verify. **3** *control one's temper*: restrain, check, curb, subdue, repress, hold back, contain.
▪ *noun* **1** *have full control*: power, charge, authority, command, mastery, government, rule, direction, management, oversight, supervision, superintendence, discipline, guidance. **2** *controls on spending*: restraint, check, curb, repression. **3** *fiddle with the controls*: instrument, dial, switch, button, knob, lever.

controversial *adjective* contentious, polemical, disputed, doubtful, questionable, debatable, disputable.

controversy *noun* debate, discussion, war of words, polemic, dispute, disagreement, argument, quarrel, squabble, wrangle, strife, contention, dissension.
F3 accord, agreement.

convenience *noun* **1** *the convenience of everything being in one place/for the convenience of our guests*: accessibility, availability, handiness, usefulness, use, utility, serviceability, service, benefit, advantage, help, suitability, fitness. **2** *all modern conveniences*: facility, amenity, appliance, gadget.
F3 1 inconvenience.

convenient *adjective* nearby, at hand, accessible, available, handy, useful, commodious, beneficial, helpful, labour-saving, adapted, fitted, suited, suitable, fit, appropriate, opportune, timely, well-timed.
F3 inconvenient, awkward.

conventional *adjective* traditional, orthodox, formal, correct, proper, prevalent, prevailing, accepted, received, expected, unoriginal, ritual, routine, usual, customary, regular, standard, normal, ordinary, straight, stereotyped, hidebound, pedestrian, commonplace, common, run-of-the-mill.
F3 unconventional, unusual, exotic.

converge *verb* focus, concentrate, approach, merge, coincide, meet, join, combine, gather.
F3 diverge, disperse.

conversation *noun* talk, chat, gossip, discussion, discourse, dialogue, exchange, communication, chinwag (*infml*), tête-à-tête.

convert *verb* **1** *convert the loft into a third bedroom*: alter, change, turn, transform, adapt, modify, remodel, restyle, revise, reorganize. **2** *convert them to Catholicism*: win over, convince, persuade, reform, proselytize.

convict *verb* condemn, sentence, imprison.
▪ *noun* criminal, felon, culprit, prisoner.

conviction *noun* assurance, confidence, fervour, earnestness, certainty, firmness, persuasion, view, opinion, belief, faith, creed, tenet, principle.

convince *verb* assure, persuade, sway, win over, bring round, reassure, satisfy.

convincing *adjective* persuasive, cogent, powerful, telling, impressive, credible, plausible, likely, probable, conclusive, incontrovertible.
F3 unconvincing, improbable.

convulsion *noun* **1** *have convulsions*: fit, seizure, paroxysm, spasm, cramp, contraction, tic, tremor. **2** *a convulsion of anger*: eruption, outburst, furore, disturbance, commotion, tumult, agitation, turbulence, upheaval.

cook *verb* concoct, prepare.

cool *adjective* **1** *a cool breeze/ climate*: chilly, fresh, breezy, nippy (*infml*), cold, chilled, iced, refreshing. **2** *a cool exterior*: calm, unruffled, unexcited, composed, self-possessed, level-headed, unemotional, quiet, relaxed, laid-back (*infml*). **3** *a cool reception*: unfriendly, unwelcoming, cold, frigid, lukewarm, half-hearted, unenthusiastic, apathetic, uninterested, unresponsive, uncommunicative, reserved, distant, aloof, standoffish.

F3 **1** warm, hot. **2** excited, angry. **3** friendly, welcoming.

▪ *verb* chill, refrigerate, ice, freeze, fan.

F3 warm, heat.

co-operate *verb* collaborate, work together, play ball (*infml*), help, assist, aid, contribute, participate, combine, unite, conspire.

co-operation *noun* helpfulness, assistance, participation, collaboration, teamwork, unity, co-ordination, give-and-take.

F3 opposition, rivalry, competition.

co-operative *adjective* helpful, supportive, obliging, accommodating, willing.

F3 unco-operative, rebellious.

co-ordinate *verb* organize, arrange, systematize, tabulate, integrate, mesh, synchronize, harmonize, match, correlate, regulate.

cope *verb* manage, carry on, survive, get by, make do.

copy *noun* duplicate, carbon copy, photocopy, Photostat®, Xerox®, facsimile, reproduction, print, tracing, transcript, transcription, replica, model, pattern, archetype, representation, image, likeness, counterfeit, forgery, fake, imitation, borrowing, plagiarism, crib.

F3 original.

▪ *verb* duplicate, photocopy, reproduce, print, trace, transcribe, forge, counterfeit, simulate, imitate, impersonate, mimic, ape, parrot, repeat, echo, mirror, follow, emulate, borrow, plagiarize, crib.

cord *noun* string, twine, rope, line, cable, flex, connection, link, bond, tie.

core *noun* kernel, nucleus, heart, centre, middle, nub, crux, essence, gist, nitty-gritty (*infml*).

F3 surface, exterior.

corner *noun* **1** *round the corner*: angle, joint, crook, bend, turning. **2** *a shady corner of the garden*: nook, cranny, niche, recess, alcove, cavity, hole, hideout, hide-away, retreat.

corpse *noun* body, stiff (*slang*), carcase, skeleton, remains, cadaver.

correct *verb* rectify, put right,

right, emend, remedy, cure, debug, redress, adjust, regulate, improve, amend.

▪ *adjective* **1** *the correct answer/correct in every detail*: right, accurate, precise, exact, strict, true, truthful, word-perfect, faultless, flawless. **2** *the correct way to address the queen*: proper, acceptable, OK (*infml*), standard, regular, just, appropriate, fitting.

F3 **1** incorrect, wrong, inaccurate.

correspond *verb* **1** *their version of events doesn't correspond with ours*: match, fit, answer, conform, tally, square, agree, concur, coincide, correlate, accord, harmonize, dovetail, complement. **2** *corresponded with her over a number of years*: communicate, write.

corresponding *adjective* matching, complementary, reciprocal, interrelated, analogous, equivalent, similar, identical.

corrode *verb* erode, wear away, eat away, consume, waste, rust, oxidize, tarnish, impair, deteriorate, crumble, disintegrate.

corrupt *adjective* rotten, unscrupulous, unprincipled, unethical, immoral, fraudulent, shady (*infml*), dishonest, bent (*infml*), crooked (*infml*), untrustworthy, depraved, degenerate, dissolute.

F3 ethical, virtuous, upright, honest, trustworthy.

▪ *verb* contaminate, pollute, adulterate, taint, defile (*fml*), debase, pervert, deprave, lead astray, lure, bribe, suborn.

F3 purify.

corruption *noun* unscrupulousness, immorality, impurity, depravity, degeneration, degradation, perversion, distortion, dishonesty, crookedness (*infml*), fraud, shadiness (*infml*), bribery, extortion, vice, wickedness, iniquity (*fml*), evil.

F3 honesty, virtue.

cosmetic *adjective* superficial, surface.

F3 essential.

cosmetics *noun* make-up, grease paint.

cosmopolitan *adjective* worldly, worldly-wise, well-travelled, sophisticated, urbane, international, universal.

F3 insular, parochial, rustic.

cost *noun* **1** *the cost of bread/high running costs*: expense, outlay, payment, disbursement (*fml*), expenditure, charge, price, rate, amount, figure, worth. **2** *to my cost*: detriment, harm, injury, hurt, loss, deprivation, sacrifice, penalty, price.

costly *adjective* **1** *costly jewellery*: expensive, dear, pricey (*infml*), exorbitant, excessive, lavish, rich, splendid, valuable, precious, priceless. **2** *a costly mistake*: harmful, damaging, disastrous, catastrophic, loss-making.

F3 **1** cheap, inexpensive.

costume *noun* outfit, uniform, livery, robes, vestments, dress, clothing, get-up (*infml*), fancy dress.

cosy *adjective* snug, comfortable, comfy (*infml*), warm, sheltered, secure, homely, intimate.
F3 uncomfortable, cold.

council *noun* committee, panel, board, cabinet, ministry, parliament, congress, assembly, convention, conference.

counsel *noun* **1** *give good counsel*: advice, suggestion, recommendation, guidance, direction, information, consultation, deliberation, consideration, forethought. **2** *counsel for the defence*: lawyer, advocate, solicitor, attorney, barrister.
▪ *verb* advise, warn, caution, suggest, recommend, advocate, urge, exhort, guide, direct, instruct.

count *verb* **1** *counting sheep/count up to 100*: number, enumerate, list, include, reckon, calculate, compute, tell, check, add, total, tot up, score. **2** *that doesn't count*: matter, signify, qualify. **3** *count yourself lucky*: consider, regard, deem, judge, think, reckon, hold.
▪ *noun* numbering, enumeration, poll, reckoning, calculation, computation, sum, total, tally.

counter *adjective* contrary, opposite, opposing, conflicting, contradictory, contrasting, opposed, against, adverse.
▪ *verb* parry, resist, offset, answer, respond, retaliate, retort, return, meet.

counteract *verb* neutralize, counterbalance, offset, countervail, act against, oppose, resist, hinder, check, thwart, frustrate, foil, defeat, undo, negate, annul, invalidate.
F3 support, assist.

counterfeit *verb* fake, forge, fabricate, copy, imitate, impersonate, pretend, feign, simulate, sham.
▪ *adjective* fake, false, phoney (*infml*), forged, copied, fraudulent, bogus, pseudo, sham, spurious, imitation, artificial, simulated, feigned, pretended.
F3 genuine, authentic, real.

counterpart *noun* equivalent, opposite number, complement, supplement, match, fellow, mate, twin, duplicate, copy.

countless *adjective* innumerable, myriad, numberless, unnumbered, untold, incalculable, infinite, endless, immeasurable, measureless, limitless.
F3 finite, limited.

country *noun* **1** *a foreign country/several European countries*: state, nation, people, kingdom, realm, principality. **2** *a walk in the country*: countryside, green belt, farmland, provinces, sticks (*infml*), backwoods, wilds. **3** *difficult country for smaller vehicles*: terrain, land, territory.
F3 **2** town, city.

▪ *adjective* rural, provincial, agrarian, rustic, agricultural, pastoral, bucolic (*fml*), landed.
F∃ urban.

countryside *noun* landscape, scenery, country, green belt, farmland, outdoors.

county *noun* shire, province, region, area, district.

couple *noun* pair, brace, twosome, duo.

coupon *noun* voucher, token, slip, check, ticket, certificate.

courage *noun* bravery, pluck, guts (*infml*), fearlessness, dauntlessness, heroism, gallantry, valour, boldness, audacity, nerve, daring, resolution, fortitude, spirit, mettle.
F∃ cowardice, fear.

courageous *adjective* brave, plucky, fearless, dauntless, indomitable, heroic, gallant, valiant, lion-hearted, hardy, bold, audacious, daring, intrepid, resolute.
F∃ cowardly, afraid.

course *noun* **1** *English/computer course*: curriculum, syllabus, classes, lessons, lectures, studies. **2** *the course of events*: flow, movement, advance, progress, development, furtherance, order, sequence, series, succession, progression. **3** *during the course of the trial*: duration, time, period, term, passage. **4** *along the river's course*: direction, way, path, track, road, route, channel, trail, line, circuit, orbit, trajectory, flight path. **5** *course of action*: plan, schedule, programme, policy, procedure, method, mode.

court *noun* **1** *the highest court in the land*: law-court, bench, bar, tribunal, trial, session. **2** *number six Meadow Court*: courtyard, yard, quadrangle, square, cloister, forecourt, enclosure. **3** *the king's court*: entourage, attendants, retinue, suite, train, cortège.

courteous *adjective* polite, civil, respectful, well-mannered, well-bred, ladylike, gentlemanly, gracious, obliging, considerate, attentive, gallant, courtly, urbane, debonair, refined, polished.
F∃ discourteous, impolite, rude.

courtesy *noun* politeness, civility, respect, manners, breeding, graciousness, consideration, attention, gallantry, urbanity.
F∃ discourtesy, rudeness.

cove *noun* bay, bight, inlet, estuary, firth, fiord, creek.

cover *verb* **1** *covered her face*: hide, conceal, obscure, shroud, veil, screen, mask, disguise, camouflage. **2** *covered with mud*: coat, spread, daub, plaster, encase, wrap, envelop, clothe, dress. **3** *covered the young plants*: shelter, protect, shield, guard, defend. **4** *cover a topic*: deal with, treat, consider, examine, investigate, encompass, embrace, incorporate, embody, involve, include, contain, comprise.
F∃ **1** uncover. **2** strip. **3** expose. **4** exclude.

▪ *noun* **1** *a book/bed/dust cover*: coating, covering, top, lid, veil, screen, mask, front, façade, jacket, wrapper, case, envelope, clothing, dress, bedspread, canopy. **2** *take cover/give cover*: shelter, refuge, protection, shield, guard, defence, concealment, disguise, camouflage.

covering *noun* layer, coat, coating, blanket, film, veneer, skin, crust, shell, casing, housing, wrapping, clothing, top, protection, mask, overlay, cover, shelter, roof.

cover-up *noun* concealment, whitewash, smokescreen, front, façade, pretence, conspiracy, complicity.

coward *noun* craven, faint-heart, chicken (*infml*), scaredy-cat, wimp (*infml*), renegade, deserter.
F3 hero.

cowardice *noun* cowardliness, faint-heartedness, timorousness, spinelessness.
F3 courage, valour.

cowardly *adjective* faint-hearted, craven, fearful, timorous, scared, unheroic, chicken-hearted, chicken-livered, chicken (*infml*), yellow (*infml*), spineless, weak, weak-kneed, soft (*infml*).
F3 brave, courageous, bold.

cower *verb* crouch, grovel, skulk, shrink, flinch, cringe, quail, tremble, shake, shiver.

crack *verb* **1** *ice cracking/cracked a plate*: split, burst, fracture, break, snap, shatter, splinter, chip. **2** *thunder roared and lightening cracked*: explode, burst, pop, crackle, snap, crash, clap, slap, whack (*infml*). **3** *crack a code*: decipher, work out, solve.
▪ *noun* **1** *a crack in the marble*: break, fracture, split, rift, gap, crevice, fissure, chink, line, flaw, chip. **2** *the crack of the whip*: explosion, burst, pop, snap, crash, clap, blow, smack, slap, whack (*infml*). **3** *what did you mean by that crack?*: joke, quip, witticism, gag (*infml*), wisecrack, gibe, dig.
▪ *adjective* (*infml*) first-class, first-rate, top-notch (*infml*), excellent, superior, choice, hand-picked.

cradle *noun* cot, crib, bed.

craft *noun* **1** *arts and crafts/the craft of boat-building*: skill, expertise, mastery, talent, knack, ability, aptitude, dexterity, cleverness, art, handicraft, handiwork. **2** *learning his craft*: trade, business, calling, vocation, job, occupation, work, employment. **3** *a sturdy little craft*: vessel, boat, ship, aircraft, spacecraft, spaceship.

crafty *adjective* sly, cunning, artful, wily, devious, subtle, scheming, calculating, designing, deceitful, fraudulent, sharp, shrewd, astute, canny.
F3 artless, naive.

cram *verb* stuff, jam, ram, force, press, squeeze, crush, compress, pack, crowd, overfill, glut, gorge.

cramped *adjective* narrow, tight, uncomfortable, restricted,

confined, crowded, packed, squashed, squeezed, overcrowded, jam-packed, congested.
E3 spacious.

crash *noun* **1** *car crash*: accident, collision, bump, smash, pile-up, smash-up (*infml*), wreck. **2** *fell to the ground with a crash*: bang, clash, clatter, clang, thud, thump, boom, thunder, racket, din. **3** *the stock-market crash*: collapse, failure, ruin, downfall, bankruptcy, depression.
▪ *verb* **1** *crashed into the wall*: collide, hit, knock, bump, bang. **2** *crashing into a thousand pieces*: break, fracture, smash, dash, shatter, splinter, shiver, fragment, disintegrate. **3** *the stock market crashed*: fall, topple, pitch, plunge, collapse, fail, fold (up), go under, go bust (*infml*).

crave *verb* hunger for, thirst for, long for, yearn for, pine for, hanker after, fancy (*infml*), desire, want, need, require.
E3 dislike.

craving *noun* appetite, hunger, thirst, longing, yearning, hankering, lust, desire, urge.
E3 dislike, distaste.

crawl *verb* **1** *crawled under the table*: creep, inch, edge, slither, wriggle. **2** *crawl to the boss*: grovel, cringe, toady, fawn, flatter, suck up (*infml*).

craze *noun* fad, novelty, fashion, vogue, mode, trend, rage (*infml*), thing (*infml*), obsession, preoccupation, mania, frenzy, passion, infatuation, enthusiasm.

crazy *adjective* **1** *a crazy person/idea*: mad, insane, lunatic, unbalanced, deranged, demented, crazed, zany, potty (*infml*), barmy (*infml*), daft (*infml*), off one's head (*infml*), silly, foolish, idiotic, senseless, unwise, imprudent, nonsensical, absurd, ludicrous, ridiculous, preposterous, outrageous, half-baked, impracticable, irresponsible, wild, berserk. **2** (*infml*) *crazy about golf*: enthusiastic, fanatical, zealous, ardent, passionate, infatuated, enamoured, smitten, mad, wild.
E3 **1** sane, sensible. **2** indifferent.

creak *verb* squeak, groan, grate, scrape, rasp, scratch, grind, squeal, screech.

crease *noun* fold, line, pleat, tuck, wrinkle, pucker, ruck, crinkle, corrugation, ridge, groove.
▪ *verb* fold, pleat, wrinkle, pucker, crumple, rumple, crinkle, crimp, corrugate, ridge.

create *verb* invent, coin, formulate, compose, design, devise, concoct, hatch, originate, initiate, found, establish, set up, institute, cause, occasion, produce, generate, engender, make, form, appoint, install, invest, ordain.
E3 destroy.

creative *adjective* artistic, inventive, original, imaginative, inspired, visionary, talented, gifted, clever, ingenious,

resourceful, fertile, productive.
F3 unimaginative.

creator *noun* maker, inventor, designer, architect, author, originator, initiator.

creature *noun* animal, beast, bird, fish, organism, being, mortal, individual, person, man, woman, body, soul.

credibility *noun* integrity, reliability, trustworthiness, plausibility, probability.
F3 implausibility.

credit *noun* acknowledgement, recognition, thanks, approval, commendation, praise, acclaim, tribute, glory, fame, prestige, distinction, honour, reputation, esteem, estimation.
F3 discredit, shame.
▪ *verb* believe, swallow (*infml*), accept, subscribe to, trust, rely on.
F3 disbelieve.

creed *noun* belief, faith, persuasion, credo, catechism, doctrine, principles, tenets, articles, canon, dogma.

creep *verb* inch, edge, tiptoe, steal, sneak, slink, crawl, slither, worm, wriggle, squirm, grovel, writhe.

creepy *adjective* eerie, spooky, sinister, threatening, frightening, scary, terrifying, hair-raising, nightmarish, macabre, gruesome, horrible, unpleasant, disturbing.

crest *noun* **1** *the crest of the hill*: ridge, crown, top, peak, summit, pinnacle, apex, head. **2** *crest of feathers on a helmet*: tuft, tassel, plume, comb, mane. **3** *the family crest*: insignia, device, symbol, emblem, badge.

crevice *noun* crack, fissure, split, rift, cleft, slit, chink, cranny, gap, hole, opening, break.

crew *noun* team, party, squad, troop, corps, company, gang, band, bunch, crowd, mob, set, lot, posse (*infml*).

crime *noun* law-breaking, lawlessness, delinquency, offence, felony, misdemeanour, misdeed, wrongdoing, misconduct, transgression, violation, sin, iniquity (*fml*), vice, villainy, wickedness, atrocity, outrage.

criminal *noun* law-breaker, crook, felon, delinquent, offender, outlaw, wrongdoer, miscreant (*fml*), culprit, convict, prisoner.
▪ *adjective* illegal, unlawful, illicit, lawless, wrong, culpable, indictable, crooked (*infml*), bent (*infml*), dishonest, corrupt, wicked, scandalous, deplorable.
F3 legal, lawful, honest, upright.

cringe *verb* shrink, recoil, shy, start, flinch, wince, quail, tremble, quiver, cower, crouch, bend, bow, stoop, grovel, crawl, creep.

cripple *verb* lame, paralyse, disable, handicap, injure, maim, mutilate, damage, impair, spoil, ruin, destroy, sabotage, weaken, incapacitate, debilitate.

crippled *adjective* lame, paralysed, disabled, handicapped, incapacitated.

crisis *noun* emergency, extremity,

crunch (*infml*), catastrophe, disaster, calamity, dilemma, quandary, predicament, difficulty, trouble, problem.

crisp *adjective* **1** *a crisp biscuit*: crispy, crunchy, brittle, crumbly, firm, hard. **2** *crisp autumn day*: bracing, invigorating, refreshing, fresh, brisk.

F3 **1** soggy, limp, flabby. **2** muggy.

criterion *noun* standard, norm, touchstone, benchmark, yardstick, measure, gauge, rule, principle, canon, test.

critic *noun* reviewer, commentator, analyst, pundit, authority, expert, judge, censor, carper, fault-finder, attacker, knocker (*infml*).

critical *adjective* **1** *at the critical moment*: crucial, vital, essential, all-important, momentous, decisive, urgent, pressing, serious, grave, dangerous, perilous. **2** *a critical study*: analytical, diagnostic, penetrating, probing, discerning, perceptive. **3** *make critical remarks*: derogatory, uncomplimentary, disparaging, disapproving, censorious, carping, fault-finding, nit-picking (*infml*).

F3 **1** unimportant. **3** complimentary, appreciative.

criticism *noun* **1** *received much criticism*: condemnation, disapproval, disparagement (*fml*), fault-finding, censure, blame, brickbat, flak (*infml*). **2** *literary criticism*: review, critique, assessment, evaluation, appraisal, judgement, analysis, commentary, appreciation.

F3 **1** praise, commendation.

criticize *verb* **1** *criticize her work*: condemn, slate (*infml*), slam (*infml*), knock (*infml*), disparage (*fml*), carp, find fault (with), censure, blame. **2** *criticize a literary work*: review, assess, evaluate, appraise, judge, analyse.

F3 **1** praise, commend.

crook *noun* criminal, thief, robber, swindler, cheat, shark (*infml*), rogue, villain, con man (*infml*).

crooked *adjective* **1** *a crooked nose*: askew, skew-whiff (*infml*), awry, lopsided, asymmetric, irregular, uneven, off-centre, tilted, slanting, bent, angled, hooked, curved, bowed, warped, distorted, misshapen, deformed, twisted, tortuous, winding, zigzag. **2** (*infml*) *something crooked about this business/a crooked lawyer*: illegal, unlawful, illicit, criminal, nefarious, dishonest, deceitful, bent (*infml*), corrupt, fraudulent, shady (*infml*), shifty, underhand, treacherous, unscrupulous, unprincipled, unethical.

F3 **1** straight. **2** straight, honest.

crop *noun* growth, yield, produce, fruits, harvest, vintage, gathering.
▪ *verb* cut, snip, clip, shear, trim, pare, prune, lop, shorten, curtail.

cross *adjective* irritable, annoyed, angry, vexed, shirty (*infml*), bad-tempered, ill-tempered, crotchety,

grumpy, grouchy, irascible, crabby, short, snappy, snappish, surly, sullen, fractious, fretful, impatient.
F3 placid, pleasant.
▪ *verb* **1** *cross the river*: go across, traverse, ford, bridge, span. **2** *our paths cross now and again*: intersect, meet, criss-cross, lace, intertwine. **3** *crossing French cattle with British ones*: crossbreed, interbreed, mongrelize, hybridize, cross-fertilize, cross-pollinate, blend, mix. **4** *don't cross him*: thwart, frustrate, foil, hinder, impede, obstruct, block, oppose.
▪ *noun* **1** *a cross on a chain*: crucifix. **2** *a collie/golden retriever cross*: crossbreed, hybrid, mongrel, blend, mixture, amalgam, combination.

crouch *verb* squat, kneel, stoop, bend, bow, hunch, duck, cower, cringe.

crowd *noun* **1** *a crowd of demonstrators*: throng, multitude, host, mob, masses, populace, people, public, riff-raff, rabble, horde, swarm, flock, herd, pack, press, crush, squash, assembly, company, group, bunch, lot. **2** *kick the ball into the crowd*: spectators, gate, attendance, audience. **3** *not one of our crowd*: set, circle, clique.
▪ *verb* gather, congregate, muster, huddle, mass, throng, swarm, flock, surge, stream, push, shove, elbow, jostle, press, squeeze, bundle, pile, pack, congest, cram, compress.

crowded *adjective* full, filled, packed, jammed, jam-packed, congested, cramped, crammed, overcrowded, overpopulated, busy, teeming, swarming, overflowing.
F3 empty, deserted.

crown *noun* **1** *a crown of thorns*: coronet, diadem, tiara, circlet, wreath, garland. **2** *the crown of the hill*: top, tip, apex, crest, summit, pinnacle, peak, acme.
▪ *verb* enthrone, anoint, adorn, festoon, honour, dignify, reward.

crucial *adjective* urgent, pressing, vital, essential, key, pivotal, central, important, momentous, decisive, critical, trying, testing, searching.
F3 unimportant, trivial.

crude *adjective* **1** *crude oil*: raw, unprocessed, unrefined, rough, coarse, unfinished, unpolished. **2** *a crude dwelling*: rough, natural, primitive, makeshift. **3** *a crude remark*: vulgar, coarse, rude, indecent, obscene, gross, dirty, lewd.
F3 **1** refined, finished. **3** polite, decent.

cruel *adjective* fierce, ferocious, vicious, savage, barbarous, bloodthirsty, murderous, cold-blooded, sadistic, brutal, inhuman, inhumane, unkind, malevolent, spiteful, callous, heartless, unfeeling, merciless, pitiless, flinty, hard-hearted, stony-hearted, implacable, ruthless, remorseless, relentless, unrelenting, inexorable, grim, hellish, atrocious, bitter, harsh, severe, cutting, painful, excruciating.

F3 kind, compassionate, merciful.

cruelty *noun* ferocity, viciousness, savagery, barbarity, bloodthirstiness, murderousness, violence, sadism, brutality, inhumanity, spite, venom, callousness, heartlessness, hard-heartedness, mercilessness, ruthlessness, tyranny, harshness, severity.

F3 kindness, compassion, mercy.

crumble *verb* fragment, break up, decompose, disintegrate, decay, degenerate, deteriorate, collapse, crush, pound, grind, powder, pulverize.

crusade *noun* campaign, drive, push, movement, cause, undertaking, expedition, holy war, jihad.

crush *verb* **1** *crush the garlic cloves*: squash, compress, squeeze, press, pulp, break, smash, pound, pulverize, grind, crumble. **2** *crushing her dress*: crumple, wrinkle. **3** *the rebels were crushed*: conquer, vanquish (*fml*), demolish, devastate, overpower, overwhelm, overcome, quash, quell, subdue, put down, humiliate, shame, abash.

crust *noun* surface, exterior, outside, covering, coat, coating, layer, film, skin, rind, shell, scab, incrustation, caking, concretion.

cry *verb* **1** *cry pathetically*: weep, sob, blubber, wail, bawl, whimper, snivel. **2** *crying for help*: shout, call, exclaim, roar, bellow, yell, scream, shriek, screech, yelp.

▪ *noun* **1** *have a good cry*: weep, sob, blubber, wail, bawl, whimper, snivel. **2** *a cry for help*: shout, call, plea, exclamation, roar, bellow, yell, scream, shriek, yelp.

cuddle *verb* hug, embrace, clasp, hold, nurse, nestle, snuggle, pet, fondle, caress.

cuddly *adjective* cuddlesome, lovable, huggable, plump, soft, warm, cosy.

cue *noun* signal, sign, nod, hint, suggestion, reminder, prompt, incentive, stimulus.

culprit *noun* guilty party, offender, wrongdoer, miscreant (*fml*), law-breaker, criminal, felon, delinquent.

cult *noun* **1** *religious cults*: sect, denomination, school, movement, party, faction. **2** *become something of a cult*: craze, fad, fashion, vogue, trend.

cultivate *verb* **1** *cultivating the land/rice*: farm, till, work, plough, grow, sow, plant, tend, harvest. **2** *cultivating new talent*: foster, nurture, cherish, help, aid, support, encourage, promote, further, work on, develop, train, prepare, polish, refine, improve, enrich.

F3 **2** neglect.

cultural *adjective* artistic, aesthetic, liberal, civilizing, humanizing, enlightening, educational, edifying, improving, enriching, elevating.

culture *noun* **1** *ancient cultures/ Western culture*: civilization, society, lifestyle, way of life, customs, mores. **2** *a man of culture*: cultivation, taste, education, enlightenment, breeding, gentility, refinement, politeness, urbanity.

cultured *adjective* cultivated, civilized, advanced, enlightened, educated, well-read, well-informed, scholarly, highbrow, well-bred, refined, polished, genteel, urbane.

F3 uncultured, uneducated, ignorant.

cunning *adjective* crafty, sly, artful, wily, tricky, devious, subtle, deceitful, guileful, sharp, shrewd, astute, canny, knowing, deep, imaginative, ingenious, skilful, deft, dexterous, sneaky.

F3 naive, ingenuous, gullible.

▪ *noun* craftiness, slyness, artfulness, trickery, deviousness, subtlety, deceitfulness, guile, sharpness, shrewdness, astuteness, ingenuity, cleverness, adroitness.

cup *noun* mug, tankard, beaker, goblet, chalice, trophy.

curb *verb* restrain, constrain, restrict, contain, control, check, moderate, bridle, muzzle, suppress, subdue, repress, inhibit, hinder, impede, hamper, retard.

F3 encourage, foster.

curdle *verb* coagulate, congeal, clot, thicken, turn, sour, ferment.

cure *verb* heal, remedy, correct, restore, repair, mend, relieve, ease, alleviate, help.

▪ *noun* remedy, antidote, panacea, medicine, specific, corrective, restorative, healing, treatment, therapy, alleviation, recovery.

curiosity *noun* **1** *his curiosity irritated her*: inquisitiveness, nosiness, prying, snooping, interest. **2** *a bit of a curiosity*: oddity, rarity, freak, phenomenon, spectacle.

curious *adjective* **1** *the neighbours are too curious about our activities*: inquisitive, nosey, prying, meddlesome, questioning, inquiring, interested. **2** *a curious sight*: odd, queer, funny (*infml*), strange, peculiar, bizarre, mysterious, puzzling, extraordinary, unusual, rare, unique, novel, exotic, unconventional, unorthodox, quaint.

F3 1 uninterested, indifferent. **2** ordinary, usual, normal.

curl *verb* crimp, frizz, wave, ripple, bend, curve, meander, loop, turn, twist, wind, wreathe, twine, coil, spiral, corkscrew, scroll.

F3 uncurl.

▪ *noun* wave, kink, swirl, twist, ringlet, coil, spiral, whorl.

curly *adjective* wavy, kinky, curling, spiralled, corkscrew, curled, crimped, permed, frizzy, fuzzy.

F3 straight.

currency *noun* **1** *European currencies*: money, legal tender, coinage, coins, notes, bills. **2** *give currency to their beliefs*: acceptance, publicity, popularity, vogue, circulation, prevalence, exposure.

current *adjective* present, ongoing, existing, contemporary, present-day, modern, fashionable, up-to-date, up-to-the-minute, trendy (*infml*), popular, widespread, prevalent, common, general, prevailing, reigning, accepted.
F3 obsolete, old-fashioned.
▪ *noun* draught, stream, jet, flow, drift, tide, course, trend, tendency, undercurrent, mood, feeling.

curse *noun* **1** *shouting curses*: swear word, oath, expletive, obscenity, profanity, blasphemy. **2** *put a curse on someone/congestion is the curse of city life*: jinx, anathema, bane, evil, plague, scourge, affliction, trouble, torment, ordeal, calamity, disaster.
F3 **2** blessing, advantage.
▪ *verb* swear, blaspheme, condemn, denounce, fulminate (*fml*).

curtain *noun* blind, screen, backdrop, hanging, drapery, tapestry.

curve *verb* bend, arch, arc, bow, bulge, hook, crook, turn, wind, twist, spiral, coil.
▪ *noun* bend, turn, arc, trajectory, loop, camber, curvature.

curved *adjective* bent, arched, bowed, rounded, humped, convex, concave, crooked, twisted, sweeping, sinuous, serpentine.
F3 straight.

cushion *noun* pad, buffer, shock absorber, bolster, pillow, headrest, hassock.
▪ *verb* soften, deaden, dampen, absorb, muffle, stifle, suppress, lessen, mitigate, protect, bolster, support.

custody *noun* **1** *be granted custody of the children*: keeping, possession, charge, care, safekeeping, protection, preservation, custodianship, trusteeship, guardianship, supervision. **2** *in police custody*: detention, confinement, imprisonment, incarceration.

custom *noun* tradition, usage, use, habit, routine, procedure, practice, policy, way, manner, style, form, convention, etiquette, formality, observance, ritual.

customary *adjective* traditional, conventional, accepted, established, habitual, routine, regular, usual, normal, ordinary, everyday, familiar, common, general, popular, fashionable, prevailing.
F3 unusual, rare.

customer *noun* client, patron, regular, punter (*infml*), consumer, shopper, buyer, purchaser, prospect.

cut *verb* **1** *cut hair/the cake/my finger/a hole in something*: clip, trim, crop, shear, mow, shave, pare, chop, hack, hew, slice, carve,

divide, part, split, bisect, dock, lop, sever, prune, excise, incise, penetrate, pierce, stab, wound, nick, gash, slit, slash, lacerate, score, engrave, chisel, sculpt. **2** *cutting prices*: reduce, decrease, lower, shorten, curtail.
▪ *noun* **1** *a deep cut*: incision, wound, nick, gash, slit, slash, rip, laceration. **2** *spending cuts*: reduction, decrease, lowering, cutback, saving, economy.
cutting *adjective* sharp, keen, pointed, trenchant (*fml*), incisive, wounding, stinging, mordant (*fml*), caustic, acid, scathing, sarcastic, malicious.
▪ *noun* clipping, extract, piece.
cycle *noun* circle, round, rotation, revolution, series, sequence, phase, period, era, age, epoch, aeon.
cylinder *noun* column, barrel, drum, reel, bobbin, spool, spindle.
cynic *noun* sceptic, doubter, pessimist, killjoy, spoilsport (*infml*), scoffer, knocker (*infml*).
cynical *adjective* sceptical, doubtful, doubting, distrustful, disillusioned, disenchanted, pessimistic, negative, scornful, derisive, contemptuous, sneering, scoffing, mocking, sarcastic, sardonic, ironic.

Dd

dab *verb* pat, tap, daub, swab, wipe.
daft *adjective* **1** *a daft thing to say*: foolish, crazy, silly, stupid, absurd, dotty (*infml*), idiotic, inane. **2** (*infml*) *he's gone daft*: insane, mad, lunatic, simple, crazy, mental, potty (*infml*). **3** (*infml*) *daft about her*: infatuated.
F3 **1** sensible. **2** sane.
daily *adjective* regular, routine, everyday, customary, common, commonplace, ordinary, diurnal (*fml*).
dainty *adjective* **1** *dainty little thing*: delicate, elegant, exquisite, refined, fine, graceful, neat, charming, delectable, petite. **2** *a dainty eater*: fastidious, fussy, particular, scrupulous, nice (*fml*).
F3 **1** gross, clumsy.
dam *noun* barrier, barrage, embankment, blockage, obstruction, hindrance.
▪ *verb* block, confine, restrict, check, barricade, staunch, stem, obstruct.
damage *noun* harm, injury, hurt, destruction, devastation, loss, suffering, mischief, mutilation,

impairment, detriment.
F3 repair.
▪ *verb* harm, injure, hurt, spoil, ruin, impair, mar, wreck, deface, mutilate, weaken, tamper with, play havoc with, incapacitate.
F3 mend, repair, fix.

damp *noun* dampness, moisture, clamminess, dankness, humidity, wet, dew, drizzle, fog, mist, vapour.
F3 dryness.
▪ *adjective* moist, wet, clammy, dank, humid, dewy, muggy, drizzly, misty, soggy.
F3 dry, arid.

dampen *verb* **1** *dampen the cloth*: moisten, wet, spray. **2** *dampen their enthusiasm*: discourage, dishearten, deter, dash, dull, deaden, restrain, check, depress, dismay, reduce, lessen, moderate, decrease, diminish, muffle, stifle, smother.
F3 1 dry. **2** encourage.

dance *noun* ball, hop (*infml*), knees-up (*infml*), social, shindig (*infml*).

danger *noun* **1** *in danger of falling*: insecurity, endangerment, jeopardy, precariousness, liability, vulnerability. **2** *the dangers of smoking*: risk, threat, peril, hazard, menace.
F3 1 safety, security. **2** safety.

dangerous *adjective* unsafe, insecure, risky, threatening, breakneck, hairy (*infml*), hazardous, perilous, precarious, reckless, treacherous, vulnerable, menacing, exposed, alarming, critical, severe, serious, grave, daring, nasty.
F3 safe, secure, harmless.

dangle *verb* hang, droop, swing, sway, flap, trail.

dare *verb* **1** *wouldn't dare ask him*: risk, venture, brave, hazard, adventure, endanger, stake, gamble. **2** *daring her to jump*: challenge, defy, goad, provoke, taunt.

daring *adjective* bold, adventurous, intrepid, fearless, brave, plucky, audacious, dauntless, reckless, rash, impulsive, valiant.
F3 cautious, timid, afraid.
▪ *noun* boldness, fearlessness, courage, bravery, nerve, audacity, guts (*infml*), intrepidity, defiance, pluck, rashness, spirit, grit, gall, prowess.
F3 caution, timidity, cowardice.

dark *adjective* **1** *a dark room*: unlit, overcast, black, dim, unilluminated, shadowy, murky, cloudy, dusky, dingy. **2** *a dark mood*: gloomy, grim, cheerless, dismal, bleak, forbidding, sombre, sinister, mournful, ominous, menacing, drab. **3** *dark secrets*: hidden, mysterious, obscure, secret, unintelligible, enigmatic, cryptic, abstruse (*fml*).
F3 1 light. **2** bright, cheerful. **3** comprehensible.
▪ *noun* **1** *scared of the dark*: darkness, dimness, night, night-time, nightfall, gloom, dusk, twilight, murkiness. **2** *stay in the*

dark: concealment, secrecy, obscurity.
F3 **1** light. **2** openness.

dart *verb* dash, bound, sprint, flit, flash, fly, rush, run, race, spring, tear.
▪ *noun* bolt, arrow, barb, shaft.

dash *verb* **1** *must dash*: rush, dart, hurry, race, sprint, run, bolt, tear. **2** *dashing the boat against the rocks*: smash, strike, lash, pound, throw, crash, hurl, fling. **3** *dash their hopes*: crush, smash, shatter, discourage, disappoint, dampen, confound, blight, ruin, destroy, spoil, frustrate.
▪ *noun* **1** *a dash of lemon juice*: drop, pinch, touch, flavour, soupçon, suggestion, hint, bit, little. **2** *make a dash for the bus*: sprint, dart, bolt, rush, spurt, race, run.

data *noun* information, documents, facts, input, statistics, figures, details, materials.

date *noun* **1** *an earlier/later date*: time, age, period, era, stage, epoch. **2** *have a date with destiny*: appointment, engagement, assignation, meeting, rendezvous.

daunt *verb* discourage, dishearten, put off, deter, intimidate, overawe, unnerve, alarm, dismay, frighten, scare.
F3 encourage.

dawdle *verb* delay, loiter, lag, hang about, dally, trail, potter, dilly-dally (*infml*).
F3 hurry.

dawn *noun* **1** *get up at dawn*: sunrise, daybreak, morning, daylight. **2** *the dawn of a new era of prosperity*: beginning, start, emergence, onset, origin, birth, advent.
F3 **1** dusk. **2** end.

day *noun* **1** *during the day*: daytime, daylight. **2** *in the days of Henry VIII*: age, period, time, date, era, generation, epoch.
F3 **1** night.

daydream *noun* fantasy, imagining, reverie, castles in the air, pipe dream, vision, musing, wish, dream, figment.

daze *verb* stun, stupefy, shock, bewilder, confuse, baffle, dumbfound, amaze, surprise, startle, perplex, astonish, flabbergast (*infml*), astound, stagger.

dazzle *verb* **1** *bright sunlight dazzled him*: daze, blind, confuse, blur. **2** *dazzled the audience with their skill*: fascinate, impress, overwhelm, awe, overawe, amaze, astonish, bewitch, stupefy.

dead *adjective* **1** *dead on arrival at hospital*: lifeless, deceased, inanimate, defunct, departed, late, gone. **2** *fingers went dead*: unresponsive, apathetic, dull, indifferent, insensitive, numb, cold, frigid, lukewarm, torpid. **3** *dead centre*: exact, absolute, perfect, unqualified, utter, outright, complete, entire, total, downright.
F3 **1** alive. **2** lively.

deaden *verb* reduce, blunt,

muffle, lessen, quieten, suppress, weaken, numb, diminish, stifle, alleviate, anaesthetize, desensitize, smother, check, abate, allay, dampen, hush, mute, paralyse.
F3 heighten.

deadlock *noun* standstill, stalemate, checkmate, impasse, dead end, halt.

deadly *adjective* **1** *deadly poison*: lethal, fatal, dangerous, venomous, destructive, pernicious, malignant, murderous, mortal. **2** *a deadly aim*: unerring, effective, true.
F3 1 harmless.

deaf *adjective* **1** *go deaf*: hard of hearing, stone-deaf. **2** *deaf to their pleas*: unconcerned, indifferent, unmoved, oblivious, heedless, unmindful.
F3 2 aware, conscious.

deafening *adjective* piercing, ear-splitting, booming, resounding, thunderous, roaring.
F3 quiet.

deal *noun* **1** *cause a great deal of trouble*: quantity, amount, extent, degree, portion, share. **2** *a better deal*: agreement, contract, understanding, pact, transaction, bargain, buy. **3** *it's your deal*: round, hand, distribution.
▪ *verb* **1** *deal the cards/deal out punishment*: apportion, distribute, share, dole out, divide, allot, dispense, assign, mete out, give, bestow. **2** *dealing in antiques*: trade, negotiate, traffic, bargain, treat.

dealer *noun* trader, merchant, wholesaler, marketer, merchandiser.

dear *adjective* **1** *my dear friend*: loved, beloved, treasured, valued, cherished, precious, favourite, esteemed, intimate, close, darling, familiar. **2** *a car was too dear so I bought a bike*: expensive, high-priced, costly, overpriced, pricey (*infml*).
F3 1 disliked, hated. **2** cheap.
▪ *noun* beloved, loved one, precious, darling, treasure.

death *noun* **1** *cause many deaths/death by hanging*: decease, end, finish, loss, demise, departure, fatality, cessation, passing, expiration, dissolution. **2** *the death of communism*: destruction, ruin, undoing, downfall, annihilation, extermination, extinction, obliteration, eradication.
F3 1 life, birth.

debatable *adjective* questionable, uncertain, disputable, contestable, controversial, arguable, open to question, doubtful, contentious, undecided, unsettled, problematical, dubious, moot.
F3 unquestionable, certain, incontrovertible.

debate *verb* **1** *debating the point*: dispute, argue, discuss, contend, wrangle. **2** *debating whether to go*: consider, deliberate, ponder, reflect, meditate on, mull over, weigh.
▪ *noun* discussion, argument,

controversy, disputation, deliberation, reflection, consideration, contention, dispute, polemic.

debris *noun* remains, ruins, rubbish, waste, wreck, wreckage, litter, fragments, rubble, trash, pieces, bits, sweepings, drift.

debt *noun* indebtedness, obligation, debit, arrears, due, liability, duty, bill, commitment, claim, score.
F3 credit, asset.

debut *noun* introduction, launching, beginning, entrance, presentation, inauguration, première, appearance, initiation.

decadent *adjective* corrupt, debased, debauched, depraved, dissolute, immoral, degenerate, degraded, self-indulgent, decaying, declining.
F3 moral.

decay *verb* **1** *plant material decays to form compost*: rot, go bad, putrefy, decompose, spoil, perish, mortify. **2** *this area is slowly decaying*: decline, deteriorate, disintegrate, corrode, crumble, waste away, degenerate, wear away, dwindle, shrivel, wither, sink.
F3 2 flourish, grow.

deceased *adjective* dead, departed, former, late, lost, defunct, expired, gone, finished, extinct.

deceit *noun* deception, pretence, cheating, misrepresentation, fraud, duplicity (*fml*), trickery, fraudulence, double-dealing, underhandedness, fake, guile, sham, subterfuge, swindle, treachery, hypocrisy, artifice, ruse, cunning, slyness, craftiness, imposition, shift, abuse.
F3 honesty, openness, frankness.

deceitful *adjective* dishonest, deceptive, deceiving, false, insincere, untrustworthy, double-dealing, fraudulent, two-faced (*infml*), treacherous, duplicitous, guileful, tricky (*infml*), underhand, sneaky, counterfeit, crafty, hypocritical, designing, illusory.
F3 honest, open.

deceive *verb* mislead, delude, cheat, betray, fool, take in (*infml*), trick, dissemble (*fml*), hoax, con (*infml*), have on (*infml*), take for a ride (*infml*), double-cross, dupe, kid (*infml*), swindle, impose upon, bamboozle (*infml*), two-time (*infml*), lead on, outwit, hoodwink, beguile, ensnare, camouflage, abuse.

decent *adjective* **1** *not decent*: respectable, proper, fitting, decorous, chaste, seemly, suitable, modest, appropriate, presentable, pure, fit, becoming, befitting, nice. **2** *very decent of you*: kind, obliging, courteous, helpful, generous, polite, gracious. **3** *a decent salary/ effort*: adequate, acceptable, satisfactory, reasonable, sufficient, tolerable, competent.
F3 1 indecent. **2** disobliging.

deception *noun* deceit, pretence, trick, cheat, fraud, lie, dissembling (*fml*), deceptiveness,

insincerity, con (*infml*), sham, fallacy, subterfuge, artifice, hypocrisy, bluff, treachery, hoax, fraudulence, duplicity (*fml*), ruse, snare, leg-pull (*infml*), illusion, wile, guile, craftiness, cunning.
E3 openness, honesty.

deceptive *adjective* dishonest, false, fraudulent, misleading, unreliable, illusive, fake, illusory, spurious, mock, fallacious, ambiguous, specious.
E3 genuine, artless, open.

decide *verb* choose, determine, resolve, reach a decision, settle, elect, opt, judge, adjudicate, conclude, fix, purpose, decree.

decidedly *adverb* definitely, certainly, undeniably, indisputably, absolutely, undisputedly, unmistakably, unquestionably, positively, unambiguously, distinctly, emphatically.

decipher *verb* decode, unscramble, crack, construe, interpret, make out (*infml*), figure out (*infml*), understand.

decision *noun* **1** *the final decision*: result, conclusion, outcome, verdict, finding, settlement, judgement, arbitration, ruling. **2** *act with decision*: determination, decisiveness, firmness, resolve, purpose.
E3 **2** indecision.

decisive *adjective* **1** *have decisive evidence*: conclusive, definite, definitive, absolute, final. **2** *he's usually very decisive*: resolute, determined, decided, positive, firm, forceful, forthright, strong-minded. **3** *a decisive moment in history*: significant, critical, crucial, influential, momentous, fateful.
E3 **1** inconclusive. **2** indecisive, hesitant. **3** insignificant.

declaration *noun* **1** *a declaration of guilt*: affirmation, acknowledgement, assertion, statement, testimony, attestation, disclosure, profession, revelation. **2** *a public declaration*: announcement, notification, pronouncement, edict, proclamation, manifesto.

declare *verb* **1** *declare that it was so*: affirm, assert, claim, profess, maintain, state, attest (*fml*), certify, confess, confirm, disclose, reveal, show, aver, swear, testify, witness, validate. **2** *declared his intention*: announce, proclaim, pronounce, decree, broadcast.

decline *noun* deterioration, dwindling, lessening, decay, degeneration, weakening, worsening, failing, downturn, diminution, falling-off, recession, slump, abatement.
E3 improvement, rise.
■ *verb* **1** *decline his invitation*: refuse, reject, turn down, deny, forgo. **2** *decline in value/her health is declining*: diminish, decrease, dwindle, lessen, fall, sink, wane, flag.

decode *verb* decipher, interpret, crack (*infml*), figure out (*infml*), unscramble, translate,

transliterate, uncipher.
⇔ encode.

decorate *verb* **1** *decorate the tree*: ornament, adorn, beautify, embellish, trim, deck, grace, enrich, prettify, trick out. **2** *decorating the bedroom*: renovate, do up (*infml*), paint, paper, colour, refurbish.

decoration *noun* **1** *Christmas decorations/a style with little decoration*: ornament, frill, adornment, ornamentation, trimming, embellishment, beautification, garnish, flourish, enrichment, elaboration, scroll, bauble. **2** *a decoration for valour*: award, medal, order, badge, garland, crown, colours, ribbon, laurel, star, emblem.

decoy *noun* lure, trap, enticement, inducement, ensnarement, pretence, attraction, bait.

decrease *verb* lessen, lower, diminish, dwindle, decline, fall off, reduce, subside, abate, cut down, contract, drop, ease, shrink, taper, wane, slim, slacken, peter out, curtail.
⇔ increase.
▪ *noun* lessening, reduction, decline, falling-off, dwindling, loss, diminution, abatement, cutback, contraction, downturn, shrinkage, subsidence.
⇔ increase.

decree *noun* order, command, law, ordinance, regulation, ruling, statute, act, edict, fiat, proclamation, mandate, precept (*fml*).
▪ *verb* order, command, rule, lay down, dictate, decide, determine, ordain, prescribe, proclaim, pronounce.

decrepit *adjective* dilapidated, run-down, rickety, broken-down, worn-out, tumbledown, clapped-out (*infml*).

dedicate *verb* **1** *dedicating himself to his studies*: devote, commit, assign, give over to, pledge, present, offer, sacrifice, surrender. **2** *dedicating the church to St Agnes*: consecrate, bless, sanctify, set apart, hallow. **3** *dedicated the book to her husband*: inscribe, address.

dedicated *adjective* devoted, committed, enthusiastic, single-minded, whole-hearted, single-hearted, zealous, given over to, purposeful.
⇔ uncommitted, apathetic.

dedication *noun* **1** *shows exceptional dedication*: commitment, devotion, single-mindedness, whole-heartedness, allegiance, attachment, adherence, faithfulness, loyalty, self-sacrifice. **2** *dedication of the chapel*: consecration, hallowing, presentation. **3** *a dedication to his parents*: inscription, address.
⇔ **1** apathy.

deduce *verb* derive, infer, gather, conclude, reason, surmise, understand, draw, glean.

deduct *verb* subtract, take away, remove, reduce by, decrease by,

knock off (*infml*), withdraw.
E3 add.

deduction *noun* **1** *powers of deduction/my deduction is that he is guilty*: inference, reasoning, finding, conclusion, corollary, assumption, result. **2** *the deduction of tax*: subtraction, reduction, decrease, diminution, abatement, withdrawal, discount, allowance.
E3 **2** addition, increase.

deed *noun* **1** *the deeds of the knights of old*: action, act, achievement, performance, exploit, feat, fact, truth, reality. **2** *a deed of sale*: document, contract, record, title, transaction, indenture (*fml*).

deep *adjective* **1** *a deep gorge*: bottomless, unplumbed, fathomless, cavernous, yawning. **2** *his books are too deep for me to understand*: obscure, mysterious, difficult, recondite (*fml*), abstruse, esoteric. **3** *a deep person*: wise, perceptive, discerning, profound, learned, astute. **4** *a deep sleep*: intense, serious, earnest, extreme. **5** *a deep groan/voice*: low, bass, resonant, booming.
E3 **1** shallow, open. **2** clear, plain, open. **3** superficial. **4** light. **5** high.

defeat *verb* **1** *defeat one's enemies*: conquer, beat, overpower, subdue, overthrow, worst, repel, subjugate, overwhelm, rout, ruin, trounce, thrash (*infml*), thump (*infml*), quell, vanquish (*fml*). **2** *the problem defeated him*: frustrate, confound, get the better of, disappoint, foil, thwart, baffle, checkmate.
▪ *noun* **1** *heavy defeat on the battlefield*: conquest, beating, rout, repulsion, subjugation, vanquishment (*fml*), thrashing (*infml*). **2** *defeat on a specific issue*: frustration, failure, setback, downfall, thwarting, disappointment, checkmate.

defect *noun* imperfection, fault, flaw, deficiency, failing, mistake, inadequacy, blemish, error, bug (*infml*), shortcoming, want, weakness, frailty, lack, spot, absence, taint.

defective *adjective* faulty, imperfect, out of order, flawed, deficient, broken, abnormal.
E3 in order, operative.

defence *noun* **1** *the castle provided defence against attack*: protection, resistance, security, fortification, cover, safeguard, shelter, guard, shield, deterrence, barricade, bastion, immunity, bulwark, rampart, buttress. **2** *evidence offered in his defence*: justification, explanation, excuse, argument, exoneration, plea, vindication, pleading, alibi, case.
E3 **1** attack, assault. **2** accusation.

defenceless *adjective* unprotected, undefended, unarmed, unguarded, vulnerable, exposed, helpless, powerless.
E3 protected, guarded.

defend *verb* **1** *defending their borders*: protect, guard, safeguard, shelter, fortify, secure, shield, screen, cover, contest. **2** *a lawyer defending the accused*: support, stand up for, stand by, uphold, endorse, vindicate, champion, argue for, speak up for, justify, plead.

F3 **1** attack. **2** accuse.

defer *verb* delay, postpone, put off, adjourn, hold over, shelve, suspend, procrastinate, prorogue (*fml*), protract, waive.

defiant *adjective* challenging, resistant, antagonistic, aggressive, rebellious, insubordinate, disobedient, intransigent, bold, contumacious (*fml*), insolent, obstinate, unco-operative, provocative.

F3 compliant, submissive.

deficiency *noun* **1** *a vitamin deficiency*: shortage, lack, inadequacy, scarcity, insufficiency, dearth, want, scantiness, absence, deficit. **2** *highlight the deficiencies in the system*: imperfection, shortcoming, weakness, fault, defect, flaw, failing, frailty.

F3 **1** excess, surfeit. **2** perfection.

deficit *noun* shortage, shortfall, deficiency, loss, arrears, lack, default.

F3 excess.

define *verb* **1** *defining the boundaries of the estate*: bound, limit, delimit, demarcate, mark out. **2** *define the meaning*: explain, characterize, describe, interpret, expound, determine, designate, specify, spell out, detail.

definite *adjective* **1** *a definite job offer*: certain, settled, sure, positive, fixed, decided, assured, determined, guaranteed. **2** *his answer was a quite definite 'no'*: clear, clear-cut, exact, precise, specific, explicit, particular, obvious, marked.

F3 **1** indefinite. **2** vague.

definitely *adverb* positively, surely, unquestionably, absolutely, certainly, categorically, undeniably, clearly, doubtless, unmistakably, plainly, obviously, indeed, easily.

definition *noun* **1** *the definition of boundaries*: delineation, demarcation, delimitation. **2** *a dictionary definition*: explanation, description, interpretation, exposition, clarification, elucidation. **3** *gives the picture definition*: distinctness, clarity, precision, clearness, focus, contrast, sharpness.

definitive *adjective* decisive, conclusive, final, authoritative, standard, correct, ultimate, reliable, exhaustive, perfect, exact, absolute, complete.

F3 interim.

deflect *verb* deviate, diverge, turn (aside), swerve, veer, sidetrack, twist, avert, wind, glance off, bend, ricochet.

deformed *adjective* distorted, misshapen, contorted, disfigured, crippled, crooked, bent, twisted, warped, buckled, defaced, mangled, maimed, marred, ruined, mutilated.

defraud *verb* cheat, swindle, dupe, fleece, sting (*infml*), rip off (*infml*), do (*infml*), diddle (*infml*), rob, trick, con (*infml*), rook, deceive, delude, mislead, fool, embezzle, beguile.

deft *adjective* adept, handy, dexterous, nimble, skilful, adroit, agile, expert, nifty (*infml*), proficient, able, neat, clever.
F3 clumsy, awkward.

defy *verb* **1** *defy the authorities*: challenge, confront, resist, dare, brave, face, repel, spurn, beard, flout, withstand, disregard, scorn, despise, defeat, provoke, thwart. **2** *his writings defy categorization*: elude, frustrate, baffle, foil.
F3 **1** obey. **2** permit.

degenerate *verb* decline, deteriorate, sink, decay, rot, slip, worsen, regress, fall off, lapse, decrease.
F3 improve.

degrade *verb* dishonour, disgrace, debase, abase, shame, humiliate, humble, discredit, demean, lower, weaken, impair, deteriorate, cheapen, adulterate, corrupt.
F3 exalt.

degree *noun* **1** *of high degree*: grade, class, rank, order, position, standing, status. **2** *to a great degree*: extent, measure, range, stage, step, level, intensity, standard.

deign *verb* condescend, stoop, lower oneself, consent, demean oneself.

deity *noun* god, goddess, divinity, godhead, idol, demigod, demigoddess, power, immortal.

dejected *adjective* downcast, despondent, depressed, downhearted, disheartened, down, low, melancholy, disconsolate, sad, miserable, cast down, gloomy, glum, crestfallen, dismal, wretched, doleful, morose, spiritless.
F3 cheerful, high-spirited, happy.

delay *noun* hold-up, check, setback, postponement, interruption, pause, lull, interval, wait.
▪ *verb* **1** *delay progress*: obstruct, hinder, impede, hold up, check, hold back, set back, stop, halt, detain. **2** *delay the wedding*: defer, put off, postpone, procrastinate, suspend, shelve, hold over, stall. **3** *don't delay, buy today*: dawdle, linger, lag, loiter, dilly-dally (*infml*), tarry, hang back (*infml*).
F3 **1** accelerate. **2** bring forward. **3** hurry.

delegate *noun* representative, agent, envoy, messenger, deputy, ambassador, commissioner.
▪ *verb* authorize, appoint, depute, charge, commission, assign, empower, entrust, devolve, consign, designate, nominate, name, hand over.

delete *verb* erase, remove, cross out, cancel, rub out, strike (out), obliterate, edit (out), blot out, efface (*fml*), expunge (*fml*).
F3 add, insert.

deliberate *adjective* **1** *a deliberate mistake*: intentional, planned, calculated, prearranged, premeditated, willed, conscious, designed, considered, advised. **2** *deliberate way of speaking*: careful, unhurried, thoughtful, methodical, cautious, circumspect *(fml)*, studied, prudent, slow, ponderous, measured, heedful.
F3 1 unintentional, accidental. **2** hasty.

delicacy *noun* **1** *treat the matter with some delicacy*: sensitivity, subtlety, finesse, tact, discrimination, niceness. **2** *provided guests with local delicacies*: titbit, dainty, taste, sweetmeat, savoury, relish.
F3 1 tactlessness.

delicate *adjective* **1** *delicate lace*: fine, fragile, dainty, exquisite, flimsy, elegant, graceful. **2** *a delicate child*: frail, weak, ailing, faint. **3** *delicate workmanship*: sensitive, scrupulous, discriminating, careful, accurate, precise.
F3 1 coarse, clumsy. **2** healthy.

delicious *adjective* **1** *the food was delicious*: appetizing, palatable, tasty, delectable, scrumptious (*infml*), mouth-watering, succulent, savoury. **2** *a delicious breeze*: enjoyable, pleasant, agreeable, delightful.
F3 1 unpalatable. **2** unpleasant.

delight *noun* bliss, happiness, joy, pleasure, ecstasy, enjoyment, gladness, rapture, transport, gratification, jubilation.
F3 disgust, displeasure.
▪ *verb* please, charm, gratify, enchant, tickle, thrill, ravish.
F3 displease, dismay.

delighted *adjective* charmed, elated, happy, pleased, enchanted, captivated, ecstatic, thrilled, overjoyed, jubilant, joyous.
F3 disappointed, dismayed.

delightful *adjective* charming, enchanting, captivating, enjoyable, pleasant, thrilling, agreeable, pleasurable, engaging, attractive, pleasing, gratifying, entertaining, fascinating.
F3 nasty, unpleasant.

delirious *adjective* demented, raving, incoherent, beside oneself, deranged, frenzied, light-headed, wild, mad, frantic, insane, crazy, ecstatic.
F3 sane.

deliver *verb* **1** *deliver a parcel*: convey, bring, send, give, carry, supply. **2** *deliver him to the court*: surrender, hand over, relinquish, yield, transfer, grant, entrust, commit. **3** *deliver a speech*: utter, speak, proclaim, pronounce. **4** *deliver a blow*: administer, inflict, direct. **5** *deliver us from evil*: set free, liberate, release, emancipate.

delivery *noun* **1** *the delivery of letters and parcels*: conveyance, consignment, dispatch, transmission, transfer, surrender. **2** *a halting delivery*: articulation, enunciation, speech, utterance, intonation, elocution. **3** *an easy delivery*: childbirth, labour, confinement.

delude *verb* deceive, mislead, beguile, dupe, take in, trick, hoodwink, hoax, cheat, misinform.

delusion *noun* illusion, hallucination, fancy, misconception, misapprehension, deception, misbelief, fallacy.

demand *verb* **1** *demanded that he come/demand payment*: ask, request, call for, insist on, solicit, claim, exact. **2** *demands your strict attention*: necessitate, need, require, involve.
▪ *noun* **1** *a demand from the boss*: request, question, claim, order, inquiry, desire, interrogation. **2** *no demand for their products*: need, necessity, call.

demanding *adjective* hard, difficult, challenging, exacting, taxing, tough, exhausting, wearing, back-breaking, insistent, pressing, urgent, trying.
F3 easy, undemanding, easy-going.

demeanour *noun* bearing, manner, deportment, conduct, behaviour, air.

democratic *adjective* self-governing, representative, egalitarian, autonomous, popular, populist, republican.

demolish *verb* **1** *demolishing the building*: destroy, dismantle, knock down, pull down, flatten, bulldoze, raze, tear down, level. **2** *demolish the opposition*: ruin, defeat, destroy, annihilate, wreck, overturn, overthrow.
F3 **1** build up.

demonstrate *verb* **1** *demonstrates the efficiency of the police*: show, display, prove, establish, exhibit, substantiate, manifest, testify to, indicate. **2** *demonstrated the technique*: show, explain, illustrate, describe, teach. **3** *students demonstrating*: protest, march, parade, rally, picket, sit in.

demonstration *noun* **1** *sufficient demonstration of his stupidity*: proof, confirmation, affirmation, substantiation, validation, evidence, testimony, manifestation, expression. **2** *demonstration of how a computer works*: display, exhibition, explanation, illustration, description, exposition, presentation, test, trial. **3** *an anti-war demonstration*: protest, march, demo (*infml*), rally, picket, sit-in, parade.

demonstrative *adjective* affectionate, expressive, expansive, emotional, open, loving.
F3 reserved, cold, restrained.

demoralize *verb* discourage, dishearten, dispirit, undermine, depress, deject, crush, lower, disconcert.
F3 encourage.

den *noun* lair, hideout, hole, retreat, study, hide-away, shelter, sanctuary, haunt.

denial *noun* **1** *issue an outright denial*: contradiction, negation, dissent, repudiation, disavowal, disclaimer, dismissal, renunciation. **2** *denial of their rights*: refusal, rebuff, rejection, prohibition, veto.

denote *verb* indicate, stand for, signify, represent, symbolize, mean, express, designate, typify, mark, show, imply.

denounce *verb* condemn, censure, accuse, revile, decry, attack, inform against, betray, impugn (*fml*), vilify (*fml*), fulminate (*fml*).

F3 acclaim, praise.

dense *adjective* **1** *a dense forest*: compact, thick, compressed, condensed, close, close-knit, heavy, solid, opaque, packed, impenetrable, crowded. **2** *he can sometimes be a bit dense*: stupid, thick (*infml*), crass, dull, slow, slow-witted.

F3 1 thin, sparse. **2** quick-witted, clever.

dent *noun* hollow, depression, dip, concavity, indentation, crater, dimple, dint, pit.

▪ *verb* depress, bend, push in, buckle, crumple, indent.

deny *verb* **1** *deny the accusation*: contradict, oppose, refute, disagree with, disaffirm, disprove. **2** *denied her faith/her own brother*: disown, disclaim, renounce, repudiate, recant. **3** *deny them basic human rights*: refuse, turn down, forbid, reject, withhold, rebuff, veto.

F3 1 admit. **3** allow.

depart *verb* **1** *he departed soon afterwards/departing from Southampton*: go, leave, withdraw, exit, make off, quit, decamp, take one's leave, absent oneself, set off, remove, retreat, migrate, escape, disappear, retire, vanish, do a bunk (*infml*). **2** *departing from the script*: deviate, digress, differ, diverge, swerve, veer.

F3 1 arrive, return. **2** keep to.

department *noun* **1** *a government department*: division, branch, subdivision, section, sector, office, station, unit. **2** *not my department*: sphere, realm, province, domain, field, area, concern, responsibility, speciality, line.

departure *noun* **1** *the departure of several colleagues*: exit, going, leave-taking, removal, withdrawal, retirement, exodus. **2** *a departure from the usual rules*: deviation, digression, divergence, variation, innovation, branching (out), difference, change, shift, veering.

F3 1 arrival, return.

dependable *adjective* reliable, trustworthy, steady, trusty, responsible, faithful, unfailing, sure, honest, conscientious, certain.

F3 unreliable, fickle.

dependent *adjective* **1** *a dependent infant/dependent on his parents*: reliant, helpless, weak, immature, vulnerable. **2** *whether* *we go or not is dependent on the weather*: conditional on, determined by, decided by, dictated by, subject to, contingent on (*fml*).

F3 1 independent.

depend on *verb* **1** *depend on his income*: rely upon, count on, bank on (*infml*), calculate on, reckon on (*infml*), build upon, trust in, lean on, expect. **2** *depends on several factors*: hinge on, rest on, revolve around, be contingent upon (*fml*), hang on.

depict *verb* portray, illustrate, delineate, sketch, outline, draw, picture, paint, trace, describe, characterize, detail.

deport *verb* expel, banish, exile, extradite, transport, expatriate, oust.

depose *verb* demote, dethrone, downgrade, dismiss, unseat, topple, disestablish, displace, oust.

deposit *verb* **1** *deposits its eggs on a leaf*: lay, drop, place, put, settle, dump (*infml*), park, precipitate (*fml*), sit, locate. **2** *deposit funds in a savings account*: save, store, hoard, bank, amass, consign, entrust, lodge, file.

▪ *noun* **1** *muddy deposits which formed the rocks*: sediment, accumulation, dregs, precipitate (*fml*), lees, silt. **2** *put down a deposit*: security, stake, down payment, pledge, retainer, instalment, part payment, money.

depot *noun* **1** *an arms depot*: storehouse, store, warehouse, depository, repository, arsenal. **2** *a bus depot*: station, garage, terminus.

depreciate *verb* devalue, deflate, downgrade, decrease, reduce, lower, drop, fall, lessen, decline, slump.

F3 appreciate.

depress *verb* deject, sadden, dishearten, discourage, oppress, upset, daunt.

F3 cheer.

depressed *adjective* dejected, low-spirited, melancholy, dispirited, sad, unhappy, low, down, downcast, disheartened, fed up (*infml*), miserable, moody, cast down, discouraged, glum, downhearted, distressed, despondent, morose, crestfallen, pessimistic.

F3 cheerful.

depressing *adjective* dejecting, dismal, bleak, gloomy, saddening, cheerless, dreary, disheartening, sad, melancholy, sombre, grey, black, daunting, discouraging, heartbreaking, distressing, hopeless.

F3 cheerful, encouraging.

depression *noun* **1** *go into a deep depression*: dejection, despair, despondency, melancholy, low spirits, sadness, gloominess, doldrums, blues (*infml*), glumness, dumps (*infml*), hopelessness. **2** *economic depression*: recession, slump, stagnation, hard times, decline, inactivity. **3** *a depression in*

the rock: indentation, hollow, dip, concavity, dent, dimple, valley, pit, sink, dint, bowl, cavity, basin, impression, dish, excavation.
F3 **1** cheerfulness. **2** prosperity, boom. **3** convexity, protuberance (*fml*).

deprive *verb* **1** *depriving them of their land*: dispossess, strip, divest, denude, bereave, expropriate (*fml*), rob. **2** *depriving him of sweets*: deny, withhold, refuse.
F3 **1** endow. **2** provide.

deprived *adjective* poor, needy, underprivileged, disadvantaged, impoverished, destitute, lacking, bereft.
F3 prosperous.

depth *noun* **1** *the depth of the water*: deepness, profoundness, extent, measure, drop. **2** *the farthest depths*: lowest point, remotest area, bed, floor, bottom, deep, abyss. **3** *a mind of great depth*: wisdom, insight, discernment, penetration. **4** *depth of feeling*: intensity, strength, seriousness.
F3 **1** shallowness. **2** surface.

deputize *verb* represent, stand in for, substitute, replace, understudy, double.

deputy *noun* representative, agent, delegate, proxy, substitute, second-in-command, ambassador, commissioner, lieutenant, surrogate, subordinate, assistant, locum.

derelict *adjective* abandoned, neglected, deserted, forsaken, desolate, discarded, dilapidated, ruined.

derive *verb* **1** *derive some benefit*: gain, obtain, get, draw, extract, receive, procure, acquire, borrow. **2** *deriving from a French word*: originate, arise, spring, flow, emanate, descend, proceed, stem, issue, follow, develop.

derogatory *adjective* insulting, pejorative, offensive, disparaging, depreciative, critical, defamatory, injurious.
F3 flattering.

descend *verb* **1** *descending from 30,000 feet*: drop, go down, fall, plummet, plunge, tumble, swoop, sink, arrive, alight, dismount, dip, slope, subside. **2** *descending into farce*: degenerate, deteriorate. **3** *descend to their level*: condescend, deign, stoop. **4** *descended from apes*: originate, proceed, spring, stem.
F3 **1** ascend, rise.

descendants *noun* offspring, children, issue, progeny (*fml*), successors, lineage, line, seed (*fml*).

descent *noun* **1** *a steep descent*: fall, drop, plunge, dip, decline, incline, slope. **2** *their descent into poverty*: comedown, debasement, degradation. **3** *of Norman descent*: ancestry, parentage, heredity, family tree, genealogy, lineage, extraction, origin.
F3 **1** ascent, rise.

describe *verb* portray, depict, delineate, illustrate, characterize, specify, draw, define, detail, explain, express, tell, narrate, outline, relate, recount, present, report, sketch.

description *noun* **1** *a good description of the thief*: portrayal, representation, account, characterization, delineation, depiction, sketch, presentation, report, outline, explanation, exposition, narration. **2** *a vehicle of some description*: sort, type, kind, variety, specification, order.

descriptive *adjective* illustrative, explanatory, expressive, detailed, graphic, colourful, pictorial, vivid.

desert[1] *noun* /**dez**-ert/ wasteland, wilderness, wilds, void.

desert[2] *verb* /di-**zert**/ abandon, forsake, leave, maroon, strand, decamp, defect, give up, renounce, relinquish, jilt, abscond, quit.

F3 stand by, support.

deserted *adjective* abandoned, forsaken, empty, derelict, desolate, godforsaken, neglected, underpopulated, stranded, isolated, bereft, vacant, betrayed, lonely, solitary, unoccupied.

F3 populous.

deserter *noun* runaway, absconder, escapee, truant, renegade, defector, traitor, fugitive, betrayer, apostate, backslider, delinquent.

deserve *verb* earn, be worthy of, merit, be entitled to, warrant, justify, win, rate, incur.

deserved *adjective* due, earned, merited, justifiable, warranted, right, rightful, well-earned, suitable, proper, fitting, fair, just, appropriate, apt, legitimate, apposite.

F3 gratuitous, undeserved.

deserving *adjective* worthy, estimable, exemplary, praiseworthy, admirable, commendable, laudable, righteous.

F3 undeserving, unworthy.

design *noun* **1** *a design for the garden*: blueprint, draft, pattern, plan, prototype, sketch, drawing, outline, model, guide. **2** *of a different design*: style, shape, form, figure, structure, organization, arrangement, composition, construction, motif.

▪ *verb* **1** *was designed to float*: plan, plot, intend, devise, purpose, aim, scheme, shape. **2** *design a dress*: sketch, draft, outline, draw (up). **3** *designing a computer program*: invent, originate, conceive, create, think up, develop, construct, fashion, form, model, fabricate, make.

designer *noun* deviser, originator, maker, stylist, inventor, creator, contriver, fashioner, architect, author.

desirable *adjective* **1** *find it desirable to accept his offer*: advantageous, profitable, worthwhile, advisable, appropriate, expedient, beneficial, preferable, sensible, eligible, good, pleasing. **2** *a*

desirable woman: attractive, alluring, seductive, fetching, tempting.
F3 **1** undesirable. **2** unattractive.

desire *verb* **1** *desire his approval*: ask, request, petition, solicit. **2** *does madam desire anything further?*: want, wish for, covet, long for, need, crave, hunger for, yearn for, fancy (*infml*), hanker after.
▪ *noun* want, longing, wish, need, yearning, craving, hankering, appetite, aspiration.

desolate *adjective* **1** *a desolate landscape*: deserted, uninhabited, abandoned, bare, arid, unfrequented, barren, bleak, gloomy, dismal, dreary, lonely, god-forsaken, forsaken, waste, depressing. **2** *left feeling desolate*: forlorn, bereft, depressed, dejected, forsaken, lonely, despondent, distressed, melancholy, miserable, gloomy, disheartened, dismal, downcast, solitary, wretched.
F3 **1** populous. **2** cheerful.

despair *noun* despondency, gloom, hopelessness, desperation, anguish, wretchedness, inconsolableness, melancholy, misery.
F3 cheerfulness, resilience.
▪ *verb* lose heart, lose hope, give up, give in, collapse, surrender.
F3 hope.

despatch *see* **dispatch**.

desperate *adjective* **1** *a desperate situation*: hopeless, inconsolable, wretched, despondent, abandoned. **2** *a desperate act*: reckless, rash, impetuous, audacious, daring, dangerous, do-or-die, foolhardy, risky, hazardous, hasty, precipitate (*fml*), wild, violent, frantic, frenzied, determined. **3** *a desperate hurry*: critical, acute, serious, severe, extreme, urgent.
F3 **1** hopeful. **2** cautious.

desperately *adverb* dangerously, critically, gravely, hopelessly, seriously, severely, badly, dreadfully, fearfully, frightfully.

desperation *noun* **1** *desperation in his voice*: despair, despondency, anguish, hopelessness, misery, agony, distress, pain, sorrow, trouble, worry, anxiety. **2** *driven to desperation*: recklessness, rashness, frenzy, madness, hastiness.

despicable *adjective* contemptible, vile, worthless, detestable, disgusting, mean, wretched, disgraceful, disreputable, shameful, reprobate.
F3 admirable, noble.

despise *verb* scorn, deride, look down on, disdain, condemn, spurn, undervalue, slight, revile, deplore, dislike, detest, loathe.
F3 admire.

despite *preposition* in spite of, notwithstanding, regardless of, in the face of, undeterred by, against, defying.

despondent *adjective* depressed, dejected, disheartened, downcast, down, low, gloomy, glum, discouraged, miserable, melancholy, sad, sorrowful, doleful, despairing, heart-broken, inconsolable, mournful, wretched.

F3 cheerful, heartened, hopeful.

destination *noun* journey's end, terminus, station, stop.

destined *adjective* **1** *destined to be a success*: fated, doomed, inevitable, predetermined, ordained, certain, foreordained, meant, unavoidable, inescapable, intended, designed, appointed. **2** *goods destined for the United States*: bound, directed, en route, headed, heading, scheduled, assigned, booked.

destiny *noun* fate, doom, fortune, karma, lot, portion (*fml*), predestiny, kismet.

destroy *verb* **1** *destroy the city/the environment*: demolish, ruin, raze, devastate, ravage, shatter, wreck, smash. **2** *destroyed his career/their trust*: ruin, wreck, nullify, undo, undermine, waste, smash, crush. **3** *the dog had to be destroyed*: kill, dispatch, slay (*fml*), annihilate, eliminate.

F3 **1** build up. **3** create.

destruction *noun* **1** *the destruction of the city*: ruin, devastation, shattering, crushing, wreckage, demolition, defeat, downfall, overthrow, ruination, desolation, undoing, wastage, havoc, ravagement. **2** *destruction of thousands of rare species*: annihilation, extermination, eradication, elimination, extinction, slaughter, massacre, end, liquidation, nullification.

F3 **2** creation.

destructive *adjective* devastating, damaging, catastrophic, disastrous, deadly, harmful, fatal, disruptive, lethal, ruinous, detrimental, hurtful, malignant, nullifying, slaughterous.

F3 creative.

detach *verb* separate, disconnect, unfasten, disjoin, cut off, disengage, remove, undo, uncouple, sever, dissociate, isolate, loosen, free, unfix, unhitch, segregate, divide, disentangle, estrange.

F3 attach.

detachment *noun* **1** *display a certain detachment*: aloofness, remoteness, coolness, unconcern, indifference, impassivity, disinterestedness, neutrality, impartiality, objectivity, fairness. **2** *detachment of the wings*: separation, disconnection, disunion, disengagement.

detail *noun* particular, item, factor, element, aspect, component, feature, point, specific, ingredient, attribute, count, respect, technicality, complication, intricacy, triviality, fact, thoroughness, elaboration, meticulousness, refinement, nicety.

▪ *verb* list, enumerate, itemize, specify, catalogue, recount, relate.

detailed *adjective* comprehensive, exhaustive, full, blow-by-blow (*infml*), thorough, minute, exact, specific, particular, itemized, intricate, elaborate, complex, complicated, meticulous, descriptive.
☒ cursory, general.

detain *verb* delay, hold (up), hinder, impede, check, retard, slow, stay, stop.

detect *verb* **1** *detect gas*: notice, ascertain, note, observe, perceive, recognize, discern, distinguish, identify, sight, spot, spy. **2** *detecting the culprits*: uncover, catch, discover, disclose, expose, find, track down, unmask, reveal.

detective *noun* investigator, private eye (*infml*), sleuth (*infml*), sleuth-hound (*infml*).

detention *noun* detainment, custody, confinement, imprisonment, restraint, incarceration, constraint, quarantine.
☒ release.

deter *verb* discourage, put off, inhibit, intimidate, dissuade, daunt, turn off (*infml*), check, caution, warn, restrain, hinder, frighten, disincline, prevent, prohibit, stop.
☒ encourage.

deteriorate *verb* **1** *the weather/their relationship deteriorated*: worsen, decline, degenerate, depreciate, go downhill (*infml*), fail, fall off, lapse, slide, relapse, slip. **2** *the building is deteriorating rapidly*: decay, disintegrate, decompose, weaken, fade.
☒ **1** improve. **2** progress.

determination *noun* resoluteness, tenacity, firmness, will-power, perseverance, persistence, purpose, backbone, guts (*infml*), grit (*infml*), steadfastness, single-mindedness, will, insistence, conviction, dedication, drive, fortitude.
☒ irresolution.

determine *verb* **1** *she determined that she wasn't cut out for the job*: decide, settle, resolve, make up one's mind, choose, conclude, fix on, elect, clinch, finish. **2** *to determine what had happened*: discover, establish, find out, ascertain, identify, check, detect, verify. **3** *will determine the result*: affect, influence, govern, control, dictate, direct, guide, regulate, ordain.

determined *adjective* resolute, firm, purposeful, strong-willed, single-minded, persevering, persistent, strong-minded, steadfast, tenacious, dogged, insistent, intent, fixed, convinced, decided, unflinching.
☒ irresolute, wavering.

deterrent *noun* hindrance, impediment, obstacle, repellent, check, bar, discouragement, obstruction, curb, restraint, difficulty.
☒ incentive, encouragement.

detest *verb* hate, abhor, loathe, abominate, execrate (*fml*), dislike,

recoil from, deplore, despise.
≠ adore, love.

detour *noun* deviation, diversion, indirect route, circuitous route, roundabout route, digression, byroad, byway, bypath, bypass.

detract *verb* diminish, subtract from, take away from, reduce, lessen, lower, devaluate, depreciate, belittle, disparage (*fml*).
≠ add to, enhance, praise.

devastating *adjective* **1** *devastating storms*: destructive, disastrous. **2** *a devastating argument*: effective, incisive, overwhelming, stunning.

devastation *noun* destruction, desolation, havoc, ruin, wreckage, ravages, demolition, annihilation, pillage, plunder, spoliation.

develop *verb* **1** *develop further*: advance, evolve, expand, progress, foster, flourish, mature, prosper, branch out. **2** *developing his argument*: elaborate, amplify, augment, enhance, unfold. **3** *developed the steam engine*: create, invent, acquire, contract, begin, generate. **4** *what developed after that*: result, come about, grow, ensue, arise, follow, happen.

development *noun* **1** *rapid development*: growth, evolution, advance, blossoming, elaboration, furtherance, progress, unfolding, expansion, extension, spread, increase, improvement, maturity, promotion, refinement, issue. **2** *a new development*: occurrence, happening, event, change, outcome, situation, result, phenomenon.

deviate *verb* diverge, veer, turn (aside), digress, swerve, vary, differ, depart, stray, yaw, wander, err, go astray, go off the rails (*infml*), drift, part.

deviation *noun* divergence, aberration, departure, abnormality, irregularity, variance, variation, digression, eccentricity, anomaly, deflection, alteration, disparity, discrepancy, detour, fluctuation, change, quirk, shift, freak.
≠ conformity, regularity.

device *noun* tool, implement, appliance, gadget, contrivance, contraption (*infml*), apparatus, utensil, instrument, machine.

devil *noun* demon, Satan, fiend, evil spirit, arch-fiend, Lucifer, imp, Evil One, Prince of Darkness, Adversary, Beelzebub, Mephistopheles, Old Nick (*infml*), Old Harry (*infml*).

devious *adjective* **1** *a devious plan/person*: underhand, deceitful, dishonest, disingenuous, double-dealing, scheming, tricky (*infml*), insidious, insincere, calculating, cunning, evasive, wily, sly, slippery (*infml*), surreptitious, treacherous, misleading. **2** *by devious means/a devious route*: indirect, circuitous, rambling, roundabout, wandering, winding, tortuous, erratic.
≠ **2** straightforward.

devise *verb* invent, contrive, plan, plot, design, conceive, arrange, formulate, imagine, scheme, construct, concoct, forge, frame, project, shape, form.

devote *verb* dedicate, consecrate, commit, give oneself, set apart, set aside, reserve, apply, allocate, allot, sacrifice, enshrine, assign, appropriate, surrender, pledge.

devoted *adjective* dedicated, ardent, committed, loyal, faithful, devout, loving, staunch, steadfast, true, constant, fond, unswerving, tireless, concerned, attentive, caring.

F3 indifferent, disloyal.

devotee *noun* enthusiast, fan (*infml*), fanatic, addict, aficionado, follower, supporter, zealot, adherent, admirer, disciple, buff (*infml*), freak (*infml*).

devotion *noun* **1** *his devotion to duty*: dedication, commitment, consecration, ardour, loyalty, allegiance, adherence, zeal, support, love, passion, fervour, fondness, attachment, adoration, affection, faithfulness, reverence, steadfastness, regard, earnestness. **2** *religious devotion*: devoutness, piety, godliness, faith, holiness, spirituality.

F3 1 inconstancy. **2** irreverence.

devour *verb* **1** *devoured everything on the table*: eat, consume, guzzle, gulp, gorge, gobble, bolt, wolf down, swallow, stuff (*infml*), cram, polish off (*infml*), gourmandize (*fml*), feast on, relish, revel in. **2** *green spaces devoured by the ever-expanding city*: destroy, consume, absorb, engulf, ravage, dispatch.

devout *adjective* **1** *a devout plea*: sincere, earnest, devoted, fervent, genuine, staunch, steadfast, ardent, passionate, serious, whole-hearted, constant, faithful, intense, heartfelt, zealous, unswerving, deep, profound. **2** *a devout Catholic*: pious, godly, religious, reverent, prayerful, saintly, holy, orthodox.

F3 1 insincere. **2** irreligious.

diabolical *adjective* devilish, fiendish, demonic, hellish, evil, infernal, wicked, vile, dreadful, outrageous, shocking, disastrous, excruciating, atrocious.

diagnose *verb* identify, determine, recognize, pinpoint, distinguish, analyse, explain, isolate, interpret, investigate.

diagnosis *noun* identification, verdict, explanation, conclusion, answer, interpretation, analysis, opinion, investigation, examination, scrutiny.

diagonal *adjective* oblique, slanting, cross, crosswise, sloping, crooked, angled, cornerways.

diagram *noun* plan, sketch, chart, drawing, figure, representation, schema, illustration, outline, graph, picture, layout, table.

dial *noun* circle, disc, face, clock, control.

▪ *verb* phone, ring, call (up).

dialect *noun* idiom, language, regionalism, patois, provincialism, vernacular, argot, jargon, accent, lingo (*infml*), speech, diction.

dialogue *noun* **1** *enter into a dialogue with them*: conversation, interchange, discourse, communication, talk, exchange, discussion, converse, debate, conference. **2** *write the dialogue for the school play*: lines, script.

diary *noun* journal, day-book, logbook, chronicle, yearbook, appointment book, engagement book.

dictate *verb* **1** *dictate a letter*: say, speak, utter, announce, pronounce, transmit. **2** *dictate the terms*: command, order, direct, decree, instruct, rule.

▪ *noun* command, decree, precept (*fml*), principle, rule, direction, injunction, edict, order, ruling, statute, requirement, ordinance, law, bidding, mandate, ultimatum, word.

dictator *noun* despot, autocrat, tyrant, supremo (*infml*), Big Brother (*infml*).

dictatorial *adjective* tyrannical, despotic, totalitarian, authoritarian, autocratic, oppressive, imperious, domineering, bossy (*infml*), absolute, repressive, overbearing, arbitrary, dogmatic.

E3 democratic, egalitarian, liberal.

dictionary *noun* lexicon, glossary, thesaurus, vocabulary, wordbook, encyclopedia, concordance.

die *verb* **1** *die young*: decease, perish, pass away, expire, depart, breathe one's last, peg out (*infml*), snuff it (*infml*), bite the dust (*infml*), kick the bucket (*infml*). **2** *sound of their voices died away*: dwindle, fade, ebb, sink, wane, wilt, wither, peter out, decline, decay, finish, lapse, end, disappear, vanish, subside. **3** (*infml*) *dying for an ice cream*: long for, pine for, yearn, desire.

E3 **1** live.

diet *noun* **1** *a healthy diet*: food, nutrition, provisions, sustenance, rations, foodstuffs, subsistence. **2** *go on a diet*: fast, abstinence, regimen.

▪ *verb* lose weight, slim, fast, reduce, abstain, weight-watch (*infml*).

differ *verb* **1** *his views differ from mine*: vary, diverge, deviate, depart from, contradict, contrast. **2** *we differ on the subject of exercise*: disagree, argue, conflict, oppose, dispute, dissent, be at odds with, clash, quarrel, fall out, debate, contend, take issue.

E3 **1** conform. **2** agree.

difference *noun* **1** *no difference between them*: dissimilarity, unlikeness, discrepancy, divergence, diversity, variation, variety, distinctness, distinction, deviation, differentiation, contrast, disparity, singularity, exception. **2** *settle their differences*:

disagreement, clash, dispute, conflict, contention, controversy. **3** *split the difference*: remainder, rest.
⇄ **1** conformity. **2** agreement.

different *adjective* **1** *different from mine*: dissimilar, unlike, contrasting, divergent, inconsistent, deviating, at odds, clashing, opposed. **2** *different colours*: varied, various, diverse, miscellaneous, assorted, disparate, many, numerous, several, sundry, other. **3** *he has always felt different*: unusual, unconventional, unique, distinct, distinctive, extraordinary, individual, original, special, strange, separate, peculiar, rare, bizarre, anomalous.
⇄ **1** similar. **2** same. **3** conventional.

differentiate *verb* distinguish, tell apart, discriminate, contrast, separate, mark off, individualize, particularize.

difficult *adjective* **1** *a difficult journey*: hard, laborious, demanding, arduous, strenuous, tough, wearisome, uphill, formidable. **2** *a difficult problem*: complex, complicated, intricate, involved, abstruse, obscure, dark, knotty, thorny, problematical, perplexing, abstract, baffling, intractable. **3** *a difficult child*: unmanageable, perverse, troublesome, trying, unco-operative, tiresome, stubborn, obstinate, intractable.
⇄ **1** easy. **2** straightforward. **3** manageable.

difficulty *noun* **1** *in great difficulty*: hardship, trouble, labour, arduousness, painfulness, trial, tribulation, awkwardness. **2** *in financial difficulties*: predicament, dilemma, quandary, perplexity, embarrassment, plight, distress, fix (*infml*), mess (*infml*), jam (*infml*), spot (*infml*), hiccup (*infml*), hang-up. **3** *encounter many difficulties*: problem, obstacle, hindrance, hurdle, impediment, objection, opposition, block, complication, pitfall, protest, stumbling block.
⇄ **1** ease.

dig *verb* **1** *dig a hole*: excavate, penetrate, burrow, mine, quarry, scoop, tunnel, till, gouge, delve, pierce. **2** *digging me in the ribs*: poke, prod. **3** *digging for clues*: investigate, probe, go into, research, search.

digest *verb* **1** *digest one's food*: absorb, assimilate, incorporate, process, dissolve. **2** *have to digest this information*: take in, absorb, understand, assimilate, grasp, study, consider, contemplate, meditate, ponder.

dignified *adjective* stately, solemn, imposing, majestic, noble, august, lordly, lofty, exalted, formal, distinguished, grave, impressive, reserved, honourable.
⇄ undignified, lowly.

dignity *noun* stateliness, propriety, solemnity, decorum, courtliness, grandeur, loftiness, majesty, honour, eminence, importance, nobility, self-respect, self-esteem, standing, poise, respectability, greatness, status, pride.

digress *verb* diverge, deviate, stray, wander, go off at a tangent, drift, depart, ramble.

dilapidated *adjective* ramshackle, shabby, broken-down, neglected, tumbledown, uncared-for, rickety, decrepit, crumbling, run-down, worn-out, ruined, decayed, decaying.

dilemma *noun* quandary, conflict, predicament, problem, catch-22 (*infml*), difficulty, puzzle, embarrassment, perplexity, plight.

diligent *adjective* assiduous (*fml*), industrious, hardworking, conscientious, painstaking, busy, attentive, tireless, careful, meticulous, persevering, persistent, studious.
F3 negligent, lazy.

dilute *verb* adulterate, water down, thin (out), attenuate (*fml*), weaken, diffuse, diminish, decrease, lessen, reduce, temper, mitigate.
F3 concentrate.

dim *adjective* **1** *a dim corner/a dim light*: dark, dull, dusky, cloudy, shadowy, gloomy, sombre, dingy, lacklustre, feeble. **2** *a dim outline*: indistinct, blurred, hazy, ill-defined, obscure, misty, unclear, foggy, fuzzy, vague, faint, weak. **3** *he's too dim to understand*: stupid, dense, obtuse, thick (*infml*), doltish.
F3 **1** bright. **2** distinct. **3** bright, intelligent.
■ *verb* darken, dull, obscure, cloud, blur, fade, tarnish, shade.
F3 brighten, illuminate.

dimension(s) *noun* extent, measurement, measure, size, scope, magnitude, largeness, capacity, mass, scale, range, bulk, importance, greatness.

diminish *verb* **1** *the light diminished*: decrease, lessen, reduce, lower, contract, decline, shrink, dwindle, recede, taper off, wane, weaken, abate, fade, sink, subside, ebb, slacken, cut. **2** *diminishing her efforts*: belittle, disparage (*fml*), deprecate (*fml*), devalue.
F3 **1** increase. **2** exaggerate.

diminutive *adjective* undersized, small, tiny, little, miniature, minute, infinitesimal, wee, petite, midget, mini (*infml*), teeny (*infml*), teeny-weeny (*infml*), Lilliputian, dinky (*infml*), pint-size(d) (*infml*), pygmy, pocket(-sized).
F3 big, large, oversized.

din *noun* noise, row, racket, clash, clatter, clamour, pandemonium, uproar, commotion, crash, hullabaloo (*infml*), hubbub, outcry, shout, babble.
F3 quiet, calm.

dine *verb* eat, feast, sup, lunch, banquet, feed.

dingy *adjective* dark, drab, grimy, murky, faded, dull, dim, shabby, soiled, discoloured, dirty, dreary, gloomy, seedy, sombre, obscure, run-down, colourless, dusky, worn.

F3 bright, clean.

dinner *noun* meal, supper, tea (*infml*), banquet, feast, spread, repast (*fml*).

dip *verb* **1** *dipping his biscuit in his tea*: plunge, immerse, submerge, duck, dunk, bathe, douse, sink. **2** *dip below the horizon*: descend, decline, drop, fall, subside, slump, sink, lower.

▪ *noun* **1** *a dip in the road*: hollow, basin, decline, hole, concavity, incline, depression, fall, slope, slump, lowering. **2** *go for a quick dip*: bathe, immersion, plunge, soaking, ducking, swim, drenching, infusion, dive.

diplomacy *noun* **1** *learn to use a little diplomacy when dealing with sensitive issues*: tact, tactfulness, finesse, delicacy, discretion, savoir-faire, subtlety, skill, craft. **2** *international diplomacy*: statecraft, statesmanship, politics, negotiation, manoeuvring.

diplomat *noun* go-between, mediator, negotiator, ambassador, consul, envoy, conciliator, peacemaker, moderator, politician.

diplomatic *adjective* tactful, politic, discreet, judicious (*fml*), subtle, sensitive, prudent.

F3 tactless.

dire *adjective* **1** *a dire warning*: desperate, urgent, grave, drastic, crucial, extreme, alarming, ominous. **2** (*infml*) *the music was dire*: disastrous, dreadful, awful, appalling, calamitous, catastrophic.

direct *verb* **1** *direct the company*: control, manage, run, administer, organize, lead, govern, regulate, superintend, supervise. **2** *directing us to stay where we were*: instruct, command, order, charge. **3** *directed me to the next set of shelves*: guide, lead, conduct, point. **4** *directed the missiles at the main cities*: aim, point, focus, turn.

▪ *adjective* **1** *a direct route*: straight, undeviating, through, uninterrupted. **2** *a direct approach*: straightforward, outspoken, blunt, frank, unequivocal, sincere, candid, honest, explicit.

F3 **1** circuitous. **2** equivocal.

direction *noun* **1** *direction of traffic*: control, administration, management, government, supervision, guidance, leadership. **2** *go in the other direction*: route, way, line, road.

directions *noun* instructions, guidelines, orders, briefing, guidance, recommendations, indication, plan.

directly *adverb* **1** *will be back directly*: immediately, instantly, promptly, right away, speedily, forthwith, instantaneously, quickly, soon, presently, straightaway, straight. **2** *spoke very directly*: frankly, bluntly, candidly, honestly.

director *noun* manager, head, boss, chief, controller, executive, principal, governor, leader, organizer, supervisor, administrator, producer, conductor.

dirt *noun* **1** *dig in the dirt*: earth, soil, clay, dust, mud. **2** *covered in dirt*: filth, grime, muck, mire, excrement, stain, smudge, slime, tarnish.

dirty *adjective* filthy, grimy, grubby, mucky, soiled, unwashed, foul, messy, muddy, polluted, squalid, dull, miry, scruffy, shabby, sullied, clouded, dark.
F3 clean.

disability *noun* handicap, impairment, disablement, disorder, inability, incapacity, infirmity.

disable *verb* cripple, lame, incapacitate, damage, handicap, impair, debilitate, disqualify, weaken, immobilize, invalidate, paralyse, prostrate.

disabled *adjective* handicapped, incapacitated, impaired, infirm, crippled, lame, immobilized, maimed, weak, weakened, paralysed, wrecked.
F3 able, able-bodied.

disadvantage *noun* drawback, snag, hindrance, handicap, impediment, inconvenience, flaw, nuisance, weakness, trouble.
F3 advantage, benefit.

disadvantaged *adjective* deprived, underprivileged, poor, handicapped, impoverished, struggling.
F3 privileged.

disagree *verb* **1** *disagree about how to go about it*: dissent, oppose, quarrel, argue, bicker, fall out (*infml*), wrangle, fight, squabble, contend, dispute, contest, object. **2** *the two sets of readings disagree*: conflict, clash, diverge, contradict, counter, differ, deviate, depart, run counter to, vary.
F3 1 agree. **2** correspond.

disagreeable *adjective* **1** *disagreeable old man*: bad-tempered, ill-humoured, difficult, peevish, rude, surly, churlish, irritable, contrary, cross, brusque. **2** *a disagreeable taste*: disgusting, offensive, repulsive, repellent, obnoxious, unsavoury, objectionable, nasty.
F3 1 amiable, pleasant. **2** agreeable.

disagreement *noun* **1** *had a disagreement over who should drive*: dispute, argument, conflict, altercation (*fml*), quarrel, clash, dissent, falling-out, contention, strife, misunderstanding, squabble, tiff (*infml*), wrangle. **2** *the disagreement in the figures is quite significant*: difference, variance, unlikeness, disparity, discrepancy, deviation, discord, dissimilarity, incompatibility, divergence, diversity, incongruity.
F3 1 agreement, harmony. **2** similarity.

disappear *verb* **1** *spots will disappear gradually*: vanish, wane, recede, fade, evaporate, dissolve, ebb. **2** *they disappeared as soon as the police arrived*: go, depart, withdraw, retire, flee, fly, escape, scarper (*infml*), hide. **3** *dinosaurs disappeared millions of years ago*: end, expire, perish, pass.
≠ **1** appear. **3** emerge.

disappearance *noun* vanishing, fading, evaporation, departure, loss, going, passing, melting, desertion, flight.
≠ appearance, manifestation.

disappointed *adjective* let down, frustrated, thwarted, disillusioned, dissatisfied, miffed (*infml*), upset, discouraged, disgruntled, disheartened, distressed, down-hearted, saddened, despondent, depressed.
≠ pleased, satisfied.

disappointment *noun* **1** *couldn't hide her disappointment*: frustration, dissatisfaction, disenchantment, disillusionment, displeasure, discouragement, distress, regret. **2** *the match was a bit of a disappointment*: failure, let-down, setback, comedown, blow, misfortune, fiasco, disaster, calamity, washout (*infml*), damp squib (*infml*), swiz (*infml*), swizzle (*infml*).
≠ **1** pleasure, satisfaction, delight. **2** success.

disapproval *noun* censure, condemnation, criticism, displeasure, reproach, objection, dissatisfaction, denunciation, dislike.
≠ approval, approbation (*fml*).

disapprove of *verb* censure, condemn, blame, take exception to, object to, deplore, denounce, disparage (*fml*), dislike, reject, spurn.
≠ approve of.

disarray *noun* disorder, confusion, chaos, mess, muddle, shambles (*infml*), tangle, disorganization, clutter, untidiness, unruliness, jumble, indiscipline, upset.
≠ order.

disaster *noun* calamity, catastrophe, misfortune, reverse, tragedy, blow, accident, act of God, cataclysm, debacle, mishap, failure, flop (*infml*), fiasco, ruin, stroke, trouble, mischance, ruination.
≠ success, triumph.

disastrous *adjective* calamitous, catastrophic, cataclysmic, devastating, ruinous, tragic, unfortunate, dreadful, dire, terrible, destructive, ill-fated, fatal, miserable.
≠ successful, auspicious.

disband *verb* disperse, break up, scatter, dismiss, demobilize, part company, separate, dissolve.
≠ assemble, muster.

disbelief *noun* unbelief, incredulity, doubt, scepticism, suspicion, distrust, mistrust, rejection.
≠ belief.

disc *noun* **1** *the bright disc of the sun*: circle, face, plate, ring. **2** *awarded a gold disc*: record, album, LP, CD.

discard *verb* reject, abandon, dispose of, get rid of, jettison, dispense with, cast aside, ditch (*infml*), dump (*infml*), drop, scrap, shed, remove, relinquish.
F retain, adopt.

discern *verb* perceive, make out, observe, detect, recognize, see, ascertain, notice, determine, discover, descry, discriminate, distinguish, differentiate, judge.

discernible *adjective* perceptible, noticeable, detectable, appreciable, distinct, observable, recognizable, visible, apparent, clear, obvious, plain, patent, manifest, discoverable.
F imperceptible.

discerning *adjective* discriminating, perceptive, astute, clear-sighted, sensitive, shrewd, wise, sharp, subtle, sagacious (*fml*), penetrating, acute, piercing, critical, eagle-eyed.
F dull, obtuse.

discharge *verb* **1** *discharge the prisoner*: liberate, free, pardon, release, clear, absolve, exonerate, acquit, relieve, dismiss. **2** *discharge one's duty*: execute, carry out, perform, fulfil, dispense. **3** *discharging a gun*: fire, shoot, let off, detonate, explode. **4** *discharged him for incompetence*: sack (*infml*), remove, fire (*infml*), expel, oust, eject.
F **1** detain. **2** neglect. **4** appoint.
▪ *noun* **1** *his discharge from prison*: liberation, release, acquittal, exoneration. **2** *discharge from the chemical plant*: emission, secretion, ejection. **3** *the discharge of his duty*: execution, accomplishment, fulfilment.
F **1** confinement, detention. **2** absorption. **3** neglect.

disciple *noun* follower, convert, proselyte, adherent, believer, devotee, supporter, learner, pupil, student, acolyte.

discipline *noun* **1** *military discipline*: training, exercise, drill, practice. **2** *harsh discipline*: punishment, chastisement, correction. **3** *the discipline of his painting technique*: strictness, restraint, regulation, self-control, orderliness. **4** *an expert in that discipline*: subject, area of study, field of study, branch, speciality.
F **3** indiscipline.
▪ *verb* **1** *he will be severely disciplined*: punish, chastise, chasten, penalize, reprimand, castigate (*fml*). **2** *moral rules that discipline their behaviour*: check, control, constrain, correct, restrain, govern.

disclose *verb* **1** *disclose details of the case*: divulge, make known, reveal, tell, confess, let slip, relate, publish, communicate, impart, leak (*infml*). **2** *opens up disclosing the brightly-coloured centre*: expose, reveal, uncover, lay bare, unveil.
F **1**, **2** conceal.

discomfort *noun* ache, pain, uneasiness, malaise, trouble, distress, disquiet, hardship, vexation, irritation, annoyance.
F3 comfort, ease.

disconcerting *adjective* disturbing, confusing, upsetting, unnerving, alarming, bewildering, off-putting (*infml*), distracting, embarrassing, awkward, baffling, perplexing, dismaying, bothersome.

disconnect *verb* cut off, disengage, uncouple, sever, separate, detach, unplug, unhook, part, divide.
F3 attach, connect.

discontent *noun* uneasiness, dissatisfaction, disquiet, restlessness, fretfulness, unrest, impatience, vexation, regret.
F3 content.

discontented *adjective* dissatisfied, fed up (*infml*), disgruntled, unhappy, browned off (*infml*), cheesed off (*infml*), disaffected, miserable, exasperated, complaining.
F3 contented, satisfied.

discontinue *verb* stop, end, finish, cease, break off, terminate, halt, drop, suspend, abandon, cancel, interrupt.
F3 continue.

discord *noun* **1** *discord amongst the back-benchers*: dissension, disagreement, discordance, clashing, disunity, incompatibility, conflict, difference, dispute, contention, friction, division, opposition, strife, split, wrangling. **2** *harmony and discord*: dissonance, disharmony, cacophony (*fml*), jangle, jarring, harshness.
F3 **1** concord, agreement. **2** harmony.

discount *verb* **1** *discount his version of events*: disregard, ignore, overlook, disbelieve, gloss over. **2** *discounting many items of stock*: reduce, deduct, mark down, knock off (*infml*).
▪ *noun* reduction, rebate, allowance, cut, concession, deduction, mark-down.

discourage *verb* **1** *discouraged by the exam results*: dishearten, dampen, dispirit, depress, demoralize, dismay, unnerve, deject, disappoint. **2** *discourage visitors*: deter, dissuade, hinder, put off, restrain, prevent.
F3 **1** hearten. **2** encourage.

discover *verb* **1** *discover a hidden valley*: find, uncover, unearth, dig up, disclose, reveal, light on, locate, trace. **2** *discover the truth*: ascertain, determine, realize, notice, recognize, perceive, see, find out, spot, discern, learn, detect. **3** *discovered penicillin*: originate, invent, pioneer.
F3 **1** miss. **2** conceal, cover (up).

discovery *noun* **1** *a new discovery*: breakthrough, find, origination, introduction, innovation, invention, exploration. **2** *their discovery of the facts*: disclosure, detection, revelation, location.

discredit *verb* disparage (*fml*), dishonour, degrade, defame (*fml*), disgrace, slander, slur, smear, reproach, vilify (*fml*).
F honour.

discreditable *adjective* dishonourable, disreputable, disgraceful, reprehensible, scandalous, blameworthy, shameful, infamous, degrading, improper.
F creditable.

discreet *adjective* tactful, careful, diplomatic, politic, prudent, cautious, delicate, judicious (*fml*), reserved, wary, sensible.
F tactless, indiscreet.

discrepancy *noun* difference, disparity, variance, variation, inconsistency, dissimilarity, discordance, divergence, disagreement, conflict, inequality.

discretion *noun* **1** *had too much discretion to mention it*: tact, diplomacy, judiciousness, caution, prudence, wisdom, circumspection, discernment, judgement, care, carefulness, consideration, wariness. **2** *I will leave the choice at your discretion*: choice, freedom, preference, will, wish.
F 1 indiscretion, imprudence.

discriminate *verb* distinguish, differentiate, discern, tell apart, make a distinction, segregate, separate.
F confuse, confound.

discriminating *adjective* discerning, fastidious, selective, critical, perceptive, particular, tasteful, astute, sensitive, cultivated.

discrimination *noun* **1** *racial discrimination*: bias, prejudice, intolerance, unfairness, bigotry, favouritism, inequity (*fml*), racism, sexism. **2** *his choice shows discrimination*: discernment, judgement, acumen, perception, acuteness, insight, penetration, subtlety, keenness, refinement, taste.

discuss *verb* debate, talk about, confer, argue, consider, deliberate, converse, consult, examine.

discussion *noun* debate, conference, argument, conversation, dialogue, exchange, consultation, discourse, deliberation, consideration, analysis, review, examination, scrutiny, seminar, symposium.

disdainful *adjective* scornful, contemptuous, derisive, haughty, aloof, arrogant, supercilious, sneering, superior, proud, insolent.
F respectful.

disease *noun* illness, sickness, ill-health, infirmity, complaint, disorder, ailment, indisposition, malady, condition, affliction, infection, epidemic.
F health.

diseased *adjective* sick, ill, unhealthy, ailing, unsound, contaminated, infected.
F healthy.

disembark *verb* land, arrive, alight, debark.
F3 embark.

disentangle *verb* **1** *disentangle the ropes*: loose, free, extricate, disconnect, untangle, disengage, detach, unravel, separate, unfold. **2** *disentangle the situation*: resolve, clarify, simplify.
F3 **1** entangle.

disfigure *verb* deface, blemish, mutilate, scar, mar, deform, distort, damage, spoil.
F3 adorn, embellish.

disgrace *noun* shame, ignominy, disrepute, dishonour, disfavour, humiliation, defamation (*fml*), discredit, scandal, reproach, slur, stain.
F3 honour, esteem.
▪ *verb* shame, dishonour, abase, defame (*fml*), humiliate, disfavour, stain, discredit, reproach, slur, sully (*fml*), taint, stigmatize.
F3 honour, respect.

disgraceful *adjective* shameful, dishonourable, disreputable, ignominious, scandalous, shocking, unworthy, dreadful, appalling.
F3 honourable, respectable.

disguise *verb* **1** *disguised as a beggar*: conceal, cover, camouflage, mask, hide, dress up, cloak, screen, veil, shroud. **2** *disguised the truth*: falsify, deceive, dissemble (*fml*), misrepresent, fake, fudge.
F3 **1** reveal, expose.
▪ *noun* concealment, camouflage, cloak, cover, costume, mask, front, façade, masquerade, deception, pretence, travesty, screen, veil.

disgust *verb* offend, displease, nauseate, revolt, sicken, repel, outrage, put off.
F3 delight, please.
▪ *noun* revulsion, repulsion, repugnance, distaste, aversion, abhorrence (*fml*), nausea, loathing, detestation, hatred.

disgusted *adjective* repelled, repulsed, revolted, offended, appalled, outraged.
F3 attracted, delighted.

disgusting *adjective* repugnant, repellent, revolting, offensive, sickening, nauseating, odious, foul, unappetizing, unpleasant, vile, obscene, abominable, detestable, objectionable, nasty.
F3 delightful, pleasant.

dish *noun* plate, bowl, platter, food, recipe.

dishearten *verb* discourage, dispirit, dampen, cast down, depress, dismay, dash, disappoint, deject, daunt, crush, deter.
F3 encourage, hearten.

dishevelled *adjective* tousled, unkempt, uncombed, untidy, bedraggled, messy, ruffled, slovenly, disordered.
F3 neat, tidy.

dishonest *adjective* untruthful, fraudulent, deceitful, false, lying, deceptive, double-dealing, cheating, crooked (*infml*), treacherous, unprincipled,

swindling, shady (*infml*), corrupt, disreputable.
F3 honest, trustworthy, scrupulous.

dishonesty *noun* deceit, falsehood, fraud, criminality, falsity, cheating, treachery, trickery, duplicity (*fml*), shadiness (*infml*).
F3 honesty, truthfulness.

dishonour *verb* disgrace, shame, humiliate, debase, defile (*fml*), degrade, defame (*fml*), discredit, demean, debauch.
F3 honour.
▪ *noun* disgrace, abasement (*fml*), humiliation, shame, degradation, discredit, disrepute, indignity, ignominy, reproach, slight, slur, scandal, insult, disfavour, outrage, aspersion (*fml*), abuse, discourtesy.
F3 honour.

disillusioned *adjective* disenchanted, disabused, undeceived, disappointed.

disinfect *verb* sterilize, fumigate, sanitize, decontaminate, cleanse, purify, purge, clean.
F3 contaminate, infect.

disintegrate *verb* break up, decompose, fall apart, crumble, rot, moulder, separate, splinter.

disinterested *adjective* unbiased, neutral, impartial, unprejudiced, dispassionate, detached, uninvolved, open-minded, equitable, even-handed, unselfish.
F3 biased, concerned.

disjointed *adjective* incoherent, aimless, confused, disordered, loose, unconnected, bitty, rambling, fitful, spasmodic.
F3 coherent.

dislike *verb* hate, detest, object to, loathe, abhor, abominate, disapprove, shun, despise, scorn.
F3 like, favour.
▪ *noun* hatred, disapproval, distaste, loathing, abhorrence (*fml*), antipathy.

dislodge *verb* displace, eject, remove, oust, extricate, shift, move, uproot.

disloyal *adjective* treacherous, faithless, false, traitorous, two-faced (*infml*), unfaithful, apostate, unpatriotic.
F3 loyal, trustworthy.

dismal *adjective* dreary, gloomy, depressing, bleak, cheerless, dull, drab, low-spirited, melancholy, sad, sombre, lugubrious, forlorn, despondent, dark, sorrowful, long-faced (*infml*), hopeless, discouraging.
F3 cheerful, bright.

dismantle *verb* demolish, take apart, disassemble, strip.
F3 assemble, put together.

dismay *noun* consternation, alarm, distress, apprehension, agitation, dread, fear, trepidation, fright, horror, terror, discouragement, disappointment.
F3 boldness, encouragement.

dismiss *verb* **1** *the class was dismissed*: discharge, free, let go, release, send away. **2** *dismiss*

employees: sack (*infml*), make redundant, lay off, fire (*infml*). **3** *dismiss it from your mind*: discount, disregard, reject, repudiate, set aside, shelve, spurn, banish.
F3 **2** appoint. **3** retain, accept.

disobey *verb* contravene, infringe, violate, transgress, flout, disregard, defy, ignore, resist, rebel.
F3 obey.

disorder *noun* **1** *try to sort out the disorder*: confusion, chaos, muddle, disarray, mess, untidiness, shambles (*infml*), clutter, disorganization, jumble. **2** *charged with public disorder*: disturbance, tumult, riot, confusion, commotion, uproar, fracas, brawl, fight, clamour, quarrel. **3** *a disorder of the nervous system*: illness, complaint, disease, sickness, disability, ailment, malady, affliction.
F3 **1** neatness, order. **2** law and order, peace.

disorderly *adjective* **1** *in disorderly piles*: disorganized, confused, chaotic, irregular, messy, untidy. **2** *a disorderly crowd of fans*: unruly, undisciplined, unmanageable, obstreperous, rowdy, turbulent, rebellious, lawless.
F3 **1** neat, tidy. **2** well-behaved.

disorganized *verb* **1** *a disorganized pile of papers*: confused, jumbled, chaotic, shambolic (*infml*), disordered, disturbed, disarranged, muddled. **2** *his life is so disorganized*: unmethodical, careless, unorganized, unsystematic, unstructured.

disown *verb* repudiate, renounce, disclaim, deny, cast off, disallow, reject, abandon.
F3 accept, acknowledge.

disparaging *adjective* derisive, derogatory, mocking, scornful, critical, insulting, snide (*infml*).
F3 flattering, praising.

dispatch, **despatch** *verb* send, transmit, forward, consign.
F3 receive.

dispense *verb* **1** *dispense medicines*: distribute, give out, apportion, allot, allocate, assign. **2** *dispense justice*: administer, apply, implement, enforce, discharge, execute, operate, mete out.

disperse *verb* scatter, dispel, spread, distribute, diffuse, dissolve, break up, dismiss, separate.
F3 gather.

displace *verb* **1** *displacing some slates*: dislodge, move, shift, misplace, disturb, dislocate. **2** *displacing his rivals*: depose, oust, remove, replace, dismiss, discharge, supplant, eject, evict, succeed, supersede.

display *verb* **1** *display goods for sale*: show, present, demonstrate, exhibit. **2** *display irritation*: betray, disclose, reveal, show, expose. **3** *displaying her tan*: show off, flourish, parade, flaunt.
F3 **1** conceal. **2** disguise.

▪ *noun* show, exhibition, demonstration, presentation, parade, spectacle, revelation, array.

displeasure *noun* offence, annoyance, disapproval, irritation, resentment, disfavour, anger, indignation, wrath.
F3 pleasure.

dispose of *verb* **1** *dispose of the matter quickly*: deal with, decide, settle. **2** *dispose of waste*: get rid of, discard, scrap, destroy, dump (*infml*), jettison.
F3 2 keep.

disposition *noun* character, nature, temperament, inclination, make-up, bent, leaning, predisposition, constitution, habit, spirit, tendency, proneness.

disproportionate *adjective* unequal, uneven, incommensurate, excessive, unreasonable.
F3 balanced.

disprove *verb* refute, rebut, confute, discredit, invalidate, contradict, expose.
F3 confirm, prove.

dispute *verb* /dis-**pyoot**/ argue, debate, question, contend, challenge, discuss, doubt, contest, contradict, deny, quarrel, clash, wrangle, squabble.
F3 agree.
▪ *noun* /**dis**-pyoot/ argument, debate, disagreement, controversy, conflict, contention, quarrel, wrangle, feud, strife, squabble.
F3 agreement, settlement.

disqualify *verb* debar, preclude, rule out, disentitle, eliminate, prohibit.
F3 qualify, accept.

disquiet *noun* anxiety, worry, concern, nervousness, uneasiness, restlessness, alarm, distress, fretfulness, fear, disturbance, trouble, unrest.
F3 calm, reassurance.

disregard *verb* **1** *if you have paid please disregard this letter*: ignore, overlook, discount, neglect, pass over, disobey, make light of, turn a blind eye to (*infml*), brush aside. **2** *disregarding the fans who had waited all night*: slight, snub, despise, disdain, disparage (*fml*).
F3 1 heed, pay attention to. **2** respect.

disrepair *noun* dilapidation, deterioration, decay, collapse, ruin, shabbiness.
F3 good repair.

disreputable *adjective* disgraceful, discreditable, dishonourable, unrespectable, notorious, scandalous, infamous, shameful, shady, base, contemptible, low, mean, shocking.
F3 respectable.

disrespectful *adjective* rude, discourteous, impertinent, impolite, impudent, insolent, uncivil, unmannerly, cheeky, insulting, irreverent, contemptuous.
F3 polite, respectful.

disrupt *verb* disturb, disorganize, confuse, interrupt, break up, unsettle, intrude, upset.

dissatisfaction *noun* discontent, displeasure, dislike, discomfort, disappointment, frustration, annoyance, irritation, exasperation, regret, resentment.
F3 satisfaction.

dissect *verb* **1** *dissect the frog*: dismember, anatomize. **2** *dissecting the evidence*: analyse, investigate, scrutinize, examine, inspect, pore over.

dissent *verb* disagree, differ, protest, object, refuse, quibble.
F3 assent.
▪ *noun* disagreement, difference, dissension, discord, resistance, opposition, objection.
F3 agreement, conformity.

disservice *noun* disfavour, injury, wrong, bad turn, harm, unkindness, injustice.
F3 favour.

dissident *noun* dissenter, protester, nonconformist, rebel, agitator, revolutionary.
F3 assenter.

dissimilar *adjective* unlike, different, divergent, disparate, unrelated, incompatible, mismatched, diverse, various, heterogeneous (*fml*).
F3 similar, like.

dissolute *adjective* dissipated, debauched, degenerate, depraved, wanton, abandoned, corrupt, immoral, licentious, lewd, wild.
F3 restrained, virtuous.

dissolve *verb* **1** *when all the sugar has dissolved*: evaporate, disintegrate, liquefy, melt. **2** *dissolved into dust*: decompose, disintegrate, disperse, break up, disappear, crumble. **3** *dissolve the marriage*: end, terminate, separate, sever, divorce.

dissuade *verb* deter, discourage, put off, disincline.
F3 persuade.

distance *noun* space, interval, gap, extent, range, reach, length, width.
F3 closeness.

distant *adjective* **1** *distant stars*: far, faraway, far-flung, out-of-the-way, remote, outlying, abroad, dispersed. **2** *he is always a little distant with strangers*: aloof, cool, reserved, standoffish, formal, cold, restrained, stiff.
F3 **1** close. **2** approachable.

distaste *noun* dislike, aversion, repugnance, disgust, revulsion, loathing, abhorrence (*fml*).
F3 liking.

distasteful *adjective* disagreeable, offensive, unpleasant, objectionable, repulsive, obnoxious, repugnant, unsavoury, loathsome, abhorrent (*fml*).
F3 pleasing.

distinct *adjective* **1** *two distinct languages*: separate, different, detached, individual, dissimilar. **2** *a distinct lack of enthusiasm*: clear, plain, evident, obvious, apparent,

marked, definite, noticeable, recognizable.
F 2 indistinct, vague.

distinction *noun* **1** *made no distinction between rich and poor*: differentiation, discrimination, discernment, separation, difference, dissimilarity, contrast. **2** *an obvious distinction*: characteristic, peculiarity, individuality, feature, quality, mark. **3** *a man of distinction*: renown, fame, celebrity, prominence, eminence, importance, reputation, greatness, honour, prestige, repute, superiority, worth, merit, excellence, quality.
F 3 unimportance, obscurity.

distinctive *adjective* characteristic, distinguishing, individual, peculiar, different, unique, singular, special, original, extraordinary, idiosyncratic.
F ordinary, common.

distinguish *verb* **1** *distinguish one from the other*: differentiate, tell apart, discriminate, determine, categorize, characterize, classify. **2** *distinguish his features*: discern, perceive, identify, ascertain, make out, recognize, see, discriminate.

distinguished *adjective* famous, eminent, celebrated, well-known, acclaimed, illustrious, notable, noted, renowned, famed, honoured, outstanding, striking, marked, extraordinary, conspicuous.
F insignificant, obscure, unimpressive.

distort *verb* **1** *distorting the image*: deform, contort, bend, misshape, disfigure, twist, warp. **2** *distorting the facts*: falsify, misrepresent, pervert, slant, colour, garble.

distract *verb* divert, sidetrack, deflect, occupy.

distracted *adjective* confused, disconcerted, bewildered, confounded, disturbed, perplexed, puzzled.

distraught *adjective* agitated, anxious, overwrought, upset, distressed, distracted, beside oneself, worked up, frantic, hysterical, raving, mad, wild, crazy.
F calm, untroubled.

distress *noun* **1** *his distress was obvious*: anguish, grief, misery, sorrow, heartache, affliction, suffering, torment, wretchedness, sadness, worry, anxiety, desolation, pain, agony. **2** *financial distress*: adversity, hardship, poverty, need, privation (*fml*), destitution, misfortune, trouble, difficulties, trial.
F 1 content. **2** comfort, ease.
▪ *verb* upset, afflict, grieve, disturb, trouble, sadden, worry, torment, harass, harrow, pain, agonize, bother.
F comfort.

distribute *verb* **1** *distribute the money to children's charities*: dispense, allocate, dole out, dish out, share, deal, divide, apportion. **2** *distribute the leaflets*: deliver,

hand out, spread, issue, circulate, diffuse, disperse, scatter.
F3 **2** collect.

distribution *noun* **1** *distribution of aid*: allocation, division, sharing. **2** *the distribution of goods*: circulation, spreading, scattering, delivery, dissemination, supply, dealing, handling.
F3 **2** collection.

district *noun* region, area, quarter, neighbourhood, locality, sector, precinct, parish, locale, community, vicinity, ward.

distrust *verb* mistrust, doubt, disbelieve, suspect, question.
F3 trust.
▪ *noun* mistrust, doubt, disbelief, suspicion, misgiving, wariness, scepticism, question, qualm.
F3 trust.

disturb *verb* **1** *disturbing his rest*: disrupt, interrupt, distract. **2** *disturbed by the news*: agitate, unsettle, upset, distress, worry, fluster, annoy, bother. **3** *disturbing the neat piles of papers*: disarrange, disorder, confuse, upset.
F3 **2** reassure. **3** order.

disturbance *noun* **1** *causing a disturbance*: disruption, agitation, interruption, intrusion, upheaval, upset, confusion, annoyance, bother, trouble, hindrance. **2** *a disturbance in the town centre*: disorder, uproar, commotion, tumult, turmoil, fracas, fray, brawl, riot.
F3 **1** peace. **2** order.

disuse *noun* neglect, decay, abandonment, discontinuance.
F3 use.

ditch *noun* trench, dyke, channel, gully, furrow, moat, drain, level, watercourse.

dither *verb* hesitate, shilly-shally (*infml*), waver, vacillate.

dive *verb* plunge, plummet, dip, submerge, jump, leap, nose-dive, fall, drop, swoop, descend, pitch.
▪ *noun* plunge, lunge, header, jump, leap, nose-dive, swoop, dash, spring.

diverge *verb* **1** *the veins diverge to form capillaries*: divide, branch, fork, separate, spread, split. **2** *diverging from the matter at hand*: deviate, digress, stray, wander. **3** *this is where opinions diverge*: differ, vary, disagree, dissent, conflict.
F3 **1** converge. **3** agree.

diverse *adjective* various, varied, varying, sundry, different, differing, assorted, dissimilar, miscellaneous, discrete, separate, several, distinct.
F3 similar, identical.

diversify *verb* vary, change, expand, branch out, spread out, alter, mix, assort.

diversion *noun* **1** *a diversion off the motorway*: deviation, detour. **2** *a puppet theatre and other diversions*: amusement, entertainment, distraction, pastime, recreation, relaxation, play, game.

divert *verb* **1** *diverting the stream*: deflect, redirect, reroute, sidetrack, avert, distract, switch. **2** *tried to divert them by singing songs*: amuse, entertain, occupy, distract, interest.

divide *verb* **1** *divide the orange into segments*: split, separate, part, cut, break up, detach, bisect, disconnect. **2** *dividing the money equally*: distribute, share, allocate, deal out, allot, apportion. **3** *dividing families*: disunite, separate, estrange, alienate. **4** *divide the men from the boys*: classify, group, sort, grade, segregate.

F3 **1** join. **2** collect. **3** unite.

divine *adjective* **1** *his powers are almost divine*: godlike, superhuman, supernatural, celestial, heavenly, angelic, spiritual. **2** *divine worship*: holy, sacred, sanctified, consecrated, transcendent, exalted, glorious, religious, supreme.

F3 **1** human. **2** mundane.

division *noun* **1** *the division of cells*: separation, detaching, parting, cutting, disunion. **2** *division of his estate amongst his children*: distribution, sharing, allotment. **3** *head of the sales division*: section, sector, segment, part, department, branch.

F3 **1** union. **2** collection. **3** whole.

divorce *noun* dissolution, annulment, break-up, split-up, rupture, separation, breach, disunion.

▪ *verb* separate, part, annul, split up, sever, dissolve, divide, dissociate.

F3 marry, unite.

divulge *verb* disclose, reveal, communicate, tell, leak (*infml*), impart, confess, betray, uncover, let slip, expose, publish, proclaim.

dizzy *adjective* **1** *feeling dizzy*: giddy, faint, light-headed, woozy (*infml*), shaky, reeling. **2** *dizzy with excitement*: confused, bewildered, dazed, muddled.

do *verb* **1** *do a play*: perform, carry out, execute, accomplish, achieve, fulfil, implement, complete, undertake, work, put on, present, conclude, end, finish. **2** *don't know what to do*: behave, act, conduct oneself. **3** *do the repairs*: fix, prepare, organize, arrange, deal with, look after, manage, produce, make, create, cause, proceed. **4** *that'll do nicely*: suffice, satisfy, serve.

▪ *noun* function, affair, event, gathering, party, occasion.

docile *adjective* tractable, co-operative, manageable, submissive, obedient, amenable, controlled, obliging.

F3 truculent, unco-operative.

dock *noun* harbour, wharf, quay, boat-yard, pier, waterfront, marina.

▪ *verb* anchor, moor, drop anchor, land, berth, put in, tie up.

doctor *noun* physician, general practitioner, GP, medic (*infml*), medical officer, consultant, clinician.

▪ *verb* alter, tamper with, falsify, misrepresent, pervert, adulterate, change, disguise, dilute.

doctrine *noun* dogma, creed, belief, tenet, principle, teaching, precept (*fml*), conviction, opinion, canon.

document *noun* paper, certificate, deed, record, report, form, instrument (*fml*).

dodge *verb* avoid, elude, evade, swerve, side-step, shirk, shift.

▪ *noun* trick, ruse, ploy, wile, scheme, stratagem, machination, manoeuvre.

dog *noun* hound, cur, mongrel, canine, puppy, pup, bitch, mutt (*infml*), pooch (*infml*).

▪ *verb* pursue, follow, trail, track, tail, hound, shadow, plague, harry, haunt, trouble, worry.

Breeds of dog include:

Afghan hound, alsatian, basset-hound, beagle, Border collie, borzoi, bulldog, bull-mastiff, bull-terrier, cairn terrier, chihuahua, chow, cocker spaniel, collie, corgi, dachshund, Dalmatian, Doberman pinscher, foxhound, fox-terrier, German Shepherd, golden retriever, Great Dane, greyhound, husky, Irish wolfhound, Jack Russell, King Charles spaniel, Labrador, lhasa apso, lurcher, Maltese, Old English sheepdog, Pekingese, pit bull terrier, pointer, poodle, pug, Rottweiler, saluki, sausage-dog (*infml*), schnauzer, Scottie (*infml*), Scottish terrier, Sealyham, setter, sheltie, shih tzu, springer spaniel, St Bernard, terrier, West Highland terrier, whippet, wolfhound, Yorkshire terrier.

---

dogged *adjective* determined, resolute, persistent, persevering, intent, tenacious, firm, steadfast, staunch, single-minded, indefatigable, steady, unshakable, stubborn, obstinate, relentless, unyielding.

F3 irresolute, apathetic.

dogma *noun* doctrine, creed, belief, precept (*fml*), principle, article (of faith), credo, tenet, conviction, teaching, opinion.

dogmatic *adjective* opinionated, assertive, authoritative, positive, doctrinaire, dictatorial, doctrinal, categorical, emphatic, overbearing, arbitrary.

dole out *verb* distribute, allocate, hand out, dish out, apportion, allot, mete out, share, divide, deal, issue, ration, dispense, administer, assign.

domain *noun* **1** *the king's domain*: dominion, kingdom, realm, territory, region, empire, lands, province. **2** *his particular domain*: field, area, speciality, concern, department, sphere, discipline, jurisdiction.

domestic *adjective* **1** *domestic chores/animals*: home, family, household, home-loving, stay-at-home, homely, house-trained, tame, pet, private. **2** *domestic affairs*: internal, indigenous, native.

domesticate *verb* tame, house-train, break, train, accustom, familiarize.

dominant *adjective* **1** *a dominant leader*: authoritative, controlling, governing, ruling, powerful, assertive, influential. **2** *the dominant species*: principal, main, outstanding, chief, important, predominant, primary, prominent, leading, pre-eminent, prevailing, prevalent, commanding.
F3 **1** submissive. **2** subordinate.

dominate *verb* **1** *the team dominates the Premiership*: control, domineer, govern, rule, direct, monopolize, master, lead, overrule, prevail, overbear, tyrannize. **2** *dominating the landscape*: overshadow, eclipse, dwarf.

donate *verb* give, contribute, present, bequeath, bestow, confer, subscribe.
F3 receive.

donation *noun* gift, present, offering, grant, gratuity, largess(e), contribution, presentation, subscription, alms, benefaction (*fml*), bequest.

done *adjective* **1** *the job's done*: finished, over, accomplished, completed, ended, concluded, settled, realized, executed. **2** *not the done thing*: conventional, acceptable, proper. **3** *the meat's done*: cooked, ready.

donor *noun* giver, donator, benefactor, contributor, philanthropist, provider, fairy godmother (*infml*).
F3 beneficiary.

doom *noun* fate, fortune, destiny, portion, lot, destruction, catastrophe, downfall, ruin, death, death-knell.

doomed *adjective* condemned, damned, fated, ill-fated, ill-omened, cursed, destined, hopeless, luckless, ill-starred.

door *noun* opening, entrance, entry, exit, doorway, portal, hatch.

dormant *adjective* **1** *a dormant volcano*: inactive, asleep, sleeping, inert, resting, slumbering, sluggish, torpid, hibernating, fallow, comatose. **2** *her talent lay dormant*: latent, unrealized, potential, undeveloped, undisclosed.
F3 **1** active, awake. **2** realized, developed.

dose *noun* measure, dosage, amount, portion, quantity, draught, potion, prescription, shot (*infml*).

dot *noun* point, spot, speck, mark, fleck, circle, pin-point, atom, decimal point, full stop, iota, jot.

double *adjective* dual, twofold, twice, duplicate, twin, paired, doubled, coupled.
F3 single, half.
▪ *verb* duplicate, enlarge, increase, repeat, multiply, fold, magnify.
▪ *noun* twin, duplicate, copy, clone, replica, doppelgänger, lookalike, spitting image (*infml*), ringer (*infml*), image, counterpart, impersonator.

doubt *verb* **1** *doubt his motives*: distrust, mistrust, query, question, suspect, fear. **2** *I don't doubt his ability*: be uncertain, be dubious, hesitate, vacillate, waver.
≠ **1** believe, trust.
▪ *noun* **1** *have doubts about him*: distrust, suspicion, mistrust, scepticism, reservation, misgiving, incredulity, apprehension, hesitation. **2** *no doubt about the accuracy of his statement*: uncertainty, difficulty, confusion, ambiguity, problem, indecision, perplexity, dilemma, quandary.
≠ **1** trust, faith. **2** certainty, belief.

doubtful *adjective* **1** *doubtful about his future*: uncertain, unsure, undecided, suspicious, irresolute, wavering, hesitant, vacillating, tentative, sceptical. **2** *writing of doubtful origin*: dubious, questionable, unclear, ambiguous, vague, obscure, debatable.
≠ **1** certain, decided. **2** definite, settled.

downfall *noun* fall, ruin, failure, collapse, destruction, disgrace, debacle, undoing, overthrow.

downright *adjective, adverb* absolute(ly), outright, plain(ly), utter(ly), clear(ly), complete(ly), out-and-out, frank(ly), explicit(ly).

downward *adjective* descending, declining, downhill, sliding, slipping.
≠ upward.

doze *verb* sleep, nod off, drop off, snooze (*infml*), kip (*infml*).

drab *adjective* dull, dingy, dreary, dismal, gloomy, flat, grey, lacklustre, cheerless, sombre, shabby.
≠ bright, cheerful.

draft *verb* draw (up), outline, sketch, plan, design, formulate, compose.
▪ *noun* outline, sketch, plan, delineation, abstract, rough, blueprint.

drag *verb* **1** *drag the box to the other room*: draw, pull, haul, lug, tug, trail, tow. **2** *time dragging by*: go slowly, creep, crawl, lag.

drain *noun* channel, conduit, culvert, duct, outlet, trench, ditch, pipe, sewer.
▪ *verb* **1** *drained the tank*: empty, remove, evacuate, draw off, strain, dry, milk, bleed. **2** *draining into the sea*: discharge, trickle, flow out, leak, ooze. **3** *draining his energy*: exhaust, consume, sap, use up, deplete, drink up, swallow.
≠ **1** fill.

drama *noun* **1** *study drama*: play, acting, theatre, show, spectacle, stage-craft, scene, melodrama. **2** *what's all the drama about?*: excitement, crisis, turmoil.

dramatic *adjective* **1** *a dramatic landscape*: exciting, striking, stirring, thrilling, marked, significant, expressive, impressive. **2** *a dramatic announcement*: histrionic, exaggerated, melodramatic, flamboyant.

drape *verb* cover, wrap, hang, fold, drop, suspend.

drastic *adjective* extreme, radical, strong, forceful, severe, harsh, far-reaching, desperate, dire.
F3 moderate, cautious.

draught *noun* puff, current, influx, flow.

draw *verb* **1** *draw a crowd*: attract, allure, entice, bring in, influence, persuade, elicit. **2** *a caravan drawn by two horses*: pull, drag, haul, tow, tug. **3** *draw a diagram*: delineate, map out, sketch, portray, trace, pencil, depict, design, outline. **4** *the teams drew*: tie, be equal, be even.
F3 1 repel. **2** push.
▪ *noun* tie, stalemate, dead-heat.

drawback *noun* disadvantage, snag, hitch, obstacle, impediment, hindrance, difficulty, flaw, fault, fly in the ointment (*infml*), catch, stumbling block, nuisance, trouble, defect, handicap, deficiency, imperfection.
F3 advantage, benefit.

drawing *noun* sketch, picture, outline, representation, delineation, portrayal, illustration, cartoon, graphic, portrait.

dread *verb* fear, shrink from, quail, cringe at, flinch, shy, shudder, tremble.
▪ *noun* fear, apprehension, misgiving, trepidation, dismay, alarm, horror, terror, fright, disquiet, worry, qualm.
F3 confidence, security.

dreadful *adjective* awful, terrible, frightful, horrible, appalling, dire, shocking, ghastly, horrendous, tragic, grievous, hideous, tremendous.
F3 wonderful, comforting.

dream *noun* **1** *have a bad dream/see them in his dreams*: vision, illusion, reverie, trance, fantasy, daydream, nightmare, hallucination, delusion, imagination. **2** *achieve his dream*: aspiration, wish, hope, ambition, desire, pipe-dream, ideal, goal, design, speculation.
▪ *verb* imagine, envisage, fancy, fantasize, daydream, hallucinate, conceive, visualize, conjure up, muse.

dreary *adjective* **1** *a dreary job*: boring, tedious, uneventful, dull, humdrum, routine, monotonous, wearisome, commonplace, colourless, lifeless. **2** *a dreary prospect*: gloomy, depressing, drab, dismal, bleak, sombre, sad, mournful.
F3 1 interesting. **2** cheerful.

dregs *noun* **1** *wash the dregs from the teacups*: sediment, deposit, residue, lees, grounds, scum, dross, trash, waste. **2** *the dregs of society*: outcasts, rabble, riff-raff, scum, down-and-outs.

drench *verb* soak, saturate, steep, wet, douse, souse, immerse, inundate, duck, flood, imbue, drown.

dress *verb* **1** *dress for dinner*: clothe, put on, garb, rig, robe, wear, don, decorate, deck, garnish, trim, adorn, fit, drape. **2** *dressing the turkey/the shop window*:

arrange, adjust, dispose, prepare, groom, straighten. **3** *dressing his wounds*: bandage, tend, treat.
E3 1 strip, undress.

dribble *verb* **1** *water dribbling down the walls*: trickle, drip, leak, run, seep, drop, ooze. **2** *dribbling saliva*: drool, slaver, slobber, drivel.

drift *noun* **1** *snow forming drifts*: accumulation, mound, pile, bank, mass, heap. **2** *a gradual drift towards democracy*: trend, tendency, course, direction, flow, movement, current, rush, sweep. **3** *get someone's drift*: meaning, intention, implication, gist, tenor, thrust, significance, aim, design, scope.
▪ *verb* **1** *drift past*: wander, waft, stray, float, freewheel, coast. **2** *snow drifting*: gather, accumulate, pile up, drive.

drill *verb* **1** *drilling the new recruits*: teach, train, instruct, coach, practise, school, rehearse, exercise, discipline. **2** *drill teeth/a hole*: bore, pierce, penetrate, puncture, perforate.

drink *noun* **1** *a cool drink*: beverage, liquid, refreshment, draught, sip, swallow, swig (*infml*), gulp. **2** *serve drinks/the demon drink*: alcohol, spirits, booze (*infml*), liquor, tipple (*infml*), tot, the bottle (*infml*).
▪ *verb* **1** *drinks only water*: imbibe, swallow, sip, drain, down, gulp, swig (*infml*), knock back (*infml*), sup, quaff, absorb, swill. **2** *he sometimes drinks after work*: get drunk, booze (*infml*), tipple (*infml*), indulge, carouse, revel.

drip *noun* drop, trickle, dribble, leak, bead, tear.
▪ *verb* drop, dribble, trickle, plop, percolate, drizzle, splash, sprinkle, weep.

drive *verb* **1** *driven by steam/greed*: direct, control, manage, operate, run, handle, motivate. **2** *he drove me to do it*: force, compel, impel, coerce, constrain, press, push, urge, dragoon, goad, guide, oblige. **3** *drive a tractor/driving home*: steer, motor, propel, ride, travel.
▪ *noun* **1** *need plenty of drive and enthusiasm*: energy, enterprise, ambition, initiative, get-up-and-go (*infml*), vigour, motivation, determination. **2** *a drive to improve standards*: campaign, crusade, appeal, effort, action. **3** *a long drive*: excursion, outing, journey, ride, spin, trip, jaunt.

drop *noun* **1** *a drop of water*: droplet, bead, tear, drip, bubble, globule, trickle. **2** *a few drops of vanilla essence*: dash, pinch, spot, sip, trace, dab. **3** *a drop in exports*: fall, decline, falling-off, lowering, downturn, decrease, reduction, slump, plunge, deterioration. **4** *a steep drop to the sea*: descent, precipice, slope, chasm, abyss.
▪ *verb* **1** *dropped to the ground/prices dropping*: fall, sink, decline, plunge, plummet, tumble, dive, descend, lower, droop, depress, diminish. **2** *drop the subject*: abandon, forsake, desert, give up,

relinquish, reject, leave, renounce, throw over, repudiate, cease, discontinue, quit.
F3 **1** rise.

drown *verb* **1** *nearly drowned while swimming/heavy rain drowning the garden*: submerge, immerse, inundate, go under, flood, sink, deluge, engulf, drench. **2** *loud music drowning their voices*: overwhelm, overpower, overcome, swamp, wipe out, extinguish.

drowsy *adjective* sleepy, tired, lethargic, nodding, dreamy, dozy, somnolent (*fml*).
F3 alert, awake.

drudgery *noun* labour, donkey-work (*infml*), hack-work, slog (*infml*), grind (*infml*), slavery, sweat, sweated labour, toil, skivvying, chore.

drug *noun* medication, medicine, remedy, potion.
▪ *verb* medicate, sedate, tranquillize, dope (*infml*), anaesthetize, dose, knock out (*infml*), stupefy, deaden, numb.

drum *verb* beat, pulsate, tap, throb, thrum, tattoo, reverberate, rap.

dry *adjective* **1** *a dry throat/too dry to grow crops*: arid, parched, thirsty, dehydrated, desiccated, barren. **2** *the book was as dry as dust*: boring, dull, dreary, tedious, monotonous. **3** *dry humour*: ironic, cynical, droll, deadpan, sarcastic, cutting.
F3 **1** wet. **2** interesting.
▪ *verb* dehydrate, parch, desiccate, drain, shrivel, wither.
F3 soak.

dual *adjective* double, twofold, duplicate, duplex, binary, combined, paired, twin, matched.

dubious *adjective* **1** *was a bit dubious about it*: doubtful, uncertain, undecided, unsure, wavering, unsettled, suspicious, sceptical, hesitant. **2** *a dubious character*: questionable, debatable, unreliable, ambiguous, suspect, obscure, fishy (*infml*), shady (*infml*).
F3 **1** certain. **2** trustworthy.

duck *verb* **1** *duck down behind the wall*: crouch, stoop, bob, bend. **2** *duck out of one's responsibilities*: avoid, dodge, evade, shirk, sidestep.

due *adjective* **1** *the payment is due*: owed, owing, payable, unpaid, outstanding, in arrears. **2** *praise where praise is due*: rightful, fitting, appropriate, proper, merited, deserved, justified, suitable. **3** *give the due amount of attention to*: adequate, enough, sufficient, ample, plenty of. **4** *another train is due*: expected, scheduled.
F3 **1** paid. **3** inadequate.
▪ *adverb* exactly, direct(ly), precisely, straight, dead (*infml*).

dull *adjective* **1** *found it very dull*: boring, uninteresting, unexciting, flat, dreary, monotonous, tedious, uneventful, humdrum, unimaginative, dismal, lifeless, plain, insipid, heavy. **2** *a dull corner/dull weather*: dark, gloomy,

drab, murky, indistinct, grey, cloudy, lacklustre, opaque, dim, overcast. **3** *too dull to work out the answer*: unintelligent, dense, dim, dimwitted (*infml*), thick (*infml*), stupid, slow.
F3 **1** interesting, exciting. **2** bright. **3** intelligent, clever.
dumb *adjective* silent, mute, soundless, speechless, tongue-tied, inarticulate, mum (*infml*).
dumbfounded *adjective* astonished, amazed, astounded, overwhelmed, speechless, taken aback, thrown (*infml*), startled, overcome, confounded, flabbergasted (*infml*), staggered, confused, bowled over, dumb, floored (*infml*), paralysed.
dump *verb* **1** *dumped it on the floor*: deposit, drop, offload, throw down, let fall, unload, empty out, discharge, park. **2** *dump it overboard*: get rid of, scrap, throw away, dispose of, ditch, tip, jettison.
▪ *noun* rubbish-tip, junk-yard, rubbish-heap, tip.
duplicate *adjective* identical, matching, twin, twofold, corresponding, matched.
▪ *noun* copy, replica, reproduction, photocopy, carbon (copy), match, facsimile.
▪ *verb* copy, reproduce, repeat, photocopy, double, clone, echo.
dusk *noun* twilight, sunset, nightfall, evening, sundown, gloaming, darkness, dark, gloom, shadows, shade.
F3 dawn, brightness.
dutiful *adjective* obedient, respectful, conscientious, devoted, filial, reverential, submissive.
duty *noun* **1** *have a duty to perform/do one's duty*: obligation, responsibility, assignment, calling, charge, role, task, job, business, function, work, office, service. **2** *his duty to his king*: obedience, respect, loyalty. **3** *pay duty on imports*: tax, toll, tariff, levy, customs, excise.
dwell *verb* live, inhabit, reside, stay, settle, populate, people, lodge, rest, abide (*fml*).
dwindle *verb* diminish, decrease, decline, lessen, subside, ebb, fade, weaken, taper off, tail off, shrink, peter out, fall, wane, waste away, die out, wither, shrivel, disappear.
F3 increase, grow.
dye *noun* colour, colouring, stain, pigment, tint, tinge.
dying *adjective* moribund, passing, final, going, mortal, not long for this world, perishing, failing, fading, vanishing.
F3 reviving.
dynamic *adjective* forceful, powerful, energetic, vigorous, go-ahead, high-powered, driving, self-starting, spirited, vital, lively, active.
F3 inactive, apathetic.

Ee

eager *adjective* **1** *eager to begin*: keen, enthusiastic, fervent, intent, earnest, zealous. **2** *eager for news*: longing, yearning.
1 unenthusiastic, indifferent.

early *adjective* **1** *early symptoms*: forward, advanced, premature, untimely, undeveloped. **2** *early theatre*: primitive, ancient, primeval.
▪ *adverb* ahead of time, in good time, beforehand, in advance, prematurely.
late.

earn *verb* **1** *earn a good salary*: receive, obtain, make, get, draw, bring in (*infml*), gain, realize, gross, reap. **2** *have earned one's reputation*: deserve, merit, warrant, win, rate.
1 spend, lose.

earnest *adjective* **1** *an earnest attempt/promise*: resolute, firm, serious, sincere, solemn, grave, heartfelt. **2** *an earnest pupil*: devoted, ardent, conscientious, keen, fervent, eager, enthusiastic, steady.
1 frivolous, flippant. **2** apathetic.

earth *noun* **1** *all over the Earth*: world, planet, globe, sphere. **2** *planted in the earth*: land, ground, soil, clay, loam, sod, humus.

ease *noun* **1** *ease of doing*: facility, effortlessness, skilfulness, deftness, dexterity, naturalness, cleverness. **2** *living in ease*: comfort, contentment, peace, affluence, repose, leisure, relaxation, rest, quiet, happiness.
1 difficulty. **2** discomfort.
▪ *verb* **1** *ease the pain*: alleviate, moderate, lessen, lighten, relieve, mitigate, abate, relent, allay, assuage (*fml*), relax, comfort, calm, soothe, facilitate, smooth. **2** *ease it into position*: inch, steer, slide, slip.
1 aggravate, intensify, worsen.

easily *adverb* **1** *fits easily into the space*: effortlessly, comfortably, readily, simply. **2** *easily the best*: by far, undoubtedly, indisputably, definitely, certainly, doubtless(ly), clearly, far and away, undeniably, simply, surely, probably, well.
1 laboriously.

easy *adjective* **1** *an easy task*: effortless, simple, uncomplicated, undemanding, straightforward, manageable, cushy (*infml*). **2** *an easy pace*: relaxed, carefree, easy-going, comfortable, informal,

calm, natural, leisurely.
F3 **1** difficult, demanding, exacting. **2** tense, uneasy.

eat *verb* **1** *eat breakfast/eat at 8 o'clock*: consume, feed, swallow, devour, chew, scoff (*infml*), munch, dine, trough (*slang*), ingest (*fml*). **2** *rust eating away the metal*: corrode, erode, wear away, decay, rot, crumble, dissolve.

eccentric *adjective* odd, peculiar, abnormal, unconventional, strange, quirky, weird, way-out (*infml*), queer, outlandish, idiosyncratic, bizarre, freakish, erratic, singular, dotty (*infml*).
F3 conventional, orthodox, normal.

echo *verb* **1** *voices echoing in the empty room*: reverberate, resound, repeat, ring. **2** *echoing what he had said*: imitate, copy, reproduce, mirror, resemble, reflect, reiterate, mimic.

eclipse *noun* **1** *an eclipse of the sun*: obscuration, overshadowing, darkening, shading, dimming. **2** *the eclipse of Britain as a great power*: decline, failure, fall, loss.
▪ *verb* **1** *the sun eclipsed by the moon*: blot out, obscure, cloud, veil, darken, dim. **2** *eclipsing his older brother's achievements*: outdo, overshadow, outshine, surpass, transcend.

economic *adjective* **1** *economic growth*: commercial, business, industrial. **2** *an economic review*: financial, budgetary, fiscal, monetary. **3** *an economic proposition*: profitable, profit-making, money-making, productive, cost-effective, viable.

economical *adjective* **1** *a very economical housekeeper*: thrifty, careful, prudent, saving, sparing, frugal. **2** *a more economical model of car*: cheap, inexpensive, low-priced, reasonable, cost-effective, modest, efficient.
F3 **1** wasteful. **2** expensive, uneconomical.

economize *verb* save, cut back, tighten one's belt (*infml*), cut costs.
F3 waste, squander.

ecstasy *noun* delight, rapture, bliss, elation, joy, euphoria, frenzy, exaltation, fervour.
F3 misery, torment.

edge *noun* **1** *the edge of the table/sea/sink*: border, rim, boundary, limit, brim, threshold, brink, fringe, margin, outline, side, verge, line, perimeter, periphery, lip. **2** *the local athlete had the edge over the other competitors*: advantage, superiority, force.
▪ *verb* creep, inch, ease, sidle.

edgy *adjective* on edge, nervous, tense, anxious, ill at ease, keyed-up, touchy, irritable.
F3 calm.

edible *adjective* eatable, palatable, digestible, wholesome, good, harmless.
F3 inedible.

edit *verb* correct, emend, revise, rewrite, reorder, rearrange, adapt, check, compile, rephrase, select, polish, annotate, censor.

educate *verb* teach, train, instruct, tutor, coach, school, inform, cultivate, edify, drill, improve, discipline, develop.

educated *adjective* learned, taught, schooled, trained, knowledgeable, informed, instructed, lettered, cultured, civilized, tutored, refined, well-bred.

F3 uneducated, uncultured.

education *noun* teaching, training, schooling, tuition, tutoring, coaching, guidance, instruction, cultivation, culture, scholarship, improvement, enlightenment, knowledge, nurture, development.

Educational establishments include:

kindergarten, nursery school, infant school; primary school, middle school, combined school, community school, foundation school, secondary school, secondary modern, upper school, high school, grammar school, grant-maintained school, preparatory school, public school, private school; sixth-form college, college, city technical college, CTC, technical college, university; academy, adult-education centre, boarding-school, business school, convent school, finishing school, secretarial college, seminary, summer school, Sunday school.

---

eerie *adjective* weird, strange, uncanny, spooky (*infml*), creepy, frightening, scary, spine-chilling.

effect *noun* **1** *the effects of the changes*: outcome, result, conclusion, consequence, upshot, aftermath, issue. **2** *have greater effect*: power, force, impact, efficacy, impression, strength. **3** *words to that effect*: meaning, significance, import.

▪ *verb* cause, execute, create, achieve, accomplish, perform, produce, make, initiate, fulfil, complete.

effective *adjective* **1** *an effective remedy*: efficient, efficacious, productive, adequate, capable, useful. **2** *when the measures become effective*: operative, in force, functioning, current, active. **3** *an effective argument*: striking, impressive, forceful, cogent, powerful, persuasive, convincing, telling.

F3 **1** ineffective, powerless.

efficient *adjective* effective, competent, proficient, skilful, capable, able, productive, adept, well-organized, businesslike, powerful, well-conducted.

F3 inefficient, incompetent.

effort *noun* **1** *too much effort involved*: exertion, strain, application, struggle, trouble, energy, toil, striving, pains, travail (*fml*). **2** *make a good effort*: attempt, try, go (*infml*), endeavour, shot (*infml*), stab. **3** *the result of their efforts*: work, achievement, accomplishment, feat, exploit, production, creation, deed, product.

egotistic *adjective* egoistic, egocentric, self-centred, self-important, conceited, vain, swollen-headed (*infml*), bigheaded (*infml*), boasting, bragging.

humble.

eject *verb* oust, evict, throw out, drive out, turn out, expel, remove, banish, deport, dismiss, exile, kick out (*infml*), fire (*infml*), sack (*infml*).

elaborate *adjective* **1** *elaborate plans*: detailed, careful, thorough, exact, extensive, painstaking, precise, perfected, minute, laboured, studied. **2** *elaborate design*: intricate, complex, complicated, involved, ornamental, ornate, fancy, decorated, ostentatious, showy, fussy.

2 simple, plain.

elapse *verb* pass, lapse, go by, slip away.

elastic *adjective* pliable, flexible, stretchable, supple, resilient, yielding, springy, rubbery, pliant, plastic, bouncy, buoyant.

rigid.

elated *adjective* exhilarated, excited, euphoric, ecstatic, exultant, jubilant, overjoyed, joyful.

despondent, downcast.

elbow *verb* jostle, nudge, push, shove, bump, crowd, knock, shoulder.

elder *adjective* older, senior, first-born, ancient.

younger.

elderly *adjective* aging, aged, old, hoary, senile.

young, youthful.

elect *verb* choose, pick, opt for, select, vote for, prefer, adopt, designate, appoint, determine.
▪ *adjective* choice, élite, chosen, designated, designate, picked, prospective, selected, to be, preferred, hand-picked.

electric *adjective* electrifying, exciting, stimulating, thrilling, charged, dynamic, stirring, tense, rousing.

unexciting, flat.

electrify *verb* thrill, excite, shock, invigorate, animate, stimulate, stir, rouse, fire, jolt, galvanize, amaze, astonish, astound, stagger.

bore.

elegant *adjective* stylish, chic, fashionable, modish, smart, refined, polished, genteel, smooth, tasteful, fine, exquisite, beautiful, graceful, handsome, delicate, neat, artistic.

inelegant, unrefined, unfashionable.

element *noun* factor, component, constituent, ingredient, member, part, piece, fragment, feature, trace.

whole.

elementary *adjective* **1** *an elementary mistake*: simple, rudimentary, clear, easy, straightforward, uncomplicated.

2 *his elementary education*: basic, fundamental, primary, introductory.
F3 2 advanced.

eliminate *verb* remove, get rid of, cut out, take out, exclude, delete, dispense with, rub out, omit, reject, disregard, dispose of, drop, do away with, eradicate, expel, extinguish, stamp out, exterminate, knock out, kill, murder.
F3 include, accept.

élite *noun* best, elect, aristocracy, upper classes, nobility, gentry, crème de la crème, establishment, high society.
▪ *adjective* choice, best, exclusive, selected, first-class, aristocratic, noble, upper-class.

elongated *adjective* lengthened, extended, prolonged, protracted, stretched, long.

elusive *adjective* **1** *an elusive quality*: indefinable, intangible, unanalysable, subtle, puzzling, baffling, transient, transitory. **2** *an elusive criminal*: evasive, shifty, slippery, tricky.

embargo *noun* restriction, ban, prohibition, restraint, proscription, bar, barrier, interdiction (*fml*), impediment, check, hindrance, blockage, stoppage, seizure.

embark *verb* board (ship), go aboard, take ship.
F3 disembark.

embarrass *verb* disconcert, mortify, show up, fluster, humiliate, shame, distress.

embarrassment *noun* **1** *suffer from acute embarrassment*: discomposure, self-consciousness, chagrin, mortification, humiliation, shame, awkwardness, confusion, bashfulness. **2** *financial embarrassment*: difficulty, constraint, predicament, distress, discomfort.

embellish *verb* adorn, ornament, decorate, deck, dress up, beautify, gild, garnish, festoon, elaborate, embroider, enrich, exaggerate, enhance, varnish, grace.
F3 simplify, denude.

emblem *noun* symbol, sign, token, representation, logo, insignia, device, crest, mark, badge, figure.

embodiment *noun* incarnation, personification, exemplification, expression, epitome, example, incorporation, realization, representation, manifestation, concentration.

embrace *verb* **1** *embrace each other*: hug, clasp, cuddle, hold, grasp, squeeze. **2** *embracing several topics*: include, encompass, incorporate, contain, comprise, cover, involve. **3** *embracing the new faith*: accept, take up, welcome.

embryo *noun* nucleus, germ, beginning, root.

emerge *verb* **1** *see what will emerge at the next meeting*: arise, rise, surface, appear, develop, crop up (*infml*), transpire, turn up, materialize. **2** *emerging from the entrance*: emanate, issue, proceed.

emergency *noun* crisis, danger, difficulty, exigency (*fml*), predicament, plight, pinch, strait, quandary.

emigrate *verb* migrate, relocate, move, depart.

emit *verb* discharge, issue, eject, emanate, exude, give out, give off, diffuse, radiate, release, shed, vent.
F3 absorb.

emotion *noun* feeling, passion, sensation, sentiment, ardour, fervour, warmth, reaction, vehemence, excitement.

emotional *adjective* **1** *she gets too emotional*: feeling, passionate, sensitive, responsive, ardent, tender, warm, roused, demonstrative, excitable, enthusiastic, fervent, impassioned, moved, sentimental, zealous, hot-blooded, heated, tempestuous, overcharged, temperamental, fiery. **2** *an emotional welcome*: emotive, moving, poignant, thrilling, touching, stirring, heart-warming, exciting, pathetic.
F3 1 unemotional, cold, detached, calm.

emphasis *noun* stress, weight, significance, importance, priority, underscoring, accent, force, power, prominence, pre-eminence, attention, intensity, strength, urgency, positiveness, insistence, mark, moment.

emphasize *verb* stress, accentuate, underline, highlight, accent, feature, dwell on, weight, point up, spotlight, play up, insist on, press home, intensify, strengthen, punctuate.
F3 play down, understate.

emphatic *adjective* forceful, positive, insistent, certain, definite, decided, unequivocal, absolute, categorical, earnest, marked, pronounced, significant, strong, striking, vigorous, distinct, energetic, forcible, important, impressive, momentous, powerful, punctuated, telling, vivid, graphic, direct.
F3 tentative, hesitant, understated.

employ *verb* **1** *employing school-leavers*: engage, hire, take on, enlist, commission, recruit. **2** *employing new techniques*: use, utilize, make use of, apply, bring to bear, ply, exercise.

employment *noun* **1** *have some form of employment*: job, work, occupation, situation, business, calling, profession, line (*infml*), vocation, trade, pursuit, craft. **2** *the employment of school-leavers*: enlistment, employ, engagement, hire.
F3 1 unemployment.

empower *verb* authorize, warrant, enable, license, sanction, permit, entitle, commission, delegate, qualify.

empty *adjective* **1** *an empty space/house/landscape*: vacant,

void, unoccupied, uninhabited, unfilled, deserted, bare, hollow, desolate, blank, clear. **2** *an empty gesture*: futile, aimless, meaningless, senseless, trivial, vain, worthless, useless, insubstantial, ineffective, insincere.
F3 **1** full. **2** meaningful.
▪ *verb* drain, exhaust, discharge, clear, evacuate, vacate, pour out, unload, void, gut.
F3 fill.

enable *verb* equip, qualify, empower, authorize, sanction, warrant, allow, permit, prepare, fit, facilitate, license, commission, endue (*fml*).
F3 prevent, inhibit, forbid.

enact *verb* **1** *enact a law*: decree, ordain, order, authorize, command, legislate, sanction, ratify, pass, establish. **2** *enact a play*: act (out), perform, play, portray, represent, depict.
F3 **1** repeal, rescind.

enchanting *adjective* captivating, charming, fascinating, attractive, alluring, appealing, delightful, enthralling, bewitching, spellbinding, hypnotic.
F3 repellent.

enclose *verb* encircle, encompass, surround, fence, hedge, hem in, bound, encase, embrace, envelop, confine, hold, shut in, wrap, pen, cover, circumscribe, incorporate, include, insert, contain, comprehend.

encompass *verb* **1** *encompassing her waist*: encircle, circle, ring, surround, gird, envelop, circumscribe, hem in, enclose, hold. **2** *encompassing the whole of mankind*: include, cover, embrace, contain, comprise, admit, incorporate, involve, embody, comprehend.

encounter *verb* meet, come across, run into (*infml*), happen on, chance upon, run across, confront, face, experience.
▪ *noun* **1** *an encounter with death*: meeting, brush, confrontation, rendezvous. **2** *a titanic encounter between two champions*: clash, fight, combat, conflict, contest, battle, set-to (*infml*), dispute, engagement, action, skirmish, run-in, collision.

encourage *verb* **1** *encouraged them to continue*: hearten, exhort, stimulate, spur, reassure, rally, inspire, incite, egg on (*infml*), buoy up, cheer, urge, rouse, comfort, console. **2** *a scheme to encourage tourism in the area*: promote, advance, aid, boost, forward, further, foster, support, help, strengthen.
F3 **1** discourage, depress. **2** discourage.

encouraging *adjective* heartening, promising, hopeful, reassuring, stimulating, uplifting, auspicious, cheering, comforting, bright, rosy, cheerful, satisfactory.
F3 discouraging.

encroach *verb* intrude, invade,

impinge, trespass, infringe, usurp, overstep, make inroads, muscle in (*infml*).

end *noun* **1** *the end of the war*: finish, conclusion, termination, close, completion, cessation, culmination, dénouement. **2** *the ends of the earth*: extremity, boundary, edge, limit, tip. **3** *a cigarette end*: remainder, tip, butt, left-over, remnant, stub, scrap, fragment. **4** *with only one end in mind*: aim, object, objective, purpose, intention, goal, point, reason, design. **5** *to that end*: result, outcome, consequence, upshot. **6** *the end was swift*: death, demise, destruction, extermination, downfall, doom, ruin, dissolution.
F3 **1** beginning, start. **6** birth.
▪ *verb* **1** *ending the speech with a joke*: finish, close, cease, conclude, stop, terminate, complete, culminate, wind up. **2** *ending their lives*: destroy, annihilate, exterminate, extinguish, ruin, abolish, dissolve.
F3 **1** begin, start.

endanger *verb* imperil, hazard, jeopardize, risk, expose, threaten, compromise.
F3 protect.

endearing *adjective* lovable, charming, appealing, attractive, winsome, delightful, enchanting.

endeavour *verb* attempt, try, strive, aim, aspire, undertake, venture, struggle, labour, take pains.
▪ *noun* attempt, effort, go (*infml*), try, shot (*infml*), stab (*infml*), undertaking, enterprise, aim, venture.

ending *noun* end, close, finish, completion, termination, conclusion, culmination, climax, resolution, consummation, dénouement, finale, epilogue.
F3 beginning, start.

endless *adjective* **1** *the endless universe*: infinite, boundless, unlimited, measureless. **2** *endless love*: everlasting, ceaseless, perpetual, constant, continual, continuous, undying, eternal, interminable, monotonous.
F3 **1** finite, limited. **2** temporary.

endorse *verb* **1** *endorse a candidate*: approve, sanction, authorize, support, back, affirm, ratify, confirm, vouch for, advocate, warrant, recommend, subscribe to, sustain, adopt. **2** *endorse a cheque*: sign, countersign.

endurance *noun* fortitude, patience, staying power, stamina, resignation, stoicism, tenacity, perseverance, resolution, stability, persistence, strength, toleration.

endure *verb* **1** *endure hardship*: bear, stand, put up with, tolerate, weather, brave, cope with, face, go through, experience, submit to, suffer, sustain, swallow, undergo, withstand, stick, stomach, allow, permit, support. **2** *a love that will endure for ever*: last, abide (*fml*), remain, live, survive, stay, persist, hold, prevail.

enemy *noun* adversary, opponent, foe (*fml*), rival, antagonist, the opposition, competitor, opposer, other side.
E3 friend, ally.

energetic *adjective* lively, vigorous, active, animated, dynamic, spirited, tireless, zestful, brisk, strong, forceful, potent, powerful, strenuous, high-powered.
E3 lethargic, sluggish, inactive, idle.

energy *noun* liveliness, vigour, activity, animation, drive, dynamism, get-up-and-go (*infml*), life, spirit, verve, vivacity, vitality, zest, zeal, ardour, fire, efficiency, force, forcefulness, zip (*infml*), strength, power, intensity, exertion, stamina.
E3 lethargy, inertia, weakness.

enforce *verb* impose, administer, implement, apply, execute, discharge, insist on, compel, oblige, urge, carry out, constrain, require, coerce, prosecute, reinforce.

engage *verb* **1** *engaging in debate*: participate, take part, embark on, take up, practise, involve. **2** *engaged by her beauty*: attract, allure, draw, captivate, charm, catch. **3** *engaging their attention*: occupy, engross, absorb, busy, tie up, grip. **4** *engage a new cook*: employ, hire, appoint, take on, enlist, enrol, commission, recruit, contract. **5** *engage first gear*: interlock, mesh, interconnect, join, interact, attach. **6** *engage the enemy*: fight, battle with, attack, take on, encounter, assail, combat.
E3 2 repel. **4** dismiss, discharge. **5** disengage.

engaged *adjective* **1** *he's engaged until 5 o'clock*: occupied, busy, engrossed, immersed, absorbed, preoccupied, involved, employed. **2** *the engaged couple*: promised, betrothed (*fml*), pledged, spoken for, committed. **3** *an engaged tone*: busy, tied up, unavailable.

engagement *noun* **1** *have several pressing engagements*: appointment, meeting, date, arrangement, assignation, fixture, rendezvous. **2** *announce their engagement*: promise, pledge, betrothal (*fml*), commitment, obligation, assurance, vow, troth (*fml*).

engaging *adjective* charming, attractive, appealing, captivating, pleasing, delightful, winsome, lovable, likable, pleasant, fetching, fascinating, agreeable.
E3 repulsive, repellent.

engine *noun* motor, machine, mechanism, appliance, contraption, apparatus, device, instrument, tool, locomotive, dynamo.

engineer *verb* plan, contrive, devise, manoeuvre, cause, manipulate, control, bring about, mastermind, originate, orchestrate, effect, plot, scheme, manage, create, rig.

engrave *verb* **1** *engrave a printing*

plate: inscribe, cut, carve, chisel, etch, chase. **2** *engraved on her mind*: imprint, impress, fix, stamp, lodge, ingrain.

engraving *noun* print, impression, inscription, carving, etching, woodcut, plate, block, cutting, chiselling, mark.

engross *verb* absorb, occupy, engage, grip, hold, preoccupy, rivet, fascinate, captivate, enthral, arrest, involve, intrigue.
bore.

enhance *verb* heighten, intensify, increase, improve, elevate, magnify, swell, exalt, raise, lift, boost, strengthen, reinforce, embellish.
reduce, minimize.

enigmatic *adjective* mysterious, puzzling, cryptic, obscure, strange, perplexing.
simple, straightforward.

enjoy *verb* **1** *enjoy dancing*: take pleasure in, delight in, appreciate, like, relish, revel in, rejoice in, savour. **2** *enjoy a benefit*: have, possess, be endowed with.
1 dislike, hate. **2** lack.

enjoyable *adjective* pleasant, agreeable, delightful, pleasing, gratifying, entertaining, amusing, fun, delicious, good, satisfying.
disagreeable.

enjoyment *noun* pleasure, delight, amusement, gratification, entertainment, relish, joy, fun, happiness, diversion, indulgence, recreation, zest, satisfaction.
displeasure.

enlarge *verb* increase, expand, augment, add to, grow, extend, magnify, inflate, swell, wax, stretch, multiply, develop, amplify, blow up, widen, broaden, lengthen, heighten, elaborate.
diminish, shrink.

enlighten *verb* instruct, edify, educate, inform, illuminate, teach, counsel, apprise, advise.
confuse.

enlightened *adjective* informed, aware, knowledgeable, educated, civilized, cultivated, refined, sophisticated, conversant (*fml*), wise, reasonable, liberal, open-minded, literate.
ignorant, confused.

enlist *verb* engage, enrol, register, sign up, recruit, conscript, employ, volunteer, join (up), gather, muster, secure, obtain, procure, enter.

enormous *adjective* huge, immense, vast, gigantic, massive, colossal, gross, gargantuan, monstrous, mammoth, jumbo (*infml*), tremendous, prodigious.
small, tiny.

enough *adjective* sufficient, adequate, ample, plenty, abundant.
▪ *noun* sufficiency, adequacy, plenty, abundance.
insufficiency.
▪ *adverb* sufficiently, adequately, reasonably, tolerably, passably, moderately, fairly, satisfactorily, amply.

enquire *see* **inquire**.

enquiry *see* **inquiry**.

enrage *verb* incense, infuriate, anger, madden, provoke, incite, inflame, exasperate, irritate, rile.
≠ calm, placate.

enrol *verb* register, enlist, sign on, sign up, join up, recruit, engage, admit.

ensemble *noun* **1** *a wedding ensemble*: outfit, costume, get-up (*infml*), rig-out (*infml*). **2** *an ensemble of singers and musicians*: group, band, company, troupe, chorus.

ensue *verb* follow, issue, proceed, succeed, result, arise, happen, turn out, befall, flow, derive, stem.
≠ precede.

ensure *verb* certify, guarantee, warrant, protect, guard, safeguard, secure.

entail *verb* involve, necessitate, occasion, require, demand, cause, give rise to, lead to, result in.

entangle *verb* enmesh, ensnare, embroil, involve, implicate, snare, tangle, entrap, trap, catch, mix up, knot, ravel, muddle.
≠ disentangle.

enter *verb* **1** *enter the room*: come in, go in, arrive, insert, introduce, board, penetrate. **2** *enter their names*: record, log, note, register, take down, inscribe. **3** *before entering university*: join, embark upon, enrol, enlist, set about, sign up, participate, commence, start, begin.
≠ **1** depart. **2** delete.

enterprise *noun* **1** *disapprove of the entire enterprise*: undertaking, venture, project, plan, effort, operation, programme, endeavour. **2** *show a lot of enterprise*: initiative, resourcefulness, drive, boldness, adventurousness, get-up-and-go (*infml*), push, energy, enthusiasm, spirit. **3** *start a new enterprise*: business, company, firm, establishment, concern.
≠ **2** apathy.

enterprising *adjective* venturesome, adventurous, bold, daring, go-ahead, imaginative, resourceful, self-reliant, enthusiastic, energetic, keen, ambitious, aspiring, spirited, active.
≠ unenterprising, lethargic.

entertain *verb* **1** *entertaining them with magic tricks*: amuse, divert, please, delight, cheer. **2** *entertaining visitors*: receive, have guests, accommodate, put up, treat. **3** *entertain hopes of promotion*: harbour, countenance, contemplate, consider, imagine, conceive.
≠ **1** bore. **3** reject.

entertaining *adjective* amusing, diverting, fun, delightful, interesting, pleasant, pleasing, humorous, witty.
≠ boring.

entertainment *noun* **1** *get their entertainment at the cinema*: amusement, diversion, recreation, enjoyment, play, pastime, fun, sport, distraction, pleasure. **2** *plan a lavish entertainment*: show, spectacle, performance, extravaganza.

Forms of entertainment include:
CD, cinema, DVD, radio, television, video; cabaret, casino, concert, dance, disco, karaoke, musical, music hall, night club, opera, pantomime, recital, revue, theatre, variety show; barbecue, carnival, circus, fair, festival, fête, firework party, gymkhana, laser show, magic show, pageant, Punch-and-Judy show, puppet show, rodeo, waxworks, zoo.

enthral *verb* captivate, entrance, enchant, fascinate, charm, beguile, thrill, intrigue, hypnotize, mesmerize, engross.
F3 bore.

enthusiast *noun* devotee, zealot, admirer, fan (*infml*), supporter, follower, buff (*infml*), freak (*infml*), fanatic, fiend (*infml*), lover.

enthusiastic *adjective* keen, ardent, eager, fervent, vehement, passionate, warm, whole-hearted, zealous, vigorous, spirited, earnest, devoted, avid, excited, exuberant.
F3 unenthusiastic, apathetic.

entice *verb* tempt, lure, attract, seduce, lead on, draw, coax, persuade, induce, sweet-talk (*infml*).

entire *adjective* complete, whole, total, full, intact, perfect.
F3 incomplete, partial.

entirely *adverb* completely, wholly, totally, fully, utterly, unreservedly, absolutely, in toto, thoroughly, altogether, perfectly, solely, exclusively, every inch.
F3 partially.

entitle *verb* **1** *entitling her to certain privileges*: authorize, qualify, empower, enable, allow, permit, license, warrant. **2** *the novel entitled 'Bleak House'*: name, call, term, title, style, christen, dub, label, designate.

entrance[1] *noun* /**en**-trans/ **1** *gain entrance to the castle*: access, admission, admittance, entry, entrée. **2** *the entrance of the United States into the war*: arrival, appearance, debut, initiation, introduction, start. **3** *the front/rear entrance*: opening, way in, door, doorway, gate.
F3 **2** departure. **3** exit.

entrance[2] *verb* /in-**trahns**/ *entrancing the audience*: charm, enchant, enrapture, captivate, bewitch, spellbind, fascinate, delight, ravish, transport, hypnotize, mesmerize.
F3 repel.

entrant *noun* **1** *entrants for the race/exam*: competitor, candidate, contestant, contender, entry, participant, player. **2** *a new entrant into the convent*: novice, beginner, newcomer, initiate, convert, probationer.

entry *noun* **1** *made a dramatic entry*: entrance, appearance, admittance, admission, access, entrée, introduction. **2** *at the entry to the building*: opening, entrance,

door, doorway, access, threshold, way in, passage, gate. **3** *an entry in his diary*: record, item, minute, note, memorandum, statement, account. **4** *a late entry into the race*: entrant, competitor, contestant, candidate, participant, player.
F3 **2** exit.

envelop *verb* /in-**vel**-op/ wrap, enfold, enwrap, encase, cover, swathe, shroud, engulf, enclose, encircle, encompass, surround, cloak, veil, blanket, conceal, obscure, hide.

envelope *noun* wrapper, wrapping, cover, case, casing, sheath, covering, shell, skin, jacket, coating.

enviable *adjective* desirable, privileged, favoured, blessed, fortunate, lucky, advantageous, sought-after, excellent, fine.
F3 unenviable.

envious *adjective* covetous, jealous, resentful, green (with envy), dissatisfied, grudging, jaundiced, green-eyed (*infml*).

environment *noun* surroundings, conditions, circumstances, milieu, atmosphere, habitat, situation, element, medium, background, ambience, setting, context, territory, domain.

envoy *noun* agent, representative, ambassador, diplomat, messenger, legate, emissary, minister, delegate, deputy, courier, intermediary.

envy *noun* covetousness, jealousy, resentfulness, resentment, dissatisfaction, grudge, ill-will, malice, spite.
▪ *verb* covet, resent, begrudge, grudge, crave.

epidemic *noun* plague, outbreak, spread, rash, upsurge, wave.

episode *noun* **1** *an unfortunate episode in her life*: incident, event, occurrence, happening, occasion, circumstance, experience, adventure, matter, business. **2** *the next episode of the soap opera*: instalment, part, chapter, passage, section, scene.

equal *adjective* **1** *of equal strength*: identical, the same, alike, like, equivalent, corresponding, commensurate, comparable. **2** *all things being equal*: even, uniform, regular, unvarying, balanced, matched. **3** *equal to the task*: competent, able, adequate, fit, capable, suitable.
F3 **1** different. **2** unequal. **3** unsuitable.
▪ *noun* peer, counterpart, equivalent, coequal, match, parallel, twin, fellow.
▪ *verb* match, parallel, correspond to, balance, square with, tally with, equalize, equate, rival, level, even.

equality *noun* **1** *demonstrating equality between the two systems*: uniformity, evenness, equivalence, correspondence, balance, parity, par, symmetry, proportion, identity, sameness, likeness. **2** *equality of treatment*:

impartiality, fairness, justice, egalitarianism.
☒ 2 inequality.
equalize *verb* level, even up, match, equal, equate, draw level, balance, square, standardize, compensate, smooth.
equip *verb* provide, fit out, supply, furnish, prepare, arm, fit up, kit out, stock, endow, rig, dress, array, deck out.
equipment *noun* apparatus, gear (*infml*), supplies, tackle, rig-out (*infml*), tools, material, furnishings, baggage, outfit, paraphernalia, stuff (*infml*), things, accessories, furniture.
equivalent *adjective* equal, same, similar, substitutable, corresponding, alike, comparable, interchangeable, even, tantamount, twin.
☒ unlike, different.
era *noun* age, epoch, period, date, day, days, time, aeon, stage, century.
erase *verb* obliterate, rub out, expunge (*fml*), delete, blot out, cancel, efface (*fml*), get rid of, remove, eradicate.
erect *adjective* upright, straight, vertical, upstanding, standing.
▪ *verb* build, construct, put up, establish, set up, elevate, assemble, found, form, institute, initiate, raise, rear, lift, mount, pitch, create.
erode *verb* wear away, eat away, wear down, corrode, abrade, consume, grind down, disintegrate, deteriorate, spoil.
erosion *noun* wear, corrosion, abrasion, attrition, denudation, disintegration, deterioration, destruction, undermining.
errand *noun* commission, charge, mission, assignment, message, task, job, duty.
erratic *adjective* changeable, variable, fitful, fluctuating, inconsistent, irregular, unstable, shifting, inconstant, unpredictable, unreliable, aberrant (*fml*), abnormal, eccentric, desultory, meandering.
☒ steady, consistent, stable.
error *noun* mistake, inaccuracy, slip, slip-up (*infml*), blunder, howler (*infml*), gaffe, faux pas, solecism (*fml*), lapse, miscalculation, misunderstanding, misconception, misapprehension, misprint, oversight, omission, fallacy, flaw, fault, wrong.
erupt *verb* break out, explode, belch, discharge, burst, gush, spout, eject, expel, emit, flare up.
eruption *noun* **1** *volcanic eruptions/a sudden eruption of violence*: outburst, discharge, ejection, emission, explosion, flare-up. **2** *a skin eruption*: rash, outbreak, inflammation.
escalate *verb* increase, intensify, grow, accelerate, rise, step up, heighten, raise, spiral, magnify, enlarge, expand, extend, mount, ascend, climb, amplify.
☒ decrease, diminish.

escapade *noun* adventure, exploit, fling, prank, caper, romp, spree, lark (*infml*), antic, stunt, trick.

escape *verb* **1** *escape from prison*: get away, break free, run away, bolt, abscond, flee, fly, decamp, break loose, break out, do a bunk (*infml*), flit, slip away, shake off, slip. **2** *escape serious injury*: avoid, evade, elude, dodge, skip, shun. **3** *gas escaping into the atmosphere*: leak, seep, flow, drain, gush, issue, discharge, ooze, trickle, pour forth, pass.

escort *noun* **1** *her escort for the evening*: companion, chaperon(e), partner, attendant, aide, squire, guide, bodyguard, protector. **2** *the king's official escort*: entourage, company, retinue, suite, train, guard, convoy, cortège.

▪ *verb* accompany, partner, chaperon(e), guide, lead, usher, conduct, guard, protect.

especially *adverb* **1** *especially in the nineteenth century*: chiefly, mainly, principally, primarily, pre-eminently, above all. **2** *especially clever*: particularly, specially, markedly, notably, exceptionally, outstandingly, expressly, supremely, uniquely, unusually, strikingly, very.

essay *noun* composition, dissertation, paper, article, assignment, thesis, piece, commentary, critique, discourse, treatise, review, leader, tract.

essence *noun* **1** *what is the essence of his style?*: nature, being, quintessence, substance, soul, spirit, core, centre, heart, meaning, quality, significance, life, entity, crux, kernel, marrow, pith, character, characteristics, attributes, principle. **2** *almond essence*: concentrate, extract, distillation, spirits.

essential *adjective* **1** *the essential message of his poem*: fundamental, basic, intrinsic, inherent, principal, main, key, characteristic, definitive, typical, constituent. **2** *an essential job*: crucial, indispensable, necessary, vital, requisite, required, needed, important.

E3 **1** incidental. **2** dispensable, inessential.

▪ *noun* necessity, prerequisite, must, requisite, sine qua non (*fml*), requirement, basic, fundamental, necessary, principle.

E3 inessential.

establish *verb* **1** *establish a colony*: set up, found, start, form, institute, create, organize, inaugurate, introduce, install, plant, settle, secure, lodge, base. **2** *establish the truth*: prove, substantiate, demonstrate, authenticate, ratify, verify, validate, certify, confirm, affirm.

E3 **1** uproot. **2** refute.

establishment *noun* **1** *the establishment of rail links*: formation, setting up, founding, creation, foundation, installation, institution, inauguration. **2** *an* *eating establishment*: business, company, firm, institute, organization, concern, institution, enterprise.

estate *noun* **1** *left his entire estate to his younger son*: possessions, effects, assets, belongings, holdings, property, goods, lands. **2** *a country estate/housing estate*: area, development, land, manor.

estimate *verb* assess, reckon, evaluate, calculate, gauge, guess, value, conjecture, consider, judge, think, number, count, compute, believe.

▪ *noun* reckoning, valuation, judgement, guess, approximation, assessment, estimation, evaluation, computation, opinion.

estimation *noun* **1** *a rough estimation of the costs involved*: judgement, opinion, belief, consideration, estimate, view, evaluation, assessment, reckoning, conception, calculation, computation. **2** *he rose in our estimation*: respect, regard, appreciation, esteem, credit.

estuary *noun* inlet, mouth, firth, fjord, creek, arm, sea loch.

eternal *adjective* **1** *eternal bliss*: unending, endless, ceaseless, everlasting, never-ending, infinite, limitless, immortal, undying, imperishable. **2** *eternal truths*: unchanging, timeless, enduring, lasting, perennial, abiding. **3** (*infml*) *eternal quarrelling*: constant, continuous, perpetual, incessant, interminable.

F3 **1** ephemeral, temporary. **2** changeable.

eternity *noun* **1** *the eternity of God*: everlastingness, endlessness, everlasting, infinity, timelessness, perpetuity, imperishability, immutability. **2** *last for an eternity*: ages, age, aeon.

ethical *adjective* moral, principled, just, right, proper, virtuous, honourable, fair, upright, righteous, seemly, honest, good, correct, commendable, fitting, noble.

F3 unethical.

ethics *noun* moral values, morality, principles, standards, code, moral philosophy, rules, beliefs, propriety, conscience, equity.

ethnic *adjective* racial, native, indigenous, traditional, tribal, folk, cultural, national, aboriginal.

etiquette *noun* code, formalities, standards, correctness, conventions, customs, protocol, rules, manners, politeness, courtesy, civility, decorum, ceremony, decency.

euphemism *noun* evasion, polite term, substitution, genteelism, politeness, understatement.

euphoria *noun* elation, ecstasy, bliss, rapture, high spirits, well-being, high (*infml*), exhilaration, exultation, joy, intoxication, jubilation, transport, glee, exaltation, enthusiasm, cheerfulness.

F3 depression, despondency.

evacuate *verb* leave, depart, withdraw, quit, remove, retire from, clear (out) (*infml*), abandon, desert, forsake, vacate, decamp, relinquish.

evade *verb* **1** *evade one's responsibilities*: elude, avoid, escape, dodge, shirk, steer clear of, shun, sidestep, duck (*infml*), balk, skive (*infml*), fend off, chicken out (*infml*), cop out (*infml*). **2** *evade a question*: equivocate, fence, prevaricate, fudge, parry, quibble, hedge.

F3 1 confront, face.

evaluate *verb* value, assess, appraise, estimate, reckon, calculate, gauge, judge, rate, size up, weigh, compute, rank.

evaporate *verb* vaporize, disappear, dematerialize, vanish, melt (away), dissolve, disperse, dispel, dissipate, fade.

evasion *noun* avoidance, escape, dodge, equivocation, excuse, prevarication, put-off, trickery, subterfuge, shirking.

F3 frankness, directness.

evasive *adjective* equivocating, indirect, prevaricating, devious, shifty (*infml*), unforthcoming, slippery (*infml*), misleading, deceitful, deceptive, cagey (*infml*), oblique, secretive, tricky, cunning.

F3 direct, frank.

eve *noun* day before, verge, brink, edge, threshold.

even *adjective* **1** *an even surface*: level, flat, smooth, horizontal, flush, parallel, plane. **2** *an even pace*: steady, unvarying, constant, regular, uniform. **3** *scores are even*: equal, balanced, matching, same, similar, like, symmetrical, fifty-fifty, level, side by side, neck and neck (*infml*).

F3 1 uneven. **3** unequal.

▪ *verb* smooth, flatten, level, match, regularize, balance, equalize, align, square, stabilize, steady, straighten.

evening *noun* nightfall, dusk, eve, eventide, twilight, sunset, sundown.

event *noun* **1** *events in history*: happening, occurrence, incident, occasion, affair, circumstance, episode, eventuality, experience, matter, case, adventure, business, fact, possibility, milestone. **2** *stage an event*: game, match, competition, contest, tournament, engagement.

eventful *adjective* busy, exciting, lively, active, full, interesting, remarkable, significant, memorable, momentous, historic, crucial, critical, notable, noteworthy, unforgettable.

F3 dull, ordinary.

eventual *adjective* final, ultimate, resulting, concluding, ensuing, future, later, subsequent, prospective, projected, planned, impending.

eventually *adverb* finally, ultimately, at last, in the end, at length, subsequently, after all, sooner or later.

ever *adverb* **1** *yours ever*: always, evermore, for ever, perpetually, constantly, at all times, continually, endlessly. **2** *don't ever do that again*: at any time, in any case, in any circumstances, at all, on any account.
F3 **1** never.

everlasting *adjective* eternal, undying, never-ending, endless, immortal, infinite, imperishable, constant, permanent, perpetual, indestructible, timeless.
F3 temporary, transient.

everybody *noun* everyone, one and all, each one, all and sundry, the whole world.

everyday *adjective* ordinary, common, commonplace, day-to-day, familiar, run-of-the-mill, regular, plain, routine, usual, workaday, common-or-garden (*infml*), normal, customary, stock, accustomed, conventional, daily, habitual, monotonous, frequent, simple, informal.
F3 unusual, exceptional, special.

everywhere *adverb* all around, all over, throughout, far and near, far and wide, high and low, left, right and centre (*infml*).

evidence *noun* **1** *the evidence of his own eyes/written evidence*: proof, verification, confirmation, affirmation, grounds, substantiation, documentation, data. **2** *give evidence in court*: testimony, declaration. **3** *evidence of water on Mars*: indication, manifestation, suggestion, sign, mark, hint, demonstration, token.

evident *adjective* clear, obvious, manifest, apparent, plain, patent, visible, conspicuous, noticeable, clear-cut, unmistakable, perceptible, distinct, discernible, tangible, incontestable, indisputable, incontrovertible.

evil *adjective* **1** *an evil dictator*: wicked, wrong, sinful, bad, immoral, vicious, vile, malevolent, iniquitous, cruel, base, corrupt, heinous (*fml*), malicious, malignant, devilish, depraved, mischievous, satanic. **2** *an evil influence*: harmful, pernicious, destructive, deadly, detrimental, hurtful, poisonous. **3** *come the evil day*: disastrous, ruinous, calamitous, catastrophic, adverse, dire, inauspicious. **4** *an evil smell*: offensive, noxious, foul.
▪ *noun* **1** *do evil*: wickedness, wrongdoing, wrong, immorality, badness, sin, sinfulness, vice, viciousness, iniquity (*fml*), depravity, baseness, corruption, malignity, mischief, heinousness. **2** *deliver us from evil*: adversity, affliction, calamity, disaster, misfortune, suffering, sorrow, ruin, catastrophe, blow, curse, distress, hurt, harm, ill, injury, misery, woe.

evolve *verb* develop, grow, increase, mature, progress, unravel, expand, enlarge, emerge, descend, derive, result, elaborate.

exact *adjective* **1** *an exact amount/account*: precise, accurate, correct, faithful, literal, flawless, faultless, right, true, veracious (*fml*), definite, explicit, detailed, specific, strict, unerring, close, factual, identical, express, word-perfect, blow-by-blow (*infml*). **2** *she's very exact*: careful, scrupulous, particular, rigorous, methodical, meticulous, orderly, painstaking.

F **1** inexact, imprecise.

exacting *adjective* demanding, difficult, hard, laborious, arduous, rigorous, taxing, tough, harsh, painstaking, severe, strict, unsparing.

F easy.

exactly *adverb* **1** *at two o'clock exactly/copy it exactly*: precisely, accurately, literally, faithfully, correctly, specifically, rigorously, scrupulously, veraciously, verbatim, carefully, faultlessly, unerringly, strictly, to the letter, particularly, methodically, explicitly, expressly, dead (*infml*). **2** *exactly so*: absolutely, definitely, precisely, indeed, certainly, truly, quite, just, unequivocally.

F **1** inaccurately, roughly.

exaggerate *verb* overstate, overdo, magnify, overemphasize, emphasize, embellish, embroider, enlarge, amplify, oversell, pile it on (*infml*).

F understate.

examination *noun* **1** *examination of the evidence*: inspection, enquiry, scrutiny, study, survey, search, analysis, exploration, investigation, probe, appraisal, observation, research, review, scan, once-over (*infml*), perusal, check, check-up, audit, critique. **2** *a French examination*: test, exam, quiz, questioning, cross-examination, cross-questioning, trial, inquisition, interrogation, viva.

examine *verb* **1** *examine the body*: inspect, investigate, scrutinize, study, survey, analyse, explore, enquire, consider, probe, review, scan, check (out), ponder, pore over, sift, vet, weigh up, appraise, assay, audit, peruse, case (*slang*). **2** *examining them on their knowledge of anatomy*: test, quiz, question, cross-examine, cross-question, interrogate, grill (*infml*), catechize (*fml*).

example *noun* instance, case, case in point, illustration, exemplification, sample, specimen, model, pattern, ideal, archetype, prototype, standard, type, lesson, citation.

exasperate *verb* infuriate, annoy, anger, incense, irritate, madden, provoke, get on someone's nerves, enrage, irk, rile, rankle, rouse, get to (*infml*), goad, vex.

F appease, pacify.

exceed *verb* surpass, outdo, outstrip, beat, better, pass, overtake, top, outshine, eclipse, outreach, outrun, transcend, cap, overdo, overstep.

excel *verb* **1** *excelling all previous records*: surpass, outdo, beat, outclass, outperform, outrank, eclipse, better. **2** *excel at sports*: be excellent, succeed, shine, stand out, predominate.

excellence *noun* superiority, pre-eminence, distinction, merit, supremacy, quality, worth, fineness, eminence, goodness, greatness, virtue, perfection, purity.

excellent *adjective* superior, first-class, first-rate, prime, superlative, unequalled, outstanding, surpassing, remarkable, distinguished, great (*infml*), good, exemplary, select, superb, admirable, commendable, top-notch (*infml*), splendid, noteworthy, notable, fine, wonderful, worthy.
E3 inferior, second-rate.

except *preposition* excepting, but, apart from, other than, save, omitting, not counting, leaving out, excluding, except for, besides, bar, minus, less.

exception *noun* oddity, anomaly, deviation, rarity, abnormality, irregularity, peculiarity, inconsistency, special case, quirk.

exceptional *adjective* **1** *this case is exceptional*: abnormal, unusual, anomalous, strange, odd, irregular, extraordinary, peculiar, special, rare, uncommon. **2** *an exceptional violinist*: outstanding, remarkable, phenomenal, prodigious, notable, noteworthy, superior, unequalled, marvellous.
E3 **1** normal. **2** mediocre.

excerpt *noun* extract, passage, portion, section, selection, quote, quotation, part, citation, scrap, fragment.

excess *noun* **1** *an excess of energy*: surfeit, overabundance, glut, plethora, superfluity, superabundance, surplus, overflow, overkill, remainder, left-over. **2** *the excesses of the imperial court*: overindulgence, dissipation (*fml*), immoderateness, intemperance, extravagance, unrestraint, debauchery.
E3 **1** deficiency. **2** restraint.
▪ *adjective* extra, surplus, spare, redundant, remaining, residual, left-over, additional, superfluous, supernumerary.
E3 inadequate.

excessive *adjective* immoderate, inordinate, extreme, undue, uncalled-for, disproportionate, unnecessary, unneeded, superfluous, unreasonable, exorbitant, extravagant, steep (*infml*).
E3 insufficient.

exchange *verb* barter, change, trade, swap, switch, replace, interchange, convert, commute, substitute, reciprocate, bargain, bandy.
▪ *noun* **1** *the exchange of vows*: switch, interchange, swap, replacement, substitution, reciprocity. **2** *currency exchange*: trade, commerce, dealing, market, traffic, barter, bargain.

excitable *adjective* temperamental, volatile,

passionate, emotional, highly-strung, fiery, hot-headed, hasty, nervous, hot-tempered, irascible, quick-tempered, sensitive, susceptible.
F3 calm, stable.

excite *verb* **1** *excites the emotions*: move, agitate, disturb, upset, touch, stir up, thrill, elate, turn on (*infml*), impress. **2** *exciting a response*: arouse, rouse, animate, awaken, fire, inflame, kindle, motivate, stimulate, engender, inspire, instigate, incite, induce, ignite, galvanize, generate, provoke, sway, quicken (*fml*), evoke.
F3 **1** calm.

excited *adjective* aroused, roused, stimulated, stirred, thrilled, elated, enthusiastic, eager, moved, high (*infml*), worked up, wrought-up, overwrought, restless, frantic, frenzied, wild.
F3 calm, apathetic.

exciting *adjective* stimulating, stirring, intoxicating, exhilarating, thrilling, rousing, moving, enthralling, electrifying, nail-biting (*infml*), cliff-hanging (*infml*), striking, sensational, provocative, inspiring, interesting.
F3 dull, unexciting.

exclaim *verb* cry (out), declare, blurt (out), call, yell, shout, proclaim, utter.

exclude *verb* **1** *excluding VAT*: omit, leave out, disallow, refuse, reject, ignore, rule out, eliminate. **2** *excluding them from school*: expel, eject, evict, excommunicate, ban, bar, keep out, shut out, prohibit, veto, proscribe, forbid, blacklist, ostracize.
F3 **1** include. **2** admit.

exclusive *adjective* **1** *the exclusive right*: sole, single, unique, only, undivided, unshared, whole, total, peculiar. **2** *an exclusive restaurant*: restricted, limited, closed, private, narrow, restrictive, choice, select, cliquey, discriminative, chic, classy (*infml*), elegant, fashionable, posh (*infml*), snobbish.

excuse *verb* /eks-**kyooz**/ **1** *can't excuse such behaviour*: forgive, pardon, overlook, absolve, acquit, exonerate, tolerate, ignore, indulge. **2** *excusing him from games*: release, free, discharge, liberate, let off, relieve, spare, exempt.
F3 **1** criticize. **2** punish.
▪ *noun* /eks-**kyoos**/ justification, explanation, grounds, defence, plea, alibi, reason, apology, pretext, pretence, exoneration, evasion, cop-out (*infml*).

execute *verb* **1** *executed the murderer*: put to death, kill, liquidate, hang, electrocute, shoot, guillotine, decapitate, behead. **2** *execute a command*: carry out, do, perform, accomplish, achieve, fulfil, complete, discharge, effect, sign, enact, deliver, enforce, finish, render, serve, implement, administer, consummate, realize, dispatch, expedite, validate.

executive *noun* **1** *a decision by the executive*: administration, management, government, leadership, hierarchy. **2** *the chief executive*: administrator, manager, organizer, leader, controller, director, governor, official.
▪ *adjective* administrative, managerial, controlling, supervisory, regulating, decision-making, governing, organizing, directing, directorial, organizational, leading, guiding.

exemplify *verb* illustrate, demonstrate, show, instance, represent, typify, manifest, embody, epitomize, exhibit, depict, display.

exempt *verb* excuse, release, relieve, let off, free, absolve, discharge, dismiss, liberate, spare.
▪ *adjective* excused, not liable, immune, released, spared, absolved, discharged, excluded, free, liberated, clear.
F3 liable.

exercise *verb* **1** *exercise a bit of self-control*: use, utilize, employ, apply, exert, practise, wield, try, discharge. **2** *must exercise regularly*: train, drill, work out (*infml*), keep fit.
▪ *noun* **1** *a military exercise/violin exercises*: training, drill, practice, task, lesson, work, discipline. **2** *take regular exercise/do one's exercises*: activity, physical jerks (*infml*), work-out (*infml*), aerobics, labour.

exert *verb* use, utilize, employ, apply, exercise, bring to bear, wield, expend.

exertion *noun* effort, industry, labour, toil, work, struggle, diligence, assiduousness (*fml*), perseverance, pains, endeavour, attempt, strain, travail (*fml*), trial.
F3 idleness, rest.

exhaust *verb* **1** *exhaust the supply of oxygen*: consume, empty, deplete, drain, sap, spend, waste, squander, dissipate, impoverish, use up, finish, dry, bankrupt. **2** *exhausting himself*: tire (out), weary, fatigue, tax, strain, weaken, overwork, wear out.
F3 1 renew. **2** refresh.
▪ *noun* emission, exhalation, discharge, fumes.

exhausted *adjective* **1** *exhausted by the climb*: tired (out), dead tired, dead-beat (*infml*), all in (*infml*), done (in) (*infml*), fatigued, weak, washed-out, whacked (*infml*). **2** *the mine/supply is exhausted*: empty, finished, depleted, spent, used up, drained, dry, worn out, void.
F3 1 fresh, vigorous.

exhausting *adjective* tiring, strenuous, taxing, gruelling, arduous, hard, laborious, backbreaking, draining, severe, testing, punishing, formidable, debilitating.
F3 refreshing.

exhaustion *noun* fatigue, tiredness, weariness, debility, feebleness, jet-lag.

F3 freshness, liveliness.

exhaustive *adjective* comprehensive, all-embracing, all-inclusive, far-reaching, complete, extensive, encyclopedic, full-scale, thorough, full, in-depth, intensive, detailed, definitive, all-out, sweeping.
F3 incomplete, restricted.

exhibit *verb* display, show, present, demonstrate, manifest, expose, parade, reveal, express, disclose, indicate, air, flaunt, offer.
F3 conceal.
▪ *noun* display, exhibition, show, illustration, model.

exhibition *noun* display, show, demonstration, exhibit, presentation, manifestation, spectacle, exposition, expo (*infml*), showing, fair, performance, airing, representation, showcase.

exile *noun* **1** *in exile/the exile of Napoleon to Elba*: banishment, deportation, expatriation, expulsion, ostracism, transportation. **2** *an exile from his homeland*: expatriate, refugee, émigré, deportee, outcast.
▪ *verb* banish, expel, deport, expatriate, drive out, ostracize, oust.

exist *verb* **1** *existing on the surface of the planet*: be, live, abide (*fml*), continue, endure, have one's being, breathe, prevail. **2** *exist on a diet of rice*: subsist, survive.

existence *noun* **1** *man's existence*: being, life, reality, actuality, continuance, continuation, endurance, survival, breath, subsistence. **2** *throughout existence*: creation, the world.
F3 **1** death, non-existence.

exit *noun* **1** *make a rapid exit*: departure, going, retreat, withdrawal, leave-taking, retirement, farewell, exodus. **2** *leave by a side exit*: door, way out, doorway, gate, vent.
F3 **1** entrance, arrival. **2** entrance.

exotic *adjective* **1** *an exotic holiday/exotic fruits*: foreign, alien, imported, introduced. **2** *an exotic mixture*: unusual, striking, different, unfamiliar, extraordinary, bizarre, curious, strange, fascinating, colourful, peculiar, outlandish.
F3 **1** native. **2** ordinary.

expand *verb* **1** *expand the boundaries of knowledge*: stretch, swell, widen, lengthen, thicken, magnify, multiply, inflate, broaden, blow up, open out, fill out, fatten. **2** *the universe is expanding/expanding the company*: increase, grow, extend, enlarge, develop, amplify, spread, branch out, diversify, elaborate.
F3 **1** contract.

expanse *noun* extent, space, area, breadth, range, stretch, sweep, field, plain, tract.

expect *verb* **1** *expect the money soon*: anticipate, await, look forward to, hope for, look for, bank on, bargain for, envisage, predict, forecast, contemplate, project, foresee. **2** *expect you to comply*: require, want, wish, insist on, demand, rely on, count on. **3** *expect you're right*: suppose, surmise, assume, believe, think, presume, imagine, reckon, guess (*infml*), trust.

expectant *adjective* **1** *an expectant silence*: awaiting, anticipating, hopeful, in suspense, ready, apprehensive, anxious, watchful, eager, curious. **2** *an expectant mother*: pregnant, expecting (*infml*), with child (*fml*).

expedition *noun* journey, excursion, trip, voyage, tour, exploration, trek, safari, hike, sail, ramble, raid, quest, pilgrimage, mission, crusade.

expel *verb* **1** *expelling the invaders/expel them from school*: drive out, eject, evict, banish, throw out, ban, bar, oust, exile, expatriate. **2** *expelling waste into the sea*: discharge, evacuate, void, cast out.

expend *verb* **1** *expending precious energy*: consume, use (up), dissipate, exhaust, employ. **2** *expending many thousands of dollars*: spend, pay, disburse (*fml*), fork out (*infml*).

1 conserve. **2** save.

expenditure *noun* spending, expense, outlay, outgoings, disbursement (*fml*), payment, output.

income.

expense *noun* spending, expenditure, disbursement (*fml*), outlay, payment, loss, cost, charge.

expensive *adjective* dear, high-priced, costly, exorbitant, extortionate, steep (*infml*), extravagant, lavish.

cheap, inexpensive.

experience *noun* **1** *have some experience of children*: knowledge, familiarity, know-how, involvement, participation, practice, understanding. **2** *an interesting experience*: incident, event, episode, happening, encounter, occurrence, adventure.

1 inexperience.

▪ *verb* undergo, go through, live through, suffer, feel, endure, encounter, face, meet, know, try, perceive, sustain.

experienced *adjective* **1** *an experienced teacher*: practised, knowledgeable, familiar, capable, competent, well-versed, expert, accomplished, qualified, skilled, tried, trained, professional. **2** *an experienced soldier*: seasoned, wise, veteran.

1 inexperienced, unskilled.

experiment *noun* trial, test, investigation, experimentation, research, examination, trial run, venture, trial and error, attempt, procedure, proof.

▪ *verb* try, test, investigate, examine, research, sample, verify.

experimental *adjective* trial, test, exploratory, empirical, tentative, provisional, speculative, pilot, preliminary, trial-and-error.

expert *noun* specialist, connoisseur, authority, professional, pro (*infml*), dab hand (*infml*), maestro, virtuoso.
▪ *adjective* proficient, adept, skilled, skilful, knowledgeable, experienced, able, practised, professional, masterly, specialist, qualified, virtuoso.
F3 amateurish, novice.

expertise *noun* expertness, proficiency, skill, skilfulness, know-how, knack (*infml*), knowledge, mastery, dexterity, virtuosity.
F3 inexperience.

explain *verb* **1** *explaining his theory*: interpret, clarify, describe, define, make clear, elucidate, simplify, resolve, solve, spell out, translate, unfold, unravel, untangle, illustrate, demonstrate, disclose, expound, teach. **2** *explain yourself*: justify, excuse, account for, rationalize.
F3 1 obscure, confound.

explanatory *adjective* descriptive, interpretive, explicative, demonstrative, expository (*fml*), justifying.

explicit *adjective* **1** *give explicit instructions*: clear, distinct, exact, categorical, absolute, certain, positive, precise, specific, unambiguous, express, definite, declared, detailed, stated. **2** *an explicit portrayal*: open, direct, frank, outspoken, straightforward, unreserved, plain.
F3 1 implicit, unspoken, vague.

explode *verb* **1** *exploding a bomb*: blow up, burst, go off, set off, detonate, discharge, blast, erupt. **2** *explode the myth*: discredit, disprove, give the lie to, debunk, invalidate, refute, rebut, repudiate.
F3 2 prove, confirm.

exploit *noun* deed, feat, adventure, achievement, accomplishment, attainment, stunt.
▪ *verb* **1** *exploit an opportunity*: use, utilize, capitalize on, profit by, turn to account, take advantage of, cash in on, make capital out of. **2** *exploiting children*: misuse, abuse, oppress, ill-treat, impose on, manipulate, rip off (*infml*), fleece (*infml*).

explore *verb* **1** *explore the possibilities*: investigate, examine, inspect, research, scrutinize, probe, analyse. **2** *exploring the island*: travel, tour, search, reconnoitre, prospect, scout, survey.

explosion *noun* detonation, blast, burst, outburst, discharge, eruption, bang, outbreak, clap, crack, fit, report.

explosive *adjective* unstable, volatile, sensitive, tense, fraught, charged, touchy, overwrought, dangerous, hazardous, perilous, stormy.
F3 stable, calm.

expose *verb* reveal, show, exhibit,

display, disclose, uncover, bring to light, present, manifest, detect, divulge, unveil, unmask, denounce.
F3 conceal.

exposed *adjective* bare, open, revealed, laid bare, unprotected, vulnerable, exhibited, on display, on show, on view, shown, susceptible.
F3 covered, sheltered.

express *verb* **1** *expressing himself clearly*: articulate, verbalize, utter, voice, say, speak, state, communicate, pronounce, tell, assert, declare, put across, formulate, intimate, testify, convey. **2** *expressing disapproval*: show, manifest, exhibit, disclose, divulge, reveal, indicate, denote, depict, embody. **3** *expressing the horrors of war*: symbolize, stand for, represent, signify, designate.
▪ *adjective* **1** *against his express wishes*: specific, explicit, exact, definite, clear, categorical, precise, distinct, clear-cut, certain, plain, manifest, particular, stated, unambiguous. **2** *an express train*: fast, speedy, rapid, quick, high-speed, non-stop.
F3 1 vague.

expression *noun* **1** *a puzzled expression*: look, air, aspect, countenance, appearance, mien (*fml*). **2** *the artist's expression of emotion*: representation, manifestation, demonstration, indication, exhibition, embodiment, show, sign, symbol, style. **3** *a clear expression of his wishes*: utterance, verbalization, communication, articulation, statement, assertion, announcement, declaration, pronouncement, speech. **4** *put some expression into your voice*: tone, intonation, delivery, diction, enunciation, modulation. **5** *a Scottish expression*: phrase, term, turn of phrase, saying, set phrase, idiom.

expressionless *adjective* dull, blank, dead-pan, impassive, straight-faced, poker-faced (*infml*), inscrutable, empty, vacuous, glassy.
F3 expressive.

expressive *adjective* eloquent, meaningful, forceful, telling, revealing, informative, indicative, communicative, demonstrative, emphatic, moving, poignant, lively, striking, suggestive, significant, thoughtful, vivid, sympathetic.

expulsion *noun* ejection, eviction, exile, banishment, removal, discharge, exclusion, dismissal.

exquisite *adjective* **1** *an exquisite collection of jade ornaments*: beautiful, attractive, dainty, delicate, charming, elegant, delightful, lovely, pleasing. **2** *an exquisite emerald*: perfect, flawless, fine, excellent, choice, precious, rare, outstanding. **3** *exquisite taste*: refined, discriminating, meticulous, sensitive, impeccable. **4** *the pain was exquisite*: intense, keen, sharp, poignant.

≠ **1** ugly. **2** flawed. **3** unrefined.

extend *verb* **1** *extending to fifty acres*: spread, stretch, reach, continue. **2** *extending his power*: enlarge, increase, expand, develop, amplify, lengthen, widen, elongate, draw out, protract, prolong, spin out, unwind.

≠ **2** contract, shorten.

extension *noun* **1** *extension of the empire*: enlargement, increase, stretching, broadening, widening, lengthening, expansion, elongation, development, enhancement, protraction, continuation. **2** *an extension to the house*: addition, supplement, appendix, annexe, addendum (*fml*). **3** *ask for an extension*: delay, postponement.

extensive *adjective* **1** *an extensive review*: broad, comprehensive, far-reaching, large-scale, thorough, widespread, universal, extended, all-inclusive, general, pervasive, prevalent. **2** *an extensive building*: large, huge, roomy, spacious, vast.

≠ **1** restricted, narrow. **2** small.

extent *noun* **1** *the extent of the universe*: dimension(s), amount, magnitude, expanse, size, area, bulk, degree, breadth, quantity, spread, stretch, volume, width, measure, duration, term, time. **2** *the extent of his knowledge*: limit, bounds, lengths, range, reach, scope, compass, sphere, play, sweep.

exterior *noun* outside, surface, covering, coating, face, façade, shell, skin, finish, externals, appearance.

≠ inside, interior.

▪ *adjective* outer, outside, outermost, surface, external, superficial, surrounding, outward, peripheral, extrinsic.

≠ inside, interior.

exterminate *verb* annihilate, eradicate, destroy, eliminate, massacre, abolish, wipe out.

external *adjective* outer, surface, outside, exterior, superficial, outward, outermost, apparent, visible, extraneous, extrinsic, extramural, independent.

≠ internal.

extinct *adjective* **1** *dinosaurs became extinct*: defunct, dead, gone, obsolete, ended, exterminated, terminated, vanished, lost, abolished. **2** *extinct volcano*: extinguished, quenched, inactive, out.

≠ **1** living.

extinguish *verb* **1** *extinguished the flames*: put out, blow out, snuff out, stifle, smother, douse, quench. **2** *extinguishing all life*: annihilate, exterminate, eliminate, destroy, kill, eradicate, erase, expunge (*fml*), abolish, remove, end, suppress.

extra *adjective* **1** *an extra room*: additional, added, auxiliary, supplementary, new, more, further,

ancillary, fresh, other. **2** *have no extra time to spare*: excess, spare, superfluous, supernumerary, surplus, unused, unneeded, leftover, reserve, redundant.
F3 1 integral. **2** essential.
▪ *noun* addition, supplement, extension, accessory, appendage, bonus, complement, adjunct, addendum (*fml*), attachment.
▪ *adverb* especially, exceptionally, remarkably, extraordinarily, particularly, unusually, extremely.

extract *verb* /eks-**trakt**/ **1** *extract a tooth*: remove, take out, draw out, exact, uproot, withdraw. **2** *extract some benefit*: derive, draw, distil, obtain, get, gather, glean, wrest (*fml*), wring, elicit.
F3 1 insert.
▪ *noun* /**eks**-trakt/ **1** *lime extract*: distillation, essence, juice. **2** *an extract from the play*: excerpt, passage, selection, clip, cutting, quotation, abstract, citation.

extraordinary *adjective* remarkable, unusual, exceptional, notable, noteworthy, outstanding, unique, special, strange, peculiar, rare, surprising, amazing, wonderful, unprecedented, marvellous, fantastic, significant, particular.
F3 commonplace, ordinary.

extravagant *adjective* **1** *extravagant lifestyle*: profligate, prodigal, spendthrift, thriftless, wasteful, reckless. **2** *extravagant behaviour*: immoderate, flamboyant, preposterous, outrageous, ostentatious, pretentious, lavish, ornate, flashy (*infml*), fanciful, fantastic, wild. **3** *charge extravagant prices*: exorbitant, expensive, excessive, costly.
F3 1 thrifty. **2** moderate. **3** reasonable.

extreme *adjective* **1** *extreme cold*: intense, great, immoderate, inordinate, utmost, utter, out-and-out, maximum, acute, downright, extraordinary, exceptional, greatest, highest, unreasonable, remarkable. **2** *the extreme corners of the universe*: farthest, far-off, faraway, distant, endmost, outermost, remotest, uttermost, final, last, terminal, ultimate. **3** *extreme views*: radical, zealous, extremist, fanatical. **4** *extreme punishment*: drastic, dire, uncompromising, stern, strict, rigid, severe, harsh.
F3 1 mild. **3** moderate.
▪ *noun* extremity, limit, maximum, ultimate, utmost, excess, top, pinnacle, peak, height, end, climax, depth, edge, termination.

eye *noun* **1** *an eye for a bargain*: appreciation, discrimination, discernment, perception, recognition. **2** *it looks odd to my eye*: viewpoint, opinion, judgement, mind.
▪ *verb* look at, watch, regard, observe, stare at, gaze at, glance at, view, scrutinize, scan, examine, peruse, study, survey, inspect, contemplate.

fable *noun* allegory, parable, story, tale, yarn, myth, legend, fiction, fabrication, invention, lie, untruth, falsehood, tall story, old wives' tale.

fabric *noun* **1** *a cotton fabric*: cloth, material, textile, stuff, web, texture. **2** *the fabric of society*: structure, framework, construction, make-up, constitution, organization, infrastructure, foundations.

fabulous *adjective* **1** *a fabulous holiday*: wonderful, marvellous, fantastic (*infml*), superb, breathtaking, spectacular, phenomenal, amazing, astounding, unbelievable, incredible, inconceivable, terrific (*infml*), cool (*infml*). **2** *a fabulous beast*: mythical, legendary, fabled, fantastic, fictitious, invented, imaginary.
E3 **2** real.

face *noun* **1** *a pretty face*: features, countenance, visage, physiognomy. **2** *modern farming has changed the face of the countryside*: look, appearance, expression, air. **3** *a building with a face of white marble*: exterior, outside, surface, cover, front, façade, aspect, side.
▪ *verb* **1** *facing south/the river*: be opposite, give on to, front, overlook. **2** *face danger*: confront, face up to, deal with, cope with, tackle, brave, defy, oppose, encounter, meet, experience.

facet *noun* surface, plane, side, face, aspect, angle, point, feature, characteristic.

facetious *adjective* flippant, frivolous, playful, jocular, jesting, tongue-in-cheek, funny, amusing, humorous, comical, witty.
E3 serious.

facilities *noun* amenities, services, conveniences, resources, prerequisites, equipment, mod cons (*infml*), means, opportunities.

fact *noun* **1** *facts and figures*: information, datum, detail, particular, specific, point, item, circumstance, event, incident, occurrence, happening, act, deed, fait accompli. **2** *the fact of the matter*: reality, actuality, truth.
E3 **2** fiction.

factor *noun* cause, influence, circumstance, contingency, consideration, element, ingredient, component, part, point, aspect, fact, item, detail.

factual *adjective* true, historical, actual, real, genuine, authentic, correct, accurate, precise, exact, literal, faithful, close, detailed, unbiased, objective.
F3 false, fictitious, imaginary, fictional.

fad *noun* craze, rage (*infml*), mania, fashion, mode, vogue, trend, whim, fancy, affectation.

fade *verb* **1** *fade in the strong sunlight*: discolour, bleach, blanch, blench, pale, whiten, dim, dull. **2** *fade into obscurity*: decline, fall, diminish, dwindle, ebb, wane, disappear, vanish, flag, weaken, droop, wilt, wither, shrivel, perish, die.

fail *verb* **1** *the plot failed/fail an exam/his business failed*: go wrong, miscarry, misfire, flop, miss, flunk (*infml*), fall through, come to grief, collapse, fold (*infml*), go bankrupt, go bust (*infml*), go under, founder, sink, decline, fall, weaken, dwindle, fade, wane, peter out, cease, die. **2** *fail to pay the bill*: omit, neglect, forget. **3** *failed her parents*: let down, disappoint, leave, desert, abandon, forsake.
F3 1 succeed, prosper.

failing *noun* weakness, foible, fault, defect, imperfection, flaw, blemish, drawback, deficiency, shortcoming, failure, lapse, error.
F3 strength, advantage.

failure *noun* **1** *the play was a failure*: flop, wash-out (*infml*), fiasco, disappointment. **2** *the failure of his business*: loss, defeat, downfall, decline, decay, deterioration, ruin, bankruptcy, crash, collapse, breakdown, stoppage. **3** *a failure of the system*: failing, shortcoming, deficiency.
F3 1 success. **2** prosperity.

faint *adjective* **1** *a faint line/sound/light*: slight, weak, feeble, soft, low, hushed, muffled, subdued, faded, bleached, light, pale, dull, dim, hazy, indistinct, vague. **2** *feel faint*: dizzy, giddy, woozy (*infml*), light-headed, weak, feeble, exhausted.
F3 1 strong, clear.
▪ *verb* black out, pass out, swoon, collapse, flake out (*infml*), keel over (*infml*), drop.
▪ *noun* blackout, swoon, collapse, unconsciousness.

fair[1] *adjective* **1** *a fair contest/assessment/man*: just, equitable, square, even-handed, dispassionate, impartial, objective, disinterested, unbiased, unprejudiced, right, proper, lawful, legitimate, honest, trustworthy, upright, honourable. **2** *he's not dark, he's fair*: fair-haired, fair-headed, blond(e), light. **3** *fair weather*: fine, dry, sunny, bright, clear, cloudless, unclouded. **4** *not good, but fair*: average, moderate, middling, not bad, all right, OK (*infml*), satisfactory, adequate, acceptable, tolerable, reasonable, passable, mediocre, so-so (*infml*).
F3 1 unfair. **2** dark. **3** inclement, cloudy. **4** excellent, poor.

fair[2] *noun* show, exhibition, exposition, expo (*infml*), market, bazaar, fête, festival, carnival, gala.

faith *noun* **1** *faith in himself*: belief, credit, trust, reliance, dependence, conviction, confidence, assurance. **2** *people of many faiths*: religion, denomination, persuasion, church, creed, dogma. **3** *in good faith*: faithfulness, fidelity, loyalty, allegiance, honour, sincerity, honesty, truthfulness.

⇄ **1** mistrust. **3** unfaithfulness, treachery.

faithful *adjective* **1** *a faithful companion*: loyal, devoted, staunch, steadfast, constant, trusty, reliable, dependable, true. **2** *a faithful copy*: accurate, precise, exact, strict, close, true, truthful.

⇄ **1** disloyal, treacherous. **2** inaccurate, vague.

fake *noun* forgery, copy, reproduction, replica, imitation, simulation, sham, hoax, fraud, phoney (*infml*), impostor, charlatan.

▪ *adjective* forged, counterfeit, false, spurious, phoney (*infml*), pseudo, bogus, assumed, affected, sham, artificial, simulated, mock, imitation, reproduction.

⇄ genuine.

▪ *verb* forge, fabricate, counterfeit, copy, imitate, simulate, feign, sham, pretend, put on, affect, assume.

fall *verb* **1** *fell to earth/fell from a great height*: descend, go down, drop, slope, incline, slide, sink, dive, plunge, plummet, nose-dive. **2** *she fell and broke her wrist*: tumble, stumble, trip, topple, keel over, collapse, slump, crash. **3** *crime rate is falling*: decrease, lessen, decline, diminish, dwindle, fall off, subside.

⇄ **2** rise. **3** increase.

▪ *noun* **1** *have a fall/a fall in prices*: tumble, descent, slope, incline, dive, plunge, decrease, reduction, lessening, drop, decline, dwindling, slump, crash. **2** *the fall of Rome*: defeat, conquest, overthrow, downfall, collapse, surrender, capitulation.

false *adjective* **1** *a false assumption*: wrong, incorrect, mistaken, erroneous, inaccurate, invalid, inexact, misleading, faulty, fallacious. **2** *false eyelashes/a false name*: unreal, artificial, synthetic, imitation, simulated, mock, fake, counterfeit, forged, feigned, pretended, sham, bogus, assumed, fictitious. **3** *be false to one's principles*: disloyal, unfaithful, faithless, lying, deceitful, insincere, hypocritical, two-faced, double-dealing, treacherous, unreliable.

⇄ **1** true, right. **2** real, genuine. **3** faithful, reliable.

falsify *verb* alter, cook (*infml*), tamper with, doctor, distort, pervert, misrepresent, misstate, forge, counterfeit, fake.

falter *verb* totter, stumble,

stammer, stutter, hesitate, waver, vacillate, flinch, quail, shake, tremble, flag, fail.

fame *noun* renown, celebrity, stardom, prominence, eminence, illustriousness, glory, honour, esteem, reputation, name.
F3 infamy.

familiar *adjective* **1** *a familiar sight*: everyday, routine, household, common, ordinary, well-known, recognizable. **2** *don't like to get too familiar with clients*: intimate, close, confidential, friendly, informal, free, free-and-easy, relaxed. **3** *familiar with the procedure*: aware, acquainted, abreast, knowledgeable, versed, conversant (*fml*).
F3 1 unfamiliar, strange. **2** formal, reserved. **3** unfamiliar, ignorant.

familiarity *noun* **1** *a relaxed familiarity among friends*: intimacy, liberty, closeness, friendliness, sociability, openness, naturalness, informality. **2** *familiarity with the procedures*: awareness, acquaintance, experience, knowledge, understanding, grasp.

familiarize *verb* accustom, acclimatize, school, train, coach, instruct, prime, brief.

family *noun* **1** *her close family*: relatives, relations, kin, kindred, kinsmen, people, folk (*infml*), ancestors, forebears, children, offspring, issue, progeny (*fml*), descendants. **2** *a family of aristocrats*: clan, tribe, race, dynasty, house, pedigree, ancestry, parentage, descent, line, lineage, extraction, blood, stock, birth.

Members of a family include:
ancestor, forebear, forefather, descendant, offspring, heir; husband, wife, spouse, parent, father, dad (*infml*), daddy (*infml*), old man (*infml*), mother, mum (*infml*), mummy (*infml*), mom (*US infml*), grandparent, grandfather, grandmother, granny (*infml*), nanny (*infml*), grandchild, son, daughter, brother, half-brother, sister, half-sister, sibling, uncle, aunt, nephew, niece, cousin, stepfather, stepmother, foster-parent, foster-child.

---

famine *noun* starvation, hunger, destitution, want, scarcity, death.
F3 plenty.

famous *adjective* well-known, famed, renowned, celebrated, noted, great, distinguished, illustrious, eminent, honoured, acclaimed, glorious, legendary, remarkable, notable, prominent, signal.
F3 unheard-of, unknown, obscure.

fan[1] *noun* extractor fan, ventilator, air-conditioner, blower, propeller, vane.
▪ *verb* cool, ventilate, air, air-condition, air-cool, blow, refresh.

fan[2] *noun* enthusiast, admirer, supporter, follower, adherent, devotee, lover, buff (*infml*), fiend (*infml*), freak (*infml*).

fanatic *noun* zealot, devotee, enthusiast, addict, fiend (*infml*), freak (*infml*), maniac, visionary, bigot, extremist, militant, activist.

fanatical *adjective* overenthusiastic, extreme, passionate, zealous, fervent, burning, mad, wild, frenzied, rabid, obsessive, single-minded, bigoted, visionary.
F∃ moderate, unenthusiastic.

fanciful *adjective* imaginary, mythical, fabulous, fantastic, visionary, romantic, fairy-tale, airy-fairy, vaporous, whimsical, wild, extravagant, curious.
F∃ real, ordinary.

fancy *verb* **1** *fancy a nice piece of cheese*: like, be attracted to, take a liking to, take to, go for, prefer, favour, desire, wish for, long for, yearn for. **2** *he fancied himself as a bit of an actor*: think, conceive, imagine, dream of, picture, conjecture, believe, suppose, reckon, guess.
F∃ 1 dislike.
▪ *adjective* elaborate, ornate, decorated, ornamented, rococo, baroque, elegant, extravagant, fantastic, fanciful, far-fetched.
F∃ plain.
▪ *noun* idea, notion, whim.

fantastic *adjective* **1** *a fantastic sight*: wonderful, marvellous, sensational, superb, excellent, first-rate, tremendous, terrific, great (*infml*), incredible, unbelievable, overwhelming, enormous, extreme, cool (*infml*). **2** *fantastic creatures*: strange, weird, odd, exotic, outlandish, fanciful, fabulous, imaginative, visionary.
F∃ 1 ordinary. **2** real.

fantasy *noun* dream, daydream, reverie, pipe-dream, nightmare, vision, hallucination, illusion, mirage, apparition, invention, fancy, flight of fancy, delusion, misconception, imagination, unreality.
F∃ reality.

far *adverb* a long way, a good way, miles (*infml*), much, greatly, considerably, extremely, decidedly, incomparably.
F∃ near, close.
▪ *adjective* distant, far-off, faraway, far-flung, outlying, remote, out-of-the-way, god-forsaken, removed, far-removed, further, opposite, other.
F∃ nearby, close.

farce *noun* **1** *tragedy and farce*: comedy, slapstick, buffoonery, satire, burlesque. **2** *the whole thing was a farce*: travesty, sham, parody, joke, mockery, ridiculousness, absurdity, nonsense.

fare *noun* charge, cost, price, fee, passage.

far-fetched *adjective* implausible, improbable, unlikely, dubious, incredible, unbelievable, fantastic, preposterous, crazy, unrealistic.
F∃ plausible.

farm *noun* ranch, farmstead, grange, homestead, station, land,

holding, acreage, acres.
▪ *verb* cultivate, till, work the land, plant, operate.

fascinate *verb* absorb, engross, intrigue, delight, charm, captivate, spellbind, enthral, rivet, transfix, hypnotize, mesmerize.
F3 bore, repel.

fascination *noun* interest, attraction, lure, magnetism, pull, charm, enchantment, spell, sorcery, magic.
F3 boredom, repulsion.

fashion *noun* **1** *the latest fashion(s)*: vogue, trend, mode, style, fad, craze, rage (*infml*), latest (*infml*), custom, convention. **2** *in the same fashion*: manner, way, method, mode, style, shape, form, pattern, line, cut, look, appearance, type, sort, kind.
▪ *verb* create, form, shape, mould, model, design, fit, tailor, alter, adjust, adapt, suit.

fashionable *adjective* chic, smart, elegant, stylish, modish, à la mode, in vogue, trendy (*infml*), in, all the rage (*infml*), popular, prevailing, current, latest, up-to-the-minute, contemporary, modern, up-to-date.
F3 unfashionable.

fast[1] *adjective* quick, swift, rapid, brisk, accelerated, speedy, nippy (*infml*), hasty, hurried, flying.
F3 slow, unhurried.
▪ *adverb* quickly, swiftly, rapidly, speedily, like a flash, like a shot, hastily, hurriedly, apace, presto.
F3 slowly, gradually.

fast[2] *verb* go hungry, diet, starve, abstain.

fasten *verb* fix, affix, attach, clamp, grip, anchor, rivet, nail, pin, clip, tack, seal, close, shut, lock, bolt, secure, tie, bind, chain, link, interlock, connect, join, unite, do up, button, lace, buckle.
F3 unfasten, untie.

fat *adjective* plump, obese, tubby, stout, corpulent, portly, round, rotund, paunchy, pot-bellied, overweight, heavy, beefy, solid, chubby, podgy, fleshy, flabby, gross.
F3 thin, slim, poor.

fatal *adjective* deadly, lethal, mortal, killing, incurable, malignant, terminal, final, destructive, calamitous, catastrophic, disastrous.
F3 harmless.

fate *noun* destiny, providence, chance, future, fortune, horoscope, stars, lot, doom, end, outcome, ruin, destruction, death.

father *noun* parent, begetter (*fml*), procreator (*fml*), progenitor (*fml*), sire (*fml*), papa, dad (*infml*), daddy (*infml*), old man (*infml*), patriarch, elder, forefather, ancestor, forebear, predecessor.

fathom *verb* understand, comprehend, grasp, see, work out, get to the bottom of, interpret.

fatigue *noun* tiredness, weariness, exhaustion, lethargy, listlessness, lassitude, weakness, debility.
F3 energy.

■ *verb* tire, wear out, weary, exhaust, drain, weaken, debilitate.

fault *noun* **1** *we like her despite her faults*: defect, flaw, blemish, imperfection, deficiency, shortcoming, weakness, failing, foible, negligence, omission, oversight. **2** *a fault in the system*: error, mistake, blunder, slip-up (*infml*), slip, lapse, misdeed, offence, wrong, sin. **3** *it's your fault*: responsibility, accountability, liability, culpability.

■ *verb* find fault with, pick holes in, criticize, knock (*infml*), impugn (*fml*), censure, blame, call to account.

F3 praise.

faultless *adjective* perfect, flawless, unblemished, spotless, immaculate, unsullied, pure, blameless, exemplary, model, correct, accurate.

F3 faulty, imperfect, flawed.

faulty *adjective* imperfect, defective, flawed, blemished, damaged, impaired, out of order, broken, wrong.

F3 faultless.

favour *noun* **1** *find favour with some powerful people*: approval, esteem, support, backing, sympathy, goodwill, patronage, favouritism, preference, partiality. **2** *he did me a favour*: kindness, service, good turn, courtesy.

F3 **1** disapproval.

■ *verb* **1** *favoured the Labour candidate*: prefer, choose, opt for, like, approve, support, back, advocate, champion. **2** *favouring poorer workers*: help, assist, aid, benefit, promote, encourage.

F3 **1** dislike. **2** mistreat.

favourable *adjective* beneficial, advantageous, helpful, fit, suitable, convenient, timely, opportune, good, fair, promising, auspicious, hopeful, positive, encouraging, complimentary, enthusiastic, friendly, amicable, well-disposed, kind, sympathetic, understanding, reassuring.

F3 unfavourable, unhelpful, negative.

favourite *adjective* preferred, favoured, pet, best-loved, dearest, beloved, esteemed, chosen.

F3 hated.

■ *noun* preference, choice, pick, pet, blue-eyed boy, teacher's pet, the apple of one's eye, darling, idol.

F3 bête noire, pet hate.

favouritism *noun* nepotism, preferential treatment, preference, partiality, one-sidedness, partisanship, bias, injustice.

F3 impartiality.

fear *noun* alarm, fright, terror, horror, panic, agitation, worry, anxiety, consternation, concern, dismay, distress, uneasiness, qualms, misgivings, apprehension, trepidation, dread, foreboding, awe, phobia, nightmare.

F3 courage, bravery, confidence.

■ *verb* take fright, shrink from, dread, shudder at, tremble, worry, suspect, anticipate, expect, foresee, respect, venerate.

fearful *adjective* **1** *fearful of the outcome*: frightened, afraid, scared, alarmed, nervous, anxious, tense, uneasy, apprehensive, hesitant, nervy, panicky. **2** *a fearful storm*: terrible, fearsome, dreadful, awful, frightful, atrocious, shocking, appalling, monstrous, gruesome, hideous, ghastly, horrible.
⇄ **1** brave, courageous, fearless. **2** wonderful, delightful.

feat *noun* exploit, deed, act, accomplishment, achievement, attainment, performance.

feature *noun* **1** *one of its most appealing features*: aspect, facet, point, factor, attribute, quality, property, trait, lineament, characteristic, peculiarity, mark, hallmark, speciality, highlight. **2** *a magazine feature*: column, article, report, story, piece, item, comment.
▪ *verb* **1** *featuring the best of British craftsmanship*: show, present, promote, emphasize, highlight, spotlight, play up. **2** *featured in several of his films*: appear, figure, participate, act, perform, star.

fee *noun* charge, terms, bill, account, pay, remuneration, payment, retainer, subscription, reward, recompense, hire, toll.

feeble *adjective* **1** *a feeble voice*: weak, faint, exhausted, frail, delicate, puny, sickly, infirm, powerless, helpless. **2** *a feeble excuse/attempt*: inadequate, lame, poor, thin, flimsy, ineffective, incompetent, indecisive.
⇄ **1** strong, powerful.

feed *verb* **1** *enough to feed everyone*: nourish, cater for, provide for, supply, sustain, suckle, nurture, foster, strengthen, fuel. **2** *cattle feeding contentedly*: graze, pasture, eat, dine.
▪ *noun* food, fodder, forage, pasture, silage.

feel *verb* **1** *feel pain*: experience, go through, undergo, suffer, endure. **2** *felt the texture*: touch, finger, handle, manipulate, hold. **3** *feel soft*: seem, appear. **4** *feel it is too soon*: think, believe, consider, reckon, judge. **5** *felt a presence*: sense, perceive, notice, observe, know.
▪ *noun* **1** *the feel of silk*: texture, surface, finish, touch. **2** *has a feel of home*: sense, impression, feeling, quality.

feeling *noun* **1** *a feeling of freedom/have a feeling about someone*: sensation, perception, sense, instinct, hunch, suspicion, inkling, impression, idea, notion, opinion, view, point of view. **2** *show their feelings*: emotion, passion, intensity, warmth, compassion, sympathy, understanding, pity, concern, affection, fondness, sentiment, sentimentality, susceptibility, sensibility, sensitivity, appreciation. **3** *a feeling of space and light*: air, aura, atmosphere, mood, quality.

fell *verb* cut down, hew, knock down, strike down, floor, level, flatten, raze, demolish.

fellow *noun* person, man, boy, chap (*infml*), bloke (*infml*), guy (*infml*), individual, character.

female *adjective* feminine, she-, girlish, womanly.
F3 male.

feminine *adjective* female, womanly, ladylike, graceful, gentle, tender.
F3 masculine.

fence *noun* barrier, railing, paling, wall, hedge, windbreak, guard, defence, barricade, stockade, rampart.
▪ *verb* surround, encircle, bound, hedge, wall, enclose, pen, coop, confine, restrict, separate, protect, guard, defend, fortify.

fend for *verb* look after, take care of, shift for, support, maintain, sustain, provide for.

ferocious *adjective* vicious, savage, fierce, wild, barbarous, barbaric, brutal, inhuman, cruel, sadistic, murderous, bloodthirsty, violent, merciless, pitiless, ruthless.
F3 gentle, mild, tame.

ferry *verb* transport, ship, convey, carry, take, shuttle, taxi, drive, run, move, shift.

fertile *adjective* fruitful, productive, generative, yielding, prolific, teeming, abundant, plentiful, rich, lush, luxuriant, fat.
F3 infertile, barren, sterile, unproductive.

fertilize *verb* **1** *fertilizing the eggs*: inseminate, pollinate. **2** *fertilize land*: enrich, feed, dress, compost, manure, dung.

festival *noun* celebration, commemoration, anniversary, jubilee, holiday, feast, gala, fête, carnival, fiesta, party, merrymaking, entertainment, festivities.

festive *adjective* celebratory, festal, holiday, gala, carnival, happy, joyful, merry, hearty, cheery, jolly, jovial, cordial, convivial.
F3 gloomy, sombre, sober.

festivity *noun* celebration, jubilation, feasting, banqueting, fun, enjoyment, pleasure, entertainment, sport, amusement, merriment, merrymaking, revelry, jollity, joviality, conviviality.

fetch *verb* get, collect, bring, carry, transport, deliver, escort.

fever *noun* feverishness, (high) temperature, delirium.

feverish *adjective* **1** *feeling feverish*: delirious, hot, burning, flushed. **2** *feverish activity*: excited, impatient, agitated, restless, nervous, frenzied, frantic, overwrought, hectic, hasty, hurried.
F3 **1** cool. **2** calm.

few *adjective* scarce, rare, uncommon, sporadic, infrequent, sparse, thin, scant, scanty, meagre, inconsiderable, inadequate, insufficient, in short supply.
F3 many.

fibre *noun* filament, strand, thread, nerve, sinew, pile.

fickle *adjective* inconstant, disloyal, unfaithful, faithless, treacherous, unreliable, unpredictable, changeable, capricious, mercurial, irresolute, vacillating.
F3 constant, steady, stable.

fictional *adjective* literary, invented, made-up, imaginary, make-believe, legendary, mythical, mythological, fabulous, non-existent, unreal.
F3 factual, real.

fictitious *adjective* false, untrue, invented, made-up, fabricated, apocryphal, imaginary, non-existent, bogus, counterfeit, spurious, assumed, supposed.
F3 true, genuine.

fiddle *verb* **1** *fiddling with her necklace*: play, tinker, toy, trifle, tamper, mess around, meddle, interfere, fidget. **2** *fiddling the books*: cheat, swindle, diddle, cook the books (*infml*), juggle, manoeuvre, racketeer, graft.

fidget *verb* squirm, wriggle, shuffle, twitch, jerk, jump, fret, fuss, bustle, fiddle, mess about, play around.

field *noun* **1** *a field of corn/a football field*: grassland, meadow, pasture, paddock, playing-field, ground, pitch, green. **2** *not my field/an expert in the field*: territory, area, province, domain, sphere, environment, department, discipline, speciality, line, forte.

fiend *noun* **1** *you little fiend!*: evil spirit, demon, devil, monster. **2** *a health fiend*: enthusiast, fanatic, addict, devotee, freak (*infml*), nut (*infml*).

fiendish *adjective* devilish, diabolical, infernal, wicked, malevolent, cunning, cruel, inhuman, savage, monstrous, unspeakable.

fierce *adjective* **1** *a fierce fighter*: ferocious, vicious, savage, cruel, brutal, merciless, aggressive, dangerous, murderous, frightening, menacing, threatening, stern, grim, relentless. **2** *fierce criticism*: intense, passionate, raging, wild, strong, powerful, relentless.
F3 gentle, kind, calm.

fiery *adjective* **1** *a fiery sun*: burning, afire, flaming, aflame, blazing, ablaze, red-hot, glowing, aglow, flushed, hot, torrid, sultry. **2** *a fiery temperament*: passionate, inflamed, ardent, fervent, impatient, excitable, impetuous, impulsive, hot-headed, fierce, violent, heated.
F3 **1** cold. **2** impassive.

fight *noun* **1** *a hard fight/a street fight*: bout, contest, duel, combat, action, battle, war, hostilities, brawl, scrap, scuffle, tussle, struggle, skirmish, set-to, clash, engagement, brush, encounter, conflict, fray, free-for-all, fracas, riot, fisticuffs. **2** *have a fight with the boss*: quarrel, row, argument, dispute. **3** *the fight for freedom*:

campaign, battle, struggle, crusade, drive.

▪ *verb* **1** *fight a battle/an opponent*: wrestle, box, fence, joust, brawl, scrap, scuffle, tussle, skirmish, combat, battle, do battle, war, wage war, clash, cross swords, engage, grapple, struggle, strive, contend. **2** *the brothers seem to fight continuously*: quarrel, argue, dispute, squabble, bicker, wrangle. **3** *fight the proposals*: oppose, contest, campaign against, resist, withstand, defy, stand up to.

fighter *noun* combatant, contestant, contender, disputant, boxer, wrestler, pugilist, prizefighter, soldier, trouper, mercenary, warrior, man-at-arms, swordsman, gladiator.

figure *noun* **1** *write the amount in figures*: number, numeral, digit, integer, sum, amount. **2** *a figure in the distance/have the figure of a supermodel*: shape, form, outline, silhouette, body, frame, build, physique. **3** *public figure*: dignitary, celebrity, personality, character, person. **4** *see figure 5 below*: diagram, illustration, picture, drawing, sketch, image, representation, symbol.

▪ *verb* feature, appear, crop up.

file[1] *verb* rub (down), sand, abrade, scour, scrape, grate, rasp, hone, whet, shave, plane, smooth, polish.

file[2] *verb* record, register, note, enter, process, store, classify, categorize, pigeonhole, catalogue.

▪ *noun* folder, dossier, portfolio, binder, case, record, documents, data, information.

file[3] *verb* march, troop, parade, stream, trail.

▪ *noun* line, queue, column, row, procession, cortège, train, string, stream, trail.

fill *verb* **1** *fill the trolley with groceries/crowds of people filling the narrow streets*: stock, supply, furnish, satisfy, pack, crowd, cram, stuff, load, congest, block, clog, plug, bung, cork, stop, close, seal. **2** *happy children's voices filled the air*: pervade, imbue, permeate, soak, impregnate. **3** *fill a post*: take up, hold, occupy, discharge, fulfil.

F3 **1** empty, drain.

film *noun* **1** *a black-and-white film*: motion picture, picture, movie (*infml*), video, DVD, feature film, blockbuster (*infml*), short, documentary. **2** *a thin film of dust/grease*: layer, covering, dusting, coat, coating, glaze, skin, membrane, tissue, sheet, veil, screen, cloud, mist, haze.

▪ *verb* photograph, shoot, video, videotape.

filter *verb* strain, sieve, sift, screen, refine, purify, clarify, percolate, ooze, seep, leak, trickle, dribble.

filth *noun* dirt, grime, muck, dung, excrement, faeces, sewage, refuse, rubbish, garbage, trash, slime, sludge, effluent, pollution, contamination, corruption, impurity, uncleanness, foulness,

sordidness, squalor.
F3 cleanness, cleanliness, purity.

filthy *adjective* dirty, soiled, unwashed, grimy, grubby, mucky, muddy, slimy, sooty, unclean, impure, foul, gross, sordid, squalid, vile, low, mean, base, contemptible, despicable.
F3 clean, pure.

final *adjective* last, latest, closing, concluding, finishing, end, ultimate, terminal, dying, last-minute, eventual, conclusive, definitive, decisive, definite, incontrovertible, irreversible.
F3 first, initial.

finale *noun* end, conclusion, close, curtain, epilogue, climax, dénouement, culmination, crowning glory.

finalize *verb* conclude, finish, complete, round off, resolve, settle, agree, decide, close, clinch, sew up (*infml*), wrap up (*infml*).

finally *adverb* lastly, in conclusion, ultimately, eventually, at last, at length, in the end, conclusively, once and for all, for ever, irreversibly, irrevocably, definitely.

finance *noun* economics, money management, accounting, banking, investment, stock market, business, commerce, trade, money, funding, sponsorship, subsidy.
▪ *verb* pay for, fund, sponsor, back, support, underwrite, guarantee, subsidize, capitalize, float, set up.

finances *noun* accounts, affairs, budget, bank account, income, revenue, liquidity, resources, assets, capital, wealth, money, cash, funds, wherewithal.

financial *adjective* monetary, money, pecuniary, economic, fiscal, budgetary, commercial.

find *verb* **1** *find the source of the Nile/find the answer*: discover, locate, track down, trace, retrieve, recover, unearth, uncover, expose, reveal, come across, chance on, stumble on, meet, encounter, detect, recognize, notice, observe, perceive, realize, learn. **2** *find peace*: attain, achieve, win, reach, gain, obtain, get. **3** *find it difficult*: consider, think, judge, declare.

fine[1] *adjective* **1** *a fine young man*: excellent, outstanding, exceptional, superior, exquisite, splendid, magnificent, brilliant, beautiful, handsome, attractive, elegant, lovely, nice, good. **2** *fine thread/stitching*: thin, slender, sheer, gauzy, powdery, flimsy, fragile, delicate, dainty. **3** *it all seems fine*: satisfactory, acceptable, all right, OK (*infml*). **4** *fine weather*: bright, sunny, clear, cloudless, dry, fair.
F3 2 thick, coarse.

fine[2] *noun* penalty, punishment, forfeit, forfeiture, damages.

finish *verb* **1** *finishing the job*: end, terminate, stop, cease, complete, accomplish, achieve, fulfil, discharge, deal with, do, conclude, close, wind up, settle, round off, top off, culminate, perfect.

2 *finished the milk*: use (up), consume, devour, eat, drink, exhaust, drain, empty.

1 begin, start.

▪ *noun* **1** *in at the finish*: end, termination, completion, conclusion, close, ending, finale, culmination. **2** *gives the wood a good finish*: surface, appearance, texture, grain, polish, shine, gloss, lustre, smoothness.

1 beginning, start, commencement.

fire *noun* flames, blaze, bonfire, conflagration, inferno, burning, combustion.

▪ *verb* **1** *fire a missile*: shoot, launch, set off, let off, detonate, explode, discharge. **2** (*infml*) *fired his press officer*: dismiss, discharge, sack (*infml*), eject.

firm[1] *adjective* **1** *a firm mattress*: dense, compressed, compact, concentrated, set, solid, hard, unyielding, stiff, rigid, inflexible. **2** *a firm foundation*: fixed, embedded, fast, tight, secure, fastened, anchored, immovable, motionless, stationary, steady, stable, sturdy, strong. **3** *firm control*: adamant, unshakable, resolute, determined, dogged, unwavering, strict, constant, steadfast, staunch, dependable, true, sure, convinced, definite, settled, committed.

1 soft, flabby. **2** unsteady. **3** hesitant.

firm[2] *noun* company, corporation, business, enterprise, concern, house, establishment, institution, organization, association, partnership, syndicate, conglomerate.

first *adjective* **1** *the first day at school/not know the first thing about it*: initial, opening, introductory, preliminary, elementary, primary, basic, fundamental. **2** *the first humans*: original, earliest, earlier, prior, primitive, primeval, oldest, eldest, senior. **3** *Scotland's first minister*: chief, main, key, cardinal, principal, head, leading, ruling, sovereign, highest, uppermost, paramount, prime, predominant, pre-eminent.

1 last, final.

▪ *adverb* initially, to begin with, to start with, at the outset, beforehand, originally, in preference, rather, sooner.

fish *verb* angle, trawl, delve, hunt, seek, invite, solicit.

fit[1] *adjective* **1** *fit for use*: suitable, appropriate, apt, fitting, correct, right, proper, ready, prepared, able, capable, competent, qualified, eligible, worthy. **2** *fit and well*: healthy, well, able-bodied, in good form, in good shape, sound, sturdy, strong, robust, hale and hearty.

1 unsuitable, unworthy. **2** unfit.

▪ *verb* **1** *the key fits the lock/fits the description*: match, correspond, conform, follow, agree, concur, tally, suit, harmonize, go, belong, dovetail, interlock, join, meet, arrange, place, position, accommodate. **2** *fit the job to the person, not the person to the job*: alter, modify, change, adjust, adapt, tailor, shape, fashion.

fit[2] *noun* seizure, convulsion, spasm, paroxysm, attack, outbreak, bout, spell, burst, surge, outburst, eruption, explosion.

fitting *adjective* apt, appropriate, suitable, fit, correct, right, proper, seemly, meet (*fml*), desirable, deserved.

unsuitable, improper.

fix *verb* **1** *fixing it to the wall*: fasten, secure, tie, bind, attach, join, connect, link, couple, anchor, pin, nail, rivet, stick, glue, cement, set, harden, solidify, stiffen, stabilize, plant, root, implant, embed, establish, install, place, locate, position. **2** *fix a date*: arrange, set, specify, define, agree on, decide, determine, settle, resolve, finalize. **3** *fix the broken chair*: mend, repair, correct, rectify, adjust, restore.

1 move, shift. **3** damage.

fixed *adjective* decided, settled, established, definite, arranged, planned, set, firm, rigid, inflexible, steady, secure, fast, rooted, permanent.

variable.

fizzy *adjective* effervescent, sparkling, aerated, carbonated, gassy, bubbly, bubbling, frothy, foaming.

flabby *adjective* fleshy, soft, yielding, flaccid, limp, floppy, drooping, hanging, sagging, slack, loose, lax, weak, feeble.

firm, strong.

flag *verb* lessen, diminish, decline, fall (off), abate, subside, sink, slump, dwindle, peter out, fade, fail, weaken, slow, falter, tire, weary, wilt, droop, sag, flop, faint, die.

revive.

flair *noun* skill, ability, aptitude, faculty, gift, talent, facility, knack, mastery, genius, feel, taste, discernment, acumen, style, elegance, stylishness, panache.

inability, ineptitude.

flake *noun* scale, peeling, paring, shaving, sliver, wafer, chip, splinter.

flamboyant *adjective* showy, ostentatious, flashy, gaudy, colourful, brilliant, dazzling, striking, extravagant, rich, elaborate, ornate, florid.

modest, restrained.

flame *noun* fire, blaze, light, brightness, heat, warmth.

flammable *adjective* inflammable, ignitable, combustible.

non-flammable, incombustible, flameproof, fire-resistant.

flap *verb* flutter, vibrate, wave, agitate, shake, wag, swing, swish, thrash, beat.

▪ *noun* **1** *a flap of skin*: fold, fly, lapel, tab, lug, tag, tail, skirt, aileron. **2** (*infml*) *in a flap*: panic, state (*infml*), fuss, commotion, fluster, agitation, flutter, dither, tizzy (*infml*).

flare *verb* **1** *fire flared from the burning wells*: flame, burn, blaze, glare, flash, flicker, burst, explode, erupt. **2** *nostrils flaring*: broaden, widen, flare out, spread out, splay.

flash *noun* beam, ray, shaft, spark, blaze, flare, burst, streak, gleam, glint, flicker, twinkle, sparkle, shimmer.
▪ *verb* **1** *lightning flashed*: beam, shine, light up, flare, blaze, glare, gleam, glint, flicker, twinkle, sparkle, glitter, shimmer. **2** *the train flashed past*: streak, fly, dart, race, dash.

flat[1] *adjective* **1** *a flat plain/roof/colour*: level, plane, even, smooth, uniform, unbroken, horizontal, low. **2** *in a flat tone*: dull, boring, monotonous, tedious, uninteresting, unexciting, stale, lifeless, dead, spiritless, lacklustre. **3** *a flat refusal*: absolute, utter, total, unequivocal, categorical, positive, unconditional, unqualified, point-blank, direct, straight, explicit, plain, final. **4** *a flat tyre*: punctured, burst, deflated, collapsed.
E3 **1** bumpy, vertical. **3** equivocal.

flat[2] *noun* apartment, penthouse, maisonette, tenement, flatlet, rooms, suite, bed-sit(ter).

flatten *verb* **1** *flatten the ground with a roller*: smooth, iron, press, roll, crush, squash, compress, level, even out. **2** *flattened him with one punch*: knock down, prostrate, floor, fell, demolish, raze, overwhelm, subdue.

flatter *verb* praise, compliment, sweet-talk (*infml*), adulate, fawn, butter up (*infml*), wheedle, humour, play up to, court, curry favour with, soft-soap.
E3 criticize.

flavour *noun* **1** *a sweet/fruity flavour*: taste, tang, smack, savour, relish, zest, zing (*infml*), aroma, odour. **2** *has something of the flavour of an old cowboy movie*: quality, property, character, style, aspect, feeling, feel, atmosphere.
▪ *verb* season, spice, ginger up, infuse, imbue.

flaw *noun* defect, imperfection, fault, blemish, spot, mark, speck, crack, crevice, fissure, cleft, split, rift, break, fracture, weakness, shortcoming, failing, fallacy, lapse, slip, error, mistake.

flawed *adjective* imperfect, defective, faulty, blemished, marked, damaged, spoilt, marred, cracked, chipped, broken, unsound, fallacious, erroneous.
E3 flawless, perfect.

flee *verb* run away, bolt, fly, take flight, take off, make off, cut and run, escape, get away, decamp, abscond, leave, depart, withdraw, retreat, vanish, disappear.
E3 stay.

flesh *noun* body, tissue, fat, muscle, brawn, skin, meat, pulp, substance, matter, physicality.

flex *verb* bend, bow, curve, angle, ply, double up, tighten, contract.

☒ straighten, extend.
▪ *noun* cable, wire, lead, cord.

flexible *adjective* **1** *flexible rod/limbs*: bendable, bendy (*infml*), pliable, pliant, plastic, malleable, mouldable, elastic, stretchy, springy, yielding, supple, lithe, limber, double-jointed, mobile. **2** *adopt a flexible approach*: adaptable, adjustable, amenable, accommodating, variable, open, manageable, agreeable.
☒ **1** inflexible, rigid. **2** inflexible.

flick *verb* hit, strike, rap, tap, touch, dab, flip, jerk, whip, lash.

flicker *verb* flash, blink, wink, twinkle, sparkle, glimmer, shimmer, gutter, flutter, vibrate, quiver, waver.
▪ *noun* flash, gleam, glint, twinkle, glimmer, spark, trace, drop, iota, atom, indication.

flight *noun* **1** *powered flight*: flying, aviation, aeronautics, air transport, air travel. **2** *a transatlantic flight*: journey, trip, voyage.

flimsy *adjective* thin, fine, light, slight, insubstantial, ethereal, fragile, delicate, shaky, rickety, makeshift, weak, feeble, meagre, inadequate, shallow, superficial, trivial, poor, unconvincing, implausible.
☒ sturdy.

flinch *verb* wince, start, cringe, cower, quail, tremble, shake, quake, shudder, shiver, shrink, recoil, draw back, shy away, duck, shirk, withdraw, retreat, flee.

fling *verb* throw, hurl, pitch, lob, toss, chuck (*infml*), cast, sling, catapult, launch, propel, send, let fly, heave, jerk.

flip *noun, verb* flick, spin, twirl, twist, turn, toss, jerk, flap.

flippant *adjective* facetious, light-hearted, frivolous, superficial, offhand, flip, glib, pert, saucy (*infml*), cheeky (*infml*), impudent, impertinent, rude, disrespectful, irreverent.
☒ serious, respectful.

flirt *verb* chat up, make up to, lead on, philander, dally.

flit *verb* dart, speed, flash, fly, wing, flutter, whisk, skim, slip, pass, bob, dance.

float *verb* glide, sail, swim, bob, drift, waft, hover, hang.
☒ sink.

flock *verb* herd, swarm, troop, converge, mass, bunch, cluster, huddle, crowd, throng, group, gather, collect, congregate.
▪ *noun* herd, pack, crowd, throng, multitude, mass, bunch, cluster, group, gathering, assembly, congregation.

flood *verb* **1** *the river burst its banks, flooding the surrounding farmland*: deluge, inundate, soak, drench, saturate, fill, overflow, immerse, submerge, engulf, swamp, overwhelm, drown. **2** *water flooding into the lock*: flow, pour, stream, rush, surge, gush.
▪ *noun* deluge, inundation, downpour, torrent, flow, tide, stream, rush, spate, outpouring,

overflow, glut, excess, abundance, profusion.

F3 drought, trickle, dearth.

floor *noun* **1** *a wooden floor*: flooring, ground, base, basis. **2** *on the third floor*: storey, level, stage, landing, deck, tier.

▪ *verb* (*infml*) defeat, overwhelm, beat, stump (*infml*), frustrate, confound, perplex, baffle, puzzle, bewilder, disconcert, throw.

flop *noun* failure, non-starter, fiasco, debacle, wash-out (*infml*), disaster.

▪ *verb* **1** *the play flopped*: fail, misfire, fall flat, founder, fold. **2** *hair flopping over her eyes/flop down on the floor*: droop, hang, dangle, sag, drop, fall, topple, tumble, slump, collapse.

flounder *verb* wallow, struggle, grope, fumble, blunder, stagger, stumble, falter.

flourish *verb* **1** *the business flourished*: thrive, grow, wax, increase, flower, blossom, bloom, develop, progress, get on, do well, prosper, succeed, boom. **2** *flourishing a big stick*: brandish, wave, shake, twirl, swing, display, wield, flaunt, parade, vaunt.

F3 **1** decline, languish, fail.

▪ *noun* display, parade, show, gesture, wave, sweep, fanfare, ornament, decoration, panache, pizzazz (*infml*).

flout *verb* defy, disobey, violate, break, disregard, spurn, reject, scorn, jeer at, scoff at, mock, ridicule.

F3 obey, respect, regard.

flow *verb* **1** *a river flowing to the sea/words flowing from his pen*: circulate, ooze, trickle, ripple, bubble, well, spurt, squirt, gush, spill, run, pour, cascade, rush, stream, teem, flood, overflow, surge, sweep, move, drift, slip, slide, glide, roll, swirl. **2** *flowing from our original discussion*: originate, derive, arise, spring, emerge, issue, result, proceed, emanate.

▪ *noun* course, flux, tide, current, drift, outpouring, stream, deluge, cascade, spurt, gush, flood, spate, abundance, plenty.

flower *noun* bloom, blossom, bud, floret.

▪ *verb* bud, burgeon, bloom, blossom, open, come out.

Flowers include:

African violet, alyssum, anemone, aster, aubrietia, azalea, begonia, bluebell, busy lizzie, calendula, candytuft, carnation, chrysanthemum, cornflower, cowslip, crocus, cyclamen, daffodil, dahlia, daisy, delphinium, forget-me-not, foxglove, freesia, fuchsia, gardenia, geranium, gladiolus, hollyhock, hyacinth, iris, lily, lily-of-the-valley, lobelia, lupin, marigold, narcissus, nasturtium, nemesia, nicotiana, night-scented stock, orchid, pansy, petunia, phlox, pink, poinsettia, polyanthus, poppy, primrose, primula, rose, salvia, snapdragon, snowdrop, stock, sunflower, sweet pea, sweet william, tulip, verbena, viola, violet, wallflower, zinnia. *See also* **plant**.

---

flowery *adjective* florid, ornate, elaborate, fancy, baroque, rhetorical.
F3 plain, simple.

fluctuate *verb* vary, change, alter, shift, rise and fall, seesaw, ebb and flow, alternate, swing, sway, oscillate, vacillate, waver.

fluent *adjective* flowing, smooth, easy, effortless, articulate, eloquent, voluble, glib, ready.
F3 broken, inarticulate, tongue-tied.

fluffy *adjective* furry, fuzzy, downy, feathery, fleecy, woolly, hairy, shaggy, velvety, silky, soft.

fluid *noun* liquid, solution, liquor, juice, gas, vapour.
▪ *adjective* **1** *fluid lava*: liquid, liquefied, aqueous, watery, running, runny, melted, molten. **2** *a fluid situation*: variable, changeable, unstable, inconstant, shifting, mobile, adjustable, adaptable, flexible, open. **3** *fluid movements*: flowing, smooth, graceful.
F3 **1** solid. **2** stable.

flurry *noun* **1** *a sudden flurry of snow*: burst, outbreak, spell, spurt, gust, blast, squall. **2** *a flurry of activity*: bustle, hurry, fluster, fuss, to-do, commotion, tumult, whirl, disturbance, stir, flap (*infml*).

flush *verb* **1** *flushing with embarrassment*: blush, go red, redden, crimson, colour, burn, glow, suffuse. **2** *flush the impurities out*: cleanse, wash, rinse, hose, swab, clear, empty, evacuate.

fluster *verb* bother, upset, embarrass, disturb, perturb, agitate, ruffle, discompose, confuse, confound, unnerve, put off, disconcert, rattle (*infml*), distract.
F3 calm.

flutter *verb* flap, wave, beat, bat, flicker, vibrate, palpitate, agitate, shake, tremble, quiver, shiver, ruffle, ripple, twitch, toss, waver, fluctuate.

fly *verb* **1** *fly from tree to tree*: take off, rise, ascend, mount, soar, glide, float, hover, flit, wing. **2** *flew down the road*: race, sprint, dash, tear, rush, hurry, speed, zoom, shoot, dart, career.

foam *noun* froth, lather, suds, head, bubbles, effervescence.
▪ *verb* froth, lather, bubble, effervesce, fizz, boil, seethe.

focus *noun* focal point, target, centre, heart, core, nucleus, kernel, crux, hub, axis, linchpin, pivot, hinge.
▪ *verb* converge, meet, join, centre, concentrate, aim, direct, fix, spotlight, home in, zoom in, zero in (*infml*).

foggy *adjective* misty, hazy, smoggy, cloudy, murky, dark, shadowy, dim, indistinct, obscure.
F3 clear.

foil *verb* defeat, outwit, frustrate, thwart, baffle, counter, nullify,

stop, check, obstruct, block, circumvent, elude.
F3 abet.

fold *verb* bend, ply, double, overlap, tuck, pleat, crease, crumple, crimp, crinkle.
▪ *noun* bend, turn, layer, ply, overlap, tuck, pleat, crease, knife-edge, line, wrinkle, furrow, corrugation.

follow *verb* **1** *night follows day*: come after, succeed, come next, replace, supersede, supplant. **2** *following the scent*: chase, pursue, go after, hunt, track, trail, shadow, tail, hound, catch. **3** *Mary's lamb follows her everywhere*: accompany, go (along) with, escort, attend, tag along with. **4** *doesn't necessarily follow*: result, ensue, develop, emanate, arise. **5** *follow the rules*: obey, comply with, adhere to, heed, mind, observe, conform to, carry out, practise. **6** *can't follow these instructions*: grasp, understand, comprehend, fathom.
F3 **1** precede. **3** abandon, desert. **5** disobey.

follower *noun* attendant, retainer, helper, companion, sidekick (*infml*), apostle, disciple, pupil, imitator, emulator, adherent, hanger-on (*infml*), believer, convert, backer, supporter, admirer, fan, devotee, freak (*infml*), buff (*infml*).
F3 leader, opponent.

following *adjective* subsequent, next, succeeding, successive, resulting, ensuing, consequent, later.
F3 previous.
▪ *noun* followers, suite, retinue, entourage, circle, fans, supporters, support, backing, patronage, clientele, audience, public.

folly *noun* foolishness, stupidity, senselessness, rashness, recklessness, irresponsibility, indiscretion, craziness, madness, lunacy, insanity, idiocy, imbecility, silliness, absurdity, nonsense.
F3 wisdom, prudence, sanity.

fond of *adjective* partial to, attached to, enamoured of, keen on, addicted to, hooked on.

food *noun* foodstuffs, comestibles (*fml*), eatables (*infml*), provisions, stores, rations, eats (*infml*), grub (*infml*), nosh (*infml*), refreshment, sustenance, nourishment, nutrition, nutriment, subsistence, feed, fodder, diet, fare, cooking, cuisine, menu, board, table, larder.

fool *noun* blockhead, fat-head, nincompoop (*infml*), ass (*infml*), chump (*infml*), ninny (*infml*), clot (*infml*), dope (*infml*), twit (*infml*), nitwit (*infml*), nit (*infml*), dunce, dimwit, simpleton, halfwit, idiot, imbecile, moron, dupe, sucker (*infml*), mug (*infml*), stooge, clown, buffoon, jester.
▪ *verb* deceive, take in, delude, mislead, dupe, gull, hoodwink, put one over on (*infml*), trick, hoax, con (*infml*), cheat, swindle, diddle (*infml*), string along (*infml*), have on (*infml*), kid (*infml*), tease, joke.

foolhardy *adjective* rash, reckless, imprudent, ill-advised, irresponsible.
cautious, prudent.

foolish *adjective* stupid, senseless, unwise, ill-advised, ill-considered, short-sighted, half-baked, daft (*infml*), crazy, mad, insane, idiotic, moronic, hare-brained, half-witted, simple-minded, simple, unintelligent, inept, inane, silly, absurd, ridiculous, ludicrous, nonsensical.
wise, prudent.

foolproof *adjective* idiot-proof, infallible, fail-safe, sure, certain, sure-fire (*infml*), guaranteed.
unreliable.

foot *noun* **1** *an animal's foot*: paw, hoof, pad, trotter, leg, toe, sole, heel. **2** *the foot of the hill*: bottom, far end, limit, foundation, base.
2 head, top, summit.

forbid *verb* prohibit, disallow, ban, proscribe, interdict (*fml*), veto, refuse, deny, outlaw, debar, exclude, rule out, preclude, prevent, block, hinder, inhibit.
allow, permit, approve.

forbidden *adjective* prohibited, banned, proscribed, taboo, vetoed, outlawed, out of bounds.

forbidding *adjective* stern, formidable, awesome, daunting, off-putting, uninviting, menacing, threatening, ominous, sinister, frightening.
approachable, congenial.

force *verb* **1** *forced to leave*: compel, make, oblige, necessitate, urge, coerce, constrain, press, pressurize, lean on (*infml*), press-gang, bulldoze, drive, propel, push, thrust. **2** *forced a confession from him*: prise, wrench, wrest (*fml*), extort, exact, wring.
▪ *noun* **1** *using force to get what they want*: compulsion, impulse, influence, coercion, constraint, pressure, duress, violence, aggression. **2** *the force of his will*: power, might, strength, intensity, effort, energy, vigour, drive, dynamism, stress, emphasis. **3** *a large force of infantry*: army, troop, body, corps, regiment, squadron, battalion, division, unit, detachment, patrol.
2 weakness.

forced *adjective* unnatural, stiff, wooden, stilted, laboured, strained, false, artificial, contrived, feigned, affected, insincere.
spontaneous, sincere.

forceful *adjective* strong, mighty, powerful, potent, effective, compelling, convincing, persuasive, cogent, telling, weighty, urgent, emphatic, vehement, forcible, dynamic, energetic, vigorous.
weak, feeble.

foreboding *noun* misgiving, anxiety, worry, dread, apprehension, fear, omen, sign, token, premonition, warning, prediction, prognostication, intuition, feeling.

forecast *verb* predict, prophesy, foretell, foresee, anticipate,

expect, estimate, calculate.
▪ *noun* prediction, prophecy, expectation, prognosis, outlook, projection, guess, guesstimate (*infml*).

forefront *noun* front, front line, firing line, van, vanguard, lead, fore, avant-garde, cutting edge.
⇔ rear.

foreign *adjective* alien, immigrant, imported, international, external, outside, overseas, exotic, faraway, distant, remote, strange, unfamiliar, unknown, uncharacteristic, incongruous, extraneous, borrowed.
⇔ native, indigenous.

foremost *adjective* first, leading, front, chief, main, principal, primary, cardinal, paramount, central, highest, uppermost, supreme, prime, pre-eminent.

foresee *verb* envisage, anticipate, expect, forecast, predict, prophesy, prognosticate, foretell, forebode, divine.

foresight *noun* anticipation, planning, forethought, far-sightedness, vision, caution, prudence, circumspection, care, readiness, preparedness, provision, precaution.
⇔ improvidence.

forever *adverb* continually, constantly, persistently, incessantly, perpetually, endlessly, eternally, always, evermore, for all time, permanently.

forfeit *verb* lose, give up, surrender, relinquish, sacrifice, forgo, renounce, abandon.
▪ *noun* loss, surrender, confiscation, fine, sequestration, penalty, damages.

forge *verb* **1** *forge an agreement*: make, mould, cast, shape, form, fashion, beat out, hammer out, work, create, invent. **2** *forge a document*: fake, counterfeit, falsify, copy, imitate, simulate, feign.

forgery *noun* fake, counterfeit, copy, replica, reproduction, imitation, dud (*infml*), phoney (*infml*), sham, fraud.
⇔ original.

forget *verb* omit, fail, neglect, let slip, overlook, disregard, ignore, lose sight of, dismiss, think no more of, unlearn.
⇔ remember, recall, recollect.

forgetful *adjective* absent-minded, dreamy, inattentive, oblivious, negligent, lax, heedless.
⇔ attentive, heedful.

forgive *verb* pardon, absolve, excuse, exonerate, exculpate (*fml*), acquit, remit, let off, overlook, condone.
⇔ punish, censure.

forgiving *adjective* merciful, clement, lenient, tolerant, forbearing, indulgent, kind, humane, compassionate, soft-hearted, mild.
⇔ merciless, censorious, harsh.

fork *verb* split, divide, part, separate, diverge, branch (off).

forlorn *adjective* deserted, abandoned, forsaken, forgotten, bereft, friendless, lonely, lost, homeless, destitute, desolate, hopeless, unhappy, miserable, wretched, helpless, pathetic, pitiable.

F3 cheerful.

form *verb* **1** *form circles/letters*: shape, mould, model, fashion, make, manufacture, produce, create, found, establish, build, construct, assemble, put together, arrange, organize. **2** *a nest formed from twigs and moss*: comprise, constitute, make up, compose. **3** *scum forming on the surface of the water*: appear, take shape, materialize, crystallize, grow, develop.

▪ *noun* **1** *in the form of a dove*: appearance, shape, mould, cast, cut, outline, silhouette, figure, build, frame, structure, format, model, pattern, design, arrangement, organization, system. **2** *a form of punishment*: type, kind, sort, order, species, variety, genre, style, manner, nature, character, description. **3** *the sixth form*: class, year, grade, stream. **4** *on top form*: health, fitness, fettle, condition, spirits. **5** *know the form*: etiquette, protocol, custom, convention, ritual, behaviour, manners. **6** *fill in a form*: questionnaire, document, paper, sheet.

formal *adjective* **1** *formal clothes/a formal occasion*: official, ceremonial, stately, solemn, conventional, orthodox, correct, fixed, set, regular. **2** *rather formal in his manner*: prim, starchy, stiff, strict, rigid, precise, exact, punctilious, ceremonious, stilted, reserved.

F3 **2** informal, casual.

formality *noun* custom, convention, ceremony, ritual, procedure, matter of form, bureaucracy, red tape, protocol, etiquette, form, correctness, propriety, decorum, politeness.

F3 informality.

formation *noun* **1** *rock formations*: structure, construction, composition, constitution, configuration, format, organization, arrangement, grouping, pattern, design, figure. **2** *formation of a new political alliance*: creation, generation, production, manufacture, appearance, development, establishment.

former *adjective* past, ex-, one-time, sometime, late, departed, old, old-time, ancient, bygone, earlier, prior, previous, preceding, antecedent, foregoing, above.

F3 current, present, future, following.

formerly *adverb* once, previously, earlier, before, at one time, lately.

F3 currently, now, later.

formidable *adjective* daunting, challenging, intimidating, threatening, frightening, terrifying, terrific, frightful, fearful, great, huge, tremendous, prodigious, impressive, awesome, overwhelming, staggering.

formula *noun* recipe, prescription, proposal, blueprint, code, wording, rubric, rule, principle, form, procedure, technique, method, way.

forthcoming *adjective* **1** *their forthcoming wedding*: impending, imminent, approaching, coming, future, prospective, projected, expected. **2** *she wasn't very forthcoming*: communicative, talkative, chatty, conversational, sociable, informative, expansive, open, frank, direct.

F3 **2** reticent, reserved.

forthright *adjective* direct, straightforward, blunt, frank, candid, plain, open, bold, outspoken.

F3 devious, secretive.

fortunate *adjective* lucky, providential, happy, felicitous (*fml*), prosperous, successful, well-off, timely, well-timed, opportune, convenient, propitious, advantageous, favourable, auspicious.

F3 unlucky, unfortunate, unhappy.

fortune *noun* **1** *make his/a fortune*: wealth, riches, treasure, mint (*infml*), pile (*infml*), income, means, assets, estate, property, possessions, affluence, prosperity, success. **2** *fortune did not favour them*: luck, chance, accident, providence, fate, destiny, doom, lot, portion, life, history, future.

forward *adjective* **1** *the forward edge/movement*: first, head, front, fore, foremost, leading, onward, progressive, go-ahead, forward-looking, enterprising. **2** *that child is becoming too forward*: confident, assertive, pushy (*infml*), bold, audacious, brazen, brash, barefaced, cheeky (*infml*), impudent, impertinent, fresh (*infml*), familiar, presumptuous.

F3 **1** backward, retrograde. **2** shy, modest.

▪ *adverb* forwards, ahead, on, onward, out, into view.

▪ *verb* **1** *forward his career*: advance, promote, further, foster, encourage, support, back, favour, help, assist, aid, facilitate, accelerate, speed, hurry, hasten, expedite. **2** *forward mail to her new address*: dispatch, send (on), post, transport, ship.

F3 **1** impede, obstruct, hinder, slow.

foster *verb* raise, rear, bring up, nurse, care for, take care of, nourish, feed, sustain, support, promote, advance, encourage, stimulate, cultivate, nurture, cherish, entertain, harbour.

F3 neglect, discourage.

foul *adjective* **1** *a foul smell*: dirty, filthy, unclean, tainted, polluted, contaminated, rank, fetid, stinking, smelly, putrid, rotten, nauseating, offensive, repulsive, revolting, disgusting, squalid. **2** *foul language*: obscene, lewd, smutty, indecent, coarse, vulgar, gross, blasphemous, abusive. **3** *a*

foul thing to have done: nasty, disagreeable, wicked, vicious, vile, base, abhorrent (*fml*), disgraceful, shameful. **4** *foul weather*: bad, unpleasant, rainy, wet, stormy, rough.
OPP 1 clean. **4** fine.
▪ *verb* dirty, soil, stain, sully (*fml*), defile (*fml*), taint, pollute, contaminate.
OPP clean.

found *verb* **1** *found a children's charity*: start, originate, create, initiate, institute, inaugurate, set up, establish, endow, organize. **2** *founded on careful research*: base, ground, bottom, rest, settle, fix, plant, raise, build, erect, construct.

foundation *noun* **1** *the statement has no foundation in truth*: base, foot, bottom, ground, bedrock, substance, basis, footing. **2** *the foundation of a new college*: setting up, establishment, institution, inauguration, endowment, organization, groundwork.

founder[1] *noun* originator, initiator, father, mother, benefactor, creator, author, architect, designer, inventor, maker, builder, constructor, organizer.

founder[2] *verb* sink, go down, submerge, subside, collapse, break down, fall, come to grief, fail, misfire, miscarry, fall through, come to nothing.

fountain *noun* spray, jet, spout, spring, well, wellspring, reservoir, waterworks.

fracture *noun* break, crack, fissure, cleft, rupture, split, rift, rent, schism, breach, gap, opening.
▪ *verb* break, crack, rupture, split, splinter, chip.
OPP join.

fragile *adjective* brittle, breakable, frail, delicate, flimsy, dainty, fine, slight, insubstantial, weak, feeble, infirm.
OPP robust, tough, durable.

fragment *noun* piece, bit, part, portion, fraction, particle, crumb, morsel, scrap, remnant, shred, chip, splinter, shiver, sliver, shard.

fragrance *noun* perfume, scent, smell, odour, aroma, bouquet.

fragrant *adjective* perfumed, scented, sweet-smelling, sweet, balmy, aromatic, odorous.

frail *adjective* delicate, brittle, breakable, fragile, flimsy, insubstantial, slight, puny, weak, feeble, infirm, vulnerable.
OPP robust, tough, strong.

frailty *noun* weakness, foible, failing, deficiency, shortcoming, fault, defect, flaw, blemish, imperfection, fallibility, susceptibility.
OPP strength, robustness, toughness.

frame *verb* **1** *framing an idea*: compose, formulate, conceive, devise, contrive, concoct, cook up, plan, map out, sketch, draw up, draft, shape, form, model, fashion, mould, forge, assemble, put

together, build, construct, fabricate, make. **2** *her face was framed by golden curls*: surround, enclose, box in, case, mount.
▪ *noun* **1** *built on a steel frame*: structure, fabric, framework, skeleton, carcase, shell, casing, chassis, construction, bodywork, body, build, form. **2** *a picture frame*: mount, mounting, setting, surround, border, edge.

framework *noun* structure, fabric, bare bones, skeleton, shell, frame, outline, plan, foundation, groundwork.

frank *adjective* honest, truthful, sincere, candid, blunt, open, free, plain, direct, forthright, straight, straightforward, downright, outspoken.
F3 insincere, evasive.

frankly *adverb* to be frank, to be honest, in truth, honestly, candidly, bluntly, openly, freely, plainly, directly, straight.
F3 insincerely, evasively.

frantic *adjective* agitated, overwrought, fraught, desperate, beside oneself, furious, raging, mad, wild, raving, frenzied, berserk, hectic.
F3 calm, composed.

fraud *noun* **1** *charged with fraud*: deceit, deception, guile, cheating, swindling, double-dealing, sharp practice, fake, counterfeit, forgery, sham, hoax, trick. **2** (*infml*) *the healer turned out to be a fraud*: charlatan, impostor, pretender, phoney (*infml*), bluffer, hoaxer, cheat, swindler, double-dealer, con man (*infml*).

frayed *adjective* ragged, tattered, worn, threadbare, unravelled.

freak *noun* **1** *a freak of nature*: monster, mutant, monstrosity, malformation, deformity, irregularity, anomaly, abnormality, aberration, oddity, curiosity, quirk, caprice, vagary, twist, turn. **2** (*infml*) *a cricket freak*: enthusiast, fanatic, addict, devotee, fan, buff (*infml*), fiend (*infml*), nut (*infml*).
▪ *adjective* abnormal, atypical, unusual, exceptional, odd, queer, bizarre, aberrant (*fml*), capricious, erratic, unpredictable, unexpected, surprise, chance, fortuitous (*fml*), flukey (*infml*).
F3 normal, common.

free *adjective* **1** *the free peoples of the world/she was free at last*: at liberty, at large, loose, unattached, unrestrained, liberated, emancipated, independent, democratic, self-governing. **2** *free time/is this seat free?*: spare, available, idle, unemployed, vacant, unoccupied, empty. **3** *free tickets*: gratis, without charge, free of charge, complimentary, on the house. **4** *a free run to the coast*: clear, unobstructed, unimpeded, open. **5** *free with money*: generous, liberal, open-handed, lavish, charitable, hospitable.
F3 **1** imprisoned, confined, restricted. **2** busy, occupied.
▪ *verb* release, let go, loose, turn loose, set free, untie, unbind,

unchain, unleash, liberate, emancipate, rescue, deliver, save, ransom, disentangle, disengage, extricate, clear, rid, relieve, unburden, exempt, absolve, acquit.
F3 imprison, confine.

freedom *noun* **1** *freedom from oppression*: liberty, emancipation, deliverance, release, exemption, immunity, impunity. **2** *win their freedom*: independence, autonomy, self-government, home rule. **3** *allow them a certain amount of freedom*: range, scope, play, leeway, latitude, licence, privilege, power, free rein, free hand, opportunity, informality.
F3 **1** captivity, confinement. **3** restriction.

freely *adverb* **1** *come freely*: readily, willingly, voluntarily, spontaneously, easily. **2** *give freely*: generously, liberally, lavishly, extravagantly, amply, abundantly. **3** *speak freely*: frankly, candidly, unreservedly, openly, plainly.
F3 **2** grudgingly. **3** evasively, cautiously.

freeze *verb* **1** *the sea froze*: ice over, ice up, glaciate, congeal, solidify, harden, stiffen. **2** *freeze the meat*: deep-freeze, ice, refrigerate, chill, cool. **3** *freeze wages*: stop, suspend, fix, immobilize, hold.
▪ *noun* **1** *a sudden freeze*: frost, freeze-up. **2** *a freeze on production*: stoppage, halt, standstill, shutdown, suspension, interruption, postponement, stay, embargo, moratorium.

freezing *adjective* icy, frosty, glacial, arctic, polar, Siberian, wintry, raw, bitter, biting, cutting, penetrating, numbing, cold, chilly.
F3 hot, warm.

freight *noun* cargo, load, lading, pay-load, contents, goods, merchandise, consignment, shipment, transportation, conveyance, carriage, haulage.

frenzied *adjective* frantic, frenetic, hectic, feverish, desperate, furious, wild, uncontrolled, mad, demented, hysterical.
F3 calm, composed.

frenzy *noun* **1** *drive him into a frenzy*: turmoil, agitation, distraction, derangement, madness, lunacy, mania, hysteria, delirium, fever. **2** *in a frenzy of activity*: burst, fit, spasm, paroxysm, convulsion, seizure, outburst, transport, passion, rage, fury.
F3 **1** calm, composure.

frequent *adjective* **1** *frequent storms*: numerous, countless, incessant, constant, continual, persistent, repeated, recurring, regular. **2** *a frequent visitor*: common, commonplace, everyday, familiar, usual, customary.
F3 **1** infrequent.
▪ *verb* visit, patronize, attend, haunt, hang out at (*infml*), associate with, hang about with (*infml*), hang out with (*infml*).

fresh *adjective* **1** *fresh supplies*: additional, other, supplementary, extra, more, further. **2** *a fresh approach*: new, novel, innovative, original, different, unconventional, modern, up-to-date, recent, latest. **3** *a fresh breeze*: refreshing, bracing, invigorating, brisk, crisp, keen, cool, fair, bright, clear, pure. **4** *fresh fruit*: raw, natural, unprocessed. **5** *feeling fresh and clean*: refreshed, revived, restored, renewed, rested, invigorated, energetic, vigorous, lively, alert. **6** *don't be so fresh!*: pert, saucy (*infml*), cheeky (*infml*), disrespectful, impudent, insolent, bold, brazen, forward, familiar, presumptuous.

F3 **2** old, hackneyed. **4** dried, processed. **5** tired, stale.

freshen *verb* **1** *a cool breeze freshening the humid air*: air, ventilate, purify. **2** *change the water to freshen the flowers*: refresh, restore, revitalize, reinvigorate, liven, enliven, spruce up.

F3 **2** tire.

fret *verb* worry, agonize, brood, pine.

friction *noun* **1** *some friction between workers and management*: disagreement, dissension, dispute, disharmony, conflict, antagonism, hostility, opposition, rivalry, animosity, ill feeling, bad blood, resentment. **2** *damage caused by friction*: rubbing, chafing, irritation, abrasion, scraping, grating, rasping, erosion, wearing away, resistance.

friend *noun* mate (*infml*), pal (*infml*), chum (*infml*), buddy (*infml*), crony (*infml*), intimate, confidant(e), bosom friend, soul mate, comrade, ally, partner, sidekick (*infml*), associate, companion, playmate, pen-friend, acquaintance, well-wisher, supporter.

F3 enemy, opponent.

friendly *adjective* **1** *friendly neighbours*: amiable, affable, genial, kind, kindly, neighbourly, helpful, sympathetic, fond, affectionate, familiar, intimate, close, matey (*infml*), pally (*infml*), chummy (*infml*), companionable, sociable, outgoing, approachable, receptive, amicable, peaceable, well-disposed, favourable. **2** *a friendly atmosphere*: convivial, congenial, cordial, welcoming, warm.

F3 **1** hostile, unsociable. **2** cold.

friendship *noun* closeness, intimacy, familiarity, affinity, rapport, attachment, affection, fondness, love, harmony, concord, goodwill, friendliness, alliance, fellowship, camaraderie, comradeship.

F3 enmity, animosity.

fright *noun* shock, scare, alarm, consternation, dismay, dread, apprehension, trepidation, fear, terror, horror, panic.

frighten *verb* alarm, daunt, unnerve, dismay, intimidate, terrorize, scare, startle, scare stiff, terrify, petrify, horrify, appal, shock.

reassure, calm.

frightening *adjective* alarming, daunting, formidable, fearsome, scary, terrifying, hair-raising, bloodcurdling, spine-chilling, petrifying, traumatic.

frightful *adjective* unpleasant, disagreeable, awful, dreadful, fearful, terrible, appalling, shocking, harrowing, unspeakable, dire, grim, ghastly, hideous, horrible, horrid, grisly, macabre, gruesome.

pleasant, agreeable.

frilly *adjective* ruffled, crimped, gathered, frilled, trimmed, lacy, fancy, ornate.

plain.

fringe *noun* **1** *on the fringes of society/the town*: margin, periphery, outskirts, edge, perimeter, limits, borderline. **2** *a fringe of lace*: border, edging, trimming, tassel, frill, valance.

▪ *adjective* unconventional, unorthodox, unofficial, alternative, avant-garde.

conventional, mainstream.

fritter *verb* waste, squander, dissipate, idle, misspend, blow (*infml*).

frolic *verb* gambol, caper, romp, play, lark around, rollick, make merry, frisk, prance, cavort, dance.

front *noun* **1** *the front of the building*: face, aspect, frontage, façade, outside, exterior, facing, cover, obverse, top, head, lead, vanguard, forefront, front line, foreground, forepart, bow. **2** *put on a front*: pretence, show, air, appearance, look, expression, manner, façade, cover, mask, disguise, pretext, cover-up.

1 back, rear.

▪ *adjective* fore, leading, foremost, head, first.

back, rear, last.

frontier *noun* border, boundary, borderline, limit, edge, perimeter, confines, marches, bounds, verge.

frosty *adjective* **1** *a frosty morning*: icy, frozen, freezing, frigid, wintry, cold, chilly. **2** *a frosty reception*: unfriendly, unwelcoming, cool, aloof, standoffish, stiff, discouraging.

warm.

froth *noun* bubbles, effervescence, foam, lather, suds, head, scum.

frown *noun* scowl, glower, dirty look (*infml*), glare, grimace.

▪ *verb* scowl, glower, lour, glare, grimace.

frozen *adjective* iced, chilled, icy, icebound, ice-covered, arctic, ice-cold, frigid, freezing, numb, solidified, stiff, rigid, fixed.

warm.

frugal *adjective* thrifty, penny-wise, parsimonious, careful, provident, saving, economical, sparing, meagre.

wasteful, generous.

fruit

Varieties of fruit include:
apple, Bramley, Cox's Orange Pippin, crab apple, Golden Delicious, Granny Smith; pear, Conference, William; orange, Jaffa, clementine, mandarin, satsuma, Seville, tangerine; apricot, avocado, cherry, damson, gooseberry, goosegog (*infml*), grape, greengage, nectarine, peach, plum, rhubarb, sloe, tomato; banana, date, fig, grapefruit, guava, lemon, lime, kiwi fruit, kumquat, lychee, mango, olive, papaya, pawpaw, pineapple, pomegranate, star fruit, Ugli® fruit; melon, cantaloupe, Galia, honeydew, watermelon; bilberry, blackberry, blueberry, boysenberry, cranberry, elderberry, loganberry, raspberry, strawberry; blackcurrant, redcurrant.

fruitful *adjective* **1** *a lush and fruitful land*: fertile, rich, teeming, plentiful, abundant, prolific, productive. **2** *a fruitful meeting*: rewarding, profitable, advantageous, beneficial, worthwhile, well-spent, useful, successful.
F3 **1** barren. **2** fruitless.

fruitless *adjective* unsuccessful, abortive, useless, futile, pointless, vain, idle, hopeless, barren, sterile.
F3 fruitful, successful, profitable.

frustrate *verb* **1** *frustrating their hopes for promotion*: thwart, foil, baffle, block, check, spike, defeat, circumvent, forestall, counter, nullify, neutralize, inhibit. **2** *frustrated by his failure*: disappoint, discourage, dishearten, depress.
F3 **1** further, promote. **2** encourage.

fuel *noun* combustible, propellant, motive power.
▪ *verb* incite, inflame, fire, encourage, fan, feed, nourish, sustain, stoke up.
F3 discourage, damp down.

fugitive *noun* escapee, runaway, deserter, refugee.

fulfil *verb* complete, finish, conclude, consummate, perfect, realize, achieve, accomplish, perform, execute, discharge, implement, carry out, comply with, observe, keep, obey, conform to, satisfy, fill, answer.
F3 fail, break.

fulfilment *noun* completion, perfection, consummation, realization, achievement, accomplishment, success, performance, execution, discharge, implementation, observance, satisfaction.
F3 failure.

full *adjective* **1** *full of water/people*: filled, loaded, packed, crowded, crammed, stuffed, jammed. **2** *the full range of colours*: entire, whole, intact, total, complete, unabridged, unexpurgated. **3** *a full report/list*: thorough, comprehensive, exhaustive, all-inclusive, broad,

vast, extensive, ample, generous, abundant, plentiful, copious, profuse. **4** *a full sound*: rich, resonant, loud, deep, clear, distinct. **5** *at full speed*: maximum, top, highest, greatest, utmost.
F3 1 empty. **2** partial, incomplete. **3** selective. **4** thin, reedy.

full-grown *adjective* adult, grown-up, of age, mature, ripe, developed, full-blown, full-scale.
F3 young, undeveloped, immature.

fully *adverb* completely, totally, utterly, wholly, entirely, thoroughly, altogether, quite, positively, without reserve, perfectly.
F3 partly.

fumble *verb* grope, feel, bungle, botch, mishandle, mismanage.

fume *verb* **1** *the volcano fumed*: smoke, smoulder, boil, steam. **2** *fume with indignation*: rage, storm, rant, rave, seethe.

fumes *noun* exhaust, smoke, gas, vapour, haze, fog, smog, pollution.

fun *noun* enjoyment, pleasure, amusement, entertainment, diversion, distraction, recreation, play, sport, game, foolery, tomfoolery, horseplay, skylarking, romp, merrymaking, mirth, jollity, jocularity, joking, jesting.

function *noun* **1** *what's his function?*: role, part, office, duty, charge, responsibility, concern, job, task, occupation, business, activity, purpose, use. **2** *a formal function*: reception, party, gathering, affair, do (*infml*), dinner, luncheon.
▪ *verb* work, operate, run, go, serve, act, perform, behave.

functional *adjective* working, operational, practical, useful, utilitarian, utility, plain, hard-wearing.
F3 useless, decorative.

fund *noun* pool, kitty, treasury, repository, storehouse, store, reserve, stock, hoard, cache, stack, mine, well, source, supply.
▪ *verb* finance, capitalize, endow, subsidize, underwrite, sponsor, back, support, promote, float.

fundamental *adjective* basic, primary, first, rudimentary, elementary, underlying, integral, central, principal, cardinal, prime, main, key, essential, indispensable, vital, necessary, crucial, important.

funds *noun* money, finance, backing, capital, resources, savings, wealth, cash.

funeral *noun* burial, interment, entombment, cremation, obsequies, wake.

funnel *verb* channel, direct, convey, move, transfer, pass, pour, siphon, filter.

funny *adjective* **1** *a funny story*: humorous, amusing, entertaining, comic, comical, silly, hilarious, witty, facetious, droll, farcical, laughable, ridiculous, absurd. **2** *funny behaviour*: odd, strange, peculiar, curious, queer, weird, unusual, remarkable, puzzling, perplexing, mysterious, suspicious, dubious.

F3 **1** serious, solemn, sad. **2** normal, ordinary, usual.

furious *adjective* **1** *he was furious with us*: angry, mad (*infml*), up in arms (*infml*), livid, enraged, infuriated, incensed, raging, fuming, boiling. **2** *a furious wind*: violent, wild, fierce, intense, vigorous, frantic, boisterous, stormy, tempestuous.

F3 **1** calm, pleased.

furnish *verb* equip, fit out, decorate, rig, stock, provide, supply, afford, grant, give, offer, present.

F3 divest.

furniture *noun* equipment, appliances, furnishings, fittings, fitments, household goods, movables, possessions, effects, things.

furrow *noun* groove, channel, trench, hollow, rut, track, line, crease, wrinkle.

▪ *verb* seam, flute, corrugate, groove, crease, wrinkle, draw together, knit.

further *adjective* more, additional, supplementary, extra, fresh, new, other.

▪ *verb* advance, forward, promote, champion, push, encourage, foster, help, aid, assist, ease, facilitate, speed, hasten, accelerate, expedite.

F3 stop, frustrate.

furthermore *adverb* moreover, what's more, in addition, further, besides, also, too, as well, additionally.

furthest *adjective* farthest, furthermost, remotest, outermost, outmost, extreme, ultimate, utmost, uttermost.

F3 nearest.

furtive *adjective* surreptitious, sly, stealthy, secretive, underhand, hidden, covert, secret.

F3 open.

fury *noun* anger, rage, wrath, frenzy, madness, passion, vehemence, fierceness, ferocity, violence, wildness, turbulence, power.

F3 calm, peacefulness.

fusion *noun* melting, smelting, welding, union, synthesis, blending, coalescence, amalgamation, integration, merger, federation.

fuss *noun* bother, trouble, hassle (*infml*), palaver, to-do (*infml*), hoo-ha (*infml*), furore, squabble, row, commotion, stir, fluster, confusion, upset, worry, agitation, flap (*infml*), excitement, bustle, flurry, hurry.

F3 calm.

▪ *verb* complain, grumble, fret, worry, flap (*infml*), take pains, bother, bustle, fidget.

fussy *adjective* **1** *fussy about what she eats*: particular, fastidious, scrupulous, finicky, pernickety, difficult, hard to please, choosy (*infml*), discriminating. **2** *a fussy pattern*: fancy, elaborate, ornate, cluttered.

F3 **1** casual, uncritical. **2** plain.

futile *adjective* pointless, useless,

worthless, vain, idle, wasted, fruitless, profitless, unavailing, unsuccessful, abortive, unprofitable, unproductive, barren, empty, hollow, forlorn.
F3 fruitful, profitable.
future *noun* hereafter, tomorrow, outlook, prospects, expectations.
F3 past.
▪ *adjective* prospective, designate, to be, fated, destined, to come, forthcoming, in the offing, impending, coming, approaching, expected, planned, unborn, later, subsequent, eventual.
F3 past.
fuzzy *adjective* **1** *fuzzy hair*: frizzy, fluffy, furry, woolly, fleecy, downy, velvety, napped. **2** *a fuzzy outline*: blurred, unfocused, ill-defined, unclear, vague, faint, hazy, shadowy, woolly, muffled, distorted.
F3 2 clear, distinct.

G

gadget *noun* tool, appliance, device, contrivance, contraption, thing, thingumajig (*infml*), invention, novelty, gimmick.
gaiety *noun* **1** *the gaiety of the occasion*: happiness, glee, cheerfulness, joie de vivre, jollity, merriment, mirth, hilarity, fun, merrymaking, revelry, festivity, celebration, joviality, high spirits, light-heartedness, liveliness. **2** *the gaiety of their costumes*: brightness, brilliance, sparkle, colour, colourfulness, show, showiness.
F3 1 sadness. **2** drabness.
gaily *adverb* **1** *whistling gaily as he worked*: happily, joyfully, merrily, blithely. **2** *gaily coloured costumes*: brightly, brilliantly, colourfully, flamboyantly.
F3 1 sadly. **2** dully.
gain *verb* **1** *gain a place at university*: secure, net, obtain, acquire, procure, reap, harvest, win, capture. **2** *shares gained 20%*: earn, make, produce, gross, net, clear, profit, yield, bring in. **3** *gain one's objective*: reach, arrive at, come to, get to, attain, achieve, realize. **4** *gain speed*: increase, pick up, gather, collect, advance, progress, improve.
F3 1 lose. **2** lose. **4** reduce.
gale *noun* wind, squall, storm, hurricane, tornado, typhoon, cyclone.
gallant *adjective* chivalrous, gentlemanly, courteous, polite, gracious, courtly, noble, dashing,

heroic, valiant, brave, courageous, fearless, dauntless, bold, daring.
F3 ungentlemanly, cowardly.

gallop *verb* bolt, run, sprint, race, career, fly, dash, tear, speed, zoom, shoot, dart, rush, hurry, hasten.
F3 amble.

gamble *verb* bet, wager, have a flutter (*infml*), try one's luck, punt, play, game, stake, chance, take a chance, risk, hazard, venture, speculate, back.

game[1] *noun* **1** *enjoy sports and games*: recreation, play, sport, pastime, diversion, distraction, entertainment, amusement, fun, frolic, romp, joke, jest. **2** *the Olympic Games*: competition, contest, match, round, tournament, event, meeting. **3** *shoot wild game*: game birds, animals, meat, flesh, prey, quarry, bag, spoils.

game[2] *adjective* **1** *game for anything*: willing, inclined, ready, prepared, eager. **2** *a game attempt*: bold, daring, intrepid, brave, courageous, fearless, resolute, spirited.
F3 **1** unwilling. **2** cowardly.

gang *noun* group, band, ring, pack, herd, mob, crowd, circle, clique, coterie, set, lot, posse, team, crew, squad, shift, party.

gap *noun* **1** *gap in the clouds*: space, blank, void, hole, opening, crack, chink, crevice, cleft, breach, rift, divide, divergence, difference. **2** *gap in the conversation*: break, interruption, recess, pause, lull, interlude, intermission, interval.

gape *verb* **1** *gaping at the TV*: stare, gaze, gawp (*infml*), goggle, gawk (*infml*). **2** *beaks gaping*: open, yawn, part, split, crack.

garbled *adjective* confused, muddled, jumbled, scrambled, mixed up.

gash *verb* cut, wound, slash, slit, incise, lacerate, tear, rend, split, score, gouge.
▪ *noun* cut, wound, slash, slit, incision, laceration, tear, rent, split, score, gouge.

gasp *verb* pant, puff, blow, breathe, wheeze, choke, gulp.
▪ *noun* pant, puff, blow, breath, gulp, exclamation.

gate *noun* barrier, door, doorway, gateway, opening, entrance, exit, access, passage.

gather *verb* **1** *gathering at the concert venue*: congregate, convene, muster, rally, round up, assemble, collect, group, amass, accumulate, hoard, stockpile, heap, pile up, build. **2** *I gather he's leaving*: infer, deduce, conclude, surmise, assume, understand, learn, hear. **3** *gathering the fabric at the waist*: fold, pleat, tuck, pucker. **4** *gather flowers/information*: pick, pluck, cull, select, reap, harvest, glean.
F3 **1** scatter, dissipate.

gathering *noun* assembly, convocation (*fml*), convention, meeting, round-up, rally, get-together, jamboree, party, group, company, congregation, mass, crowd, throng, turnout.

gauge *verb* estimate, guess, judge, assess, evaluate, value, rate, reckon, figure, calculate, compute, count, measure, weigh, determine, ascertain.
▪ *noun* **1** *the gauge of excellence*: standard, norm, criterion, benchmark, yardstick, rule, guideline, indicator, measure, meter, test, sample, example, model, pattern. **2** *a wider gauge of barrel*: size, magnitude, measure, capacity, bore, calibre, thickness, width, span, extent, scope, height, depth, degree.

gaunt *adjective* haggard, hollow-eyed, angular, bony, thin, lean, lank, skinny, scraggy, scrawny, skeletal, emaciated, wasted.
F∃ plump.

gaze *verb* stare, contemplate, regard, watch, view, look, gape, wonder.
▪ *noun* stare, look.

gear *noun* **1** *lifting gear*: equipment, kit, outfit, tackle, apparatus, tools, instruments, accessories. **2** *engage first gear*: gearwheel, cogwheel, cog, gearing, mechanism, machinery, works. **3** *(infml) pack their gear*: belongings, possessions, things, stuff *(infml)*, baggage, luggage, paraphernalia. **4** *(infml) trendy gear*: clothes, clothing, garments, attire, dress, garb *(infml)*, togs *(infml)*, get-up *(infml)*.

gem *noun* gemstone, precious stone, stone, jewel, treasure, prize, masterpiece, pièce de résistance.

general *adjective* **1** *a general statement*: broad, blanket, sweeping, all-inclusive, comprehensive, universal, global, total, across-the-board, widespread, prevalent, extensive, overall, panoramic. **2** *a general feeling of ill-ease*: vague, ill-defined, indefinite, imprecise, inexact, approximate, loose, unspecific. **3** *the general opinion*: usual, regular, normal, typical, ordinary, everyday, customary, conventional, common, public.
F∃ **1** particular, limited. **2** specific. **3** rare.

generally *adverb* usually, normally, as a rule, by and large, on the whole, mostly, mainly, chiefly, broadly, commonly, universally.

generate *verb* produce, engender, whip up, arouse, cause, bring about, give rise to, create, originate, initiate, make, form, breed, propagate.
F∃ prevent.

generation *noun* **1** *the younger/older generation*: age group, age, era, epoch, period, time. **2** *generation of profits*: production, creation, origination, formation, genesis, procreation, reproduction, propagation, breeding.

generosity *noun* liberality, munificence, open-handedness, bounty, charity, magnanimity, philanthropy, kindness, big-

heartedness, benevolence, goodness.
meanness, selfishness.

generous *adjective* **1** *a generous gesture*: liberal, free, bountiful, open-handed, unstinting, unsparing, lavish. **2** *a generous person*: magnanimous, charitable, philanthropic, public-spirited, unselfish, kind, big-hearted, benevolent, good, high-minded, noble. **3** *a generous allowance*: ample, full, plentiful, abundant, overflowing, copious.
1 mean, miserly. **2** selfish. **3** meagre.

genial *adjective* affable, amiable, friendly, convivial, cordial, kindly, kind, warm-hearted, warm, hearty, jovial, jolly, cheerful, happy, good-natured, easy-going (*infml*), agreeable, pleasant.
cold.

genius *noun* **1** *she's a mathematical genius*: virtuoso, maestro, master, past master, expert, adept, egghead (*infml*), intellectual, mastermind, brain, intellect. **2** *Einstein's genius*: intelligence, brightness, brilliance, ability, aptitude, gift, talent, flair, knack, bent, inclination, propensity, capacity, faculty.

gentle *adjective* **1** *a gentle person*: kind, kindly, amiable, tender, soft-hearted, compassionate, sympathetic, merciful, mild, placid, calm, tranquil. **2** *a gentle slope*: gradual, slow, easy, smooth, moderate, slight, light, imperceptible. **3** *a gentle breeze*: soothing, peaceful, serene, quiet, soft, balmy.
1 unkind, rough. **3** harsh, wild.

genuine *adjective* real, actual, natural, pure, original, authentic, veritable (*fml*), true, bona fide, legitimate, honest, sincere, frank, candid, earnest.
artificial, false, insincere.

geography

Terms used in geography include:
archipelago, base level, bergschrund, chorography, cirque, col, continental drift, deforestation, denudation, ecosystem, effluent, equator, erosion, estuary, fjord, floodplain, glacial, glaciate, glaciation, hanging valley, headwaters, ice cap, inlet, line of latitude, line of longitude, Mercator's projection, meridian, moraine, oxbow lake, peneplain, permafrost, plateau, plate tectonics, prime meridian, prograde, ria, roche moutonnée, shield volcano, shott, stratum, taiga, tributary, tundra, water cycle, weathering, zenithal projection.

---

germ *noun* **1** *catch germs*: micro-organism, microbe, bacterium, bacillus, virus, bug (*infml*). **2** *the germ of an idea*: beginning, start, origin, source, cause, spark, rudiment, nucleus, root, seed, embryo, bud, sprout.

germinate *verb* bud, sprout,

shoot, develop, grow, swell.

gesticulate *verb* wave, signal, gesture, indicate, sign.

gesture *noun* act, action, movement, motion, indication, sign, signal, wave, gesticulation.

get *verb* **1** *get a job/rise/letter*: obtain, acquire, procure, come by, receive, earn, gain, win, secure, achieve, realize. **2** *it's getting dark*: become, turn, go, grow. **3** *get him to help*: persuade, coax, induce, urge, influence, sway. **4** *getting home*: move, go, come, reach, arrive. **5** *get the newspaper/get a bite to eat*: fetch, collect, pick up, take, catch, capture, seize, grab. **6** *get mumps*: contract, catch, pick up, develop, come down with.

F3 **1** lose. **4** leave.

ghastly *adjective* awful, dreadful, frightful, terrible, grim, gruesome, hideous, horrible, horrid, loathsome, repellent, shocking, appalling.

F3 delightful, attractive.

ghost *noun* spectre, phantom, spook (*infml*), apparition, visitant, spirit, wraith, soul, shade, shadow.

ghostly *adjective* eerie, spooky (*infml*), creepy, supernatural, unearthly, ghostlike, spectral, wraith-like, phantom, illusory.

giant *noun* monster, titan, colossus, ogre, Goliath, Hercules.
▪ *adjective* gigantic, colossal, titanic, mammoth, jumbo (*infml*), humungous (*infml*), king-size, huge, enormous, immense, vast, large.

gibe, **jibe** *noun* jeer, sneer, mockery, ridicule, taunt, derision, scoff, dig (*infml*), crack (*infml*), poke, quip.

gift *noun* **1** *birthday gifts*: present, offering, donation, contribution, bounty, largess, gratuity, tip, bonus, freebie (*infml*), legacy, bequest, endowment. **2** *have a real gift*: talent, genius, flair, aptitude, bent, knack, power, faculty, attribute, ability, capability, capacity.

gifted *adjective* talented, adept, skilful, expert, masterly, skilled, accomplished, able, capable, clever, intelligent, bright, brilliant.

gigantic *adjective* huge, enormous, immense, vast, giant, colossal, titanic, mammoth, gargantuan, humungous (*infml*), Brobdingnagian.

F3 tiny, Lilliputian.

giggle *verb, noun* titter, snigger, chuckle, chortle, laugh.

gimmick *noun* attraction, ploy, stratagem, ruse, scheme, trick, stunt, dodge, device, contrivance, gadget.

gingerly *adverb* tentatively, hesitantly, warily, cautiously, carefully, delicately.

F3 boldly, carelessly.

girl *noun* lass, young woman, girlfriend, sweetheart, daughter.

gist *noun* pith, essence, marrow, substance, matter, meaning, significance, import, sense, idea, drift, direction, point, nub, core, quintessence.

give *verb* **1** *giving the prizes*: present, award, confer, offer, lend, donate, contribute, provide, supply, furnish, grant, bestow, endow, gift, make over, hand over, deliver, entrust, commit, devote. **2** *give news*: communicate, transmit, impart, utter, announce, declare, pronounce, publish, set forth. **3** *must give you that*: concede, allow, admit, yield, give way, surrender. **4** *give trouble*: cause, occasion, make, produce, do, perform. **5** *give under their weight*: sink, yield, bend, give way, break, collapse, fall.
F3 **1** take, withhold. **5** withstand.

given *adjective* **1** *a given number*: specified, particular, definite. **2** *given to sudden rages*: inclined, disposed, likely, liable, prone.

glad *adjective* **1** *glad to hear you are better*: pleased, delighted, gratified, contented, happy, joyful, merry, cheerful, cheery, bright. **2** *glad to help*: willing, eager, keen, ready, inclined, disposed.
F3 **1** sad, unhappy. **2** unwilling, reluctant.

glamorous *adjective* smart, elegant, attractive, beautiful, gorgeous, enchanting, captivating, alluring, appealing, fascinating, exciting, dazzling, glossy, colourful.
F3 plain, drab, boring.

glamour *noun* attraction, allure, appeal, fascination, charm, magic, beauty, elegance, glitter, prestige.

glance *verb* peep, peek, glimpse, view, look, scan, skim, leaf, flip, thumb, dip, browse.
▪ *noun* peep, peek, glimpse, look.

glare *verb* **1** *she was glaring at us*: glower, look daggers, frown, scowl, stare. **2** *blinded by the sunlight glaring off the water*: dazzle, blaze, flame, flare, shine, reflect.

glaring *adjective* blatant, flagrant, open, conspicuous, manifest, patent, obvious, outrageous, gross.
F3 hidden, concealed, minor.

glaze *verb* coat, enamel, gloss, varnish, lacquer, polish, burnish.
▪ *noun* coat, coating, finish, enamel, varnish, lacquer, polish, shine, lustre, gloss.

gleam *noun, verb* glint, flash, beam, ray, flicker, glimmer, shimmer, sparkle, glitter, gloss, glow.

glib *adjective* fluent, easy, facile, quick, ready, talkative, plausible, insincere, smooth, slick, suave, smooth-tongued.
F3 tongue-tied, implausible.

glide *verb* slide, slip, skate, skim, fly, float, drift, sail, coast, roll, run, flow.

glimmer *verb* glow, shimmer, glisten, glitter, sparkle, twinkle, wink, blink, flicker, gleam, shine.
▪ *noun* **1** *the faint glimmer of moonlight*: glow, shimmer, sparkle, twinkle, flicker, glint, gleam. **2** *not a glimmer of hope*: trace, hint, suggestion, grain.

glimpse *noun* peep, peek, squint, glance, look, sight, sighting, view.

■ *verb* spy, espy, spot, catch sight of, sight, view.

glint *verb* flash, gleam, shine, reflect, glitter, sparkle, twinkle, glimmer.

■ *noun* flash, gleam, shine, reflection, glitter, sparkle, twinkle, glimmer.

glisten *verb* shine, gleam, glint, glitter, sparkle, twinkle, glimmer, shimmer.

glitter *verb* sparkle, spangle, scintillate, twinkle, shimmer, glimmer, glisten, glint, gleam, flash, shine.

■ *noun* sparkle, coruscation, scintillation, twinkle, shimmer, glimmer, glint, gleam, flash, shine, lustre, sheen, brightness, radiance, brilliance, splendour, showiness, glamour.

gloat *verb* triumph, glory, exult, rejoice, revel in, relish, crow, boast, vaunt, rub it in (*infml*).

global *adjective* universal, worldwide, international, general, all-encompassing, total, thorough, exhaustive, comprehensive, all-inclusive, encyclopedic, wide-ranging.

F3 parochial, limited.

globe *noun* world, earth, planet, sphere, ball, orb, round.

gloom *noun* **1** *gloom descended on the company*: depression, low spirits, despondency, dejection, sadness, unhappiness, glumness, melancholy, misery, desolation, despair. **2** *see nothing through the gloom*: dark, darkness, shade, shadow, dusk, twilight, dimness, obscurity, cloud, cloudiness, dullness.

F3 **1** cheerfulness, happiness. **2** brightness.

gloomy *adjective* **1** *feel gloomy about the results*: depressed, down, low, despondent, dejected, downcast, dispirited, down-hearted, sad, miserable, glum, morose, pessimistic, cheerless, dismal, depressing. **2** *a gloomy corner*: dark, sombre, shadowy, dim, obscure, overcast, dull, dreary.

F3 **1** cheerful. **2** bright.

glorious *adjective* **1** *a glorious victory*: illustrious, eminent, distinguished, famous, renowned, noted, great, noble, splendid, magnificent, grand, majestic, triumphant. **2** *a glorious summer day*: fine, bright, radiant, shining, brilliant, dazzling, beautiful, gorgeous, superb, excellent, wonderful, marvellous, delightful, heavenly.

F3 **1** unknown.

gloss *noun* polish, varnish, lustre, sheen, shine, brightness, brilliance, show, appearance, semblance, surface, front, façade, veneer, window-dressing.

glossy *adjective* shiny, sheeny, lustrous, sleek, silky, smooth, glassy, polished, burnished, glazed, enamelled, bright, shining, brilliant.

F3 matt.

glow *noun* light, gleam, glimmer,

radiance, luminosity, brightness, vividness, brilliance, splendour.
▪ *verb* **1** *lamp glowing in the window*: shine, radiate, gleam, glimmer, burn, smoulder. **2** *their faces glowed*: flush, blush, colour, redden.

glowing *adjective* **1** *glowing embers*: bright, luminous, vivid, vibrant, rich, warm, flushed, red, flaming. **2** *a glowing report*: complimentary, enthusiastic, ecstatic, rhapsodic, rave (*infml*).
⇄ **1** dull, colourless. **2** restrained.

glue *noun* adhesive, gum, paste, size, cement.
▪ *verb* stick, affix, gum, paste, seal, bond, cement, fix.

glut *noun* surplus, excess, superfluity, surfeit, overabundance, superabundance, saturation, overflow.
⇄ scarcity, lack.

glutton *noun* gourmand, gourmandizer (*fml*), guzzler, gorger, gobbler, pig.
⇄ ascetic.

gnaw *verb* **1** *mice gnawed a hole in the bag*: bite, nibble, munch, chew, eat, devour, consume, erode, wear. **2** *thought gnawing away at the back of his mind*: worry, niggle, fret, trouble, plague, nag, prey, haunt.

go *verb* **1** *go to school/go immediately*: move, pass, advance, progress, proceed, make for, travel, journey, start, begin, depart, leave, take one's leave, retreat, withdraw, disappear, vanish. **2** *the engine was still going*: operate, function, work, run, act, perform. **3** *going from left to right*: extend, spread, stretch, reach, span, continue, unfold. **4** *time goes quickly*: pass, elapse, lapse, roll on.
⇄ **2** break down, fail.
▪ *noun* **1** *have a go*: attempt, try, shot (*infml*), bash (*infml*), stab (*infml*), turn. **2** *full of go*: energy, get-up-and-go (*infml*), vitality, life, spirit, dynamism, effort.

goad *verb* prod, prick, spur, impel, push, drive, provoke, incite, instigate, arouse, stimulate, prompt, urge, nag, hound, harass, annoy, irritate, vex.

go-ahead *noun* permission, authorization, clearance, green light (*infml*), sanction, assent, consent, OK (*infml*), agreement.
⇄ ban, veto, embargo.
▪ *adjective* enterprising, pioneering, progressive, ambitious, up-and-coming, dynamic, energetic.
⇄ unenterprising, sluggish.

goal *noun* target, mark, objective, aim, intention, object, purpose, end, ambition, aspiration.

gobble *verb* bolt, guzzle, gorge, cram, stuff (*infml*), devour, consume, put away (*infml*), swallow, gulp.

golden *adjective* **1** *golden hair*: gold, gilded, gilt, yellow, blond(e), fair, bright, shining, lustrous. **2** *their golden years*: prosperous, successful, glorious, excellent, happy, joyful, favourable, auspicious, promising, rosy.

good *adjective* **1** *a good service/worker/degree*: acceptable, satisfactory, pleasant, agreeable, nice, enjoyable, pleasing, commendable, excellent, great (*infml*), super (*infml*), first-class, first-rate, superior, advantageous, beneficial, favourable, auspicious, helpful, useful, worthwhile, profitable, appropriate, suitable, fitting. **2** *good at her job*: competent, proficient, skilled, expert, accomplished, professional, skilful, clever, talented, gifted, fit, able, capable, dependable, reliable. **3** *good of you*: kind, considerate, gracious, benevolent, charitable, philanthropic. **4** *a good man*: virtuous, exemplary, moral, upright, honest, trustworthy, worthy, righteous. **5** *you've been a good boy today*: well-behaved, obedient, well-mannered. **6** *have a good look*: thorough, complete, whole, substantial, considerable.
F3 **1** bad, poor. **2** incompetent. **3** unkind, inconsiderate. **4** wicked, immoral. **5** naughty, disobedient.
▪ *noun* **1** *the good and the bad in everyone*: virtue, morality, goodness, righteousness, right. **2** *it's no good*: use, purpose, avail, advantage, profit, gain, worth, merit, usefulness, service. **3** *for your own good*: welfare, well-being, interest, sake, behalf, benefit, convenience.

goodbye *noun* farewell, adieu, au revoir, valediction, leave-taking, parting.

good-natured *adjective* kind, kindly, kind-hearted, sympathetic, benevolent, helpful, neighbourly, gentle, good-tempered, approachable, friendly, tolerant, patient.
F3 ill-natured.

goodness *noun* virtue, uprightness, rectitude, honesty, probity (*fml*), kindness, compassion, graciousness, goodwill, benevolence, unselfishness, generosity, friendliness, helpfulness.
F3 badness, wickedness.

goods *noun* **1** *all their worldly goods*: property, chattels (*fml*), effects, possessions, belongings, paraphernalia, stuff (*infml*), things, gear (*infml*). **2** *sell their goods at the market*: merchandise, wares, commodities, stock, freight.

goodwill *noun* benevolence, kindness, generosity, favour, friendliness, friendship, zeal.
F3 ill-will.

gorge *noun* canyon, ravine, gully, defile (*fml*), chasm, abyss, cleft, fissure, gap, pass.
▪ *verb* feed, guzzle, gobble, devour, bolt, wolf, gulp, swallow, cram, stuff (*infml*), fill, sate, surfeit, glut, overeat.
F3 fast.

gorgeous *adjective* magnificent, splendid, grand, glorious, superb, fine, rich, sumptuous, luxurious,

brilliant, dazzling, showy, glamorous, attractive, beautiful, handsome, good-looking, delightful, pleasing, lovely, enjoyable, good.
F3 dull, plain.

gory *adjective* bloody, sanguinary, bloodstained, blood-soaked, grisly, brutal, savage, murderous.

gossip *noun* **1** *don't listen to gossip*: idle talk, prattle, chitchat, tittle-tattle, rumour, hearsay, report, scandal. **2** *the local gossip*: gossip-monger, scandalmonger, whisperer, prattler, babbler, chatterbox, nosey parker (*infml*), busybody, talebearer, tell-tale, tattler.
▪ *verb* talk, chat, natter, chatter, gabble, tell tales, prattle, tattle, whisper, rumour.

gouge *verb* chisel, cut, hack, incise, score, groove, scratch, claw, gash, slash, dig, scoop, hollow, extract.

gourmet *noun* gastronome, epicure, epicurean, connoisseur, bon vivant.

govern *verb* **1** *governing most of Europe*: rule, reign, direct, manage, superintend, supervise, oversee, preside, lead, head, command, influence, guide, conduct, steer, pilot. **2** *govern one's temper*: dominate, master, control, regulate, curb, check, restrain, contain, quell, subdue, tame, discipline.

government *noun* **1** *blame the government*: administration, executive, ministry, Establishment, authorities, powers that be, state, régime. **2** *government by the people*: rule, sovereignty, sway, direction, management, superintendence, supervision, surveillance, command, charge, authority, guidance, conduct, domination, dominion, control, regulation, restraint.

governor *noun* ruler, commissioner, administrator, executive, director, manager, leader, head, chief, commander, superintendent, supervisor, overseer, controller, boss.

gown *noun* robe, dress, frock, dressing-gown, habit, costume.

grab *verb* seize, snatch, take, nab (*infml*), pluck, snap up, catch hold of, grasp, clutch, grip, catch, bag (*infml*), capture, collar (*infml*), commandeer, appropriate, usurp, annex.

grace *noun* **1** *move with grace*: gracefulness, poise, beauty, attractiveness, loveliness, shapeliness, elegance, tastefulness, refinement, polish, breeding, manners, etiquette, decorum, decency, courtesy, charm. **2** *the grace of God*: kindness, kindliness, compassion, consideration, goodness, virtue, generosity, charity, benevolence, goodwill, favour, forgiveness, indulgence, mercy, leniency, pardon, reprieve. **3** *say grace*: blessing, benediction,

thanksgiving, prayer.
2 cruelty, harshness.

graceful *adjective* easy, flowing, smooth, supple, agile, deft, natural, slender, fine, tasteful, elegant, beautiful, charming, suave.
graceless, awkward, clumsy, ungainly.

gracious *adjective* elegant, refined, polite, courteous, well-mannered, considerate, sweet, obliging, accommodating, kind, compassionate, kindly, benevolent, generous, magnanimous, charitable, hospitable, forgiving, indulgent, lenient, mild, clement, merciful.
ungracious.

grade *noun* rank, status, standing, station, place, position, level, stage, degree, step, rung, notch, mark, brand, quality, standard, condition, size, order, group, class, category.
▪ *verb* sort, arrange, categorize, order, group, class, rate, size, rank, range, classify, evaluate, assess, value, mark, brand, label, pigeonhole, type.

gradient *noun* slope, incline, hill, bank, rise, declivity (*fml*).

gradual *adjective* slow, leisurely, unhurried, easy, gentle, moderate, regular, even, measured, steady, continuous, progressive, step-by-step.
sudden, precipitate (*fml*).

gradually *adverb* little by little, bit by bit, imperceptibly, inch by inch, step by step, progressively, by degrees, piecemeal, slowly, gently, cautiously, gingerly, moderately, evenly, steadily.

graduate *verb* pass, qualify.

graft *noun* implant, implantation, transplant, splice, bud, sprout, shoot, scion.
▪ *verb* engraft, implant, insert, transplant, join, splice.

grain *noun* **1** *a grain of sand*: bit, piece, fragment, scrap, morsel, crumb, granule, particle, molecule, atom, jot, iota, mite, speck, modicum, trace. **2** *making flour from the grain*: seed, kernel, corn, cereals. **3** *the grain of the wood*: texture, fibre, weave, pattern, marking, surface.

grand *adjective* majestic, regal, stately, splendid, magnificent, glorious, superb, sublime, fine, excellent, outstanding, first-rate, impressive, imposing, striking, monumental, large, noble, lordly, lofty, pompous, pretentious, grandiose, ambitious.
humble, common, poor.

grandeur *noun* majesty, stateliness, pomp, state, dignity, splendour, magnificence, nobility, greatness, illustriousness, importance.
humbleness, lowliness, simplicity.

grandiose *adjective* pompous, pretentious, high-flown, lofty, ambitious, extravagant, ostentatious, showy, flamboyant, grand, majestic, stately,

magnificent, impressive, imposing, monumental.
F3 unpretentious.

grant *verb* **1** *grant them leave to appeal*: give, donate, present, award, confer, bestow, impart, transmit, dispense, apportion, assign, allot, allocate, provide, supply. **2** *grant that it is likely*: admit, acknowledge, concede, allow, permit, consent to, agree to, accede to.
F3 1 withhold. **2** deny.
▪ *noun* allowance, subsidy, concession, award, bursary, scholarship, gift, donation, endowment, bequest, annuity, pension, honorarium.

graph *noun* diagram, chart, table, grid.

graphic *adjective* vivid, descriptive, expressive, striking, telling, lively, realistic, explicit, clear, lucid, specific, detailed, blow-by-blow, visual, pictorial, diagrammatic, illustrative.
F3 vague, impressionistic.

grapple *verb* seize, grasp, snatch, grab, grip, clutch, clasp, hold, wrestle, tussle, struggle, contend, fight, combat, clash, engage, encounter, face, confront, tackle, deal with, cope with.
F3 release, avoid, evade.

grasp *verb* **1** *grasping the rope in both hands*: hold, clasp, clutch, grip, grapple, seize, snatch, grab, catch. **2** *grasp a concept*: understand, comprehend, get (*infml*), follow, see, realize.
▪ *noun* **1** *a firm grasp*: grip, clasp, hold, embrace, clutches, possession, control, power. **2** *a good grasp of grammar*: understanding, comprehension, apprehension, mastery, familiarity, knowledge.

grasping *adjective* avaricious, greedy, rapacious, acquisitive, mercenary, mean, selfish, miserly, close-fisted, tight-fisted, parsimonious.
F3 generous.

grass *noun* turf, lawn, green, grassland, field, meadow, pasture, prairie, pampas, savanna, steppe.

grate *verb* **1** *grate the cheese*: grind, shred, mince, pulverize, rub, rasp, scrape. **2** *grate on one's nerves*: jar, set one's teeth on edge, annoy, irritate, aggravate (*infml*), get on one's nerves, vex, irk, exasperate.

grateful *adjective* thankful, appreciative, indebted, obliged, obligated, beholden.
F3 ungrateful.

gratify *verb* satisfy, fulfil, indulge, pander to, humour, favour, please, gladden, delight, thrill.
F3 frustrate, thwart.

grating[1] *adjective* harsh, rasping, scraping, squeaky, strident, discordant, jarring, annoying, irritating, unpleasant, disagreeable.
F3 harmonious, pleasing.

grating[2] *noun* grate, grill, grid, lattice, trellis.

gratitude *noun* gratefulness,

thankfulness, thanks, appreciation, acknowledgement, recognition, indebtedness, obligation.
F3 ingratitude, ungratefulness.

gratuitous *adjective* wanton, unnecessary, needless, superfluous, unwarranted, unjustified, groundless, undeserved, unprovoked, uncalled-for, unasked-for, unsolicited, voluntary, free, gratis, complimentary.
F3 justified, provoked.

grave[1] *noun* burial-place, tomb, vault, crypt, sepulchre, mausoleum, pit, barrow, tumulus, cairn.

grave[2] *adjective* **1** *a grave mistake*: important, significant, weighty, momentous, serious, critical, vital, crucial, urgent, acute, severe, dangerous, hazardous. **2** *look grave*: solemn, dignified, sober, sedate, serious, thoughtful, pensive, grim, long-faced, quiet, reserved, subdued, restrained.
F3 **1** trivial, light, slight. **2** cheerful.

gravity *noun* **1** *realize the gravity of their predicament*: importance, significance, seriousness, urgency, acuteness, severity, danger. **2** *the gravity of his expression*: solemnity, dignity, sobriety, seriousness, thoughtfulness, sombreness, reserve, restraint. **3** *force of gravity*: gravitation, attraction, pull, weight, heaviness.
F3 **1** triviality. **2** levity.

graze *verb* scratch, scrape, skin, abrade, rub, chafe, shave, brush, skim, touch.
▪ *noun* scratch, scrape, abrasion.

grease *noun* oil, lubrication, fat, lard, dripping, tallow.

greasy *adjective* oily, fatty, lardy, buttery, smeary, slimy, slippery, smooth, waxy.

great *adjective* **1** *a great house/the Great Plains*: large, big, huge, enormous, massive, colossal, gigantic, mammoth, immense, vast, impressive. **2** *with great care*: considerable, pronounced, extreme, excessive, inordinate. **3** *a great actor*: famous, renowned, celebrated, illustrious, eminent, distinguished, prominent, noteworthy, notable, remarkable, outstanding, grand, glorious, fine. **4** *a great discovery*: important, significant, serious, major, principal, primary, main, chief, leading. **5** *(infml) that's great!*: excellent, first-rate, superb, wonderful, marvellous, tremendous, terrific, fantastic (*infml*), cool (*infml*), wicked (*infml*).
F3 **1** small. **2** slight. **3** unknown. **4** unimportant, insignificant.

greedy *adjective* **1** *a greedy boy*: hungry, starving, ravenous, gluttonous, gourmandizing (*fml*), voracious, insatiable. **2** *greedy for money and power*: acquisitive, covetous, desirous, craving, eager, impatient, avaricious, grasping, selfish.
F3 **1** abstemious.

green *adjective* **1** *a green field*: grassy, leafy, verdant, unripe, unseasoned, tender, fresh, budding, blooming, flourishing. **2** *too green to know better*: immature, naive, unsophisticated, ignorant, inexperienced, untrained, raw, new, recent, young. **3** *green issues*: ecological, environmental, eco-friendly, environmentally aware.
▪ *noun* common, lawn, grass, turf.

greenhouse *noun* glasshouse, hothouse, conservatory, pavilion, vinery, orangery.

greet *verb* hail, salute, acknowledge, address, accost, meet, receive, welcome.
ignore.

greeting *noun* salutation, acknowledgement, wave, hallo, the time of day, address, reception, welcome.

greetings *noun* regards, respects, compliments, salutations, best wishes, good wishes, love.

gregarious *adjective* sociable, outgoing, extrovert, friendly, affable, social, convivial, cordial, warm.
unsociable.

grey *adjective* **1** *a grey colour/day*: neutral, colourless, pale, ashen, leaden, dull, cloudy, overcast, dim, dark, murky. **2** *a grey industrial landscape*: gloomy, dismal, cheerless, depressing, dreary, bleak.

grief *noun* sorrow, sadness, unhappiness, depression, dejection, desolation, distress, misery, woe, heartbreak, mourning, bereavement, heartache, anguish, agony, pain, suffering, affliction, trouble, regret, remorse.
happiness, delight.

grievance *noun* complaint, moan (*infml*), grumble (*infml*), resentment, objection, protest, charge, wrong, injustice, injury, damage, trouble, affliction, hardship, trial, tribulation.

grieve *verb* **1** *grieving for his dead wife*: sorrow, mope, lament, mourn, wail, cry, weep. **2** *grieves me that he didn't take my advice*: sadden, upset, dismay, distress, afflict, pain, hurt, wound.
1 rejoice. **2** please, gladden.

grim *adjective* **1** *a grim sight*: unpleasant, horrible, horrid, ghastly, gruesome, grisly, sinister, frightening, fearsome, terrible, shocking. **2** *a grim expression*: stern, severe, harsh, dour, forbidding, surly, sullen, morose, gloomy, depressing, unattractive.
1 pleasant. **2** attractive.

grimace *noun* frown, scowl, pout, smirk, sneer, face.
▪ *verb* make a face, pull a face, frown, scowl, pout, smirk, sneer.

grind *verb* crush, pound, pulverize, powder, mill, grate, scrape, gnash, rut, abrade, sand, file, smooth, polish, sharpen, whet.

grip *noun* hold, grasp, clasp, embrace, clutches, control, power.

▪ *verb* **1** *grip the rock*: hold, grasp, clasp, clutch, seize, grab, catch. **2** *gripped by the film*: fascinate, thrill, enthral, spellbind, mesmerize, hypnotize, rivet, engross, absorb, involve, engage, compel.

grisly *adjective* gruesome, gory, grim, macabre, horrid, horrible, ghastly, awful, frightful, terrible, dreadful, abominable, appalling, shocking.

F3 delightful.

grit *noun* gravel, pebbles, shingle, sand, dust.

▪ *verb* clench, gnash, grate, grind.

groan *noun* moan, sigh, cry, whine, wail, lament, complaint, objection, grumble, protest, outcry.

F3 cheer.

▪ *verb* moan, sigh, cry, whine, wail, lament, complain, object, protest, grumble.

F3 cheer.

groom *verb* **1** *grooming the horses*: smarten, neaten, tidy, spruce up, clean, brush, curry, preen, dress. **2** *groomed for her new post*: prepare, train, school, educate, drill.

groove *noun* furrow, rut, track, slot, channel, gutter, trench, hollow, indentation, score.

F3 ridge.

grope *verb* feel, fumble, scrabble, flounder, cast about, fish, search, probe.

gross *adjective* **1** *gross misconduct*: serious, grievous, blatant, flagrant, glaring, obvious, plain, sheer, utter, outright, shameful, shocking. **2** *don't be so gross!*: obscene, lewd, improper, indecent, offensive, rude, coarse, crude, vulgar, tasteless. **3** *a gross body*: fat, obese, overweight, big, large, huge, colossal, hulking, bulky, heavy. **4** *gross earnings*: inclusive, all-inclusive, total, aggregate, entire, complete, whole.

F3 **3** slight. **4** net.

grotesque *adjective* bizarre, odd, weird, unnatural, freakish, monstrous, hideous, ugly, unsightly, misshapen, deformed, distorted, twisted, fantastic, fanciful, extravagant, absurd, surreal, macabre.

F3 normal, graceful.

ground *noun* **1** *feet on the ground*: bottom, foundation, surface, land, terrain, dry land, terra firma, earth, soil, clay, loam, dirt, dust. **2** *football ground*: field, pitch, stadium, arena, park.

groundless *adjective* baseless, unfounded, unsubstantiated, unsupported, empty, imaginary, false, unjustified, unwarranted, unprovoked, uncalled-for.

F3 well-founded, reasonable, justified.

grounds[1] *noun* land, terrain, holding, estate, property, territory, domain, gardens, park, campus, surroundings, fields, acres.

grounds[2] *noun* base, foundation, justification, excuse, vindication, reason, motive, inducement, cause, occasion, call, score, account, argument, principle, basis.

group *noun* band, gang, pack, team, crew, troop, squad, detachment, party, faction, set, circle, clique, club, society, association, organization, company, gathering, congregation, crowd, collection, bunch, clump, cluster, conglomeration, constellation, batch, lot, combination, formation, grouping, class, classification, category, genus, species.

▪ *verb* **1** *grouped around their parents*: gather, collect, assemble, congregate, mass, cluster, clump, bunch. **2** *group them according to size*: sort, range, arrange, marshal, organize, order, class, classify, categorize, band, link, associate.

grovel *verb* crawl, creep, ingratiate oneself, toady, suck up (*infml*), flatter, fawn, cringe, cower, kowtow, defer, demean oneself.

grow *verb* **1** *grow in size*: increase, rise, expand, enlarge, swell, spread, extend, stretch, develop, proliferate, mushroom. **2** *grow from seed*: originate, arise, issue, spring, germinate, shoot, sprout, bud, flower, mature, develop, progress, thrive, flourish, prosper. **3** *grow crops*: cultivate, farm, produce, propagate, breed, raise. **4** *grow cold*: become, get, go, turn.

F3 **1** decrease, shrink.

growl *verb* snarl, snap, yap, rumble, roar.

grown-up *adjective* adult, mature, of age, full-grown, fully-fledged.

F3 young, immature.

▪ *noun* adult, man, woman.

F3 child.

growth *noun* **1** *the growth in prosperity*: increase, rise, extension, enlargement, expansion, spread, proliferation, development, evolution, progress, advance, improvement, success, prosperity. **2** *a cancerous growth*: tumour, lump, swelling, protuberance (*fml*), outgrowth.

F3 **1** decrease, decline, failure.

grub *noun* maggot, worm, larva, pupa, caterpillar, chrysalis.

grudge *noun* resentment, bitterness, envy, jealousy, spite, malice, enmity, antagonism, hate, dislike, animosity, ill-will, hard feelings, grievance.

F3 favour.

▪ *verb* begrudge, resent, envy, covet, dislike, take exception to, object to, mind.

grudging *adjective* reluctant, unwilling, hesitant, half-hearted, unenthusiastic, resentful, envious, jealous.

gruelling *adjective* hard, difficult, taxing, demanding, tiring, exhausting, laborious, arduous, strenuous, backbreaking, harsh, severe, tough, punishing.

F3 easy.

gruesome *adjective* horrible, disgusting, repellent, repugnant, repulsive, hideous, grisly,

macabre, grim, ghastly, awful, terrible, horrific, shocking, monstrous, abominable.
F3 pleasant.

gruff *adjective* **1** *a gruff manner*: curt, brusque, abrupt, blunt, rude, surly, sullen, grumpy, bad-tempered. **2** *a gruff voice*: rough, harsh, rasping, guttural, throaty, husky, hoarse.
F3 **1** friendly, courteous.

grumble *verb* complain, moan, whine, bleat, grouch, gripe, mutter, murmur, carp, find fault.

grumpy *adjective* bad-tempered, ill-tempered, crotchety, crabbed, cantankerous, cross, irritable, surly, sullen, sulky, grouchy, discontented.
F3 contented.

guarantee *noun* warranty, insurance, assurance, promise, word of honour, pledge, oath, bond, security, collateral, surety, endorsement, testimonial.
▪ *verb* assure, promise, pledge, swear, vouch for, answer for, warrant, certify, underwrite, endorse, secure, protect, insure, ensure, make sure, make certain.

guard *verb* protect, safeguard, save, preserve, shield, screen, shelter, cover, defend, patrol, police, escort, supervise, oversee, watch, look out, mind, beware.
▪ *noun* **1** *an armed guard*: protector, defender, custodian, warder, escort, bodyguard, minder (*infml*), watchman, lookout, sentry, picket, patrol, security. **2** *a guard against infection*: protection, safeguard, defence, wall, barrier, screen, shield, bumper, buffer, pad.

guarded *adjective* cautious, wary, careful, watchful, discreet, non-committal, reticent, reserved, secretive, cagey (*infml*).
F3 communicative, frank.

guardian *noun* trustee, curator, custodian, keeper, warden, protector, preserver, defender, champion, guard, warder, escort, attendant.

guess *verb* speculate, conjecture, predict, estimate, judge, reckon, work out, suppose, assume, surmise, think, believe, imagine, fancy, feel, suspect.
▪ *noun* prediction, estimate, speculation, conjecture, supposition, assumption, belief, fancy, idea, notion, theory, hypothesis, opinion, feeling, suspicion, intuition.

guesswork *noun* speculation, conjecture, estimation, reckoning, supposition, assumption, surmise, intuition.

guest *noun* visitor, caller, boarder, lodger, resident, patron, regular.

guidance *noun* leadership, direction, management, control, teaching, instruction, advice, counsel, counselling, help, instructions, directions, guidelines, indications, pointers, recommendations.

guide *verb* lead, conduct, direct, navigate, point, steer, pilot, manoeuvre, usher, escort, accompany, attend, control, govern, manage, oversee, supervise, superintend, advise, counsel, influence, educate, teach, instruct, train.

▪ *noun* **1** *a tour guide*: leader, courier, navigator, pilot, helmsman, steersman, usher, escort, chaperon(e), attendant, companion, adviser, counsellor, mentor, guru, teacher, instructor. **2** *a guide to the Lake District*: manual, handbook, guidebook, catalogue, directory. **3** *the lighthouse serves as a guide to ships*: indication, pointer, signpost, sign, marker. **4** *serve as a guide to others*: guideline, example, model, standard, criterion.

guilt *noun* **1** *he confessed his guilt*: culpability, responsibility, blame, disgrace, dishonour. **2** *a feeling of guilt*: guilty conscience, conscience, shame, self-condemnation, self-reproach, regret, remorse, contrition.
F3 **1** innocence, righteousness. **2** shamelessness.

guilty *adjective* **1** *the guilty party*: culpable, responsible, blamable, blameworthy, offending, wrong, sinful, wicked, criminal, convicted. **2** *feel guilty*: conscience-stricken, ashamed, shamefaced, sheepish, sorry, regretful, remorseful, contrite, penitent, repentant.
F3 **1** innocent, guiltless, blameless. **2** shameless.

gulf *noun* bay, bight, basin, gap, opening, separation, rift, split, breach, cleft, chasm, gorge, abyss, void.

gullible *adjective* credulous, suggestible, impressionable, trusting, unsuspecting, foolish, naive, green, unsophisticated, innocent.
F3 astute.

gully *noun* channel, watercourse, gutter, ditch, ravine.

gulp *verb* swallow, swig, swill, knock back (*infml*), bolt, wolf (*infml*), gobble, guzzle, devour, stuff (*infml*).
F3 sip, nibble.

▪ *noun* swallow, swig, draught, mouthful.

gum *noun* adhesive, glue, paste, cement.

▪ *verb* stick, glue, paste, fix, cement, seal, clog.

gun *noun* firearm, handgun, pistol, revolver, shooter (*infml*), rifle, shotgun, bazooka, howitzer, cannon.

gurgle *verb* bubble, babble, burble, murmur, ripple, lap, splash, crow.

▪ *noun* babble, murmur, ripple.

gush *verb* **1** *oil gushing from the bore hole*: flow, run, pour, stream, cascade, flood, rush, burst, spurt, spout, jet, well. **2** *'how splendid you look!' she gushed*: enthuse, chatter, babble, jabber, go on (*infml*).

▪ *noun* flow, outflow, stream, torrent, cascade, flood, tide, rush, burst, outburst, spurt, spout, jet.

gust *noun* blast, burst, rush, flurry, blow, puff, breeze, wind, gale, squall.

gusto *noun* zest, relish, appreciation, enjoyment, pleasure, delight, enthusiasm, exuberance, élan, verve, zeal.
E3 distaste, apathy.

gut *verb* **1** *gut a fish*: disembowel, draw, clean (out). **2** (*infml*) *gut the house*: strip, clear, empty, rifle, ransack, plunder, loot, sack, ravage.

guts *noun* **1** *remove the guts from the game*: intestines, bowels, viscera, entrails, insides, innards (*infml*), belly, stomach. **2** (*infml*) *have a lot of guts*: courage, bravery, pluck, grit, nerve, mettle.

gutter *noun* drain, sluice, ditch, trench, trough, channel, duct, conduit, passage, pipe, tube.

habit *noun* custom, usage, practice, routine, rule, second nature, way, manner, mode, wont, inclination, tendency, bent, mannerism, quirk, addiction, dependence, fixation, obsession, weakness.

habitat *noun* home, abode (*fml*), domain, element, environment, surroundings, locality, territory, terrain.

hack *verb* cut, chop, hew, notch, gash, slash, lacerate, mutilate, mangle.

hackneyed *adjective* stale, overworked, tired, worn-out, time-worn, threadbare, unoriginal, corny (*infml*), clichéd, stereotyped, stock, banal, trite, commonplace, common, pedestrian, uninspired.
E3 original, new, fresh.

haggle *verb* bargain, negotiate, barter, wrangle, squabble, bicker, quarrel, dispute.

hail *verb* greet, address, acknowledge, salute, wave, signal to, flag down, shout, call, acclaim, cheer, applaud, honour, welcome.

hair-raising *adjective* frightening, scary, terrifying, horrifying, shocking, bloodcurdling, spine-chilling, eerie, alarming, startling, thrilling.

hairstyle *noun* style, coiffure, hairdo (*infml*), cut, haircut, set, perm (*infml*), barnet (*infml*).

hairy *adjective* hirsute, bearded, shaggy, bushy, fuzzy, furry, woolly.
E3 bald, clean-shaven.

half *noun* fifty per cent, bisection, hemisphere, semicircle, section,

segment, portion, share, fraction.
▪ *adjective* semi-, halved, divided, fractional, part, partial, incomplete, moderate, limited.
F3 whole.
▪ *adverb* partly, partially, incompletely, moderately, slightly.
F3 completely.

half-hearted *adjective* lukewarm, cool, weak, feeble, passive, apathetic, uninterested, indifferent, neutral.
F3 whole-hearted, enthusiastic.

hall *noun* hallway, corridor, passage, passageway, entrance-hall, foyer, vestibule, lobby, concert-hall, auditorium, chamber, assembly room.

hallmark *noun* stamp, mark, trademark, brand-name, sign, indication, symbol, emblem, device, badge.

hallucination *noun* illusion, mirage, vision, apparition, dream, daydream, fantasy, figment, delusion.

halt *verb* stop, draw up, pull up, pause, wait, rest, break off, discontinue, cease, desist, quit, end, terminate, check, stem, curb, obstruct, impede.
F3 start, continue.
▪ *noun* stop, stoppage, arrest, interruption, break, pause, rest, standstill, end, close, termination.
F3 start, continuation.

halve *verb* bisect, cut in half, split in two, divide, split, share, cut down, reduce, lessen.

hammer *verb* hit, strike, beat, drum, bang, bash, pound, batter, knock, drive, shape, form, make.
▪ *noun* mallet, gavel.

hamper *verb* hinder, impede, obstruct, slow down, hold up, frustrate, thwart, prevent, handicap, hamstring, shackle, cramp, restrict, curb, restrain.
F3 aid, facilitate.

hand *noun* **1** *holding it in his hand*: fist, palm, paw (*infml*), mitt (*infml*). **2** *give me a hand*: help, aid, assistance, support, participation, part, influence. **3** *a farm hand*: worker, employee, operative, workman, labourer, farm-hand, hireling.
▪ *verb* give, pass, offer, submit, present, yield, deliver, transmit, conduct, convey.

handbook *noun* manual, instruction book, guide, guidebook, companion.

handful *noun* few, sprinkling, scattering, smattering.
F3 a lot, many.

handicap *noun* obstacle, block, barrier, impediment, stumbling block, hindrance, drawback, disadvantage, restriction, limitation, penalty, disability, impairment, defect, shortcoming.
F3 assistance, advantage.
▪ *verb* impede, hinder, disadvantage, hold back, retard, hamper, burden, encumber, restrict, limit, disable.
F3 help, assist.

handiwork *noun* work, doing, responsibility, achievement, product, result, design, invention, creation, production, skill, workmanship, craftsmanship, artisanship.

handle *noun* grip, handgrip, knob, stock, shaft, hilt.
▪ *verb* **1** *don't handle the fruit*: touch, finger, feel, fondle, pick up, hold, grasp. **2** *handle a situation*: tackle, treat, deal with, manage, cope with, control, supervise.

handout *noun* leaflet, circular, bulletin, statement, press release, literature.

handsome *adjective* **1** *a handsome youth*: good-looking, attractive, fair, personable, elegant. **2** *a handsome amount*: generous, liberal, large, considerable, ample.
1 ugly, unattractive. **2** mean.

handwriting *noun* writing, script, hand, fist (*infml*), penmanship, scrawl, calligraphy.

handy *adjective* **1** *keep it handy/a handy guide*: available, to hand, ready, at hand, near, accessible, convenient, practical, useful, helpful. **2** *he's quite handy about the house*: skilful, proficient, expert, skilled, clever, practical.
1 inconvenient. **2** clumsy.

hang *verb* **1** *hang from a branch/long hair hanging down over his eyes*: suspend, dangle, swing, drape, drop, flop, droop, sag, trail. **2** *hang a picture*: fasten, attach, fix, stick. **3** *hang in the air*: float, drift, hover, linger, remain, cling.

hanker *verb* crave, hunger for, thirst for, wish for, desire, yearn for, pine for, long for, want, need.

haphazard *adjective* random, chance, casual, arbitrary, hit-or-miss, unsystematic, disorganized, disorderly, careless, slapdash, slipshod.
methodical, orderly.

happen *verb* occur, take place, arise, crop up, develop, materialize (*infml*), come about, result, ensue, follow, turn out, transpire.

happening *noun* occurrence, phenomenon, event, incident, episode, occasion, adventure, experience, accident, chance, circumstance, case, affair.

happiness *noun* joy, joyfulness, gladness, cheerfulness, contentment, pleasure, delight, glee, elation, bliss, ecstasy, euphoria.
unhappiness, sadness.

happy *adjective* **1** *very happy to see her*: joyful, jolly, merry, cheerful, glad, pleased, delighted, thrilled, elated, satisfied, content, contented. **2** *a happy coincidence*: lucky, fortunate, felicitous (*fml*), favourable, apt, appropriate, fitting.
1 unhappy, sad, discontented. **2** unfortunate, inappropriate.

harass *verb* pester, badger, harry, plague, torment, persecute, exasperate, vex, annoy, irritate, bother, disturb, nag, hassle (*infml*), trouble, worry, stress, tire, wear out, exhaust, fatigue.

harbour *noun* port, dock, quay,

wharf, marina, mooring, anchorage, haven, shelter.
▪ *verb* **1** *harbour a criminal*: hide, conceal, protect, shelter. **2** *harbour a grudge*: hold, retain, cling to, entertain, foster, nurse, nurture, cherish, believe, imagine.

hard *adjective* **1** *a hard surface*: solid, firm, unyielding, tough, strong, dense, impenetrable, stiff, rigid, inflexible. **2** *found the exam quite hard*: difficult, arduous, strenuous, laborious, tiring, exhausting, backbreaking, complex, complicated, involved, knotty, baffling, puzzling, perplexing. **3** *a hard taskmaster*: harsh, severe, strict, callous, unfeeling, unsympathetic, cruel, pitiless, merciless, ruthless, unrelenting, distressing, painful, unpleasant, heartless.
F3 **1** soft, yielding. **2** easy, simple. **3** kind, pleasant.
▪ *adverb* industriously, diligently, assiduously (*fml*), doggedly, steadily, laboriously, strenuously, earnestly, keenly, intently, strongly, violently, intensely, energetically, vigorously.

harden *verb* solidify, set, freeze, bake, stiffen, strengthen, reinforce, fortify, buttress, brace, steel, nerve, toughen, season, accustom, train.
F3 soften, weaken.

hard-hearted *adjective* callous, unfeeling, cold, hard, stony, heartless, unsympathetic, cruel, inhuman, pitiless, merciless.
F3 soft-hearted, kind, merciful.

hardly *adverb* barely, scarcely, just, only just, not quite, not at all, by no means.

hardship *noun* misfortune, adversity, trouble, difficulty, affliction, distress, suffering, trial, tribulation, want, need, privation (*fml*), austerity, poverty, destitution, misery.
F3 ease, comfort, prosperity.

hard-working *adjective* industrious, diligent, assiduous (*fml*), conscientious, zealous, busy, energetic.
F3 idle, lazy.

hardy *adjective* strong, tough, sturdy, robust, vigorous, fit, sound, healthy.
F3 weak, unhealthy.

harm *noun* damage, loss, injury, hurt, detriment, ill, misfortune, wrong, abuse.
F3 benefit.
▪ *verb* damage, impair, blemish, spoil, mar, ruin, hurt, injure, wound, ill-treat, maltreat, abuse, misuse.
F3 benefit, improve.

harmful *adjective* damaging, detrimental, pernicious, noxious, unhealthy, unwholesome, injurious, dangerous, hazardous, poisonous, toxic, destructive.
F3 harmless, safe.

harmless *adjective* safe, innocuous, non-toxic, inoffensive, gentle, innocent.
F3 harmful, dangerous, destructive.

harmonious *adjective* **1** *harmonious sounds*: melodious, tuneful, musical, sweet-sounding. **2** *harmonious colours/relationship*: matching, co-ordinated, balanced, compatible, like-minded, agreeable, cordial, amicable, peaceable, friendly, sympathetic.
F3 **1** discordant. **2** inharmonious.

harmonize *verb* match, co-ordinate, balance, fit in, suit, tone, blend (in), correspond, agree, reconcile, accommodate, adapt, arrange, compose.
F3 clash.

harmony *noun* **1** *the harmony of his playing*: tunefulness, tune, melody, euphony. **2** *live in harmony*: agreement, unanimity, accord, concord, unity, compatibility, like-mindedness, peace, goodwill, rapport, sympathy, understanding, amicability, friendliness, co-operation, co-ordination, balance, symmetry, correspondence, conformity.
F3 **1** discord. **2** conflict.

harness *noun* tackle, gear, equipment, reins, straps, tack.
▪ *verb* control, channel, use, utilize, exploit, make use of, employ, mobilize, apply.

harsh *adjective* **1** *a harsh punishment*: severe, strict, Draconian, unfeeling, cruel, hard, pitiless, austere, Spartan, bleak, grim, comfortless. **2** *a harsh sound*: rough, coarse, rasping, croaking, guttural, grating, jarring, discordant, strident, raucous, sharp, shrill, unpleasant. **3** *harsh colour*: bright, dazzling, glaring, gaudy, lurid.
F3 **1** lenient. **2** soft. **3** subdued.

harvest *noun* **1** *an early harvest*: harvest-time, ingathering, reaping, collection. **2** *a good harvest of grapes*: crop, yield, return, produce, fruits, result, consequence.
▪ *verb* reap, mow, pick, gather, collect, accumulate, amass.

haste *noun* hurry, rush, hustle, bustle, speed, velocity, rapidity, swiftness, quickness, briskness, urgency, rashness, recklessness, impetuosity.
F3 slowness.

hasten *verb* hurry, rush, make haste, run, sprint, dash, tear, race, fly, bolt, accelerate, speed (up), quicken, expedite, dispatch, precipitate (*fml*), urge, press, advance, step up.
F3 dawdle, delay.

hasty *adjective* hurried, rushed, impatient, headlong, rash, reckless, heedless, thoughtless, impetuous, impulsive, hot-headed, fast, quick, rapid, swift, speedy, brisk, prompt, short, brief, cursory.
F3 slow, careful, deliberate.

hatch *verb* **1** *hatching her eggs*: incubate, brood, breed. **2** *hatch a plot*: concoct, formulate, originate, think up, dream up, conceive, devise, contrive, plot, scheme, design, plan, project.

hate *verb* dislike, despise, detest, loathe, abhor, abominate, execrate (*fml*).

F3 like, love.

▪ *noun* hatred, aversion, dislike, loathing, abhorrence (*fml*), abomination.

F3 liking, love.

hatred *noun* hate, aversion, dislike, detestation, loathing, repugnance, revulsion, abhorrence (*fml*), abomination, execration (*fml*), animosity, ill-will, antagonism, hostility, enmity, antipathy.

F3 liking, love.

haul *verb* pull, heave, tug, draw, tow, drag, trail, move, transport, convey, carry, cart, lug, hump (*infml*).

F3 push.

▪ *noun* loot, booty, plunder, swag (*slang*), spoils, takings, gain, yield, find.

haunt *verb* **1** *haunting the art galleries*: frequent, patronize, visit. **2** *memories haunted her*: plague, torment, trouble, disturb, recur, prey on, beset, obsess, possess.

▪ *noun* resort, hangout (*infml*), stamping-ground, den, meeting-place, rendezvous.

haunting *adjective* memorable, unforgettable, persistent, recurrent, evocative, nostalgic, poignant.

have *verb* **1** *have a job*: own, possess, get, obtain, gain, acquire, procure, secure, receive, accept, keep, hold. **2** *have a good time/a heart attack*: feel, experience, enjoy, suffer, undergo, endure, put up with. **3** *have two bedrooms*: contain, include, comprise, incorporate, consist of. **4** *have a baby*: give birth to, bear.

F3 **1** lack.

havoc *noun* chaos, confusion, disorder, disruption, damage, destruction, ruin, wreck, rack and ruin, devastation, waste, desolation.

haywire *adjective* wrong, tangled, out of control, crazy, mad, wild, chaotic, confused, disordered, disorganized, topsy-turvy.

hazard *noun* risk, danger, peril, jeopardy, threat, death-trap, accident, chance.

F3 safety.

hazardous *adjective* risky, dangerous, unsafe, perilous, precarious, insecure, chancy, difficult, tricky.

F3 safe, secure.

hazy *adjective* misty, foggy, smoky, clouded, cloudy, milky, fuzzy, blurred, ill-defined, veiled, obscure, dim, faint, unclear, indistinct, vague, indefinite, uncertain.

F3 clear, bright, definite.

head *noun* **1** *bump his head/all in his head/have a good head on her shoulders*: skull, cranium, brain, mind, mentality, brains (*infml*), intellect, intelligence, understanding, thought. **2** *the*

head of the school: leader, chief, captain, commander, boss, director, manager, superintendent, principal, head teacher, ruler.
E3 2 subordinate.
▪ *verb* lead, rule, govern, command, direct, manage, run, superintend, oversee, supervise, control, guide, steer.

heading *noun* title, name, headline, rubric, caption, section, division, category, class.

headlong *adjective* hasty, precipitate (*fml*), impetuous, impulsive, rash, reckless, dangerous, breakneck, head-first.
▪ *adverb* head first, hurriedly, hastily, precipitately, rashly, recklessly, heedlessly, thoughtlessly, wildly.

headquarters *noun* HQ, base (camp), head office, nerve centre.

headstrong *adjective* stubborn, obstinate, intractable, pigheaded, wilful, self-willed, perverse, contrary.
E3 tractable, docile.

headway *noun* advance, progress, way, improvement.

heal *verb* cure, remedy, mend, restore, treat, soothe, salve, settle, reconcile, patch up.

health *noun* fitness, constitution, form, shape, trim, fettle, condition, tone, state, healthiness, good condition, well-being, welfare, soundness, robustness, strength, vigour.
E3 illness, infirmity.

healthy *adjective* **1** *a healthy child/stay healthy*: well, fit, good, fine, in condition, in good shape, in fine fettle, sound, sturdy, robust, strong, vigorous, hale and hearty, blooming, flourishing, thriving. **2** *healthy food*: wholesome, nutritious, nourishing, bracing, invigorating, healthful.
E3 1 ill, sick, infirm.

heap *noun* pile, stack, mound, mountain, lot, mass, accumulation, collection, hoard, stockpile, store.
▪ *verb* pile, stack, mound, bank, build, amass, accumulate, collect, gather, hoard, stockpile, store, load, burden, shower, lavish.

hear *verb* **1** *hear him calling*: listen, catch, pick up, overhear, eavesdrop, heed, pay attention. **2** *I heard she's going to Australia*: learn, find out, discover, ascertain, understand, gather. **3** *hear the case*: judge, try, examine, investigate.

hearing *noun* **1** *said in his hearing*: earshot, sound, range, reach, ear, perception. **2** *a preliminary hearing*: trial, inquiry, investigation, inquest, audition, interview, audience.

hearsay *noun* rumour, word of mouth, talk, gossip, tittle-tattle, report, buzz (*infml*).

heart *noun* **1** *have no heart*: soul, mind, character, disposition, nature, temperament, feeling, emotion, sentiment, love, tenderness, compassion,

sympathy, pity. **2** *lose heart*: courage, bravery, boldness, spirit, resolution, determination. **3** *the heart of the countryside/the matter*: centre, middle, core, kernel, nucleus, nub, crux, essence.
F3 2 cowardice. **3** periphery.

heartbreaking *adjective* distressing, sad, tragic, harrowing, heart-rending, pitiful, agonizing, grievous, bitter, disappointing.
F3 heartwarming, heartening.

heartbroken *adjective* broken-hearted, desolate, sad, miserable, dejected, despondent, downcast, crestfallen, disappointed, dispirited, grieved, crushed.
F3 delighted, elated.

hearten *verb* comfort, console, reassure, cheer (up), buck up (*infml*), encourage, boost, inspire, stimulate, rouse, pep up (*infml*).
F3 dishearten, depress, dismay.

heartfelt *adjective* deep, profound, sincere, honest, genuine, earnest, ardent, fervent, whole-hearted, warm.
F3 insincere, false.

heartless *adjective* unfeeling, uncaring, cold, hard, hard-hearted, callous, unkind, cruel, inhuman, brutal, pitiless, merciless.
F3 kind, considerate, sympathetic, merciful.

hearty *adjective* **1** *a hearty welcome/laugh*: enthusiastic, whole-hearted, unreserved, heartfelt, sincere, genuine, warm, friendly, cordial, jovial, cheerful, ebullient, exuberant, boisterous, energetic, vigorous. **2** *a hearty breakfast*: large, sizable, substantial, filling, ample, generous.
F3 1 half-hearted, cool, cold.

heat *noun* hotness, warmth, sultriness, closeness, high temperature.
F3 cold(ness).
▪ *verb* warm, boil, toast, cook, bake, roast, reheat, warm up, inflame, excite, animate, rouse, stimulate, flush, glow.
F3 cool, chill.

heave *verb* **1** *heave the piano up a flight of stairs*: pull, haul, drag, tug, raise, lift, hitch, hoist, lever, rise, surge. **2** *heave a brick through the window*: throw, fling, hurl, cast, toss, chuck, let fly.

heavy *adjective* **1** *a heavy load/a heavy chocolate pudding*: weighty, hefty, ponderous, burdensome, massive, large, bulky, solid, dense, stodgy. **2** *heavy work*: hard, difficult, tough, arduous, laborious, strenuous, demanding, taxing, harsh, severe.
F3 1 light. **2** easy.

hectic *adjective* busy, frantic, frenetic, chaotic, fast, feverish, excited, heated, furious, wild.
F3 leisurely.

hedge *noun* hedgerow, screen, windbreak, barrier, fence, dike, boundary.

heed *verb* listen, pay attention, mind, note, regard, observe, follow, obey.
F3 ignore, disregard.

heedless *adjective* oblivious, unthinking, careless, negligent, rash, reckless, inattentive, unobservant, thoughtless, unconcerned.
F3 mindful, attentive.

hefty *adjective* heavy, weighty, big, large, burly, hulking, beefy, brawny, strong, powerful, vigorous, robust, strapping, solid, substantial, massive, colossal, bulky, unwieldy.
F3 slight, small.

height *noun* **1** *the height of Everest*: highness, altitude, elevation, tallness, loftiness, stature. **2** *when the sun is at its height*: top, summit, peak, pinnacle, apex, crest, crown, zenith, apogee, culmination, climax, extremity, maximum, limit, ceiling.
F3 1 depth.

heighten *verb* raise, elevate, increase, add to, magnify, intensify, strengthen, sharpen, improve, enhance.
F3 lower, decrease, diminish.

helm *noun* tiller, wheel, driving seat, reins, saddle, command, control, leadership, direction.

help *verb* **1** *can you help me, please*: aid, assist, lend a hand, serve, be of use, collaborate, co-operate, back, stand by, support. **2** *shouting won't help the situation*: improve, ameliorate (*fml*), relieve, alleviate, mitigate, ease, facilitate.
F3 1 hinder. **2** worsen.
▪ *noun* aid, assistance, collaboration, co-operation, support, advice, guidance, service, use, utility, avail, benefit.
F3 hindrance.

helper *noun* assistant, deputy, auxiliary, subsidiary, attendant, right-hand man, PA, mate, partner, associate, colleague, collaborator, accomplice, aide, ally, supporter, second.

helpful *adjective* **1** *made some helpful comments*: useful, practical, constructive, worthwhile, valuable, beneficial, advantageous. **2** *a helpful person*: co-operative, obliging, neighbourly, friendly, caring, considerate, kind, sympathetic, supportive.
F3 1 useless, futile.

helping *noun* serving, portion, share, ration, amount, plateful, piece, dollop (*infml*).

helpless *adjective* weak, feeble, powerless, dependent, vulnerable, exposed, unprotected, defenceless, abandoned, friendless, destitute, forlorn, incapable, incompetent, infirm, disabled, paralysed.
F3 strong, independent, competent.

hem *noun* edge, border, margin, fringe, trimming.

herald *noun* messenger, courier, harbinger, forerunner, precursor, omen, token, signal, sign, indication.
▪ *verb* announce, proclaim, broadcast, advertise, publicize,

trumpet, pave the way, precede, usher in, show, indicate, promise.

herd *noun* flock, swarm, pack, press, crush, mass, horde, throng, multitude, crowd, mob, the masses, rabble.

hereditary *adjective* inherited, bequeathed, handed down, family, ancestral, inborn, inbred, innate, natural, congenital, genetic.

heritage *noun* history, past, tradition, culture.

hero *noun* protagonist, lead, celebrity, star, superstar, idol, paragon, goody (*infml*), champion, conqueror.

heroic *adjective* brave, courageous, fearless, dauntless, undaunted, lion-hearted, stout-hearted, valiant, bold, daring, intrepid, adventurous, gallant, chivalrous, noble, selfless.
⇄ cowardly, timid.

heroism *noun* bravery, courage, valour, boldness, daring, intrepidity, gallantry, prowess, selflessness.
⇄ cowardice, timidity.

hesitant *adjective* hesitating, reluctant, half-hearted, uncertain, unsure, indecisive, irresolute, vacillating, wavering, tentative, wary, shy, timid, halting, stammering, stuttering.
⇄ decisive, resolute, confident, fluent.

hesitate *verb* pause, delay, wait, be reluctant, be unwilling, think twice, hold back, shrink from, scruple, boggle, demur, vacillate, waver, be uncertain, dither, shilly-shally, falter, stumble, halt, stammer, stutter.
⇄ decide.

hesitation *noun* pause, delay, reluctance, unwillingness, hesitance, scruple(s), qualm(s), misgivings, doubt, second thoughts, vacillation, uncertainty, indecision, irresolution, faltering, stumbling, stammering, stuttering.
⇄ eagerness, assurance.

heyday *noun* peak, prime, flush, bloom, flowering, golden age, boom time.

hidden *adjective* **1** *a hidden door*: concealed, covered, shrouded, veiled, disguised, camouflaged, unseen, secret. **2** *hidden meaning*: obscure, dark, occult, secret, covert, close, cryptic, mysterious, abstruse (*fml*), mystical, latent, ulterior.
⇄ **1** showing, apparent. **2** obvious.

hide[1] *verb* **1** *hiding the key/truth*: conceal, cover, cloak, shroud, veil, screen, mask, disguise, camouflage, obscure, shadow, eclipse, bury, stash (*infml*), secrete (*fml*), withhold, keep dark, suppress. **2** *hid behind some rocks*: take cover, shelter, lie low, go to ground, hole up (*infml*).
⇄ **1** reveal, show, display.

hide[2] *noun* skin, pelt, fell, fur, leather.

hideous *adjective* ugly, repulsive, grotesque, monstrous, horrid, ghastly, awful, dreadful, frightful,

terrible, grim, gruesome, macabre, terrifying, shocking, appalling, disgusting, revolting, horrible.
F3 beautiful, attractive.

hiding *noun* beating, flogging, whipping, caning, spanking, thrashing, walloping (*infml*).

hiding-place *noun* hide-away, hideout, lair, den, hole, hide, cover, refuge, haven, sanctuary, retreat.

hierarchy *noun* pecking order, ranking, grading, scale, series, ladder, echelons, strata.

high *adjective* **1** *a high cliff*: tall, lofty, elevated, soaring, towering. **2** *a high wind*: great, strong, intense, extreme. **3** *a high official*: important, influential, powerful, eminent, distinguished, prominent, chief, leading, senior. **4** *a high voice*: high-pitched, soprano, treble, sharp, shrill, piercing. **5** *a high price*: expensive, dear, costly, exorbitant, excessive.
F3 **1** low, short. **2** light, gentle. **3** lowly. **4** deep. **5** cheap.

highlight *noun* high point, high spot, peak, climax, best, cream.
▪ *verb* underline, emphasize, stress, accentuate, play up, point up, spotlight, illuminate, show up, set off, focus on, feature.

highly *adverb* very, greatly, considerably, decidedly, extremely, immensely, tremendously, exceptionally, extraordinarily, enthusiastically, warmly, well.

highly-strung *adjective* sensitive, neurotic, nervy, jumpy, edgy, temperamental, excitable, restless, nervous, tense.
F3 calm.

high-spirited *adjective* boisterous, bouncy, exuberant, bold, effervescent, frolicsome, ebullient, sparkling, vibrant, vivacious, lively, energetic, spirited, dashing, daring.
F3 quiet, sedate.

hijack *verb* commandeer, expropriate (*fml*), skyjack, seize, take over.

hike *verb* ramble, walk, trek, tramp, trudge, plod.
▪ *noun* ramble, walk, trek, tramp, march.

hilarious *adjective* funny, amusing, comical, side-splitting, hysterical (*infml*), uproarious, noisy, rollicking, merry, jolly, jovial.
F3 serious, grave.

hill *noun* **1** *rolling hills*: hillock, knoll, mound, prominence, eminence, elevation, foothill, down, fell, mountain, height. **2** *a steep hill*: slope, incline, gradient, ramp, rise, ascent, acclivity (*fml*), drop, descent, declivity (*fml*).

hinder *verb* hamper, obstruct, impede, encumber, handicap, hamstring, hold up, delay, retard, slow down, hold back, check, curb, stop, prevent, frustrate, thwart, oppose.
F3 help, aid, assist.

hindrance *noun* obstruction, impediment, handicap, encumbrance, obstacle, stumbling block, barrier, bar, check, restraint, restriction,

limitation, difficulty, drag, snag, hitch, drawback, disadvantage, inconvenience, deterrent.
F3 help, aid, assistance.

hinge *verb* centre, turn, revolve, pivot, hang, depend, rest.

hint *noun* **1** *give them a hint*: tip, advice, suggestion, help, clue, inkling, suspicion, tip-off, reminder, indication, sign, pointer, mention, allusion, intimation, insinuation, implication, innuendo. **2** *a hint of garlic*: touch, trace, tinge, taste, dash, soupçon, speck.
▪ *verb* suggest, prompt, tip off, indicate, imply, insinuate, intimate, allude, mention.

hire *verb* rent, let, lease, charter, commission, book, reserve, employ, take on, sign up, engage, appoint, retain.
F3 dismiss, fire (*infml*).
▪ *noun* rent, rental, fee, charge, cost, price.

historic *adjective* momentous, consequential, important, significant, epoch-making, notable, remarkable, outstanding, extraordinary, celebrated, renowned, famed, famous.
F3 unimportant, insignificant, unknown.

historical *adjective* real, actual, authentic, factual, documented, recorded, attested, verifiable.
F3 legendary, fictional.

history *noun* **1** *characters from history*: past, olden days, days of old, antiquity. **2** *a history of the twentieth century*: chronicle, record, annals, archives, chronology, account, narrative, story, tale, saga, biography, life, autobiography, memoirs.

hit *verb* **1** *hit the ball*: strike, knock, tap, smack, slap, thrash, whack (*infml*), bash, thump, clout, punch, belt (*infml*), wallop (*infml*), beat, batter. **2** *hit his head*: bump, collide with, bang, crash, smash, damage, harm.
▪ *noun* **1** *several good hits to make 20 more runs*: stroke, shot, blow, knock, tap, slap, smack, bash, bump, collision, impact, crash, smash. **2** *be a great hit*: success, triumph, winner (*infml*).
F3 **2** failure.

hitch *noun* delay, hold-up, trouble, problem, difficulty, mishap, setback, hiccup, drawback, snag, catch, impediment, hindrance.
▪ *verb* **1** *hitch the horse to the wagon*: fasten, attach, tie, harness, yoke, couple, connect, join, unite. **2** *hitching up her dress*: pull, heave, yank (*infml*), tug, jerk, hoist, hike (up) (*infml*).
F3 **1** unhitch, unfasten.

hoard *noun* collection, accumulation, mass, heap, pile, fund, reservoir, supply, reserve, store, stockpile, cache, treasure-trove.
▪ *verb* collect, gather, amass, accumulate, save, put by, lay up, store, stash away (*infml*), stockpile, keep, treasure.
F3 use, spend, squander.

hoarse *adjective* husky, croaky, throaty, guttural, gravelly, gruff, growling, rough, harsh, rasping, grating, raucous, discordant.
F3 clear, smooth.

hoax *noun* trick, prank, practical joke, put-on (*infml*), joke, leg-pull (*infml*), spoof, fake, fraud, deception, bluff, humbug, cheat, swindle, con (*infml*).

hobble *verb* limp, stumble, falter, stagger, totter, dodder, shuffle.

hobby *noun* pastime, diversion, recreation, relaxation, pursuit, sideline.

hoist *verb* lift, elevate, raise, erect, jack up, winch up, heave, rear, uplift.

hold *verb* **1** *hold her hand*: grip, grasp, clutch, clasp, embrace, have, own, possess, keep, retain. **2** *hold a meeting*: conduct, carry on, continue, call, summon, convene, assemble. **3** *hold fifty passengers*: bear, support, sustain, carry, comprise, contain, accommodate. **4** *holding him for questioning*: imprison, detain, stop, arrest, check, curb, restrain.
F3 **1** drop. **4** release, free, liberate.
▪ *noun* **1** *keep a tight hold*: grip, grasp, clasp, embrace. **2** *have a hold over him*: influence, power, sway, mastery, dominance, authority, control, leverage.

hole *noun* **1** *a hole in the pipe*: aperture, opening, orifice, pore, puncture, perforation, eyelet, tear, split, vent, outlet, shaft, slot, gap, breach, break, crack, fissure, fault, defect, flaw. **2** *a hole in the ground*: dent, dimple, depression, hollow, cavity, crater, pit, excavation, cavern, cave, chamber, pocket, niche, recess, burrow, nest, lair, retreat.

holiday *noun* vacation, recess, leave, time off, day off, break, rest, half-term, bank-holiday, feast-day, festival, celebration, anniversary.

hollow *adjective* **1** *a hollow tube*: empty, vacant, unfilled, concave, indented, depressed, sunken, deep, cavernous. **2** *a hollow victory*: false, artificial, deceptive, insincere, meaningless, empty, vain, futile, fruitless, worthless.
F3 **1** solid. **2** real.
▪ *noun* hole, pit, well, cavity, crater, excavation, cavern, cave, depression, concavity, basin, bowl, cup, dimple, dent, indentation, groove, channel, trough, valley.

holy *adjective* **1** *holy ground*: sacred, hallowed, consecrated, sanctified, dedicated, blessed, venerated, revered, spiritual, divine, evangelical. **2** *a holy man*: pious, religious, devout, godly, God-fearing, saintly, virtuous, good, righteous, faithful, pure, perfect.
F3 **1** unsanctified. **2** impious, irreligious.

home *noun* residence, domicile, dwelling-place, abode (*fml*), base, house, pied-à-terre, hearth, fireside, birthplace, home town,

home ground, territory, habitat, element.
▪ *adjective* domestic, household, family, internal, local, national, inland.
☒ foreign, international.

homeless *adjective* itinerant, travelling, nomadic, wandering, vagrant, rootless, unsettled, displaced, dispossessed, evicted, exiled, outcast, abandoned, forsaken, destitute, down-and-out.

homely *adjective* homelike, homey, comfortable, cosy, snug, relaxed, informal, friendly, intimate, familiar, everyday, ordinary, domestic, natural, plain, simple, modest, unassuming, unpretentious, unsophisticated, folksy, homespun.
☒ grand, formal.

honest *adjective* **1** *an honest answer*: truthful, sincere, frank, candid, blunt, outspoken, direct, straight, outright, forthright, straightforward, plain, simple, open, above-board, legitimate, legal, lawful, on the level (*infml*), fair, just, impartial, objective. **2** *an honest citizen*: law-abiding, virtuous, upright, ethical, moral, high-minded, scrupulous, honourable, reputable, respectable, reliable, trustworthy, true, genuine, real.
☒ **1** dishonest. **2** dishonourable.

honorary *adjective* unpaid, unofficial, titular, nominal, in name only, honorific, formal.
☒ paid.

honour *noun* **1** *the honour of his family*: reputation, good name, repute, renown, distinction, esteem, regard, respect, credit, dignity, self-respect, pride, integrity, morality, decency, rectitude, probity (*fml*). **2** *military honours*: award, accolade, commendation, acknowledgement, recognition, tribute, privilege. **3** *in her honour*: praise, acclaim, homage, admiration, reverence, worship, adoration.
☒ **1** dishonour, disgrace.
▪ *verb* **1** *honouring the saint*: praise, acclaim, exalt, glorify, pay homage to, decorate, crown, celebrate, commemorate, remember, admire, esteem, respect, revere, worship, prize, value. **2** *honour a promise*: keep, observe, respect, fulfil, carry out, discharge, execute, perform.
☒ **1** dishonour, disgrace.

honourable *adjective* great, eminent, distinguished, renowned, respected, worthy, prestigious, trusty, reputable, respectable, virtuous, upright, upstanding, straight, honest, trustworthy, true, sincere, noble, principled, moral, ethical, fair, just, right, proper, decent.
☒ dishonourable, unworthy, dishonest.

hop *verb* jump, leap, spring, bound, vault, skip, dance, prance, frisk.

hope *noun* hopefulness,

optimism, ambition, aspiration, wish, desire, longing, dream, expectation, anticipation, prospect, promise, belief, confidence, assurance, conviction, faith.
F3 pessimism, despair.
▪ *verb* aspire, wish, desire, long, expect, await, look forward, anticipate, contemplate, foresee, believe, trust, rely, reckon on, assume.
F3 despair.

hopeful *adjective* **1** *hopeful that it will turn out well*: optimistic, bullish (*infml*), confident, assured, expectant, sanguine, cheerful, buoyant. **2** *a hopeful sign*: encouraging, heartening, reassuring, favourable, auspicious, promising, rosy, bright.
F3 1 pessimistic, despairing. **2** discouraging.

hopeless *adjective* **1** *felt hopeless about the future*: pessimistic, defeatist, negative, despairing, demoralized, downhearted, dejected, despondent, forlorn, wretched. **2** *a hopeless dream*: unattainable, unachievable, impracticable, impossible, vain, foolish, futile, useless, pointless. **3** *a hopeless failure/case*: worthless, poor, helpless, lost, irremediable, irreparable, incurable.
F3 1 hopeful, optimistic. **2** possible. **3** curable.

horde *noun* band, gang, pack, herd, drove, flock, swarm, crowd, mob, throng, multitude, host.

horizon *noun* skyline, vista, prospect, compass, range, scope, perspective.

horrible *adjective* unpleasant, disagreeable, nasty, unkind, horrid, disgusting, revolting, offensive, repulsive, hideous, grim, ghastly, awful, dreadful, frightful, fearful, terrible, abominable, shocking, appalling, horrific.
F3 pleasant, agreeable, lovely, attractive.

horrific *adjective* horrifying, shocking, appalling, awful, dreadful, ghastly, gruesome, terrifying, frightening, scary, harrowing, bloodcurdling.

horrify *verb* shock, outrage, scandalize, appal, disgust, sicken, dismay, alarm, startle, scare, frighten, terrify.
F3 please, delight.

horror *noun* **1** *recoil in horror*: shock, outrage, disgust, revulsion, repugnance, abhorrence (*fml*), loathing, dismay, consternation, alarm, fright, fear, terror, panic, dread, apprehension. **2** *the horrors of war*: ghastliness, awfulness, frightfulness, hideousness.
F3 1 approval, delight.

hospitable *adjective* friendly, sociable, welcoming, receptive, cordial, amicable, congenial, convivial, genial, kind, gracious, generous, liberal.
F3 inhospitable, unfriendly, hostile.

hostile *adjective* belligerent, warlike, ill-disposed, unsympathetic, unfriendly, inhospitable, inimical, antagonistic, opposed, adverse, unfavourable, contrary, opposite.
F3 friendly, welcoming, favourable.

hot *adjective* **1** *a hot climate/hot soup*: warm, heated, fiery, burning, scalding, blistering, scorching, roasting, baking, boiling, steaming, sizzling, sweltering, sultry, torrid, tropical. **2** *a hot curry*: spicy, peppery, piquant, sharp, pungent, strong.
F3 **1** cold, cool. **2** mild.

hotel *noun* boarding-house, guest-house, pension, motel, inn, public house, pub (*infml*), hostel.

hotheaded *adjective* headstrong, impetuous, impulsive, hasty, rash, reckless, fiery, volatile, hot-tempered, quick-tempered.
F3 cool, calm.

hound *verb* chase, pursue, hunt (down), drive, goad, prod, chivvy, nag, pester, badger, harry, harass, persecute.

house *noun* **1** *rows of neat little houses*: building, dwelling, residence, home. **2** *the house of Stuart*: dynasty, family, clan, tribe.
▪ *verb* **1** *soldiers housed with local families*: lodge, quarter, billet, board, accommodate, put up, take in, shelter, harbour. **2** *housing the crown jewels*: hold, contain, protect, cover, sheathe, place, keep, store.

Types of house include:
bungalow, cottage, council house, detached, pied-à-terre, prefab (*infml*), semi-detached, semi (*infml*), terraced, thatched cottage, town house; apartment, bedsit, condominium (*US*), duplex (*US*), flat, granny flat, maisonette, penthouse, studio; chalet, croft, farmhouse, grange, hacienda, hall, homestead, lodge, manor, manse, mansion, parsonage, ranch house, rectory, shack, shanty, treehouse, vicarage, villa; hut, igloo, log cabin, tepee, wigwam, yurt. *See also* **accommodation**; **building**.

---

household *noun* family, family circle, house, home, ménage, establishment, set-up.
▪ *adjective* domestic, home, family, ordinary, plain, everyday, common, familiar, well-known, established.

hover *verb* **1** *a hawk hovering above*: hang, poise, float, drift, fly, flutter, flap. **2** *he hovered by the door*: pause, linger, hang about, hesitate, waver, fluctuate, seesaw.

however *adverb, conjunction* nevertheless, nonetheless, still, yet, even so, notwithstanding, though, anyhow.

howl *noun, verb* wail, cry, shriek, scream, shout, yell, roar, bellow, bay, yelp, hoot, moan, groan.

hub *noun* centre, middle, focus, focal point, axis, pivot, linchpin, nerve centre, core, heart.

hubbub *noun* noise, racket, din, clamour, commotion, disturbance, riot, uproar, hullabaloo, rumpus, confusion, disorder, tumult, hurly-burly, chaos, pandemonium.
peace, quiet.

huddle *noun* **1** *sheep stood in a huddle by the gate*: cluster, clump, knot, mass, crowd, muddle, jumble. **2** *go into a huddle*: conclave, conference, meeting.
▪ *verb* cluster, gravitate, converge, meet, gather, congregate, crowd, flock, throng, press, cuddle, snuggle, nestle, curl up, crouch, hunch.
disperse.

hue *noun* colour, shade, tint, dye, tinge, nuance, tone, complexion, aspect, light.

huff *noun* pique, sulks, mood, bad mood, anger, rage, passion.

hug *verb* embrace, cuddle, squeeze, enfold, hold, clasp, clutch, grip, cling to, enclose.
▪ *noun* embrace, cuddle, squeeze, clasp, hold, clinch.

huge *adjective* immense, vast, enormous, massive, colossal, titanic, giant, gigantic, mammoth, monumental, tremendous, great, big, large, bulky, unwieldy.
tiny, minute.

hum *verb* buzz, whirr, purr, drone, thrum, croon, sing, murmur, mumble, throb, pulse, vibrate.

human *adjective* **1** *he's only human*: mortal, fallible, susceptible, reasonable, rational. **2** *he's quite human once you get to know him*: kind, considerate, understanding, humane, compassionate.
2 inhuman.
▪ *noun* human being, mortal, homo sapiens, man, woman, child, person, individual, body, soul.

humane *adjective* kind, compassionate, sympathetic, understanding, kind-hearted, good-natured, gentle, tender, loving, mild, lenient, merciful, forgiving, forbearing, kindly, benevolent, charitable, humanitarian, good.
inhumane, cruel.

humanitarian *adjective* benevolent, charitable, philanthropic, public-spirited, compassionate, humane, altruistic, unselfish.
selfish, self-seeking.

humanity *noun* **1** *affecting the whole of humanity*: human race, humankind, mankind, womankind, mortality, people. **2** *the humanity of their actions*: humaneness, kindness, compassion, fellow-feeling, understanding, tenderness, benevolence, generosity, goodwill.
2 inhumanity, cruelty.

humble *adjective* **1** *try to be humble*: meek, submissive, unassertive, self-effacing, polite, respectful, deferential, servile, subservient, sycophantic, obsequious. **2** *their humble home*: lowly, low, mean, insignificant,

unimportant, common, commonplace, ordinary, plain, simple, modest, unassuming, unpretentious, unostentatious.
F3 **1** proud, assertive. **2** important, pretentious.
▪ *verb* bring down, lower, bring low, abase, demean, sink, discredit, disgrace, shame, humiliate, mortify, chasten, crush, deflate, subdue, belittle.
F3 exalt.

humdrum *adjective* boring, tedious, monotonous, routine, dull, dreary, uninteresting, uneventful, ordinary, mundane, everyday, commonplace.
F3 lively, unusual, exceptional.

humid *adjective* damp, moist, dank, clammy, sticky, muggy, sultry, steamy.
F3 dry.

humiliate *verb* mortify, embarrass, confound, crush, break, deflate, chasten, shame, disgrace, discredit, degrade, demean, humble, bring low.
F3 dignify, exalt.

humility *noun* meekness, submissiveness, deference, self-abasement (*fml*), servility, humbleness, lowliness, modesty, unpretentiousness.
F3 pride, arrogance, assertiveness.

humorous *adjective* funny, amusing, comic, entertaining, witty, satirical, jocular, facetious, playful, waggish, droll, whimsical, comical, farcical, zany (*infml*), ludicrous, absurd, hilarious, side-splitting.
F3 serious, humourless.

humour *noun* wit, drollery, jokes, jesting, badinage, repartee, facetiousness, satire, comedy, farce, fun, amusement.
▪ *verb* go along with, comply with, accommodate, gratify, indulge, pamper, spoil, favour, please, mollify, flatter.

hunch *noun* premonition, presentiment, intuition, suspicion, feeling, impression, idea, guess.
▪ *verb* hump, bend, curve, arch, stoop, crouch, squat, huddle, draw in, curl up.

hunger *noun* **1** *die from hunger*: hungriness, emptiness, starvation, malnutrition, famine, appetite, ravenousness. **2** *hunger for power*: desire, craving, longing, yearning, itch, thirst.

hungry *adjective* **1** *feel hungry*: starving, peckish (*infml*), empty, hollow, famished, ravenous. **2** *hungry for knowledge*: desirous, craving, longing, aching, thirsty, eager, avid.
F3 **1** satisfied, full.

hunt *verb* **1** *police hunting the killer*: chase, pursue, hound, dog, stalk, track, trail. **2** *hunt for her umbrella*: seek, look for, search, scour, rummage, forage, investigate.
▪ *noun* chase, pursuit, search, quest, investigation.

hurdle *noun* jump, fence, wall, hedge, barrier, barricade, obstacle, obstruction, stumbling block, hindrance, impediment, handicap, problem, snag, difficulty, complication.

hurl *verb* throw, toss, fling, sling, catapult, project, propel, fire, launch, send.

hurried *adjective* rushed, hectic, hasty, precipitate *(fml)*, speedy, quick, swift, rapid, passing, brief, short, cursory, superficial, shallow, careless, slapdash.
leisurely.

hurry *verb* rush, dash, fly, get a move on *(infml)*, hasten, quicken, speed up, hustle, push.
slow down, delay.
▪ *noun* rush, haste, quickness, speed, urgency, hustle, bustle, flurry, commotion.
leisureliness, calm.

hurt *verb* **1** *my leg hurts*: ache, pain, throb, sting, smart. **2** *hurt her head*: injure, wound, maltreat, ill-treat, bruise, cut, burn, torture, maim, disable. **3** *hurt his chances*: damage, impair, harm, mar, spoil. **4** *hurts me when he behaves like that*: upset, sadden, grieve, distress, afflict, offend, wound, annoy.
▪ *noun* pain, soreness, discomfort, suffering, injury, wound, damage, harm, distress, sorrow.
▪ *adjective* **1** *how many people were hurt?*: injured, wounded, bruised, grazed, cut, scarred, maimed. **2** *hurt feelings*: upset, sad, saddened, distressed, aggrieved, annoyed, offended, affronted, wounded.

hurtful *adjective* upsetting, wounding, vicious, cruel, mean, unkind, nasty, malicious, spiteful, catty, derogatory, scathing, cutting.
kind.

hurtle *verb* dash, tear, race, fly, shoot, speed, rush, charge, plunge, dive, crash, rattle.

hush *verb* quieten, silence, still, settle, compose, calm, soothe, subdue.
disturb, rouse.
▪ *noun* quietness, silence, peace, stillness, repose, calm, calmness, tranquillity, serenity.
noise, clamour.
▪ *interjection* quiet, hold your tongue, shut up *(infml)*, not another word.

husky *adjective* hoarse, croaky, croaking, low, throaty, guttural, gruff, rasping, rough, harsh.

hustle *verb* hasten, rush, hurry, bustle, force, push, shove, thrust, bundle, elbow, jostle.

hut *noun* cabin, shack, shanty, booth, shed, lean-to, shelter, den.

hybrid *adjective* crossbred, mongrel, composite, combined, mixed, heterogeneous *(fml)*, compound.
pure-bred.

hygiene *noun* sanitariness, sanitation, sterility, disinfection, cleanliness, purity, wholesomeness.
insanitariness.

hygienic *adjective* sanitary, sterile, aseptic, germ-free,

disinfected, clean, pure, salubrious (*fml*), healthy, wholesome.
F3 unhygienic, insanitary.
hypnotic *adjective* mesmerizing, soporific (*fml*), sleep-inducing, spellbinding, fascinating, compelling, irresistible, magnetic.
hypnotize *verb* mesmerize, spellbind, bewitch, enchant, entrance, fascinate, captivate, magnetize.
hypocritical *adjective* insincere, two-faced, self-righteous, double-dealing, false, hollow, deceptive, spurious, deceitful, dissembling (*fml*), pharisaic(al) (*fml*).
F3 sincere, genuine.
hypothetical *adjective* theoretical, imaginary, supposed, assumed, proposed, conjectural, speculative.
F3 real, actual.
hysterical *adjective* **1** *become hysterical*: frantic, frenzied, berserk, uncontrollable, mad, raving, crazed, demented, overwrought, neurotic. **2** (*infml*) *hysterical laughter/the show's hysterical*: hilarious, uproarious, side-splitting, priceless (*infml*), rich (*infml*).
F3 **1** calm, composed, self-possessed.

ice *noun* frost, rime, icicle, glacier, iciness, frostiness, coldness, chill.
icon *noun* image, representation, symbol, idol, portrait.
icy *adjective* **1** *icy wind*: ice-cold, arctic, polar, glacial, freezing, frozen, raw, bitter, biting, cold, chill, chilly. **2** *icy roads*: frosty, slippery, glassy, frozen, icebound, frostbound. **3** *an icy silence*: hostile, cold, stony, cool, indifferent, aloof, distant, formal.
F3 **1** hot. **3** friendly, warm.
idea *noun* **1** *have an idea*: thought, concept, notion, theory, hypothesis, guess, conjecture, belief, opinion, view, viewpoint, judgement, conception, vision, image, impression, perception, interpretation, understanding, inkling, suspicion, clue. **2** *a good idea*: brainwave, suggestion, proposal, proposition, plan, scheme, recommendation, design.
ideal *noun* perfection, epitome, acme, paragon, exemplar, example, model, pattern, archetype, prototype, type, image, criterion, standard, principle.
▪ *adjective* perfect, dream,

utopian, best, optimum, optimal, supreme, highest, model, archetypal.

idealistic *adjective* perfectionist, utopian, visionary, romantic, quixotic, starry-eyed, optimistic, unrealistic, impractical, impracticable.

F3 realistic, pragmatic.

identical *adjective* same, self-same, indistinguishable, interchangeable, twin, duplicate, like, alike, corresponding, matching, equal, equivalent.

F3 different.

identify *verb* recognize, know, pick out, single out, distinguish, perceive, make out, discern, notice, detect, diagnose, name, label, tag, specify, pinpoint, place, catalogue, classify.

identity *noun* individuality, particularity, singularity, uniqueness, self, personality, character, existence.

idiosyncrasy *noun* characteristic, peculiarity, singularity, oddity, eccentricity, freak, quirk, habit, mannerism, trait, feature.

idiot *noun* fool, blockhead, fathead, nincompoop (*infml*), ass (*infml*), chump (*infml*), ninny (*infml*), clot (*infml*), dope (*infml*), twit (*infml*), nitwit (*infml*), nit (*infml*), dunce, dimwit, simpleton, halfwit, imbecile, moron, dupe, sucker (*infml*), mug (*infml*).

idiotic *adjective* foolish, stupid, silly, absurd, senseless, daft (*infml*), lunatic, insane, foolhardy, harebrained, halfwitted, moronic, cretinous, crazy.

F3 sensible, sane.

idle *adjective* **1** *machines lying idle/he's been idle for three months*: inactive, inoperative, unused, unoccupied, unemployed, jobless, redundant. **2** *an idle layabout*: lazy, work-shy, indolent. **3** *idle talk*: empty, trivial, casual, futile, vain, pointless, unproductive.

F3 **1** active. **2** busy.

idol *noun* icon, effigy, image, graven image, god, deity, fetish, favourite, darling, hero, heroine, pin-up, superstar, heart-throb (*infml*).

idolize *verb* hero-worship, lionize, exalt, glorify, worship, venerate, revere, admire, adore, love, dote on.

F3 despise.

idyllic *adjective* perfect, idealized, heavenly, delightful, charming, picturesque, pastoral, rustic, unspoiled, peaceful, happy.

F3 unpleasant.

ignite *verb* set fire to, set alight, catch fire, flare up, burn, conflagrate, fire, kindle, touch off, spark off.

F3 quench.

ignorance *noun* unintelligence, illiteracy, unawareness, unconsciousness, oblivion, innocence, unfamiliarity, inexperience, naivety.

F3 knowledge, wisdom.

ignorant *adjective* uneducated,

illiterate, unread, untaught, untrained, inexperienced, stupid, clueless (*infml*), uninitiated, unenlightened, uninformed, ill-informed, unwitting, unaware, unconscious, oblivious.
F3 educated, knowledgeable, clever, wise.

ignore *verb* disregard, take no notice of, shut one's eyes to, overlook, pass over, neglect, omit, reject, snub, cold-shoulder.
F3 notice, observe.

ill *adjective* sick, poorly, unwell, indisposed, laid up, ailing, off-colour, out of sorts (*infml*), under the weather (*infml*), seedy, queasy, diseased, unhealthy, infirm, frail.
F3 well.

illegal *adjective* unlawful, illicit, criminal, wrong, forbidden, prohibited, banned, outlawed, unauthorized, under-the-counter, black-market, unconstitutional, wrongful.
F3 legal, lawful.

illegible *adjective* unreadable, indecipherable, scrawled, obscure, faint, indistinct.
F3 legible.

illicit *adjective* illegal, unlawful, criminal, wrong, illegitimate, improper, forbidden, prohibited, unauthorized, unlicensed, black-market, contraband, ill-gotten, under-the-counter, furtive, clandestine.
F3 legal, permissible.

illness *noun* disease, disorder, complaint, ailment, sickness, ill-health, ill-being, indisposition, infirmity, disability, affliction.

ill-treat *verb* maltreat, abuse, injure, harm, damage, neglect, mistreat, mishandle, misuse, wrong, oppress.

illusion *noun* apparition, mirage, hallucination, figment, fantasy, fancy, delusion, misapprehension, misconception, error, fallacy.
F3 reality, truth.

illusory *adjective* illusive, deceptive, misleading, apparent, seeming, deluding, delusive, unreal, unsubstantial, sham, false, fallacious, untrue, mistaken.
F3 real.

illustrate *verb* draw, sketch, depict, picture, show, exhibit, demonstrate, exemplify, explain, interpret, clarify, elucidate, illuminate, decorate, ornament, adorn.

illustration *noun* picture, plate, half-tone, photograph, drawing, sketch, figure, representation, decoration.

image *noun* **1** *an image in his mind*: idea, notion, concept, impression, perception. **2** *images of the saints*: representation, likeness, picture, portrait, icon, effigy, figure, statue, idol, replica, reflection.

imaginary *adjective* imagined, fanciful, illusory, hallucinatory, visionary, pretend, make-believe, unreal, non-existent, fictional, fabulous, legendary, mythological, made-up, invented, fictitious,

assumed, supposed, hypothetical.
F3 real.

imagination *noun* imaginativeness, creativity, inventiveness, originality, inspiration, insight, ingenuity, resourcefulness, enterprise, wit, vision, mind's eye, fancy, illusion.
F3 unimaginativeness, reality.

imaginative *adjective* creative, inventive, innovative, original, inspired, visionary, ingenious, clever, resourceful, enterprising, fanciful, fantastic, vivid.
F3 unimaginative.

imagine *verb* **1** *imagining what it would be like*: picture, visualize, envisage, conceive, fancy, fantasize, pretend, make believe, conjure up, dream up, think up, invent, devise, create, plan, project. **2** *I imagine so*: think, believe, judge, suppose, guess, conjecture, assume, take it, gather.

imitate *verb* copy, emulate, follow, ape, mimic, impersonate, take off, caricature, parody, send up, spoof, mock, parrot, repeat, echo, mirror, duplicate, reproduce, simulate, counterfeit, forge.

imitation *noun* copy, duplicate, reproduction, replica, simulation, counterfeit, fake, forgery, sham, likeness, resemblance, reflection, dummy.
▪ *adjective* artificial, synthetic, man-made, ersatz, fake, phoney (*infml*), mock, pseudo, reproduction, simulated, sham, dummy.
F3 genuine.

immaculate *adjective* perfect, unblemished, flawless, faultless, impeccable, spotless, clean, spick and span, pure, unsullied, undefiled, untainted, stainless, blameless, innocent.
F3 blemished, stained, contaminated.

immature *adjective* young, under-age, adolescent, juvenile, childish, puerile (*fml*), infantile, babyish, raw, crude, callow, inexperienced, green, unripe, undeveloped.
F3 mature.

immediate *adjective* **1** *an immediate response*: instant, instantaneous, direct, prompt, swift, current, present, existing, urgent, pressing. **2** *our immediate neighbours*: nearest, next, adjacent, near, close, recent.
F3 **1** delayed. **2** distant.

immediately *adverb* now, straight away, right away, at once, instantly, directly, forthwith, without delay, promptly, unhesitatingly.
F3 eventually, never.

immense *adjective* vast, great, huge, enormous, massive, giant, gigantic, tremendous, monumental.
F3 tiny, minute.

immerse *verb* plunge, submerge, submerse, sink, duck, dip, douse, bathe.

immigrant *noun* incomer, settler, newcomer, alien.
emigrant.

imminent *adjective* impending, forthcoming, in the offing, approaching, coming, near, close, looming, menacing, threatening, brewing, in the air.
remote, far-off.

immoral *adjective* unethical, wrong, bad, sinful, evil, wicked, unscrupulous, unprincipled, dishonest, corrupt, depraved, degenerate, dissolute, lewd, indecent, pornographic, obscene, impure.
moral, right, good.

immortal *adjective* undying, imperishable, eternal, everlasting, perpetual, endless, ceaseless, lasting, enduring, abiding, timeless, ageless.
mortal.

immune *adjective* invulnerable, insusceptible, resistant, proof, protected, safe, exempt, free, clear.
susceptible.

immunize *verb* vaccinate, inoculate, inject, protect, safeguard.

impact *noun* **1** *the impact of the reforms*: effect, consequences, repercussions, impression, power, influence, significance, meaning. **2** *flung forward by the impact*: collision, crash, smash, bang, bump, blow, knock, contact, jolt, shock, brunt.

impair *verb* damage, harm, injure, hinder, mar, spoil, worsen, undermine, weaken, reduce, lessen, diminish, blunt.
improve, enhance.

impartial *adjective* objective, dispassionate, detached, disinterested, neutral, non-partisan, unbiased, unprejudiced, open-minded, fair, fair-minded, just, equitable, even-handed, equal.
biased, prejudiced.

impassive *adjective* expressionless, calm, composed, unruffled, unconcerned, cool, unfeeling, unemotional, unmoved, imperturbable, unexcitable, stoical, indifferent, dispassionate.
responsive, moved.

impatient *adjective* eager, keen, restless, fidgety, fretful, edgy, irritable, snappy, hot-tempered, quick-tempered, intolerant, brusque, abrupt, impetuous, hasty, precipitate (*fml*), headlong.
patient.

impeccable *adjective* perfect, faultless, precise, exact, flawless, unblemished, stainless, immaculate, pure, irreproachable, blameless, innocent.
faulty, flawed, corrupt.

impede *verb* hinder, hamper, obstruct, block, clog, slow, retard, hold up, delay, check, curb, restrain, thwart, disrupt, stop, bar.
aid, promote, further.

impediment *noun* hindrance, obstacle, obstruction, barrier, bar,

block, stumbling block, snag, difficulty, handicap, check, curb, restraint, restriction.
F3 aid.

impel *verb* urge, force, oblige, compel, constrain, drive, propel, push, spur, goad, prompt, stimulate, excite, instigate, motivate, inspire, move.
F3 deter, dissuade.

impending *adjective* imminent, forthcoming, approaching, coming, close, near, looming, menacing, threatening.
F3 remote.

impenetrable *adjective* **1** *impenetrable jungle*: solid, thick, dense, impassable. **2** *impenetrable logic*: unintelligible, incomprehensible, unfathomable, baffling, mysterious, cryptic, enigmatic, obscure, dark, inscrutable.
F3 **1** accessible. **2** understandable.

imperceptible *adjective* inappreciable, indiscernible, inaudible, faint, slight, negligible, infinitesimal, microscopic, minute, tiny, small, fine, subtle, gradual.
F3 perceptible, obvious.

imperfect *adjective* faulty, flawed, defective, damaged, broken, chipped, deficient, incomplete.
F3 perfect.

impersonal *adjective* formal, official, businesslike, bureaucratic, faceless, aloof, remote, distant, detached, neutral, objective, dispassionate, cold, frosty, glassy.
F3 informal, friendly.

impersonate *verb* imitate, mimic, take off, parody, ape, caricature, mock, masquerade as, pose as, act, portray.

impetuous *adjective* impulsive, spontaneous, unplanned, unpremeditated, hasty, precipitate (*fml*), rash, reckless, thoughtless, unthinking.
F3 cautious, wary, circumspect (*fml*).

impetus *noun* impulse, momentum, force, energy, power, drive, boost, push, spur, stimulus, incentive, motivation.

impinge *verb* hit, touch (on), affect, influence, encroach, infringe, intrude, trespass, invade.

implement *noun* tool, instrument, utensil, gadget, device, apparatus, appliance.
▪ *verb* enforce, effect, bring about, carry out, execute, discharge, perform, do, fulfil, complete, accomplish, realize.

implicate *verb* involve, embroil, entangle, incriminate, compromise, include, concern, connect, associate.
F3 exonerate.

implication *noun* inference, insinuation, suggestion, meaning, significance, ramification, repercussion.

imply *verb* suggest, insinuate, hint, intimate, mean, signify, point to, indicate, involve, require.
F3 state.

importance *noun* momentousness, significance, consequence, substance, matter, concern, interest, usefulness, value, worth, weight, influence, mark, prominence, eminence, distinction, esteem, prestige, status, standing.
F3 unimportance.

important *adjective* momentous, noteworthy, significant, meaningful, relevant, material, salient, urgent, vital, essential, key, primary, major, substantial, valuable, seminal, weighty, serious, grave, far-reaching.
F3 unimportant, insignificant, trivial.

impose *verb* **1** *imposing taxes*: introduce, institute, enforce, promulgate, exact, levy, set, fix, put, place, lay, inflict, burden, encumber, saddle. **2** *impose on their hospitality*: intrude, butt in, encroach, trespass, obtrude, force oneself, presume, take liberties.

imposing *adjective* impressive, striking, grand, stately, majestic, dignified.
F3 unimposing, modest.

impossible *adjective* hopeless, impracticable, unworkable, unattainable, unachievable, unobtainable, insoluble, unreasonable, unacceptable, inconceivable, unthinkable, preposterous, absurd, ludicrous, ridiculous.
F3 possible.

impostor *noun* fraud, fake, phoney (*infml*), quack, charlatan, impersonator, pretender, con man (*infml*), swindler, cheat, rogue.

impress *verb* **1** *tried to impress me*: strike, move, touch, affect, influence, stir, inspire, excite, grab (*infml*). **2** *must impress on them the importance of this*: stamp, imprint, mark, indent, instil, inculcate.

impression *noun* **1** *get the impression he doesn't want to come*: feeling, awareness, consciousness, sense, illusion, idea, notion, opinion, belief, conviction, suspicion, hunch, memory, recollection. **2** *do an impression of someone*: impersonation, imitation, take-off, parody, send-up. **3** *make a good impression*: effect, impact, influence.

impressionable *adjective* naive, gullible, susceptible, vulnerable, sensitive, responsive, open, receptive.

impressive *adjective* striking, imposing, grand, powerful, effective, stirring, exciting, moving, touching.
F3 unimpressive, uninspiring.

imprison *verb* jail, incarcerate, intern, detain, send down (*infml*), put away (*infml*), lock up, cage, confine, shut in.
F3 release, free.

impromptu *adjective* improvised, extempore (*fml*), ad-lib, off the cuff, unscripted,

unrehearsed, unprepared, spontaneous.
⇄ rehearsed.
▪ *adverb* extempore (*fml*), ad lib, off the cuff, off the top of one's head, spontaneously, on the spur of the moment.

improper *adjective* wrong, incorrect, irregular, unsuitable, inappropriate, inopportune, incongruous, out of place, indecent, rude, vulgar, unseemly, unbecoming, shocking.
⇄ proper, appropriate, decent.

improve *verb* better, ameliorate (*fml*), enhance, polish, touch up, mend, rectify, correct, amend, reform, upgrade, increase, rise, pick up, develop, look up, advance, progress, get better, recover, recuperate, rally, perk up, mend one's ways, turn over a new leaf.
⇄ worsen, deteriorate, decline.

improvement *noun* betterment, amelioration (*fml*), enhancement, rectification, correction, amendment, reformation, increase, rise, upswing, gain, development, advance, progress, furtherance, recovery, rally.
⇄ deterioration, decline.

improvise *verb* **1** *improvised a stage using a curtain*: contrive, devise, concoct, invent, throw together, make do. **2** *an actor who improvises a lot*: extemporize (*fml*), ad-lib, play by ear, vamp.

impudent *adjective* impertinent, cheeky (*infml*), saucy (*infml*), bold, forward, shameless, cocky, insolent, rude, presumptuous, fresh.
⇄ polite.

impulse *noun* urge, wish, desire, inclination, whim, notion, instinct, feeling, passion.

impulsive *adjective* impetuous, rash, reckless, hasty, quick, spontaneous, automatic, instinctive, intuitive.
⇄ cautious, premeditated.

impurity *noun* adulteration, contamination, pollution, infection, corruption, dirtiness, contaminant, dirt, filth, foreign body, mark, spot.
⇄ purity.

inability *noun* incapability, incapacity, powerlessness, impotence, inadequacy, weakness, handicap, disability.
⇄ ability.

inaccessible *adjective* isolated, remote, unfrequented, unapproachable, unget-at-able (*infml*), unreachable, unattainable.
⇄ accessible.

inaccurate *adjective* incorrect, wrong, erroneous, mistaken, faulty, flawed, defective, imprecise, inexact, loose, unreliable, unfaithful, untrue.
⇄ accurate, correct.

inadequate *adjective* **1** *an inadequate supply of food*: insufficient, short, wanting, deficient, scanty, sparse, meagre, niggardly. **2** *feel inadequate/an inadequate attempt*: incompetent,

incapable, unequal, unqualified, ineffective, faulty, defective, imperfect, unsatisfactory.
F3 **1** adequate. **2** satisfactory.

inane *adjective* senseless, foolish, stupid, unintelligent, silly, idiotic, fatuous, frivolous, trifling, puerile (*fml*), mindless, vapid, empty, vacuous, vain, worthless, futile.
F3 sensible.

inappropriate *adjective* unsuitable, inapt, ill-suited, ill-fitted, irrelevant, incongruous, out of place, untimely, ill-timed, tactless, improper, unseemly, unbecoming, unfitting.
F3 appropriate, suitable.

incapable *adjective* unable, powerless, impotent, helpless, weak, feeble, unfit, unsuited, unqualified, incompetent, inept, inadequate, ineffective.
F3 capable.

incentive *noun* bait, lure, enticement, carrot (*infml*), sweetener (*infml*), reward, encouragement, inducement, reason, motive, impetus, spur, stimulus, motivation.
F3 disincentive, discouragement, deterrent.

incessant *adjective* ceaseless, unceasing, endless, never-ending, interminable, continual, persistent, constant, perpetual, eternal, everlasting, continuous, unbroken, unremitting, non-stop.
F3 intermittent, sporadic, periodic, temporary.

incidence *noun* frequency, commonness, prevalence, extent, range, amount, degree, rate, occurrence.

incident *noun* occurrence, happening, event, episode, adventure, affair, occasion, instance.

incidental *adjective* accidental, chance, random, minor, non-essential, secondary, subordinate, subsidiary, ancillary, supplementary, accompanying, attendant, related, contributory.
F3 important, essential.

incite *verb* prompt, instigate, rouse, foment, stir up, whip up, work up, excite, animate, provoke, stimulate, spur, goad, impel, drive, urge, encourage, egg on (*infml*).
F3 restrain.

incline *verb* /in-**klain**/ dispose, influence, persuade, affect, bias, prejudice.
▪ *noun* /**in**-klain/ slope, gradient, ramp, hill, rise, ascent, acclivity (*fml*), dip, descent, declivity (*fml*).

inclined *adjective* liable, likely, given, apt, disposed, of a mind, willing.

include *verb* comprise, incorporate, embody, comprehend, contain, enclose, embrace, encompass, cover, subsume, take in, add, allow for, take into account, involve, rope in.
F3 exclude, omit, eliminate.

inclusive *adjective* comprehensive, full, all-in, all-inclusive, all-embracing, blanket, across-the-board, general, catch-

all, overall, sweeping.
⇄ exclusive, narrow.

income *noun* revenue, returns, proceeds, gains, profits, interest, takings, receipts, earnings, pay, salary, wages, means.
⇄ expenditure, expenses.

incompatible *adjective* irreconcilable, contradictory, conflicting, at variance, inconsistent, clashing, mismatched, unsuited.
⇄ compatible.

incompetent *adjective* incapable, unable, unfit, inefficient, inexpert, unskilful, bungling, stupid, useless, ineffective.
⇄ competent, able.

incomplete *adjective* deficient, lacking, short, unfinished, abridged, partial, part, fragmentary, broken, imperfect, defective.
⇄ complete, exhaustive.

incongruous *adjective* inappropriate, unsuitable, out of place, out of keeping, inconsistent, conflicting, incompatible, irreconcilable, contradictory, contrary.
⇄ consistent, compatible.

inconsiderate *adjective* unkind, uncaring, unconcerned, selfish, self-centred, intolerant, insensitive, tactless, rude, thoughtless, unthinking, careless, heedless.
⇄ considerate.

inconsistent *adjective* **1** *a fact that is inconsistent with their theory*: conflicting, at variance, at odds, incompatible, contradictory, contrary, incongruous, discordant. **2** *he can be very inconsistent*: changeable, variable, irregular, unpredictable, varying, unstable, unsteady, inconstant, fickle.
⇄ **2** constant.

inconspicuous *adjective* hidden, concealed, camouflaged, plain, ordinary, unobtrusive, discreet, low-key, modest, unassuming, quiet, retiring, insignificant.
⇄ conspicuous, noticeable, obtrusive.

inconvenience *noun* awkwardness, difficulty, annoyance, nuisance, hindrance, drawback, bother, trouble, fuss, upset, disturbance, disruption.
⇄ convenience.

inconvenient *adjective* awkward, ill-timed, untimely, inopportune, unsuitable, difficult, embarrassing, annoying, troublesome, unwieldy, unmanageable.
⇄ convenient.

incorporate *verb* include, embody, contain, subsume, take in, absorb, assimilate, integrate, combine, unite, merge, blend, mix, fuse, coalesce, consolidate.
⇄ separate.

increase *verb* /in-**krees**/ raise, boost, add to, improve, enhance, advance, step up, intensify, strengthen, heighten, grow, develop, build up, wax, enlarge,

extend, prolong, expand, spread, swell, magnify, multiply, proliferate, rise, mount, soar, escalate.
F3 decrease, reduce, decline.
▪ *noun* /**in**-krees/ rise, surge, upsurge, upturn, gain, boost, addition, increment, advance, step-up, intensification, growth, development, enlargement, extension, expansion, spread, proliferation, escalation.
F3 decrease, reduction, decline.

incredible *adjective* unbelievable, improbable, implausible, far-fetched, preposterous, absurd, impossible, inconceivable, unthinkable, unimaginable, extraordinary, amazing, astonishing, astounding.
F3 credible, believable.

incredulous *adjective* unbelieving, disbelieving, unconvinced, sceptical, doubting, distrustful, suspicious, dubious, doubtful, uncertain.
F3 credulous.

incriminate *verb* inculpate, implicate, involve, accuse, charge, impeach, indict, point the finger at, blame.
F3 exonerate.

incur *verb* suffer, sustain, provoke, arouse, bring upon oneself, expose oneself to, meet with, run up, gain, earn.

incurable *adjective* terminal, fatal, untreatable, inoperable, hopeless.
F3 curable.

indebted *adjective* obliged, grateful, thankful.

indecent *adjective* improper, immodest, impure, indelicate, offensive, obscene, pornographic, lewd, licentious, vulgar, coarse, crude, dirty, filthy, foul, gross, outrageous, shocking.
F3 decent, modest.

indecisive *adjective* undecided, irresolute, undetermined, vacillating, wavering, in two minds, hesitating, faltering, tentative, uncertain, unsure, doubtful, inconclusive, indefinite, indeterminate, unclear.
F3 decisive.

indeed *adverb* really, actually, in fact, certainly, positively, truly, undeniably, undoubtedly, to be sure.

indefinite *adjective* unknown, uncertain, unsettled, unresolved, undecided, undetermined, undefined, unspecified, unlimited, ill-defined, vague, indistinct, unclear, obscure, ambiguous, imprecise, inexact, loose, general.
F3 definite, limited, clear.

indefinitely *adverb* for ever, eternally, endlessly, continually, ad infinitum.

independence *noun* autonomy, self-government, self-determination, self-rule, home rule, sovereignty, freedom, liberty, individualism, separation.
F3 dependence.

independent *adjective* **1** *an independent nation*: autonomous,

self-governing, self-determining, sovereign, absolute, non-aligned, neutral, impartial, unbiased. **2** *a very independent person*: free, liberated, unconstrained, individualistic, unconventional, self-sufficient, self-supporting, self-reliant, unaided.
1 dependent.

indestructible *adjective* unbreakable, durable, tough, strong, lasting, enduring, abiding, permanent, eternal, everlasting, immortal, imperishable.
breakable, mortal.

indicate *verb* register, record, show, reveal, display, manifest, point to, designate, specify, point out, mark, signify, mean, denote, express, suggest, imply.

indication *noun* mark, sign, manifestation, evidence, symptom, signal, warning, omen, intimation, suggestion, hint, clue, note, explanation.

indifferent *adjective* **1** *indifferent to their distress*: uninterested, unenthusiastic, unexcited, apathetic, unconcerned, unmoved, uncaring, unsympathetic, cold, cool, distant, aloof, detached, uninvolved, neutral, disinterested. **2** *an indifferent meal*: mediocre, average, middling, passable, moderate, fair, ordinary.
1 interested, caring. **2** excellent.

indigenous *adjective* native, aboriginal, original, local, home-grown.
foreign.

indignant *adjective* annoyed, angry, irate, heated, fuming, livid, furious, incensed, infuriated, exasperated, outraged.
pleased, delighted.

indignation *noun* annoyance, anger, ire, wrath, rage, fury, exasperation, outrage, scorn, contempt.
pleasure, delight.

indirect *adjective* **1** *an indirect route*: roundabout, circuitous, wandering, rambling, winding, meandering, zigzag, tortuous. **2** *an indirect effect*: secondary, incidental, unintended, subsidiary, ancillary.
1 direct. **2** primary.

indiscreet *adjective* tactless, undiplomatic, impolitic, injudicious, imprudent, unwise, foolish, rash, reckless, hasty, careless, heedless, unthinking.
discreet, cautious.

indiscriminate *adjective* general, sweeping, wholesale, random, haphazard, hit or miss, aimless, unsystematic, unmethodical, mixed, motley, miscellaneous.
selective, specific, precise.

indispensable *adjective* vital, essential, basic, key, crucial, imperative, required, requisite, needed, necessary.
dispensable, unnecessary.

indistinct *adjective* unclear, ill-defined, blurred, fuzzy, misty, hazy,

shadowy, obscure, dim, faint, muffled, confused, unintelligible, vague, woolly, ambiguous, indefinite.
F3 distinct, clear.

individual *noun* person, being, creature, party, body, soul, character, fellow.
▪ *adjective* distinctive, characteristic, idiosyncratic, peculiar, singular, unique, exclusive, special, personal, own, proper, respective, several, separate, distinct, specific, personalized, particular, single.
F3 collective, shared, general.

individuality *noun* character, personality, distinctiveness, peculiarity, singularity, uniqueness, separateness, distinction.
F3 sameness.

induce *verb* **1** *inducing a violent response*: cause, effect, bring about, occasion, give rise to, lead to, incite, instigate, prompt, provoke, produce, generate. **2** *induce him to stay*: coax, prevail upon, encourage, press, persuade, talk into, move, influence, draw, tempt.
F3 **2** discourage, deter.

indulge *verb* gratify, satisfy, humour, pander to, go along with, give in to, yield to, favour, pet, cosset, mollycoddle, pamper, spoil, treat, regale.

indulgence *noun* extravagance, luxury, excess, immoderation, intemperance, favour, tolerance.

indulgent *adjective* tolerant, easy-going (*infml*), lenient, permissive, generous, liberal, kind, fond, tender, understanding, patient.
F3 strict, harsh.

industry *noun* **1** *the steel industry*: business, trade, commerce, manufacturing, production. **2** *the industry of the worker ants*: industriousness, diligence, application, effort, labour, toil, persistence, perseverance, determination.

inedible *adjective* uneatable, unpalatable, indigestible, harmful, noxious, poisonous, deadly.
F3 edible.

ineffective *adjective* useless, worthless, vain, idle, futile, unavailing, fruitless, unproductive, unsuccessful, powerless, impotent, ineffectual, inadequate, weak, feeble, inept, incompetent.
F3 effective, effectual.

inefficient *adjective* uneconomic, wasteful, money-wasting, time-wasting, incompetent, inexpert, unworkmanlike, slipshod, sloppy, careless, negligent.
F3 efficient.

inept *adjective* awkward, clumsy, bungling, incompetent, unskilful, inexpert, foolish, stupid.
F3 competent, skilful.

inequality *noun* unequalness, difference, diversity, dissimilarity, disparity, unevenness,

disproportion, bias, prejudice.
equality.

inert *adjective* immobile, motionless, unmoving, still, inactive, inanimate, lifeless, dead, passive, unresponsive, apathetic, dormant, idle, lazy, lethargic, sluggish, torpid, sleepy.
lively, animated.

inertia *noun* immobility, stillness, inactivity, passivity, unresponsiveness, apathy, idleness, laziness, lethargy, torpor, listlessness.
activity, liveliness.

inevitable *adjective* unavoidable, inescapable, necessary, definite, certain, sure, decreed, ordained, destined, fated, automatic, assured, fixed, unalterable, irrevocable, inexorable.
avoidable, uncertain, alterable.

inexperienced *adjective* inexpert, untrained, unskilled, amateur, probationary, apprentice, unfamiliar, unacquainted, unaccustomed, new, fresh, raw, callow, young, immature, naive, unsophisticated, innocent.
experienced, mature.

inexplicable *adjective* unexplainable, unaccountable, strange, mystifying, puzzling, baffling, mysterious, enigmatic, unfathomable, incomprehensible, incredible, unbelievable, miraculous.
explicable.

infallible *adjective* accurate, unerring, unfailing, foolproof, fail-safe, sure-fire (*infml*), certain, sure, reliable, dependable, trustworthy, sound, perfect, faultless, impeccable.
fallible.

infamous *adjective* notorious, ill-famed, disreputable, disgraceful, shameful, shocking, outrageous, scandalous, wicked, iniquitous.
illustrious, glorious.

infancy *noun* babyhood, childhood, youth.
adulthood.

infant *noun* baby, toddler, tot (*infml*), child, babe (*fml*), babe in arms (*fml*).
adult.

infantile *adjective* babyish, childish, puerile (*fml*), juvenile, young, youthful, adolescent, immature.
adult, mature.

infatuated *adjective* besotted, obsessed, enamoured, smitten (*infml*), crazy (*infml*), spellbound, mesmerized, captivated, fascinated, enraptured, ravished.
indifferent, disenchanted.

infect *verb* contaminate, pollute, defile (*fml*), taint, blight, poison, corrupt, pervert, influence, affect, touch, inspire.

infectious *adjective* contagious, communicable, transmissible, infective, catching, spreading, epidemic, virulent, deadly, contaminating, polluting, defiling, corrupting.

infer *verb* derive, extrapolate,

deduce, conclude, assume, presume, surmise, gather, understand.

inferior *adjective* **1** *an inferior position*: lower, lesser, minor, secondary, junior, subordinate, subsidiary, second-class, low, humble, menial. **2** *an inferior product*: substandard, second-rate, mediocre, bad, poor, unsatisfactory, slipshod, shoddy.
F3 **1** superior. **2** excellent.
▪ *noun* subordinate, junior, underling (*infml*), minion, vassal, menial.
F3 superior.

infest *verb* swarm, teem, throng, flood, overrun, invade, infiltrate, penetrate, permeate, pervade, ravage.

infinite *adjective* limitless, unlimited, boundless, unbounded, endless, never-ending, inexhaustible, bottomless, innumerable, numberless, uncountable, countless, untold, incalculable, inestimable, immeasurable, unfathomable, vast, immense, enormous, huge, absolute, total.
F3 finite, limited.

infinity *noun* eternity, perpetuity, limitlessness, boundlessness, endlessness, inexhaustibility, countlessness, immeasurableness, vastness, immensity.
F3 finiteness, limitation.

infirm *adjective* weak, feeble, frail, ill, unwell, poorly, sickly, failing, faltering, unsteady, shaky, wobbly, doddery, lame.
F3 healthy, strong.

inflame *verb* anger, enrage, infuriate, incense, exasperate, madden, provoke, stimulate, excite, rouse, arouse, agitate, foment, kindle, ignite, fire, heat, fan, fuel, increase, intensify, worsen, aggravate.
F3 cool, quench.

inflammable *adjective* flammable, combustible, burnable.
F3 non-flammable, incombustible, flameproof.

inflammation *noun* soreness, painfulness, tenderness, swelling, abscess, infection, redness, heat, rash, sore, irritation.

inflate *verb* blow up, pump up, blow out, puff out, swell, distend, bloat, expand, enlarge, increase, boost, exaggerate.
F3 deflate.

inflation *noun* expansion, increase, rise, escalation, hyperinflation.
F3 deflation.

inflict *verb* impose, enforce, perpetrate, wreak, administer, apply, deliver, deal, mete out, lay, burden, exact, levy.

influence *noun* power, sway, rule, authority, domination, mastery, hold, control, direction, guidance, bias, prejudice, pull, pressure, effect, impact, weight, importance, prestige, standing.
▪ *verb* dominate, control,

manipulate, direct, guide, manoeuvre, change, alter, modify, affect, impress, move, stir, arouse, rouse, sway, persuade, induce, incite, instigate, prompt, motivate, dispose, incline, bias, prejudice, predispose.

influential *adjective* dominant, controlling, leading, authoritative, charismatic, persuasive, convincing, compelling, inspiring, moving, powerful, potent, effective, telling, strong, weighty, momentous, important, significant, instrumental, guiding.
F3 ineffective, unimportant.

influx *noun* inflow, inrush, invasion, arrival, stream, flow, rush, flood, inundation.

inform *verb* tell, advise, notify, communicate, impart, leak, tip off, acquaint, fill in (*infml*), brief, instruct, enlighten, illuminate.

informal *adjective* unofficial, unceremonious, casual, relaxed, easy, free, natural, simple, unpretentious, familiar, colloquial.
F3 formal, solemn.

information *noun* facts, data, input, gen (*infml*), bumf (*infml*), intelligence, news, report, bulletin, communiqué, message, word, advice, notice, briefing, instruction, knowledge, dossier, database, databank, clues, evidence.

informative *adjective* educational, instructive, edifying, enlightening, illuminating, revealing, forthcoming, communicative, chatty, gossipy, newsy, helpful, useful, constructive.
F3 uninformative.

informed *adjective* **1** *we'll keep you informed*: familiar, conversant (*fml*), acquainted, enlightened, briefed, primed, posted, up to date, abreast, au fait, in the know (*infml*). **2** *an informed opinion*: well-informed, authoritative, expert, versed, well-read, erudite, learned, knowledgeable, well-researched.
F3 **1** ignorant, unaware.

infuriate *verb* anger, vex, enrage, incense, exasperate, madden, provoke, rouse, annoy, irritate, rile, antagonize.
F3 calm, pacify.

ingenious *adjective* clever, shrewd, cunning, crafty, skilful, masterly, imaginative, creative, inventive, resourceful, original, innovative.
F3 unimaginative.

ingrained *adjective* fixed, rooted, deep-rooted, deep-seated, entrenched, immovable, ineradicable, permanent, inbuilt, inborn, inbred.

ingratiate *verb* curry favour, flatter, creep, crawl, grovel, fawn, get in with.

ingratitude *noun* ungratefulness, thanklessness, unappreciativeness, ungraciousness.
F3 gratitude, thankfulness.

ingredient *noun* constituent, element, factor, component, part.

inhabit *verb* live, dwell, reside, occupy, possess, colonize, settle, people, populate, stay.

inhabitant *noun* resident, dweller, citizen, native, occupier, occupant, inmate, tenant, lodger.

inherit *verb* succeed to, accede to, assume, come into, be left, receive.

inheritance *noun* legacy, bequest, heritage, birthright, heredity, descent, succession.

inhibit *verb* discourage, repress, hold back, suppress, curb, check, restrain, hinder, impede, obstruct, interfere with, frustrate, thwart, prevent, stop, stanch, stem.
encourage, assist.

inhibited *adjective* repressed, self-conscious, shy, reticent, withdrawn, reserved, guarded, subdued.
uninhibited, open, relaxed.

inhibition *noun* repression, hang-up (*infml*), self-consciousness, shyness, reticence, reserve, restraint, curb, check, hindrance, impediment, obstruction, bar.
freedom.

inhuman *adjective* barbaric, barbarous, animal, bestial, vicious, savage, sadistic, cold-blooded, brutal, cruel, inhumane.
human.

inhumane *adjective* unkind, insensitive, callous, unfeeling, heartless, cold-hearted, hard-hearted, pitiless, ruthless, cruel, brutal, inhuman.
humane, kind, compassionate.

initial *adjective* first, beginning, opening, introductory, inaugural, original, primary, early, formative.
final, last.

initially *adverb* at first, at the beginning, to begin with, to start with, originally, first, firstly, first of all.
finally, in the end.

initiate *verb* begin, start, commence, originate, pioneer, institute, set up, introduce, launch, open, inaugurate, instigate, activate, trigger, prompt, stimulate, cause.

initiative *noun* **1** *show some initiative*: energy, drive, dynamism, get-up-and-go (*infml*), ambition, enterprise, resourcefulness, inventiveness, originality, innovativeness. **2** *a government initiative*: suggestion, recommendation, action, lead, first move, first step.

inject *verb* **1** *injected into the vein*: inoculate, vaccinate. **2** *inject a little humour into the discussion*: introduce, insert, add, bring, infuse, instil.

injure *verb* hurt, harm, damage, impair, spoil, mar, ruin, disfigure, deface, mutilate, wound, cut, break, fracture, maim, disable, cripple, lame, ill-treat, maltreat, abuse, offend, wrong, upset, put out.

injury *noun* wound, cut, lesion,

fracture, trauma, hurt, mischief, ill, harm, damage, impairment, ruin, disfigurement, mutilation, ill-treatment, abuse, insult, offence, wrong, injustice.

injustice *noun* unfairness, inequality, disparity, discrimination, oppression, bias, prejudice, one-sidedness, partisanship, partiality, favouritism, wrong, iniquity (*fml*).
F3 justice, fairness.

inkling *noun* suspicion, idea, notion, faintest (*infml*), glimmering, clue, hint, intimation, suggestion, allusion, indication, sign, pointer.

inlet *noun* bay, cove, creek, fjord, opening, entrance, passage.

inn *noun* public house, pub (*infml*), local (*infml*), tavern, hostelry, hotel.

innate *adjective* inborn, inbred, inherent, intrinsic, native, natural, instinctive, intuitive.
F3 acquired, learnt.

inner *adjective* internal, interior, inside, inward, innermost, central, middle, concealed, hidden, secret, private, personal, intimate, mental, psychological, spiritual, emotional.
F3 outer, outward.

innocent *adjective* **1** *innocent of the crime*: guiltless, blameless, irreproachable, unimpeachable, honest, upright, virtuous, righteous, faultless, impeccable, stainless, spotless, immaculate, unsullied, untainted, uncontaminated, pure, chaste, virginal, inoffensive, harmless, innocuous. **2** *too innocent to understand*: artless, guileless, ingenuous, naive, green, inexperienced, fresh, natural, simple, unsophisticated, unworldly, childlike, credulous, gullible, trusting.
F3 **1** guilty. **2** experienced.

innuendo *noun* insinuation, aspersion (*fml*), slur, whisper, hint, intimation, suggestion, implication.

inoculation *noun* vaccination, immunization, protection, injection, shot (*infml*), jab (*infml*).

inoffensive *adjective* harmless, innocuous, innocent, peaceable, mild, unobtrusive, unassertive, quiet, retiring.
F3 offensive, harmful, provocative.

inquire, **enquire** *verb* ask, question, quiz, query, investigate, look into, probe, examine, inspect, scrutinize, search, explore.

inquiry, **enquiry** *noun* question, query, investigation, inquest, hearing, inquisition, examination, inspection, scrutiny, study, survey, poll, search, probe, exploration.

inquisitive *adjective* curious, questioning, probing, searching, prying, peeping, snooping, nosey, interfering, meddlesome, intrusive.

insane *adjective* mad, crazy, mentally ill, lunatic, mental

(*slang*), demented, deranged, unhinged, disturbed.
E3 sane.

insanity *noun* madness, craziness, lunacy, mental illness, neurosis, psychosis, mania, dementia, derangement, folly, stupidity, senselessness, irresponsibility.
E3 sanity.

insatiable *adjective* unquenchable, unsatisfiable, ravenous, voracious, immoderate, inordinate.

inscription *noun* engraving, epitaph, caption, legend, lettering, words, writing, signature, autograph, dedication.

insect

Insects include:
cranefly, daddy longlegs (*infml*), dragonfly, fly, gnat, horsefly, locust, mayfly, midge, mosquito, tsetse-fly; butterfly, red admiral, cabbage-white, moth, tiger moth; bee, bumblebee, hornet, wasp; aphid, blackfly, greenfly, froghopper, lacewing, ladybird, lady bug (*US*), water boatman, whitefly; beetle, cockroach, roach (*US*), earwig, grasshopper, cricket, cicada, flea, glow-worm, leatherjacket, louse, nit, stick insect, termite, woodworm, weevil, woodlouse.

insecure *adjective* **1** *feeling insecure*: anxious, worried, nervous, uncertain, unsure, afraid. **2** *an insecure position*: unsafe, dangerous, hazardous, perilous, precarious, unsteady, shaky, loose, unprotected, defenceless, exposed, vulnerable.
E3 **1** confident, self-assured. **2** secure, safe.

insensitive *adjective* hardened, tough, resistant, impenetrable, impervious, immune, insusceptible, thick-skinned, unfeeling, impassive, indifferent, unaffected, unmoved, untouched, uncaring, unconcerned, callous, thoughtless, tactless, crass.
E3 sensitive.

inseparable *adjective* indivisible, indissoluble, inextricable, close, intimate, bosom, devoted.
E3 separable.

insert *verb* put, place, put in, stick in, push in, introduce, implant, embed, engraft, set, inset, let in, interleave, intercalate, interpolate, interpose.

inside *noun* interior, content, contents, middle, centre, heart, core.
E3 outside.
▪ *adverb* within, indoors, internally, inwardly, secretly, privately.
E3 outside.
▪ *adjective* interior, internal, inner, innermost, inward, secret, classified, confidential, private.

insides *noun* entrails, guts, intestines, bowels, innards (*infml*), organs, viscera, belly, stomach.

insight *noun* awareness, knowledge, comprehension, understanding, grasp, apprehension, perception, intuition, sensitivity, discernment, judgement, acumen, penetration, observation, vision, wisdom, intelligence.

insignificant *adjective* unimportant, irrelevant, meaningless, inconsequential, minor, trivial, trifling, petty, paltry, small, tiny, insubstantial, inconsiderable, negligible, non-essential.
F3 significant, important.

insincere *adjective* hypocritical, two-faced, double-dealing, lying, untruthful, dishonest, deceitful, devious, unfaithful, faithless, untrue, false, feigned, pretended, phoney (*infml*), hollow.
F3 sincere.

insinuate *verb* imply, suggest, allude, hint, intimate, get at (*infml*), indicate.

insipid *adjective* tasteless, flavourless, unsavoury, dry, unappetizing, watery, weak, bland, wishy-washy (*infml*), colourless, drab, dull, monotonous, boring, lifeless, uninteresting, tame, flat, spiritless, characterless, trite, unimaginative.
F3 tasty, spicy, piquant, appetizing.

insist *verb* demand, require, urge, stress, emphasize, repeat, reiterate, dwell on, harp on, assert, maintain, claim, contend, hold (*fml*), vow, swear, persist, stand firm.

insistent *adjective* demanding, importunate (*fml*), emphatic, forceful, pressing, urgent, dogged, tenacious, persistent, persevering, relentless, unrelenting, unremitting, incessant.

insolent *adjective* rude, abusive, insulting, disrespectful, cheeky (*infml*), impertinent, impudent, saucy (*infml*), bold, forward, fresh, presumptuous, arrogant, defiant, insubordinate.
F3 polite, respectful.

insoluble *adjective* unsolvable, unexplainable, inexplicable, incomprehensible, unfathomable, impenetrable, obscure, mystifying, puzzling, perplexing, baffling.
F3 explicable.

inspect *verb* check, vet, look over, examine, search, investigate, scrutinize, study, scan, survey, superintend, supervise, oversee, visit.

inspection *noun* check, check-up, examination, scrutiny, scan, study, survey, review, search, investigation, supervision, visit.

inspiration *noun* **1** *lacking inspiration*: creativity, imagination, genius, muse, influence, encouragement, stimulation, motivation, spur, stimulus. **2** *a flash of inspiration*: idea, brainwave, insight, illumination, revelation, awakening.

inspire *verb* encourage, hearten, influence, impress, animate, enliven, quicken (*fml*), galvanize, fire, kindle, stir, arouse, trigger, spark off, prompt, spur, motivate, provoke, stimulate, excite, exhilarate, thrill, enthral, enthuse, imbue, infuse.

inspiring *adjective* encouraging, heartening, uplifting, invigorating, stirring, rousing, stimulating, exciting, exhilarating, thrilling, enthralling, moving, affecting, memorable, impressive.
F3 uninspiring, dull.

instability *noun* unsteadiness, shakiness, vacillation, wavering, irresolution, uncertainty, unpredictability, changeableness, variability, fluctuation, volatility, capriciousness, fickleness, inconstancy, unreliability, insecurity, unsafeness, unsoundness.
F3 stability.

install *verb* fix, fit, lay, put, place, position, locate, site, situate, station, plant, settle, establish, set up, introduce, institute, inaugurate, invest, induct, ordain.

instalment *noun* **1** *pay in instalments*: payment, repayment, portion. **2** *find out in the next instalment*: episode, chapter, part, section, division.

instant *noun* flash, twinkling, trice, moment, tick (*infml*), split second, second, minute, time, occasion.
▪ *adjective* instantaneous, immediate, on-the-spot, direct, prompt, urgent, unhesitating, quick, fast, rapid, swift.
F3 slow.

instead *adverb* alternatively, preferably, rather.

instil *verb* infuse, imbue, insinuate, introduce, inject, implant, inculcate, impress, din into (*infml*).

instinct *noun* intuition, sixth sense, gut reaction (*infml*), impulse, urge, feeling, hunch, flair, knack, gift, talent, feel, faculty, ability, aptitude, predisposition, tendency.

instinctive *adjective* natural, native, inborn, innate, inherent, intuitive, impulsive, involuntary, automatic, mechanical, reflex, spontaneous, immediate, unthinking, unpremeditated, gut (*infml*), visceral.
F3 conscious, voluntary, deliberate.

institute *noun* school, college, academy, conservatory, foundation, institution.

instruct *verb* **1** *instructing them in safety procedures*: teach, educate, tutor, coach, train, drill, ground, school, discipline. **2** *instructed him to remain where he was*: order, command, direct, mandate, tell, inform, notify, advise, counsel, guide.

instruction *noun* **1** *follow the instructions*: direction, recommendation, advice, guidance, information, order, command, injunction, mandate, directive, ruling. **2** *religious instruction*: education, schooling, lesson(s), tuition, teaching, training, coaching, drilling, grounding, preparation.

instructive *adjective* informative, educational, edifying, enlightening, illuminating, helpful, useful.

☒ unenlightening.

instrument *noun* tool, implement, utensil, appliance, gadget, contraption, device, contrivance, apparatus, mechanism.

Musical instruments include:
balalaika, banjo, cello, clarsach, double bass, guitar, harp, hurdy-gurdy, lute, lyre, mandolin, sitar, spinet, ukulele, viola, violin, fiddle (*infml*), zither; accordion, concertina, squeeze-box (*infml*), clavichord, harmonium, harpsichord, keyboard, melodeon, organ, Wurlitzer®, piano, grand piano, Pianola®, player-piano, synthesizer, virginals; bagpipes, bassoon, bugle, clarinet, cor anglais, cornet, didgeridoo, euphonium, fife, flugelhorn, flute, French horn, harmonica, horn, kazoo, mouth-organ, oboe, Pan-pipes, piccolo, recorder, saxophone, sousaphone, trombone, trumpet, tuba, uillean pipes; castanets, cymbal, glockenspiel, maracas, marimba, tambourine, triangle, tubular bells, xylophone; bass drum, bodhran, bongo, kettledrum, snare-drum, tenor-drum, timpani, tom-tom.

---

instrumental *adjective* active, involved, contributory, conducive, influential, useful, helpful, auxiliary, subsidiary.

☒ obstructive, unhelpful.

insufferable *adjective* intolerable, unbearable, detestable, loathsome, dreadful, impossible.

☒ pleasant, tolerable.

insufficient *adjective* inadequate, short, deficient, lacking, sparse, scanty, scarce.

☒ sufficient, excessive.

insular *adjective* parochial, provincial, cut off, detached, isolated, remote, withdrawn, inward-looking, blinkered, closed, narrow-minded, narrow, limited, petty.

☒ cosmopolitan.

insulate *verb* cushion, pad, lag, cocoon, protect, shield, shelter, isolate, separate, cut off.

insult *verb* abuse, call names, disparage (*fml*), revile, libel, slander, slight, snub, injure, affront, offend, outrage.

☒ compliment, praise.

▪ *noun* abuse, rudeness, insolence, defamation (*fml*), libel, slander, slight, snub, affront, indignity, offence, outrage.

☒ compliment, praise.

insurance *noun* cover, protection, safeguard, security, provision, assurance, indemnity, guarantee, warranty, policy, premium.

intact *adjective* unbroken, all in one piece, whole, complete,

integral, entire, perfect, sound, undamaged, unhurt, uninjured.
F3 broken, incomplete, damaged.

intangible *adjective* insubstantial, imponderable, elusive, fleeting, airy, shadowy, vague, indefinite, abstract, unreal, invisible.
F3 tangible, real.

integral *adjective* intrinsic, constituent, elemental, basic, fundamental, necessary, essential, indispensable.
F3 extra, additional, unnecessary.

integrate *verb* assimilate, merge, join, unite, combine, amalgamate, incorporate, coalesce, fuse, knit, mesh, mix, blend, harmonize.
F3 divide, separate.

integrity *noun* honesty, uprightness, probity (*fml*), incorruptibility, purity, morality, principle, honour, virtue, goodness, righteousness.
F3 dishonesty.

intellect *noun* mind, brain(s), brainpower, intelligence, genius, reason, understanding, sense, wisdom, judgement.
F3 stupidity.

intellectual *adjective* academic, scholarly, intelligent, studious, thoughtful, cerebral, mental, highbrow, cultural.
F3 lowbrow.
▪ *noun* thinker, academic, highbrow, egghead, mastermind, genius.
F3 lowbrow.

intelligence *noun* **1** *high/low intelligence*: intellect, reason, wit(s), brain(s) (*infml*), brainpower, cleverness, brightness, aptitude, quickness, alertness, discernment, perception, understanding, comprehension. **2** *military intelligence*: information, facts, data, lowdown (*infml*), knowledge, findings, news, report, warning, tip-off.
F3 1 stupidity, foolishness.

intelligent *adjective* clever, bright, smart, brainy (*infml*), quick, alert, quick-witted, sharp, acute, knowing, knowledgeable, well-informed, thinking, rational, sensible.
F3 unintelligent, stupid, foolish.

intend *verb* aim, have a mind, contemplate, mean, propose, plan, project, scheme, plot, design, purpose, resolve, determine, destine, mark out, earmark, set apart.

intense *adjective* great, deep, profound, strong, powerful, forceful, fierce, harsh, severe, acute, sharp, keen, eager, earnest, ardent, fervent, fervid, passionate, vehement, energetic, violent, intensive, concentrated, heightened.
F3 moderate, mild, weak.

intensify *verb* increase, step up, escalate, heighten, hot up (*infml*), fire, boost, fuel, aggravate, add to, strengthen, reinforce, sharpen, whet, quicken (*fml*), deepen, concentrate, emphasize, enhance.
F3 reduce, weaken.

intensive *adjective* concentrated, thorough, exhaustive, comprehensive, detailed, in-depth, thoroughgoing, all-out, intense.
F3 superficial.

intent *adjective* determined, resolved, resolute, set, bent, concentrated, eager, earnest, committed, steadfast, fixed, alert, attentive, concentrating, preoccupied, engrossed, wrapped up, absorbed, occupied.
F3 absent-minded, distracted.

intention *noun* aim, purpose, object, end, point, target, goal, objective, idea, plan, design, view, intent, meaning.

intentional *adjective* designed, wilful, conscious, planned, deliberate, prearranged, premeditated, calculated, studied, intended, meant.
F3 unintentional, accidental.

intercede *verb* mediate, arbitrate, intervene, plead, entreat, beseech, speak.

intercept *verb* head off, ambush, interrupt, cut off, stop, arrest, catch, take, seize, check, block, obstruct, delay, frustrate, thwart.

interchangeable *adjective* reciprocal, equivalent, similar, identical, the same, synonymous, standard.
F3 different.

interest *noun* **1** *a matter of little interest*: importance, significance, note, concern. **2** *attracting the interest of the police*: attention, notice, curiosity, involvement, participation, care, concern. **3** *leisure interests*: activity, pursuit, pastime, hobby, diversion, amusement.
▪ *verb* concern, involve, touch, move, attract, appeal to, divert, amuse, occupy, engage, absorb, engross, fascinate, intrigue.
F3 bore.

interested *adjective* attentive, curious, absorbed, engrossed, fascinated, enthusiastic, keen, attracted.
F3 uninterested, indifferent, apathetic.

interesting *adjective* attractive, appealing, entertaining, engaging, absorbing, engrossing, fascinating, intriguing, compelling, gripping, stimulating, thought-provoking, curious, unusual.
F3 uninteresting, boring, monotonous, tedious.

interfere *verb* **1** *interfere with someone else's business*: intrude, poke one's nose in (*infml*), pry, butt in, interrupt, intervene, meddle, tamper. **2** *interfere with the proceedings*: hinder, hamper, obstruct, block, impede, handicap, cramp, inhibit, conflict, clash.
F3 **2** assist.

interim *adjective* temporary, provisional, stopgap, makeshift, improvised, stand-in, acting, caretaker.
▪ *noun* meantime, meanwhile, interval.

interior *adjective* **1** *interior view/ life*: internal, inside, inner, central, inward, mental, spiritual, private, secret, hidden. **2** *interior design*: home, domestic.

F3 **1** exterior, external.

▪ *noun* inside, centre, middle, core, heart, depths.

F3 exterior, outside.

intermediate *adjective* midway, halfway, in-between, mean, middle, mid, median, intermediary, intervening, transitional.

F3 extreme.

intermission *noun* interval, entr'acte, interlude, break, recess, rest, respite, breather (*infml*), breathing-space, pause, lull, let-up (*infml*), remission, suspension, interruption, halt, stop, stoppage, cessation.

intermittent *adjective* occasional, periodic, sporadic, spasmodic, fitful, erratic, irregular, broken.

F3 continuous, constant.

internal *adjective* inside, inner, interior, inward, intimate, private, personal, domestic, in-house.

F3 external.

international *adjective* global, worldwide, intercontinental, cosmopolitan, universal, general.

F3 national, local, parochial.

interpret *verb* explain, expound, elucidate, clarify, throw light on, define, paraphrase, translate, render, decode, decipher, solve, make sense of, understand, construe, read, take.

interpretation *noun* explanation, clarification, analysis, translation, rendering, version, performance, reading, understanding, sense, meaning.

interrogate *verb* question, quiz, examine, cross-examine, grill, give the third degree, pump, debrief.

interrupt *verb* intrude, barge in (*infml*), butt in, interject, break in, heckle, disturb, disrupt, interfere, obstruct, check, hinder, hold up, stop, halt, suspend, discontinue, cut off, disconnect, punctuate, separate, divide, cut, break.

interruption *noun* intrusion, interjection, disturbance, disruption, obstruction, impediment, obstacle, hitch, pause, break, halt, stop, stoppage, suspension, discontinuance, disconnection, separation, division.

interval *noun* interlude, intermission, break, rest, pause, delay, wait, interim, meantime, meanwhile, gap, opening, space, distance, period, spell, time, season.

intervene *verb* step in, mediate, arbitrate, interfere, interrupt, intrude.

intervention *noun* involvement, interference, intrusion, mediation, agency, intercession.

interview *noun* audience, consultation, talk, dialogue, meeting, conference, press

conference, oral examination.
▪ *verb* question, interrogate, examine, vet.

intestines *noun* bowels, guts, entrails, insides, innards (*infml*), offal, viscera, vitals.

intimacy *noun* friendship, closeness, familiarity, confidence, confidentiality, privacy.
F3 distance.

intimate *adjective* friendly, informal, familiar, cosy, warm, affectionate, dear, bosom, close, near, confidential, secret, private, personal, internal, innermost, deep, penetrating, detailed, exhaustive.
F3 unfriendly, cold, distant.

intimidate *verb* daunt, cow, overawe, appal, dismay, alarm, scare, frighten, terrify, threaten, menace, terrorize, bully, browbeat, bulldoze, coerce, pressure, pressurize, lean on (*infml*).

intolerable *adjective* unbearable, unendurable, insupportable, unacceptable, insufferable, impossible.
F3 tolerable.

intolerant *adjective* impatient, prejudiced, bigoted, narrow-minded, small-minded, opinionated, dogmatic, illiberal, uncharitable.
F3 tolerant.

intonation *noun* modulation, tone, accentuation, inflection.

intoxicating *adjective* **1** *intoxicating liquor*: alcoholic, strong. **2** *an intoxicating atmosphere*: exciting, stimulating, heady, exhilarating, thrilling.
F3 2 sobering.

intrepid *adjective* bold, daring, brave, courageous, plucky, valiant, lion-hearted, fearless, dauntless, undaunted, stout-hearted, stalwart, gallant, heroic.
F3 cowardly, timid.

intricate *adjective* elaborate, fancy, ornate, rococo, complicated, complex, sophisticated, involved, convoluted, tortuous, tangled, entangled, knotty, perplexing, difficult.
F3 simple, plain, straightforward.

intriguing *adjective* fascinating, puzzling, tantalizing, attractive, charming, captivating.

introduce *verb* institute, begin, start, commence, establish, found, inaugurate, launch, open, bring in.
F3 end, conclude.

introduction *noun* **1** *introduction of new taxes*: institution, beginning, start, commencement, establishment, inauguration, launch, presentation, debut, initiation. **2** *the introduction to the book*: foreword, preface, preamble, prologue, preliminaries, overture, prelude, lead-in, opening.
F3 1 removal, withdrawal. **2** appendix, conclusion.

introductory *adjective* preliminary, preparatory, opening, inaugural, first, initial, early, elementary, basic.

introverted *adjective* introspective, inward-looking, self-centred, withdrawn, shy, reserved, quiet.
F3 extroverted.

intrude *verb* interrupt, butt in, meddle, interfere, violate, infringe, encroach, trespass.
F3 withdraw, stand back.

intruder *noun* trespasser, prowler, burglar, raider, invader, infiltrator, interloper, gatecrasher.

intuition *noun* instinct, sixth sense, perception, discernment, insight, hunch, feeling, gut feeling (*infml*).
F3 reasoning.

invade *verb* enter, penetrate, infiltrate, burst in, descend on, attack, raid, seize, occupy, overrun, swarm over, infest, pervade, encroach, infringe, violate.
F3 withdraw, evacuate.

invalid[1] *noun* /**in**-va-id/ patient, convalescent.
▪ *adjective* sick, ill, poorly, ailing, sickly, weak, feeble, frail, infirm, disabled, bedridden.
F3 healthy.

invalid[2] *adjective* /in-**val**-id/ false, fallacious, unsound, ill-founded, unfounded, baseless, illogical, irrational, unscientific, wrong, incorrect.
F3 legal.

invaluable *adjective* priceless, inestimable, incalculable, precious, valuable, useful.
F3 worthless, cheap.

invariably *adverb* always, without exception, without fail, unfailingly, consistently, regularly, habitually.
F3 never.

invasion *noun* attack, offensive, onslaught, raid, incursion, foray, breach, penetration, infiltration, intrusion, encroachment, infringement, violation.
F3 withdrawal, evacuation.

invent *verb* conceive, think up, design, discover, create, originate, formulate, frame, devise, contrive, improvise, fabricate, make up, concoct, cook up, trump up, imagine, dream up.

invention *noun* design, creation, brainchild, discovery, development, device, gadget.

inventive *adjective* imaginative, creative, innovative, original, ingenious, resourceful, fertile, inspired, gifted, clever.

inventor *noun* designer, discoverer, creator, originator, author, architect, maker, scientist, engineer.

invert *verb* upturn, turn upside down, overturn, capsize, upset, transpose, reverse.
F3 right.

invertebrate

Invertebrates include:
sponges: calcareous, glass, horny; *jellyfish, corals and sea anemones*: box jellyfish, dead-men's fingers, Portuguese man-of-war, sea pansy, sea gooseberry, sea wasp, Venus's girdle; *echinoderms*: brittle star,

crown-of-thorns, feather star, sand dollar, sea cucumber, sea lily, sea urchin, starfish; *worms*: annelid worm, arrow worm, blood fluke, bristle worm, earthworm, eelworm, flatworm, fluke, hookworm, leech, liver fluke, lugworm, peanut worm, pinworm, ragworm, ribbonworm, roundworm, sea mouse, tapeworm, threadworm; *crustaceans*: acorn barnacle, barnacle, brine shrimp, crayfish, daphnia, fairy shrimp, fiddler crab, fish louse, goose barnacle, hermit crab, krill, lobster, mantis shrimp, mussel shrimp, pill bug, prawn, sand hopper, seed shrimp, spider crab, spiny lobster, tadpole shrimp, water flea, whale louse, woodlouse; centipede, millipede, velvet worm. *See also* **insect**; **mollusc**.

---

invest *verb* spend, lay out, put in, sink.

investigate *verb* inquire into, look into, consider, examine, study, inspect, scrutinize, analyse, go into, probe, explore, search, sift.

investigation *noun* inquiry, inquest, hearing, examination, study, research, survey, review, inspection, scrutiny, analysis, probe, exploration, search.

investment *noun* asset, speculation, venture, stake, contribution, outlay, expenditure, transaction.

invigorate *verb* vitalize, energize, animate, enliven, liven up, quicken (*fml*), strengthen, fortify, brace, stimulate, inspire, exhilarate, perk up, refresh, freshen, revitalize, rejuvenate.
F≡ tire, weary, dishearten.

invincible *adjective* unbeatable, unconquerable, insuperable, insurmountable, indomitable, unassailable, impregnable, impenetrable, invulnerable, indestructible.
F≡ beatable.

invisible *adjective* unseen, out of sight, hidden, concealed, disguised, inconspicuous, indiscernible, imperceptible, infinitesimal, microscopic, imaginary, non-existent.
F≡ visible.

invitation *noun* request, solicitation, call, summons, temptation, enticement, allurement, encouragement, inducement, provocation, incitement, challenge.

invite *verb* ask, call, summon, welcome, encourage, lead, draw, attract, tempt, entice, allure, bring on, provoke, ask for, request, solicit, seek.

inviting *adjective* welcoming, appealing, attractive, tempting, seductive, enticing, alluring, pleasing, delightful, captivating, fascinating, intriguing, tantalizing.
F≡ uninviting, unappealing.

involuntary *adjective* spontaneous, unconscious, automatic, mechanical, reflex, instinctive, conditioned,

impulsive, unthinking, blind, uncontrolled, unintentional.
F3 deliberate, intentional.

involve *verb* **1** *involve some careful thought*: require, necessitate, mean, imply, entail. **2** *involve the family*: include, incorporate, embrace, cover, take in, affect, concern.
F3 **2** exclude.

involved *adjective* complicated, complex, intricate, elaborate, tangled, knotty, tortuous, confusing.
F3 simple.

involvement *noun* concern, interest, responsibility, association, connection, participation, implication, entanglement.

inward *adjective* incoming, entering, inside, interior, internal, inner, innermost, inmost, personal, private, secret, confidential.
F3 outward, external.

irate *adjective* annoyed, irritated, indignant, up in arms, angry, enraged, mad (*infml*), furious, infuriated, incensed, worked up, fuming, livid, exasperated.
F3 calm, composed.

iron *adjective* rigid, inflexible, adamant, determined, hard, steely, tough, strong.
F3 pliable, weak.
▪ *verb* press, smooth, flatten.

ironic *adjective* ironical, sarcastic, sardonic, scornful, contemptuous, derisive, sneering, scoffing, mocking, satirical, wry, paradoxical.

irony *noun* sarcasm, mockery, satire, paradox, contrariness, incongruity.

irrational *adjective* unreasonable, unsound, illogical, absurd, crazy, wild, foolish, silly, senseless, unwise.
F3 rational.

irregular *adjective* **1** *at irregular intervals*: variable, fluctuating, wavering, erratic, fitful, intermittent, sporadic, spasmodic, occasional, random, haphazard, disorderly, unsystematic. **2** *this is quite irregular*: abnormal, unconventional, unorthodox, improper, unusual, exceptional, anomalous.
F3 **1** regular. **2** conventional.

irrelevant *adjective* immaterial, beside the point, inapplicable, inappropriate, unrelated, unconnected, inconsequent, peripheral, tangential.
F3 relevant.

irreplaceable *adjective* indispensable, essential, vital, unique, priceless, peerless, matchless, unmatched.
F3 replaceable.

irresistible *adjective* overwhelming, overpowering, unavoidable, inevitable, inescapable, uncontrollable, potent, compelling, imperative, pressing, urgent, tempting, seductive, ravishing, enchanting, charming, fascinating.
F3 resistible, avoidable.

irresponsible *adjective* unreliable, untrustworthy, careless, negligent, thoughtless, heedless, ill-considered, rash, reckless, wild, carefree, light-hearted, immature.
F∃ responsible, cautious.

irreverent *adjective* impious, godless, irreligious, profane, sacrilegious, blasphemous.
F∃ reverent.

irritable *adjective* cross, bad-tempered, ill-tempered, crotchety, crusty, cantankerous, crabby, testy, short-tempered, snappish, snappy, short, impatient, touchy, edgy, prickly, peevish, fretful, fractious, tetchy.
F∃ good-tempered, cheerful.

irritate *verb* **1** *try not to irritate her*: annoy, get on one's nerves, aggravate (*infml*), bother, harass, rouse, provoke, rile, anger, vex, enrage, infuriate, incense, exasperate, peeve, put out. **2** *irritating the skin*: inflame, chafe, rub, tickle, itch.
F∃ 1 please, gratify.

irritation *noun* displeasure, dissatisfaction, annoyance, aggravation, provocation, anger, vexation, indignation, fury, exasperation, irritability, crossness, testiness, snappiness, impatience.
F∃ pleasure, satisfaction, delight.

isolate *verb* set apart, sequester, seclude, keep apart, segregate, quarantine, insulate, cut off, detach, remove, disconnect, separate, divorce, alienate, shut out, ostracize, exclude.
F∃ assimilate, incorporate.

isolated *adjective* **1** *an isolated community*: remote, out-of-the-way, outlying, god-forsaken, deserted, unfrequented, secluded, detached, cut off, lonely, solitary, single. **2** *an isolated occurrence*: unique, special, exceptional, atypical, unusual, freak, abnormal, anomalous.
F∃ 1 populous. **2** typical.

issue *noun* **1** *a political issue*: matter, affair, concern, problem, point, subject, topic, question, debate, argument, dispute, controversy. **2** *a special issue of stamps*: publication, release, distribution, supply, delivery, circulation, promulgation, broadcast, announcement. **3** *last week's issue*: copy, number, instalment, edition, impression, printing.
▪ *verb* **1** *issue a statement/summons*: publish, release, distribute, supply, deliver, give out, deal out, circulate, promulgate, broadcast, announce, put out, emit, produce. **2** *issuing from a mountain lake*: originate, stem, spring, rise, emerge, burst forth, gush, flow, proceed, emanate, arise.

itch *verb* tickle, irritate, tingle, prickle, crawl.
▪ *noun* **1** *scratch an itch*: itchiness, tickle, irritation, prickling. **2** *an itch*

to travel: eagerness, keenness, desire, longing, yearning, hankering, craving.

item *noun* object, article, thing, piece, component, ingredient, element, factor, point, detail, particular, aspect, feature, consideration, matter.

itinerant *adjective* travelling, peripatetic, roving, roaming, wandering, rambling, nomadic, migratory, rootless, unsettled.
F3 stationary, settled.

itinerary *noun* route, course, journey, tour, circuit, plan, programme, schedule.

jab *verb* poke, prod, dig, nudge, stab, push, elbow, lunge, punch, tap, thrust.

jaded *adjective* fatigued, exhausted, dulled, played-out, tired, tired out, weary, spent, bored, fagged (*infml*).
F3 fresh, refreshed.

jagged *adjective* uneven, irregular, notched, indented, rough, serrated, saw-edged, toothed, ragged, pointed, ridged, craggy, barbed, broken.
F3 even, smooth.

jail *noun* prison, jailhouse, custody, lock-up, penitentiary, guardhouse, inside (*infml*), nick (*infml*), clink (*slang*).
▪ *verb* imprison, incarcerate, lock up, put away, send down, confine, detain, intern, impound, immure.

jam[1] *verb* **1** *jamming them into a tiny space*: cram, pack, wedge, squash, squeeze, press, crush, crowd, congest, ram, stuff, confine, force. **2** *jamming the road/the door jammed*: block, clog, obstruct, stall, stick.
▪ *noun* **1** *trying to clear the jam*: crush, crowd, press, congestion, pack, mob, throng, bottle-neck, traffic jam, obstruction, gridlock. **2** *in a bit of a jam*: predicament, trouble, quandary, plight, fix (*infml*).

jam[2] *noun* conserve, preserve, jelly, spread, marmalade.

jar[1] *noun* pot, container, vessel, receptacle, crock, pitcher, urn, vase, flagon, jug, mug.

jar[2] *verb* **1** *jarred her spine*: jolt, agitate, rattle, shake, vibrate, jangle, rock, disturb, discompose. **2** *a harsh voice jarring on the ears of the listeners*: annoy, irritate, grate, nettle (*infml*), offend, upset, irk.

jargon *noun* **1** *legal jargon*: parlance, cant, argot, vernacular, idiom. **2** *full of meaningless jargon*: nonsense, gobbledegook (*infml*), mumbo-jumbo (*infml*), gibberish.

jaunty *adjective* sprightly, lively, perky, breezy, buoyant, high-spirited, self-confident, carefree, airy, cheeky, debonair, dapper, smart, showy, spruce.
F3 depressed, dowdy.

jealous *adjective* **1** *jealous of her sister*: envious, green (*infml*), green-eyed (*infml*), covetous, grudging, resentful. **2** *a jealous husband/wife*: suspicious, wary, distrustful, anxious, possessive, protective.
F3 1 contented, satisfied.

jeer *verb* mock, scoff, taunt, jibe, ridicule, sneer, deride, make fun of, chaff, barrack, twit, knock (*infml*), heckle, banter, boo.
▪ *noun* mockery, derision, ridicule, taunt, jibe, sneer, scoff, abuse, catcall, dig (*infml*), hiss, hoot.

jeopardize *verb* endanger, imperil, risk, hazard, venture, gamble, chance, threaten, menace, expose, stake.
F3 protect, safeguard.

jerk *noun, verb* jolt, tug, twitch, jar, jog, yank, wrench, pull, pluck, lurch, throw, thrust, shrug.

jerky *adjective* fitful, twitchy, spasmodic, jumpy, jolting, convulsive, disconnected, bumpy, bouncy, shaky, rough, unco-ordinated, uncontrolled, incoherent.
F3 smooth.

jet *noun* gush, spurt, spout, spray, spring, sprinkler, sprayer, fountain, flow, stream, squirt.

jetty *noun* breakwater, pier, dock, groyne, quay, wharf.

jewel *noun* gem, precious stone, gemstone, ornament, rock (*infml*).

jibe *see* **gibe**.

jilt *verb* abandon, reject, desert, discard, brush off, ditch (*infml*), drop, spurn, betray.

jingle *verb* clink, tinkle, ring, chime, chink, jangle, clatter, rattle.
▪ *noun* **1** *the jingle of bells*: clink, tinkle, ringing, clang, rattle, clangour. **2** *a catchy jingle*: rhyme, verse, song, tune, ditty, doggerel, melody, poem, chant, chorus.

jinx *noun* (*infml*) spell, curse, evil eye, hex, voodoo, hoodoo, black magic, gremlin (*infml*), charm, plague.

job *noun* **1** *she has a good job*: work, employment, occupation, position, post, situation, profession, career, calling, vocation, trade, métier, capacity, business, livelihood. **2** *it's a difficult job*: task, chore, duty, responsibility, charge, commission, mission, activity, affair, concern, proceeding, project, enterprise, office, pursuit, role, undertaking, venture, province, part, place, share, errand, function, contribution, stint, assignment, consignment.

jobless *adjective* unemployed, out of work, laid off, on the dole (*infml*), inactive, redundant.
F3 employed.

jog *verb* **1** *jogged his arm*: jolt, jar, bump, jostle, jerk, joggle, nudge, poke, shake, prod, bounce, push, rock. **2** *jogged her memory*: prompt, remind, stir, arouse, activate, stimulate. **3** *jogs to work every morning*: run, trot.
▪ *noun* **1** *gave her arm a jog*: jolt, bump, jerk, nudge, shove, push, poke, prod, shake. **2** *go for a jog*: run, trot.

join *verb* **1** *join the two pieces together*: unite, connect, combine, conjoin, attach, link, amalgamate, fasten, merge, marry, couple, yoke, tie, splice, knit, cement, add, adhere, annex. **2** *where it joins the neighbouring estate*: abut, adjoin, border (on), verge on, touch, meet, coincide, march with. **3** *join a club*: associate, affiliate, accompany, ally, enlist, enrol, enter, sign up, team.
F3 **1** divide, separate. **3** leave.

joint *noun* junction, connection, union, juncture, intersection, hinge, knot, articulation, seam.
▪ *adjective* combined, common, communal, joined, shared, united, collective, amalgamated, mutual, co-operative, co-ordinated, consolidated, concerted.

joke *noun* **1** *crack a few jokes*: jest, quip, crack (*infml*), gag (*infml*), witticism, wisecrack (*infml*), one-liner (*infml*), pun, hoot, whimsy, yarn. **2** *play a joke on him*: trick, jape, lark, prank, spoof, fun.
▪ *verb* jest, quip, clown, fool, pun, wisecrack (*infml*), kid (*infml*), tease, banter, mock, laugh, frolic, gambol.

joker *noun* comedian, comic, wit, humorist, jester, trickster, wag, clown, buffoon, kidder (*infml*), droll, card (*infml*), character, sport.

jolly *adjective* jovial, merry, cheerful, playful, hearty, happy, exuberant.
F3 sad.

jolt *verb* **1** *jolting his arm*: jar, jerk, jog, bump, jostle, knock, bounce, shake, push. **2** *jolted by the news*: upset, startle, shock, surprise, stun, discompose, disconcert, disturb.
▪ *noun* **1** *a sudden jolt*: jar, jerk, jog, bump, blow, impact, lurch, shake. **2** *gave her a bit of a jolt*: shock, surprise, reversal, setback, start.

jostle *verb* push, shove, jog, bump, elbow, hustle, jolt, crowd, shoulder, joggle, shake, squeeze, throng.

jot *verb* write down, take down, note, list, record, scribble, register, enter.

journal *noun* newspaper, periodical, magazine, paper, publication, review, weekly, monthly, register, chronicle, diary, gazette, daybook, log, record.

journalist *noun* reporter, news-writer, hack, correspondent, editor, columnist, feature-writer, commentator, broadcaster, contributor.

journey *noun* voyage, trip, travel, expedition, passage, trek, tour, ramble, outing, wanderings, safari, progress.

jovial *adjective* jolly, cheery, merry, affable, cordial, genial.
F3 gloomy.

joy *noun* happiness, gladness, delight, pleasure, bliss, ecstasy, elation, joyfulness, exultation, gratification, rapture.
F3 despair, grief.

joyful *adjective* happy, pleased, delighted, glad, elated, ecstatic, triumphant.
F3 sorrowful.

jubilant *adjective* joyful, rejoicing, overjoyed, delighted, elated, triumphant, exuberant, excited, euphoric, thrilled.

judge *noun* **1** *a High Court judge*: justice, Law Lord, magistrate, arbiter, adjudicator, arbitrator, mediator, moderator, referee, umpire, beak (*infml*). **2** *a good judge of wine*: connoisseur, authority, expert, evaluator, assessor, critic.
▪ *verb* **1** *judging the case*: adjudicate, arbitrate, try, referee, umpire, decree, mediate, examine, sentence, review, rule, find. **2** *judge if it is safe*: ascertain, determine, decide, assess, appraise, evaluate, estimate, value, distinguish, discern, reckon, believe, think, consider, conclude, rate.

judgement *noun* **1** *deliver his judgement*: verdict, sentence, ruling, decree, conclusion, decision, arbitration, finding, result, mediation, order. **2** *good judgement*: discernment, discrimination, understanding, wisdom, prudence, common sense, sense, intelligence, taste, shrewdness, penetration, enlightenment. **3** *judgement of the risks and benefits*: assessment, evaluation, appraisal, estimate, opinion, view, belief, diagnosis. **4** *a harsh judgement*: conviction, damnation, punishment, retribution, doom, fate, misfortune.

juggle *verb* alter, change, manipulate, falsify, rearrange, rig, doctor (*infml*), cook (*infml*), disguise.

juice *noun* liquid, fluid, extract, essence, sap, secretion, nectar, liquor.

juicy *adjective* **1** *a juicy orange*: succulent, moist, lush, watery. **2** (*infml*) *some juicy gossip*: interesting, colourful, sensational, racy, risqué, suggestive, lurid.
F3 **1** dry.

jumble *verb* disarrange, confuse, disorganize, mix (up), muddle, shuffle, tangle.
F3 order.
▪ *noun* disorder, disarray, confusion, mess, chaos, mix-up, muddle, clutter, mixture, hotch-potch, mishmash (*infml*), medley.

jump *verb* **1** *jumping the gate*: leap, spring, bound, vault, clear, bounce, skip, hop, prance, frolic, gambol. **2** *nearly jumped out of his skin*: start, flinch, jerk, recoil, jump out of one's skin (*infml*), wince, quail. **3** *jumped a few verses*: omit, leave out, miss, skip, pass over, bypass, disregard, ignore, avoid, digress.

jumpy *adjective* nervous, anxious, agitated, apprehensive, jittery, tense, edgy, fidgety, shaky.
F3 calm, composed.

junction *noun* joint, join, joining, connection, juncture, union, intersection, linking, coupling, meeting-point, confluence.

junior *adjective* younger, minor, lesser, lower, subordinate, secondary, subsidiary, inferior.
F3 senior.

junk *noun* rubbish, refuse, trash, debris, garbage, waste, scrap, litter, clutter, oddments, rummage, dregs, wreckage.

just *adjective* **1** *a just ruler*: fair, equitable, impartial, unbiased, unprejudiced, fair-minded, even-handed, objective, righteous, upright, virtuous, honourable, good, honest, irreproachable. **2** *a just punishment*: deserved, merited, fitting, well-deserved, appropriate, suitable, due, proper, reasonable, rightful, lawful, legitimate.
F3 **1** unjust. **2** undeserved.

justice *noun* **1** *can see the justice in that*: fairness, equity, impartiality, objectivity, equitableness, justness, legitimacy, honesty, right, justifiableness, reasonableness, rectitude. **2** *trying to get justice/flee justice*: legality, law, penalty, recompense, reparation, satisfaction.
F3 **1** injustice, unfairness.

justifiable *adjective* defensible, excusable, warranted, reasonable, justified, lawful, legitimate, acceptable, explainable, forgivable, pardonable, understandable, valid, well-founded, right, proper, explicable, fit, tenable.

justify *verb* vindicate, exonerate, warrant, substantiate, defend, acquit, absolve, excuse, forgive, explain, pardon, validate, uphold, sustain, support, maintain, establish.

jut *verb* project, protrude, stick out, overhang, extend.
F3 recede.

juvenile *noun* child, youth, minor, young person, youngster, adolescent, teenager, boy, girl, kid (*infml*), infant.
▪ *adjective* young, youthful, immature, childish, puerile (*fml*), infantile, adolescent, babyish, unsophisticated.
F3 mature.

keen *adjective* **1** *a keen gardener*: eager, avid, fervent, enthusiastic, earnest, devoted, diligent, industrious. **2** *a keen mind*: astute, shrewd, clever, perceptive, wise, discerning, quick, deep, sensitive. **3** *keen eyesight/understanding*: sharp, piercing, penetrating, incisive, acute, pointed.
F3 **1** apathetic. **2** superficial. **3** dull.

keep *verb* **1** *keep the receipt*: retain, hold, preserve, hold on to, hang on to, store, stock, possess, amass, accumulate, collect, stack, conserve, deposit, heap, pile, place, maintain, furnish. **2** *keep walking/in step*: carry on, keep on, continue, persist, remain. **3** *keep pigs and chickens/keep two houses*: look after, tend, care for, have charge of, have custody of, maintain, provide for, subsidize, support, sustain, be responsible for, foster, mind, protect, shelter, guard, defend, watch (over), shield, safeguard, feed, nurture, manage. **4** *keep us waiting*: detain, delay, retard, check, hinder, hold (up), impede, obstruct, prevent, block, curb, interfere with, restrain, limit, inhibit, deter, hamper, keep back, control, constrain, arrest, withhold. **5** *keep to the rules/keep faith with*: observe, comply with, respect, obey, fulfil, adhere to, recognize, keep up, keep faith with, commemorate, celebrate, hold, maintain, perform, perpetuate, mark, honour.
▪ *noun* subsistence, board, livelihood, living, maintenance, support, upkeep, means, food, nourishment, nurture.

key *noun* **1** *the key to the mystery*: clue, cue, indicator, pointer, explanation, sign, answer, solution, interpretation, means, secret. **2** *a key to the symbols*: guide, glossary, translation, legend, code, table, index.
▪ *adjective* important, essential, vital, crucial, necessary, principal, decisive, central, chief, main, major, leading, basic, fundamental.

kick *verb* **1** *kick a ball*: boot, hit, strike, jolt. **2** (*infml*) *kicking the habit*: give up, quit, stop, leave off, abandon, desist from, break.

kid *noun* (*infml*) child, youngster, youth, juvenile, infant, girl, boy, teenager, lad, nipper (*infml*), tot (*infml*).

kidnap *verb* abduct, capture, seize, hold to ransom, snatch, hijack, steal.

kill *verb* slaughter, murder, slay (*fml*), put to death, exterminate, assassinate, do to death, do in (*infml*), bump off (*infml*), finish off, massacre, execute, eliminate, destroy, dispatch, do away with (*infml*), butcher, annihilate, liquidate (*infml*).

kind *noun* sort, type, class, category, set, variety, character, genus, genre, style, brand, family, breed, race, nature, persuasion, description, species, stamp, temperament, manner.
▪ *adjective* benevolent, kind-hearted, kindly, good-hearted, good-natured, helpful, obliging, humane, generous, compassionate, charitable, amiable, friendly, congenial, soft-hearted, thoughtful, warm, warm-hearted, considerate, courteous, sympathetic, tender-hearted, understanding, lenient, mild, hospitable, gentle, indulgent, neighbourly, tactful, giving, good, loving, gracious.
E3 cruel, inconsiderate, unhelpful.

kindly *adjective* benevolent, kind, compassionate, charitable, good-natured, helpful, warm, generous, cordial, favourable, giving, indulgent, pleasant, sympathetic, tender, gentle, mild, patient, polite.
E3 cruel, uncharitable.

kindness *noun* **1** *thank them for their kindness*: benevolence, kindliness, charity, magnanimity, compassion, generosity, hospitality, humanity, loving-kindness (*fml*), courtesy, friendliness, good will, goodness, grace, indulgence, tolerance, understanding, gentleness. **2** *did me a kindness*: favour, good turn, assistance, help, service.
E3 **1** cruelty, inhumanity. **2** disservice.

king *noun* monarch, ruler, sovereign, majesty, emperor, chief, chieftain, prince, supremo (*infml*), leading light (*infml*).

kingdom *noun* monarchy, sovereignty, reign, realm, empire, dominion, commonwealth, nation, principality, state, country, domain, dynasty, province, sphere, territory, land, division.

kiosk *noun* booth, stall, stand, news-stand, bookstall, cabin, box, counter.

kiss *verb* **1** *kiss and cuddle*: caress, peck (*infml*), smooch (*infml*), neck (*infml*), snog (*slang*). **2** *the cue ball kissed the pink*: touch, graze, glance, brush, lick, scrape, fan.
▪ *noun* peck (*infml*), smack (*infml*), smacker (*infml*).

kit *noun* equipment, gear, strip, apparatus, supplies, tackle, provisions, outfit, implements, set, tools, trappings, rig, instruments, paraphernalia, utensils, effects, luggage, baggage.

knack *noun* flair, faculty, facility, hang (*infml*), bent, skill, talent, genius, gift, trick, propensity, ability, expertise, skilfulness, forte, capacity, handiness, dexterity, quickness, turn.

knife *noun* blade, cutter, carver, dagger, penknife, pocket-knife, switchblade, jack-knife, flick-knife, machete.
▪ *verb* cut, rip, slash, stab, pierce, wound.

knit *verb* **1** *the bones are knitting well*: join, unite, secure, connect, tie, fasten, link, mend, interlace, intertwine. **2** *knit a cardigan*: knot, loop, crotchet, weave. **3** *knitting his brows*: wrinkle, furrow.

knock *verb* hit, strike, rap, thump, pound, slap, smack.
▪ *noun* blow, box, rap, thump, cuff, clip, pounding, hammering, slap, smack.

knot *verb* tie, secure, bind, entangle, tangle, knit, entwine, ravel, weave.
▪ *noun* **1** *a reef knot*: tie, bond, joint, fastening, loop, splice, hitch. **2** *a knot of people*: bunch, cluster, clump, group.

know *verb* **1** *know French*: understand, comprehend, apprehend, perceive, notice, be aware, fathom, experience, realize, see, undergo. **2** *I know George*: be acquainted with, be familiar with, recognize, identify. **3** *know a good wine*: distinguish, discriminate, discern, differentiate, make out, tell.

knowledge *noun* **1** *have the knowledge but not the experience*: learning, scholarship, erudition, education, schooling, instruction, tuition, information, enlightenment, know-how. **2** *a good knowledge of wine*: acquaintance, familiarity, awareness, cognizance, intimacy, consciousness. **3** *test your knowledge*: understanding, comprehension, cognition, apprehension, recognition, judgement, discernment, ability, grasp, wisdom, intelligence.
⇄ **1**, **3** ignorance.

knowledgeable *adjective* educated, scholarly, learned, well-informed, lettered, intelligent, well-read.
⇄ ignorant.

known *adjective* acknowledged, recognized, well-known, noted, obvious, patent, plain, admitted, familiar, avowed, commonplace, published, confessed, celebrated, famous.

L

label *noun* **1** *the maker's label*: tag, ticket, docket, mark, marker, sticker, trademark. **2** *give him the label 'delinquent'*: description, categorization, identification, characterization, classification, badge, brand.
▪ *verb* **1** *labelling their goods*: tag, mark, stamp. **2** *labelled him a liar*: define, describe, classify, categorize, characterize, identify, class, designate, brand, call, dub, name.

labour *noun* **1** *hard labour*: work, task, job, chore, toil, effort, exertion, drudgery, grind (*infml*), slog (*infml*), sweat (*infml*). **2** *hire new labour*: workers, employees, workforce, labourers. **3** *in labour*: childbirth, birth, delivery, labour pains, contractions.
F3 **1** ease, leisure. **2** management.
▪ *verb* **1** *laboured for six days*: work, toil, drudge, slave, strive, endeavour, struggle, grind (*infml*), sweat (*infml*), plod, travail (*fml*). **2** *labour the point*: overdo, overemphasize, dwell on, elaborate, overstress, strain.
F3 **1** laze, idle, lounge.

lack *noun* need, want, scarcity, shortage, insufficiency, dearth, deficiency, absence, scantiness, vacancy, void, privation (*fml*), deprivation, destitution, emptiness.
F3 abundance, profusion.
▪ *verb* need, want, require, miss.

lag *verb* dawdle, loiter, hang back, linger, straggle, trail, saunter, delay, shuffle, tarry, idle, dally.
F3 hurry, lead.

lake *noun* lagoon, reservoir, loch, mere, tarn, lough.

lame *adjective* **1** *become/go lame*: crippled, limping, hobbling. **2** *a lame excuse*: weak, feeble, flimsy, inadequate, unsatisfactory, poor, pathetic (*infml*).
F3 **2** convincing.

lament *noun* lamentation, dirge, elegy, requiem, threnody (*fml*), complaint, moan, wail.
▪ *verb* mourn, bewail, bemoan, grieve, sorrow, weep, wail, complain, deplore, regret.
F3 rejoice, celebrate.

land *noun* **1** *reach land*: earth, (solid) ground, terra firma. **2** *till the land*: dirt, earth, soil. **3** *buy land*: property, grounds, estate, real estate (*US*), country, countryside, farmland, tract. **4** *a foreign land*: country, nation, region, territory, province.

■ *verb* **1** *land on the runway*: alight, disembark, dock, berth, touch down, come to rest, arrive, deposit, wind up, end up, drop, settle, turn up. **2** *land a big contract*: obtain, secure, gain, get, acquire, net, capture, achieve, win.

landscape *noun* scene, scenery, view, panorama, outlook, vista, prospect, countryside, aspect.

language *noun* **1** *learn languages*: speech, tongue, dialect, lingo (*infml*). **2** *medical language*: vocabulary, terminology, parlance, jargon. **3** *the language of love*: talk, conversation, discourse. **4** *use complicated language*: wording, style, phraseology, phrasing, expression, utterance, diction.

Terms used when talking about language include:

argot, brogue, buzz word, colloquialism, creole, dialect, etymology, idiom, jargon, journalese, legalese, lingua franca, linguistics, orthography, phonetics, patois, pidgin, semantics, slang, syntax, vernacular.

---

lap[1] *verb* drink, sip, sup, lick.

lap[2] *noun* circuit, round, orbit, tour, loop, course, circle, distance.

lapse *noun* **1** *an unfortunate lapse on his part*: error, slip, mistake, negligence, omission, oversight, fault, failing, indiscretion, aberration, backsliding, relapse. **2** *a lapse in demand*: fall, descent, decline, drop, deterioration. **3** *a lapse of a few weeks*: break, gap, interval, lull, interruption, intermission, pause.

■ *verb* **1** *lapsed into a coma*: decline, fall, sink, drop, deteriorate, slide, slip, fail, worsen, degenerate, backslide. **2** *policy lapsed*: expire, run out, end, stop, terminate.

large *adjective* **1** *a large nose/ country/amount*: big, huge, immense, massive, vast, sizable, great, giant, gigantic, bulky, enormous, king-sized, broad, considerable, monumental, substantial, whopping (*infml*), mega (*infml*). **2** *large house/ grounds*: extensive, generous, liberal, roomy, plentiful, spacious, capacious, grand, sweeping, grandiose.

F3 **1** small, tiny. **2** modest.

largely *adverb* mainly, principally, chiefly, generally, primarily, predominantly, mostly, considerably, by and large, widely, extensively, greatly.

lash *verb* **1** *lashing the horses*: whip, flog, beat, hit, thrash, strike, scourge. **2** *lash out at someone*: attack, criticize, lay into, scold.

last[1] *adjective* final, ultimate, closing, latest, rearmost, terminal, furthest, concluding, remotest, utmost, extreme, conclusive, definitive.

F3 first, initial.

■ *adverb* finally, ultimately, behind, after.

F3 first, firstly.

last[2] *verb* continue, endure, remain, persist, keep (on), survive, hold out, carry on, wear, stay, hold on, stand up, abide (*fml*).
F3 cease, stop, fade.

late *adjective* **1** *late for work*: overdue, behind, behind-hand, slow, unpunctual, delayed, last-minute. **2** *his late wife*: former, previous, departed, dead, deceased, past, preceding, old.
F3 1 early, punctual.

lately *adverb* recently, of late, latterly.

later *adverb* next, afterwards, subsequently, after, successively.
F3 earlier.

latter *adjective* last-mentioned, last, later, closing, concluding, ensuing, succeeding, successive, second.
F3 former.

laugh *verb* chuckle, giggle, guffaw, snigger, titter, chortle, split one's sides, fall about (*infml*), crease up (*infml*).
▪ *noun* giggle, chuckle, snigger, titter, guffaw, chortle, lark, scream (*infml*), hoot (*infml*), joke.

laughable *adjective* ridiculous, absurd, ludicrous, preposterous, nonsensical, derisory, derisive.
F3 serious.

laughter *noun* laughing, giggling, chuckling, chortling, guffawing, tittering, hilarity, amusement, merriment, mirth, glee, convulsions.

launch *verb* **1** *launch a rocket*: propel, dispatch, discharge, send off, project, float, set in motion, throw, fire. **2** *launch a campaign*: begin, commence, start, embark on, establish, found, open, initiate, inaugurate, introduce, instigate.

lavatory *noun* toilet, loo (*infml*), WC, bathroom, cloakroom, washroom, water-closet (*old*), public convenience, ladies (*infml*), gents (*infml*), urinal, powder-room.

lavish *adjective* **1** *give it lavish praise*: abundant, plentiful, profuse, unlimited, prolific. **2** *lavish in her gifts to charity*: generous, liberal, open-handed, extravagant, thriftless, prodigal, immoderate, intemperate, unstinting.
F3 1 scant. **2** frugal, thrifty.

law *noun* **1** *a law against trespass/the law of the land*: rule, act, decree, edict, order, statute, regulation, command, ordinance, charter, constitution, enactment. **2** *a law of physics*: principle, axiom, criterion, standard, precept (*fml*), formula, code, canon. **3** *work at the law/go to law*: jurisprudence, legislation, litigation.

lawsuit *noun* litigation, suit, action, proceedings, case, prosecution, dispute, process, trial, argument, contest, cause.

lawyer *noun* solicitor, barrister, advocate, attorney, counsel, QC, brief (*infml*).

lax *adjective* casual, careless, easy-going, slack, lenient, negligent, remiss.
F3 strict.

lay *verb* **1** *lay the book down*: put, place, deposit, set down, settle, lodge, plant, set, leave. **2** *lay the table for dinner*: arrange, position, set out, locate, devise, prepare, present. **3** *lay the blame firmly on them*: attribute, ascribe, assign, charge.

layer *noun* **1** *a thin layer of snow*: cover, coating, coat, covering, film, blanket, mantle, sheet, lamina. **2** *a layer of peat*: stratum, seam, thickness, tier, bed, plate.

layout *noun* arrangement, design, outline, plan, sketch, draft, map.

laze *verb* idle, loaf (*infml*), lounge, sit around, lie around, loll, relax, veg (*infml*).

lazy *adjective* idle, slothful, slack, work-shy, inactive, lethargic.
≠ industrious.

lead *verb* **1** *lead him by the hand*: guide, conduct, escort, steer, pilot, usher. **2** *lead the country*: rule, govern, head, preside over, direct, supervise. **3** *leads me to believe*: influence, persuade, incline. **4** *leading by three lengths*: come/be/go first, surpass, outdo, excel, outstrip, transcend. **5** *lead a quiet life*: pass, spend, live, undergo.
≠ **1** follow.

▪ *noun* **1** *have a five-point lead*: advantage, edge, priority, precedence, first place, start, van, vanguard. **2** *follow the lead of the United States*: guidance, direction, leadership, example, model. **3** *give the police a lead*: clue, hint, indication, guide, tip, suggestion. **4** *the lead in the movie*: title role, starring part, principal.

leader *noun* head, chief, director, ruler, principal, commander, captain, boss (*infml*), superior, chieftain, ringleader, guide, conductor.
≠ follower.

leadership *noun* direction, control, command, management, authority, guidance, domination, pre-eminence, premiership, administration, sway, directorship.

leading *adjective* main, principal, chief, primary, first, supreme, outstanding, foremost, dominant, ruling, superior, greatest, highest, governing, pre-eminent, number one.
≠ subordinate.

league *noun* **1** *the football league*: association, confederation, alliance, union, federation, confederacy, coalition, combination, band, syndicate, guild, consortium, cartel, combine, partnership, fellowship, compact. **2** *not in the same league*: category, class, level, group.

leak *verb* **1** *water leaking out of the tank*: seep, drip, ooze, escape, spill, trickle, percolate, exude, discharge. **2** *leak the information to the press*: divulge, disclose, reveal, let slip, make known, make public, tell, give away, pass on.

▪ *noun* **1** *a leak in the gutter*: crack, hole, opening, puncture, crevice, chink. **2** *leaks of harmful gases*:

leakage, leaking, seepage, drip, oozing, percolation. **3** *a government leak*: disclosure, divulgence.

lean[1] *verb* **1** *leaning to the left*: slant, slope, bend, tilt, list, tend. **2** *leaning against the wall*: recline, prop, rest. **3** *lean towards the opposite view*: incline, favour, prefer.

lean[2] *adjective* **1** *a lean athlete*: thin, skinny, bony, gaunt, lank, angular, slim, scraggy, scrawny, emaciated. **2** *lean times*: scanty, inadequate, bare, barren.
1 fat. **2** plentiful.

leap *verb* **1** *leaping the wall*: jump (over), bound, spring, vault, clear, skip, hop, bounce, caper, gambol. **2** *prices leaping upwards*: soar, surge, increase, rocket, escalate, rise.
2 drop, fall.
▪ *noun* **1** *in one leap*: jump, bound, spring, vault, hop, skip, caper. **2** *a leap in the price of oil*: increase, upsurge, upswing, surge, rise, escalation.

learn *verb* **1** *learns quickly*: grasp, comprehend, understand, master, acquire, pick up, gather, assimilate, discern. **2** *learn a poem*: memorize, learn by heart. **3** *learn about his misfortune*: discover, find out, ascertain, hear, detect, determine.

learner *noun* novice, beginner, student, trainee, pupil, scholar, apprentice.

learning *noun* scholarship, erudition, education, schooling, knowledge, information, letters, study, wisdom, tuition, culture, edification, research.

lease *verb* let, loan, rent, hire, sublet, charter.

least *adjective* smallest, lowest, minimum, fewest, slightest, poorest.
most.

leave[1] *verb* **1** *he left around midnight*: depart, go, go away, set out, take off, decamp, exit, move, quit, retire, withdraw, disappear, do a bunk (*infml*), clear off (*infml*). **2** *leave school*: abandon, desert, forsake, give up, drop, relinquish, renounce, pull out, surrender, desist, cease. **3** *leave him money in her will*: assign, commit, entrust, consign, bequeath, will, hand down, leave behind, give over, transmit.
1 arrive. **3** receive.

leave[2] *noun* **1** *get leave to go*: permission, authorization, consent, allowance, sanction, concession, dispensation, indulgence, liberty, freedom. **2** *take a few days' leave*: holiday, time off, vacation, sabbatical, furlough.
1 refusal, rejection.

lecture *noun* **1** *gives lectures on anatomy*: discourse, address, lesson, speech, talk, instruction. **2** *gave him a lecture*: reprimand, rebuke, reproof, scolding, harangue, censure, chiding, telling-off (*infml*), talking-to (*infml*), dressing-down (*infml*).

▪ *verb* **1** *invited to lecture at the university*: talk, teach, hold forth, speak, expound, address. **2** *she's always lecturing me about being late*: reprimand, reprove, scold, admonish, harangue, chide, censure, tell off (*infml*).

left *adjective* left-hand, port, sinistral.

F3 right.

leg *noun* **1** *broke her leg*: limb, member, shank, pin (*infml*), stump (*infml*). **2** *a leg at each corner*: support, prop, upright, brace. **3** *the last leg of the journey*: stage, part, section, portion, stretch, segment, lap.

legacy *noun* bequest, endowment, gift, heritage, heritance, inheritance, birthright, estate, heirloom.

legal *adjective* **1** *is it legal?*: lawful, legitimate, permissible, sanctioned, allowed, authorized, allowable, legalized, constitutional, valid, warranted, above board, proper, rightful. **2** *a legal inquiry*: judicial, judiciary, forensic.

F3 **1** illegal.

legalize *verb* legitimize, license, permit, sanction, allow, authorize, warrant, validate, approve.

legend *noun* **1** *the legend of St George*: myth, story, tale, folk-tale, fable, fiction, narrative. **2** *displaying the legend 'Buy British'*: inscription, caption, key, motto.

legendary *adjective* **1** *legendary monsters*: mythical, fabulous, story-book, fictitious, traditional. **2** *a legendary win*: famous, celebrated, renowned, well-known, illustrious.

legislate *verb* enact, ordain, authorize, codify, constitutionalize, prescribe, establish.

legislation *noun* law, statute, regulation, bill, act, charter, authorization, ruling, measure.

legitimate *adjective* **1** *a legitimate claim*: legal, lawful, authorized, statutory, rightful, proper, correct, real, acknowledged. **2** *have a legitimate reason to call*: reasonable, sensible, admissible, acceptable, justifiable, warranted, well-founded, valid, true.

F3 **1** illegal, illegitimate. **2** invalid.

leisure *noun* relaxation, rest, spare time, time off, ease, freedom, liberty, recreation, retirement, holiday, vacation.

F3 work.

leisurely *adjective* unhurried, slow, relaxed, comfortable, easy, unhasty, tranquil, restful, gentle, carefree, laid-back (*infml*), lazy, loose.

F3 rushed, hectic.

lend *verb* **1** *lend him the money*: loan, advance. **2** *lends truth to his statement*: give, grant, bestow, provide, furnish, confer, supply, impart, contribute.

F3 **1** borrow.

length *noun* **1** *the length of a piece of string*: extent, distance, measure, reach, piece, portion, section, segment. **2** *a short length of time*: duration, period, term, stretch, space, span.

lengthen *verb* stretch, extend, elongate, draw out, prolong, protract, spin out, eke (out), pad out, increase, expand, continue.

E reduce, shorten.

lengthy *adjective* long, prolonged, protracted, extended, lengthened, overlong, long-drawn-out, long-winded, rambling, diffuse, verbose, drawn-out, interminable.

E brief, concise.

lessen *verb* decrease, reduce, diminish, lower, ease, abate, contract, die down, dwindle, lighten, slow down, weaken, shrink, abridge, de-escalate, erode, minimize, narrow, moderate, slack, flag, fail, deaden, impair.

E grow, increase.

lesser *adjective* lower, secondary, inferior, smaller, subordinate, slighter, minor.

E greater.

lesson *noun* **1** *a piano lesson*: class, period, instruction, lecture, tutorial, teaching, coaching. **2** *finish your lessons before watching TV*: assignment, exercise, homework, practice, task, drill. **3** *a lesson to us all*: example, model, warning, deterrent.

let *verb* **1** *let him go*: permit, allow, give leave, give permission, authorize, consent to, agree to, sanction, grant, OK, enable, tolerate. **2** *let the flat*: lease, hire, rent.

E 1 prohibit, forbid.

lethal *adjective* fatal, deadly, deathly, mortal, dangerous, poisonous, noxious, destructive, devastating.

E harmless, safe.

letter *noun* **1** *send him a letter*: note, message, line, missive (*fml*), epistle (*fml*), dispatch, communication, acknowledgement, chit. **2** *a capital letter*: character, symbol, sign, grapheme.

level *adjective* **1** *make sure it's level*: flat, smooth, even, flush, horizontal, aligned, plane. **2** *the teams were level at half-time*: equal, balanced, even, on a par, neck and neck, matching, uniform.

E 1 uneven. **2** unequal.

▪ *verb* **1** *levelling the buildings*: demolish, destroy, devastate, flatten, knock down, raze, pull down, bulldoze, tear down, lay low. **2** *level the ground/score*: even out, flush, plane, smooth, equalize. **3** *level criticism/a gun at*: direct, point.

▪ *noun* **1** *at the same level*: height, elevation, altitude. **2** *the next level up*: position, rank, status, class, degree, grade, standard, standing, plane, echelon, layer, stratum, storey, stage, zone.

lever *verb* force, prise, pry, raise, dislodge, jemmy, shift, move, heave.

▪ *noun* bar, crowbar, jemmy, joy-stick, handle.

liability *noun* **1** *the insurers accepted liability*: accountability, duty, obligation, responsibility, onus. **2** *assets and liabilities*: debt, arrears, indebtedness. **3** *a bit of a liability*: drawback, disadvantage, hindrance, impediment, drag (*infml*).

liable *adjective* **1** *liable to lose his temper*: inclined, likely, apt, disposed, prone, tending, susceptible. **2** *liable for any damage*: responsible, answerable, accountable, amenable.

liar *noun* falsifier, perjurer, deceiver, fibber (*infml*).

libel *noun* defamation (*fml*), slur, smear, slander, vilification (*fml*), aspersion (*fml*), calumny (*fml*).
▪ *verb* defame (*fml*), slur, smear, slander, vilify (*fml*), malign.

liberty *noun* **1** *give them their liberty*: freedom, emancipation, release, independence, autonomy. **2** *liberty to roam*: licence, permission, sanction, right, authorization, dispensation, franchise. **3** *take liberties*: familiarity, disrespect, overfamiliarity, presumption, impertinence, impudence.
≠ **1** imprisonment. **3** respect.

licence *noun* **1** *a driving licence*: permission, permit, leave, warrant, authorization, authority, certificate, charter. **2** *licence to roam*: right, entitlement, privilege, dispensation, carte blanche, freedom, liberty, exemption, independence.
≠ **1** prohibition. **2** restriction.

license *verb* permit, allow, authorize, certify, warrant, entitle, empower, sanction, commission, accredit (*fml*).
≠ ban, prohibit.

lick *verb* tongue, touch, wash, lap, taste, dart, flick, flicker, play over, smear, brush.

lie[1] *verb* perjure, misrepresent, fabricate, falsify, fib (*infml*), invent, equivocate, prevaricate, forswear oneself (*fml*).
▪ *noun* falsehood, untruth, falsification, fabrication, invention, fiction, deceit, fib (*infml*), falsity, white lie, prevarication, whopper (*infml*), porky (*infml*).
≠ truth.

lie[2] *verb* be, exist, dwell, belong, extend, remain.

life *noun* **1** *a long and happy life*: being, existence, animation, breath, viability, entity, soul. **2** *the life of the parliament*: duration, course, span, career. **3** *full of life*: liveliness, vigour, vitality, vivacity, verve, zest, energy, élan, spirit, sparkle, activity.

lifeless *adjective* **1** *her lifeless body*: dead, deceased, defunct, cold, unconscious, inanimate, insensible, stiff. **2** *feel lifeless*: lethargic, listless, sluggish, dull, apathetic, passive, insipid, colourless, slow. **3** *a lifeless desert*: barren, bare, empty, desolate, arid.

OPP **1** alive. **2** lively. **3** fertile.

lifelike *adjective* realistic, true-to-life, real, true, vivid, natural, authentic, faithful, exact, graphic.
OPP unrealistic, unnatural.

lifelong *adjective* lifetime, long-lasting, long-standing, persistent, lasting, enduring, abiding, permanent, constant.
OPP impermanent, temporary.

lift *verb* **1** *she lifted the chair*: raise, elevate, hoist, upraise. **2** *it lifted their spirits*: uplift, exalt, buoy up, boost. **3** *the ban was lifted*: revoke, cancel, relax.
OPP **1** drop. **2** lower.

light[1] *noun* **1** *full of light*: illumination, brightness, brilliance, luminescence, radiance, glow, ray, shine, glare, gleam, glint, lustre, flash, blaze. **2** *bring a light*: lamp, lantern, lighter, match, torch, candle, bulb, beacon. **3** *at first light*: day, daybreak, daylight, daytime, dawn, sunrise. **4** *see the light*: enlightenment, explanation, elucidation, understanding.
OPP **1** darkness. **3** night.
▪ *verb* **1** *light the fire*: ignite, fire, set alight, set fire to, kindle. **2** *lighting up the sky*: illuminate, light up, lighten, brighten, animate, cheer, switch on, turn on, put on.
OPP **1** extinguish. **2** darken.
▪ *adjective* **1** *a light corner*: illuminated, bright, brilliant, luminous, glowing, shining, well-lit, sunny. **2** *light skin/hair*: pale, pastel, fair, blond, blonde, bleached, faded, faint.
OPP **1** dark. **2** dark, colourful.

light[2] *adjective* **1** *light as a feather*: weightless, insubstantial, delicate, airy, buoyant, flimsy, feathery, slight. **2** *light punishment*: trivial, inconsiderable, trifling, inconsequential, worthless. **3** *a light mood*: cheerful, cheery, carefree, lively, merry, blithe. **4** *light entertainment*: amusing, funny, humorous, frivolous, witty, pleasing.
OPP **1** heavy, weighty. **2** important, serious. **3** solemn. **4** serious.

lighten[1] *verb* illuminate, illumine, brighten, light up, shine.
OPP darken.

lighten[2] *verb* **1** *lightening his burden*: ease, lessen, unload, lift, relieve, reduce, mitigate, alleviate. **2** *lightening their hearts*: brighten, cheer, encourage, hearten, inspirit, uplift, gladden, revive, elate, buoy up, inspire.
OPP **1** burden. **2** depress.

light-hearted *adjective* cheerful, joyful, jolly, happy-go-lucky, bright, carefree, untroubled, merry, sunny, glad, elated, jovial, playful.
OPP sad, unhappy, serious.

like[1] *adjective* similar, resembling, alike, same, identical, equivalent, akin, corresponding, related, relating, parallel, allied, analogous, approximating.
OPP unlike, dissimilar.

like[2] *verb* **1** *like a good film/like her immensely*: enjoy, delight in, care

for, admire, appreciate, hold dear, love, esteem, cherish, prize, relish, revel in, approve, take (kindly) to. **2** *would you like coffee or tea?*: prefer, choose, select, feel inclined, go for (*infml*), desire, want, wish.
1 dislike. **2** reject.

likeable *adjective* pleasing, appealing, agreeable, charming, engaging, winsome, pleasant, amiable, congenial, attractive, sympathetic.
unpleasant, disagreeable.

likelihood *noun* likeliness, probability, possibility, chance, prospect, liability.
improbability, unlikeliness.

likely *adjective* **1** *it is likely to rain*: probable, possible, anticipated, expected, liable, prone, tending, predictable, odds-on (*infml*), inclined, foreseeable. **2** *a likely explanation*: credible, believable, plausible, feasible, reasonable. **3** *a likely candidate*: promising, hopeful, pleasing, appropriate, proper, suitable.
1, **2** unlikely. **3** unsuitable.
▪ *adverb* probably, presumably, like as not, in all probability, no doubt, doubtlessly.

liken *verb* compare, equate, match, parallel, relate, juxtapose, associate, set beside.

likeness *noun* **1** *bears a remarkable likeness to the one I lost*: similarity, resemblance, affinity, correspondence. **2** *a likeness of the king*: image, representation, copy, reproduction, replica, facsimile, effigy, picture, portrait, photograph, counterpart.
1 dissimilarity, unlikeness.

likewise *adverb* similarly, also, moreover, furthermore, in addition, further, besides, by the same token, too.

liking *noun* fondness, affection, preference, partiality, affinity, predilection, penchant, taste, attraction, love, appreciation, proneness, propensity, inclination, tendency, bias, desire, weakness, fancy, soft spot (*infml*).
dislike, aversion, hatred.

limb *noun* arm, leg, member, appendage, branch, projection, offshoot, wing, fork, extension, part, spur, extremity, bough.

limelight *noun* fame, celebrity, spotlight, stardom, recognition, renown, attention, prominence, publicity, public eye.

limit *noun* **1** *the outer limits of the solar system*: boundary, bound, border, frontier, confines, edge, brink, threshold, verge, brim, end, perimeter, rim, compass, termination, ultimate, utmost, terminus, extent. **2** *a limit on spending/a time limit*: check, curb, restraint, restriction, limitation, ceiling, maximum, cut-off point, saturation point, deadline.
▪ *verb* check, curb, restrict, restrain, constrain, confine, demarcate, delimit, bound, hem in, ration, specify, hinder.

limitation *noun* **1** *a limitation on*

imports: check, restriction, curb, control, constraint, restraint, delimitation, demarcation, block. **2** *has its limitations*: inadequacy, shortcoming, disadvantage, drawback, condition, qualification, reservation.
F3 **1** extension.

limited *adjective* restricted, circumscribed, constrained, controlled, confined, checked, defined, finite, fixed, minimal, narrow, inadequate, insufficient.
F3 limitless.

limp[1] *verb* hobble, falter, stumble, hop, shuffle, shamble.

limp[2] *adjective* **1** *a limp handshake*: flabby, drooping, flaccid, floppy, loose, slack, relaxed, lax, soft, flexible, pliable, limber. **2** *feel weak and limp*: tired, weary, exhausted, spent, weak, worn out, lethargic, debilitated, enervated.
F3 **1** stiff. **2** vigorous.

line[1] *noun* **1** *draw a line*: stroke, band, bar, stripe, mark, strip, rule, dash, strand, streak, underline, score, scratch. **2** *a line of people/ cars*: row, rank, queue, file, column, sequence, series, procession, chain, trail. **3** *the front line*: limit, boundary, border, borderline, edge, frontier, demarcation. **4** *plastic line*: string, rope, cord, cable, thread, filament, wire. **5** *the line of her chin*: profile, contour, outline, silhouette, figure, formation, configuration. **6** *lines on his face*: crease, wrinkle, furrow, groove, corrugation. **7** *his line of sight*: course, path, direction, track, route, axis. **8** *take a different line*: approach, avenue, course (of action), belief, ideology, policy, system, position, practice, procedure, method, scheme. **9** *in a different line (of work)*: occupation, business, trade, profession, vocation, job, activity, interest, employment, department, calling, field, province, forte, area, pursuit, specialization, specialty, specialism, speciality. **10** *the female line*: ancestry, family, descent, extraction, lineage, pedigree, stock, race, breed.

line[2] *verb* fill, pad, stuff, reinforce.

linger *verb* loiter, delay, dally, tarry, wait, remain, stay, hang on, lag, procrastinate, dawdle, dilly-dally (*infml*), idle, stop, endure, hold out, last, persist, survive.
F3 leave, rush.

lining *noun* inlay, interfacing, padding, backing, stiffening.

link *noun* **1** *could find no link to the other crimes*: connection, bond, tie, association, joint, relationship, tie-up, union, knot, liaison, attachment, communication. **2** *a link in the chain*: part, piece, element, member, constituent, component, division.
▪ *verb* connect, join, couple, tie, fasten, unite, bind, amalgamate, merge, associate, ally, bracket, identify, relate, yoke, attach, hook up, join forces, team up.
F3 separate, unfasten.

lip *noun* edge, brim, border, brink, rim, margin, verge.

liquid *noun* liquor, fluid, juice, drink, sap, solution, lotion.
▪ *adjective* fluid, flowing, liquefied, watery, wet, runny, melted, molten, thawed, clear, smooth.
F3 solid.

list *noun* catalogue, roll, inventory, register, enumeration, schedule, index, listing, record, file, directory, table, tabulation, tally, series, syllabus, invoice.
▪ *verb* enumerate, register, itemize, catalogue, index, tabulate, record, file, enrol, enter, note, bill, book, set down, write down.

listen *verb* hark, attend, pay attention, hear, heed, hearken, hang on (someone's) words, prick up one's ears, take notice, lend an ear, eavesdrop, overhear, give ear.

listless *adjective* sluggish, lethargic, languid, torpid, enervated, spiritless, limp, lifeless, inert, inactive, impassive, indifferent, uninterested, vacant, apathetic, indolent, depressed, bored, heavy.
F3 energetic, enthusiastic.

literal *adjective* **1** *a literal translation*: verbatim, word-for-word, strict, close, actual, precise, faithful, exact, accurate, factual, true, genuine, unexaggerated. **2** *a literal interpretation*: prosaic, unimaginative, uninspired, matter-of-fact, down-to-earth, humdrum.
F3 **1** imprecise, loose. **2** imaginative.

literature *noun* **1** *English literature*: writings, letters, paper(s). **2** *get all the available literature*: information, leaflet(s), pamphlet(s), circular(s), brochure(s), handout(s), bumf (*infml*).

Types of literature include:
allegory, autobiography, biography, comedy, drama, epic, essay, fiction, lampoon, novel, novella, parody, pastiche, poetry, prose, saga, satire, tragedy, verse. *See also* **poem**; **story**.

Terms used in literature include:
alliteration, assonance, bathos, blank verse, couplet, epigram, epilogue, free verse, genre, imagery, irony, metaphor, metre, motif, onomatopoeia, oxymoron, narrator, plot, prologue, protagonist, rhyme, rhythm, simile, stanza, sub-plot.

---

litter *noun* **1** *clear up other people's litter*: rubbish, debris, refuse, waste, mess, disorder, clutter, confusion, disarray, untidiness, junk (*infml*), muck, jumble, fragments, shreds. **2** *a litter of pups*: offspring, young, progeny (*fml*), brood, family.
▪ *verb* strew, scatter, mess up, disorder, clutter.
F3 tidy.

little *adjective* **1** *a little man/car/creature*: small, short, tiny, wee

(*infml*), minute, teeny (*infml*), diminutive, miniature, infinitesimal, mini, microscopic, petite, pint-size(d) (*infml*), slender. **2** *a little pause*: short-lived, brief, fleeting, passing, transient. **3** *had little water/money*: insufficient, sparse, scant, meagre, paltry, skimpy. **4** *a little detail*: insignificant, inconsiderable, negligible, trivial, petty, trifling, unimportant.
E3 1 big. **2** lengthy. **3** ample. **4** considerable.
▪ *adverb* barely, hardly, scarcely, rarely, seldom, infrequently, not much.
E3 frequently.
▪ *noun* bit, dash, pinch, spot, trace, drop, dab, speck, touch, taste, particle, hint, fragment, modicum, trifle.
E3 lot.

live[1] *verb* /liv/ **1** *live for seventy years*: be, exist, breathe, draw breath. **2** *his achievements will live on after his death*: last, endure, continue, remain, persist, survive. **3** *live in a tent*: dwell, inhabit, reside, lodge, abide (*fml*). **4** *live a quiet life*: pass, spend, lead.
E3 1 die. **2** cease, disappear.

live[2] *adjective* /laiv/ **1** *live births*: alive, living, existent. **2** *he's a live wire*: lively, vital, active, energetic, dynamic, alert, vigorous. **3** *live electric cable*: burning, glowing, blazing, ignited. **4** *live issue*: relevant, current, topical, pertinent, controversial, pressing.
E3 1 dead. **2** apathetic.

lively *adjective* **1** *lively discussion*: animated, alert, active, energetic, spirited, vivacious, vigorous, sprightly, spry, agile, nimble, quick, keen. **2** *she's very lively for her age*: cheerful, blithe, merry, frisky, perky, breezy, chirpy (*infml*), frolicsome. **3** *a lively market*: busy, bustling, brisk, crowded, eventful, exciting, buzzing. **4** *a lively scene*: vivid, bright, colourful, stimulating, stirring, invigorating, racy, refreshing, sparkling.
E3 1 moribund, apathetic. **2** lethargic. **3** inactive. **4** dull.

liven *verb* enliven, vitalize, put life into, rouse, invigorate, animate, energize, brighten, stir (up), buck up (*infml*), pep up (*infml*), perk up (*infml*), hot up (*infml*).
E3 dishearten.

living *adjective* alive, breathing, existing, live, current, extant, operative, strong, vigorous, active, lively, vital, animated.
E3 dead, sluggish.
▪ *noun* livelihood, maintenance, support, income, subsistence, sustenance, work, job, occupation, profession, benefice, way of life.

load *noun* **1** *carry heavy loads*: burden, onus, encumbrance, weight, pressure, oppression, millstone. **2** *spilling its load*: cargo, consignment, shipment, goods, lading, freight.
▪ *verb* **1** *she arrived loaded with packages*: burden, weigh down, encumber, overburden, oppress,

trouble, weight, saddle with. **2** *load the crates into the van*: pack, pile, heap, freight, fill, stack.

loan *noun* advance, credit, mortgage, allowance.
▪ *verb* lend, advance, credit, allow.

lobby *verb* campaign for, press for, demand, persuade, call for, urge, push for, influence, solicit, pressure, promote.
▪ *noun* **1** *the hotel lobby*: vestibule, foyer, porch, anteroom, hall, hallway, waiting room, entrance hall, corridor, passage. **2** *the tobacco lobby*: pressure group, campaign, ginger group.

local *adjective* regional, provincial, community, district, neighbourhood, parochial, vernacular, small-town, limited, narrow, restricted, parish(-pump).
F3 national.
▪ *noun* **1** *one of the locals*: inhabitant, citizen, resident, native. **2** (*infml*) *go down the local*: pub.

locate *verb* **1** *can't locate the file*: find, discover, unearth, run to earth (*infml*), track down, detect, lay one's hands on (*infml*), pinpoint, identify. **2** *located near the station*: situate, settle, fix, establish, place, put, set, seat.

location *noun* position, situation, place, locus, whereabouts, venue, site, locale, bearings, spot, point.

lock *noun* fastening, bolt, clasp, padlock.
▪ *verb* **1** *lock the gates*: fasten, secure, bolt, latch, seal, shut. **2** *locking the two pieces together*: join, unite, engage, link, mesh, entangle, entwine, clench. **3** *locking arms*: clasp, hug, embrace, grasp, encircle, enclose, clutch, grapple.
F3 unlock.

lodge *noun* hut, cabin, cottage, chalet, shelter, retreat, den, gatehouse, house, hunting-lodge, meeting-place, club, haunt.
▪ *verb* **1** *lodging with an elderly couple*: live, stay, reside. **2** *house that lodged two whole families*: accommodate, put up (*infml*), quarter, board, billet, shelter. **3** *lodged between the boards*: fix, imbed, implant, get stuck. **4** *lodge funds in the account/lodge a complaint*: deposit, place, put, submit, register.

log *noun* **1** *put some logs on the fire*: timber, trunk, block, chunk. **2** *the captain's log*: record, diary, journal, logbook, daybook, account, tally.
▪ *verb* record, register, write up, note, book, chart, tally.

logic *noun* reasoning, reason, sense, deduction, rationale, argumentation.

logical *adjective* reasonable, rational, reasoned, coherent, consistent, valid, sound, well-founded, clear, sensible, deducible, methodical, well-organized.
F3 illogical, irrational.

loiter *verb* dawdle, hang about, idle, linger, dally, dilly-dally (*infml*), delay, mooch, lag, saunter.

lone *adjective* single, sole, one, only, isolated, solitary, separate, separated, unattached, unaccompanied, unattended.
≠ accompanied.

lonely *adjective* **1** *a lonely old woman*: alone, friendless, lonesome, solitary, abandoned, forsaken, companionless, unaccompanied, destitute. **2** *a lonely farmhouse*: isolated, uninhabited, remote, out-of-the-way, unfrequented, secluded, abandoned, deserted, forsaken, desolate.
≠ 1 popular. **2** accessible.

long *adjective* lengthy, extensive, extended, expanded, prolonged, protracted, stretched, spread out, sustained, expansive, far-reaching, long-drawn-out, interminable, slow.
≠ brief, short, fleeting, abbreviated.

longing *noun* craving, desire, yearning, hungering, hankering, yen, thirst, wish, urge, coveting, aspiration, ambition.

long-winded *adjective* lengthy, overlong, prolonged, diffuse, verbose, wordy, voluble, long-drawn-out, discursive, repetitious, rambling, tedious.
≠ brief, terse.

look *verb* **1** *looking through the window*: watch, see, observe, view, survey, regard, gaze, study, stare, examine, inspect, scrutinize, glance, contemplate, scan, peep, gawp (*infml*). **2** *looking very smart*: seem, appear, show, exhibit, display.
▪ *noun* **1** *take a good look*: view, survey, inspection, examination, observation, sight, review, once-over (*infml*), glance, glimpse, gaze, peek. **2** *has a frightening look*: appearance, aspect, manner, semblance, mien (*fml*), expression, bearing, face, complexion.

look-alike *noun* double, replica, twin, spitting image (*infml*), living image, clone, spit (*infml*), dead ringer (*infml*), doppelgänger.

loom *verb* appear, emerge, take shape, menace, threaten, impend, hang over, dominate, tower, overhang, rise, soar, overshadow, overtop.

loop *noun* hoop, ring, circle, noose, coil, eyelet, loophole, spiral, curve, curl, kink, twist, whorl, twirl, turn, bend.
▪ *verb* coil, encircle, roll, bend, circle, curve round, turn, twist, spiral, connect, join, knot, fold, braid.

loophole *noun* let-out, escape, evasion, excuse, pretext, plea, pretence.

loose *adjective* **1** *a loose tooth*: free, unfastened, untied, movable, unattached, insecure, wobbly. **2** *loose clothing*: slack, lax, baggy, hanging. **3** *a loose description*: imprecise, vague, inexact, ill-defined, indefinite, inaccurate, indistinct.
≠ 1 firm, secure. **2** tight. **3** precise.

loosen *verb* **1** *loosen his collar*: ease, relax, loose, slacken, undo, unbind, untie, unfasten. **2** *loosening his tongue*: free, set free, release, let go, let out, deliver.
F3 **1** tighten.

loot *verb* plunder, pillage, rob, sack, rifle, raid, maraud, ransack, ravage.
▪ *noun* spoils, booty, plunder, haul, swag (*infml*), prize.

lopsided *adjective* asymmetrical, unbalanced, askew, off balance, uneven.
F3 balanced, symmetrical.

lord *noun* **1** *my noble lords*: peer, noble, earl, duke, count, baron. **2** *the lord of all he surveys*: master, ruler, superior, overlord, leader, commander, governor, king.

lose *verb* **1** *lose his pen*: mislay, misplace, forget, miss, forfeit. **2** *lose money*: waste, squander, dissipate, use up, exhaust, expend, drain. **3** *lose the race*: fail, fall short, suffer defeat.
F3 **1** find. **2** make, gain. **3** win.

loss *noun* **1** *loss of liberty*: deprivation, disadvantage, defeat, failure, losing, bereavement, damage, destruction, ruin, hurt. **2** *have large losses*: waste, depletion, disappearance, deficiency, deficit.
F3 gain.

lost *adjective* **1** *lost property*: mislaid, missing, vanished, disappeared, misplaced, astray. **2** *look lost*: confused, disoriented, bewildered, puzzled, baffled, perplexed, preoccupied. **3** *lost time*: wasted, squandered, ruined, destroyed.
F3 **1** found.

lot *noun* **1** *lots of food/a lot of people*: large amount, great number, many, a quantity, a good/great deal, shedload (*infml*). **2** *an interesting lot*: collection, batch, assortment, quantity, group, set, crowd. **3** *accept our lot*: share, portion, allowance, ration, quota, part, piece, parcel.

lotion *noun* ointment, balm, cream, salve.

loud *adjective* **1** *a loud voice*: noisy, deafening, booming, resounding, ear-piercing, ear-splitting, piercing, thundering, blaring, clamorous, vociferous. **2** *a loud tie*: garish, gaudy, glaring, flashy, brash, showy, ostentatious, tasteless.
F3 **1** quiet. **2** subdued.

lounge *verb* relax, loll, idle, laze, waste time, kill time, lie about, take it easy, sprawl, recline, lie back, slump.
▪ *noun* sitting room, living room, drawing room, day room, parlour.

lovable *adjective* adorable, endearing, winsome, captivating, charming, engaging, attractive, fetching, sweet, lovely, pleasing, delightful.
F3 detestable, hateful.

love *verb* **1** *he loves his children*: adore, cherish, dote on, treasure, hold dear, idolize, worship. **2** *I love dancing*: like, take pleasure in,

enjoy, delight in, appreciate, desire, fancy.
≠ detest, hate.
▪ *noun* adoration, affection, fondness, attachment, regard, liking, amorousness, ardour, devotion, adulation, passion, rapture, tenderness, warmth, inclination, infatuation, delight, enjoyment, soft spot (*infml*), weakness, taste, friendship.
≠ detestation, hate, loathing.

lovely *adjective* beautiful, charming, delightful, attractive, enchanting, pleasing, pleasant, pretty, adorable, agreeable, enjoyable, sweet, winning, exquisite.
≠ ugly, hideous.

loving *adjective* amorous, affectionate, devoted, doting, fond, ardent, passionate, warm, warm-hearted, tender.

low *adjective* **1** *a low wall*: short, small, squat, stunted, little, shallow, deep, depressed, sunken. **2** *supplies are low*: inadequate, deficient, poor, sparse, meagre, paltry, scant, insignificant. **3** *feeling a bit low*: unhappy, depressed, downcast, gloomy. **4** *a low trick*: base, coarse, vulgar, mean, contemptible. **5** *low prices*: cheap, inexpensive, reasonable. **6** *low lighting*: subdued, muted, soft.
≠ **1** high. **2** plentiful. **3** cheerful. **4** honourable. **5** exorbitant, high. **6** harsh.

lower *adjective* inferior, lesser, subordinate, secondary, minor, second-class, low-level, lowly, junior.
≠ higher.
▪ *verb* **1** *lower the flag*: drop, depress, sink, descend, let down. **2** *lowering interest rates*: reduce, decrease, cut, lessen, diminish.
≠ **1** raise. **2** increase, raise.

lowly *adjective* humble, low-born, obscure, poor, plebeian, plain, simple, modest, ordinary, inferior, meek, mild, mean, submissive, subordinate.
≠ lofty, noble.

loyal *adjective* true, faithful, steadfast, staunch, devoted, trustworthy, sincere, patriotic.
≠ disloyal, treacherous.

loyalty *noun* allegiance, faithfulness, fidelity, devotion, steadfastness, constancy, trustworthiness, reliability, patriotism.
≠ disloyalty, treachery.

luck *noun* **1** *trust to luck*: chance, fortune, accident, fate, fortuity (*fml*), fluke (*infml*), destiny. **2** *have the luck to be in the right place at the right time*: good fortune, success, break (*infml*), godsend.
≠ **1** design. **2** misfortune.

lucky *adjective* fortunate, favoured, auspicious, successful, prosperous, timely, jammy (*infml*).
≠ unlucky.

lukewarm *adjective* cool, half-hearted, apathetic, tepid, indifferent, unenthusiastic, uninterested, unresponsive, unconcerned.

lull *verb* soothe, subdue, calm, hush, pacify, quieten down, quiet, quell, compose.
F3 agitate.
▪ *noun* calm, peace, quiet, tranquillity, stillness, let-up, pause, hush, silence.
F3 agitation.

lump *noun* **1** *a lump of sugar/rock*: mass, cluster, clump, clod, ball, bunch, piece, chunk, cake, hunk, nugget, wedge. **2** *a lump on his head*: swelling, growth, bulge, bump, protuberance (*fml*), protrusion, tumour, nodule.
▪ *verb* collect, mass, gather, cluster, combine, coalesce, group, consolidate, unite.

lunge *verb* thrust, jab, stab, pounce, plunge, pitch into, charge, dart, dash, dive, poke, strike (at), fall upon, grab (at), hit (at), leap.

lure *verb* tempt, entice, draw, attract, allure, seduce, ensnare, lead on.
▪ *noun* temptation, enticement, attraction, bait, inducement.

lurk *verb* skulk, prowl, lie in wait, crouch, lie low, hide, snoop.

luxurious *adjective* sumptuous, opulent, lavish, de luxe, plush, magnificent, splendid, expensive, costly, self-indulgent, pampered.
F3 austere, spartan.

luxury *noun* sumptuousness, opulence, hedonism, splendour, affluence, richness, magnificence, pleasure, indulgence, gratification, comfort, extravagance, satisfaction.
F3 austerity.

M*m*

machine *noun* instrument, device, contrivance, tool, mechanism, engine, apparatus, appliance.

machinery *noun* **1** *farm machinery*: instruments, mechanism, tools, apparatus, equipment, tackle, gear. **2** *the machinery of government*: organization, channels, structure, system, procedure.

mad *adjective* **1** *went mad with grief*: insane, lunatic, unbalanced, psychotic, deranged, demented, out of one's mind, crazy (*infml*), nuts (*infml*), barmy (*infml*), bonkers (*infml*). **2** (*infml*) *she got really mad*: angry, furious, enraged, infuriated, incensed. **3** *a mad idea*: irrational, illogical, unreasonable, absurd, preposterous, foolish, crazy (*infml*). **4** *mad about cars/*

football: fanatical, enthusiastic, infatuated, ardent.
E3 **1** sane. **2** calm. **3** sensible. **4** apathetic.

madden *verb* anger, enrage, infuriate, incense, exasperate, provoke, annoy, irritate.
E3 calm, pacify.

madly *adverb* **1** *rolling his eyes madly*: insanely, dementedly, hysterically, wildly. **2** *waving her arms about madly*: excitedly, frantically, furiously, recklessly, violently, energetically, rapidly, hastily, hurriedly. **3** *madly in love*: intensely, extremely, exceedingly, fervently, devotedly.

magazine *noun* **1** *a fashion magazine*: journal, periodical, paper, weekly, monthly, quarterly. **2** *a magazine of bullets*: arsenal, storehouse, ammunition dump, depot, ordnance.

magic *noun* **1** *black/white magic*: sorcery, enchantment, occultism, black art, witchcraft, wizardry, spell, necromancy. **2** *perform magic*: conjuring, illusion, sleight of hand, legerdemain, trickery. **3** *islands have a certain indefinable magic*: charm, fascination, glamour, allure.
▪ *adjective* charming, enchanting, bewitching, fascinating, spellbinding.

magician *noun* sorcerer, miracle-worker, conjuror, enchanter, enchantress, wizard, witch, warlock, spellbinder, wonder-worker.

magnetic *adjective* attractive, alluring, fascinating, charming, mesmerizing, seductive, irresistible, entrancing, captivating, gripping, absorbing, charismatic.
E3 repellent, repulsive.

magnificent *adjective* splendid, grand, imposing, impressive, glorious, gorgeous, brilliant, excellent, majestic, superb, sumptuous, noble, elegant, fine, rich.
E3 modest, humble, poor.

magnify *verb* enlarge, amplify, increase, expand, intensify, boost, enhance, greaten, heighten, deepen, build up, exaggerate, dramatize, overemphasize, overplay, overstate, overdo, blow up (*infml*).
E3 belittle, play down.

magnitude *noun* **1** *the magnitude of a star*: size, extent, measure, amount, expanse, dimensions, mass, proportions, quantity, volume, bulk, largeness, space, strength, amplitude. **2** *a decision of great magnitude*: importance, consequence, significance, weight, greatness, moment, intensity.

mail *noun* post, letters, correspondence, packages, parcels, delivery.
▪ *verb* post, send, dispatch, forward.

maim *verb* mutilate, wound, incapacitate, injure, disable, hurt, impair, cripple, lame.

main *adjective* principal, chief, leading, first, foremost, predominant, pre-eminent, primary, prime, supreme, paramount, central, cardinal, outstanding, essential, critical, crucial, necessary, vital.
F3 minor, unimportant, insignificant.
▪ *noun* pipe, duct, conduit, channel, cable, line.

mainly *adverb* primarily, principally, chiefly, in the main, mostly, on the whole, for the most part, generally, in general, especially, as a rule, above all, largely, overall.

maintain *verb* **1** *maintain the same rate of production*: carry on, continue, keep (up), sustain, retain. **2** *work to maintain one's family*: care for, conserve, look after, take care of, preserve, support, finance, supply. **3** *maintains that he never received the letter*: assert, affirm, claim, contend, declare, hold (*fml*), state, insist, believe, fight for.
F3 2 neglect. **3** deny.

maintenance *noun* **1** *long-term maintenance of low inflation*: continuation, continuance, perpetuation. **2** *house required constant maintenance*: care, conservation, preservation, support, repairs, protection, upkeep, running. **3** *paying child maintenance*: keep, subsistence, living, livelihood, allowance, alimony.
F3 2 neglect.

majestic *adjective* magnificent, grand, dignified, noble, royal, stately, splendid, imperial, impressive, exalted, imposing, regal, sublime, superb, lofty, monumental, pompous.
F3 lowly, unimpressive, unimposing.

major *adjective* greater, chief, main, larger, bigger, higher, leading, outstanding, notable, supreme, uppermost, significant, crucial, important, key, keynote, great, senior, older, superior, pre-eminent, vital, weighty.
F3 minor, unimportant, trivial.

majority *noun* bulk, mass, preponderance, most, greater part.
F3 minority.

make *verb* **1** *make cars/cakes/music*: create, manufacture, fabricate, construct, build, produce, put together, originate, compose, form, shape. **2** *made trouble/a scene/a mistake*: cause, bring about, effect, accomplish, occasion, give rise to, generate, render, perform. **3** *they made him do it*: coerce, force, oblige, constrain, compel, prevail upon, pressurize, press, require. **4** *made her a partner in the firm*: appoint, elect, designate, nominate, ordain, install. **5** *make money/a profit*: earn, gain, net, obtain, acquire. **6** *two plus two makes four*: compose, constitute, comprise, add up to, amount to.
▪ *noun* brand, sort, type, style,

variety, manufacture, model, mark, kind, form, structure.

make-believe *noun* pretence, imagination, fantasy, unreality, play-acting, role-play, dream, charade.
≠ reality.

makeshift *adjective* temporary, improvised, rough and ready, provisional, substitute, stop-gap, expedient, make-do.
≠ permanent.

make-up *noun* cosmetics, paint, powder, maquillage, war paint (*infml*).

male *adjective* masculine, manly, virile, boyish, he-.
≠ female.

malice *noun* malevolence, enmity, animosity, ill-will, hatred, hate, spite, vindictiveness, bitterness.
≠ love.

malicious *adjective* malevolent, ill-natured, malign, spiteful, venomous, vicious, vengeful, evil-minded, bitter, resentful.
≠ kind, friendly.

mammal

Mammals include:
aardvark, anteater, antelope, ape, armadillo, baboon, badger, bat, bear, beaver, bull, bushbaby, camel, cat, chimpanzee, chipmunk, cow, deer, dog, dolphin, dromedary, duck-billed platypus, dugong, echidna, elephant, fox, gerbil, gibbon, giraffe, goat, gorilla, guinea pig, hamster, hare, hedgehog, hippopotamus, horse, human being, hyena, kangaroo, koala, lemming, lemur, leopard, lion, manatee, marmoset, marmot, mole, mongoose, monkey, mouse, opossum, orang-utan, otter, panda, pig, porcupine, porpoise, rabbit, raccoon, rat, rhinoceros, sea cow, seal, sea lion, sheep, shrew, skunk, sloth, squirrel, tapir, tiger, vole, wallaby, walrus, weasel, whale, wolf, zebra. *See also* **animal**; **cat**; **dog**; **marsupial**; **rodent**.

man *noun* **1** *don't know that man*: male, gentleman, fellow, bloke (*infml*), chap (*infml*), guy (*infml*). **2** *all men are created equal*: human being, person, individual, adult, human. **3** *the evolution of man*: humanity, humankind, mankind, human race, people, Homo sapiens, mortals.
▪ *verb* staff, crew, take charge of, operate, occupy.

manage *verb* **1** *managed the task quite easily*: accomplish, succeed, bring about, bring off, effect. **2** *managing a small workforce*: administer, direct, run, command, govern, preside over, rule, superintend, supervise, oversee, conduct. **3** *manage money*: control, influence, deal with, handle, operate, manipulate, guide. **4** *can't manage on less than £200 per week*: cope, fare, survive, get by, get along, get on, make do.
≠ **1** fail. **2** mismanage.

management *noun* **1** *the overall management of the project*:

administration, direction, control, government, command, running, superintendence, supervision, charge, care, handling. **2** *management versus unions*: managers, directors, directorate, executive, executives, governors, board, bosses (*infml*), supervisors. **F3** **1** mismanagement. **2** workers.

manager *noun* director, executive, administrator, controller, superintendent, supervisor, overseer, governor, organizer, head, boss (*infml*).

mangle *verb* mutilate, disfigure, mar, maim, spoil, butcher, destroy, deform, wreck, twist, maul, distort, crush, cut, hack, tear, rend.

mania *noun* **1** *suffer from persecution mania*: madness, insanity, lunacy, psychosis, derangement, disorder, aberration, craziness (*infml*), frenzy. **2** *have a mania for collecting Chinese porcelain*: passion, craze, rage, obsession, compulsion, enthusiasm, fad (*infml*), infatuation, fixation, craving.

Manias (by name of disorder) include:

dipsomania (*alcohol*), bibliomania (*books*), ailuromania (*cats*), demomania (*crowds*), necromania (*dead bodies*), thanatomania (*death*), cynomania (*dogs*), narcomania (*drugs*), pyromania (*fire-raising*), anthomania (*flowers*), hippomania (*horses*), mythomania (*lying and exaggerating*), egomania (*oneself*), ablutomania (*personal cleanliness*), hedonomania (*pleasure*), megalomania (*power*), theomania (*religion*), monomania (*single idea or thing*), kleptomania (*stealing*), tomomania (*surgery*), logomania (*talking*), ergomania (*work*). *See also* **phobia**.

---

maniac *noun* **1** *attacked by a maniac*: lunatic, madman, madwoman, psychotic, psychopath, loony (*infml*), nutter (*infml*). **2** *a bit of a fitness maniac*: enthusiast, fan (*infml*), fanatic, fiend (*infml*), freak (*infml*).

manipulate *verb* **1** *manipulating the clay/an audience*: handle, control, wield, operate, use, manoeuvre, influence, engineer, guide, direct, steer, negotiate, work. **2** *manipulate the figures*: falsify, rig, juggle with, doctor (*infml*), cook (*infml*), fiddle (*infml*).

manner *noun* **1** *address him in the correct manner*: way, method, means, fashion, style, procedure, process, form. **2** *her manner is a little offhand*: behaviour, conduct, bearing, demeanour, air, appearance, look, character.

mannerism *noun* idiosyncrasy, peculiarity, characteristic, quirk, trait, feature, foible, habit.

manners *noun* behaviour, conduct, demeanour, etiquette, politeness, bearing, courtesy, formalities, social graces, p's and q's.

manoeuvre *noun* **1** *an overtaking manoeuvre*: move, movement, operation. **2** *a political manoeuvre*: action, exercise, plan, ploy, plot, ruse, stratagem, machination, gambit, tactic, trick, scheme, dodge (*infml*).

▪ *verb* move, manipulate, handle, guide, pilot, steer, navigate, jockey, direct, drive.

manual *noun* handbook, guide, guidebook, instructions, Bible, vade-mecum, directions.

▪ *adjective* hand-operated, by hand, physical, human.

automatic.

manufacture *verb* make, produce, construct, build, fabricate, create, assemble, mass-produce, turn out, process, forge, form.

many *adjective* numerous, countless, lots of (*infml*), manifold (*fml*), various, varied, sundry, diverse, umpteen (*infml*).

few.

march *verb* walk, stride, parade, pace, file, tread, stalk.

▪ *noun* **1** *advance at a slow march*: step, pace, stride. **2** *the long march home*: walk, trek, hike, footslog (*infml*). **3** *a peace march*: procession, parade, demonstration, demo (*infml*).

margin *noun* allowance, play, leeway, latitude, scope, room, space, surplus, extra.

marginal *adjective* borderline, peripheral, negligible, minimal, insignificant, minor, slight, doubtful, low, small.

central, core.

marital *adjective* conjugal, matrimonial, married, wedded, nuptial (*fml*), connubial (*fml*).

maritime *adjective* marine, nautical, naval, seafaring, sea, seaside, oceanic, coastal.

mark *noun* **1** *leave marks on the table/skin/paintwork*: spot, stain, blemish, blot, blotch, smudge, dent, impression, scar, scratch, bruise, line. **2** *a mark of good quality*: symbol, sign, indication, emblem, brand, stamp, token, characteristic, feature, proof, evidence, badge. **3** *hit the mark*: target, goal, aim, objective, purpose.

▪ *verb* **1** *marked the paintwork*: stain, blemish, blot, smudge, dent, scar, scratch, bruise. **2** *marked with a kite symbol*: brand, label, stamp, characterize, identify, distinguish. **3** *marking the exam papers*: evaluate, assess, correct, grade.

marked *adjective* noticeable, obvious, conspicuous, evident, pronounced, distinct, decided, emphatic, considerable, remarkable, apparent, glaring.

unnoticeable, slight.

marriage *noun* matrimony, wedlock, wedding, nuptials (*fml*).

divorce.

marry *verb* wed, join in matrimony, tie the knot (*infml*), get hitched (*infml*), get spliced (*infml*).

divorce.

marsh *noun* marshland, bog, swamp, fen, morass, quagmire, slough.

marsupial

Marsupials include:
bandicoot, cuscus, kangaroo, rat kangaroo, tree kangaroo, wallaroo, koala, marsupial anteater, marsupial mouse, marsupial mole, marsupial rat, opossum, pademelon, phalanger, Tasmanian devil, Tasmanian wolf, wallaby, rock wallaby, wombat.

marvel *noun* wonder, miracle, phenomenon, prodigy, spectacle, sensation, genius.
▪ *verb* wonder, gape, gaze, be amazed at.

marvellous *adjective* **1** *had a marvellous holiday*: wonderful, excellent, splendid, superb, magnificent, terrific (*infml*), super, fantastic (*infml*). **2** *a marvellous sight*: extraordinary, amazing, astonishing, astounding, miraculous, remarkable, surprising, unbelievable, incredible, glorious.
F3 **1** terrible, awful. **2** ordinary, run-of-the-mill.

masculine *adjective* male, manlike, manly, mannish, virile, macho, strong, muscular, powerful, vigorous.
F3 feminine, girly (*infml*).

mash *verb* crush, pulp, beat, pound, pulverize, pummel, grind, smash.

mask *noun* disguise, camouflage, façade, front, concealment, cover-up, cover, guise, pretence, semblance, cloak, veil, blind, show, veneer, visor.

mass *noun* **1** *a mass of rubbish/ masses of clothes*: heap, pile, load, accumulation, aggregate, collection, conglomeration, combination, entirety, whole, totality, sum, lot, group, batch, bunch. **2** *moved forward in a mass*: multitude, throng, troop, crowd, band, horde, mob. **3** *the greater mass of the population*: majority, body, bulk. **4** *measure its mass*: size, dimension, magnitude, immensity. **5** *forming a solid mass*: lump, piece, chunk, block, hunk.
▪ *adjective* widespread, large-scale, extensive, comprehensive, general, indiscriminate, popular, across-the-board, sweeping, wholesale, blanket.
F3 limited, small-scale.
▪ *verb* collect, gather, assemble, congregate, crowd, rally, cluster, muster, swarm, throng.
F3 separate.

massacre *noun* slaughter, murder, extermination, carnage, butchery, holocaust, bloodbath, annihilation, killing.
▪ *verb* slaughter, butcher, murder, mow down, wipe out, exterminate, annihilate, kill, decimate.

massive *adjective* huge, immense, enormous, vast, colossal, gigantic, big, bulky, monumental, solid, substantial, heavy, large-scale, extensive, whopping (*infml*).
F3 tiny, small.

master *noun* **1** *obey one's master*: ruler, chief, governor, head, lord, captain, boss (*infml*), employer, commander, controller, director, manager, superintendent, overseer, principal, overlord, owner. **2** *a chess master*: expert, genius, virtuoso, past master, maestro, dab hand (*infml*), ace (*infml*), pro (*infml*). **3** *the science master*: teacher, tutor, instructor, schoolmaster, guide, guru, preceptor (*fml*).
F3 **1** servant, underling. **2** amateur. **3** learner, pupil.
▪ *adjective* chief, principal, main, leading, foremost, prime, predominant, controlling, great, grand.
F3 subordinate.
▪ *verb* **1** *master one's fear*: conquer, defeat, subdue, subjugate, vanquish (*fml*), triumph over, overcome, quell, rule, control. **2** *master the basics*: learn, grasp, acquire, get the hang of (*infml*), manage.

masterful *adjective* arrogant, authoritative, domineering, overbearing, high-handed, despotic, dictatorial, autocratic, bossy (*infml*), tyrannical, powerful.
F3 humble, servile.

masterly *adjective* expert, skilled, skilful, dexterous, adept, adroit, first-rate, ace (*infml*), excellent, superb, superior, supreme.
F3 inept, clumsy.

masterpiece *noun* masterwork, magnum opus, pièce de résistance, jewel.

match *noun* **1** *a football/hockey match*: contest, competition, bout, game, test, trial. **2** *meet one's match*: equal, equivalent, peer, counterpart, fellow, mate, rival, copy, double, replica, look-alike, twin, duplicate.
▪ *verb* **1** *match its speed*: equal, compare, measure up to, rival, compete, oppose, contend, vie, pit against. **2** *colour matches your eyes*: fit, go with, accord, agree, suit, correspond, harmonize, tally, co-ordinate, blend, adapt, go together, relate, tone with, accompany. **3** *matching the girls up with suitable partners*: join, marry, unite, mate, link, couple, combine, ally, pair, yoke, team.
F3 **2** clash. **3** separate.

matching *adjective* corresponding, comparable, equivalent, like, identical, co-ordinating, similar, duplicate, same, twin.
F3 clashing.

mate *noun* **1** *my best mate*: friend, companion, comrade, pal (*infml*), colleague, partner, fellow-worker, co-worker, associate, buddy (*infml*), chum (*infml*). **2** *find a mate for life*: spouse, partner, husband, wife. **3** *a carpenter's mate*: assistant, helper, subordinate.

material *noun* **1** *material from the*

comet's tail: stuff, substance, body, matter. **2** *a material similar to velvet*: fabric, textile, cloth. **3** *it would make good material for a novel*: information, facts, data, evidence, constituents, work, notes.

mathematics

Terms used in mathematics include:

acute angle, addition, algebra, algorithm, analysis, angle, apex, approximate, arc, area, arithmetic, arithmetic progression, asymmetrical, average, axis, axis of symmetry, bar chart, bar graph, base, bearing, binary, binomial, breadth, calculus, cardinal number, Cartesian co-ordinates, circumference, coefficient, combination, complement, complementary angle, complex number, concave, concentric circles, congruent, conjugate angles, constant, converse, convex, co-ordinate, correlation, cosine, cross-section, cube, cube root, cuboid, curve, decimal, degree, denominator, determinant, diagonal, diameter, differentiation, distribution, dividend, division, equation, equidistant, even number, exponent, exponential, factor, factorial, Fibonacci sequence, formula, fraction, function, geometric progression, geometry, gradient, graph, helix, histogram, horizontal, hyperbola, hypotenuse, infinity, integer, integration, intersecting, irrational number, line graph, locus, logarithm, longitude, magic square, matrix, maximum, mean, measure, median, Möbius strip, mode, modulus, multiple, natural logarithm, natural number, negative number, numerator, oblique angle, obtuse angle, ordinal number, origin, parabola, parallel lines, parallel planes, parameter, percentage, percentile, perimeter, permutation, perpendicular, pi, pie chart, plane figure, positive number, prime number, prism, probability, product, proportion, protractor, Pythagoras' theorem, quadrant, quadratic equation, quadrilateral, quartile, quotient, radian, radius, ratio, rational number, real number, reciprocal, recurring decimal, reflex angle, remainder, right-angle, right-angled triangle, root, rotation, rotational symmetry, scalar, sector, segment, set, simultaneous equation, sine, square, square root, statistics, subset, subtraction, supplementary angle, symmetry, tangent, tangram, three-dimensional, triangulation, trigonometry, unit, universal set, variable, variance, vector, velocity, Venn diagram, vertex, vertical, volume, whole number. *See also* **shape**.

matter *noun* **1** *a very serious matter*: subject, issue, topic, question, affair, business,

concern, event, episode, incident. **2** *what's the matter?*: trouble, problem, difficulty, worry. **3** *organic matter*: substance, stuff, material, body, content.
▪ *verb* count, be important, make a difference, mean something.

matter-of-fact *adjective* unemotional, prosaic, emotionless, straightforward, sober, unimaginative, flat, deadpan (*infml*).
F3 emotional.

mature *adjective* **1** *a mature young man/attitude*: adult, grown-up, grown, full-grown, fully fledged, complete, perfect, perfected, well-thought-out. **2** *mature wood*: ripe, ripened, seasoned, mellow, ready.
F3 1 childish. **2** immature.
▪ *verb* grow up, come of age, develop, mellow, ripen, perfect, age, bloom, fall due.

maximum *adjective* greatest, highest, largest, biggest, most, utmost, supreme.
F3 minimum.
▪ *noun* most, top (point), utmost, upper limit, peak, pinnacle, summit, height, ceiling, extremity, zenith.
F3 minimum.

maybe *adverb* perhaps, possibly, perchance (*fml*).
F3 definitely.

meagre *adjective* scanty,sparse, inadequate, deficient, skimpy, paltry, negligible, poor.
F3 ample.

meal

Meals include:
afternoon tea, banquet, barbecue, barbie (*infml*), blow-out (*slang*), breakfast, brunch, buffet, cream tea, dinner, elevenses (*infml*), evening meal, feast, fork supper, harvest supper, high tea, lunch, luncheon, picnic, snack, spread, supper, take-away, tea, tea break, tea party, tiffin, TV dinner, wedding breakfast.

mean[1] *adjective* **1** *too mean to spend the money*: miserly, niggardly, parsimonious, selfish, tight (*infml*), tight-fisted, stingy (*infml*), penny-pinching (*infml*). **2** *a mean thing to say*: unkind, unpleasant, nasty, bad-tempered, cruel.
F3 1 generous. **2** kind.

mean[2] *verb* **1** *what does this word mean?*: signify, represent, denote, stand for, symbolize, suggest, indicate, imply. **2** *what do you mean to do?*: intend, aim, propose, design. **3** *it will mean severe cutbacks*: cause, give rise to, involve, entail.

meaning *noun* **1** *the meaning of the phrase*: significance, sense, import, implication, gist, trend, explanation, interpretation. **2** *what's the meaning of this behaviour?*: aim, intention, purpose, object, idea. **3** *gives her life some meaning*: value, worth, point.

meaningful *adjective* **1** *a*

meaningful look: expressive, significant, suggestive, warning, pointed. **2** *meaningful employment*: important, relevant, valid, useful, worthwhile, material, purposeful, serious.

F3 2 unimportant, worthless.

meaningless *adjective* **1** *a meaningless statement*: senseless, pointless, purposeless, useless, insignificant, aimless, futile, insubstantial, trifling, trivial. **2** *a meaningless existence*: empty, hollow, vacuous, vain, worthless, nonsensical, absurd.

F3 1 important, meaningful. **2** worthwhile.

means *noun* **1** *the means of production/a means of travel*: method, mode, way, medium, course, agency, process, instrument, channel, vehicle. **2** *a man of means/have the means to buy a house*: resources, funds, money, income, wealth, riches, substance, wherewithal, fortune, affluence.

measure *noun* **1** *short measure*: size, quantity, magnitude, amount, degree, extent, range, scope. **2** *a tape measure/a measure of efficiency*: rule, gauge, scale, standard, criterion, norm, touchstone, yardstick, test, meter. **3** *introduce new measures to control imports*: step, course, action, deed, procedure, method, act, bill, statute. **4** *has had his fair measure of bad luck*: portion, ration, share, allocation, quota, proportion.

■ *verb* quantify, evaluate, assess, weigh, value, gauge, judge, sound, fathom, determine, calculate, estimate, plumb, survey, compute, measure out, measure off.

measurement *noun* **1** *take the measurements of the hall*: dimension, size, extent, amount, magnitude, area, capacity, height, depth, length, width, weight, volume. **2** *a good measurement of the scheme's success*: assessment, evaluation, estimation, computation, calculation, calibration, gauging, judgement, appraisal, appreciation, survey.

mechanical *adjective* automatic, involuntary, instinctive, routine, habitual, impersonal, emotionless, cold, matter-of-fact, unfeeling, lifeless, dead, dull.

F3 conscious.

mechanism *noun* **1** *the clock's mechanism*: machine, machinery, engine, appliance, instrument, tool, motor, works, workings, gadget, device, apparatus, contrivance, gears, components. **2** *find some mechanism for making quick payments*: means, method, agency, process, procedure, system, technique, medium, structure, operation, functioning, performance.

meddle *verb* interfere, intervene, pry, snoop (*infml*), intrude, butt in, tamper.

medicinal *adjective* therapeutic, healing, remedial, curative, restorative, medical.

medicine *noun* medication, drug, cure, remedy, medicament, prescription, pharmaceutical, panacea.

medium[1] *adjective* average, middle, median, mean, medial, intermediate, middling, midway, standard, fair.

medium[2] *noun* **1** *a medium for informing local people*: means, agency, channel, vehicle, instrument, way, mode, form, avenue, organ *(fml)*. **2** *a spiritual medium*: psychic, spiritualist, spiritist, clairvoyant.

meek *adjective* modest, long-suffering, forbearing, humble, docile, patient, unassuming, unpretentious, resigned, gentle, peaceful, tame, timid, submissive, spiritless.
F3 arrogant, assertive, rebellious.

meet *verb* **1** *met him in the street*: encounter, come across, run across, run into, chance on, bump into *(infml)*. **2** *met with an accident*: experience, encounter, face, go through, undergo, endure. **3** *meet at the station*: gather, collect, assemble, congregate, convene. **4** *meet the target*: fulfil, satisfy, match, answer, measure up to, equal, discharge, perform. **5** *meet in the middle*: join, converge, come together, connect, cross, intersect, touch, abut, unite.
F3 **3** scatter. **5** diverge.

meeting *noun* **1** *their first meeting*: encounter, confrontation, rendezvous, engagement, assignation, introduction, tryst *(fml)*. **2** *call a meeting of the council*: assembly, gathering, congregation, conference, convention, rally, get-together, forum, conclave, session. **3** *a meeting of minds*: convergence, confluence, junction, intersection, union.

mellow *adjective* **1** *tastes warm and mellow*: mature, smooth, ripe, juicy, full-flavoured, sweet, tender, mild. **2** *became more mellow as he got older*: genial, cordial, affable, pleasant, relaxed, easy-going, placid, serene, tranquil, cheerful, happy, jolly. **3** *a mellow sound*: melodious, rich, rounded, soft.
F3 **1** unripe. **2** cold. **3** harsh.
▪ *verb* mature, ripen, improve, sweeten, soften, temper, season, perfect.

melodramatic *adjective* histrionic, theatrical, overdramatic, exaggerated, overemotional, sensational, hammy *(infml)*.

melt *verb* liquefy, dissolve, thaw, fuse, deliquesce *(fml)*.
F3 freeze, solidify.

member *noun* adherent, associate, subscriber, representative, comrade, fellow.

memento *noun* souvenir, keepsake, remembrance, reminder, token, memorial, record, relic.

memoirs *noun* reminiscences, recollections, autobiography, life story, diary, chronicles, annals, journals, records, confessions, experiences.

memorable *adjective* unforgettable, remarkable, significant, impressive, notable, noteworthy, extraordinary, important, outstanding, momentous.
F3 forgettable, trivial, unimportant.

memorial *noun* remembrance, monument, souvenir, memento, record, stone, plaque, mausoleum.

memorize *verb* learn, learn by heart, commit to memory, remember.
F3 forget.

memory *noun* recall, retention, recollection, remembrance, reminiscence, commemoration.
F3 forgetfulness.

menace *noun* **1** *voice full of menace*: intimidation, threat, terrorism, warning. **2** *combat the menace of drinking and driving*: danger, peril, hazard, jeopardy, risk. **3** *cats are becoming a menace*: nuisance, annoyance, pest.

mend *verb* **1** *mend a road/tear/shoes*: repair, renovate, restore, refit, fix, patch, cobble, darn, heal. **2** *he's mending slowly*: recover, get better, improve. **3** *mend the mistakes of the past*: remedy, correct, rectify, reform, revise.
F3 1 break. **2** deteriorate. **3** destroy.

mental *adjective* **1** *mental exercises/processes*: intellectual, abstract, conceptual, cognitive, cerebral, theoretical, rational. **2** *(infml) go mental*: mad, insane, lunatic, crazy, unbalanced, deranged, psychotic, disturbed, loony *(infml)*.
F3 1 physical. **2** sane.

mentality *noun* frame of mind, attitude, character, disposition, personality, psychology, outlook.

mention *verb* refer to, speak of, allude to, touch on, name, cite, acknowledge, bring up, report, make known, impart, declare, communicate, broach, divulge, disclose, intimate, point out, reveal, state, hint at, quote.
▪ *noun* reference, allusion, citation, observation, recognition, remark, acknowledgement, announcement, notification, tribute, indication.

merchant *noun* trader, dealer, broker, trafficker, wholesaler, retailer, seller, shopkeeper, vendor.

merciful *adjective* compassionate, forgiving, forbearing, humane, lenient, sparing, tender-hearted, pitying, gracious, humanitarian, kind, liberal, sympathetic, generous, mild.
F3 hard-hearted, merciless.

merciless *adjective* pitiless, relentless, unmerciful, ruthless, hard-hearted, hard, heartless, implacable, inhumane, unforgiving, remorseless, unpitying, unsparing, severe, cruel, callous, inhuman.
F3 compassionate, merciful.

mercy *noun* compassion, clemency, forgiveness, forbearance, leniency, pity, humanitarianism, kindness, grace.
F3 cruelty, harshness.

mere *adjective* sheer, plain, simple, bare, utter, pure, absolute, complete, stark, unadulterated, common, paltry, petty.

merge *verb* join, unite, combine, converge, amalgamate, blend, coalesce, mix, intermix, mingle, melt into, fuse, meet, meld, incorporate, consolidate.

merit *noun* worth, excellence, value, quality, good, goodness, virtue, asset, credit, advantage, strong point, talent, justification, due, claim.
F3 fault.
▪ *verb* deserve, be worthy of, earn, justify, warrant.

merry *adjective* jolly, light-hearted, mirthful, joyful, happy, convivial, festive, cheerful, glad.
F3 gloomy, melancholy, sober.

mesh *noun* net, network, netting, lattice, web, tangle, entanglement, snare, trap.

mess *noun* **1** *clearing up the mess after the party*: chaos, untidiness, disorder, disarray, confusion, muddle, jumble, clutter, disorganization, mix-up, shambles (*infml*). **2** *got himself into a mess financially*: difficulty, trouble, predicament, fix (*infml*), jam (*infml*), pickle (*infml*).
F3 **1** order, tidiness.

message *noun* **1** *got an urgent message*: communication, bulletin, dispatch, communiqué, report, missive (*fml*), errand, letter, memorandum, note, notice, cable, fax, e-mail, text. **2** *the message in the song*: meaning, idea, point, theme, moral.

messenger *noun* courier, emissary, envoy, go-between, herald, runner, carrier, bearer, harbinger, agent, ambassador.

messy *adjective* untidy, unkempt, dishevelled, disorganized, chaotic, sloppy, slovenly, confused, dirty, grubby, muddled, cluttered.
F3 neat, ordered, tidy.

method *noun* **1** *teaching methods*: way, approach, means, course, manner, mode, fashion, process, procedure, route, technique, style, plan, scheme, programme. **2** *need to apply some method to your work*: organization, order, structure, system, pattern, form, planning, regularity, routine.

methodical *adjective* systematic, structured, organized, ordered, orderly, tidy, regular, planned, efficient, disciplined, businesslike, deliberate, neat, scrupulous, precise, meticulous, painstaking.
F3 chaotic, irregular, confused.

meticulous *adjective* precise, scrupulous, exact, punctilious, fussy, detailed, accurate, thorough, fastidious, painstaking, strict.
F3 careless, slapdash.

middle *adjective* central, halfway, mean, median, inner, intermediate, inside, intervening.
▪ *noun* centre, halfway point, mid-point, mean, heart, core, midst, inside, bull's eye.
F3 extreme, end, edge, beginning, border.

midget *noun* person of restricted growth, pygmy, dwarf, Tom Thumb.
F3 giant.

midst *noun* middle, centre, mid-point, heart, hub, interior.

migrate *verb* move, resettle, relocate, wander, roam, rove, journey, emigrate, travel, voyage, trek, drift.

mild *adjective* **1** *mild manners*: gentle, calm, peaceable, placid, tender, soft, good-natured, kind, amiable, lenient, compassionate. **2** *mild weather*: calm, temperate, warm, balmy, clement, fair, pleasant. **3** *mild curry*: bland, mellow, smooth, subtle, soothing.
F3 **1** harsh, fierce. **2** stormy. **3** strong.

militant *adjective* aggressive, belligerent, vigorous, fighting, warring.
F3 pacifist, peaceful.
▪ *noun* activist, combatant, fighter, struggler, warrior, aggressor, belligerent.

military *adjective* martial, armed, soldierly, warlike, service.

milk *verb* drain, bleed, tap, extract, draw off, exploit, use, express, press, pump, siphon, squeeze, wring.

milky *adjective* white, milk-white, chalky, opaque, clouded, cloudy.

mill *noun* **1** *woollen mill/steel mill*: factory, plant, works, workshop, foundry. **2** *pepper mill*: grinder, crusher, quern, roller.

mimic *verb* imitate, parody, caricature, take off (*infml*), ape, parrot, impersonate, echo, mirror, simulate, look like.

mind *noun* **1** *using your mind*: intelligence, intellect, brains, reason, sense, understanding, wits, mentality, thinking, thoughts, grey matter (*infml*), head, genius, concentration, attention, spirit, psyche. **2** *come to mind*: memory, remembrance, recollection. **3** *we're of the same mind*: opinion, view, point of view, belief, attitude, judgement, feeling, sentiment. **4** *have a good mind to object*: inclination, disposition, tendency, will, wish, intention, desire.
▪ *verb* **1** *didn't mind the noise*: care, object, take offence, resent, disapprove, dislike. **2** *mind the step*: regard, heed, pay attention, pay heed to, note, obey, listen to, comply with, follow, observe, be careful, watch. **3** *minding the shop*: look after, take care of, watch over, guard, have charge of, keep an eye on (*infml*).

mindless *adjective* thoughtless, senseless, illogical, irrational, stupid, foolish, gratuitous, negligent.
F3 thoughtful, intelligent.

mine *noun* **1** *a coal/gold/diamond mine*: pit, colliery, coalfield, excavation, vein, seam, shaft, trench, deposit. **2** *a mine of information*: supply, source, stock, store, reserve, fund, hoard, treasury, wealth.
▪ *verb* excavate, dig for, dig up, delve, quarry, extract, unearth, tunnel, remove, undermine.

mingle *verb* **1** *joy mingled with a touch of regret*: mix, intermingle, intermix, combine, blend, merge, unite, alloy, coalesce, join, compound. **2** *mingling with the crowd*: associate, socialize, circulate, hobnob (*infml*), rub shoulders (*infml*).

miniature *adjective* tiny, small, scaled-down, minute, diminutive, baby, pocket-size(d), pint-size(d) (*infml*), little, mini (*infml*).
F3 giant.

minimal *adjective* least, smallest, minimum, slightest, littlest, negligible, minute, token.

minimize *verb* **1** *minimize the risk of failure*: reduce, decrease, diminish. **2** *minimized his achievements*: belittle, make light of, make little of, disparage (*fml*), deprecate (*fml*), discount, play down, underestimate, underrate.
F3 1 maximize.

minimum *noun* least, lowest point, slightest, bottom.
F3 maximum.
▪ *adjective* minimal, least, lowest, slightest, smallest, littlest, tiniest.
F3 maximum.

minister *noun* **1** *a government minister*: official, office-holder, politician, dignitary, diplomat, ambassador, delegate, envoy, consul, cabinet minister, agent, aide, administrator, executive. **2** *a local minister conducted the service*: clergyman, clergywoman, churchman, churchwoman, cleric, parson, priest, pastor, vicar, preacher, ecclesiastic (*fml*), divine.

minor *adjective* lesser, secondary, smaller, inferior, subordinate, subsidiary, junior, younger, insignificant, inconsiderable, negligible, petty, trivial, trifling, second-class, unclassified, slight, light.
F3 major, significant, important.

minute[1] *noun* /**min**-it/ moment, second, instant, flash, jiffy (*infml*), tick (*infml*).

minute[2] *adjective* /mai-**nyoot**/ tiny, infinitesimal, minuscule, microscopic, miniature, inconsiderable, negligible, small.
F3 gigantic, huge.

miraculous *adjective* wonderful, marvellous, phenomenal, extraordinary, amazing, astounding, astonishing, unbelievable, supernatural, incredible, inexplicable, unaccountable, superhuman.
F3 natural, normal.

mirror *noun* glass, looking-glass, reflector.
▪ *verb* reflect, echo, imitate, copy, represent, show, depict, mimic.

misbehave *verb* offend, transgress, trespass (*fml*), get up to mischief, mess about (*infml*), muck about (*infml*), play up (*infml*), act up (*infml*).

miscellaneous *adjective* mixed, varied, various, assorted, diverse, diversified, sundry, motley, jumbled, indiscriminate.

mischievous *adjective* **1** *a mischievous child*: naughty, impish, rascally, roguish, playful, teasing. **2** *a mischievous lie*: malicious, evil, spiteful, vicious, wicked, pernicious, destructive, injurious.
F3 **1** well-behaved, good. **2** kind.

miserable *adjective* **1** *the news made him miserable*: unhappy, sad, dejected, despondent, downcast, heartbroken, wretched, distressed, crushed. **2** *a miserable wet day*: cheerless, depressing, dreary, impoverished, shabby, gloomy, dismal, forlorn, joyless. **3** *a miserable state of affairs*: contemptible, despicable, ignominious, detestable, disgraceful, deplorable, shameful.
F3 **1** cheerful, happy. **2** pleasant.

misery *noun* **1** *her expression was one of complete misery*: unhappiness, sadness, suffering, distress, depression, despair, gloom, grief, wretchedness, affliction. **2** *lived a life of misery in terrible conditions*: privation (*fml*), hardship, deprivation, poverty, want, oppression, destitution. **3** (*infml*) *don't be such an old misery!*: spoilsport, pessimist, killjoy, wet blanket (*infml*).
F3 **1** contentment. **2** comfort.

misfortune *noun* bad luck, mischance, mishap, ill-luck, setback, reverse, calamity, catastrophe, disaster, blow, accident, tragedy, trouble, hardship, trial, tribulation.
F3 luck, success.

misguided *adjective* misled, misconceived, ill-considered, ill-advised, ill-judged, imprudent, rash, misplaced, deluded, foolish, erroneous.
F3 sensible, wise.

misinterpret *verb* misconstrue, misread, misunderstand, mistake, distort, garble.

misjudge *verb* miscalculate, mistake, misinterpret, misconstrue, misunderstand, overestimate, underestimate.

mislay *verb* lose, misplace, miss, lose sight of.

mislead *verb* misinform, misdirect, deceive, delude, lead astray, fool.

misleading *adjective* deceptive, confusing, unreliable, ambiguous, biased, loaded, evasive, tricky (*infml*).
F3 unequivocal, authoritative, informative.

miss *verb* **1** *missed his chance/ missed the point*: fail, miscarry, lose, let slip, let go, omit, overlook, pass over, slip, leave out, mistake, trip, misunderstand, err. **2** *just missed a pedestrian/missed a couple of pages*: avoid, escape,

evade, dodge, forego, skip, bypass, circumvent. **3** *missing his family*: pine for, long for, yearn for, regret, grieve for, mourn, sorrow for, want, wish, need, lament.
▪ *noun* failure, error, blunder, mistake, omission, oversight, fault, flop (*infml*), fiasco.

missile *noun* projectile, shot, guided missile, arrow, shaft, dart, rocket, bomb, shell, flying bomb, grenade, torpedo, weapon.

missing *adjective* absent, lost, lacking, gone, mislaid, unaccounted-for, wanting, disappeared, astray, strayed, misplaced.
F3 found, present.

mission *noun* **1** *a peace mission*: task, undertaking, assignment, operation, campaign, crusade, business, errand. **2** *his mission in life*: calling, duty, purpose, vocation, raison d'être, aim, goal, quest, pursuit, charge, office, job, work.

mist *noun* haze, fog, vapour, smog, cloud, condensation, film, spray, drizzle, dew, steam, veil, dimness.

mistake *noun* error, inaccuracy, slip, slip-up (*infml*), oversight, lapse, blunder, clanger (*infml*), boob (*infml*), gaffe, fault, faux pas, solecism (*fml*), indiscretion, misjudgement, miscalculation, misunderstanding, misprint, misspelling, misreading, mispronunciation, howler (*infml*).
▪ *verb* misunderstand, misapprehend, misconstrue, misjudge, misread, miscalculate, confound, confuse, slip up, blunder, err.

mistaken *adjective* wrong, incorrect, erroneous, inaccurate, inexact, untrue, inappropriate, ill-judged, inauthentic, false, deceived, deluded, misinformed, misled, faulty.
F3 correct, right.

mistreat *verb* abuse, ill-treat, ill-use, maltreat, harm, hurt, batter, injure, knock about, molest.

misty *adjective* hazy, foggy, cloudy, blurred, fuzzy, murky, smoky, unclear, dim, indistinct, obscure, opaque, vague, veiled.
F3 clear.

misunderstanding *noun* **1** *a misunderstanding of the instructions*: mistake, error, misapprehension, misconception, misjudgement, misinterpretation, misreading, mix-up. **2** *they've had a slight misunderstanding*: disagreement, argument, dispute, conflict, clash, difference, breach, quarrel, discord, rift.
F3 **1** understanding. **2** agreement.

misuse *noun* mistreatment, maltreatment, abuse, harm, ill-treatment, misapplication, misappropriation, waste, perversion, corruption, exploitation.
▪ *verb* abuse, misapply, misemploy, ill-use, ill-treat, harm, mistreat, wrong, distort, injure, corrupt, pervert, waste, squander,

misappropriate, exploit, dissipate.

mix *verb* **1** *mix the ingredients in a bowl*: combine, blend, mingle, intermingle, intermix, amalgamate, compound, homogenize, synthesize, merge, join, unite, coalesce, fuse, incorporate, fold in. **2** *doesn't mix with the locals much*: associate, consort, fraternize, socialize, mingle, join, hobnob (*infml*).
F3 **1** divide, separate.

mixed *adjective* **1** *of mixed race*: combined, hybrid, mingled, crossbred, mongrel, blended, composite, compound, incorporated, united, alloyed, amalgamated, fused. **2** *mixed biscuits*: assorted, varied, miscellaneous, diverse, diversified, motley. **3** *have mixed feelings*: ambivalent, equivocal, conflicting, contradicting, uncertain.

mixture *noun* mix, blend, combination, amalgamation, amalgam, compound, conglomeration, composite, coalescence, alloy, brew, synthesis, union, fusion, concoction, cross, hybrid, assortment, variety, miscellany, medley, mélange, mixed bag, pot-pourri, jumble, hotchpotch.

moan *verb* **1** *women crying and moaning*: lament, wail, sob, weep, howl, groan, whimper, mourn, grieve. **2** (*infml*) *always moaning about something*: complain, grumble, whine, whinge (*infml*), gripe (*infml*), carp.
F3 **1** rejoice.

mob *noun* crowd, mass, throng, multitude, horde, host, swarm, gathering, group, collection, flock, herd, pack, set, tribe, troop, company, crew, gang.
▪ *verb* crowd, crowd round, surround, swarm round, jostle, overrun, set upon, besiege, descend on, throng, pack, pester, charge.

mobile *adjective* **1** *a mobile home*: moving, movable, portable, peripatetic, travelling, roaming, roving, itinerant, wandering, migrant. **2** *exercises to keep the joints mobile*: flexible, agile, active, energetic, nimble. **3** *the mime artist's mobile features*: changing, changeable, ever-changing, expressive, lively.
F3 **1** immobile, static.

mock *verb* ridicule, jeer, make fun of, laugh at, disparage (*fml*), deride, scoff, sneer, taunt, scorn, tease.
▪ *adjective* imitation, counterfeit, artificial, sham, simulated, synthetic, false, fake, forged, fraudulent, bogus, phoney (*infml*), pseudo, spurious, feigned, faked, pretended, dummy, faux.

mocking *adjective* scornful, derisive, contemptuous, sarcastic, satirical, taunting, scoffing, sardonic, snide (*infml*), insulting, irreverent, impudent, disrespectful, disdainful, cynical.

model *noun* **1** *a cardboard model*

of the ship: copy, replica, representation, facsimile, imitation, mock-up. **2** *a model of what a soldier ought to be*: example, exemplar, pattern, standard, ideal, mould, prototype, template. **3** *buy the latest model*: design, style, type, version, mark. **4** *a fashion model/an artist's model*: mannequin, supermodel, dummy, sitter, subject, poser.

▪ *adjective* exemplary, perfect, typical, ideal.

▪ *verb* **1** *modelling it from clay*: make, form, fashion, mould, sculpt, carve, cast, shape, work, create, design, plan. **2** *modelling the designer's latest collection*: display, wear, show off.

moderate *adjective* **1** *the accommodation was good but the weather was only moderate*: medium, ordinary, fair, indifferent, average, middle-of-the-road, middling. **2** *take a more moderate view*: reasonable, restrained, sensible, calm, controlled, cool, mild, well-regulated.

F3 **1** exceptional. **2** immoderate.

moderately *adverb* somewhat, quite, rather, fairly, slightly, reasonably, passably, to some extent.

F3 extremely.

modern *adjective* current, contemporary, up-to-date, new, fresh, latest, late, novel, present, present-day, recent, up-to-the-minute, newfangled (*infml*), advanced, avant-garde, progressive, modernistic, innovative, inventive, state-of-the-art, go-ahead, fashionable, stylish, in vogue, in style, modish, trendy (*infml*), hip (*infml*).

F3 old-fashioned, old, out-of-date, antiquated.

modernize *verb* renovate, refurbish, rejuvenate, regenerate, streamline, revamp, renew, update, improve, do up, redesign, reform, remake, remodel, refresh, transform, modify, progress.

F3 regress.

modest *adjective* **1** *a modest man*: unassuming, humble, self-effacing, quiet, reserved, retiring, unpretentious, discreet, bashful, shy. **2** *makes a modest living*: moderate, ordinary, unexceptional, fair, reasonable, limited, small.

F3 **1** immodest, conceited. **2** exceptional, excessive.

modify *verb* **1** *modified their plans*: change, alter, redesign, revise, vary, adapt, adjust, tweak (*infml*), transform, reform, convert, improve, reorganize. **2** *modify the aggressive tone of the letter*: moderate, reduce, temper, tone down, limit, soften, qualify.

moist *adjective* damp, clammy, humid, wet, dewy, rainy, muggy, marshy, drizzly, watery, soggy.

F3 dry, arid.

moisten *verb* moisturize, dampen, damp, wet, water, lick, irrigate.

F3 dry.

moisture *noun* water, liquid, wetness, wateriness, damp, dampness, dankness, humidity, vapour, dew, mugginess, condensation, steam, spray.
☒ dryness.

mollusc

Molluscs include:
abalone, conch, cowrie, cuttlefish, clam, cockle, limpet, mussel, nautilus, nudibranch, octopus, oyster, periwinkle, scallop, sea slug, slug, freshwater snail, land snail, marine snail, squid, tusk shell, whelk. *See also* **invertebrate**.

moment *noun* second, instant, minute, split second, trice, jiffy (*infml*), tick (*infml*).

momentary *adjective* brief, short, short-lived, temporary, transient, transitory, fleeting, ephemeral, hasty, quick, passing.
☒ lasting, permanent.

momentum *noun* impetus, force, energy, impulse, drive, power, thrust, speed, velocity, impact, incentive, stimulus, urge, strength, push.

money *noun* currency, cash, legal tender, banknotes, coin, funds, capital, dough (*infml*), dosh (*infml*), riches, wealth.

mongrel *noun* cross, crossbreed, hybrid, half-breed.

monitor *noun* **1** *a computer monitor*: screen, display, VDU, recorder, scanner. **2** *the milk monitor*: supervisor, watchdog, overseer, invigilator, adviser, prefect.
▪ *verb* check, watch, keep track of, keep under surveillance, keep an eye on, follow, track, supervise, observe, note, survey, trace, scan, record, plot, detect.

monopolize *verb* dominate, take over, appropriate, corner, control, hog (*infml*), engross, occupy, preoccupy, take up, tie up.
☒ share.

monster *noun* beast, fiend, brute, barbarian, savage, villain, giant, ogre, ogress, troll, mammoth, freak, monstrosity, mutant.
▪ *adjective* huge, gigantic, giant, colossal, enormous, immense, massive, monstrous, jumbo, mammoth, vast, tremendous.
☒ tiny, minute.

monstrous *adjective* **1** *that was a monstrous thing to do*: wicked, evil, vicious, cruel, criminal, heinous (*fml*), outrageous, scandalous, disgraceful, atrocious, abhorrent (*fml*), dreadful, frightful, horrible, horrifying, terrible. **2** *a monstrous appearance*: unnatural, inhuman, freakish, grotesque, hideous, deformed, malformed, misshapen. **3** *a monstrous sum of money*: huge, enormous, colossal, gigantic, vast, immense, massive, mammoth.

monument *noun* memorial, cenotaph, headstone, gravestone, tombstone, shrine, mausoleum, cairn, barrow, cross, marker, obelisk, pillar, statue, relic, remembrance, commemoration, testament, reminder, record, memento, evidence, token.

monumental *adjective* **1** *a monumental decision*: impressive, imposing, awe-inspiring, awesome, overwhelming, significant, important, epoch-making, historic, magnificent, majestic, memorable, notable, outstanding, abiding, immortal, lasting, classic. **2** *a monumental mistake*: huge, immense, enormous, colossal, vast, tremendous, massive, great. **3** *monumental statues*: commemorative, memorial.
F3 **1** insignificant, unimportant.

mood *noun* **1** *gauge the mood of the nation*: disposition, frame of mind, state of mind, temper, humour, spirit, tenor, whim. **2** *in one of his moods*: bad temper, sulk, the sulks, pique, melancholy, depression, blues (*infml*), doldrums, dumps (*infml*).

moody *adjective* changeable, temperamental, unpredictable, capricious, irritable, short-tempered, crabby (*infml*), crotchety, crusty (*infml*), testy, touchy, morose, angry, broody, mopey, sulky, sullen, gloomy, melancholy, miserable, downcast, doleful, glum, impulsive, fickle, flighty.
F3 equable, cheerful.

moor[1] *verb* fasten, secure, tie up, drop anchor, anchor, berth, dock, make fast, fix, hitch, bind.
F3 loose.

moor[2] *noun* moorland, heath, fell, upland.

mop *verb* swab, sponge, wipe, clean, wash, absorb, soak.

mope *verb* brood, fret, sulk, pine, languish, droop, despair, grieve, idle.

moral *adjective* ethical, virtuous, good, right, principled, honourable, decent, upright, upstanding, straight, righteous, high-minded, honest, incorruptible, proper, blameless, chaste, clean-living, pure, just, noble.
F3 immoral.
▪ *noun* lesson, message, teaching, dictum, meaning, maxim, adage, precept (*fml*), saying, proverb, aphorism, epigram.

morale *noun* confidence, spirits, esprit de corps, self-esteem, state of mind, heart, mood.

morality *noun* ethics, morals, ideals, principles, standards, virtue, rectitude, righteousness, decency, goodness, honesty, integrity, justice, uprightness, propriety, conduct, manners.
F3 immorality.

morals *noun* morality, ethics, principles, standards, ideals, integrity, scruples, behaviour, conduct, habits, manners.

morbid *adjective* **1** *a morbid story of death and destruction*: ghoulish, ghastly, gruesome, macabre, hideous, horrid, grim. **2** *a morbid view of life*: gloomy, pessimistic, melancholy, sombre.

more *adjective* further, extra, additional, added, new, fresh, increased, other, supplementary, repeated, alternative, spare.
⇄ less.
▪ *adverb* further, longer, again, besides, moreover, better.
⇄ less.

moreover *adverb* furthermore, further, besides, in addition, as well, also, additionally, what is more.

mortal *adjective* **1** *his mortal remains*: worldly, earthly, bodily, human, perishable, temporal. **2** *a mortal wound*: fatal, lethal, deadly.
⇄ **1** immortal.
▪ *noun* human being, human, individual, person, being, body, creature.
⇄ immortal, god.

mortality *noun* **1** *aware of one's own mortality*: humanity, death, impermanence, perishability. **2** *a high rate of infant mortality*: fatality, death rate.
⇄ **1** immortality.

mostly *adverb* mainly, on the whole, principally, chiefly, generally, usually, largely, for the most part, as a rule.

mother *noun* parent, procreator (*fml*), progenitress (*fml*), dam, mamma (*infml*), mum (*infml*), mummy (*infml*), ma (*infml*), matriarch, ancestor, matron, old woman (*infml*).
▪ *verb* pamper, spoil, baby, indulge, overprotect, fuss over.

motherly *adjective* maternal, caring, comforting, affectionate, kind, loving, protective, warm, tender, gentle, fond.
⇄ neglectful, uncaring.

motif *noun* theme, idea, topic, concept, pattern, design, figure, form, logo, shape, device, ornament, decoration.

motion *noun* **1** *in constant motion*: movement, action, mobility, moving, activity, locomotion, travel, progress, change, flow. **2** *put forward a motion*: proposal, suggestion, recommendation, proposition.
▪ *verb* signal, gesture, gesticulate, sign, wave, nod, beckon, direct, usher.

motionless *adjective* unmoving, still, stationary, static, immobile, at a standstill, fixed, halted, at rest, resting, standing, paralysed, inanimate, lifeless, frozen, rigid, stagnant.
⇄ active, moving.

motivate *verb* prompt, incite, impel, spur, provoke, stimulate, drive, lead, stir, urge, push, propel, persuade, move, inspire, encourage, cause, trigger, induce, kindle, draw, arouse, bring.
⇄ deter, discourage.

motive *noun* ground(s), cause, reason, purpose, motivation, object, intention, urge, influence, rationale, thinking, incentive, impulse, stimulus, desire, inspiration, incitement, design, encouragement, consideration.
⇄ deterrent, disincentive.

motto *noun* saying, slogan, maxim, watchword, catchword, byword, precept (*fml*), proverb, adage, formula, rule, golden rule, dictum.

mould *noun* cast, form, die, template, pattern, matrix.
▪ *verb* **1** *moulding the clay*: forge, cast, shape, stamp, make, form, create, design, construct, sculpt, model, work. **2** *moulding young minds*: influence, direct, control.

mouldy *adjective* mildewed, blighted, musty, decaying, corrupt, rotten, fusty, putrid, bad, spoiled, stale, off.
F3 fresh, wholesome.

mound *noun* heap, pile, bank, stack.

mount *verb* **1** *mount a campaign*: produce, put on, set up, prepare, stage, exhibit, display, launch. **2** *tension was mounting*: increase, grow, accumulate, multiply, rise, intensify, soar, swell. **3** *mounting the stairs/his horse*: climb, ascend, get up, go up, get on, clamber up, scale, get astride.
F3 **2** decrease, descend. **3** descend, dismount, go down.

mountain *noun* **1** *snow-capped mountains*: height, elevation, mount, peak, mound, alp, tor, massif. **2** *a mountain of paperwork*: heap, pile, stack, mass, abundance, backlog.

mourn *verb* grieve, lament, sorrow, bemoan, miss, regret, deplore, weep, wail.
F3 rejoice.

mournful *adjective* sorrowful, sad, unhappy, desolate, grief-stricken, heavy-hearted, heartbroken, broken-hearted, cast-down, downcast, miserable, tragic, woeful, melancholy, sombre, depressed, dejected, gloomy, dismal.
F3 joyful.

mouth *noun* **1** *open one's mouth to speak*: lips, jaws, trap (*infml*), gob (*slang*). **2** *the mouth of the cave*: opening, aperture, orifice, cavity, entrance, gateway. **3** *the mouth of the river*: inlet, estuary.
▪ *verb* enunciate, articulate, utter, pronounce, whisper, form.

movable *adjective* mobile, portable, transportable, changeable, alterable, adjustable, flexible, transferable.
F3 fixed, immovable.

move *verb* **1** *move suddenly/move forward*: stir, go, advance, budge, change, proceed, progress, make strides. **2** *moving goods*: transport, carry, transfer. **3** *they're moving to London*: depart, go away, leave, decamp, migrate, remove, move house, relocate. **4** *was moved to object*: prompt, stimulate, urge, impel, drive, propel, motivate, incite, persuade, induce, inspire. **5** *moved her to tears*: affect, touch, agitate, stir, impress, excite.
▪ *noun* **1** *work out what the next move should be*: movement, motion, step, manoeuvre, action, device, stratagem. **2** *a move to the city*: removal,

relocation, migration, transfer.

movement *noun* **1** *movement of traffic*: repositioning, move, moving, relocation, activity, act, action, agitation, stirring, transfer, passage. **2** *movement towards a settlement*: change, development, advance, evolution, current, drift, flow, shift, progress, progression, trend, tendency. **3** *the Green movement*: campaign, crusade, drive, group, organization, party, faction.

moving *adjective* **1** *moving traffic*: mobile, active, in motion. **2** *a moving story*: touching, affecting, poignant, impressive, emotive, arousing, stirring, inspiring, inspirational, exciting, thrilling, persuasive, stimulating.
F3 **1** immobile. **2** unemotional.

much *adverb* greatly, considerably, a lot, frequently, often.
▪ *adjective* copious, plentiful, ample, considerable, a lot, abundant, great, substantial.

muck *noun* dirt, grime, dung, manure, mire, filth, mud, sewage, slime, gunge (*infml*), ordure, scum, sludge.

muddle *verb* **1** *muddled clean and dirty clothes*: disorganize, disorder, mix up, mess up, jumble, scramble, tangle. **2** *you're deliberately trying to muddle me*: confuse, bewilder, bemuse, perplex.
▪ *noun* chaos, confusion, disorder, mess, mix-up, jumble, clutter, tangle.

muddy *adjective* dirty, foul, miry, mucky, marshy, boggy, swampy, quaggy, grimy.
F3 clean.

muffle *verb* **1** *muffled in long scarves and woolly hats*: wrap, envelop, cloak, swathe, cover. **2** *their voices were muffled*: deaden, dull, quieten, silence, stifle, dampen, muzzle, suppress.
F3 **2** amplify.

mug *verb* set upon, attack, assault, waylay, steal from, rob, beat up, jump (on).

muggy *adjective* humid, sticky, stuffy, sultry, close, clammy, oppressive, sweltering, moist, damp.
F3 dry.

multiple *adjective* many, numerous, manifold (*fml*), various, several, sundry, collective.

multiply *verb* increase, proliferate, expand, spread, reproduce, propagate, breed, accumulate, intensify, extend, build up, augment, boost.
F3 decrease, lessen.

multitude *noun* crowd, throng, horde, swarm, mob, mass, herd, congregation, host, lot, lots, legion, public, people, populace.
F3 few, scattering.

munch *verb* eat, chew, crunch, masticate (*fml*).

murder *noun* homicide, killing, manslaughter, slaying, assassination, massacre, bloodshed.
▪ *verb* kill, slaughter, slay (*fml*),

assassinate, butcher, massacre.

murderous *adjective* homicidal, brutal, barbarous, bloodthirsty, bloody, cut-throat, killing, lethal, cruel, savage, ferocious, deadly.

murky *adjective* dark, dingy, dismal, gloomy, dreary, cheerless, dull, overcast, misty, foggy, dim, cloudy, obscure, veiled, grey.
F∃ bright, clear.

murmur *noun* mumble, muttering, whisper, undertone, undercurrent, humming, rumble, drone, buzz, hum, grumble, susurration (*fml*).
▪ *verb* mutter, mumble, whisper, buzz, hum, rumble, purr, burble.

muscular *adjective* brawny, beefy (*infml*), sinewy, athletic, powerfully built, strapping, hefty, powerful, hunky (*infml*), robust, stalwart, vigorous, strong.
F∃ puny, flabby, weak.

music

Types of music include:
acid house, ambient, ballet, ballroom, bebop, bhangra, Big Beat, bluegrass, blues, boogie-woogie, chamber, choral, classical, country-and-western, dance, disco, Dixieland, doo-wop, electronic, folk, folk rock, funk, garage, gospel, grunge, hard rock, heavy metal, hip-hop, honky-tonk, house, indie, jazz, jazz-funk, jazz-pop, jazz-rock, jive, karaoke, lounge music, muzak, nu-metal, operatic, orchestral, pop, punk rock, ragtime, rap, reggae, rhythm and blues (R & B), rock, rock'n'roll, salsa, ska, skiffle, soft rock, soul, swing, techno, thrash metal, trance, trip-hop, world music.

Terms used in music include:
accelerando, acciaccatura, accidental, acoustic, adagio, ad lib, affettuoso, agitato, al fine, al segno, alla breve, alla cappella, allargando, allegretto, allegro, alto, alto clef, amoroso, andante, animato, appoggiatura, arco, arpeggio, arrangement, a tempo, attacca, bar, bar line, baritone, bass clef, beat, bis, breve, buffo, cadence, cantabile, cantilena, chord, chromatic, clef, coda, col canto, compound time, con brio, con fuoco, con moto, consonance, contralto, counterpoint, crescendo, cross-fingering, crotchet, cue, da capo, decrescendo, demisemiquaver, descant, diatonic, diminuendo, dissonance, dolce, doloroso, dotted note, dotted rest, double bar line, double flat, double sharp, double trill, downbeat, drone, duet, duo, duplet, encore, ensemble, finale, fine, fingerboard, flat, forte, fortissimo, four-four time, fret, glissando, grave, harmonics, harmony, hemidemisemiquaver, improvisation, interval, intonation, key, key signature, langsam, larghetto, largo, leading note, ledger line, legato, lento, lyric, maestoso, maestro, major, marcato, mediant, metre, mezza voce, mezzo forte, microtone,

middle C, minim, minor, mode, moderato, modulation, molto, mordent, motif, movement, non troppo, nonet, obbligato, octave, ostinato, pentatonic, percussion, perdendo, phrase, pianissimo, piano, pitch, pizzicato, presto, prima donna, quarter tone, quartet, quaver, quintet, quintuplet, rallentando, reed, rhythm, rinforzando, ritenuto, root, scale, score, semibreve, semiquaver, semitone, semplice, sempre, senza, sequence, sextet, sextuplet, sharp, simple time, six-eight time, smorzando, solo, soprano, sostenuto, sotto voce, spiritoso, staccato, staff, stave, string, subdominant, subito, submediant, sul ponticello, supertonic, syncopation, tablature, tacet, tanto, tempo, tenor clef, tenuto, theme, three-four time, tie, timbre, time signature, tonic sol-fa, transposition, treble clef, tremolo, triad, trill, trio, triplet, tutti, two-two time, unison, upbeat, vibrato, vigoroso, virtuoso, vivace.

---

musical *adjective* tuneful, melodious, melodic, harmonious, dulcet, sweet-sounding, lyrical.
F3 discordant, unmusical.

musty *adjective* mouldy, mildewy, stale, stuffy, fusty, dank, airless, decayed, smelly.

mutation *noun* change, alteration, variation, modification, transformation, deviation, anomaly, evolution.

mute *adjective* silent, dumb, voiceless, wordless, speechless, mum (*infml*), unspoken, noiseless, unexpressed, unpronounced.
F3 vocal, talkative.

mutilate *verb* maim, injure, dismember, disable, disfigure, lame, mangle, cut to pieces, cut up, butcher.

mutiny *noun* rebellion, insurrection, revolt, revolution, rising, uprising, insubordination, disobedience, defiance, resistance, riot, strike.
▪ *verb* rebel, revolt, rise up, resist, protest, disobey, strike.

mutter *verb* mumble, murmur, rumble.

mutual *adjective* reciprocal, shared, common, joint, interchangeable, interchanged, exchanged, complementary.

mysterious *adjective* enigmatic, cryptic, mystifying, inexplicable, incomprehensible, puzzling, perplexing, obscure, strange, unfathomable, unsearchable, mystical, baffling, curious, hidden, insoluble, secret, weird, secretive, veiled, dark, furtive.
F3 straightforward, comprehensible.

mystery *noun* **1** *solve a mystery*: enigma, puzzle, secret, riddle, conundrum, question. **2** *cloaked in mystery*: obscurity, secrecy, ambiguity.

mystical *adjective* occult, arcane, mystic, esoteric, supernatural, paranormal, transcendental, metaphysical, hidden, mysterious.

mystify *verb* puzzle, bewilder, baffle, perplex, confound, confuse.

myth *noun* legend, fable, fairy tale, allegory, parable, saga, story, fiction, tradition, fancy, fantasy, superstition.

mythical *adjective* **1** *mythical beasts*: mythological, legendary, fabled, fairy-tale. **2** *his wealth turned out to be entirely mythical*: fictitious, imaginary, made-up, invented, make-believe, non-existent, unreal, pretended, fanciful.

F3 **1** historical. **2** actual, real.

mythology *noun* legend, myths, lore, tradition(s), folklore, folk tales, tales.

nag *verb* scold, berate, irritate, annoy, pester, badger, plague, torment, harass, henpeck (*infml*), harry, vex, upbraid (*fml*), goad.

nail *noun* **1** *hammer in the nail*: fastener, pin, tack, spike, skewer. **2** *long painted nails*: talon, claw.

▪ *verb* fasten, attach, secure, pin, tack, fix, join.

naive *adjective* unsophisticated, ingenuous, innocent, unaffected, artless, guileless, simple, natural, childlike, open, trusting, unsuspecting, gullible, credulous, wide-eyed.

F3 experienced, sophisticated.

naked *adjective* **1** *a naked body*: nude, bare, undressed, unclothed, uncovered, stripped, stark naked, disrobed, denuded, in the altogether (*infml*). **2** *naked aggression*: open, unadorned, undisguised, unqualified, plain, stark, overt, blatant, exposed.

F3 **1** clothed, covered. **2** hidden.

name *noun* **1** *what's your name?*: title, appellation (*fml*), designation, label, term, epithet, handle (*infml*). **2** *have a name for efficient service*: reputation, character, repute, renown, esteem, eminence, fame, honour, distinction, note.

▪ *verb* **1** *name the baby*: call, christen, baptize, term, title, entitle, dub, label, style. **2** *name your price*: designate, nominate, cite, choose, select, specify, classify, commission, appoint.

namely *adverb* that is, ie, specifically, viz, that is to say.

narrate *verb* tell, relate, report, recount, describe, unfold, recite, state, detail.

narrative *noun* story, tale, chronicle, account, history, report, detail, statement.

narrow *adjective* **1** *a narrow passage/bridge/waist/margin*: tight, confined, constricted, cramped, slim, slender, thin, fine, tapering, close. **2** *a narrow brief*: limited, restricted, circumscribed. **3** *a narrow outlook*: narrow-minded, biased, bigoted, exclusive, dogmatic.

F3 **1** wide. **2** broad. **3** broad-minded, tolerant.

▪ *verb* constrict, limit, tighten, reduce, diminish, simplify.

F3 broaden, widen, increase.

narrow-minded *adjective* illiberal, biased, bigoted, prejudiced, reactionary, small-minded, conservative, intolerant, insular, petty.

F3 broad-minded.

nasty *adjective* **1** *a nasty smell*: unpleasant, repellent, repugnant, repulsive, objectionable, offensive, disgusting, sickening, horrible, filthy, foul, polluted, obscene. **2** *a nasty remark*: malicious, mean, spiteful, vicious, malevolent.

F3 **1** agreeable, pleasant, decent. **2** benevolent, kind.

nation *noun* country, people, race, state, realm, population, community, society.

national *adjective* countrywide, civil, domestic, nationwide, state, internal, general, governmental, public, widespread, social.

▪ *noun* citizen, native, subject, inhabitant, resident.

nationalism *noun* patriotism, allegiance, loyalty, chauvinism, xenophobia, jingoism.

nationality *noun* race, nation, ethnic group, birth, tribe, clan.

native *adjective* **1** *native species/land/customs*: local, indigenous, domestic, vernacular, home, aboriginal, mother, original. **2** *native cunning*: inborn, inherent, innate, inbred, hereditary, inherited, congenital, instinctive, natural, intrinsic, natal.

▪ *noun* inhabitant, resident, national, citizen, dweller, aborigine.

F3 foreigner, outsider, stranger.

natural *adjective* **1** *in his natural voice*: ordinary, normal, common, regular, standard, usual, typical. **2** *a natural ability*: innate, inborn, instinctive, intuitive, inherent, congenital, native, indigenous. **3** *natural materials/in its natural state*: genuine, pure, authentic, unrefined, unprocessed, unmixed, real. **4** *she's always so natural*: sincere, unaffected, genuine, artless, ingenuous, guileless, simple, unsophisticated, open, candid, spontaneous.

F3 **1** unnatural. **2** acquired. **3** artificial, synthetic. **4** affected, disingenuous.

naturally *adverb* **1** *naturally, he was shocked at their behaviour*: of course, as a matter of course, simply, obviously, logically, typically, certainly, absolutely. **2** *speaking quite naturally*: normally, genuinely, instinctively, spontaneously.

nature *noun* **1** *a pleasant nature*: essence, quality, character, features, disposition, attributes, personality, make-up, constitution, temperament, mood, outlook, temper. **2** *of a different nature*: kind, sort, type, description, category, variety, style, species. **3** *not found anywhere in nature*: universe, world, creation, earth, environment. **4** *a keen interest in nature*: natural history.

naughty *adjective* **1** *a naughty child*: bad, badly behaved, mischievous, disobedient, wayward, exasperating, playful, roguish. **2** *a naughty word*: indecent, obscene, bawdy, risqué, smutty.

F3 **1** good, well-behaved. **2** decent.

nauseate *verb* sicken, disgust, revolt, repel, offend, turn one's stomach (*infml*).

nautical *adjective* naval, marine, maritime, sea-going, seafaring, sailing, oceanic, boating.

navigate *verb* steer, drive, direct, pilot, guide, handle, manoeuvre, cruise, sail, skipper, voyage, journey, cross, helm, plot, plan.

near *adjective* **1** *near neighbours*: nearby, close, bordering, adjacent, adjoining, alongside, neighbouring. **2** *the exams are near*: imminent, impending, forthcoming, coming, approaching. **3** *a near relation*: dear, familiar, close, related, intimate, akin.

F3 **1** far. **2** distant. **3** remote.

nearby *adverb* near, within reach, at close quarters, close at hand, not far away.

nearly *adverb* almost, practically, virtually, closely, approximately, more or less, as good as, just about, roughly, well-nigh.

F3 completely, totally.

neat *adjective* **1** *a neat appearance*: tidy, orderly, smart, spruce, trim, clean, spick-and-span (*infml*), shipshape. **2** *a neat trick*: deft, clever, adroit, skilful, expert.

F3 **1** untidy. **2** clumsy.

necessary *adjective* needed, required, essential, compulsory, indispensable, vital, imperative, mandatory, obligatory, needful, unavoidable, inevitable, inescapable, inexorable, certain.

F3 unnecessary, inessential, unimportant.

necessitate *verb* require, involve, entail, call for, demand, oblige, force, constrain, compel.

necessity *noun* requirement, obligation, prerequisite, essential, fundamental, need, want, compulsion, demand.

need *verb* miss, lack, want, require, demand, call for, necessitate, have need of, have to, crave.

▪ *noun* **1** *a need for caution*: call,

demand, obligation, requirement. **2** *the family's needs*: essential, necessity, requisite, prerequisite. **3** *a need for equipment*: want, lack, insufficiency, inadequacy, neediness, shortage.

needless *adjective* unnecessary, gratuitous, uncalled-for, unwanted, redundant, superfluous, useless, pointless, purposeless.
E3 necessary, essential.

needy *adjective* poor, destitute, impoverished, penniless, disadvantaged, deprived, poverty-stricken, underprivileged.
E3 affluent, wealthy, well-off.

negate *verb* **1** *negate any gains made*: nullify, annul, cancel, invalidate, undo, countermand, abrogate (*fml*), neutralize, quash, retract, reverse, revoke, rescind, wipe out, void, repeal. **2** *negating his argument*: deny, contradict, oppose, disprove, refute, repudiate.
E3 **2** affirm.

negative *adjective* **1** *a negative answer*: contradictory, contrary, denying, opposing, invalidating, neutralizing, nullifying, annulling. **2** *a negative attitude*: unco-operative, cynical, pessimistic, unenthusiastic, uninterested, unwilling.
E3 **1** affirmative, positive. **2** constructive, positive.
▪ *noun* contradiction, denial, opposite, refusal.

neglect *verb* **1** *neglect one's family*: disregard, ignore, leave alone, abandon, pass by, rebuff, scorn, disdain, slight, spurn. **2** *neglect one's duty*: forget, fail (in), omit, overlook, let slide, shirk, skimp.
E3 **1** cherish, appreciate. **2** remember.
▪ *noun* negligence, disregard, carelessness, failure, inattention, indifference, slackness, dereliction of duty, forgetfulness, heedlessness, oversight, slight, disrespect.
E3 care, attention, concern.

negligent *adjective* neglectful, inattentive, remiss, thoughtless, casual, lax, careless, indifferent, offhand, nonchalant, slack, uncaring, forgetful.
E3 attentive, careful, scrupulous.

negligible *adjective* unimportant, insignificant, small, imperceptible, trifling, trivial, minor, minute.
E3 significant.

negotiate *verb* **1** *negotiate with the union*: confer, deal, mediate, arbitrate, bargain, arrange, transact, work out, manage, settle, consult, contract. **2** *negotiate the bend*: get round, cross, surmount, traverse, pass.

neighbouring *adjective* adjacent, bordering, near, nearby, adjoining, connecting, next, surrounding.
E3 distant, remote.

neighbourly *adjective* sociable, friendly, amiable, kind, helpful, genial, hospitable, obliging, considerate, companionable.

nerve *noun* **1** *lose one's nerve*: courage, bravery, mettle, pluck, guts (*infml*), spunk (*infml*), spirit, vigour, intrepidity, daring, fearlessness, firmness, resolution, fortitude, steadfastness, will, determination, endurance, force. **2** (*infml*) *what a nerve he's got!*: audacity, impudence, cheek (*infml*), effrontery, brazenness, boldness, chutzpah (*infml*), impertinence, insolence.
F3 1 weakness. **2** timidity.

nerve-racking *adjective* harrowing, distressing, trying, stressful, tense, maddening, worrying, difficult, frightening.

nerves *noun* nervousness, tension, stress, anxiety, worry, strain, fretfulness.

nervous *adjective* highly-strung, excitable, anxious, agitated, nervy (*infml*), on edge, edgy, jumpy (*infml*), jittery (*infml*), tense, fidgety, apprehensive, neurotic, shaky, uneasy, worried, flustered, fearful.
F3 calm, relaxed.

nest *noun* **1** *an eagle's nest*: breeding-ground, den, roost, eyrie, lair. **2** *a cosy nest*: retreat, refuge, haunt, hideaway.

nestle *verb* snuggle, huddle, cuddle, curl up.

net[1] *noun* mesh, web, network, netting, open-work, lattice, lace.
▪ *verb* catch, trap, capture, bag, ensnare, entangle, nab (*infml*).

net[2] *adjective* nett, clear, after tax, final, lowest.

network *noun* system, organization, arrangement, structure, interconnections, complex, grid, net, maze, mesh, labyrinth, channels, circuitry, convolution, grill, tracks.

neutral *adjective* **1** *a neutral country*: impartial, uncommitted, unbiased, non-aligned, disinterested, unprejudiced, undecided, non-partisan, non-committal, objective, indifferent, dispassionate, even-handed. **2** *a neutral colour*: dull, nondescript, colourless, drab, expressionless, indistinct.
F3 1 biased, partisan. **2** colourful.

neutralize *verb* counteract, counterbalance, offset, negate, cancel, nullify, invalidate, undo, frustrate.

nevertheless *adverb* nonetheless, notwithstanding, still, anyway, even so, yet, however, anyhow, but, regardless.

new *adjective* **1** *a new approach/car/day/lamb*: novel, original, fresh, different, unfamiliar, unusual, brand-new, mint, unknown, unused, newborn. **2** *new technology*: modern, contemporary, current, latest, recent, up-to-date, up-to-the-minute, topical, trendy (*infml*), ultra-modern, advanced, newfangled (*infml*). **3** *the new face of politics*: changed, altered, modernized, improved, renewed, restored, redesigned. **4** *new vigour*: added, additional, extra,

more, supplementary.
F3 1 usual. **2** outdated, out-of-date. **3** old.

news *noun* report, account, information, intelligence, dispatch, communiqué, bulletin, gossip, hearsay, rumour, statement, story, word, tidings, latest, release, scandal, revelation, lowdown (*infml*), exposé, disclosure, gen (*infml*), advice.

next *adjective* **1** *the next street*: adjacent, adjoining, neighbouring, nearest, closest. **2** *the next day*: following, subsequent, succeeding, ensuing, later.
F3 2 previous, preceding.
▪ *adverb* afterwards, subsequently, later, then.

nice *adjective* **1** *a nice person*: pleasant, agreeable, delightful, charming, likable, attractive, good, kind, friendly, well-mannered, polite, respectable. **2** (*fml*) *a nice distinction*: subtle, delicate, fine, fastidious, discriminating, scrupulous, precise, exact, accurate, careful, strict.
F3 1 nasty, disagreeable, unpleasant. **2** careless.

niche *noun* **1** *a niche in the wall*: recess, alcove, hollow, nook, cubby-hole, corner, opening. **2** *find one's niche in life*: position, place, vocation, calling, métier, slot.

nick *noun* notch, indentation, chip, cut, groove, dent, scar, scratch, mark.
▪ *verb* notch, cut, dent, indent, chip, score, scratch, scar, mark, damage, snick.

nickname *noun* pet name, sobriquet (*fml*), epithet, diminutive.

night *noun* night-time, darkness, dark, dead of night.
F3 day, daytime.

nightfall *noun* sunset, dusk, twilight, evening, gloaming.
F3 dawn, sunrise.

nightmare *noun* **1** *in his worst nightmare*: bad dream, hallucination. **2** *the journey was a nightmare*: ordeal, horror, torment, trial.

nimble *adjective* agile, active, lively, sprightly, spry, smart, quick, brisk, nippy (*infml*), deft, alert, light-footed, prompt, ready, swift, quick-witted.
F3 clumsy, slow.

nip *verb* bite, pinch, squeeze, snip, clip, tweak, catch, grip, nibble.

nobility *noun* **1** *the nobility of his actions*: nobleness, dignity, grandeur, illustriousness, stateliness, majesty, magnificence, eminence, excellence, superiority, uprightness, honour, virtue, worthiness. **2** *belong to the nobility*: aristocracy, peerage, nobles, gentry, élite, lords, high society.
F3 1 baseness. **2** proletariat.

noble *adjective* **1** *a noble family*: aristocratic, high-born, titled, high-ranking, patrician, blue-blooded (*infml*). **2** *a noble brow*: magnificent, magnanimous,

splendid, stately, generous, dignified, distinguished, eminent, grand, great, honoured, honourable, imposing, impressive, majestic, virtuous, worthy, excellent, elevated, fine, gentle.
F3 **1** low-born. **2** ignoble, base, contemptible.

nod *verb* **1** *nodding and waving*: gesture, indicate, sign, signal, salute, acknowledge. **2** *he nodded but said nothing*: agree, assent.
▪ *noun* gesture, indication, sign, signal, salute, greeting, beck, acknowledgement.

noise *noun* sound, din, racket, row, clamour, clash, clatter, commotion, outcry, hubbub, uproar, cry, blare, talk, pandemonium, tumult, babble.
F3 quiet, silence.

noisy *adjective* loud, deafening, ear-splitting, clamorous, piercing, vocal, vociferous, tumultuous, boisterous, obstreperous.
F3 quiet, silent, peaceful.

nominate *verb* propose, choose, select, name, designate, submit, suggest, recommend, put up, present, elect, appoint, assign, commission, elevate, term.

nonchalant *adjective* unconcerned, detached, dispassionate, offhand, blasé, indifferent, casual, cool, collected, apathetic, careless, insouciant.
F3 concerned, careful.

none *pronoun* no-one, not any, not one, nobody, nil, zero.

nonsense *noun* rubbish, trash, drivel, balderdash, gibberish, gobbledygook, senselessness, stupidity, silliness, foolishness, folly, rot (*infml*), blather, twaddle (*infml*), ridiculousness, claptrap (*infml*), cobblers (*slang*).
F3 sense, wisdom.

non-stop *adjective* never-ending, uninterrupted, continuous, incessant, constant, endless, interminable, unending, unbroken, round-the-clock, ongoing.
F3 intermittent, occasional.

nook *noun* recess, alcove, corner, cranny, niche, cubby-hole, hideout, retreat, shelter, cavity.

norm *noun* average, mean, standard, rule, pattern, criterion, model, yardstick, benchmark, measure, reference.

normal *adjective* usual, standard, general, common, ordinary, conventional, average, regular, routine, typical, mainstream, natural, accustomed, well-adjusted, straight, rational, reasonable.
F3 abnormal, irregular, peculiar.

normality *noun* usualness, commonness, ordinariness, regularity, routine, conventionality, balance, adjustment, typicality, naturalness, reason, rationality.
F3 abnormality, irregularity, peculiarity.

normally *adverb* ordinarily, usually, as a rule, typically, commonly, characteristically.
F3 abnormally, exceptionally.

nosey *adjective* inquisitive, meddlesome, prying, interfering, snooping, curious, eavesdropping.

nostalgic *adjective* yearning, longing, wistful, emotional, regretful, sentimental, homesick.

notable *adjective* noteworthy, remarkable, noticeable, striking, extraordinary, impressive, outstanding, marked, unusual, celebrated, distinguished, famous, eminent, well-known, notorious, renowned, rare.
F3 ordinary, commonplace, usual.

notably *adverb* markedly, noticeably, particularly, remarkably, strikingly, conspicuously, distinctly, especially, impressively, outstandingly, eminently.

notch *noun* cut, nick, indentation, incision, score, groove, cleft, mark, snip.

note *noun* **1** *a note of absence*: communication, letter, message, memorandum, reminder, memo (*infml*), line, jotting, record. **2** *a note in the margin*: annotation, comment, gloss, remark. **3** *a note of distinction*: indication, signal, token, mark, symbol. **4** *of considerable note*: eminence, distinction, consequence, fame, renown, reputation. **5** *take note*: heed, attention, regard, notice, observation.
▪ *verb* **1** *noted his absence*: notice, observe, perceive, heed, detect, mark, remark, mention, see, witness. **2** *noted down the details*: record, register, write down, enter.

noted *adjective* famous, well-known, renowned, notable, celebrated, eminent, prominent, great, acclaimed, illustrious, distinguished, respected, recognized.
F3 obscure, unknown.

noteworthy *adjective* remarkable, significant, important, notable, memorable, exceptional, extraordinary, unusual, outstanding.
F3 commonplace, unexceptional, ordinary.

nothing *noun* nought, zero, nothingness, zilch (*infml*), nullity, non-existence, emptiness, void, nobody, nonentity.
F3 something.

notice *verb* note, remark, perceive, observe, mind, see, discern, distinguish, mark, detect, heed, spot.
F3 ignore, overlook.
▪ *noun* **1** *notice to quit*: notification, announcement, information, declaration, communication, intelligence, news, warning, instruction. **2** *a notice in the paper*: advertisement, poster, sign, bill. **3** *reading the notices for the play*: review, comment, criticism. **4** *take some notice*: attention, observation, awareness, note, regard, consideration, heed.

noticeable *adjective* perceptible, observable, appreciable, unmistakable, conspicuous, evident, manifest, clear, distinct,

significant, striking, plain, obvious, measurable.
E3 inconspicuous, unnoticeable.

notification *noun* announcement, information, notice, declaration, advice, warning, intelligence, message, publication, statement, communication.

notify *verb* inform, tell, advise, announce, declare, warn, acquaint, alert, publish, disclose, reveal.

notion *noun* idea, thought, concept, conception, belief, impression, view, opinion, understanding, apprehension.

notorious *adjective* infamous, disreputable, scandalous, dishonourable, disgraceful, ignominious, flagrant, well-known.

nought *noun* zero, nil, zilch (*infml*), naught, nothing, nothingness.

nourish *verb* **1** *nourishing the parched land*: nurture, feed, foster, care for, provide for, sustain, support, tend, nurse, maintain, cherish. **2** *nourishing a general sense of injustice*: strengthen, encourage, promote, cultivate, stimulate.

nourishment *noun* nutrition, food, sustenance, diet.

novel *adjective* new, original, fresh, innovative, unfamiliar, unusual, uncommon, different, imaginative, unconventional, strange.
E3 hackneyed, familiar, ordinary.
▪ *noun* fiction, story, tale, narrative, romance.

novelty *noun* **1** *the novelty of the situation*: newness, originality, freshness, innovation, unfamiliarity, uniqueness, difference, strangeness. **2** *selling toys and novelties*: gimmick, gadget, trifle, memento, knick-knack, curiosity, souvenir, trinket, bauble, gimcrack.

novice *noun* beginner, tiro, learner, pupil, trainee, probationer, apprentice, neophyte (*fml*), amateur, newcomer, rookie (*US infml*).
E3 expert.

now *adverb* **1** *do it now*: immediately, at once, directly, instantly, straight away, promptly, next. **2** *here and now*: at present, nowadays, these days.

nucleus *noun* centre, heart, nub, core, focus, kernel, pivot, basis, crux.

nude *adjective* naked, bare, undressed, unclothed, stripped, stark-naked, uncovered, starkers (*infml*), in one's birthday suit (*infml*).
E3 clothed, dressed.

nudge *verb, noun* poke, prod, shove, dig, jog, prompt, push, elbow, bump.

nuisance *noun* annoyance, inconvenience, bother, irritation, pest, pain (*infml*), drag (*infml*), bore, problem, trial, trouble, drawback.

numb *adjective* benumbed, insensitive, unfeeling, deadened, insensitive, frozen, immobilized.
F sensitive.
■ *verb* deaden, anaesthetize, freeze, immobilize, paralyse, dull, stun.
F sensitize.

number *noun* **1** *a list of numbers*: figure, numeral, digit, integer, unit. **2** *a large number*: total, sum, aggregate, collection, amount, quantity, several, many, company, crowd, multitude, throng, horde. **3** *the latest number of the magazine*: copy, issue, edition, impression, volume, printing.
■ *verb* count, calculate, enumerate, reckon, total, add, compute, include.

numerous *adjective* many, abundant, several, plentiful, copious, profuse, sundry.
F few.

nurse *verb* **1** *nurse the sick*: tend, care for, look after, treat. **2** *mother nursing her baby*: breast-feed, feed, suckle, nurture, nourish. **3** *have to nurse it along*: preserve, sustain, support, cherish, encourage, keep, foster, promote.
■ *noun* sister, matron, nursemaid, nanny.

nurture *noun* rearing, upbringing, training, care, cultivation, development, education, discipline.
■ *verb* **1** *nurture the plants*: feed, nourish, nurse, tend, care for, foster, support, sustain. **2** *nurturing the next generation*: bring up, rear, cultivate, develop, educate, instruct, train, school, discipline.

nutrition *noun* food, nourishment, sustenance.

nutritious *adjective* nourishing, nutritive, wholesome, healthful, health-giving, good, beneficial, strengthening, substantial, invigorating.
F bad, unwholesome.

O

oasis *noun* **1** *an oasis in the desert*: spring, watering-hole. **2** *an oasis of peace*: refuge, haven, island, sanctuary, retreat.

oath *noun* **1** *an oath of loyalty*: vow, pledge, promise, word, affirmation, assurance, word of honour. **2** *shouting oaths*: curse, imprecation, swear-word, profanity, expletive, blasphemy.

obedient *adjective* compliant, docile, acquiescent, submissive,

tractable, yielding, dutiful, law-abiding, deferential, respectful, subservient, observant.
disobedient, rebellious, wilful.

obese *adjective* fat, overweight, corpulent, stout, gross, plump, portly, bulky.
thin, slender, skinny.

obey *verb* **1** *obey the rules*: comply, submit, surrender, yield, be ruled by, bow to, take orders from, defer (to), give way, follow, observe, abide by, adhere to, conform, heed, keep, mind, respond. **2** *obey a command*: carry out, discharge, execute, act upon, fulfil, perform.
1 disobey.

object[1] *noun* /**ob**-jekt/ **1** *a valuable object*: thing, entity, article, body. **2** *the object of the exercise*: aim, objective, purpose, goal, target, intention, motive, end, reason, point, design. **3** *an object of fun*: target, recipient, butt, victim.

object[2] *verb* /ob-**jekt**/ protest, oppose, demur, take exception, disapprove, refuse, complain, rebut, repudiate.
agree, acquiesce.

objection *noun* protest, dissent, disapproval, opposition, demur, complaint, challenge, scruple.
agreement, assent.

objectionable *adjective* unacceptable, unpleasant, offensive, obnoxious, repugnant, disagreeable, abhorrent (*fml*), detestable, deplorable, despicable.
acceptable.

objective *adjective* impartial, unbiased, detached, unprejudiced, open-minded, equitable, dispassionate, even-handed, neutral, disinterested, just, fair.
subjective.
▪ *noun* object, aim, goal, end, purpose, ambition, mark, target, intention, design.

oblige *verb* **1** *was obliged to go*: compel, constrain, coerce, require, make, necessitate, force, bind. **2** *happy to oblige*: help, assist, accommodate, do a favour, serve, gratify, please.

obliging *adjective* accommodating, co-operative, helpful, considerate, agreeable, friendly, kind, civil.
unhelpful.

obnoxious *adjective* unpleasant, disagreeable, disgusting, loathsome, nasty, horrid, odious, repulsive, revolting, repugnant, sickening, nauseating.
pleasant.

obscene *adjective* indecent, improper, immoral, impure, filthy, dirty, bawdy, lewd, licentious, pornographic, scurrilous, suggestive, disgusting, foul, shocking, shameless, offensive.
decent, wholesome.

obscure *adjective* **1** *an obscure poet*: unknown, unimportant, little-known, unheard-of, undistinguished, nameless, inconspicuous, humble, minor. **2** *an obscure remark*: cryptic,

incomprehensible, enigmatic, recondite (*fml*), arcane, esoteric, mysterious, deep, abstruse (*fml*), confusing. **3** *shape was too obscure to make out what it was*: indistinct, unclear, indefinite, shadowy, blurred, cloudy, faint, hazy, dim, misty, shady, vague, murky, gloomy, dusky.
F3 **1** famous, renowned. **2** intelligible, straightforward. **3** clear, definite.

observant *adjective* attentive, alert, vigilant, watchful, perceptive, eagle-eyed, wide-awake, heedful.
F3 unobservant.

observation *noun* **1** *learn by observation*: attention, notice, examination, inspection, scrutiny, monitoring, study, watching, consideration, discernment. **2** *he made an interesting observation about the situation*: remark, comment, utterance, thought, statement, pronouncement, reflection, opinion, finding, note.

observe *verb* **1** *observing wildlife*: watch, see, study, notice, contemplate, keep an eye on, perceive. **2** *'that's odd,' she observed*: remark, comment, say, mention. **3** *observe the rules*: abide by, comply with, honour, keep, fulfil, celebrate, perform.
F3 **1** miss. **3** break, violate.

obsession *noun* preoccupation, fixation, idée fixe, ruling passion, compulsion, fetish, hang-up (*infml*), infatuation, mania, enthusiasm.

obsessive *adjective* consuming, compulsive, gripping, fixed, haunting, tormenting, maddening.

obsolete *adjective* outmoded, disused, out-of-date, old-fashioned, passé, dated, outworn, old, antiquated, antique, dead, extinct.
F3 modern, current, up-to-date.

obstacle *noun* barrier, bar, obstruction, impediment, hurdle, hindrance, check, snag, stumbling block, drawback, difficulty, hitch, catch, stop, interference, interruption.
F3 advantage, help.

obstinate *adjective* stubborn, inflexible, immovable, intractable, pigheaded (*infml*), unyielding, intransigent, persistent, dogged, headstrong, bloody-minded, strong-minded, self-willed, steadfast, firm, determined, wilful.
F3 flexible, tractable.

obstruct *verb* block, impede, hinder, prevent, check, frustrate, hamper, clog, choke, bar, barricade, stop, stall, retard, restrict, thwart, inhibit, hold up, curb, arrest, slow down, interrupt, interfere with, shut off, cut off, obscure.
F3 assist, further.

obstruction *noun* barrier, blockage, bar, barricade, hindrance, impediment, check, stop, stoppage, difficulty.
F3 help.

obtain *verb* acquire, get, gain,

come by, attain, procure, secure, earn, achieve.

obvious *adjective* evident, self-evident, manifest, patent, clear, plain, distinct, transparent, undeniable, unmistakable, conspicuous, glaring, apparent, open, unconcealed, visible, noticeable, perceptible, pronounced, recognizable, self-explanatory, straightforward, prominent.

F3 unclear, indistinct, obscure.

occasion *noun* **1** *on the occasion of their marriage/on each occasion*: event, occurrence, incident, time, instance, chance, case, opportunity. **2** *gave him occasion to pause*: reason, cause, excuse, justification, ground(s). **3** *it was quite an occasion*: celebration, function, affair, party.

occasional *adjective* periodic, intermittent, irregular, sporadic, infrequent, uncommon, incidental, odd, rare, casual.

F3 frequent, regular, constant.

occasionally *adverb* sometimes, on occasion, from time to time, at times, at intervals, now and then, now and again, irregularly, periodically, every so often, once in a while, off and on, infrequently.

F3 frequently, often, always.

occupant *noun* occupier, holder, inhabitant, resident, householder, tenant, user, lessee, squatter, inmate.

occupation *noun* **1** *what's his occupation?*: job, profession, work, vocation, employment, trade, post, calling, business, line, pursuit, craft, walk of life, activity. **2** *occupation of the country by the enemy*: invasion, seizure, conquest, control, takeover. **3** *take up occupation of a house*: occupancy, possession, holding, tenancy, tenure, residence, habitation, use.

occupy *verb* **1** *occupying the house next door*: inhabit, live in, possess, reside in, stay in, take possession of, own. **2** *occupied by the task*: absorb, take up, engross, engage, hold, involve, preoccupy, amuse, busy, interest. **3** *occupying the country*: invade, seize, capture, overrun, take over. **4** *occupy one's time*: fill, take up, use.

occur *verb* happen, come about, take place, transpire, turn out, chance, come to pass, materialize, befall, develop, crop up, arise, appear, turn up, obtain (*fml*), result, exist, be present, be found.

odd *adjective* **1** *odd smell/ behaviour*: unusual, strange, uncommon, peculiar, abnormal, exceptional, curious, atypical, different, queer, bizarre, eccentric, remarkable, unconventional, weird, irregular, extraordinary, outlandish, rare. **2** *odd socks*: unmatched, unpaired, single, spare, surplus, left-over, remaining, sundry, various, miscellaneous.

F3 **1** normal, usual.

oddity *noun* **1** *the oddity of his*

appearance: abnormality, peculiarity, rarity, eccentricity, idiosyncrasy, phenomenon, quirk. **2** *a bit of an oddity*: curiosity, character, freak, misfit.

odds *noun* **1** *what are the odds of rain?*: likelihood, probability, chances. **2** *against the odds*: advantage, edge, lead, superiority.

odour *noun* smell, scent, fragrance, aroma, perfume, redolence, stench, stink (*infml*), pong (*infml*).

off *adjective* **1** *this milk is off*: rotten, bad, sour, turned, rancid, mouldy, decomposed. **2** *the match is off*: cancelled, postponed. **3** *he's off somewhere*: away, absent, gone. **4** *have an off day*: substandard, below par, disappointing, unsatisfactory.

▪ *adverb* away, elsewhere, out, at a distance, apart, aside.

offence *noun* **1** *a criminal offence*: misdemeanour, transgression, violation, wrong, wrongdoing, infringement, crime, misdeed, sin, trespass (*fml*). **2** *an offence to decency*: affront, insult, injury. **3** *take offence*: resentment, indignation, pique, umbrage, outrage, hurt, hard feelings.

offend *verb* **1** *offended him by laughing*: hurt, insult, injure, affront, wrong, wound, displease, snub, upset, annoy, outrage. **2** *offending the senses*: disgust, repel, sicken. **3** *offended repeatedly*: transgress, sin, violate, err.

F3 **1** please.

offender *noun* transgressor, wrongdoer, culprit, criminal, miscreant (*fml*), guilty party, law-breaker, delinquent.

offensive *adjective* **1** *an offensive remark*: disagreeable, unpleasant, objectionable, displeasing, disgusting, odious, obnoxious, repellent, repugnant, revolting, loathsome, vile, nauseating, nasty, detestable, abominable. **2** *don't be offensive*: insolent, abusive, rude, insulting, impertinent.

F3 **1** pleasant. **2** polite.

▪ *noun* attack, assault, onslaught, invasion, raid, sortie.

offer *verb* **1** *offered him a drink*: present, make available, advance, extend, put forward, submit, suggest, hold out, provide, sell. **2** *offered his hand in marriage*: proffer, propose, bid, tender. **3** *offered their services*: volunteer, come forward, show willing (*infml*).

▪ *noun* proposal, bid, submission, tender, suggestion, proposition, overture, approach, attempt, presentation.

offering *noun* present, gift, donation, contribution.

offhand *adjective* casual, unconcerned, uninterested, take-it-or-leave-it (*infml*), brusque, abrupt, perfunctory (*fml*), informal, cavalier, careless.

▪ *adverb* impromptu, off the cuff, extempore (*fml*), off the top of one's head, immediately.

F3 calculated, planned.

office *noun* **1** *high office*: responsibility, duty, obligation, charge, commission, occupation, situation, post, employment, function, appointment, business, role, service. **2** *go into the office*: workplace, workroom, bureau.

officer *noun* official, office-holder, public servant, functionary, dignitary, bureaucrat, administrator, representative, executive, agent, appointee.

official *adjective* authorized, authoritative, legitimate, formal, licensed, accredited, certified, approved, authenticated, authentic, bona fide, proper.
F3 unofficial.
▪ *noun* office-bearer, officer, functionary, bureaucrat, executive, representative, agent.

often *adverb* frequently, repeatedly, regularly, generally, again and again, time after time, time and again, much.
F3 rarely, seldom, never.

oil *verb* grease, lubricate, anoint.

oily *adjective* greasy, fatty.

OK *adjective* acceptable, all right, fine, permitted, in order, fair, satisfactory, reasonable, tolerable, passable, not bad, good, adequate, convenient, correct, accurate.
▪ *interjection* all right, fine, very well, agreed, right, yes.

old *adjective* **1** *an old person*: aged, elderly, advanced in years, grey, senile. **2** *an old manuscript*: ancient, original, primitive, antiquated, mature. **3** *an old friend*: long-standing, long-established, time-honoured, traditional. **4** *an old model*: obsolete, old-fashioned, out-of-date, worn-out, decayed, decrepit. **5** *an old girlfriend*: former, previous, earlier, one-time, ex-.
F3 **1** young. **2** new. **4** modern. **5** current.

old-fashioned *adjective* outmoded, out-of-date, outdated, dated, unfashionable, obsolete, behind the times, antiquated, archaic, passé, obsolescent, retro (*infml*).
F3 modern, up-to-date.

omen *noun* portent, sign, warning, premonition, foreboding, augury, indication.

ominous *adjective* portentous, inauspicious, foreboding, menacing, sinister, fateful, unpromising, threatening.
F3 auspicious, favourable.

omission *noun* exclusion, gap, oversight, failure, lack, neglect, default, avoidance.

omit *verb* leave out, exclude, miss out, pass over, overlook, drop, skip, eliminate, forget, neglect, leave undone, fail, disregard, edit out.
F3 include.

once *adverb* formerly, previously, in the past, at one time, long ago, in times past, once upon a time, in the old days.

one *adjective* **1** *the one person who knows*: single, solitary, lone, individual, only. **2** *of one mind*:

united, harmonious, like-minded, whole, entire, complete, equal, identical, alike.

one-sided *adjective* **1** *a one-sided grin*: unbalanced, unequal, lopsided. **2** *a one-sided argument*: unfair, unjust, prejudiced, biased, partial, partisan. **3** *a one-sided decision*: unilateral, independent.
F∃ 1 balanced. **2** impartial. **3** bilateral, multilateral.

only *adverb* just, at most, merely, simply, purely, barely, exclusively, solely.
▪ *adjective* sole, single, solitary, lone, unique, exclusive, individual.

onset *noun* beginning, start, commencement, inception, outset, outbreak.
F∃ end, finish.

onward(s) *adverb* forward, on, ahead, in front, beyond, forth.
F∃ backward(s).

ooze *verb* seep, exude, leak, escape, dribble, drip, drop, discharge, bleed, secrete, emit, overflow with, filter, drain.

open *adjective* **1** *an open door*: unclosed, ajar, gaping, uncovered, unfastened, unlocked, unsealed, yawning, lidless. **2** *an open meeting/outlook*: unrestricted, free, unobstructed, clear, accessible, exposed, unprotected, unsheltered, vacant, wide, available. **3** *open opposition*: overt, obvious, plain, evident, manifest, noticeable, flagrant, conspicuous. **4** *an open question*: undecided, unresolved, unsettled, debatable, problematic, moot. **5** *an open manner*: frank, candid, honest, guileless, natural, ingenuous, unreserved.
F∃ 1 shut. **2** restricted. **3** hidden. **4** decided. **5** reserved.
▪ *verb* **1** *open the window/road*: unfasten, undo, unlock, uncover, unseal, unblock, uncork, clear, expose. **2** *opening her heart*: explain, divulge, disclose, lay bare. **3** *open the campaign*: begin, start, commence, inaugurate, initiate, set in motion, launch.
F∃ 1 close, shut. **2** hide. **3** end, finish.

opening *noun* **1** *an opening in the hedge*: aperture, breach, gap, orifice, break, chink, crack, fissure, cleft, chasm, hole, split, vent, rupture. **2** *the opening of discussions*: start, onset, beginning, inauguration, inception, birth, dawn, launch. **3** *looking for an opening in advertising*: opportunity, chance, occasion, break (*infml*), place, vacancy.
F∃ 2 close, end.
▪ *adjective* beginning, commencing, starting, first, inaugural, introductory, initial, early, primary.
F∃ closing.

openly *adverb* overtly, frankly, candidly, blatantly, flagrantly, plainly, unashamedly, unreservedly, glaringly, in public, in full view, shamelessly.
F∃ secretly, slyly.

operate *verb* **1** *torch operates on batteries*: function, act, perform, run, work, go. **2** *people who operate heavy machinery*: control, handle, manage, use, utilize, manoeuvre.

operation *noun* **1** *the operation of government/the machine*: functioning, action, running, motion, movement, performance, working. **2** *operation of the controls*: influence, manipulation, handling, management, use, utilization. **3** *runs an international mining operation*: undertaking, enterprise, affair, procedure, proceeding, process, business, deal, transaction, effort. **4** *a military operation*: campaign, action, task, manoeuvre, exercise.

opinion *noun* belief, judgement, view, point of view, idea, perception, stance, theory, impression, feeling, sentiment, estimation, assessment, conception, mind, notion, way of thinking, persuasion, attitude.

opponent *noun* adversary, enemy, antagonist, foe (*fml*), competitor, contestant, challenger, opposer, opposition, rival, objector, dissident.
F3 ally.

opportunity *noun* chance, opening, break (*infml*), occasion, possibility, hour, moment.

oppose *verb* **1** *opposing the plan*: resist, withstand, counter, attack, combat, contest, stand up to, take a stand against, take issue with, confront, defy, face, fight, fly in the face of, hinder, obstruct, bar, check, prevent, thwart. **2** *oppose one thing with the other*: compare, contrast, match, offset, counterbalance, play off.
F3 **1** defend, support.

opposed *adjective* in opposition, against, hostile, conflicting, opposing, opposite, antagonistic, clashing, contrary, incompatible, anti.
F3 in favour.

opposite *adjective* **1** *on the opposite bank*: facing, fronting, corresponding. **2** *opposite views*: opposed, antagonistic, conflicting, contrary, hostile, adverse, contradictory, antithetical, irreconcilable, unlike, reverse, inconsistent, different, contrasted, differing.
F3 **2** same.
▪ *noun* reverse, converse, contrary, antithesis, contradiction, inverse.
F3 same.

opposition *noun* **1** *met with a great deal of opposition*: antagonism, hostility, resistance, obstructiveness, unfriendliness, disapproval. **2** *beat the opposition*: opponent, antagonist, rival, foe (*fml*), other side.
F3 **1** co-operation, support. **2** ally, supporter.

oppression *noun* tyranny, subjugation, subjection, repression, despotism, suppression, injustice, cruelty, brutality, abuse, persecution, maltreatment, harshness, hardship.

oppressive *adjective* **1** *an oppressive atmosphere*: airless, stuffy, close, stifling, suffocating, sultry, muggy, heavy. **2** *an oppressive regime*: tyrannical, despotic, overbearing, overwhelming, repressive, harsh, unjust, inhuman, cruel, brutal, burdensome, onerous, intolerable.
F3 **1** airy. **2** just, gentle.

optimistic *adjective* confident, assured, sanguine, hopeful, positive, cheerful, buoyant, bright, idealistic, expectant, upbeat (*infml*).
F3 pessimistic.

option *noun* choice, alternative, preference, possibility, selection.

optional *adjective* voluntary, discretionary, elective, free, unforced.
F3 compulsory.

orbit *noun* circuit, cycle, circle, course, path, trajectory, track, revolution, rotation.
▪ *verb* revolve, circle, encircle, circumnavigate.

ordeal *noun* trial, test, tribulation(s), affliction, trouble(s), suffering, anguish, agony, pain, persecution, torture, nightmare.

order *noun* **1** *an order of the court*: command, directive, decree, injunction, instruction, direction, edict, ordinance, mandate, regulation, rule, precept (*fml*), law. **2** *deal with your order immediately*: requisition, request, booking, commission, reservation, application, demand. **3** *change the order*: arrangement, organization, grouping, disposition, sequence, categorization, classification, method, pattern, plan, system, array, layout, line-up, structure. **4** *restore order*: peace, quiet, calm, tranquillity, harmony, law and order, discipline. **5** *a religious order*: association, society, community, fraternity, brotherhood, sisterhood, lodge, guild, company, organization, denomination, sect, union.
F3 **3** confusion, disorder. **4** anarchy.
▪ *verb* **1** *ordered them to go*: command, instruct, direct, bid, decree, require, authorize. **2** *ordered a taxi*: request, reserve, book, apply for, requisition. **3** *ordering the books according to author*: arrange, organize, dispose, classify, group, marshal, sort out, lay out, manage, control, catalogue.

orderly *adjective* **1** *an orderly system*: ordered, systematic, neat, tidy, regular, methodical, in order, well-organized, well-regulated. **2** *orderly conduct*: well-behaved, controlled, disciplined, law-abiding.
F3 **1** chaotic. **2** disorderly.

ordinary *adjective* common, commonplace, regular, routine, standard, average, everyday, run-of-the-mill, usual, unexceptional, unremarkable, typical, normal,

customary, common-or-garden, plain, familiar, habitual, simple, conventional, modest, mediocre, indifferent, pedestrian, prosaic, undistinguished.
extraordinary, unusual.

organ *noun* device, instrument, implement, tool, element, process, structure, unit, member.

organization *noun* **1** *a religious organization*: association, institution, society, company, firm, corporation, federation, group, league, club, confederation, consortium. **2** *efficient organization/the organization of society*: arrangement, system, classification, methodology, order, formation, grouping, method, plan, structure, pattern, composition, configuration, design.

organize *verb* **1** *organize the library*: structure, co-ordinate, arrange, order, group, marshal, classify, systematize, tabulate, catalogue. **2** *organize a strike*: establish, found, set up, develop, form, frame, construct, shape, run.
1 disorganize.

origin *noun* **1** *the origin of the story*: source, spring, fount, foundation, base, cause, derivation, provenance, roots, well-spring. **2** *the origins of man*: beginning, commencement, start, inauguration, launch, dawning, creation, emergence. **3** *of Welsh origin*: ancestry, descent, extraction, heritage, family, lineage, parentage, pedigree, birth, paternity, stock.
2 end, termination.

original *adjective* **1** *the original version*: first, early, earliest, initial, primary, archetypal, rudimentary, embryonic, starting, opening, commencing, first-hand. **2** *a very original piece of work*: novel, innovative, new, creative, fresh, imaginative, inventive, unconventional, unusual, unique.
1 latest. **2** hackneyed, unoriginal.
▪ *noun* prototype, master, paradigm, model, pattern, archetype, standard, type.

originate *verb* **1** *where does it originate from?*: rise, arise, spring, stem, issue, flow, proceed, derive, come, evolve, emerge, be born. **2** *the person who originated the idea*: create, invent, inaugurate, introduce, give birth to, develop, discover, establish, begin, commence, start, set up, launch, pioneer, conceive, form, produce, generate.
1 end, terminate.

ornament *noun* decoration, adornment, embellishment, garnish, trimming, accessory, frill, trinket, bauble, jewel.

ornamental *adjective* decorative, embellishing, adorning, attractive, showy.

ornate *adjective* elaborate, ornamented, fancy, decorated, baroque, rococo, florid, flowery, fussy, busy, sumptuous.
plain.

orthodox *adjective* conformist, conventional, accepted, official, traditional, usual, well-established, established, received, customary, conservative, recognized, authoritative.
F3 nonconformist, unorthodox.

ostentatious *adjective* showy, flashy, pretentious, vulgar, loud, garish, gaudy, flamboyant, conspicuous, extravagant.
F3 restrained.

ostracize *verb* exclude, banish, exile, expel, excommunicate, reject, segregate, send to Coventry, shun, snub, boycott, avoid, cold-shoulder (*infml*), cut.
F3 accept, welcome.

other *adjective* **1** *prefer some other method*: different, dissimilar, unlike, separate, distinct, contrasting. **2** *is there any other business?*: more, further, extra, additional, supplementary, spare, alternative.

out *adjective* **1** *he's out at the moment*: away, absent, elsewhere, not at home, gone, outside, abroad. **2** *it will all be out in the open*: revealed, exposed, disclosed, public, evident, manifest.
F3 1 in. **2** concealed.

outbreak *noun* eruption, outburst, explosion, flare-up, upsurge, flash, rash, burst, epidemic.

outburst *noun* outbreak, eruption, explosion, flare-up, outpouring, burst, fit, gush, surge, storm, spasm, seizure, gale, attack, fit of temper.

outcast *noun* castaway, exile, pariah, outsider, untouchable, refugee, reject, persona non grata.

outcome *noun* result, consequence, upshot, conclusion, effect, end result.

outcry *noun* protest, complaint, protestation, objection, dissent, indignation, uproar, cry, exclamation, clamour, row, commotion, noise, hue and cry, hullabaloo (*infml*), outburst.

outdo *verb* surpass, exceed, beat, excel, outstrip, outshine, get the better of, overcome, outclass, outdistance.

outer *adjective* **1** *the outer wall*: external, exterior, outside, outward, surface, peripheral. **2** *the outer regions*: outlying, distant, remote, further.
F3 1 internal. **2** inner.

outfit *noun* clothes, costume, ensemble, get-up (*infml*), togs (*infml*), garb.

outlaw *noun* bandit, brigand, robber, desperado, highwayman, criminal, marauder, pirate, fugitive.
▪ *verb* ban, disallow, forbid, prohibit, exclude, embargo, bar, debar, banish, condemn.
F3 allow, legalize.

outlet *noun* **1** *the outlet from the boiler*: exit, way out, vent, egress, escape, opening, release, safety valve, channel. **2** *open several*

outlets nationwide: retailer, shop, store, market.
F3 1 entry, inlet.

outline *noun* **1** *an outline of the story*: summary, synopsis, précis, bare facts, sketch, thumbnail sketch, abstract. **2** *the outline of the hills*: profile, form, contour, silhouette, shape.
▪ *verb* sketch, summarize, draft, trace, rough out.

outlook *noun* **1** *have a different outlook on life*: view, viewpoint, point of view, attitude, perspective, frame of mind, angle, slant, standpoint, opinion. **2** *the outlook is good*: expectations, future, forecast, prospect, prognosis.

out-of-date *adjective* old-fashioned, unfashionable, outdated, obsolete, dated, outmoded, antiquated, passé.
F3 fashionable, modern.

output *noun* production, productivity, product, yield, manufacture, achievement.

outrage *noun* **1** *wrote letters expressing their outrage*: anger, fury, rage, indignation, shock, affront, horror. **2** *their prices are an outrage*: atrocity, offence, injury, enormity, barbarism, crime, violation, evil, scandal.
▪ *verb* anger, infuriate, affront, incense, enrage, madden, disgust, injure, offend, shock, scandalize.

outrageous *adjective* **1** *outrageous behaviour*: atrocious, abominable, shocking, scandalous, offensive, disgraceful, monstrous, heinous (*fml*), unspeakable, horrible. **2** *outrageous prices*: excessive, exorbitant, immoderate, unreasonable, extortionate, inordinate, preposterous.
F3 2 acceptable, reasonable.

outright *adjective* total, utter, absolute, complete, pure, downright, out-and-out, unqualified, unconditional, perfect, thorough, direct, definite, categorical, straightforward.
F3 ambiguous, indefinite.
▪ *adverb* **1** *win outright*: totally, absolutely, completely, utterly, thoroughly, openly, without restraint, straightforwardly, positively, directly, explicitly. **2** *killed outright*: instantaneously, at once, there and then, instantly, immediately.

outside *adjective* **1** *the outside world*: external, exterior, outer, surface, superficial, outward, extraneous, outdoor, outermost, extreme. **2** *an outside chance*: remote, marginal, distant, faint, slight, slim, negligible.
F3 1 inside.
▪ *noun* exterior, façade, front, surface, face, appearance, cover.
F3 inside.

outsider *noun* stranger, intruder, alien, non-member, non-resident, foreigner, newcomer, visitor, interloper, misfit, odd man out.

outskirts *noun* suburbs, vicinity, periphery, fringes, borders,

boundary, edge, margin.
☒ centre.

outspoken *adjective* candid, frank, forthright, blunt, unreserved, plain-spoken, direct, explicit.
☒ diplomatic, reserved.

outstanding *adjective* **1** *an outstanding success/performance*: excellent, distinguished, eminent, pre-eminent, celebrated, exceptional, superior, remarkable, prominent, superb, great, notable, impressive, striking, superlative, important, noteworthy, memorable, special, extraordinary. **2** *the amount outstanding*: owing, unpaid, due, unsettled, unresolved, uncollected, pending, payable, remaining, ongoing, leftover.
☒ **1** ordinary, unexceptional. **2** paid, settled.

outward *adjective* external, exterior, outer, outside, surface, superficial, visible, apparent, observable, evident, supposed, professed, public, obvious, ostensible.
☒ inner, private.

outwit *verb* outsmart, outthink, get the better of, trick, better, beat, dupe, cheat, deceive, defraud, swindle.

oval *adjective* egg-shaped, elliptical, ovoid, ovate.

over *adjective* finished, ended, done with, concluded, past, gone, completed, closed, in the past, settled, up, forgotten, accomplished.
▪ *adverb* **1** *two birds flew over*: above, beyond, overhead, on high. **2** *there were six left over*: extra, remaining, surplus, superfluous, left, unclaimed, unused, unwanted, in excess, in addition.
▪ *preposition* **1** *the roof over our heads*: higher than, above. **2** *over the odds*: exceeding, more than, in excess of.

overall *adjective* total, all-inclusive, all-embracing, comprehensive, inclusive, general, universal, global, broad, blanket, complete, all-over.
☒ narrow, specific.
▪ *adverb* in general, on the whole, by and large, broadly, generally speaking.

overcast *adjective* cloudy, grey, dull, dark, sombre, sunless, hazy, lowering.
☒ bright, clear.

overcharge *verb* surcharge, short-change, cheat, extort, rip off (*infml*), sting (*infml*), do (*infml*), diddle (*infml*).
☒ undercharge.

overcome *verb* conquer, defeat, beat, surmount, triumph over, vanquish (*fml*), rise above, master, overpower, overwhelm, overthrow, subdue.

overcrowded *adjective* congested, packed (out), jam-packed, crammed full, chock-full, overpopulated, overloaded, swarming.
☒ deserted, empty.

overdo *verb* exaggerate, go too

far, carry to excess, go overboard (*infml*), lay it on thick (*infml*), overindulge, overstate, overact, overplay, overwork.

overdue *adjective* late, behindhand, behind schedule, delayed, owing, unpunctual, slow.
F3 early.

overflow *verb* spill, overrun, run over, pour over, well over, brim over, bubble over, surge, flood, inundate, deluge, shower, submerge, soak, swamp, teem.

overhang *verb* jut, project, bulge, protrude, stick out, extend.

overhaul *verb* **1** *overhaul the engine*: renovate, repair, service, recondition, mend, examine, inspect, check, survey, re-examine, fix. **2** *was overhauled by a more powerful car*: overtake, pull ahead of, outpace, outstrip, gain on, pass.
▪ *noun* reconditioning, repair, renovation, check, service, examination, inspection, going-over (*infml*).

overhead *adverb* above, up above, on high, upward.
F3 below, underfoot.
▪ *adjective* elevated, aerial, overhanging, raised.

overload *verb* burden, oppress, strain, tax, weigh down, overcharge, encumber.

overlook *verb* **1** *overlooking the sea*: front on to, face, look on to, look over, command a view of. **2** *overlooked several spelling mistakes*: miss, disregard, ignore, omit, neglect, pass over, let pass, let ride. **3** *I will overlook your lateness on this occasion*: excuse, forgive, pardon, condone, wink at, turn a blind eye to.
F3 **2** notice. **3** penalize.

overpowering *adjective* overwhelming, powerful, strong, forceful, irresistible, uncontrollable, compelling, extreme, oppressive, suffocating, unbearable, nauseating, sickening.

overrule *verb* overturn, override, countermand, revoke, reject, rescind, reverse, invalidate, cancel, vote down.

overrun *verb* **1** *country was overrun by the enemy troops*: invade, occupy, infest, overwhelm, inundate, run riot, spread over, swamp, swarm over, surge over, ravage, overgrow. **2** *overrun the time allowed*: exceed, overshoot, overstep, overreach.

overshadow *verb* outshine, eclipse, excel, surpass, dominate, dwarf, put in the shade, rise above, tower above.

oversight *noun* lapse, omission, fault, error, slip-up (*infml*), mistake, blunder, carelessness, neglect.

overtake *verb* **1** *overtake a lorry*: pass, catch up with, outdistance, outstrip, draw level with, pull ahead of, overhaul. **2** *overtaken by events*: come upon, befall, happen, strike, engulf.

overthrow *verb* depose, oust, bring down, topple, unseat, displace, dethrone, conquer,

vanquish (*fml*), beat, defeat, crush, overcome, overpower, overturn, overwhelm, subdue, master, abolish, upset.
E3 install, protect, reinstate, restore.

overtone *noun* suggestion, intimation, nuance, hint, undercurrent, insinuation, connotation, association, feeling, implication, sense, flavour.

overturn *verb* **1** *car overturned*: capsize, upset, upturn, tip over, topple, overbalance, keel over, knock over, spill. **2** *overturned the decision*: overthrow, repeal, rescind, reverse, annul, abolish, destroy, quash, set aside.

overwhelm *verb* **1** *problems threatened to overwhelm them*: overcome, overpower, destroy, defeat, crush, rout, devastate. **2** *their troops were overwhelmed by a stronger force*: overrun, inundate, snow under, submerge, swamp, engulf. **3** *your generosity overwhelms me*: confuse, bowl over, stagger, floor.

overwork *verb* overstrain, overload, exploit, exhaust, overuse, overtax, strain, wear out, oppress, burden, weary.

owing *adjective* unpaid, due, owed, in arrears, outstanding, payable, unsettled, overdue.

own *adjective* personal, individual, private, particular, idiosyncratic.
▪ *verb* possess, have, hold, retain, keep, enjoy.

owner *noun* possessor, holder, landlord, landlady, proprietor, proprietress, master, mistress, freeholder.

Pp

pace *noun* step, stride, walk, gait, tread, movement, motion, progress, rate, speed, velocity, celerity, quickness, rapidity, tempo, measure.
▪ *verb* step, stride, walk, march, tramp, pound, patrol, mark out, measure.

pacify *verb* appease, conciliate, placate, mollify, calm, compose, soothe, assuage (*fml*), allay, moderate, soften, lull, still, quiet, silence, quell, crush, put down, tame, subdue.
E3 anger.

pack *noun* **1** *a pack of cigarettes*: packet, box, carton, parcel, package, bundle, burden, load, backpack, rucksack, haversack, knapsack, kitbag. **2** *a pack of*

wolves: group, company, troop, herd, flock, band, crowd, gang, mob.
▪ *verb* **1** *pack books into boxes*: wrap, parcel, package, bundle, stow, store. **2** *packed them into the theatre*: cram, stuff, crowd, throng, press, ram, wedge, compact, compress, fill, load, charge.

package *noun* parcel, pack, packet, box, carton, bale, consignment.

packed *adjective* filled, full, jam-packed, chock-a-block, crammed, crowded, congested.
≠ empty, deserted.

packet *noun* pack, carton, box, bag, package, parcel, case, container, wrapper, wrapping, packing.

pact *noun* treaty, convention, covenant, bond, alliance, cartel, contract, deal, bargain, compact, agreement, arrangement, understanding.
≠ disagreement, quarrel.

pad *verb* fill, stuff, wad, pack, wrap, line, cushion, protect.

paddle[1] *verb* row, oar, scull, propel, steer.
▪ *noun* oar, scull.

paddle[2] *verb* wade, splash, slop, dabble.

pagan *noun* heathen, atheist, unbeliever, infidel, idolater.
≠ believer.
▪ *adjective* heathen, irreligious, atheistic, godless, infidel, idolatrous.

page *noun* leaf, sheet, folio, side.

pain *noun* **1** *a pain in his stomach/ feel pain*: hurt, ache, throb, cramp, spasm, twinge, pang, stab, sting, smart, soreness, tenderness, discomfort, distress, suffering, affliction, trouble, anguish, agony, torment, torture. **2** (*infml*) *it's a pain*: nuisance, bother, bore (*infml*), annoyance, vexation, burden, headache (*infml*).
▪ *verb* hurt, afflict, torment, torture, agonize, distress, upset, sadden, grieve.
≠ please, delight, gratify.

painful *adjective* **1** *a painful wound*: sore, tender, aching, throbbing, smarting, stabbing, agonizing, excruciating. **2** *a painful experience*: unpleasant, disagreeable, distressing, upsetting, saddening, harrowing, traumatic.
≠ **1** painless, soothing. **2** pleasant, agreeable.

painkiller *noun* analgesic, anodyne, anaesthetic, palliative (*fml*), sedative, drug, remedy.

painless *adjective* pain-free, trouble-free, effortless, easy, simple, undemanding.
≠ painful, difficult.

pains *noun* trouble, bother, effort, labour, care, diligence.

painstaking *adjective* careful, meticulous, scrupulous, thorough, conscientious, diligent, assiduous (*fml*), industrious, hardworking, dedicated, devoted, persevering.
≠ careless, negligent.

paint *noun* colour, colouring,

pigment, dye, tint, stain.
▪ *verb* **1** *paint the ceiling*: colour, dye, tint, stain, lacquer, varnish, glaze, apply, daub, coat, cover, decorate. **2** *paint a portrait*: portray, depict, describe, recount, picture, represent.

Terms used in painting include:
abstract, acrylics, aquatint, canvas, chiaroscuro, collage, composition, diptych, drawing, easel, figurative, foreground, fresco, frieze, gouache, impasto, landscape, mahlstick, miniature, monochrome, montage, mural, oil painting, palette, palette knife, pastels, pastoral, perspective, pigment, pointillism, portrait, primer, sable brush, seascape, sfumato, silhouette, sketch, still life, stipple, tempera, tint, tone, triptych, trompe l'œil, turpentine, vanishing point, vignette, wash, watercolour.

---

pair *noun* couple, brace, twosome, duo, twins, two of a kind.
▪ *verb* match (up), twin, team, mate, marry, wed, splice, join, couple, link, bracket, put together.
F3 separate, part.

palatable *adjective* tasty, appetizing, eatable, edible, acceptable, satisfactory, pleasant, agreeable, enjoyable, attractive.
F3 unpalatable, unacceptable, unpleasant, disagreeable.

pale *adjective* **1** *went/look pale*: pallid, livid, ashen, ashy, white, chalky, pasty, pasty-faced, waxen, waxy, wan, sallow, anaemic. **2** *pale blue*: light, pastel, faded, washed-out, bleached, colourless, insipid, vapid, weak, feeble, faint, dim.
F3 **1** ruddy. **2** dark.

palpable *adjective* solid, substantial, material, real, touchable, tangible, visible, apparent, clear, plain, obvious, evident, manifest, conspicuous, blatant, unmistakable.
F3 impalpable, imperceptible, intangible, elusive.

paltry *adjective* meagre, derisory, contemptible, mean, low, miserable, wretched, poor, sorry, small, slight, trifling, inconsiderable, negligible, trivial, minor, petty, unimportant, insignificant, worthless.
F3 substantial, significant, valuable.

pamper *verb* cosset, coddle, mollycoddle, humour, gratify, indulge, overindulge, spoil, pet, fondle.
F3 neglect, ill-treat.

pamphlet *noun* leaflet, brochure, booklet, folder, circular, handout, notice.

pander to *verb* humour, indulge, pamper, please, gratify, satisfy, fulfil, provide, cater to.

panel *noun* board, committee, jury, team.

pang *noun* pain, ache, twinge, stab, sting, prick, stitch, gripe, spasm, throe, agony, anguish, discomfort, distress.

panic *noun* agitation, flap (*infml*),

alarm, dismay, consternation, fright, fear, horror, terror, frenzy, hysteria.
F3 calmness, confidence.
▪ *verb* lose one's nerve, lose one's head, go to pieces, flap (*infml*), overreact.
F3 relax.

panic-stricken *adjective* alarmed, frightened, horrified, terrified, petrified, scared stiff, in a cold sweat, panicky, frantic, frenzied, hysterical.
F3 relaxed, confident.

panoramic *adjective* scenic, wide, sweeping, extensive, far-reaching, widespread, overall, general, universal.
F3 narrow, restricted, limited.

pant *verb* puff, blow, gasp, wheeze, breathe, sigh, heave, throb, palpitate.

pants *noun* **1** *wearing a vest and pants*: underpants, drawers, panties, briefs, knickers (*infml*), thong, Y-fronts, boxer shorts, trunks, shorts. **2** (*US*) *he put his wallet in the back pocket of his pants*: trousers, slacks, jeans.

paper *noun* **1** *a daily paper/the Sunday papers*: newspaper, daily, broadsheet, tabloid, rag (*infml*), journal, organ (*fml*). **2** *personal/travel/legal papers*: document, credential, authorization, identification, certificate, deed. **3** *a paper on alternative medicine*: essay, composition, dissertation, thesis, treatise, article, report.

parade *noun* procession, cavalcade, motorcade, march, column, file, train, review, ceremony, spectacle, pageant, show, display, exhibition.
▪ *verb* **1** *parade down the high street*: march, process, file past. **2** *parading his recently-acquired wealth*: show, display, exhibit, show off, vaunt, flaunt, brandish.

paradise *noun* heaven, utopia, Shangri-La, Elysium, Eden, bliss, nirvana, delight.
F3 hell, Hades.

parallel *adjective* equidistant, aligned, coextensive, alongside, analogous, equivalent, corresponding, matching, like, similar, resembling.
F3 divergent, different.
▪ *noun* **1** *have no parallel*: match, equal, twin, duplicate, analogue, equivalent, counterpart. **2** *draw a parallel*: similarity, resemblance, likeness, correspondence, correlation, equivalence, analogy, comparison.

paralyse *verb* cripple, lame, disable, incapacitate, immobilize, anaesthetize, numb, deaden, freeze, transfix, halt, stop.

paralysed *adjective* paralytic, paraplegic, quadriplegic, crippled, lame, disabled, incapacitated, immobilized, numb.
F3 able-bodied.

paralysis *noun* paraplegia, quadriplegia, palsy, numbness, deadness, immobility.

paraphernalia *noun* equipment, gear (*infml*), tackle, apparatus, accessories, trappings, bits and pieces, odds and ends, belongings, effects, stuff (*infml*), things, baggage.

parcel *noun* package, packet, pack, box, carton, bundle.

parch *verb* dry (up), desiccate, dehydrate, bake, burn, scorch, sear, blister, wither, shrivel.

parched *adjective* **1** *a parched landscape*: arid, waterless, dry, dried up, dehydrated, scorched, withered, shrivelled. **2** (*infml*) *I'm absolutely parched*: thirsty, gasping (*infml*).

pardon *verb* forgive, condone, overlook, excuse, vindicate, acquit, absolve, remit, let off, reprieve, free, liberate, release.
E3 punish, discipline.
▪ *noun* forgiveness, mercy, clemency, indulgence, amnesty, excuse, acquittal, absolution, reprieve, release, discharge.
E3 punishment, condemnation.

parent *noun* father, mother, dam, sire (*fml*), progenitor (*fml*), begetter (*fml*), procreator (*fml*), guardian.

park *noun* grounds, estate, parkland, gardens, woodland, reserve, pleasure-ground.
▪ *verb* put, position, deposit, leave.

parliament *noun* legislature, senate, congress, house, assembly, convocation (*fml*), council, diet.

parody *noun* caricature, lampoon, burlesque, satire, send-up, spoof, skit, mimicry, imitation, take-off, travesty, distortion.

part *noun* **1** *have some parts missing*: component, constituent, element, factor, piece, bit, particle, fragment, scrap, segment, fraction, portion, share. **2** *a different part of the organization/country*: section, division, department, branch, sector, district, region, territory. **3** *get a part in a film*: role, character. **4** *did his part to make it a success*: duty, task, responsibility, office, function, capacity.
E3 1 whole, totality.
▪ *verb* **1** *part on the best of terms*: separate, part company, split up, break up, disband, leave, depart, withdraw, go away. **2** *part the curtains*: separate, divide, detach, disconnect, sever, split, tear, break, take apart, dismantle, come apart, disunite.

partial *adjective* **1** *a partial victory*: incomplete, limited, restricted, imperfect, fragmentary, unfinished. **2** *someone less partial should judge*: biased, prejudiced, partisan, one-sided, discriminatory, unfair, unjust, predisposed, coloured, affected.
E3 1 complete, total. **2** impartial, disinterested, unbiased, fair.

participate *verb* take part, join in, contribute, engage, be involved, enter, share, partake, co-operate, help, assist.

particle *noun* bit, piece, fragment, scrap, shred, sliver, speck, morsel, crumb, iota, whit, jot, tittle, atom, grain, drop.

particular *adjective* **1** *on that particular day*: specific, precise, exact, distinct, special, peculiar. **2** *made a particular effort to be polite*: exceptional, remarkable, notable, marked, thorough, unusual, uncommon. **3** *not very particular about hygiene*: fussy, discriminating, choosy (*infml*), finicky, fastidious.
F3 **1** general.
▪ *noun* detail, specific, point, feature, item, fact, circumstance.

particularly *adverb* especially, exceptionally, remarkably, notably, extraordinarily, unusually, uncommonly, surprisingly, in particular, specifically, explicitly, distinctly.

parting *noun* **1** *an emotional parting*: departure, going, leave-taking, farewell, goodbye, adieu. **2** *a parting of the ways*: divergence, separation, division, partition, rift, split, rupture, breaking.
F3 **1** meeting. **2** convergence.
▪ *adjective* departing, farewell, last, dying, final, closing, concluding.
F3 first.

partition *noun* **1** *build a partition in one corner*: divider, barrier, wall, panel, screen, room-divider. **2** *the partition of the country*: division, break-up, splitting, separation, parting, severance.
▪ *verb* separate, divide, subdivide, wall off, fence off, screen.

partly *adverb* somewhat, to some extent, to a certain extent, up to a point, slightly, fractionally, moderately, relatively, in part, partially, incompletely.
F3 completely, totally.

partner *noun* **1** *partner in crime*: associate, ally, confederate, colleague, team-mate, collaborator, accomplice, helper, mate, sidekick (*infml*), companion, comrade. **2** *my life partner*: spouse, husband, wife, consort, boyfriend, girlfriend, other half (*infml*), significant other.

partnership *noun* **1** *go into partnership*: alliance, confederation, affiliation, combination, union, syndicate, co-operative, association, society, corporation, company, firm, fellowship, fraternity, brotherhood, sisterhood. **2** *partnership in government*: collaboration, co-operation, participation, sharing.

party *noun* **1** *a birthday party*: celebration, festivity, social, do (*infml*), knees-up (*infml*), rave-up (*infml*), bash (*infml*), get-together, gathering, reunion, function, reception, at-home, housewarming. **2** *a search party*: team, squad, crew, gang, band, group, company, detachment. **3** *a political party*: faction, side, league, cabal, alliance, association, grouping, combination. **4** *the other party*: person, individual, litigant, plaintiff, defendant.

Kinds of party include:
acid-house party, barbecue, bash (*infml*), beanfeast (*infml*), beano (*infml*), birthday party, bunfight (*infml*), ceilidh, cocktail party, dinner party, disco, flatwarming, garden party, gathering of the clan (*infml*), Hallowe'en party, hen party, hooley (*infml*), hootenanny (*US infml*), housewarming, knees-up (*infml*), picnic, pyjama party, rave, rave-up (*infml*), shindig (*infml*), shower (*US infml*), sleepover, slumber party (*US*), social, soirée, stag party, supper party, tea party, thrash (*infml*), welcoming party. *See also* **celebration**.

pass[1] *verb* **1** *passed the other runners and went on to win*: surpass, exceed, go beyond, outdo, outstrip, overtake, leave behind. **2** *passing the time*: spend, while away, fill, occupy. **3** *time passing slowly*: go past, go by, elapse, lapse, proceed, roll, flow, run, move, go, disappear, vanish. **4** *passed him the butter/passed secrets to the enemy*: give, hand, transfer, transmit. **5** *legislation passed by parliament*: enact, ratify, validate, adopt, authorize, sanction, approve. **6** *pass an exam*: succeed, get through, qualify, graduate.

▪ *noun* permit, passport, identification, ticket, licence, authorization, warrant, permission.

pass[2] *noun* col, defile (*fml*), gorge, ravine, canyon, gap, passage.

passable *adjective* **1** *gave a passable performance*: satisfactory, acceptable, allowable, tolerable, average, ordinary, unexceptional, moderate, fair, adequate, all right, OK (*infml*), mediocre. **2** *the road is now passable*: clear, unobstructed, unblocked, open, navigable.

F3 **1** unacceptable, excellent. **2** obstructed, blocked, impassable.

passage *noun* **1** *a long unlit passage*: passageway, aisle, corridor, hall, hallway. **2** *read a short passage from the Bible*: extract, excerpt, quotation, text, paragraph, section, piece, clause, verse. **3** *book a passage to Australia*: journey, voyage, trip, crossing.

passing *adjective* ephemeral, transient, short-lived, temporary, momentary, fleeting, brief, short, cursory, hasty, quick, slight, superficial, shallow, casual, incidental.

F3 lasting, permanent.

passion *noun* feeling, emotion, love, adoration, infatuation, fondness, affection, lust, itch, desire, craving, fancy, mania, obsession, craze, eagerness, keenness, avidity, zest, enthusiasm, fanaticism, zeal, ardour, fervour, warmth, heat, fire, spirit, intensity, vehemence, anger, indignation, fury, rage, outburst.

F3 coolness, indifference, self-possession.

passionate *adjective* **1** *feel passionate about the subject*: ardent, fervent, eager, keen, avid, enthusiastic, fanatical, zealous, warm, hot, fiery, inflamed, aroused, excited, impassioned, intense, strong, fierce, vehement, violent, stormy, tempestuous, wild, frenzied. **2** *a passionate nature*: emotional, excitable, hot-headed, impetuous, impulsive, quick-tempered, irritable.
F3 1 phlegmatic, laid-back (*infml*).

passive *adjective* receptive, unassertive, submissive, docile, unresisting, non-violent, patient, resigned, long-suffering, indifferent, apathetic, lifeless, inert, inactive, non-participating.
F3 active, lively, responsive, involved.

past *adjective* **1** *the time is past*: over, ended, finished, completed, done, over and done with. **2** *past experiences*: former, previous, preceding, foregoing, late, recent. **3** *past times*: ancient, bygone, olden, early, gone, no more, extinct, defunct, forgotten.
F3 2 future.
▪ *noun* **1** *in the past*: history, former times, olden days, antiquity. **2** *know nothing about her past*: life, background, history, experience, track record.
F3 1 future.

paste *noun* adhesive, glue, gum, mastic, putty, cement.
▪ *verb* stick, glue, gum, cement, fix.

pastime *noun* hobby, activity, game, sport, recreation, play, fun, amusement, entertainment, diversion, distraction, relaxation.
F3 work, employment.

pastoral *adjective* **1** *a pastoral landscape*: rural, country, rustic, bucolic (*fml*), agricultural, agrarian, idyllic. **2** *pastoral duties/a pastoral visit*: ecclesiastical, clerical, priestly, ministerial.
F3 1 urban.

pasture *noun* grass, grassland, meadow, field, paddock, pasturage, grazing.

pasty *adjective* pale, pallid, wan, anaemic, pasty-faced, sickly, unhealthy.
F3 ruddy, healthy.

pat *verb* tap, dab, slap, touch, stroke, caress, fondle, pet.
▪ *noun* tap, dab, slap, touch, stroke, caress.

patch *noun* piece, bit, scrap, spot, area, stretch, tract, plot, lot, parcel.
▪ *verb* mend, repair, fix, cover, reinforce.

patchy *adjective* uneven, irregular, inconsistent, variable, random, fitful, erratic, sketchy, bitty, spotty, blotchy.
F3 even, uniform, regular, consistent.

path *noun* route, course, direction, way, passage, road, avenue, lane, footpath, bridleway, trail, track, walk.

pathetic *adjective* **1** *a pathetic sight*: pitiable, poor, sorry, lamentable, miserable, sad, distressing, moving, touching, poignant, plaintive, heart-rending, heartbreaking. **2** (*infml*) *a pathetic attempt at humour*: contemptible, derisory, deplorable, useless, worthless, inadequate, meagre, feeble.

≠ **1** cheerful. **2** admirable, excellent, valuable.

patience *noun* calmness, composure, self-control, restraint, tolerance, forbearance, endurance, fortitude, long-suffering, submission, resignation, stoicism, persistence, perseverance, diligence.

≠ impatience, intolerance, exasperation.

patient *adjective* calm, composed, self-possessed, self-controlled, restrained, even-tempered, mild, lenient, indulgent, understanding, forgiving, tolerant, accommodating, forbearing, long-suffering, uncomplaining, submissive, resigned, philosophical, stoical, persistent, persevering.

≠ impatient, restless, intolerant, exasperated.

▪ *noun* invalid, sufferer, case, client.

patriotic *adjective* nationalistic, chauvinistic, jingoistic, loyal, flag-waving.

patrol *verb* police, guard, protect, defend, go the rounds, tour, inspect.

patron *noun* **1** *a patron of the arts*: benefactor, philanthropist, sponsor, backer, supporter, sympathizer, advocate, champion, defender, protector, guardian, helper. **2** *the shop's regular patrons*: customer, client, frequenter, regular, shopper, buyer, purchaser, subscriber.

patronizing *adjective* condescending, stooping, overbearing, high-handed, haughty, superior, snobbish, supercilious, disdainful.

≠ humble, lowly.

patter *noun* **1** *the patter of tiny feet*: pattering, tapping, pitter-patter, beating. **2** *a salesman's patter*: chatter, gabble, jabber, line, pitch, spiel (*infml*), jargon, lingo (*infml*).

pattern *noun* **1** *a pattern of behaviour*: system, method, order, plan. **2** *a striped pattern*: decoration, ornamentation, ornament, figure, motif, design, style. **3** *was the pattern for many other schemes*: model, template, stencil, guide, original, prototype, standard, norm.

pause *verb* halt, stop, cease, discontinue, break off, interrupt, take a break, rest, wait, delay, hesitate.

▪ *noun* halt, stoppage, interruption, break, rest, breather (*infml*), lull, let-up (*infml*), respite, gap, interval, interlude, intermission, wait, delay, hesitation.

pay *verb* **1** *pay £30/the bill*: remit, settle, discharge, reward,

remunerate, recompense, reimburse, repay, refund, spend, pay out. **2** *the business didn't pay*: benefit, profit, pay off, bring in, yield, return. **3** *pay for one's mistakes*: atone, make amends, compensate, answer, suffer.
▪ *noun* remuneration, wages, salary, earnings, income, fee, stipend, honorarium, emoluments, payment, reward, recompense, compensation, reimbursement.

payment *noun* remittance, settlement, discharge, premium, outlay, advance, deposit, instalment, contribution, donation, allowance, reward, remuneration, pay, fee, hire, fare, toll.

peace *noun* **1** *enjoyed the peace of the countryside*: silence, quiet, hush, stillness, rest, relaxation, tranquillity, calm, calmness, composure, contentment. **2** *negotiate a lasting peace*: armistice, truce, ceasefire, conciliation, concord, harmony, agreement, treaty.
E3 **1** noise, disturbance. **2** war, disagreement.

peaceful *adjective* quiet, still, restful, relaxing, tranquil, serene, calm, placid, unruffled, undisturbed, untroubled, friendly, amicable, peaceable, pacific, gentle.
E3 noisy, disturbed, troubled, violent.

peak *noun* top, summit, pinnacle, crest, crown, zenith, height, maximum, climax, culmination, apex, tip, point.
E3 nadir, trough.
▪ *verb* climax, culminate, come to a head.

peal *noun* chime, carillon, toll, knell, ring, clang, ringing, crash, reverberation, rumble, roar, clap.
▪ *verb* chime, toll, ring, clang, resonate, crash, reverberate, resound, rumble, roll, roar.

peculiar *adjective* **1** *a peculiar person*: strange, odd, curious, funny, weird, bizarre, extraordinary, unusual, abnormal, exceptional, unconventional, offbeat, eccentric, way-out (*infml*), outlandish, exotic. **2** *a peculiar way of pronouncing certain words*: characteristic, distinctive, specific, particular, special, individual, personal, idiosyncratic, unique, singular.
E3 **1** ordinary, normal. **2** general, normal.

pedestrian *noun* walker, foot-traveller.

pedigree *noun* genealogy, family tree, lineage, ancestry, descent, line, family, parentage, derivation, extraction, race, breed, stock, blood.

peel *verb* pare, skin, strip, scale, flake (off).
▪ *noun* skin, rind, zest, peeling.

peep *verb* look, peek, glimpse, spy, squint, peer, emerge, issue, appear.
▪ *noun* look, peek, glimpse, glance, squint.

peer[1] *verb* look, gaze, scan, scrutinize, examine, inspect, spy, snoop, peep, squint.

peer[2] *noun* **1** *a peer of the realm*: aristocrat, noble, nobleman, lord, lady, duke, duchess, marquess, marquis, earl, count, viscount, baron. **2** *amongst one's peers*: equal, counterpart, equivalent, match, fellow.

peg *verb* fasten, secure, fix, attach, join.
▪ *noun* pin, dowel, hook, knob, marker, post, stake.

pelt *verb* **1** *pelted them with rotten fruit*: throw, hurl, bombard, shower, assail, batter, beat, hit, strike. **2** *it's pelting outside*: pour, teem, rain cats and dogs (*infml*). **3** *came pelting down the street*: rush, hurry, charge, belt (*infml*), tear, dash, speed, career.

penalize *verb* punish, discipline, correct, fine, handicap.
F3 reward.

penalty *noun* punishment, retribution, fine, forfeit, handicap, disadvantage.
F3 reward.

penetrate *verb* pierce, stab, prick, puncture, probe, sink, bore, enter, infiltrate, permeate, seep, pervade, suffuse.

penitent *adjective* repentant, contrite, sorry, apologetic, remorseful, regretful, conscience-stricken, shamefaced, humble.
F3 unrepentant, hard-hearted, callous.

penniless *adjective* poor, poverty-stricken, impoverished, destitute, bankrupt, ruined, bust, broke (*infml*), stony-broke (*infml*), skint (*infml*).
F3 rich, wealthy, affluent.

pension *noun* annuity, superannuation, allowance, benefit.

pent-up *adjective* repressed, inhibited, restrained, bottled-up, suppressed, stifled.

people *noun* persons, individuals, humans, human beings, mankind, humanity, folk, public, general public, populace, rank and file, population, inhabitants, citizens, community, society, race, nation.
▪ *verb* populate, inhabit, occupy, settle, colonize.

perceive *verb* **1** *could just perceive faint marks on the surface*: see, discern, make out, detect, discover, spot, catch sight of, notice, observe, view, remark, note, distinguish, recognize. **2** *perceiving that she was upset*: sense, feel, apprehend, learn, realize, appreciate, be aware of, know, grasp, understand, gather, deduce, conclude.

perceptible *adjective* perceivable, discernible, detectable, appreciable, distinguishable, observable, noticeable, obvious, evident, conspicuous, clear, plain, apparent, visible.
F3 imperceptible, inconspicuous.

perception *noun* sense, feeling,

impression, idea, conception, apprehension, awareness, consciousness, observation, recognition, grasp, understanding, insight, discernment, taste.

perceptive *adjective* discerning, observant, sensitive, responsive, aware, alert, quick, sharp, astute, shrewd.

E3 unobservant.

perfect *adjective* **1** *a perfect performance/trying to be perfect*: faultless, impeccable, flawless, immaculate, spotless, blameless, pure, superb, excellent, matchless, incomparable. **2** *a perfect circle*: exact, precise, accurate, right, correct, true. **3** *he would make a perfect partner for her*: ideal, model, exemplary, ultimate, consummate, expert, accomplished, experienced, skilful. **4** *felt a perfect fool*: utter, absolute, sheer, complete, entire, total.

E3 **1** imperfect, flawed, blemished. **2** inaccurate, wrong. **3** inexperienced, unskilled.

▪ *verb* fulfil, consummate, complete, finish, polish, refine, elaborate.

E3 spoil, mar.

perfection *noun* faultlessness, flawlessness, excellence, superiority, ideal, model, paragon, crown, pinnacle, acme, consummation, completion.

E3 imperfection, flaw.

perform *verb* **1** *perform a task/one's duty*: do, carry out, execute, discharge, fulfil, satisfy, complete, achieve, accomplish, bring off, pull off, effect, bring about. **2** *performing a play/Hamlet*: stage, put on, present, enact, represent, act, play, appear as. **3** *car performs well in wet conditions*: function, work, operate, behave, produce.

performance *noun* **1** *a performance of Macbeth*: show, act, play, appearance, presentation, production, interpretation, rendition, representation, portrayal, acting. **2** *in the performance of his duty*: action, deed, doing, carrying out, execution, implementation, discharge, fulfilment, completion, achievement, accomplishment. **3** *the engine's performance*: functioning, operation, behaviour, conduct.

performer *noun* actor, actress, player, artiste, entertainer.

perfume *noun* scent, fragrance, smell, odour, aroma, bouquet, sweetness, balm, essence, cologne, toilet water, incense.

perhaps *adverb* maybe, possibly, conceivably, feasibly.

perimeter *noun* circumference, edge, border, boundary, frontier, limit, bounds, confines, fringe, margin, periphery.

E3 middle, centre, heart.

period *noun* era, epoch, age, generation, date, years, time, term, season, stage, phase, stretch, turn, session, interval, space, span, spell, cycle.

perish *verb* rot, decay, decompose, disintegrate, crumble, collapse, fall, die, expire, pass away.

perishable *adjective* destructible, biodegradable, decomposable, short-lived.
F3 imperishable, durable.

perk *noun* perquisite (*fml*), fringe benefit, benefit, bonus, dividend, gratuity, tip, extra, plus (*infml*).

perk up *verb* (*infml*) brighten, cheer up, buck up (*infml*), revive, liven up, pep up (*infml*), rally, recover, improve, look up.

permanent *adjective* fixed, stable, unchanging, imperishable, indestructible, unfading, eternal, everlasting, lifelong, perpetual, constant, steadfast, perennial, long-lasting, lasting, enduring, durable.
F3 temporary, ephemeral, fleeting.

permeate *verb* pass through, soak through, filter through, seep through, penetrate, infiltrate, pervade, imbue, saturate, impregnate, fill.

permission *noun* consent, assent, agreement, approval, go-ahead, green light (*infml*), authorization, sanction, leave, warrant, permit, licence, dispensation, freedom, liberty.
F3 prohibition.

permit *verb* /per-**mit**/ allow, let, consent, agree, admit, grant, authorize, sanction, warrant, license.
F3 prohibit, forbid.

▪ *noun* /**per**-mit/ pass, passport, visa, licence, warrant, authorization, sanction, permission.
F3 prohibition.

perpendicular *adjective* vertical, upright, erect, straight, sheer, plumb.
F3 horizontal.

perpetual *adjective* eternal, everlasting, infinite, endless, unending, never-ending, interminable, ceaseless, unceasing, incessant, continuous, uninterrupted, constant, persistent, continual, repeated, recurrent, perennial, permanent, lasting, enduring, abiding, unchanging.
F3 intermittent, temporary, ephemeral, transient.

perplex *verb* puzzle, baffle, mystify, stump (*infml*), confuse, muddle, confound, bewilder, dumbfound.

persecute *verb* hound, pursue, hunt, bother, worry, annoy, pester, harass, molest, abuse, ill-treat, maltreat, oppress, tyrannize, victimize, martyr, distress, afflict, torment, torture, crucify.
F3 pamper, spoil.

persevere *verb* continue, carry on, stick at it (*infml*), keep going, soldier on, persist, plug away (*infml*), remain, stand firm, stand fast, hold on, hang on.
F3 give up, stop, discontinue.

persist *verb* remain, linger, last, endure, abide (*fml*), continue,

carry on, keep at it, persevere, insist.
OPP desist, stop.

persistent *adjective* **1** *a persistent knocking sound*: incessant, endless, never-ending, interminable, continuous, unrelenting, relentless, unremitting, constant, steady, continual, repeated, perpetual, lasting, enduring. **2** *persistent effort*: persevering, determined, resolute, dogged, tenacious, stubborn, obstinate, steadfast, zealous, tireless, unflagging, indefatigable.

person *noun* individual, being, human being, human, man, woman, body, soul, character, type.

personal *adjective* own, private, confidential, intimate, special, particular, individual, exclusive, idiosyncratic, distinctive.
OPP public, general, universal.

personality *noun* **1** *an attractive personality*: character, nature, disposition, temperament, individuality, psyche, traits, make-up, charm, charisma, magnetism. **2** *a TV personality*: celebrity, notable, personage, public figure, VIP (*infml*), star.

personify *verb* embody, epitomize, typify, exemplify, symbolize, represent, mirror.

personnel *noun* staff, workforce, workers, employees, crew, human resources, manpower, people, members.

perspective *noun* aspect, angle, slant, attitude, standpoint, viewpoint, point of view, view, vista, scene, prospect, outlook, proportion, relation.

perspire *verb* sweat, exude, secrete, swelter, drip.

persuade *verb* coax, prevail upon, lean on, cajole, wheedle, inveigle (*fml*), talk into, induce, bring round, win over, convince, convert, sway, influence, lead on, incite, prompt, urge.
OPP dissuade, deter, discourage.

persuasion *noun* **1** *used persuasion to get what she wants*: coaxing, cajolery, wheedling, inducement, enticement, pull, power, influence, conviction, conversion. **2** *of a different religious persuasion*: opinion, school (of thought), party, faction, side, conviction, faith, belief, denomination, sect.

persuasive *adjective* convincing, plausible, cogent, sound, valid, influential, forceful, weighty, effective, telling, potent, compelling, moving, touching.
OPP unconvincing.

perturb *verb* disturb, bother, trouble, upset, worry, alarm, disconcert, unsettle, discompose, ruffle, fluster, agitate, vex.
OPP reassure, compose.

perverse *adjective* contrary, wayward, wrong-headed, wilful, headstrong, stubborn, obstinate, unyielding, intransigent, disobedient, rebellious,

troublesome, unmanageable, ill-tempered, cantankerous, unreasonable, incorrect, improper.
F3 obliging, co-operative, reasonable.

pessimistic *adjective* negative, cynical, fatalistic, defeatist, resigned, hopeless, despairing, despondent, dejected, downhearted, glum, morose, melancholy, depressed, dismal, gloomy, bleak.
F3 optimistic.

pest *noun* nuisance, bother, annoyance, irritation, vexation, trial, curse, scourge, bane, blight, bug.

pester *verb* nag, badger, hound, hassle (*infml*), harass, plague, torment, provoke, worry, bother, disturb, annoy, irritate, pick on, get at (*infml*).

pet *adjective* favourite, favoured, preferred, dearest, cherished, special, particular, personal.
▪ *verb* stroke, caress, fondle, cuddle, kiss, neck (*infml*), snog (*slang*).

peter out *verb* dwindle, taper off, fade, wane, ebb, fail, cease, stop.

petition *noun* appeal, round robin, application, request, solicitation, plea, entreaty, prayer, supplication, invocation.
▪ *verb* appeal, call upon, ask, crave, solicit, bid, urge, press, implore, beg, plead, entreat, beseech, supplicate, pray.

petrified *adjective* terrified, horrified, appalled, paralysed, numb.

petty *adjective* **1** *a petty offence*: minor, unimportant, insignificant, trivial, secondary, lesser, small, little, slight, trifling, paltry, inconsiderable, negligible. **2** *don't be so petty!*: small-minded, mean, ungenerous, grudging, spiteful.
F3 **1** important, significant. **2** generous.

phantom *noun* ghost, spectre, spirit, apparition, vision, hallucination, illusion, figment.

phase *noun* stage, step, time, period, spell, season, chapter, position, point, aspect, state, condition.

phenomenal *adjective* marvellous, sensational, stupendous, amazing, remarkable, extraordinary, exceptional, unusual, unbelievable, incredible.

phenomenon *noun* **1** *a natural phenomenon*: occurrence, happening, event, incident, episode, fact, appearance, sight. **2** *a young tennis phenomenon*: wonder, marvel, miracle, prodigy, rarity, curiosity, spectacle, sensation.

philanthropy *noun* humanitarianism, public-spiritedness, altruism, unselfishness, benevolence, kind-heartedness, charity, alms-giving, patronage, generosity, liberality, open-handedness.
F3 misanthropy.

philosophical *adjective* **1** *a philosophical discussion*: metaphysical, abstract, theoretical, analytical, rational, logical, erudite, learned, wise, thoughtful. **2** *was philosophical about his failure*: resigned, patient, stoical, unruffled, calm, composed.

philosophy *noun* metaphysics, rationalism, reason, logic, thought, thinking, wisdom, knowledge, ideology, world-view, doctrine, beliefs, convictions, values, principles, attitude, viewpoint.

phobia *noun* fear, terror, dread, anxiety, neurosis, obsession, hang-up (*infml*), thing (*infml*), aversion, dislike, hatred, horror, loathing, revulsion, repulsion.
F3 love, liking.

Phobias (by name of fear) include: zoophobia (*animals*), apiphobia (*bees*), haemophobia (*blood*), ailurophobia (*cats*), necrophobia (*corpses*), demophobia/ ochlophobia (*crowds*), scotophobia (*darkness*), thanatophobia (*death*), cynophobia (*dogs*), claustrophobia (*enclosed places*), panphobia (*everything*), pyrophobia (*fire*), xenophobia (*foreigners*), bacteriophobia/ spermophobia (*germs*), phasmophobia (*ghosts*), acrophobia (*high places*), hippophobia (*horses*), entomophobia (*insects*), astraphobia (*lightning*), autophobia (*loneliness*), agoraphobia (*open spaces*), toxiphobia (*poison*), herpetophobia (*reptiles*), ophiophobia (*snakes*), tachophobia (*speed*), arachnophobia (*spiders*), triskaidekaphobia (*thirteen*), brontophobia (*thunder*), hodophobia (*travel*), hydrophobia (*water*). *See also* **mania**.

---

phone *verb* telephone, ring (up), call (up), dial, contact, get in touch, give a buzz (*infml*), give a tinkle (*infml*).

phoney *adjective* fake, counterfeit, forged, bogus, trick, false, spurious, assumed, affected, put-on, sham, pseudo, imitation.
F3 real, genuine.

photograph *noun* photo, snap, snapshot, print, shot, slide, transparency, picture, image, likeness.
▪ *verb* snap, take, film, shoot, video, record.

phrase *noun* construction, clause, idiom, expression, saying, utterance, remark.
▪ *verb* word, formulate, frame, couch, present, put, express, say, utter, pronounce.

physical *adjective* **1** *physical pain*: bodily, corporeal, fleshy, incarnate, mortal, earthly. **2** *the physical world*: material, concrete, solid, substantial, tangible, visible, real, actual.
F3 mental, spiritual.

physics

Terms used in physics include:
absolute zero, acceleration, acoustics, alpha particle, Archimedes principle, atom, beta particle, Big Bang theory, capillary action, centrifugal force, centripetal force, circuit, circuit-breaker, critical mass, cryogenics, density, diffraction, elasticity, electric current, electric discharge, electricity, electromagnetism, electron, energy, entropy, evaporation, force, formula, freezing point, frequency, friction, gamma ray, gravity, half-life, hydraulics, hydrodynamics, hydrostatics, inertia, infrared, ion, Kelvin effect, kinetic energy, laser, latent heat, lens, light emission, light intensity, longitudinal wave, luminescence, Mach number, magnetic field, magnetism, mass, mechanics, microwave, Mohs scale, molecule, neutron, nuclear, nuclear fission, nuclear fusion, nuclear physics, nucleus, optical centre, optics, oscillation, parallel motion, particle, periodic law, perpetual motion, phonon, photon, photosensitivity, polarity, potential energy, proton, quantum chromodynamics (QCD), quantum electrodynamics (QED), quantum mechanics, quantum theory, quark, radiation, radioactivity, radioisotope, reflection, refraction, relativity, resistance, resonance, semiconductor, sensitivity, separation, SI unit, specific gravity, specific heat capacity, spectroscopy, spectrum, statics, surface tension, thermodynamics, Thomson effect, transverse wave, ultrasound, ultraviolet, velocity, viscosity, visible spectrum, volume, wave, X-ray.

---

physique *noun* body, figure, shape, form, build, frame, structure, constitution, make-up.

pick *verb* **1** *pick a number*: select, choose, opt for, decide on, settle on, single out. **2** *pick strawberries*: gather, collect, pluck, harvest.
▪ *noun* **1** *take your pick*: choice, selection, option, decision, preference. **2** *the pick of the crop*: best, cream, flower, élite, elect.

picket *verb* protest, demonstrate, boycott, blockade, enclose, surround.

pickle *verb* preserve, conserve, souse, marinade, steep, cure, salt.

pictorial *adjective* graphic, diagrammatic, schematic, representational, vivid, expressive, illustrated, picturesque, scenic.

picture *noun* **1** *hang pictures on the wall*: painting, portrait, landscape, drawing, sketch, illustration, engraving, photograph, print, representation, likeness, image, effigy. **2** *gives a good picture of the overall situation*: depiction, portrayal, description, account, report, impression.
▪ *verb* **1** *picture the scene*: imagine, envisage, envision, conceive,

visualize, see. **2** *was pictured sitting on a wall*: depict, describe, represent, show, portray, draw, sketch, paint, photograph, illustrate.

picturesque *adjective* **1** *a picturesque view*: attractive, beautiful, pretty, charming, quaint, idyllic, scenic. **2** *his account was picturesque*: descriptive, graphic, vivid, colourful, striking.
F3 **1** unattractive. **2** dull.

piece *noun* **1** *a piece of orange/ fabric/the jigsaw*: fragment, bit, scrap, morsel, mouthful, bite, lump, chunk, slice, sliver, snippet, shred, offcut, sample, component, constituent, element, part, segment, section, division, fraction, share, portion, quantity. **2** *a piece in the paper*: article, item, report, study, work, composition, creation, specimen, example.

pierce *verb* penetrate, enter, stick into, puncture, drill, bore, probe, perforate, punch, prick, stab, lance, bayonet, run through, spear, skewer, spike, impale, transfix.

piercing *adjective* **1** *a piercing cry*: shrill, high-pitched, loud, ear-splitting, sharp. **2** *piercing eyes*: penetrating, probing, searching. **3** *a piercing wind*: cold, bitter, raw, biting, keen, fierce, severe, wintry, frosty, freezing. **4** *a piercing pain*: agonizing, excruciating, stabbing, lacerating.

pig *noun* **1** *pigs in the farmyard*: swine, hog, sow, boar. **2** *made a pig of herself*: glutton, gourmand.

pigeonhole *noun* compartment, niche, slot, cubby-hole, cubicle, locker, box, place, section, class, category, classification.
▪ *verb* compartmentalize, label, classify, sort, file, catalogue, alphabetize, shelve, defer.

pigment *noun* colour, hue, tint, dye, stain, paint, colouring, tincture.

pile *noun* stack, heap, mound, mountain, mass, accumulation, collection, assortment, hoard, stockpile.
▪ *verb* stack, heap, mass, amass, accumulate, build up, gather, assemble, collect, hoard, stockpile, store, load, pack, jam, crush, crowd, flock, flood, stream, rush, charge.

pilgrimage *noun* crusade, mission, expedition, journey, trip, tour.

pillar *noun* column, shaft, post, mast, pier, upright, pile, support, prop, mainstay, bastion, tower of strength.

pilot *noun* **1** *a fighter pilot*: flyer, aviator, airman. **2** *a ship's pilot*: navigator, steersman, helmsman, coxswain, captain, leader, director, guide.
▪ *verb* fly, drive, steer, direct, control, handle, manage, operate, run, conduct, lead, guide, navigate.

pin *verb* tack, nail, fix, affix, attach, join, staple, clip, fasten, secure, hold down, restrain, immobilize.

▪ *noun* tack, nail, screw, spike, rivet, bolt, peg, fastener, clip, staple, brooch.

pinch *verb* **1** *pinched her cheek*: squeeze, compress, crush, press, tweak, nip, hurt, grip, grasp. **2** (*infml*) *his bike was pinched*: steal, nick (*infml*), pilfer, filch, snatch.
▪ *noun* **1** *gave him a pinch*: squeeze, tweak, nip. **2** *a pinch of salt*: dash, soupçon, taste, bit, speck, jot, mite.

pine *verb* long, yearn, ache, sigh, grieve, mourn, wish, desire, crave, hanker, hunger, thirst.

pinnacle *noun* **1** *a rocky pinnacle*: peak, summit, top, cap, crown, crest, apex, vertex, acme, zenith, height, eminence. **2** *the pinnacle of the roof*: spire, steeple, turret, pyramid, cone, obelisk, needle.

pioneer *noun* colonist, settler, frontiersman, frontierswoman, explorer, developer, pathfinder, trail-blazer, leader, innovator, inventor, discoverer, founder.

pious *adjective* **1** *a good and pious man*: devout, godly, saintly, holy, spiritual, religious, reverent, virtuous, righteous, moral. **2** *a pious attitude*: sanctimonious, holier-than-thou (*infml*), self-righteous, goody-goody (*infml*), hypocritical.
F3 **1** impious, irreligious, irreverent.

pipe *noun* tube, hose, piping, tubing, pipeline, line, main, flue, duct, conduit, channel, passage, conveyor.

pit *noun* mine, coalmine, excavation, trench, ditch, hollow, depression, indentation, dent, hole, cavity, crater, pothole, gulf, chasm, abyss.

pitch *verb* **1** *pitching the ball*: throw, fling, toss, chuck (*infml*), lob, bowl, hurl, heave, sling, fire, launch, aim, direct. **2** *ship pitched and rolled*: plunge, dive, plummet, drop, fall headlong, tumble, lurch, roll, wallow. **3** *pitch camp*: erect, put up, set up, place, station, settle, plant, fix.
▪ *noun* **1** *cricket pitch*: ground, field, playing-field, arena, stadium. **2** *played at the correct pitch*: sound, tone, timbre, modulation, frequency, level.

pitfall *noun* danger, peril, hazard, trap, snare, stumbling block, catch, snag, drawback, difficulty.

pitiful *adjective* **1** *a pitiful example*: contemptible, despicable, low, mean, vile, shabby, deplorable, lamentable, woeful, inadequate, hopeless, pathetic (*infml*), insignificant, paltry, worthless. **2** *a pitiful wail*: piteous, doleful, mournful, distressing, heart-rending, pathetic, pitiable, sad, miserable, wretched, poor, sorry.

pity *noun* **1** *feel pity for them*: sympathy, commiseration, regret, understanding, fellow-feeling, compassion, kindness, tenderness, mercy, forbearance. **2** *what a pity!*: shame, misfortune, bad luck.

F3 **1** cruelty, anger, scorn.
▪ *verb* feel sorry for, feel for, sympathize with, commiserate with, grieve for, weep for.

pivot *noun* axis, hinge, fulcrum, axle, spindle, kingpin, linchpin, swivel, hub, focal point, centre, heart.
▪ *verb* **1** *windows that pivot inwards*: swivel, turn, spin, revolve, rotate, swing. **2** *success or failure pivots on his performance today*: depend, rely, hinge, hang, lie.

place *noun* **1** *broken in several places*: site, locale, venue, location, situation, spot, point, position. **2** *a place at table/take your place*: seat, space, room. **3** *a place on the map*: city, town, village, locality, neighbourhood, district, area, region. **4** *a big place in town*: building, property, dwelling, residence, house, flat, apartment, home.
▪ *verb* put, set, plant, fix, position, locate, situate, rest, settle, lay, stand, deposit, leave.

placid *adjective* calm, composed, unruffled, laid-back (*infml*), untroubled, cool, self-possessed, level-headed, imperturbable, phlegmatic, mild, gentle, equable, even-tempered, serene, tranquil, still, quiet, peaceful, restful.
F3 excitable, agitated, disturbed.

plague *noun* **1** *thousands died from plague*: pestilence, epidemic, disease, infection, contagion. **2** *a plague of biting flies*: nuisance, annoyance, infestation, invasion, scourge, torment.
▪ *verb* annoy, vex, bother, disturb, trouble, distress, upset, pester, harass, hound, haunt, bedevil, afflict, torment, torture, persecute.

plain *adjective* **1** *good plain cooking*: ordinary, basic, simple, unpretentious, modest, unadorned, unelaborate, restrained. **2** *it was plain to see*: obvious, evident, patent, clear, understandable, apparent, visible, unmistakable. **3** *plain speaking*: frank, candid, blunt, outspoken, direct, forthright, straightforward, unambiguous, plain-spoken, open, honest, truthful. **4** *a plain face*: unattractive, ugly, unprepossessing, unlovely. **5** *plain fabric*: unpatterned, unvariegated, uncoloured, self-coloured.
F3 **1** fancy, elaborate. **2** unclear, obscure. **3** devious, deceitful. **4** attractive, good-looking. **5** patterned.
▪ *noun* grassland, prairie, steppe, lowland, flat, plateau, tableland.

plan *noun* **1** *the plans for the extension*: blueprint, layout, diagram, chart, map, drawing, sketch, representation, design. **2** *have a cunning plan*: idea, suggestion, proposal, proposition, project, scheme, plot, system, method, procedure, strategy, programme, schedule, scenario.
▪ *verb* **1** *planning the attack*: plot, scheme, design, invent, devise, contrive, formulate, frame, draft, outline, prepare, organize,

arrange. **2** *plan to be a lawyer*: aim, intend, propose, contemplate, envisage, foresee.

plant *noun* flower, shrub, herb, bush, greenery.

▪ *verb* **1** *plant seeds*: sow, seed, bury, transplant. **2** *plant an idea in his head*: insert, put, place, set, fix, lodge, root, settle, found, establish.

Plants include:

annual, biennial, perennial; cultivar, evergreen, herbaceous plant, house plant, hybrid, pot plant, succulent; air-plant, algae, bush, cactus, cereal, grass, fern, flower, fungus, herb, lichen, moss, shrub, tree, vegetable, vine, water-plant, weed, wild flower; bulb, bush, climber, corm, sapling, seedling. *See also* **flower**.

---

plaster *verb* daub, smear, coat, cover, spread.

plate *noun* **1** *a plate of mince*: dish, platter, salver, helping, serving, portion. **2** *a colour plate*: illustration, picture, print, lithograph.

▪ *verb* coat, cover, overlay, veneer, laminate, electroplate, anodize, galvanize, platinize, gild, silver, tin.

platform *noun* stage, podium, dais, rostrum, stand.

plausible *adjective* credible, believable, reasonable, logical, likely, possible, probable, convincing, persuasive, smooth-talking, glib.

F3 implausible, unlikely, improbable.

play *verb* **1** *play games*: amuse oneself, have fun, enjoy oneself, revel, sport, romp, frolic, caper. **2** *play a part*: participate, take part, join in, compete. **3** *France played Italy*: oppose, vie with, challenge, take on. **4** *played Hamlet*: act, perform, portray, represent, impersonate.

F3 **1** work.

▪ *noun* **1** *all work and no play*: fun, amusement, entertainment, diversion, recreation, sport, game, hobby, pastime. **2** *a part in a play*: drama, tragedy, comedy, farce, show, performance.

F3 **1** work.

player *noun* **1** *a football player*: contestant, competitor, participant, sportsman, sportswoman. **2** *the players took a bow*: performer, entertainer, artiste, actor, actress, musician, instrumentalist.

playful *adjective* sportive, frolicsome, lively, spirited, mischievous, roguish, impish, puckish, kittenish, good-natured, jesting, teasing, humorous, tongue-in-cheek.

F3 serious.

plea *noun* **1** *a plea for mercy*: appeal, petition, request, entreaty, supplication, prayer, invocation. **2** *a plea of temporary insanity*: defence, justification, excuse, explanation, claim.

plead *verb* **1** *pleading with him to let them go*: beg, implore, beseech, entreat, appeal, petition, ask, request. **2** *plead ignorance*: assert, maintain, claim, allege.

pleasant *adjective* agreeable, nice, fine, lovely, delightful, charming, likable, amiable, friendly, affable, good-humoured, cheerful, congenial, enjoyable, amusing, pleasing, gratifying, satisfying, acceptable, welcome, refreshing.

F3 unpleasant, nasty, unfriendly.

please *verb* **1** *it pleases me to see them so happy*: delight, charm, captivate, entertain, amuse, cheer, gladden, humour, indulge, gratify, satisfy, content, suit. **2** *if you please*: want, will, wish, desire, like, prefer, choose, think fit.

F3 1 displease, annoy, anger, sadden.

pleased *adjective* contented, satisfied, gratified, glad, happy, delighted, thrilled, euphoric.

F3 displeased, annoyed.

pleasing *adjective* gratifying, satisfying, acceptable, good, pleasant, agreeable, nice, delightful, charming, attractive, engaging, winning.

F3 unpleasant, disagreeable.

pleasure *noun* amusement, entertainment, recreation, fun, enjoyment, gratification, satisfaction, contentment, happiness, joy, delight, comfort, solace.

F3 sorrow, pain, trouble, displeasure.

pleat *noun, verb* tuck, fold, crease, flute, crimp, gather, pucker.

plentiful *adjective* ample, abundant, profuse, copious, overflowing, lavish, generous, liberal, bountiful, fruitful, productive.

F3 scarce, scanty, rare.

plenty *noun* abundance, profusion, plethora, lots (*infml*), loads (*infml*), masses (*infml*), heaps (*infml*), piles (*infml*), stacks (*infml*), enough, sufficiency, quantity, mass, volume, fund, mine, store.

F3 scarcity, lack, want, need.

pliable *adjective* pliant, flexible, bendable, bendy (*infml*), supple, lithe, malleable, plastic, yielding, adaptable, accommodating, manageable, tractable, docile, compliant, biddable, persuadable, responsive, receptive, impressionable, susceptible.

F3 rigid, inflexible, headstrong.

plod *verb* **1** *plod through the mud*: trudge, tramp, stump, lumber, plough through. **2** *keep plodding on regardless*: drudge, labour, toil, grind, slog, persevere, soldier on.

plot *noun* **1** *the Gunpowder Plot*: conspiracy, intrigue, machination, scheme, plan, stratagem. **2** *couldn't follow the plot*: story, narrative, subject, theme, storyline, thread, outline, scenario. **3** *plot of land*: patch, tract, area, allotment, lot, parcel.

▪ *verb* **1** *plotting against him*: conspire, intrigue, machinate, scheme, hatch, lay, cook up, devise, contrive, plan, project, design, draft. **2** *plotting their route*: chart, map, mark, locate, draw, calculate.

ploy *noun* manoeuvre, stratagem, tactic, move, device, contrivance, scheme, game, trick, artifice, dodge, wile, ruse, subterfuge.

pluck *verb* **1** *plucking the feathers from the bird*: pull, draw, tug, snatch, pull off, remove, pick, collect, gather, harvest. **2** *pluck a guitar*: pick, twang, strum.

plug *noun* **1** *a bath plug*: stopper, bung, cork, spigot. **2** (*infml*) *giving his new book a plug*: advertisement, publicity, mention, puff.

▪ *verb* **1** *plug the hole*: stop (up), bung, cork, block, choke, close, seal, fill, pack, stuff. **2** (*infml*) *plugging their new album*: advertise, publicize, promote, push, mention.

plump *adjective* fat, dumpy, tubby, stout, round, rotund, portly, chubby, podgy, fleshy, full, ample, buxom.

F3 thin, skinny.

plunder *verb* loot, pillage, ravage, devastate, sack, raid, ransack, rifle, steal, rob, strip.

plunge *verb* dive, jump, nosedive, swoop, dive-bomb, plummet, descend, go down, sink, drop, fall, pitch, tumble, hurtle, career, charge, dash, rush, tear.

▪ *noun* dive, jump, swoop, descent, drop, fall, tumble, immersion, submersion.

poach *verb* steal, pilfer, appropriate, trespass, encroach, infringe.

pocket *noun* pouch, bag, envelope, receptacle, compartment, hollow, cavity.

▪ *verb* take, appropriate, help oneself to, lift, pilfer, filch, steal, nick (*infml*), pinch (*infml*).

poem

Types of poem include:

ballad, clerihew, elegy, epic, haiku, idyll, lay, limerick, lyric, madrigal, nursery-rhyme, ode, pastoral, roundelay, saga, sonnet, triolet. *See also* **literature**; **song**.

poet *noun* versifier, rhymer, rhymester, lyricist, bard, minstrel.

poetic *adjective* poetical, lyrical, moving, artistic, graceful, flowing, metrical, rhythmical, rhyming.

F3 prosaic.

poignant *adjective* moving, touching, affecting, tender, distressing, upsetting, heartbreaking, heart-rending, piteous, pathetic, sad, painful, agonizing.

point *noun* **1** *has several good points*: feature, attribute, aspect, facet, detail, particular, item, subject, topic. **2** *what's the point?*: use, purpose, motive, reason, object, intention, aim, end, goal, objective. **3** *the point of the story*: essence, crux, core, pith, gist, thrust, meaning, drift, burden. **4** *a point on the route*: place, position, situation, location, site, spot. **5** *at this point in time*: moment, instant,

juncture, stage, time, period. **6** *a point of light*: dot, spot, mark, speck, full stop.
▪ *verb* **1** *point a gun*: aim, direct, train, level. **2** *point to the culprit*: indicate, signal, show, signify, denote, designate.

point-blank *adjective* direct, forthright, straightforward, plain, explicit, open, unreserved, blunt, frank, candid.

pointed *adjective* sharp, keen, edged, barbed, cutting, incisive, trenchant (*fml*), biting, penetrating, telling.

pointless *adjective* useless, futile, vain, fruitless, aimless, unproductive, unprofitable, worthless, senseless, absurd, meaningless.
F3 useful, profitable, meaningful.

point of view *noun* opinion, view, belief, judgement, attitude, position, standpoint, viewpoint, outlook, perspective, approach, angle, slant.

poised *adjective* **1** *a poised performance*: dignified, graceful, calm, composed, unruffled, collected, self-possessed, cool, self-confident, assured. **2** *poised for action*: prepared, ready, set, waiting, expectant.

poison *noun* toxin, venom, bane, blight, cancer, malignancy, contagion, contamination, corruption.
▪ *verb* infect, contaminate, pollute, taint, adulterate, corrupt, deprave, pervert, warp.

poisonous *adjective* toxic, venomous, lethal, deadly, fatal, mortal, noxious, pernicious, malicious.

poke *verb* prod, stab, jab, stick, thrust, push, shove, nudge, elbow, dig, butt, hit, punch.
▪ *noun* prod, jab, thrust, shove, nudge, dig, butt, punch.

police *noun* police force, constabulary, the law (*infml*), the cops (*infml*).
▪ *verb* check, control, regulate, monitor, watch, observe, supervise, oversee, patrol, guard, protect, defend, keep the peace.

policy *noun* **1** *not our policy*: code of practice, rules, guidelines, procedure, method, practice, custom, protocol. **2** *government policy*: course of action, line, course, plan, programme, scheme, stance, position.

polish *verb* shine, brighten, smooth, rub, buff, burnish, clean, wax.
F3 tarnish, dull.
▪ *noun* **1** *a tin of polish*: wax, varnish. **2** *a high polish*: shine, gloss, sheen, lustre, brightness, brilliance, sparkle, smoothness, finish, glaze, veneer.
F3 **2** dullness.

polite *adjective* courteous, well-mannered, respectful, civil, well-bred, refined, cultured, gentlemanly, ladylike, gracious, obliging, thoughtful, considerate, tactful, diplomatic.
F3 impolite, discourteous, rude.

politics *noun* public affairs, civics, affairs of state, statecraft, government, diplomacy, statesmanship, political science.

Terms used in politics include: alliance, assembly, ballot, bill, cabinet, campaign, civil service, coalition, constitution, council, coup d'état, détente, devolution, election, electoral register, first minister, general election, government, green paper, Hansard, left wing, lobby, local government, majority, mandate, manifesto, nationalization, parliament, party, party line, prime minister's question time, propaganda, proportional representation, rainbow coalition, referendum, right wing, sanction, shadow cabinet, sovereignty, state, summit conference, term of office, veto, vote, welfare state, whip, three-line whip, white paper.

poll *noun* ballot, vote, voting, plebiscite, referendum, straw-poll, sampling, canvass, opinion poll, survey, census, count, tally.

pollution *noun* impurity, contamination, infection, taint, adulteration, corruption, dirtiness, foulness, defilement.
F3 purification, purity, cleanness.

pompous *adjective* self-important, arrogant, grandiose, supercilious, overbearing, imperious, magisterial, bombastic, high-flown, overblown, windy, affected, pretentious, ostentatious, stuffy.
F3 unassuming, modest, simple, unaffected.

pool[1] *noun* puddle, pond, lake, mere, tarn, watering-hole, paddling-pool, swimming-pool.

pool[2] *noun* fund, reserve, accumulation, bank, kitty, purse, pot, jackpot.
▪ *verb* contribute, chip in (*infml*), combine, amalgamate, merge, share, muck in (*infml*).

poor *adjective* **1** *a poor country*: impoverished, poverty-stricken, badly off, hard-up, broke (*infml*), stony-broke (*infml*), skint (*infml*), bankrupt, penniless, destitute, miserable, wretched, distressed, straitened, needy, lacking, deficient, insufficient, scanty, skimpy, meagre, sparse, depleted, exhausted. **2** *a poor mark*: bad, substandard, unsatisfactory, inferior, mediocre, below par, low-grade, second-rate, third-rate, shoddy, imperfect, faulty, weak, feeble, pathetic (*infml*), sorry, worthless, fruitless. **3** *the poor souls*: unfortunate, unlucky, luckless, ill-fated, unhappy, miserable, pathetic, pitiable, pitiful.
F3 **1** rich, wealthy, affluent. **2** superior, impressive. **3** fortunate, lucky.

poorly *adjective* ill, sick, unwell, indisposed, ailing, sickly, off colour, below par, out of sorts (*infml*), under the weather (*infml*), seedy, groggy, rotten (*infml*).
F3 well, healthy.

pop *verb* burst, explode, go off, bang, crack, snap.
▪ *noun* bang, crack, snap, burst, explosion.

popular *adjective* well-liked, favourite, liked, favoured, approved, in demand, sought-after, fashionable, modish, trendy (*infml*), prevailing, current, accepted, conventional, standard, stock, common, prevalent, widespread, universal, general, household, famous, well-known, celebrated, idolized.
E3 unpopular.

popularize *verb* spread, propagate, universalize, democratize, simplify.

populate *verb* people, occupy, settle, colonize, inhabit, live in, overrun.

population *noun* inhabitants, natives, residents, citizens, occupants, community, society, people, folk.

portable *adjective* movable, transportable, compact, lightweight, manageable, handy, convenient.
E3 fixed, immovable.

porter[1] *noun* bearer, carrier, baggage-attendant, baggage-handler.

porter[2] *noun* doorman, door-keeper, commissionaire, gatekeeper, janitor, caretaker, concierge.

portion *noun* share, allocation, allotment, parcel, allowance, ration, quota, measure, part, section, division, fraction, percentage, bit, fragment, morsel, piece, segment, slice, serving, helping.

portrait *noun* picture, painting, drawing, sketch, caricature, miniature, icon, photograph, likeness, image, representation, vignette, profile, characterization, description, depiction, portrayal.

portray *verb* draw, sketch, paint, illustrate, picture, represent, depict, describe, evoke, play, impersonate, characterize, personify.

pose *verb* **1** *posing for the camera*: model, sit, position. **2** *posing as a salesman*: pretend, feign, affect, put on an act, masquerade, pass oneself off, impersonate. **3** *pose a question*: set, put forward, submit, present.
▪ *noun* **1** *adopt a relaxed pose*: position, stance, air, bearing, posture, attitude. **2** *just a pose*: pretence, sham, affectation, façade, front, masquerade, role, act.

poser[1] *noun* puzzle, riddle, conundrum, brain-teaser, mystery, enigma, problem, vexed question.

poser[2] *noun* poseur, poseuse, posturer, attitudinizer, exhibitionist, show-off, pseud (*infml*), phoney (*infml*).

posh *adjective* smart, stylish, fashionable, high-class, upper-class, la-di-da (*infml*), grand, luxurious, lavish, swanky (*infml*), luxury, de luxe, up-market,

exclusive, select, classy (*infml*), swish (*infml*).
F3 inferior, cheap.

position *noun* **1** *what's the ship's position?*: place, situation, location, site, spot, point. **2** *sitting in an awkward position*: posture, stance, pose, arrangement, disposition. **3** *was offered the position of nanny*: job, post, occupation, employment, office, duty, function, role. **4** *a high position in government*: rank, grade, level, status, standing. **5** *take a position on the issue*: opinion, point of view, belief, view, outlook, viewpoint, standpoint, stand.
▪ *verb* put, place, set, fix, stand, arrange, dispose, lay out, deploy, station, locate, situate, site.

positive *adjective* **1** *positive I saw him*: sure, certain, convinced, confident, assured. **2** *positive criticism*: helpful, constructive, practical, useful, optimistic, hopeful, promising. **3** *a positive answer*: definite, decisive, conclusive, clear, unmistakable, explicit, unequivocal, express, firm, emphatic, categorical, undeniable, irrefutable, indisputable, incontrovertible. **4** *it's a positive scandal!*: absolute, utter, sheer, complete, perfect.
F3 1 uncertain. **2** negative. **3** indefinite, vague.

possess *verb* **1** *I don't possess an umbrella*: own, have, hold, enjoy, be endowed with. **2** *possessed by demons*: seize, take, obtain, acquire, take over, occupy, control, dominate, bewitch, haunt.

possessions *noun* belongings, property, things, paraphernalia, effects, goods, chattels (*fml*), movables, assets, estate, wealth, riches.

possessive *adjective* selfish, clinging, overprotective, domineering, dominating, jealous, covetous, acquisitive, grasping.
F3 unselfish, sharing.

possibility *noun* likelihood, probability, odds, chance, risk, danger, hope, prospect, potentiality, conceivability, practicability, feasibility.
F3 impossibility, impracticability.

possible *adjective* potential, promising, likely, probable, imaginable, conceivable, practicable, feasible, viable, tenable, workable, achievable, attainable, accomplishable, realizable.
F3 impossible, unthinkable, impracticable, unattainable.

possibly *adverb* perhaps, maybe, hopefully (*infml*), by any means, at all, by any chance.

post[1] *noun* pole, stake, picket, pale, pillar, column, shaft, support, baluster, upright, stanchion, strut, leg.
▪ *verb* display, stick up, pin up, advertise, publicize, announce, make known, report, publish.

post[2] *noun* office, job, employment, position, situation,

place, vacancy, appointment.
▪ *verb* station, locate, situate, position, place, put, appoint, assign, second, transfer, move, send.

post[3] *noun* mail, letters, dispatch, collection, delivery.
▪ *verb* mail, send, dispatch, transmit.

poster *noun* notice, bill, sign, placard, sticker, advertisement, announcement.

postpone *verb* put off, defer, put back, hold over, delay, adjourn, suspend, shelve, pigeonhole, freeze, put on ice.
F3 advance, forward.

postscript *noun* PS (*infml*), addition, supplement, afterthought, addendum, codicil, appendix, afterword, epilogue.
F3 introduction, prologue.

posture *noun* position, stance, pose, attitude, disposition, bearing, carriage, deportment.

potent *adjective* powerful, mighty, strong, intoxicating, pungent, effective, impressive, cogent, convincing, persuasive, compelling, forceful, dynamic, vigorous, authoritative, commanding, dominant, influential, overpowering.
F3 impotent, weak.

potential *adjective* possible, likely, probable, prospective, future, aspiring, would-be, promising, budding, embryonic, undeveloped, dormant, latent, hidden, concealed, unrealized.
▪ *noun* possibility, ability, capability, capacity, aptitude, talent, powers, resources.

potion *noun* mixture, concoction, brew, beverage, drink, draught, dose, medicine, tonic, elixir.

potter *verb* tinker, fiddle, mess about (*infml*), dabble, loiter, fritter.

pounce *verb* fall on, dive on, swoop, drop, attack, strike, ambush, spring, jump, leap, snatch, grab.

pound *verb* **1** *pounding at the door*: strike, thump, beat, drum, pelt, hammer, batter, bang, bash, smash. **2** *pounding the rock into dust*: pulverize, powder, grind, mash, crush. **3** *his heart was pounding*: throb, pulsate, palpitate, thump, thud.

pour *verb* **1** *pour a drink*: serve, decant, tip. **2** *pouring into the football ground*: spill, issue, discharge, flow, stream, run, rush, spout, spew, gush, cascade, crowd, throng, swarm.

pout *verb* scowl, glower, grimace, pull a face, sulk, mope.
F3 grin, smile.

poverty *noun* poorness, impoverishment, insolvency, bankruptcy, pennilessness, penury (*fml*), destitution, distress, hardship, privation (*fml*), need, necessity, want, lack, deficiency, shortage, inadequacy, insufficiency, depletion, scarcity, meagreness, paucity (*fml*), dearth.
F3 wealth, richness, affluence, plenty.

powdery *adjective* dusty, sandy, grainy, granular, powdered, pulverized, ground, fine, loose, dry, crumbly, friable, chalky.

power *noun* **1** *political power*: command, authority, sovereignty, rule, dominion, control, influence. **2** *powers of arrest*: right, privilege, prerogative, authorization, warrant. **3** *engine is losing power*: potency, strength, intensity, force, vigour, energy. **4** *the power of speech*: ability, capability, capacity, potential, faculty, competence.
⇄ **1** subjection. **3** weakness. **4** inability.

powerful *adjective* dominant, prevailing, leading, influential, high-powered, authoritative, commanding, potent, effective, strong, mighty, robust, muscular, energetic, forceful, telling, impressive, convincing, persuasive, compelling, winning, overwhelming.
⇄ impotent, ineffective, weak.

powerless *adjective* impotent, incapable, ineffective, weak, feeble, frail, infirm, incapacitated, disabled, paralysed, helpless, vulnerable, defenceless, unarmed.
⇄ powerful, potent, able.

practical *adjective* **1** *a practical idea/person*: realistic, sensible, commonsense, practicable, workable, feasible, down-to-earth, matter-of-fact, pragmatic, hardnosed (*infml*), hard-headed, businesslike, experienced, trained, qualified, skilled, accomplished, proficient, hands-on, applied. **2** *designed to be practical rather than beautiful*: useful, handy, serviceable, utilitarian, functional, working, everyday, ordinary.
⇄ **1** impractical, unskilled, theoretical.

practically *adverb* **1** *practically grown up*: almost, nearly, well-nigh, virtually, pretty well, all but, just about, in principle, in effect, essentially, fundamentally, to all intents and purposes. **2** *not practically possible*: realistically, sensibly, reasonably, rationally, pragmatically.

practice *noun* **1** *our normal practice*: custom, tradition, convention, usage, habit, routine, way, method, system, procedure, policy. **2** *need practice*: rehearsal, run-through, dry run, dummy run, try-out, training, drill, exercise, work-out, study, experience. **3** *in practice*: effect, reality, actuality, action, operation, performance, use, application.
⇄ **3** theory, principle.

practise *verb* **1** *practising medicine/law*: do, perform, execute, implement, carry out, apply, put into practice, follow, pursue, engage in, undertake. **2** *practising the violin*: rehearse, run through, repeat, drill, exercise, train, study, perfect.

praise *noun* approval, admiration, commendation, congratulation, compliment, flattery, adulation,

eulogy, applause, ovation, cheering, acclaim, recognition, testimonial, tribute, accolade, homage, honour, glory, worship, adoration, devotion, thanksgiving.
F3 criticism, revilement.
▪ *verb* commend, congratulate, admire, compliment, flatter, eulogize (*fml*), wax lyrical, rave over (*infml*), extol (*fml*), promote, applaud, cheer, acclaim, hail, recognize, acknowledge, pay tribute to, honour, laud (*fml*), glorify, magnify, exalt, worship, adore, bless.
F3 criticize, revile.

pray *verb* invoke, call on, supplicate, entreat, implore, plead, beg, beseech, petition, ask, request, crave, solicit.

prayer *noun* collect, litany, devotion, communion, invocation, supplication, entreaty, plea, appeal, petition, request.

preach *verb* address, lecture, harangue, pontificate, sermonize, evangelize, moralize, exhort, urge, advocate.

precarious *adjective* unsafe, dangerous, treacherous, risky, hazardous, chancy, uncertain, unsure, dubious, doubtful, unpredictable, unreliable, unsteady, unstable, shaky, wobbly, insecure, vulnerable.
F3 safe, certain, stable, secure.

precaution *noun* safeguard, security, protection, insurance, providence, forethought, caution, prudence, foresight, anticipation, preparation, provision.

precede *verb* come before, lead, come first, go before, take precedence, introduce, herald, usher in.
F3 follow, succeed.

precedent *noun* example, instance, pattern, model, standard, criterion.

precious *adjective* **1** *very precious to her*: valued, treasured, prized, cherished, beloved, dearest, darling, favourite, loved, adored, idolized. **2** *a precious stone*: valuable, expensive, costly, dear, priceless, inestimable, rare, choice, fine.

precise *adjective* exact, accurate, right, punctilious, correct, factual, faithful, authentic, literal, word-for-word, express, definite, explicit, unequivocal, unambiguous, clear-cut, distinct, detailed, blow-by-blow, minute, nice (*fml*), particular, specific, fixed, rigid, strict, careful, meticulous, scrupulous, fastidious.
F3 imprecise, inexact, ambiguous, careless.

precisely *adverb* exactly, absolutely, just so, accurately, correctly, literally, verbatim, word for word, strictly, minutely, clearly, distinctly.

precocious *adjective* forward, ahead, advanced, early, premature, mature, developed, gifted, clever, bright, smart, quick, fast.
F3 backward.

preconception *noun* presupposition, presumption, assumption, conjecture, anticipation, expectation, prejudgement, bias, prejudice.

predecessor *noun* ancestor, forefather, forebear, antecedent, forerunner, precursor.
successor, descendant.

predetermined *adjective* **1** *believe everything is predetermined*: predestined, destined, fated, doomed, ordained, foreordained. **2** *a predetermined time*: prearranged, arranged, agreed, fixed, set.

predicament *noun* situation, plight, trouble, mess, fix, spot (*infml*), quandary, dilemma, impasse, crisis, emergency.

predict *verb* foretell, prophesy, foresee, forecast, prognosticate, project.

predictable *adjective* foreseeable, expected, anticipated, likely, probable, imaginable, foreseen, foregone, certain, sure, reliable, dependable.
unpredictable, uncertain.

pre-empt *verb* anticipate, obviate, forestall.

preface *noun* foreword, introduction, preamble, prologue, prelude, preliminaries.
epilogue, postscript.

prefer *verb* favour, like better, would rather, would sooner, want, wish, desire, choose, select, pick, opt for, go for, plump for, single out, advocate, recommend, back, support, fancy, elect, adopt.
reject.

preferable *adjective* better, superior, nicer, preferred, favoured, chosen, desirable, advantageous, advisable, recommended.
inferior, undesirable.

preference *noun* **1** *this would be my preference*: favourite, first choice, choice, pick, selection, option, wish, desire. **2** *have a preference for*: liking, fancy, inclination, predilection, partiality, favouritism, preferential treatment.

preferential *adjective* better, superior, favoured, privileged, special, favourable, advantageous.
equal.

pregnant *adjective* expectant, expecting, with child (*fml*).

prejudice *noun* **1** *racial/religious prejudice*: bias, partiality, partisanship, discrimination, unfairness, injustice, intolerance, narrow-mindedness, bigotry, chauvinism, racism, sexism. **2** *without prejudice to any subsequent discussion*: harm, damage, impairment, hurt, injury, detriment, disadvantage, loss, ruin.
1 fairness, tolerance. **2** benefit, advantage.

▪ *verb* **1** *prejudicing the jury against the witness*: bias, predispose, incline, sway, influence, condition, colour, slant, distort, load, weight.

2 *prejudice his chances of getting a job*: harm, damage, impair, hinder, undermine, hurt, injure, mar, spoil, ruin, wreck.
F3 **2** benefit, help, advance.

prejudiced *adjective* biased, partial, predisposed, subjective, partisan, one-sided, discriminatory, unfair, unjust, loaded, weighted, intolerant, narrow-minded, bigoted, chauvinist, racist, sexist, jaundiced, distorted, warped, influenced, conditioned.
F3 impartial, fair, tolerant.

preliminary *adjective* preparatory, prior, advance, exploratory, experimental, trial, test, pilot, early, earliest, first, initial, primary, qualifying, inaugural, introductory, opening.
F3 final, closing.

prelude *noun* overture, introduction, preface, foreword, preamble, prologue, opening, opener, preliminary, preparation, beginning, start, commencement, precursor, curtain-raiser.
F3 finale, epilogue.

premature *adjective* early, immature, green, unripe, embryonic, half-formed, incomplete, undeveloped, abortive, hasty, ill-considered, rash, untimely, inopportune, ill-timed.
F3 late, tardy.

premeditated *adjective* planned, intended, intentional, deliberate, wilful, conscious, cold-blooded, calculated, considered, contrived, preplanned, prearranged, predetermined.
F3 unpremeditated, spontaneous.

premise *noun* proposition, statement, assertion, postulate, thesis, argument, basis, supposition, hypothesis, presupposition, assumption.

premises *noun* building, property, establishment, office, grounds, estate, site, place.

premonition *noun* presentiment, feeling, intuition, hunch, idea, suspicion, foreboding, misgiving, fear, apprehension, anxiety, worry, warning, omen, sign.

preoccupied *adjective* distracted, abstracted, absent-minded, daydreaming, absorbed, faraway, heedless, oblivious, pensive.

preparation *noun* **1** *do the preparation/in preparation for*: readiness, provision, precaution, safeguard, foundation, groundwork, spadework, basics, rudiments, preliminaries, plans, arrangements. **2** *a medical preparation*: mixture, compound, concoction, potion, medicine, lotion, application.

preparatory *adjective* preliminary, introductory, opening, initial, primary, basic, fundamental, rudimentary, elementary.

prepare *verb* **1** *preparing them for the match*: get ready, warm up, train, coach, study, make ready, adapt, adjust, plan, organize, arrange, pave the way. **2** *prepare a meal*: make, produce, construct, assemble, concoct, contrive, devise, draft, draw up, compose.

prepared *adjective* ready, waiting, set, fit, inclined, disposed, willing, planned, organized, arranged.

F3 unprepared, unready.

prescribe *verb* ordain, decree, dictate, rule, command, order, require, direct, assign, specify, stipulate, lay down, set, appoint, impose, fix, define, limit.

prescription *noun* medicine, drug, preparation, mixture, remedy, treatment.

presence *noun* **1** *the presence of oxygen in the atmosphere/in the judge's presence*: attendance, company, occupancy, residence, existence. **2** *have a certain presence*: aura, air, demeanour, bearing, carriage, appearance, poise, self-assurance, personality, charisma. **3** *could feel her presence*: nearness, closeness, proximity, vicinity.

F3 1 absence. **3** remoteness.

present[1] *adjective* /**prez**-ent/ **1** *present at the meeting*: attending, here, there, near, at hand, to hand, available, ready. **2** *at the present time*: current, contemporary, present-day, immediate, instant, existent, existing.

F3 1 absent. **2** past, out-of-date.

present[2] *verb* /pri-**zent**/ **1** *present a play*: show, display, exhibit, demonstrate, mount, stage, put on, introduce, announce. **2** *present him with the award*: award, confer, bestow, grant, give, donate, hand over, entrust, extend, hold out, offer, tender, submit.

▪ *noun* /**prez**-ent/ gift, prezzie (*infml*), offering, donation, grant, endowment, benefaction (*fml*), bounty, largess, gratuity, tip, favour.

presentable *adjective* neat, tidy, clean, respectable, decent, proper, suitable, acceptable, satisfactory, tolerable.

F3 unpresentable, untidy, shabby.

presentation *noun* **1** *presentation is important*: show, performance, production, staging, representation, display, exhibition, demonstration, talk, delivery, appearance, arrangement. **2** *made a presentation to the queen*: award, conferral, bestowal, investiture.

presently *adverb* soon, shortly, in a minute, before long, by and by.

preserve *verb* **1** *preserve our customs*: protect, safeguard, guard, defend, shield, shelter, care for, maintain, uphold, sustain, continue, perpetuate, keep, retain, conserve, save, store. **2** *preserve food*: bottle, tin, can, pickle, salt, cure, dry, smoke, treat.

F3 1 destroy, ruin.

▪ *noun* **1** *home-made preserves*: conserve, jam, marmalade, jelly, pickle. **2** *a preserve for endangered* *species*: reservation, sanctuary, game reserve, safari park.

preside *verb* chair, officiate, conduct, direct, manage, administer, control, run, head, lead, govern, rule.

press *verb* **1** *press flowers*: crush, squash, squeeze, compress, stuff, cram, crowd, push, depress. **2** *press clothes*: iron, smooth, flatten. **3** *pressed him for an answer*: urge, plead, petition, campaign, demand, insist on, compel, constrain, force, pressure, pressurize, harass.

▪ *noun* journalists, reporters, correspondents, the media, newspapers, papers, Fleet Street, fourth estate.

pressing *adjective* urgent, high-priority, burning, crucial, vital, essential, imperative, serious, important.

F3 unimportant, trivial.

pressure *noun* **1** *under pressure*: force, power, load, burden, weight, heaviness, compression, squeezing, stress, strain. **2** *the pressures of modern living*: difficulty, problem, demand, constraint, stress, obligation, urgency.

pressurize *verb* force, compel, constrain, oblige, drive, bulldoze, coerce, press, pressure, lean on (*infml*), browbeat, bully.

prestige *noun* status, reputation, standing, stature, eminence, distinction, esteem, regard, importance, authority, influence, fame, renown, kudos, credit, honour.

F3 humbleness, unimportance.

prestigious *adjective* esteemed, respected, reputable, important, influential, great, eminent, prominent, illustrious, renowned, celebrated, exalted, imposing, impressive, up-market.

F3 humble, modest.

presume *verb* **1** *presume this is correct*: assume, take it, think, believe, suppose, surmise, infer, presuppose, take for granted, count on, rely on, depend on, bank on, trust. **2** *presume to criticize*: dare, make so bold, go so far, venture, undertake.

presumptuous *adjective* bold, audacious, impertinent, impudent, insolent, over-familiar, forward, pushy (*infml*), arrogant, over-confident, conceited.

F3 humble, modest.

pretence *noun* show, display, appearance, cover, front, façade, veneer, cloak, veil, mask, guise, sham, feigning, faking, simulation, deception, trickery, wile, ruse, excuse, pretext, bluff, falsehood, deceit, fabrication, invention, make-believe, charade, acting, play-acting, posturing, posing, affectation, pretension, pretentiousness.

F3 honesty, openness.

pretend *verb* **1** *pretend to be pleased*: affect, put on, assume, feign, sham, counterfeit, fake, simulate, bluff, impersonate, pass oneself off, act, play-act, mime, go through the motions. **2** *pretending to the throne*: claim, allege, profess, purport. **3** *pretend this is a castle*: imagine, make believe, suppose.

pretentious *adjective* pompous, self-important, conceited, immodest, snobbish, affected, mannered, showy, ostentatious, extravagant, over-the-top, exaggerated, magniloquent, high-sounding, inflated, grandiose, ambitious, overambitious.
F3 modest, humble, simple, straightforward.

pretext *noun* excuse, ploy, ruse, cover, cloak, mask, guise, semblance, appearance, pretence, show.

pretty *adjective* attractive, good-looking, beautiful, fair, lovely, bonny, cute, winsome, appealing, charming, dainty, graceful, elegant, fine, delicate, nice.
F3 plain, unattractive, ugly.
▪ *adverb* fairly, somewhat, rather, quite, reasonably, moderately, tolerably.

prevail *verb* **1** *the opinion that prevails*: predominate, preponderate, abound. **2** *our soldiers will prevail*: win, triumph, succeed, overcome, overrule, reign, rule.
F3 **2** lose.

prevailing *adjective* predominant, preponderant, main, principal, dominant, controlling, powerful, compelling, influential, reigning, ruling, current, fashionable, popular, mainstream, accepted, established, set, usual, customary, common, prevalent, widespread.
F3 minor, subordinate.

prevent *verb* stop, avert, avoid, head off, ward off, stave off, intercept, forestall, anticipate, frustrate, thwart, check, restrain, inhibit, hinder, hamper, impede, obstruct, block, bar.
F3 cause, help, foster, encourage, allow.

prevention *noun* avoidance, frustration, check, hindrance, impediment, obstruction, obstacle, bar, elimination, precaution, safeguard, deterrence.
F3 cause, help.

preventive *adjective* preventative, anticipatory, pre-emptive, inhibitory, obstructive, precautionary, protective, counteractive, deterrent.
F3 causative.

previous *adjective* preceding, foregoing, earlier, prior, past, former, ex-, one-time, sometime, erstwhile.
F3 following, subsequent, later.

previously *adverb* formerly, once, earlier, before, beforehand.
F3 later.

prey *noun* quarry, victim, game, kill.

price *noun* value, worth, cost, expense, outlay, expenditure, fee, charge, levy, toll, rate, bill, assessment, valuation, estimate, quotation, figure, amount, sum, payment, reward, penalty, forfeit, sacrifice, consequences.

priceless *adjective* **1** *a priceless manuscript*: invaluable, inestimable, incalculable, expensive, costly, dear, precious, valuable, prized, treasured, irreplaceable. **2** (*infml*) *joke was priceless*: funny, amusing, comic, hilarious, riotous, side-splitting, killing (*infml*), rich (*infml*).
E3 **1** cheap, run-of-the-mill.

prick *verb* pierce, puncture, perforate, punch, jab, stab, sting, bite, prickle, itch, tingle.
▪ *noun* puncture, perforation, pinhole, stab, pang, twinge, sting, bite.

prickly *adjective* thorny, brambly, spiny, barbed, spiky, bristly, rough, scratchy.
E3 smooth.

pride *noun* **1** *pride goes before a fall*: conceit, vanity, egotism, bigheadedness, boastfulness, smugness, arrogance, self-importance, presumption, haughtiness, superciliousness, snobbery, pretentiousness. **2** *for her pride's sake*: dignity, self-respect, self-esteem, honour. **3** *take pride in something*: satisfaction, gratification, pleasure, delight.
E3 **1** humility, modesty. **2** shame.

priest *noun* minister, vicar, padre, father, man of God, man of the cloth, clergyman, clergywoman, churchman, churchwoman.

prim *adjective* prudish, strait-laced, formal, demure, proper, priggish, prissy, fussy, particular, precise, fastidious.
E3 informal, relaxed, easy-going (*infml*).

primarily *adverb* chiefly, principally, mainly, mostly, basically, fundamentally, especially, particularly, essentially.

primary *adjective* **1** *primary school*: first, earliest, original, initial, introductory, beginning, basic, fundamental, essential, radical, rudimentary, elementary, simple. **2** *primary reason*: chief, principal, main, dominant, leading, foremost, supreme, cardinal, capital, paramount, greatest, highest, ultimate.
E3 **2** secondary, subsidiary, minor.

prime *adjective* best, choice, select, quality, first-class, first-rate, excellent, top, supreme, pre-eminent, superior, senior, leading, ruling, chief, principal, main, predominant, primary.
E3 second-rate, secondary.
▪ *noun* height, peak, zenith, heyday, flower, bloom, maturity, perfection.

primitive *adjective* **1** *primitive paintings*: crude, rough, unsophisticated, uncivilized, barbarian, savage. **2** *primitive man*: early, elementary, rudimentary, primary, first, original, earliest.
E3 **1** advanced, sophisticated, civilized.

principal *adjective* main, chief, key, essential, cardinal, primary, first, foremost, leading, dominant, prime, paramount, pre-eminent, supreme, highest.
F3 minor, subsidiary, lesser, least.
▪ *noun* head, head teacher, headmaster, headmistress, chief, leader, boss, director, manager, superintendent.

principally *adverb* mainly, mostly, chiefly, primarily, predominantly, above all, particularly, especially.

principle *noun* **1** *go against all principles of morality and decency*: rule, formula, law, canon, axiom, dictum, precept (*fml*), maxim, truth, tenet, doctrine, creed, dogma, code, standard, criterion, proposition, fundamental, essential. **2** *a man of principle*: honour, integrity, rectitude, uprightness, virtue, decency, morality, morals, ethics, standards, scruples, conscience.

print *verb* mark, stamp, imprint, impress, engrave, copy, reproduce, run off, publish, issue.
▪ *noun* **1** *appear in print*: letters, characters, lettering, type, typescript, typeface, fount. **2** *find the lion's prints*: mark, impression, fingerprint, footprint. **3** *make a series of prints of the painting*: copy, reproduction, picture, engraving, lithograph, photograph, photo.

prior *adjective* earlier, preceding, foregoing, previous, former.
F3 later.

priority *noun* right of way, precedence, seniority, rank, superiority, pre-eminence, supremacy, the lead, first place, urgency.
F3 inferiority.

prison *noun* jail, nick (*infml*), clink (*slang*), cooler (*slang*), penitentiary, cell, lock-up, cage, dungeon, imprisonment, confinement, detention, custody.

prisoner *noun* captive, hostage, convict, jail-bird (*infml*), inmate, internee, detainee.

privacy *noun* secrecy, confidentiality, independence, solitude, isolation, seclusion, concealment, retirement, retreat.

private *adjective* **1** *private discussion*: secret, classified, hush-hush (*infml*), off the record, unofficial, confidential. **2** *private life*: intimate, personal, individual, own, secret, independent, solitary, reserved, withdrawn. **3** *private place*: isolated, secluded, hidden, concealed, exclusive, particular, special, separate, remote.
F3 **1** public, open.

privilege *noun* advantage, benefit, concession, birthright, title, due, right, prerogative, entitlement, freedom, liberty, franchise, licence, sanction, authority, immunity, exemption.
F3 disadvantage.

privileged *adjective* advantaged, favoured, special, sanctioned, authorized, immune, exempt, élite, honoured, ruling, powerful. ☒ disadvantaged, underprivileged.

prize *noun* reward, trophy, medal, award, winnings, jackpot, purse, premium, stake(s), honour, accolade.
▪ *adjective* best, top, first-rate, excellent, outstanding, champion, winning, prize-winning, award-winning, plum, top-notch (*infml*). ☒ second-rate.
▪ *verb* treasure, value, appreciate, esteem, revere, cherish, hold dear. ☒ despise.

probability *noun* likelihood, odds, chances, expectation, prospect, chance, possibility. ☒ improbability.

probable *adjective* likely, odds-on, expected, credible, believable, plausible, feasible, possible, apparent, seeming. ☒ improbable, unlikely.

probation *noun* apprenticeship, trial period, trial, test.

probe *verb* prod, poke, pierce, penetrate, sound, plumb, explore, examine, scrutinize, investigate, go into, look into, search, sift, test.

problem *noun* **1** *what's the problem here?*: trouble, worry, predicament, quandary, dilemma, difficulty, complication, snag. **2** *a mathematical problem*: question, poser (*infml*), puzzle, brain-teaser, conundrum, riddle, enigma.

procedure *noun* routine, process, method, system, technique, custom, practice, policy, formula, course, scheme, strategy, plan of action, move, step, action, conduct, operation, performance.

proceed *verb* **1** *permission to proceed*: advance, go ahead, move on, progress, continue, carry on, press on. **2** *proceeding from our discussions*: originate, derive, flow, start, stem, spring, arise, issue, result, ensue, follow, come. ☒ **1** stop, retreat.

proceedings *noun* **1** *court proceedings*: matters, affairs, business, dealings, transactions, report, account, minutes, records, archives, annals. **2** *watch the proceedings with interest*: events, happenings, deeds, doings, moves, steps, measures, action, course of action.

proceeds *noun* revenue, income, returns, receipts, takings, earnings, gain, profit, yield, produce. ☒ expenditure, outlay.

process *noun* **1** *the smelting process*: procedure, operation, practice, method, system, technique, means, manner, mode, way, stage, step. **2** *in the process of developing*: course, progression, advance, progress, development, evolution, formation, growth, movement, action, proceeding.

procession *noun* march, parade, cavalcade, motorcade, cortège, file, column, train, succession, series, sequence, course, run.

proclaim *verb* announce,

declare, pronounce, affirm, give out, publish, advertise, make known, profess, testify, show, indicate.

prod *verb* poke, jab, dig, elbow, nudge, push, shove, goad, spur, urge, egg on (*infml*), prompt, stimulate, motivate.

produce *verb* **1** *produce gases/ milk*: cause, occasion, give rise to, provoke, bring about, result in, effect, create, originate, invent, make, manufacture, fabricate, construct, compose, generate, yield, bear, deliver. **2** *produced a letter from his pocket*: advance, put forward, present, offer, give, supply, provide, furnish, bring out, bring forth, show, exhibit, demonstrate. **3** *produce a play*: direct, stage, mount, put on.
▪ *noun* crop, harvest, yield, output, product.

product *noun* **1** *dairy/ manufactured products*: commodity, merchandise, goods, end-product, artefact, work, creation, invention, production, output, yield, produce, fruit, return. **2** *the accident was a product of carelessness*: result, consequence, outcome, issue, upshot, offshoot, spin-off, by-product, legacy.
F3 **2** cause.

production *noun* **1** *the production of oil and gas*: making, manufacture, fabrication, construction, assembly, creation, origination, preparation, formation. **2** *an amateur production*: staging, presentation, direction, management.
F3 **1** consumption.

productive *adjective* fruitful, profitable, rewarding, valuable, worthwhile, useful, constructive, creative, inventive, fertile, rich, teeming, busy, energetic, vigorous, efficient, effective.
F3 unproductive, fruitless, useless.

productivity *noun* productiveness, yield, output, work rate, efficiency.

profession *noun* career, job, occupation, employment, business, line (of work), trade, vocation, calling, métier, craft, office, position.

professional *adjective* qualified, licensed, trained, experienced, practised, skilled, expert, masterly, proficient, competent, businesslike, efficient.
F3 amateur, unprofessional.
▪ *noun* expert, authority, specialist, pro (*infml*), master, virtuoso, dab hand (*infml*).
F3 amateur.

profile *noun* **1** *viewed in profile*: side view, outline, contour, silhouette, shape, form, figure, sketch, drawing, diagram, chart, graph. **2** *a profile of the candidate*: biography, curriculum vitae, thumbnail sketch, vignette, portrait, study, analysis, examination, survey, review.

profit *noun* gain, surplus, excess,

bottom line, revenue, return, yield, proceeds, receipts, takings, earnings, winnings, interest, advantage, benefit, use, avail, value, worth.
loss.
▪ *verb* gain, make money, pay, serve, avail, benefit.
lose.

profitable *adjective* cost-effective, economic, commercial, money-making, lucrative, remunerative, paying, rewarding, successful, fruitful, productive, advantageous, beneficial, useful, valuable, worthwhile.
unprofitable, loss-making, non-profit-making.

profound *adjective* **1** *profound sadness*: deep, great, intense, extreme, heartfelt, marked, far-reaching, extensive, exhaustive. **2** *a profound remark*: serious, weighty, penetrating, thoughtful, philosophical, wise, learned, erudite, abstruse (*fml*).
1 shallow, slight, mild.

programme *noun* **1** *a teaching/study programme*: schedule, timetable, agenda, calendar, order of events, listing, line-up, plan, scheme, project, syllabus, curriculum. **2** *radio programme*: broadcast, transmission, show, performance, production, presentation.

progress *noun* movement, progression, passage, journey, way, advance, headway, step forward, breakthrough, development, evolution, growth, increase, improvement, betterment, promotion.
recession, deterioration, decline.
▪ *verb* proceed, advance, go forward, forge ahead, make progress, make headway, come on, develop, grow, mature, blossom, improve, better, prosper, increase.
deteriorate, decline.

progression *noun* cycle, chain, string, succession, series, sequence, order, course, advance, headway, progress, development.

progressive *adjective* **1** *a progressive school*: modern, avant-garde, advanced, forward-looking, enlightened, liberal, radical, revolutionary, reformist, dynamic, enterprising, go-ahead, up-and-coming. **2** *progressive disease*: advancing, continuing, developing, growing, increasing, intensifying.
1 regressive.

prohibit *verb* forbid, ban, bar, veto, proscribe, outlaw, rule out, preclude, prevent, stop, hinder, hamper, impede, obstruct, restrict.
permit, allow, authorize.

project *noun* /**proj**-ekt/ assignment, contract, task, job, work, occupation, activity, enterprise, undertaking, venture, plan, scheme, programme, design, proposal, idea, conception.
▪ *verb* /pro-**jekt**/ **1** *project into the future*: predict, forecast, extrapolate, estimate, reckon,

calculate. **2** *missiles projected at the cities*: throw, fling, hurl, launch, propel. **3** *projecting from the surface*: protrude, stick out, bulge, jut out, overhang.

projection *noun* **1** *a projection from the wall*: protuberance (*fml*), bulge, overhang, ledge, sill, shelf, ridge. **2** *a budget projection*: prediction, forecast, extrapolation, estimate, reckoning, calculation, computation.

prolong *verb* lengthen, extend, stretch, protract, draw out, spin out, drag out, delay, continue, perpetuate.
F3 shorten.

prominent *adjective* **1** *put it in a prominent position*: noticeable, conspicuous, obvious, unmistakable, striking, eye-catching. **2** *prominent eyes*: bulging, protuberant, projecting, jutting, protruding, obtrusive. **3** *a prominent writer*: famous, well-known, celebrated, renowned, noted, eminent, distinguished, respected, leading, foremost, chief, main, important, popular, outstanding.
F3 **1** inconspicuous. **3** unknown, unimportant, insignificant.

promise *verb* **1** *promise to pay*: vow, pledge, swear, take an oath, contract, undertake, give one's word, vouch, warrant, guarantee, assure. **2** *dark clouds promising rain*: augur, presage, indicate, suggest, hint at.

▪ *noun* **1** *make a promise*: vow, pledge, oath, word of honour, bond, compact, covenant, guarantee, assurance, undertaking, engagement, commitment. **2** *show promise*: potential, ability, capability, aptitude, talent.

promising *adjective* auspicious, propitious, favourable, rosy, bright, encouraging, hopeful, talented, gifted, budding, up-and-coming.
F3 unpromising, inauspicious, discouraging.

promote *verb* **1** *promote their products/promote a healthy lifestyle*: advertise, plug (*infml*), publicize, hype (*infml*), popularize, market, sell, push, recommend, advocate, champion, endorse, sponsor, support, back, help, aid, assist, foster, nurture, further, forward, encourage, boost, stimulate, urge. **2** *promoted to head teacher*: upgrade, advance, move up, raise, elevate, exalt, honour.
F3 **1** disparage (*fml*), hinder. **2** demote.

promotion *noun* **1** *ask for/get promotion*: advancement, upgrading, rise, preferment, elevation, exaltation. **2** *an advertising promotion*: advertising, plugging (*infml*), publicity, hype (*infml*), campaign, propaganda, marketing, pushing, support, backing, furtherance, development, encouragement, boosting.

F3 **1** demotion. **2** disparagement (*fml*), obstruction.

prompt[1] *adjective* punctual, on time, immediate, instantaneous, instant, direct, quick, swift, rapid, speedy, unhesitating, willing, ready, alert, responsive, timely, early.

F3 slow, hesitant, late.

prompt[2] *verb* cause, give rise to, result in, occasion, produce, instigate, call forth, elicit, provoke, incite, urge, encourage, inspire, move, stimulate, motivate, spur, prod, remind.

F3 deter, dissuade.

prone *adjective* **1** *prone to jealousy*: likely, given, inclined, disposed, predisposed, bent, apt, liable, subject, susceptible, vulnerable. **2** *she lay prone*: face down, prostrate, flat, horizontal, full-length, stretched, recumbent.

F3 **1** unlikely, immune. **2** upright, supine.

pronounce *verb* **1** *pronounce words correctly*: say, utter, speak, express, voice, vocalize, sound, enunciate, articulate, stress. **2** *pronounced herself satisfied*: declare, announce, proclaim, decree, judge, affirm, assert.

pronounced *adjective* clear, distinct, definite, positive, decided, marked, noticeable, conspicuous, evident, obvious, striking, unmistakable, strong, broad.

F3 faint, vague.

pronunciation *noun* speech, diction, elocution, enunciation, articulation, delivery, accent, stress, inflection, intonation, modulation.

proof *noun* evidence, documentation, demonstration, verification, confirmation, corroboration, substantiation.

prop *verb* **1** *propping up the wall*: support, sustain, uphold, maintain, shore, stay, buttress, bolster, underpin, set. **2** *propped against the wall*: lean, rest, stand.
▪ *noun* support, stay, mainstay, strut, buttress, brace, truss.

propaganda *noun* advertising, publicity, hype (*infml*), indoctrination, brainwashing, disinformation.

propel *verb* move, drive, impel, force, thrust, push, shove, launch, shoot, send.

F3 stop.

proper *adjective* **1** *the proper way to do it*: right, correct, accurate, exact, precise, true, genuine, real, actual. **2** *proper behaviour*: accepted, correct, suitable, appropriate, fitting, decent, respectable, polite, formal.

F3 **1** wrong. **2** improper, indecent.

property *noun* **1** *own property*: estate, land, real estate (*US*), acres, premises, buildings, house(s), wealth, riches, resources, means, capital, assets, holding(s), belongings, possessions, effects, goods, chattels (*fml*). **2** *a property of the chemical*: feature, trait, quality, attribute, characteristic, idiosyncrasy, peculiarity, mark.

prophecy *noun* /**prof**-*es*-i/ prediction, augury, forecast, prognosis.

prophesy *verb* /**prof**-*es*-ai/ predict, foresee, augur, foretell, forewarn, forecast.

prophet *noun* seer, soothsayer, foreteller, forecaster, oracle, clairvoyant, fortune-teller.

proportion *noun* **1** *a large proportion*: percentage, fraction, part, division, share, quota, amount. **2** *in proportion*: ratio, relationship, correspondence, symmetry, balance, distribution.
F3 2 disproportion, imbalance.

proportional *adjective* proportionate, relative, commensurate, consistent, corresponding, analogous, comparable, equitable, even.
F3 disproportionate.

proposal *noun* proposition, suggestion, motion, recommendation, plan, scheme, project, design, programme, manifesto, presentation, bid, offer, tender, terms.

propose *verb* **1** *propose a motion*: suggest, recommend, move, advance, put forward, introduce, bring up, table, submit, present, offer, tender. **2** *when do you propose to leave?*: intend, mean, aim, purpose, plan, design. **3** *propose him for chairman*: nominate, put up. **4** *propose marriage*: ask to marry, ask for someone's hand (in marriage), pop the question (*infml*), go down on bended knee (*infml*).
F3 1 withdraw.

prosecute *verb* accuse, indict, sue, prefer charges, take to court, litigate, summon, put on trial, try.
F3 defend.

prospect *noun* chance, odds, probability, likelihood, possibility, hope, expectation, anticipation, outlook, future.
F3 unlikelihood.

prospective *adjective* future, -to-be, intended, designate, destined, forthcoming, approaching, coming, imminent, awaited, expected, anticipated, likely, possible, probable, potential, aspiring, would-be.
F3 current.

prosper *verb* boom, thrive, flourish, flower, bloom, succeed, get on, advance, progress, grow rich.
F3 fail.

prosperity *noun* boom, plenty, affluence, wealth, riches, fortune, well-being, luxury, the good life, success, good fortune.
F3 adversity, poverty.

prosperous *adjective* booming, thriving, flourishing, blooming, successful, fortunate, lucky, rich, wealthy, affluent, well-off, well-to-do.
F3 unfortunate, poor.

prostrate *adjective* flat, horizontal, prone, fallen, overcome, overwhelmed, crushed,

paralysed, powerless, helpless, defenceless.
F3 triumphant.

protect *verb* safeguard, defend, guard, escort, cover, screen, shield, secure, watch over, look after, care for, support, shelter, harbour, keep, conserve, preserve, save.
F3 attack, neglect.

protection *noun* **1** *protection of the environment*: care, custody, charge, guardianship, safekeeping, conservation, preservation, safety, safeguard. **2** *flood protection*: barrier, buffer, bulwark, defence, guard, shield, armour, screen, cover, shelter, refuge, security, insurance.
F3 1 neglect, attack.

protective *adjective* **1** *protective parents*: possessive, defensive, motherly, maternal, fatherly, paternal, watchful, vigilant, careful. **2** *protective clothing*: waterproof, fireproof, insulating, weatherproof.
F3 1 aggressive, threatening.

protest *noun* /**proh**-test/ objection, disapproval, opposition, dissent, complaint, protestation, outcry, appeal, demonstration.
F3 acceptance.
▪ *verb* /pro-**test**/ **1** *protest against the new road*: object, take exception, complain, appeal, demonstrate, oppose, disapprove, disagree, argue. **2** *protest one's innocence*: assert, maintain, contend, insist, profess.
F3 1 accept.

protrude *verb* stick out, poke out, come through, bulge, jut out, project, extend, stand out, obtrude.

proud *adjective* **1** *a proud man*: conceited, vain, egotistical, bigheaded, boastful, smug, complacent, arrogant, self-important, cocky, presumptuous, haughty, high and mighty, overbearing, supercilious, snooty (*infml*), snobbish, toffee-nosed (*infml*), stuck-up (*infml*). **2** *proud of his achievements*: satisfied, contented, gratified, pleased, delighted, honoured. **3** *a proud tradition*: dignified, noble, honourable, worthy, self-respecting.
F3 1 humble, modest, unassuming. **2** ashamed. **3** deferential, ignoble.

prove *verb* show, demonstrate, attest (*fml*), verify, confirm, corroborate, substantiate, bear out, document, certify, authenticate, validate, justify, establish, determine, ascertain, try, test, check, examine, analyse.
F3 disprove, discredit, falsify.

proverb *noun* saying, adage, aphorism, maxim, byword, dictum, precept (*fml*).

proverbial *adjective* axiomatic, accepted, conventional, traditional, customary, time-honoured, famous, well-known, legendary, notorious, typical, archetypal.

provide *verb* **1** *provide her with a place to stay*: supply, furnish, stock, equip, outfit, prepare for, cater, serve, present, give, contribute, yield, lend, add, bring. **2** *provide for the future*: plan for, allow, make provision, accommodate, arrange for, take precautions.
1 take, remove.

providing *conjunction* provided, with the proviso, given, as long as, on condition, on the understanding.

province *noun* region, area, district, zone, county, shire, department, territory, colony, dependency.

provincial *adjective* regional, local, rural, rustic, country.
national, cosmopolitan, urban, sophisticated.

provision *noun* **1** *make provision for old age*: plan, arrangement, preparation, measure, precaution. **2** *a provision of the contract*: stipulation, specification, proviso, condition, term, requirement.

provisional *adjective* temporary, interim, transitional, stopgap, makeshift, conditional, tentative.
permanent, fixed, definite.

provisions *noun* food, foodstuff, groceries, eatables (*infml*), sustenance, rations, supplies, stocks, stores.

proviso *noun* condition, term, requirement, stipulation, qualification, reservation, restriction, limitation, provision, clause, rider.

provocative *adjective* annoying, aggravating (*infml*), galling, outrageous, offensive, insulting, abusive.
conciliatory.

provoke *verb* **1** *don't provoke him*: annoy, irritate, rile, aggravate (*infml*), offend, insult, anger, enrage, infuriate, incense, madden, exasperate, tease, taunt. **2** *provoke debate*: cause, occasion, give rise to, produce, generate, induce, elicit, evoke, excite, inspire, move, stir, prompt, stimulate, motivate, incite, instigate.
1 please, pacify.

proximity *noun* closeness, nearness, vicinity, neighbourhood, adjacency, juxtaposition.
remoteness.

pry *verb* meddle, interfere, poke one's nose in, intrude, peep, peer, snoop, nose, ferret, dig, delve.
mind one's own business.

psychic *adjective* spiritual, supernatural, occult, mystic(al), clairvoyant, extra-sensory, telepathic, mental, psychological, intellectual, cognitive.

psychological *adjective* mental, cerebral, intellectual, cognitive, emotional, subjective, subconscious, unconscious, psychosomatic, irrational, unreal.
physical, real.

puberty *noun* pubescence, adolescence, teens, youth, growing up, maturity.

public *adjective* **1** *public buildings*:

state, national, civil, community, social, collective, communal, common, general, universal, open, unrestricted. **2** *public figure/ knowledge*: known, well-known, recognized, acknowledged, overt, open, exposed, published.

OPP 1 private, personal. **2** secret.

▪ *noun* people, nation, country, population, populace, masses, citizens, society, community, voters, electorate, followers, supporters, fans, audience, patrons, clientele, customers, buyers, consumers.

publication *noun* **1** *a new publication*: book, newspaper, magazine, periodical, booklet, leaflet, pamphlet, handbill. **2** *publication of the figures*: announcement, declaration, notification, disclosure, release, issue, printing, publishing.

publicity *noun* advertising, plug (*infml*), hype (*infml*), promotion, build-up, boost, attention, limelight, splash.

publicize *verb* advertise, plug (*infml*), hype (*infml*), promote, push, spotlight, broadcast, make known, blaze.

publish *verb* produce, print, issue, bring out, distribute, circulate, spread, diffuse.

puff *noun* **1** *not a puff of wind*: breath, waft, whiff, draught, flurry, gust, blast. **2** *a few puffs on his pipe*: pull, drag.

▪ *verb* **1** *puff and blow*: breathe, pant, gasp, gulp, wheeze, blow, waft, inflate, expand, swell. **2** *puff a cigarette*: smoke, pull, drag, draw, suck.

puffy *adjective* puffed up, inflated, swollen, bloated, distended, enlarged.

pull *verb* **1** *pull a caravan*: tow, drag, haul, draw, tug, jerk, yank (*infml*). **2** *pull a tooth*: remove, take out, extract, pull out, pluck, uproot, pull up, rip, tear. **3** *pull the crowds*: attract, draw, lure, allure, entice, tempt, magnetize. **4** *pull a muscle*: dislocate, sprain, wrench, strain.

OPP 1 push, press. **3** repel, deter, discourage.

▪ *noun* **1** *give it a pull*: tow, drag, tug, jerk, yank (*infml*). **2** *the pull of London*: attraction, lure, allurement, drawing power, magnetism, influence, weight.

pulp *noun* flesh, marrow, paste, purée, mash, mush, pap.

pulsate *verb* pulse, beat, throb, pound, hammer, drum, thud, thump, vibrate, oscillate, quiver.

pulse *noun* beat, stroke, rhythm, throb, pulsation, beating, pounding, drumming, vibration, oscillation.

pump *verb* push, drive, force, inject, siphon, draw, drain.

pun *noun* play on words, double entendre, witticism, quip.

punch[1] *verb* hit, strike, pummel, jab, bash, clout, cuff, box, thump, sock (*infml*), wallop (*infml*).

▪ *noun* **1** *a punch in the face*: blow, jab, bash, clout, thump, wallop (*infml*). **2** *has plenty of punch*: force, impact, effectiveness, drive, vigour, verve, panache.

punch[2] *verb* perforate, pierce, puncture, prick, bore, drill, stamp, cut.

punctual *adjective* prompt, on time, on the dot, exact, precise, early, in good time.
F unpunctual, late.

punctuation

Punctuation marks include:
apostrophe, asterisk, backslash, brace, brackets, colon, comma, ellipsis, exclamation mark, forward slash, full stop, hyphen, inverted commas, oblique, parentheses, period, question mark, quotation marks, quotes (*infml*), semicolon, speech marks, square brackets, star, stop, solidus.

---

puncture *noun* **1** *car had a puncture*: flat tyre, flat (*infml*), blow-out. **2** *a small puncture in the skin*: leak, hole, perforation, cut, nick.
▪ *verb* prick, pierce, penetrate, perforate, hole, cut, nick, burst, rupture, flatten, deflate.

pungent *adjective* **1** *a pungent cheese*: strong, hot, peppery, spicy, aromatic, tangy, piquant, sharp, sour, bitter, acrid, stinging. **2** *a pungent remark*: biting, caustic, cutting, keen, acute, incisive, pointed, piercing, penetrating, sarcastic, scathing.
F **1** mild, bland, tasteless.

punish *verb* penalize, discipline, correct, chastise, castigate (*fml*), scold, beat, flog, lash, cane, spank, fine, imprison.
F reward.

punishment *noun* discipline, correction, chastisement, beating, flogging, penalty, fine, imprisonment, sentence, deserts, retribution, revenge.
F reward.

puny *adjective* weak, feeble, frail, sickly, undeveloped, underdeveloped, stunted, undersized, diminutive, little, tiny, insignificant.
F strong, sturdy, large, important.

pupil *noun* student, scholar, schoolboy, schoolgirl, learner, apprentice, beginner, novice, disciple, protégé(e).
F teacher.

purchase *verb* buy, pay for, invest in (*infml*), procure, acquire, obtain, get, secure, gain, earn, win.
F sell.
▪ *noun* acquisition, buy (*infml*), investment, asset, possession, property.
F sale.

pure *adjective* **1** *pure gold*: unadulterated, unalloyed, unmixed, undiluted, neat, solid, simple, natural, real, authentic, genuine, true. **2** *pure water*: sterile, uncontaminated, unpolluted, germ-free, aseptic, antiseptic, disinfected, sterilized, hygienic, sanitary, clean, immaculate, spotless, clear. **3** *pure nonsense*: sheer, utter, complete, total, thorough, absolute, perfect, unqualified. **4** *young and pure*: chaste, virginal, undefiled, unsullied, moral, upright, virtuous, blameless, innocent.

1 impure, adulterated. **2** contaminated, polluted, impure. **4** immoral, impure.

purely *adverb* **1** *not purely accurate*: utterly, completely, totally, entirely, wholly, thoroughly, absolutely. **2** *purely out of interest*: only, simply, merely, just, solely, exclusively.

purge *verb* **1** *purged of sin*: purify, cleanse, clean out, scour, clear, absolve. **2** *purging those who didn't agree*: oust, remove, get rid of, eject, expel, root out, eradicate, exterminate, wipe out, kill.

▪ *noun* removal, ejection, expulsion, witch hunt, eradication, extermination.

purify *verb* refine, filter, clarify, clean, cleanse, decontaminate, sanitize, disinfect, sterilize, fumigate, deodorize.

contaminate, pollute, defile (*fml*).

purist *noun* pedant, literalist, formalist, stickler, quibbler, nit-picker.

puritanical *adjective* puritan, moralistic, disciplinarian, ascetic, abstemious, austere, severe, stern, strict, strait-laced, prim, proper, prudish, disapproving, stuffy, stiff, rigid, narrow-minded, bigoted, fanatical, zealous.

hedonistic, liberal, indulgent, broad-minded.

purity *noun* **1** *purity of the water*: clearness, clarity, cleanness, cleanliness, untaintedness, wholesomeness. **2** *purity of line*: simplicity, authenticity, genuineness, truth. **3** *purity of spirit*: chastity, decency, morality, integrity, rectitude, uprightness, virtue, innocence, blamelessness.

1 impurity. **3** immorality.

purpose *noun* **1** *have a purpose in life*: intention, aim, objective, end, goal, target, plan, design, vision, idea, point, object, reason, motive, rationale, principle, result, outcome. **2** *full of purpose*: determination, resolve, resolution, drive, single-mindedness, dedication, devotion, constancy, steadfastness, persistence, tenacity, zeal. **3** *what purpose will it serve?*: use, function, application, good, advantage, benefit, value.

purposeful *adjective* determined, decided, resolved, resolute, single-minded, constant, steadfast, persistent, persevering, tenacious, strong-willed, positive, firm, deliberate.

purposeless, aimless.

purse *noun* money-bag, wallet, pouch.

▪ *verb* pucker, wrinkle, draw together, close, tighten, contract, compress.

pursue *verb* **1** *pursue an activity*: perform, engage in, practise, conduct, carry on, continue, keep on, keep up, maintain, persevere in, persist in, hold to, aspire to, aim for, strive for, try for. **2** *pursued by the press*: chase, go after, follow, track, trail, shadow, tail, dog, harass, harry, hound, hunt, seek, search for, investigate, inquire into.

pursuit *noun* **1** *join the pursuit*: chase, hue and cry, tracking, stalking, trail, hunt, quest, search, investigation. **2** *interesting pursuits*: activity, interest, hobby, pastime, occupation, trade, craft, line, speciality, vocation.

push *verb* **1** *pushed along by the wind/push the button*: propel, thrust, ram, shove, jostle, elbow, prod, poke, press, depress, squeeze, squash, drive, force, constrain. **2** *pushing his products*: promote, advertise, publicize, boost, encourage, urge, egg on (*infml*), incite, spur, influence, persuade, pressurize, bully.
F3 **1** pull. **2** discourage, dissuade.
▪ *noun* **1** *gave him a push*: knock, shove, nudge, jolt, prod, poke, thrust. **2** *doesn't have much push*: energy, vigour, vitality, go (*infml*), drive, effort, dynamism, enterprise, initiative, ambition, determination.

pushy *adjective* assertive, self-assertive, ambitious, forceful, aggressive, over-confident, forward, bold, brash, arrogant, presumptuous, assuming, bossy (*infml*), in-your-face (*infml*).
F3 unassertive, unassuming.

put *verb* **1** *put it over there*: place, lay, deposit, plonk (*infml*), set, fix, settle, establish, stand, position, dispose, situate, station, post. **2** *put all the blame on me*: apply, impose, inflict, levy, assign, subject. **3** *put it another way*: word, phrase, formulate, frame, couch, express, voice, utter, state. **4** *put a suggestion*: submit, present, offer, suggest, propose.

putrid *adjective* rotten, decayed, decomposed, mouldy, off, bad, rancid, addled, corrupt, contaminated, tainted, polluted, foul, rank, fetid, stinking.
F3 fresh, wholesome.

puzzle *verb* **1** *their behaviour always puzzled him*: baffle, mystify, perplex, confound, stump (*infml*), floor (*infml*), confuse, bewilder, flummox (*infml*). **2** *puzzling over the problem*: think, ponder, meditate, consider, mull over, deliberate, figure, rack one's brains.
▪ *noun* question, poser (*infml*), brain-teaser, mind-bender, crossword, rebus, anagram, riddle, conundrum, mystery, enigma, paradox.

puzzled *adjective* baffled, mystified, perplexed, confounded, at a loss, beaten, stumped (*infml*), confused, bewildered, nonplussed, lost, at sea, flummoxed (*infml*).
F3 clear.

quagmire *noun* bog, marsh, fen, swamp, morass, quicksand.
quail *verb* recoil, back away, shy away, shrink, flinch, cringe, cower, tremble, quake, shudder, falter.
quaint *adjective* picturesque, charming, twee (*infml*), old-fashioned, antiquated, old-world, olde-worlde (*infml*), unusual, strange, odd, curious, bizarre, fanciful, whimsical.
F3 modern.
quake *verb* shake, tremble, shudder, quiver, shiver, quail, vibrate, wobble, rock, sway, move, convulse, heave.
qualification *noun* **1** *good qualifications*: certificate, diploma, training, skill, competence, ability, capability, capacity, aptitude, suitability, fitness, eligibility. **2** *without qualification*: restriction, limitation, reservation, exception, exemption, condition, caveat, provision, proviso, stipulation, modification.
qualified *adjective* certified, chartered, licensed, professional, trained, experienced, practised, skilled, accomplished, expert, knowledgeable, skilful, talented, proficient, competent, efficient, able, capable, fit, eligible.
F3 unqualified.
qualify *verb* **1** *qualify as a doctor*: train, prepare, equip, fit, pass, graduate, certify, empower, entitle, authorize, sanction, permit. **2** *qualify the last statement*: moderate, reduce, lessen, diminish, temper, soften, weaken, mitigate, ease, adjust, modify, restrain, restrict, limit, delimit, define, classify.
F3 1 disqualify.
quality *noun* **1** *has many good qualities*: property, characteristic, peculiarity, attribute, aspect, feature, trait, mark. **2** *of poor quality*: standard, grade, class, kind, sort, nature, character, calibre, status, rank, value, worth, merit, condition. **3** *shows real quality*: excellence, superiority, pre-eminence, distinction, refinement.
quantity *noun* amount, number, sum, total, aggregate, mass, lot, share, portion, quota, allotment, measure, dose, proportion, part, content, capacity, volume, weight, bulk, size, magnitude, expanse, extent, length, breadth.
quarrel *noun* row, argument,

slanging match (*infml*), wrangle, squabble, tiff, misunderstanding, disagreement, dispute, dissension, controversy, difference, conflict, clash, contention, strife, fight, scrap, brawl, feud, vendetta, schism.
F3 agreement, harmony.
▪ *verb* row, argue, bicker, squabble, wrangle, be at loggerheads, fall out, disagree, dispute, dissent, differ, be at variance, clash, contend, fight, scrap, feud.
F3 agree.

quarrelsome *adjective* argumentative, disputatious, contentious, belligerent, ill-tempered, irritable.
F3 peaceable, placid.

quarter *noun* district, sector, zone, neighbourhood, locality, vicinity, area, region, province, territory, division, section, part, place, spot, point, direction, side.
▪ *verb* station, post, billet, accommodate, put up, lodge, board, house, shelter.

quarters *noun* accommodation, lodgings, billet, digs (*infml*), residence, dwelling, habitation, domicile, rooms, barracks, station, post.

quash *verb* annul, revoke, rescind, overrule, cancel, nullify, void, invalidate, reverse, set aside, squash, crush, quell, suppress, subdue, defeat, overthrow.
F3 confirm, vindicate, reinstate.

quaver *verb* shake, tremble, quake, shudder, quiver, vibrate, pulsate, oscillate, flutter, flicker, trill, warble.

queasy *adjective* sick, ill, unwell, queer, groggy, green, nauseated, sickened, bilious, squeamish, faint, dizzy, giddy.

queen *noun* monarch, sovereign, ruler, majesty, princess, empress, consort.

queer *adjective* odd, mysterious, strange, unusual, uncommon, weird, unnatural, bizarre, eccentric, peculiar, funny, puzzling, curious, remarkable.
F3 ordinary, usual, common.

quell *verb* subdue, quash, crush, squash, suppress, put down, overcome, conquer, defeat, overpower, moderate, mitigate, allay, alleviate, soothe, calm, pacify, hush, quiet, silence, stifle, extinguish.

quench *verb* **1** *quench one's thirst*: slake, satisfy, sate, cool. **2** *quenching the flames*: extinguish, douse, put out, snuff out.

query *verb* ask, inquire, question, challenge, dispute, quarrel with, doubt, suspect, distrust, mistrust, disbelieve.
F3 accept.
▪ *noun* question, inquiry, problem, uncertainty, doubt, suspicion, scepticism, reservation, hesitation.

quest *noun* search, hunt, pursuit, investigation, inquiry, mission, crusade, enterprise, undertaking, venture, journey, voyage, expedition, exploration, adventure.

question *verb* interrogate, quiz, grill, pump, interview, examine, cross-examine, debrief, ask, inquire, investigate, probe, query, challenge, dispute, doubt, disbelieve.
▪ *noun* **1** *have a couple of questions*: query, inquiry, poser (*infml*), problem, difficulty. **2** *that's not the question we're dealing with at the moment*: issue, matter, subject, topic, point, proposal, proposition, motion, debate, dispute, controversy.

questionable *adjective* debatable, disputable, unsettled, undetermined, unproven, uncertain, arguable, controversial, vexed, dodgy (*infml*), doubtful, dubious, suspicious, suspect, shady (*infml*), fishy (*infml*), iffy (*infml*).
F3 unquestionable, indisputable, certain.

questionnaire *noun* quiz, test, survey, opinion poll.

queue *noun* line, tailback, file, crocodile, procession, train, string, succession, series, sequence, order.

quibble *verb* carp, cavil, split hairs, nit-pick, equivocate, prevaricate.
▪ *noun* complaint, objection, criticism, query.

quick *adjective* **1** *a quick look/ phone call*: fast, swift, rapid, speedy, express, hurried, hasty, cursory, fleeting, brief, prompt, ready, immediate, instant, instantaneous, sudden, brisk, nimble, sprightly, agile. **2** *she's very quick at picking things up*: clever, intelligent, quick-witted, smart, sharp, keen, shrewd, astute, discerning, perceptive, responsive, receptive.
F3 **1** slow, sluggish, lethargic. **2** unintelligent, dull.

quicken *verb* accelerate, speed, hurry, hasten, precipitate (*fml*), expedite, dispatch, advance.
F3 slow, retard.

quiet *adjective* **1** *quiet as a mouse/ in a quiet voice*: silent, noiseless, inaudible, hushed, soft, low. **2** *quiet surroundings*: peaceful, still, tranquil, serene, calm, composed, undisturbed, untroubled, placid. **3** *a quiet person*: shy, reserved, reticent, uncommunicative, taciturn, unforthcoming, retiring, withdrawn, thoughtful, subdued, meek. **4** *a quiet spot*: isolated, unfrequented, lonely, secluded, private.
F3 **1** noisy, loud. **2** excitable. **3** extrovert.
▪ *noun* quietness, silence, hush, peace, lull, stillness, tranquillity, serenity, calm, rest, repose.
F3 noise, loudness, disturbance, bustle.

quieten *verb* **1** *quieten the children*: silence, hush, mute, soften, lower, diminish, reduce, stifle, muffle, deaden, dull. **2** *he's quietened down a lot*: subdue, pacify, quell, quiet, still, smooth, calm, soothe, compose, sober.

F3 **2** disturb, agitate.
quirk *noun* freak, eccentricity, curiosity, oddity, peculiarity, idiosyncrasy, mannerism, habit, trait, foible, whim, caprice, turn, twist.
quit *verb* **1** *quit his job*: leave, depart, go, exit, decamp, desert, forsake, abandon, renounce, relinquish, surrender, give up, resign, retire, withdraw. **2** *quit smoking*: stop, cease, end, discontinue, desist, drop, give up, pack in (*infml*).
quite *adverb* **1** *quite good*: moderately, rather, somewhat, fairly, relatively, comparatively. **2** *quite awful*: utterly, absolutely, totally, completely, entirely, wholly, fully, perfectly, exactly, precisely.
quiver *verb* shake, tremble, shudder, shiver, quake, quaver, vibrate, palpitate, flutter, flicker, oscillate, wobble.
quiz *noun* questionnaire, test, examination, competition.
▪ *verb* question, interrogate, grill, pump, examine, cross-examine.
quizzical *adjective* questioning, inquiring, curious, amused, humorous, teasing, mocking, satirical, sardonic, sceptical.
quota *noun* ration, allowance, allocation, assignment, share, portion, part, slice, cut (*infml*), percentage, proportion.
quotation *noun* **1** *a quotation from Shakespeare*: citation, quote (*infml*), extract, excerpt, passage, piece, cutting, reference. **2** *a quotation from a builder*: estimate, quote (*infml*), tender, figure, price, cost, charge, rate.
quote *verb* cite, refer to, mention, name, reproduce, echo, repeat, recite, recall, recollect.

rabble *noun* crowd, throng, horde, herd, mob, masses, populace, riff-raff.
race[1] *noun* sprint, steeplechase, marathon, scramble, regatta, competition, contest, contention, rivalry, chase, pursuit, quest.
▪ *verb* run, sprint, dash, tear, fly, gallop, speed, career, dart, zoom, rush, hurry, hasten.
race[2] *noun* nation, people, tribe, clan, house, dynasty, family, kindred, ancestry, line, blood, stock, genus, species, breed.
racial *adjective* national, tribal, ethnic, folk, genealogical, ancestral, inherited, genetic.
racism *noun* racialism,

xenophobia, chauvinism, jingoism, discrimination, prejudice, bias.

racket *noun* **1** *stop that terrible racket!*: noise, din, uproar, row, fuss, outcry, clamour, commotion, disturbance, pandemonium, hurly-burly, hubbub. **2** *running a racket*: swindle, con (*infml*), fraud, fiddle, deception, trick, dodge, scheme, business, game.

radiant *adjective* **1** *radiant as if lit with a thousand candles*: bright, luminous, shining, gleaming, glowing, beaming, glittering, sparkling, brilliant, resplendent, splendid, glorious. **2** *a radiant smile*: happy, joyful, delighted, ecstatic.

F3 **1** dull. **2** miserable.

radiate *verb* **1** *heat radiating from the sun*: shine, gleam, glow, beam, shed, pour, give off, emit, emanate, diffuse, issue, disseminate, scatter, spread (out). **2** *lines radiating from a central point*: diverge, branch.

radical *adjective* **1** *radical change/ investigation*: drastic, comprehensive, thorough, sweeping, far-reaching, fundamental, thoroughgoing, complete, total, entire. **2** *radical views*: fanatical, militant, extreme, extremist, revolutionary.

F3 **1** superficial. **2** moderate.

▪ *noun* fanatic, militant, extremist, revolutionary, reformer, reformist, fundamentalist.

rage *noun* anger, wrath, fury, frenzy, tantrum, temper.

▪ *verb* fume, seethe, rant, rave, storm, thunder, explode, rampage.

ragged *adjective* **1** *ragged clothes*: frayed, torn, ripped, tattered, worn-out, threadbare, tatty, shabby, scruffy, unkempt, down-at-heel. **2** *a ragged edge*: jagged, serrated, indented, notched, rough, uneven, irregular.

raid *noun* attack, onset, onslaught, invasion, inroad, incursion, foray, sortie, strike, blitz, swoop, bust (*infml*), robbery, break-in, hold-up.

▪ *verb* loot, pillage, plunder, ransack, rifle, maraud, attack, descend on, invade, storm.

rain *noun* rainfall, precipitation, raindrops, drizzle, shower, cloudburst, downpour, deluge, torrent, storm, thunderstorm, squall.

▪ *verb* spit, drizzle, shower, pour, teem, pelt, bucket (*infml*), deluge.

raise *verb* **1** *raising defensive walls*: lift, elevate, hoist, jack up, erect, build, construct. **2** *raise prices*: increase, augment, escalate, magnify, heighten, strengthen, intensify, amplify, boost, enhance. **3** *raise funds*: get, obtain, collect, gather, assemble, rally, muster, recruit. **4** *raise a family*: bring up, rear, breed, propagate, grow, cultivate, develop. **5** *raise a subject*: bring up, broach, introduce, present, put forward, moot, suggest.

F3 **1** lower. **2** decrease, reduce. **5** suppress.

rake *verb* **1** *rake the leaves*: hoe, scratch, scrape, graze, comb, level. **2** *raking through their belongings*: search, scour, hunt, ransack. **3** *raking money in*: gather, collect, amass, accumulate.

rally *verb* **1** *rallied an army/rallied to the cause*: gather, collect, assemble, congregate, convene, muster, summon, round up, unite, marshal, organize, mobilize, reassemble, regroup, reorganize. **2** *rallied for a short time before relapsing*: recover, recuperate, revive, improve, pick up.
▪ *noun* gathering, assembly, convention, convocation (*fml*), conference, meeting, jamboree, reunion, march, demonstration.

ram *verb* **1** *ramming the car in front*: hit, strike, butt, hammer, pound, drum, crash, smash, slam. **2** *rammed his hands into his pockets*: force, drive, thrust, cram, stuff, pack, crowd, jam, wedge.

ramble *verb* **1** *rambling along the road*: walk, hike, trek, tramp, traipse, stroll, amble, saunter, straggle, wander, roam, rove, meander, wind, zigzag. **2** *he rambles on for hours*: chatter, babble, rabbit (on) (*infml*), witter (on) (*infml*), expatiate, digress, drift.
▪ *noun* walk, hike, trek, tramp, stroll, saunter, tour, trip, excursion.

rambling *adjective* **1** *a rambling rose*: spreading, sprawling, straggling, trailing. **2** *a rambling explanation*: circuitous, roundabout, digressive, wordy, long-winded, long-drawn-out, disconnected, incoherent.
F3 **2** direct.

rampage *verb* run wild, run amok, run riot, rush, tear, storm, rage, rant, rave.
▪ *noun* rage, fury, frenzy, storm, uproar, violence, destruction.

rampant *adjective* unrestrained, uncontrolled, unbridled, unchecked, wanton, excessive, fierce, violent, raging, wild, riotous, rank, profuse, rife, widespread, prevalent.

ramshackle *adjective* dilapidated, tumbledown, broken-down, crumbling, ruined, derelict, jerry-built, unsafe, rickety, shaky, unsteady, tottering, decrepit.
F3 solid, stable.

rancid *adjective* sour, off, bad, musty, stale, rank, foul, fetid, putrid, rotten.
F3 sweet.

random *adjective* arbitrary, chance, fortuitous (*fml*), casual, incidental, haphazard, irregular, unsystematic, unplanned, accidental, aimless, purposeless, indiscriminate, stray.
F3 systematic, deliberate.

range *noun* **1** *across the entire range*: scope, compass, scale, gamut, spectrum, sweep, spread, extent, distance, reach, span, limits, bounds, parameters, area, field, domain, province, sphere, orbit. **2** *a range of colours*: variety, diversity, assortment, selection, sort, kind, class, order, series, string, chain.

▪ *verb* **1** *ranges from dark to light*: extend, stretch, reach, spread, vary, fluctuate. **2** *ranging the books along the shelf*: align, arrange, order, rank, classify, catalogue.

rank *noun* **1** *high rank/an army rank*: grade, degree, class, caste, status, standing, position, station, condition, estate (*fml*), echelon, level, stratum, tier, classification, sort, type, group, division. **2** *ranks of shelves*: row, line, range, column, file, series, order, formation.

▪ *verb* grade, class, rate, place, position, range, sort, classify, categorize, order, arrange, organize, marshal.

ransack *verb* search, scour, comb, rummage, rifle, raid, sack, strip, despoil, ravage, loot, plunder, pillage.

ransom *noun* price, money, payment, pay-off, redemption, deliverance, rescue, liberation, release.

▪ *verb* buy off, redeem, deliver, rescue, liberate, free, release.

rap *verb* knock, hit, strike, tap, thump.

▪ *noun* knock, blow, tap, thump.

rapid *adjective* swift, speedy, quick, fast, express, lightning, prompt, brisk, hurried, hasty, precipitate (*fml*), headlong.

F3 slow, leisurely, sluggish.

rapport *noun* bond, link, affinity, relationship, empathy, sympathy, understanding, harmony.

rapture *noun* delight, happiness, joy, bliss, ecstasy, euphoria, exaltation.

rare *adjective* uncommon, unusual, scarce, sparse, sporadic, infrequent.

F3 common, abundant, frequent.

rarely *adverb* seldom, hardly ever, infrequently, little.

F3 often, frequently.

raring *adjective* eager, keen, enthusiastic, ready, willing, impatient, longing, itching, desperate.

rarity *noun* **1** *something of a rarity*: curiosity, curio, gem, pearl, treasure, find. **2** *sought after for its rarity*: uncommonness, unusualness, strangeness, scarcity, shortage, sparseness, infrequency.

F3 2 commonness, frequency.

rash *adjective* reckless, ill-considered, foolhardy, ill-advised, madcap, hare-brained, hot-headed, headstrong, impulsive, impetuous, hasty, headlong, unguarded, unwary, indiscreet, imprudent, careless, heedless, unthinking.

F3 cautious, wary, careful.

rate *noun* **1** *rate of change*: speed, velocity, tempo, time, ratio, proportion, relation, degree, grade, rank, rating, standard, basis, measure, scale. **2** *rate of pay/interest*: charge, fee, hire, toll, tariff, price, cost, value, worth, tax, duty, amount, figure, percentage.

▪ *verb* **1** *rated as the best in its class*: judge, regard, consider, deem, count, reckon, figure, estimate, evaluate, assess, weigh, measure, grade, rank, class, classify. **2** *don't rate it at all*: admire, respect, esteem, value, prize. **3** *rate a second look*: deserve, merit.

rather *adverb* **1** *rather funny*: moderately, relatively, slightly, a bit, somewhat, fairly, quite, pretty, noticeably, significantly, very. **2** *rather you than me*: preferably, sooner, instead.

rating *noun* class, rank, degree, status, standing, position, placing, order, grade, mark, evaluation, assessment, classification, category.

ratio *noun* percentage, fraction, proportion, relation, relationship, correspondence, correlation.

ration *noun* quota, allowance, allocation, allotment, share, portion, helping, part, measure, amount.

▪ *verb* apportion, allot, allocate, share, deal out, distribute, dole out, dispense, supply, issue, control, restrict, limit, conserve, save.

rational *adjective* logical, reasonable, sound, well-founded, realistic, sensible, clear-headed, judicious (*fml*), wise, sane, normal, balanced, lucid, reasoning, thinking, intelligent, enlightened. **E3** irrational, illogical, insane, crazy.

rattle *verb* clatter, jingle, jangle, clank, shake, vibrate, jolt, jar, bounce, bump.

raucous *adjective* harsh, rough, hoarse, husky, rasping, grating, jarring, strident, noisy, loud.

ravage *verb* destroy, devastate, lay waste, demolish, raze, wreck, ruin, spoil, damage, loot, pillage, plunder, sack, despoil.

rave *verb* rage, storm, thunder, roar, rant, ramble, babble, splutter.

ravenous *adjective* hungry, starving, starved, famished, greedy, voracious, insatiable.

raving *adjective* mad, insane, crazy, hysterical, delirious, wild, frenzied, furious, berserk.

ravishing *adjective* delightful, enchanting, charming, lovely, beautiful, gorgeous, stunning (*infml*), radiant, dazzling, alluring, seductive.

raw *adjective* **1** *raw vegetables*: uncooked, fresh. **2** *raw cotton*: unprocessed, unrefined, untreated, crude, natural. **3** *the raw truth*: plain, bare, naked, basic, harsh, brutal, realistic. **4** *raw skin*: scratched, grazed, scraped, open, bloody, sore, tender, sensitive. **5** *it's raw outside*: cold, chilly, bitter, biting, piercing, freezing, bleak. **6** *a raw recruit*: new, green, immature, callow, inexperienced, untrained, unskilled.
E3 **1** cooked, done. **2** processed, refined. **5** warm. **6** experienced, skilled.

ray *noun* beam, shaft, flash,

gleam, flicker, glimmer, glint, spark, trace, hint, indication.

reach *verb* arrive at, get to, attain, achieve, make, amount to, hit, strike, touch, contact, stretch, extend, grasp.

▪ *noun* range, scope, compass, distance, spread, extent, stretch, grasp, jurisdiction, command, power, influence.

react *verb* respond, retaliate, reciprocate, reply, answer, acknowledge, act, behave.

reaction *noun* response, effect, reply, answer, acknowledgement, feedback, counteraction, reflex, recoil, reciprocation, retaliation.

read *verb* **1** *read a book/read French*: study, peruse, pore over, scan, skim, decipher, decode, interpret, construe, understand, comprehend. **2** *read us a story*: recite, declaim, deliver, speak, utter.

readable *adjective* **1** *machine-readable language*: legible, decipherable, intelligible, clear, understandable, comprehensible. **2** *his style is very readable*: interesting, enjoyable, entertaining, gripping, unputdownable (*infml*).

F3 **1** illegible. **2** unreadable.

readily *adverb* willingly, unhesitatingly, gladly, eagerly, promptly, quickly, freely, smoothly, easily, effortlessly.

F3 unwillingly, reluctantly.

ready *adjective* **1** *ready to go*: prepared, waiting, set, fit, arranged, organized, completed, finished. **2** *ready and able*: willing, inclined, disposed, happy, game (*infml*), eager, keen. **3** *ready cash/in ready amounts*: available, to hand, present, near, accessible, convenient, handy. **4** *a ready response*: prompt, immediate, quick, sharp, astute, perceptive, alert.

F3 **1** unprepared. **2** unwilling, reluctant, disinclined. **3** unavailable, inaccessible. **4** slow.

real *adjective* actual, existing, physical, material, substantial, tangible, genuine, authentic, bona fide, official, rightful, legitimate, valid, true, factual, certain, sure, positive, veritable (*fml*), honest, sincere, heartfelt, unfeigned, unaffected.

F3 unreal, imaginary, false.

realistic *adjective* **1** *not a realistic proposal*: practical, down-to-earth, commonsense, sensible, level-headed, clear-sighted, businesslike, hard-headed, pragmatic, matter-of-fact, rational, logical, objective, detached, unsentimental, unromantic. **2** *a realistic portrayal*: lifelike, faithful, truthful, true, genuine, authentic, natural, real, real-life, graphic, representational.

F3 **1** unrealistic, impractical, irrational, idealistic.

reality *noun* truth, fact, certainty, realism, actuality, existence, materiality, tangibility, genuineness, authenticity, validity.

realize *verb* understand, comprehend, grasp, catch on, cotton on (*infml*), recognize, accept, appreciate.

really *adverb* actually, truly, honestly, sincerely, genuinely, positively, certainly, absolutely, categorically, very, indeed.

realm *noun* kingdom, monarchy, principality, empire, country, state, land, territory, area, region, province, domain, sphere, orbit, field, department.

rear *noun* back, stern, end, tail, rump, buttocks, posterior, behind, bottom, backside (*infml*).
F3 front.
▪ *adjective* back, hind, hindmost, rearmost, last.
F3 front.
▪ *verb* **1** *rear a child*: bring up, raise, breed, grow, cultivate, foster, nurse, nurture, train, educate. **2** *rearing up out of the mist*: rise, tower, soar, raise, lift.

reason *noun* **1** *the reason for his silence/their reason for leaving*: cause, motive, incentive, rationale, explanation, excuse, justification, defence, warrant, ground, basis, case, argument, aim, intention, purpose, object, end, goal. **2** *using reason*: sense, logic, reasoning, rationality, sanity, mind, wit, brain, intellect, understanding, wisdom, judgement, common sense, gumption.
▪ *verb* work out, solve, resolve, conclude, deduce, infer, think.

reasonable *adjective* **1** *a reasonable suggestion*: sensible, wise, well-advised, sane, intelligent, rational, logical, practical, sound, reasoned, well-thought-out, plausible, credible, possible, viable. **2** *a reasonable price*: acceptable, satisfactory, tolerable, moderate, average, fair, just, modest, inexpensive.
F3 **1** irrational, unreasonable. **2** exorbitant.

reassure *verb* comfort, cheer, encourage, hearten, inspirit, brace, bolster.
F3 alarm.

rebate *noun* refund, repayment, reduction, discount, deduction, allowance.

rebel *verb* /ri-**bel**/ revolt, mutiny, rise up, run riot, dissent, disobey, defy, resist, recoil, shrink.
F3 conform.
▪ *noun* /**reb**-el/ revolutionary, insurrectionary, mutineer, dissenter, nonconformist, schismatic, heretic.

rebellion *noun* revolt, revolution, coup (d'état), rising, uprising, insurrection, insurgence, mutiny, resistance, opposition, defiance, disobedience, insubordination, dissent, heresy.

rebound *verb* recoil, backfire, return, bounce, ricochet, boomerang.

recall *verb* remember, recollect, cast one's mind back, evoke, bring back.

recede *verb* go back, return, retire, withdraw, retreat, ebb, wane, sink, decline, diminish, dwindle, decrease, lessen, shrink, slacken, subside, abate.
F3 advance.

receipt *noun* **1** *issue a receipt*: voucher, ticket, slip, counterfoil, stub, acknowledgement. **2** *on receipt of your letter*: receiving, reception, acceptance, delivery.

receive *verb* **1** *received twenty pounds*: take, accept, get, obtain, derive, acquire, pick up, collect, inherit. **2** *received their guests*: admit, let in, greet, welcome, entertain, accommodate. **3** *receive a blow to the head*: experience, undergo, suffer, sustain, meet with, encounter. **4** *wasn't received favourably*: react to, respond to, hear, perceive, apprehend.
F3 1 give, donate.

recent *adjective* late, latest, current, present-day, contemporary, modern, up-to-date, new, novel, fresh, young.
F3 old, out-of-date.

recently *adverb* lately, newly, freshly.

reception *noun* **1** *got a great reception*: welcome, treatment, acceptance, admission, greeting, recognition, response, reaction, acknowledgement, receipt. **2** *attend the reception*: party, function, do (*infml*), entertainment.

receptive *adjective* open-minded, amenable, accommodating, suggestible, susceptible, sensitive, responsive, open, accessible, approachable, friendly, hospitable, welcoming, sympathetic, favourable, interested.
F3 narrow-minded, resistant, unresponsive.

recess *noun* **1** *during recess*: break, interval, intermission, rest, respite, holiday, vacation. **2** *a recess in the wall*: alcove, niche, nook, corner, bay, cavity, hollow, depression, indentation.

recession *noun* slump, depression, downturn, decline.
F3 boom, upturn.

recipe *noun* formula, prescription, ingredients, instructions, directions, method, system, procedure, technique.

reciprocate *verb* respond, reply, requite, return, exchange, swap, trade, match, equal, correspond, interchange, alternate.

recite *verb* repeat, tell, narrate, relate, recount, speak, deliver, articulate, declaim, perform, reel off, itemize, enumerate.

reckless *adjective* heedless, thoughtless, mindless, careless, negligent, irresponsible, imprudent, ill-advised, indiscreet, rash, hasty, foolhardy, daredevil, wild.
F3 cautious, wary, careful, prudent.

reckon *verb* **1** *reckoning the cost*: calculate, compute, figure out, work out, add up, total, tally, count, number, enumerate. **2** *reckoned to be quite good*: deem, regard, consider, esteem, value, rate, judge, evaluate, assess, estimate, gauge. **3** *I reckon that will be OK*: think, believe, imagine, fancy, suppose, surmise, assume, guess, conjecture.

reckoning *noun* **1** *by my reckoning*: calculation, computation, estimate. **2** *the day of reckoning*: judgement, retribution, doom.

reclaim *verb* recover, regain, recapture, retrieve, salvage, rescue, redeem, restore, reinstate, regenerate.

recognition *noun* **1** *damaged beyond all recognition*: identification, detection, discovery, recollection, recall, remembrance, awareness, perception, realization, understanding. **2** *recognition of his failings/nod in recognition*: confession, admission, acceptance, acknowledgement, gratitude, appreciation, honour, respect, greeting, salute.

recognize *verb* **1** *recognized him immediately*: identify, know, remember, recollect, recall, place, see, notice, spot, perceive. **2** *recognize I may have been wrong*: confess, own, acknowledge, accept, admit, grant, concede, allow, appreciate, understand, realize.

recollect *verb* recall, remember, cast one's mind back, reminisce.

recollection *noun* recall, remembrance, memory, souvenir, reminiscence, impression.

recommend *verb* advocate, urge, exhort, advise, counsel, suggest, propose, put forward, advance, praise, commend, plug (*infml*), endorse, approve, vouch for.
F3 disapprove.

recommendation *noun* advice, counsel, suggestion, proposal, advocacy, endorsement, approval, sanction, blessing, praise, commendation, plug (*infml*), reference, testimonial.
F3 disapproval.

reconcile *verb* reunite, conciliate, pacify, appease, placate, propitiate, accord, harmonize, accommodate, adjust, resolve, settle, square.
F3 estrange, alienate.

record *noun* /**rek**-awd/ **1** *a record of events*: register, log, report, account, minutes, memorandum, note, entry, document, file, dossier, diary, journal, memoir, history, annals, archives, documentation, evidence, testimony, trace. **2** *make a pop record*: recording, disc, single, CD, compact disc, album, release, LP. **3** *break the record*: fastest time, best performance, personal best, world record. **4** *has a good record in the industry*: background, track record, curriculum vitae, career.
▪ *verb* /ri-**kawd**/ **1** *recording dates and times*: note, enter, inscribe, write down, transcribe, register,

log, put down, enrol, report, minute, chronicle, document, keep, preserve. **2** *recording their new album*: tape-record, tape, videotape, video, cut.

recording *noun* release, performance, record, disc, CD, cassette, tape, video, DVD, MP3, Mini Disc®.

recoup *verb* recover, retrieve, regain, get back, make good, repay, refund, reimburse, compensate.

recover *verb* **1** *recover from illness*: get better, improve, pick up, rally, mend, heal, pull through, get over, recuperate, revive, convalesce, come round. **2** *recover stolen goods*: regain, get back, recoup, retrieve, retake, recapture, repossess, reclaim, restore.
F3 **1** worsen. **2** lose, forfeit.

recovery *noun* **1** *make a rapid recovery*: recuperation, convalescence, rehabilitation, mending, healing, improvement, upturn, rally, revival, restoration. **2** *recovery of the wreckage*: retrieval, salvage, reclamation, repossession, recapture.
F3 **1** worsening. **2** loss, forfeit.

recreation *noun* fun, enjoyment, pleasure, amusement, diversion, distraction, entertainment, hobby, pastime, game, sport, play, leisure, relaxation, refreshment.

recruit *verb* enlist, draft, conscript, enrol, sign up, engage, take on, mobilize, raise, gather, obtain, procure.
▪ *noun* beginner, novice, initiate, learner, trainee, apprentice, conscript, convert.

recur *verb* repeat, persist, return, reappear.

recurrent *adjective* recurring, chronic, persistent, repeated, repetitive, regular, periodic, frequent, intermittent.

recycle *verb* reuse, reprocess, reclaim, recover, salvage, save.

red *adjective* **1** *red as blood*: scarlet, vermilion, cherry, ruby, crimson, maroon, pink, reddish, bloodshot, inflamed. **2** *a red face*: ruddy, florid, glowing, rosy, flushed, blushing, embarrassed, shamefaced. **3** *red hair*: ginger, carroty, auburn, chestnut, Titian.

redden *verb* blush, flush, colour, go red, crimson.

redeem *verb* **1** *redeem a pledge*: buy back, repurchase, cash (in), exchange, change, trade, ransom, reclaim, regain, repossess, recoup, recover, recuperate, retrieve, salvage. **2** *did nothing to redeem himself*: compensate for, make up for, offset, outweigh, atone for, expiate, absolve, acquit, discharge, release, liberate, emancipate, free, deliver, rescue, save.

reduce *verb* **1** *reduce the power*: lessen, decrease, contract, shrink, slim, shorten, curtail, trim, cut, slash, discount, rebate, lower, moderate, weaken, diminish, impair. **2** *reduce her to tears/ reduced to begging*: drive, force, degrade, downgrade, demote,

humble, humiliate, impoverish, subdue, overpower, master, vanquish (*fml*).
1 increase, raise, boost.

reduction *noun* decrease, drop, fall, decline, lessening, moderation, weakening, diminution, contraction, compression, shrinkage, narrowing, shortening, curtailment, restriction, limitation, cutback, cut, discount, rebate, devaluation, depreciation, deduction, subtraction, loss.
increase, rise, enlargement.

redundant *adjective* **1** *was made redundant*: unemployed, out of work, laid off, dismissed. **2** *a redundant machine*: superfluous, surplus, excess, extra, supernumerary, unneeded, unnecessary, unwanted.
2 necessary, essential.

reel *verb* stagger, totter, wobble, rock, sway, waver, falter, stumble, lurch, pitch, roll, revolve, gyrate, spin, wheel, twirl, whirl, swirl.

refer *verb* **1** *refer it to the committee*: send, direct, point, guide, pass on, transfer, commit, deliver. **2** *refer to a catalogue*: consult, look up, turn to, resort to. **3** *refer to him by name*: allude, mention, touch on, speak of, bring up, recommend, cite, quote. **4** *what does this refer to?*: apply, concern, relate, belong, pertain.

referee *noun* umpire, judge, adjudicator, arbitrator, mediator, ref (*infml*).

reference *noun* **1** *several references to his family*: allusion, remark, mention, citation, quotation, illustration, instance, note. **2** *need at least three references*: testimonial, recommendation, endorsement, character. **3** *in reference to your letter*: relation, regard, respect, connection, bearing.

refine *verb* process, treat, purify, clarify, filter, distil, polish, hone, improve, perfect, elevate, exalt.

refined *adjective* civilized, cultured, cultivated, polished, sophisticated, urbane, genteel, gentlemanly, ladylike, well-bred, well-mannered, polite, civil, elegant, fine, delicate, subtle, precise, exact, sensitive, discriminating.
coarse, vulgar, rude.

reflect *verb* **1** *image reflected in the water*: mirror, echo, imitate, reproduce, portray, depict, show, reveal, display, exhibit, manifest, demonstrate, indicate, express, communicate. **2** *reflect on what she had done*: think, ponder, consider, mull (over), deliberate, contemplate, meditate, muse.

reflection *noun* **1** *a reflection of their views*: image, likeness, echo, impression, indication, manifestation, observation, view, opinion. **2** *on reflection*: thinking, thought, study, consideration, deliberation, contemplation, meditation, musing.

reform *verb* change, amend,

improve, ameliorate (*fml*), better, rectify, correct, mend, repair, rehabilitate, rebuild, reconstruct, remodel, revamp, renovate, restore, regenerate, reconstitute, reorganize, shake up (*infml*), revolutionize, purge.
▪ *noun* change, amendment, improvement, rectification, correction, rehabilitation, renovation, reorganization, shake-up (*infml*), purge.

refresh *verb* **1** *refreshed by the breeze*: cool, freshen, enliven, invigorate, fortify, revive, restore, renew, rejuvenate, revitalize, reinvigorate. **2** *refresh one's memory*: jog, stimulate, prompt, prod.
F3 **1** tire, exhaust.

refreshing *adjective* **1** *a refreshing drink/shower*: cool, thirst-quenching, bracing, invigorating, energizing, reviving, stimulating. **2** *a refreshing change from routine*: fresh, new, novel, different.

refreshment *noun* sustenance, food, drink, snack, revival, restoration, renewal, reanimation, reinvigoration, revitalization.

refuge *noun* sanctuary, asylum, shelter, protection, security, retreat, hideout, hide-away, resort, harbour, haven.

refugee *noun* exile, émigré, displaced person, fugitive, runaway, escapee.

refund *verb* repay, reimburse, rebate, return, restore.
▪ *noun* repayment, reimbursement, rebate, return.

refusal *noun* rejection, no, rebuff, repudiation, denial, negation.
F3 acceptance.

refuse[1] *verb* /ri-**fyooz**/ reject, turn down, decline, spurn, repudiate, rebuff, repel, deny, withhold.
F3 accept, allow, permit.

refuse[2] *noun* /**ref**-yoos/ rubbish, waste, trash, garbage, junk, litter.

refute *verb* disprove, rebut, confute, give the lie to, discredit, counter, negate.

regain *verb* recover, get back, recoup, reclaim, repossess, retake, recapture, retrieve, return to.

regal *adjective* majestic, kingly, queenly, princely, imperial, royal, sovereign, stately, magnificent, noble, lordly.

regard *verb* consider, deem, judge, rate, value, think, believe, suppose, imagine, look upon, view, observe, watch.
▪ *noun* care, concern, consideration, attention, notice, heed, respect, deference, honour, esteem, admiration, affection, love, sympathy.
F3 disregard, contempt.

regarding *preposition* with regard to, as regards, concerning, with reference to, re, about, as to.

regardless *adverb* anyway, nevertheless, nonetheless, despite everything, come what may.

regime *noun* government, rule, administration, management, leadership, command, control, establishment, system.

region *noun* land, terrain, territory, country, province, area, district, zone, sector, neighbourhood, range, scope, expanse, domain, realm, sphere, field, division, section, part, place.

Types of geographical region include:

basin, belt, coast, colony, continent, country, desert, forest, grassland, green belt, heath, hemisphere, interior, jungle, lowlands, marshland, outback, pampas, plain, prairie, riviera, savannah, scrubland, seaside, settlement, steppe, subcontinent, territory, time zone, tundra, veld, wilderness, woodland, zone.

Types of administrative region include:

bailiwick, banana republic, borough, burgh, capital city, county, county town, diocese, district, dominion, duchy, emirate, empire, free state, kingdom, municipality, nation, parish, postal district, principality, protectorate, province, realm, republic, riding, shire, state, town, township, urban district.

---

register *noun* roll, roster, list, index, catalogue, directory, log, record, chronicle, annals, archives, file, ledger, schedule, diary, almanac.
▪ *verb* **1** *register for the vote*: record, note, log, enter, inscribe, mark, list, catalogue, chronicle, enrol, enlist, sign on, check in. **2** *registering ten degrees*: show, reveal, betray, display, exhibit, manifest, express, say, read, indicate.

regret *verb* rue, repent, lament, mourn, grieve, deplore.
▪ *noun* remorse, contrition, compunction, self-reproach, shame, sorrow, grief, disappointment, bitterness.

regretful *adjective* remorseful, rueful, repentant, contrite, penitent, conscience-stricken, ashamed, sorry, apologetic, sad, sorrowful, disappointed.
F3 impenitent, unashamed.

regrettable *adjective* unfortunate, unlucky, unhappy, sad, disappointing, upsetting, distressing, lamentable, deplorable, shameful, wrong, ill-advised.
F3 fortunate, happy.

regular *adjective* **1** *a regular event/not the regular thing*: routine, habitual, typical, usual, customary, time-honoured, conventional, orthodox, correct, official, standard, normal, ordinary, common, commonplace, everyday. **2** *a regular pulse*: periodic, rhythmic, steady, constant, fixed, set, unvarying, uniform, even, level, smooth, balanced, symmetrical, orderly, systematic, methodical.
F3 **1** unusual, unconventional. **2** irregular.

regulate *verb* control, direct, guide, govern, rule, administer, manage, handle, conduct, run, organize, order, arrange, settle, square, monitor, set, adjust, tune, moderate, balance.

regulation *noun* rule, statute, law, ordinance, edict, decree, order, commandment, precept (*fml*), dictate, requirement, procedure.

rehearsal *noun* practice, drill, exercise, dry run, run-through, preparation, reading, recital, narration, account, enumeration, list.

rehearse *verb* practise, drill, train, go over, prepare, try out, repeat, recite, recount, relate.

reign *noun* rule, sway, monarchy, empire, sovereignty, supremacy, power, command, dominion, control, influence.
▪ *verb* rule, govern, command, prevail, predominate, influence.

reinforce *verb* strengthen, fortify, toughen, harden, stiffen, steel, brace, support, buttress, shore, prop, stay, supplement, augment, increase, emphasize, stress, underline.
weaken, undermine.

reinstate *verb* restore, return, replace, recall, reappoint, reinstall, re-establish.

reject *verb* /ri-**jekt**/ refuse, deny, decline, turn down, veto, disallow, condemn, despise, spurn, rebuff, jilt, exclude, repudiate, repel, renounce, eliminate, scrap, discard, jettison, cast off.
accept, choose, select.
▪ *noun* /**ree**-jekt/ failure, second, discard, cast-off.

rejoice *verb* celebrate, revel, delight, glory, exult, triumph.

relapse *verb* worsen, deteriorate, degenerate, weaken, sink, fail, lapse, revert, regress, backslide.
▪ *noun* worsening, deterioration, setback, recurrence, weakening, lapse, reversion, regression, backsliding.

relate *verb* **1** *related to each other*: link, connect, join, couple, ally, associate, correlate. **2** *a book relating their adventures*: tell, recount, narrate, report, describe, recite.

related *adjective* kindred, akin, affiliated, allied, associated, connected, linked, interrelated, interconnected, accompanying, concomitant, joint, mutual.
unrelated, unconnected.

relation *noun* **1** *a close relation*: relative, family, kin, kindred. **2** *has no relation to the events of yesterday*: link, connection, bond, relationship, correlation, comparison, similarity, affiliation, interrelation, interconnection, interdependence, regard, reference.

relations *noun* **1** *all our friends and relations*: relatives, family, kin, kindred. **2** *establish friendly relations with other countries*: relationship, terms, rapport, liaison, intercourse, affairs, dealings, interaction, communications, contact, associations, connections.

relationship *noun* bond, link, connection, association, liaison, rapport, affinity, closeness, similarity, parallel, correlation, ratio, proportion.

relative *adjective* comparative, proportional, proportionate, commensurate, corresponding, respective, appropriate, relevant, applicable, related, connected, interrelated, reciprocal, dependent.
▪ *noun* relation, family, kin.

relax *verb* slacken, loosen, lessen, reduce, diminish, weaken, lower, soften, moderate, abate, remit, relieve, ease, rest, unwind, calm, tranquillize, sedate.
F3 tighten, intensify.

relaxed *adjective* informal, casual, laid-back (*infml*), easy-going (*infml*), carefree, happy-go-lucky, cool, calm, composed, collected, unhurried, leisurely.
F3 tense, nervous, formal.

relay *verb* broadcast, transmit, communicate, send, spread, carry, supply.

release *verb* loose, unloose, unleash, unfasten, extricate, free, liberate, deliver, emancipate, acquit, absolve, exonerate, excuse, exempt, discharge, issue, publish, circulate, distribute, present, launch, unveil.
F3 imprison, detain, check.
▪ *noun* freedom, liberty, liberation, deliverance, emancipation, acquittal, absolution, exoneration, exemption, discharge, issue, publication, announcement, proclamation.
F3 imprisonment, detention.

relent *verb* give in, give way, yield, capitulate, unbend, relax, slacken, soften, weaken.

relentless *adjective* unrelenting, unremitting, incessant, persistent, unflagging, ruthless, remorseless, implacable, merciless, pitiless, unforgiving, cruel, harsh, fierce, grim, hard, punishing, uncompromising, inflexible, unyielding, inexorable.
F3 merciful, yielding.

relevant *adjective* pertinent, material, significant, germane, related, applicable, apposite, apt, appropriate, suitable, fitting, proper, admissible.
F3 irrelevant, inapplicable, inappropriate, unsuitable.

reliable *adjective* unfailing, certain, sure, dependable, responsible, trusty, trustworthy, honest, true, faithful, constant, staunch, solid, safe, sound, stable, predictable, regular.
F3 unreliable, doubtful, untrustworthy.

relic *noun* memento, souvenir, keepsake, token, survival, remains, remnant, scrap, fragment, vestige, trace.

relief *noun* **1** *relief from pain*: alleviation, cure, remedy. **2** *smile with relief*: reassurance, consolation, comfort, ease, release. **3** *famine relief*: deliverance, help, aid, assistance, support, sustenance, refreshment. **4** *relief from the merciless sun*: diversion, relaxation, rest, respite, break, breather (*infml*), remission, let-up (*infml*), abatement.

relieve *verb* **1** *relieve suffering*: alleviate, mitigate, cure, soothe, calm, reassure, console, comfort, ease. **2** *relieve overcrowding*: release, deliver, free, unburden, lighten, soften, slacken, relax.
F3 aggravate, intensify.

religion

Religions include:
Christianity, Mormonism; Baha'ism, Buddhism, Confucianism, Hinduism, Islam, Jainism, Judaism, Sikhism, Taoism, Shintoism, Zoroastrianism; druidism, paganism, Scientology, voodoo.

religious *adjective* **1** *religious texts*: sacred, holy, divine, spiritual, devotional, scriptural, theological, doctrinal. **2** *a very religious person*: devout, godly, pious, God-fearing, church-going, reverent, righteous.
F3 **1** secular. **2** irreligious, ungodly.

relish *verb* like, enjoy, savour, appreciate, revel in.
▪ *noun* **1** *hamburger with relish*: seasoning, condiment, sauce, pickle, spice, piquancy, tang. **2** *did it with a great deal of relish*: enjoyment, pleasure, delight, gusto, zest.

reluctant *adjective* unwilling, disinclined, indisposed, hesitant, slow, backward, lo(a)th, averse, unenthusiastic, grudging.
F3 willing, ready, eager.

rely *verb* depend, lean, count, bank, reckon, trust, swear by.

remain *verb* stay, rest, stand, dwell, abide (*fml*), last, endure, survive, prevail, persist, continue, linger, wait.
F3 go, leave, depart.

remainder *noun* rest, balance, surplus, excess, remnant, remains.

remaining *adjective* left, unused, unspent, unfinished, residual, outstanding, surviving, persisting, lingering, lasting, abiding.

remains *noun* **1** *she cleared the remains of the breakfast*: rest, remainder, residue, debris, dregs, leavings, leftovers, scraps, crumbs, fragments, remnants, oddments, traces, vestiges. **2** *remains of the dead*: body, corpse, relics, carcass, ashes.

remark *noun* comment, observation, opinion, reflection, mention, utterance, statement, assertion, declaration.
▪ *verb* comment, observe, note, mention, say, state, declare.

remarkable *adjective* striking, impressive, noteworthy, surprising, amazing, strange, odd, unusual, uncommon, extraordinary, phenomenal, exceptional, outstanding, notable,

conspicuous, prominent, distinguished.
F3 average, ordinary, commonplace, usual.

remedy *noun* cure, antidote, countermeasure, corrective, restorative, medicine, treatment, therapy, relief, solution, answer, panacea.
▪ *verb* correct, rectify, put right, redress, counteract, cure, heal, restore, treat, help, relieve, soothe, ease, mitigate, mend, repair, fix, solve.

remember *verb* **1** *I can't remember his name*: recall, recollect, summon up, think back, reminisce, recognize, place. **2** *remembering her lines*: memorize, learn, retain.
F3 **1** forget.

remind *verb* prompt, nudge, hint, jog one's memory, refresh one's memory, bring to mind, call to mind, call up.

reminder *noun* prompt, nudge, hint, suggestion, memorandum, memo, souvenir, memento, keepsake.

reminiscence *noun* memory, remembrance, memoir, anecdote, recollection, recall, retrospection, review, reflection.

reminiscent *adjective* suggestive, evocative, nostalgic.

remnant *noun* scrap, piece, bit, fragment, end, offcut, leftover, remainder, balance, residue, shred, trace, vestige.

remorse *noun* regret, compunction, ruefulness, repentance, penitence, contrition, self-reproach, shame, guilt, bad conscience, sorrow, grief.

remote *adjective* **1** *a remote island*: distant, far, faraway, far-off, outlying, out-of-the-way, inaccessible, god-forsaken, isolated, secluded, lonely. **2** *a remote possibility*: slight, small, slim, slender, faint, negligible, unlikely, improbable.
F3 **1** close, nearby, accessible.

remove *verb* **1** *remove a tooth/one's hat*: detach, pull off, amputate, cut off, extract, pull out, withdraw, take away, take off, strip, shed, doff. **2** *remove all trace of it*: expunge (*fml*), efface (*fml*), erase, delete, strike out, get rid of, abolish, purge, eliminate. **3** *remove the dictator*: dismiss, discharge, eject, throw out, oust, depose.

render *verb* **1** *rendered it harmless*: make, cause to be, leave. **2** *rendering thanks*: give, provide, supply, tender, present, submit, hand over, deliver.

renew *verb* **1** *renew a house*: renovate, modernize, refurbish, refit, recondition, mend, repair, overhaul, remodel, reform, transform, recreate, reconstitute, re-establish, regenerate, revive, resuscitate, refresh, rejuvenate, reinvigorate, revitalize, restore, replace, replenish, restock. **2** *renewing calls for his resignation*: repeat, restate, reaffirm, extend, prolong, continue, recommence, restart, resume.

renounce *verb* abandon, forsake, give up, resign, relinquish, surrender, discard, reject, spurn, disown, repudiate, disclaim, deny, recant, abjure.

renovate *verb* restore, renew, recondition, repair, overhaul, modernize, refurbish, refit, redecorate, do up, remodel, reform, revamp, improve.

rent *noun* rental, lease, hire, payment, fee.
▪ *verb* let, sublet, lease, hire, charter.

repair *verb* mend, fix, patch up, overhaul, service, rectify, redress, restore, renovate, renew.
▪ *noun* mend, patch, darn, overhaul, service, maintenance, restoration, adjustment, improvement.

repay *verb* refund, reimburse, compensate, recompense, reward, remunerate, pay, settle, square, get even with, retaliate, reciprocate, revenge, avenge.

repeal *verb* revoke, rescind, abrogate (*fml*), quash, annul, nullify, void, invalidate, cancel, countermand, reverse, abolish.
E enact.

repeat *verb* restate, reiterate, recapitulate, echo, quote, recite, relate, retell, reproduce, duplicate, renew, rebroadcast, reshow, replay, rerun, redo.
▪ *noun* repetition, echo, reproduction, duplicate, rebroadcast, reshowing, replay, rerun.

repeatedly *adverb* time after time, time and (time) again, again and again, over and over, frequently, often.

repel *verb* **1** *repelled their attackers*: drive back, repulse, check, hold off, ward off, parry, resist, oppose, fight, refuse, decline, reject, rebuff. **2** *the sight of it repels me*: disgust, revolt, nauseate, sicken, offend.
E **1** attract. **2** delight.

repent *verb* regret, rue, sorrow, lament, deplore, atone.

repentant *adjective* penitent, contrite, sorry, apologetic, remorseful, regretful, rueful, chastened, ashamed.
E unrepentant.

repercussion *noun* result, consequence, backlash, reverberation, echo, rebound, recoil.

repetition *noun* restatement, reiteration, recapitulation, echo, return, reappearance, recurrence, duplication, tautology.

repetitive *adjective* recurrent, monotonous, tedious, boring, dull, mechanical, unchanging, unvaried.

replace *verb* **1** *replace the lid*: put back, return, restore, make good, reinstate, re-establish. **2** *replacing the outgoing chairman*: supersede, succeed, follow, supplant, oust, deputize, substitute.

replacement *noun* substitute,

stand-in, understudy, fill-in, supply, proxy, surrogate, successor.

replenish *verb* refill, restock, reload, recharge, replace, restore, renew, supply, provide, furnish, stock, fill, top up.

replica *noun* model, imitation, reproduction, facsimile, copy, duplicate, clone.

reply *verb* answer, respond, retort, rejoin, react, acknowledge, return, echo, reciprocate, counter, retaliate.

▪ *noun* answer, response, retort, rejoinder, riposte, repartee, reaction, comeback, acknowledgement, return, echo, retaliation.

report *noun* article, piece, write-up, record, account, relation, narrative, description, story, tale, gossip, hearsay, rumour, talk, statement, communiqué, declaration, announcement, communication, information, news, word, message, note.

▪ *verb* state, announce, declare, proclaim, air, broadcast, relay, publish, circulate, communicate, notify, tell, recount, relate, narrate, describe, detail, cover, document, record, note.

reporter *noun* journalist, correspondent, columnist, newspaperman, newspaperwoman, hack, newscaster, commentator, announcer.

represent *verb* stand for, symbolize, designate, denote, mean, express, evoke, depict, portray, describe, picture, draw, sketch, illustrate, exemplify, typify, epitomize, embody, personify, appear as, act as, enact, perform, show, exhibit, be, amount to, constitute.

representation *noun* likeness, image, icon, picture, portrait, illustration, sketch, model, statue, bust, depiction, portrayal, description, account, explanation.

representative *noun* delegate, deputy, proxy, stand-in, spokesperson, spokesman, spokeswoman, ambassador, commissioner, agent, salesman, saleswoman, rep (*infml*), traveller.

▪ *adjective* typical, illustrative, exemplary, archetypal, characteristic, usual, normal, symbolic.

F3 unrepresentative, atypical.

repress *verb* inhibit, check, control, curb, restrain, suppress, bottle up, hold back, stifle, smother, muffle, silence, quell, crush, quash, subdue, overpower, overcome, master, subjugate, oppress.

repressive *adjective* oppressive, authoritarian, despotic, tyrannical, dictatorial, autocratic, totalitarian, absolute, harsh, severe, tough, coercive.

reprieve *verb* pardon, let off, spare, rescue, redeem, relieve, respite.

▪ *noun* pardon, amnesty, suspension, abeyance,

postponement, deferment, remission, respite, relief, let-up (*infml*), abatement.

reprimand *noun* rebuke, reproof, reproach, admonition, telling-off (*infml*), ticking-off (*infml*), lecture, talking-to (*infml*), dressing-down (*infml*), censure, blame.

reprisal *noun* retaliation, counter-attack, retribution, requital, revenge, vengeance.

reproach *verb* rebuke, reprove, reprimand, upbraid (*fml*), scold, chide, reprehend (*fml*), blame, censure, condemn, criticize, disparage (*fml*), defame (*fml*).

reproduce *verb* **1** *reproducing his achievements*: copy, transcribe, print, duplicate, clone, mirror, echo, repeat, imitate, emulate, match, simulate, recreate, reconstruct. **2** *animals reproduce*: breed, spawn, procreate, generate, propagate, multiply.

reproduction *noun* **1** *a reproduction of the painting*: copy, print, picture, duplicate, facsimile, replica, clone, imitation. **2** *sexual reproduction*: breeding, procreation, generation, propagation, multiplication.
F3 **1** original.

reproductive *adjective* procreative, generative, sexual, sex, genital.

reptile

Reptiles include:

adder, puff adder, grass snake, tree snake, asp, viper, rattlesnake, sidewinder, anaconda, boa constrictor, cobra, king cobra, mamba, python; lizard, chameleon, frilled lizard, gecko, iguana, monitor lizard, skink, slow-worm, worm lizard; turtle, green turtle, hawksbill turtle, snapping turtle, terrapin, tortoise, giant tortoise; alligator, crocodile. *See also* **amphibian**.

repulsive *adjective* repellent, repugnant, revolting, disgusting, nauseating, sickening, offensive, distasteful, objectionable, obnoxious, foul, vile, loathsome, abominable, abhorrent (*fml*), hateful, horrid, unpleasant, disagreeable, ugly, hideous, forbidding.
F3 attractive, pleasant, delightful.

reputable *adjective* respectable, reliable, dependable, trustworthy, upright, honourable, creditable, worthy, good, excellent, irreproachable.
F3 disreputable, infamous.

reputation *noun* honour, character, standing, stature, esteem, opinion, credit, repute, fame, renown, celebrity, distinction, name, good name, bad name, infamy, notoriety.

reputed *adjective* alleged, supposed, said, rumoured, believed, thought, considered, regarded, estimated, reckoned, held, seeming, apparent, ostensible.
F3 actual, true.

request *verb* ask for, solicit, demand, require, seek, desire, beg, entreat, supplicate, petition, appeal.

▪ *noun* appeal, call, demand, requisition, desire, application, solicitation, suit, petition, entreaty, supplication, prayer.

require *verb* **1** *is there anything you require?*: need, want, wish, desire, lack, miss. **2** *you are required to attend*: oblige, force, compel, constrain, make, ask, request, instruct, direct, order, demand, necessitate, take, involve.

requirement *noun* need, necessity, essential, must, requisite, prerequisite, demand, stipulation, condition, term, specification, proviso, qualification, provision.

rescue *verb* save, recover, salvage, deliver, free, liberate, release, redeem, ransom.

F3 capture, imprison.

▪ *noun* saving, recovery, salvage, deliverance, liberation, release, redemption, salvation.

F3 capture.

research *noun* investigation, inquiry, fact-finding, groundwork, examination, analysis, scrutiny, study, search, probe, exploration, experimentation.

▪ *verb* investigate, examine, analyse, scrutinize, study, search, probe, explore, experiment.

resemblance *noun* likeness, similarity, sameness, parity, conformity, closeness, affinity, parallel, comparison, analogy, correspondence, image, facsimile.

F3 dissimilarity.

resemble *verb* be like, look like, take after, favour, mirror, echo, duplicate, parallel.

F3 differ from.

resent *verb* grudge, begrudge, envy, take offence at, take umbrage at, take amiss, object to, grumble at, take exception to, dislike.

F3 accept, like.

resentful *adjective* grudging, envious, jealous, bitter, embittered, hurt, wounded, offended, aggrieved, put out, miffed (*infml*), peeved (*infml*), indignant, angry, vindictive.

F3 satisfied, contented.

resentment *noun* grudge, envy, jealousy, bitterness, spite, malice, ill-will, ill-feeling, animosity, hurt, umbrage, pique, displeasure, irritation, indignation, vexation, anger, vindictiveness.

F3 contentment, happiness.

reservation *noun* **1** *have some reservations about the scheme*: doubt, scepticism, misgiving, qualm, scruple, hesitation, second thought. **2** *agree without reservation*: proviso, stipulation, qualification. **3** *live on the reservation*: reserve, preserve, park, sanctuary, homeland, enclave. **4** *make a reservation*: booking, engagement, appointment.

reserve *verb* **1** *reserved for VIPs*: set apart, earmark, keep, retain, hold back, save, store, stockpile. **2** *reserve a seat*: book, engage, order, secure.

F3 1 use up.

▪ *noun* **1** *a reserve of money*: store, stock, supply, fund, stockpile, cache, hoard, savings. **2** *her reserve made her difficult to talk to*: shyness, reticence, secretiveness, coolness, aloofness, modesty, restraint. **3** *a game reserve*: reservation, preserve, park, sanctuary. **4** *he's the second reserve*: replacement, substitute, stand-in.

F3 2 friendliness, openness.

reserved *adjective* **1** *a reserved table*: booked, engaged, taken, spoken for, set aside, earmarked, meant, intended, designated, destined, saved, held, kept, retained. **2** *he's very reserved*: shy, retiring, reticent, unforthcoming, uncommunicative, secretive, silent, taciturn, unsociable, cool, aloof, standoffish, unapproachable, modest, restrained, cautious.

F3 1 unreserved, free, available. **2** friendly, open.

residence *noun* dwelling, habitation, domicile, abode (*fml*), seat, place, home, house, lodgings, quarters, hall, manor, mansion, palace, villa, country house, country seat.

resident *noun* inhabitant, citizen, local, householder, occupier, tenant, lodger, guest.

F3 non-resident.

residual *adjective* remaining, leftover, unused, unconsumed, net.

resign *verb* stand down, leave, quit, abdicate, vacate, renounce, relinquish, forgo, waive, surrender, yield, abandon, forsake.

F3 join.

resignation *noun* **1** *offered his resignation*: standing-down, abdication, retirement, departure, notice, renunciation, relinquishment. **2** *resignation to their fate*: acceptance, acquiescence, surrender, submission, non-resistance, passivity, patience, stoicism, defeatism.

F3 2 resistance.

resigned *adjective* reconciled, philosophical, stoical, patient, unprotesting, unresisting, submissive, defeatist.

F3 resistant.

resilient *adjective* **1** *resilient material*: flexible, pliable, supple, plastic, elastic, springy, bouncy. **2** *a resilient person*: strong, tough, hardy, adaptable, buoyant.

F3 1 rigid, brittle.

resist *verb* oppose, defy, confront, fight, combat, weather, withstand, repel, counteract, check, avoid, refuse.

F3 submit, accept.

resistant *adjective* **1** *resistant to change*: opposed, antagonistic, defiant, unyielding, intransigent, unwilling. **2** *water-resistant*: proof, impervious, immune,

invulnerable, tough, strong.
1 compliant, yielding.

resolute *adjective* determined, resolved, set, fixed, unwavering, staunch, firm, steadfast, relentless, single-minded, persevering, dogged, tenacious, stubborn, obstinate, strong-willed, undaunted, unflinching, bold.
irresolute, weak-willed, half-hearted.

resolution *noun* **1** *his resolution never wavered*: determination, resolve, willpower, commitment, dedication, devotion, firmness, steadfastness, persistence, perseverance, doggedness, tenacity, zeal, courage, boldness. **2** *vote on the resolution*: decision, judgement, finding, declaration, proposition, motion.
1 half-heartedness, uncertainty, indecision.

resolve *verb* decide, make up one's mind, determine, fix, settle, conclude, sort out, work out, solve.

resort *verb* go, visit, frequent, patronize, haunt.
▪ *noun* recourse, refuge, course (of action), alternative, option, chance, possibility.

resounding *adjective* **1** *a resounding bang*: resonant, reverberating, echoing, ringing, sonorous, booming, thunderous, full, rich, vibrant. **2** *a resounding victory*: decisive, conclusive, crushing, thorough.
1 faint.

resourceful *adjective* ingenious, imaginative, creative, inventive, innovative, original, clever, bright, sharp, quick-witted, able, capable, talented.

resources *noun* materials, supplies, reserves, holdings, funds, money, wealth, riches, capital, assets, property, means.

respect *noun* **1** *respect for their elders*: admiration, esteem, appreciation, recognition, honour, deference, reverence, veneration, politeness, courtesy. **2** *in every respect*: point, aspect, facet, feature, characteristic, particular, detail, sense, way, regard, reference, relation, connection.
1 disrespect.
▪ *verb* **1** *respect his judgement*: admire, esteem, regard, appreciate, value. **2** *respect the law*: obey, observe, heed, follow, honour, fulfil.
1 despise, scorn. **2** ignore, disobey.

respectable *adjective* **1** *a respectable family*: honourable, worthy, respected, dignified, upright, honest, decent, clean-living. **2** *a respectable score*: acceptable, tolerable, passable, adequate, fair, reasonable, appreciable, considerable.
1 dishonourable, disreputable. **2** inadequate, paltry.

respectful *adjective* deferential, reverential, humble, polite, well-mannered, courteous, civil.
disrespectful.

respective *adjective* corresponding, relevant, various, several, separate, individual, personal, own, particular, special.

respond *verb* answer, reply, retort, acknowledge, react, return, reciprocate.

response *noun* answer, reply, retort, comeback, acknowledgement, reaction, feedback.

F query.

responsibility *noun* fault, blame, guilt, culpability, answerability, accountability, duty, obligation, burden, onus, charge, care, trust, authority, power.

responsible *adjective* **1** *are you responsible for this mess?*: guilty, culpable, at fault, to blame, liable, answerable, accountable. **2** *a responsible adult*: dependable, reliable, conscientious, trustworthy, honest, sound, steady, sober, mature, sensible, rational. **3** *the body responsible for this*: authoritative, executive, decision-making.

F 2 irresponsible, unreliable, untrustworthy.

rest[1] *noun* **1** *get some rest*: leisure, relaxation, repose, lie-down, sleep, snooze, nap, siesta, idleness, inactivity, motionlessness, standstill, stillness, tranquillity, calm. **2** *need a rest*: break, pause, breathing-space, breather (*infml*), intermission, interlude, interval, recess, holiday, vacation, halt, cessation, lull, respite. **3** *an arm rest*: support, prop, stand, base.

F 1 action, activity. **2** work.

▪ *verb* **1** *rest for a moment*: pause, halt, stop, cease. **2** *rest in bed*: relax, repose, sit, recline, lounge, laze, lie down, sleep, snooze, doze. **3** *rested his hand on her shoulder*: lean, prop, support, stand.

F 1 continue. **2** work.

rest[2] *noun* remainder, others, balance, surplus, excess, residue, remains, leftovers, remnants.

restaurant *noun* eating-house, bistro, steakhouse, grill room, dining room, snack bar, buffet, cafeteria, café.

restful *adjective* relaxing, soothing, calm, tranquil, serene, peaceful, quiet, undisturbed, relaxed, comfortable, leisurely, unhurried.

F tiring, restless.

restless *adjective* fidgety, unsettled, disturbed, troubled, agitated, nervous, anxious, worried, uneasy, fretful, edgy, jumpy, restive, unruly, turbulent, sleepless.

F calm, relaxed, comfortable.

restore *verb* **1** *restoring law and order*: return, reinstate, rehabilitate, re-establish, reintroduce, re-enforce. **2** *restore a building*: renovate, renew, rebuild, reconstruct, refurbish, retouch, recondition, repair, mend, fix. **3** *restoring his strength*: revive, refresh, rejuvenate, revitalize, strengthen.

F 1 remove. **2** damage. **3** weaken.

restrain *verb* hold back, keep

back, suppress, subdue, repress, inhibit, check, curb, bridle, stop, arrest, prevent, bind, tie, chain, fetter, manacle, imprison, jail, confine, restrict, regulate, control, govern.
F3 encourage, liberate.

restrained *adjective* moderate, temperate, mild, subdued, muted, quiet, soft, low-key, unobtrusive, discreet, tasteful, calm, controlled, steady, self-controlled.
F3 unrestrained.

restraint *noun* moderation, inhibition, self-control, self-discipline, hold, grip, check, curb, rein, bridle, suppression, bondage, captivity, confinement, imprisonment, bonds, chains, fetters, straitjacket, restriction, control, constraint, limitation, tie, hindrance, prevention.
F3 liberty.

restrict *verb* limit, bound, demarcate, control, regulate, confine, contain, cramp, constrain, impede, hinder, hamper, handicap, tie, restrain, curtail.
F3 broaden, free.

restriction *noun* limit, bound, confine, limitation, constraint, handicap, check, curb, restraint, ban, embargo, control, regulation, rule, stipulation, condition, proviso.
F3 freedom.

result *noun* effect, consequence, sequel, repercussion, reaction, outcome, upshot, issue, end-product, fruit, score, answer, verdict, judgement, decision, conclusion.
F3 cause.
▪ *verb* follow, ensue, happen, occur, issue, emerge, arise, spring, derive, stem, flow, proceed, develop, end, finish, terminate, culminate.
F3 cause.

resume *verb* restart, recommence, reopen, reconvene, continue, carry on, go on, proceed.
F3 cease.

resurrection *noun* restoration, revival, resuscitation, renaissance, rebirth, renewal, resurgence, reappearance, return, comeback.

retain *verb* **1** *retain a copy for your files*: keep, hold, reserve, hold back, save, preserve. **2** *able to retain information*: remember, memorize, recall. **3** *retaining his services*: employ, engage, hire, commission.
F3 **1** release. **2** forget. **3** dismiss.

retaliate *verb* reciprocate, counter-attack, hit back, strike back, fight back, get one's own back, get even with, take revenge.

retire *verb* leave, depart, withdraw, retreat, recede.
F3 join, enter, advance.

retirement *noun* withdrawal, retreat, solitude, loneliness, seclusion, privacy, obscurity.

retract *verb* take back, withdraw, recant, reverse, revoke, rescind, cancel, repeal, repudiate,

disown, disclaim, deny.
assert, maintain.

retreat *verb* draw back, recoil, shrink, turn tail (*infml*), withdraw, retire, leave, depart, quit.
advance.
▪ *noun* **1** *army is in retreat*: withdrawal, departure, evacuation, flight. **2** *provide a retreat from the world*: seclusion, privacy, hideaway, den, refuge, asylum, sanctuary, shelter, haven.
1 advance, charge.

retrieve *verb* fetch, bring back, regain, get back, recapture, repossess, recoup, recover, salvage, save, rescue, redeem, restore, return.
lose.

retrograde *adjective* retrogressive, backward, reverse, negative, downward, declining, deteriorating.
progressive.

retrospect *noun* hindsight, afterthought, re-examination, review, recollection, remembrance.
prospect.

return *verb* **1** *return home*: come back, reappear, recur, go back, backtrack, regress, revert. **2** *return his letters*: give back, hand back, send back, deliver, put back, replace, restore. **3** *return a favour*: reciprocate, requite, repay, refund, reimburse, recompense.
1 leave, depart. **2** take.
▪ *noun* **1** *on his return*: reappearance, recurrence, comeback, home-coming. **2** *the return of a favour*: repayment, recompense, replacement, restoration, reinstatement, reciprocation. **3** *make a good return on their investment*: revenue, income, proceeds, takings, yield, gain, profit, reward, advantage, benefit.
1 departure, disappearance. **2** removal. **3** payment, expense, loss.

reveal *verb* expose, uncover, unveil, unmask, show, display, exhibit, manifest, disclose, divulge, betray, leak, tell, impart, communicate, broadcast, publish, announce, proclaim.
hide, conceal, mask.

revelation *noun* uncovering, unveiling, exposure, unmasking, show, display, exhibition, manifestation, disclosure, confession, admission, betrayal, giveaway, leak, news, information, communication, broadcasting, publication, announcement, proclamation.

revel in *verb* enjoy, relish, savour, delight in, thrive on, bask in, glory in, lap up, indulge in, wallow in, luxuriate in.

revenge *noun* vengeance, satisfaction, reprisal, retaliation, requital, retribution.

revenue *noun* income, return, yield, interest, profit, gain, proceeds, receipts, takings.
expenditure.

reverberate *verb* echo, re-echo,

resound, resonate, ring, boom, vibrate.

revere *verb* respect, esteem, honour, pay homage to, venerate, worship, adore, exalt.
F3 despise, scorn.

reverence *noun* respect, deference, honour, homage, admiration, awe, veneration, worship, adoration, devotion.
F3 contempt, scorn.

reverent *adjective* reverential, respectful, deferential, humble, dutiful, awed, solemn, pious, devout, adoring, loving.
F3 irreverent, disrespectful.

reversal *noun* negation, cancellation, annulment, nullification, countermanding, revocation, rescinding, repeal, reverse, turnabout, turnaround, U-turn, volte-face, upset.
F3 advancement, progress.

reverse *verb* **1** *reverse into the garage/reverse an order*: back, retreat, backtrack, undo, negate, cancel, annul, invalidate, countermand, overrule, revoke, rescind, repeal, retract, quash, overthrow. **2** *mirror reverses the image*: transpose, turn round, invert, up-end, overturn, upset, change, alter.
F3 1 advance, enforce.
▪ *noun* **1** *the reverse of the coin*: underside, back, rear, inverse, converse, contrary, opposite, antithesis. **2** *suffer a major reverse of fortunes*: misfortune, mishap, misadventure, adversity, affliction, hardship, trial, blow, disappointment, setback, check, delay, problem, difficulty, failure, defeat.

revert *verb* return, go back, resume, lapse, relapse, regress.

review *verb* **1** *review the play*: criticize, assess, evaluate, judge, weigh, discuss, examine, inspect, scrutinize, study, survey, recapitulate. **2** *review the situation*: reassess, re-evaluate, re-examine, reconsider, rethink, revise.
▪ *noun* criticism, critique, assessment, evaluation, judgement, report, commentary, examination, scrutiny, analysis, study, survey, recapitulation, reassessment, re-evaluation, re-examination, revision.

revise *verb* **1** *revise one's opinion*: change, alter, modify, amend, correct, update, adjust, edit, rewrite, reword, recast, revamp, reconsider, re-examine, review. **2** *revising for the exams*: study, learn, swot up (*infml*), cram (*infml*).

revival *noun* resuscitation, revitalization, restoration, renewal, renaissance, rebirth, reawakening, resurgence, upsurge.

revive *verb* resuscitate, reanimate, revitalize, restore, renew, refresh, animate, invigorate, quicken (*fml*), rouse, awaken, recover, rally, reawaken, rekindle, reactivate.
F3 weary.

revoke *verb* repeal, rescind,

quash, abrogate (*fml*), annul, nullify, invalidate, negate, cancel, countermand, reverse, retract, withdraw.
F3 enforce.

revolt *noun* revolution, rebellion, mutiny, rising, uprising, insurrection, putsch, coup (d'état), secession, defection.
▪ *verb* **1** *revolt against authority*: rebel, mutiny, rise, riot, resist, dissent, defect. **2** *it revolted him*: disgust, sicken, nauseate, repel, offend, shock, outrage, scandalize.
F3 **1** submit. **2** please, delight.

revolting *adjective* disgusting, sickening, nauseating, repulsive, repellent, obnoxious, nasty, horrible, foul, loathsome, abhorrent (*fml*), distasteful, offensive, shocking, appalling.
F3 pleasant, delightful, attractive, palatable.

revolution *noun* **1** *the French Revolution*: revolt, rebellion, mutiny, rising, uprising, insurrection, putsch, coup (d'état), reformation, change, transformation, innovation, upheaval, cataclysm. **2** *allow the engine to go through several revolutions*: rotation, turn, spin, cycle, circuit, round, circle, orbit, gyration.

revolutionary *noun* rebel, mutineer, insurgent, anarchist, revolutionist.
▪ *adjective* **1** *a revolutionary leader*: rebel, rebellious, mutinous, insurgent, subversive, seditious, anarchistic. **2** *revolutionary ideas*: new, innovative, avant-garde, different, drastic, radical, thoroughgoing.
F3 **1** conservative.

revolve *verb* rotate, turn, pivot, swivel, spin, wheel, whirl, gyrate, circle, orbit.

revulsion *noun* repugnance, disgust, distaste, dislike, aversion, hatred, loathing, abhorrence (*fml*), abomination.
F3 delight, pleasure, approval.

reward *noun* prize, honour, medal, decoration, bounty, pay-off, bonus, premium, payment, remuneration, recompense, repayment, requital, compensation, gain, profit, return, benefit, merit, desert, retribution.
F3 punishment.
▪ *verb* pay, remunerate, recompense, repay, requite, compensate, honour, decorate.
F3 punish.

rewarding *adjective* profitable, remunerative, lucrative, productive, fruitful, worthwhile, valuable, advantageous, beneficial, satisfying, gratifying, pleasing, fulfilling, enriching.
F3 unrewarding.

rhetoric *noun* eloquence, oratory, grandiloquence, magniloquence, bombast, pomposity, hyperbole, verbosity, wordiness.

rhetorical *adjective* oratorical, grandiloquent, magniloquent, bombastic, declamatory,

pompous, high-sounding, grand, high-flown, flowery, florid, flamboyant, showy, pretentious, artificial, insincere.
☒ simple.

rhyme *noun* poetry, verse, poem, ode, limerick, jingle, song, ditty.

rhythm *noun* beat, pulse, time, tempo, metre, measure, movement, flow, lilt, swing, accent, cadence, pattern.

rhythmic *adjective* rhythmical, metric, metrical, pulsating, throbbing, flowing, lilting, periodic, regular, steady.

rich *adjective* **1** *a rich family*: wealthy, affluent, moneyed, prosperous, well-to-do, well-off, loaded (*infml*). **2** *orchards rich in apples*: plentiful, abundant, copious, profuse, prolific, ample, full. **3** *rich food*: creamy, fatty, full-bodied, heavy, full-flavoured, strong, spicy, savoury, tasty, delicious, luscious, juicy, sweet.
☒ 1 poor, impoverished. **2** barren. **3** plain, bland.

riches *noun* wealth, affluence, money, gold, treasure, fortune, assets, property, substance, resources, means.
☒ poverty.

rickety *adjective* unsteady, wobbly, shaky, unstable, insecure, flimsy, jerry-built, decrepit, ramshackle, broken-down, dilapidated, derelict.
☒ stable, strong.

rid *verb* clear, purge, free, deliver, relieve, unburden.

riddle *noun* enigma, mystery, conundrum, brain-teaser, puzzle, poser (*infml*), problem.

riddled *adjective* perforated, pierced, punctured, full, permeated, pervaded, infested.

ride *verb* sit, move, progress, travel, journey, gallop, trot, pedal, drive, steer, control, handle, manage.
▪ *noun* journey, trip, outing, jaunt, spin, drive, lift.

ridicule *noun* satire, irony, sarcasm, mockery, jeering, scorn, derision, taunting, teasing, chaff, banter, badinage, laughter.
☒ praise.
▪ *verb* satirize, send up, caricature, lampoon, burlesque, parody, mock, make fun of, jeer, scoff, deride, sneer, tease, rib (*infml*), humiliate, taunt.
☒ praise.

ridiculous *adjective* ludicrous, absurd, nonsensical, silly, foolish, stupid, contemptible, derisory, laughable, farcical, comical, funny, hilarious, outrageous, preposterous, incredible, unbelievable.
☒ sensible.

rife *adjective* abundant, rampant, teeming, raging, epidemic, prevalent, widespread, general, common, frequent.
☒ scarce.

rift *noun* **1** *a rift in the rock*: split, breach, break, fracture, crack, fault, chink, cleft, cranny, crevice, gap, space, opening. **2** *cause a rift*

between them: disagreement, difference, separation, division, schism, alienation.
F2 unity.

right *adjective* **1** *the right answer*: correct, accurate, exact, precise, true, factual, actual, real. **2** *the right thing to do*: proper, fitting, seemly, becoming, appropriate, suitable, fit, admissible, satisfactory, reasonable, desirable, favourable, advantageous. **3** *a right decision*: fair, just, equitable, lawful, honest, upright, good, virtuous, righteous, moral, ethical, honourable.
F **1** wrong, incorrect. **2** improper, unsuitable. **3** unfair, wrong.
▪ *adverb* **1** *do it right*: correctly, accurately, exactly, precisely, factually, properly, satisfactorily, well, fairly. **2** *right to the bottom*: straight, directly, completely, utterly.
F **1** wrongly, incorrectly, unfairly.
▪ *noun* **1** *human rights*: privilege, prerogative, due, claim, business, authority, power. **2** *legal/moral rights*: justice, legality, good, virtue, righteousness, morality, honour, integrity, uprightness.
F **2** wrong.
▪ *verb* rectify, correct, put right, fix, repair, redress, vindicate, avenge, settle, straighten, stand up.

rightful *adjective* legitimate, lawful, legal, just, bona fide, true, real, genuine, valid, authorized, correct, proper, suitable, due.
F wrongful, unlawful.

rigid *adjective* stiff, inflexible, unbending, cast-iron, hard, firm, set, fixed, unalterable, invariable, austere, harsh, severe, unrelenting, strict, rigorous, stringent, stern, uncompromising, unyielding.
F flexible, elastic.

rigorous *adjective* strict, stringent, rigid, firm, exact, precise, accurate, meticulous, painstaking, scrupulous, conscientious, thorough.
F lax, superficial.

rile *verb* annoy, irritate, nettle, pique, peeve (*infml*), put out, upset, irk, vex, anger, exasperate.
F calm, soothe.

rim *noun* lip, edge, brim, brink, verge, margin, border, circumference.
F centre, middle.

ring[1] *noun* **1** *a ring of gold*: circle, round, loop, hoop, halo, band, girdle, collar, circuit, arena, enclosure. **2** *a drugs ring*: group, cartel, syndicate, association, organization, gang, crew, mob, band, cell, clique, coterie.
▪ *verb* surround, encircle, gird, circumscribe, encompass, enclose.

ring[2] *verb* **1** *the doorbell rang*: chime, peal, toll, tinkle, clink, jingle, clang, sound, resound, resonate, reverberate, buzz. **2** *asked me to ring him back*: telephone, phone, call, ring up.
▪ *noun* **1** *the ring of a bell*: chime, peal, toll, tinkle, clink, jingle,

clang. **2** *promised to give me a ring*: phone call, call, buzz (*infml*), tinkle (*infml*).

rinse *verb* swill, bathe, wash, clean, cleanse, flush, wet, dip.

riot *noun* insurrection, rising, uprising, revolt, rebellion, anarchy, lawlessness, affray, disturbance, turbulence, disorder, confusion, commotion, tumult, turmoil, uproar, row, quarrel, strife.

F3 order, calm.

▪ *verb* revolt, rebel, rise up, run riot, run wild, rampage.

rip *verb* tear, rend, split, separate, rupture, burst, cut, slit, slash, gash, lacerate, hack.

▪ *noun* tear, rent, split, cleavage, rupture, cut, slit, slash, gash, hole.

ripe *adjective* **1** *ripe fruit*: ripened, mature, mellow, seasoned, grown, developed, complete, finished, perfect. **2** *ripe for change*: ready, suitable, right, favourable, auspicious, propitious, timely, opportune.

F3 2 untimely, inopportune.

ripen *verb* develop, mature, mellow, season, age.

rise *verb* **1** *rising above the horizon*: go up, ascend, climb, mount, slope (up), soar, tower, grow, increase, escalate, intensify. **2** *all rise*: stand up, get up, arise, jump up, spring up. **3** *living standards are rising*: advance, progress, improve, prosper. **4** *a stream rising in the mountains*: originate, spring, flow, issue, emerge, appear.

F3 1 fall, descend. **2** sit down.

▪ *noun* **1** *over the next rise*: ascent, climb, slope, incline, hill, elevation. **2** *a rise in prices*: increase, increment, upsurge, upturn, advance, progress, improvement, advancement, promotion.

F3 1 descent, valley. **2** fall.

risk *noun* danger, peril, jeopardy, hazard, chance, possibility, uncertainty, gamble, speculation, venture, adventure.

F3 safety, certainty.

▪ *verb* endanger, imperil, jeopardize, hazard, chance, gamble, venture, dare.

risky *adjective* dangerous, unsafe, perilous, hazardous, chancy, uncertain, touch-and-go, dicey (*infml*), tricky, precarious.

F3 safe.

ritual *noun* custom, tradition, convention, usage, practice, habit, wont, routine, procedure, ordinance, prescription, form, formality, ceremony, ceremonial, solemnity, rite, sacrament, service, liturgy, observance, act.

▪ *adjective* customary, traditional, conventional, habitual, routine, procedural, prescribed, set, formal, ceremonial.

F3 informal.

rival *noun* competitor, contestant, contender, challenger, opponent, adversary, antagonist, match, equal, peer.

F3 colleague, associate.

▪ *verb* compete with, contend with,

vie with, oppose, emulate, match, equal.

F3 co-operate.

rivalry *noun* competitiveness, competition, contest, contention, conflict, struggle, strife, opposition, antagonism.

F3 co-operation.

river *noun* waterway, watercourse, tributary, stream, brook, beck, creek, estuary.

road *noun* roadway, motorway, bypass, highway, thoroughfare, street, avenue, boulevard, crescent, drive, lane, track, route, course, way, direction.

roam *verb* wander, rove, range, travel, walk, ramble, stroll, amble, prowl, drift, stray.

F3 stay.

roar *verb, noun* bellow, yell, shout, cry, bawl, howl, hoot, guffaw, thunder, crash, blare, rumble.

F3 whisper.

rob *verb* steal from, hold up, raid, burgle, loot, pillage, plunder, sack, rifle, ransack, swindle, rip off (*infml*), do (*infml*), cheat, defraud, deprive.

robbery *noun* theft, stealing, larceny, hold-up, stick-up (*infml*), heist (*infml*), raid, burglary, pillage, plunder, fraud, embezzlement, swindle, rip-off (*infml*).

robust *adjective* strong, sturdy, tough, hardy, vigorous, powerful, muscular, athletic, fit, healthy, well.

F3 weak, feeble, unhealthy.

rock[1] *noun* boulder, stone, pebble, crag, outcrop.

rock[2] *verb* sway, swing, tilt, tip, shake, wobble, roll, pitch, toss, lurch, reel, stagger, totter.

rocky *adjective* **1** *a rocky slope*: stony, pebbly, craggy, rugged, rough, hard, flinty. **2** *the chair/business is rocky*: unsteady, shaky, wobbly, staggering, tottering, unstable, unreliable, uncertain, weak.

F3 1 smooth, soft. **2** steady, stable, dependable, strong.

rod *noun* bar, shaft, strut, pole, stick, baton, wand, cane, switch, staff, mace, sceptre.

rodent

Kinds of rodent include:

agouti, bandicoot, beaver, black rat, brown rat, cane rat, capybara, cavy, chinchilla, chipmunk, cony, coypu, dormouse, ferret, fieldmouse, gerbil, gopher, grey squirrel, groundhog, guinea pig, hamster, hare, harvest mouse, hedgehog, jerboa, kangaroo rat, lemming, marmot, meerkat, mouse, muskrat, musquash, pika, porcupine, prairie dog, rabbit, rat, red squirrel, squirrel, vole, water rat, water vole, woodchuck.

rogue *noun* scoundrel, rascal, scamp, villain, miscreant (*fml*), crook (*infml*), swindler, fraud, cheat, con man (*infml*), reprobate, wastrel, ne'er-do-well.

role *noun* part, character, representation, portrayal,

impersonation, function, capacity, task, duty, job, post, position.

roll *verb* **1** *rolling a hoop*: rotate, revolve, turn, spin, wheel, twirl, whirl, gyrate, move, run, pass. **2** *rolled up into a ball*: wind, coil, furl, twist, curl, wrap, envelop, enfold, bind. **3** *the ship rolled*: rock, sway, swing, pitch, toss, lurch, reel, wallow, undulate. **4** *thunder rolled*: rumble, roar, thunder, boom, resound, reverberate.
▪ *noun* **1** *a roll of paper*: roller, cylinder, drum, reel, spool, bobbin, scroll. **2** *the electoral roll*: register, roster, census, list, inventory, index, catalogue, directory, schedule, record, chronicle, annals. **3** *roll of the dice*: rotation, revolution, cycle, turn, spin, wheel, twirl, whirl, gyration, undulation. **4** *the roll of thunder*: rumble, roar, thunder, boom, resonance, reverberation.

romance *noun* **1** *her latest romance*: love affair, affair, relationship, liaison, intrigue, passion. **2** *write romances*: love story, novel, story, tale, fairy tale, legend, idyll, fiction, fantasy. **3** *the romance of living on a tropical island*: adventure, excitement, melodrama, mystery, charm, fascination, glamour, sentiment.

romantic *adjective* **1** *a romantic figure/notion*: imaginary, fictitious, fanciful, fantastic, legendary, fairy tale, idyllic, utopian, idealistic, quixotic, visionary, starry-eyed, dreamy, unrealistic, impractical, improbable, wild, extravagant, exciting, fascinating. **2** *wrote romantic letters*: sentimental, loving, amorous, passionate, tender, fond, lovey-dovey (*infml*), soppy, mushy, sloppy.
F3 **1** real, practical. **2** unromantic, unsentimental.

room *noun* space, volume, capacity, headroom, legroom, elbow-room, scope, range, extent, leeway, latitude, margin, allowance, chance, opportunity.

Types of room include:
attic, basement, bathroom, bedroom, boudoir, boxroom, breakfast room, cellar, chamber, cloakroom, conservatory, den (*infml*), dining room, drawing room, dressing-room, en suite bathroom, family room, front room, guest room, hall, kitchen, kitchen-diner, kitchenette, landing, larder, laundry, lavatory, library, living room, loft, loo (*infml*), lounge, lounge-diner, lumber room, morning room, nursery, pantry, parlour, playroom, porch, reception room, rest room (*US*), rumpus room (*US*), salon, scullery, sitting room, spare room, study, sun lounge, toilet, utility room, WC; anteroom, assembly room, boardroom, buttery, cabin, cell, chambers, classroom, common room, consulting room, control room, courtroom, cubicle, darkroom, day room, dormitory, engine-room, fitting-room, foyer,

games room, greenroom, guardroom, laboratory, lobby, locker room, music-room, office, reading-room, recreation room, saddle-room, sick-room, smoking room, staff room, stateroom, stockroom, store-room, strongroom, studio, tack room, waiting room, washroom, workroom, workshop.

---

roomy *adjective* spacious, capacious, large, sizable, broad, wide, extensive, ample, generous.
F3 cramped, small, tiny.

root[1] *noun* **1** *edible roots*: tuber, rhizome, stem. **2** *get to the root of the problem*: origin, source, derivation, cause, starting point, fount, fountainhead, seed, germ, nucleus, heart, core, nub, essence, seat, base, bottom, basis, foundation.
▪ *verb* anchor, moor, fasten, fix, set, stick, implant, embed, entrench, establish, ground, base.

root[2] *verb* dig, delve, burrow, forage, hunt, rummage, ferret, poke, pry, nose.

roots *noun* beginning(s), origins, family, heritage, background, birthplace, home.

rope *noun* line, cable, cord, string, strand.
▪ *verb* tie, bind, lash, fasten, hitch, moor, tether.

rot *verb* decay, decompose, putrefy, fester, perish, corrode, spoil, go bad, go off, degenerate, deteriorate, crumble, disintegrate, taint, corrupt.
▪ *noun* **1** *find rot in the timbers*: decay, decomposition, putrefaction, corrosion, rust, mould. **2** (*infml*) *talking rot*: nonsense, rubbish, poppycock (*infml*), drivel, claptrap.

rotate *verb* revolve, turn, spin, gyrate, pivot, swivel, roll.

rotten *adjective* **1** *rotten wood/ fruit*: decayed, decomposed, putrid, addled, bad, off, mouldy, fetid, stinking, rank, foul, rotting, decaying, disintegrating. **2** *a rotten job*: inferior, bad, poor, inadequate, low-grade, lousy, crummy (*infml*), ropy (*infml*), mean, nasty, beastly, dirty, despicable, contemptible, dishonourable, wicked.
F3 **1** fresh. **2** good.

rough *adjective* **1** *a rough surface*: uneven, bumpy, lumpy, rugged, craggy, jagged, irregular, coarse, bristly, scratchy. **2** *rough treatment*: harsh, severe, tough, hard, cruel, brutal, drastic, extreme, brusque, curt, sharp. **3** *a rough guess*: approximate, estimated, imprecise, inexact, vague, general, cursory, hasty, incomplete, unfinished, crude, rudimentary. **4** *rough sea*: choppy, agitated, turbulent, stormy, tempestuous, violent, wild.
F3 **1** smooth. **2** mild. **3** accurate. **4** calm.

round *adjective* **1** *a round coin*: spherical, globular, ball-shaped, circular, ring-shaped, disc-shaped, cylindrical, rounded,

curved. **2** *she's rather small and round*: rotund, plump, stout, portly.
▪ *noun* **1** *a round of golf*: cycle, series, sequence, succession, period, bout, session. **2** *security guard doing his rounds*: beat, circuit, lap, course, routine.
▪ *verb* circle, skirt, flank, bypass.

roundabout *adjective* circuitous, tortuous, twisting, winding, indirect, oblique, devious, evasive.
straight, direct.

rouse *verb* wake (up), awaken, arouse, call, stir, move, start, disturb, agitate, anger, provoke, stimulate, instigate, incite, inflame, excite, galvanize, whip up.
calm.

rout *noun* defeat, conquest, overthrow, beating, thrashing, flight, stampede.
win.

route *noun* course, run, path, road, avenue, way, direction, itinerary, journey, passage, circuit, round, beat.

routine *noun* procedure, way, method, system, order, pattern, formula, practice, usage, custom, habit.
▪ *adjective* customary, habitual, usual, typical, ordinary, run-of-the-mill, normal, standard, conventional, unoriginal, predictable, familiar, everyday, banal, humdrum, dull, boring, monotonous, tedious.
unusual, different, exciting.

row[1] *noun* /roh/ line, tier, bank, rank, range, column, file, queue, string, series, sequence.

row[2] *noun* /row/ **1** *have a row with someone*: argument, quarrel, dispute, disagreement, controversy, squabble, tiff, slanging match (*infml*), fight, brawl. **2** *stop that row immediately!*: noise, racket, din, uproar, commotion, disturbance, rumpus, fracas.

rowdy *adjective* noisy, loud, rough, boisterous, disorderly, unruly, riotous, wild.
quiet, peaceful.

royal *adjective* regal, majestic, kingly, queenly, princely, imperial, monarchical, sovereign, august, grand, stately, magnificent, splendid, superb.

rub *verb* apply, spread, smear, stroke, caress, massage, knead, chafe, grate, scrape, abrade, scour, scrub, clean, wipe, smooth, polish, buff, shine.

rubbish *noun* **1** *rubbish scattered on the beach*: refuse, garbage, trash, junk, litter, waste, dross, debris, flotsam and jetsam. **2** *talking rubbish*: nonsense, drivel, claptrap, twaddle, gibberish, gobbledegook (*infml*), balderdash, poppycock (*infml*), rot (*infml*).
2 sense.

rude *adjective* **1** *was rude to the teacher*: impolite, discourteous, disrespectful, impertinent, impudent, cheeky (*infml*), insolent, offensive, insulting, abusive, ill-mannered, uncivil,

curt, brusque, abrupt, sharp, short, ill-bred, uncouth, uncivilized. **2** *made a rude noise*: obscene, vulgar, coarse, dirty, naughty, gross.
F3 1 polite, courteous, civil.

ruin *noun* **1** *the ruin of all their hopes*: destruction, devastation, wreckage, havoc, damage, disrepair, decay, disintegration, breakdown, collapse, fall, downfall, failure, defeat, overthrow, ruination, undoing. **2** *financial ruin*: insolvency, bankruptcy, crash.
F3 1 development, reconstruction.
▪ *verb* spoil, mar, botch, mess up (*infml*), damage, break, smash, shatter, wreck, destroy, demolish, raze, devastate, overwhelm, overthrow, defeat, crush, impoverish, bankrupt.
F3 develop, restore.

rule *noun* **1** *that's against the rules*: regulation, law, statute, ordinance, decree, order, direction, guide, precept (*fml*), tenet, canon, maxim, axiom, principle, formula, guideline, standard, criterion. **2** *the rule of law*: reign, sovereignty, supremacy, dominion, mastery, power, authority, command, control, influence, regime, government, leadership.
▪ *verb* **1** *rule a country*: reign, govern, command, lead, administer, manage, direct, guide, control, regulate, prevail, dominate. **2** *court ruled in our favour*: judge, adjudicate, decide, find, determine, resolve, establish, decree, pronounce.

ruling *noun* judgement, adjudication, verdict, decision, finding, resolution, decree, pronouncement.
▪ *adjective* reigning, sovereign, supreme, governing, commanding, leading, main, chief, principal, dominant, predominant, controlling.

rumour *noun* hearsay, gossip, talk, whisper, word, news, report, story, grapevine, bush telegraph.

run *verb* **1** *run for the bus*: sprint, jog, race, career, tear, dash, hurry, rush, speed, bolt, dart, scoot, scuttle. **2** *route runs through the village*: go, pass, move, proceed, issue. **3** *leave the engine running*: function, work, operate, perform. **4** *run a company*: head, lead, administer, direct, manage, superintend, supervise, oversee, control, regulate. **5** *can hear water running*: flow, stream, pour, gush.
▪ *noun* **1** *go for a run every morning*: jog, gallop, race, sprint, spurt, dash, rush. **2** *take the family for a run in the car*: drive, ride, spin, jaunt, excursion, outing, trip, journey. **3** *a run of bad luck*: sequence, series, string, chain, course.

runner *noun* jogger, sprinter, athlete, competitor, participant, courier, messenger.

running *adjective* successive, consecutive, unbroken, uninterrupted, continuous,

constant, perpetual, incessant, unceasing, moving, flowing.
☒ broken, occasional.

runny *adjective* flowing, fluid, liquid, liquefied, melted, molten, watery, diluted.
☒ solid.

run-of-the-mill *adjective* ordinary, common, everyday, average, unexceptional, unremarkable, undistinguished, unimpressive, mediocre.
☒ exceptional.

rupture *noun* split, tear, burst, puncture, break, breach, fracture, crack, separation, division, estrangement, schism, rift, disagreement, quarrel, falling-out, bust-up (*infml*).
▪ *verb* split, tear, burst, puncture, break, fracture, crack, sever, separate, divide.

rural *adjective* country, rustic, pastoral, agricultural, agrarian.
☒ urban.

rush *verb* hurry, hasten, quicken, accelerate, speed (up), press, push, dispatch, bolt, dart, shoot, fly, tear, career, dash, race, run, sprint, scramble, stampede, charge.
▪ *noun* hurry, haste, urgency, speed, swiftness, dash, race, scramble, stampede, charge, flow, surge.

rustic *adjective* pastoral, sylvan (*fml*), bucolic (*fml*), countrified, country, rural.
☒ urban.

rusty *adjective* **1** *a rusty old car*: corroded, rusted, rust-covered, oxidized, tarnished, discoloured, dull. **2** *my German is a bit rusty*: unpractised, weak, poor, deficient, dated, old-fashioned, outmoded, antiquated, stale, stiff, creaking.

ruthless *adjective* merciless, pitiless, hard-hearted, hard, heartless, unfeeling, callous, cruel, inhuman, brutal, savage, cut-throat, fierce, ferocious, relentless, unrelenting, inexorable, implacable, harsh, severe.
☒ merciful, compassionate.

sabotage *verb* damage, spoil, mar, disrupt, vandalize, wreck, destroy, thwart, scupper, cripple, incapacitate, disable, undermine, weaken.
▪ *noun* vandalism, wilful damage, impairment, disruption, wrecking, destruction.

sack *verb* dismiss, fire (*infml*), discharge, axe (*infml*), lay off, make redundant.
▪ *noun* dismissal, discharge, one's cards, notice, the boot (*infml*), the push (*infml*), the elbow (*infml*), the axe (*infml*), the chop (*infml*).

sacred *adjective* holy, divine, heavenly, blessed, hallowed, sanctified, consecrated, dedicated, religious, devotional, ecclesiastical, priestly, saintly, godly, venerable, revered, sacrosanct, inviolable.
E3 temporal, profane.

sacrifice *verb* **1** *sacrificed his precious time*: surrender, forfeit, relinquish, let go, abandon, renounce, give up, forgo. **2** *sacrificed a goat to appease the gods*: offer, kill, slaughter.

sad *adjective* **1** *don't look so sad*: unhappy, sorrowful, tearful, grief-stricken, heavy-hearted, upset, distressed, miserable, low-spirited, downcast, doleful, glum, long-faced, crestfallen, dejected, down-hearted, down (*infml*), despondent, melancholy, depressed, low, gloomy, dismal, blue (*infml*), woebegone. **2** *sad news/a sad state of affairs*: upsetting, distressing, painful, depressing, touching, poignant, heart-rending, tragic, grievous, lamentable, regrettable, sorry, unfortunate, serious, grave, disastrous.
E3 **1** happy, cheerful. **2** fortunate, lucky.

safe *adjective* **1** *is the water safe to drink?*: harmless, innocuous, non-toxic, non-poisonous, uncontaminated. **2** *make your property safe from burglars*: secure, protected, guarded, impregnable, invulnerable, immune. **3** *they were found safe and well*: unharmed, undamaged, unscathed, uninjured, unhurt, intact. **4** *take the safe course of action/a safe pair of hands*: unadventurous, cautious, prudent, conservative, sure, proven, tried, tested, sound, dependable, reliable, trustworthy.
E3 **1** dangerous, harmful, unsafe. **2** vulnerable, exposed. **4** risky.

safeguard *verb* protect, preserve, defend, guard, shield, screen, shelter, secure.
E3 endanger, jeopardize.

safety *noun* protection, refuge, sanctuary, shelter, cover, security, safeguard, immunity, impregnability, safeness, harmlessness, reliability, dependability.
E3 danger, jeopardy, risk.

sag *verb* bend, give, bag, droop, hang, fall, drop, sink, dip, decline, slump, flop, fail, flag, weaken, wilt.
E3 bulge, rise.

sail *verb* **1** *sail for France*: embark, set sail, weigh anchor, put to sea, cruise, voyage. **2** *sailed the yacht around the world*: captain, skipper, pilot, navigate, steer. **3** *it sailed over our heads*: glide, plane, sweep, float, skim, scud, fly.

sailor *noun* seafarer, mariner,

seaman, marine, rating, yachtsman, yachtswoman.

saintly *adjective* godly, pious, devout, God-fearing, holy, religious, blessed, angelic, pure, spotless, innocent, blameless, sinless, virtuous, upright, worthy, righteous.
E3 godless, unholy, wicked.

sake *noun* benefit, advantage, good, welfare, well-being, gain, profit, behalf, interest, account.

salary *noun* pay, payment, remuneration, emolument (*fml*), stipend, wages, earnings, income.

sale *noun* selling, marketing, vending, disposal, trade, traffic, transaction, deal, auction.

salty *adjective* salt, salted, saline, briny, brackish, savoury, spicy, piquant, tangy.
E3 fresh, sweet.

salute *verb* greet, acknowledge, recognize, wave, hail, address, nod, bow, honour.
▪ *noun* greeting, acknowledgement, recognition, wave, gesture, hail, address, handshake, nod, bow, tribute.

salvage *verb* save, preserve, conserve, rescue, recover, retrieve, reclaim, redeem, repair, restore.
E3 waste, abandon.

salvation *noun* deliverance, liberation, rescue, saving, preservation, redemption, reclamation.
E3 loss, damnation.

same *adjective* **1** *gave the same excuse yesterday*: identical, twin, duplicate, indistinguishable, selfsame. **2** *these words have much the same meaning*: alike, like, similar, comparable, equivalent, matching, corresponding, mutual, reciprocal, interchangeable, substitutable, synonymous. **3** *stuck to the same theme throughout*: consistent, uniform, unvarying, changeless, unchanged.
E3 **1** different. **2** different, opposite. **3** inconsistent, variable, changeable.

sample *noun* specimen, example, cross-section, model, pattern, swatch, piece, demonstration, illustration, instance, sign, indication, foretaste.
▪ *verb* try, test, taste, sip, inspect, experience.

sanctions *noun* restrictions, boycott, embargo, ban, prohibition, penalty.

sanctity *noun* holiness, sacredness, inviolability, piety, godliness, religiousness, devotion, grace, spirituality, purity, goodness, righteousness.
E3 unholiness, secularity, worldliness, godlessness.

sane *adjective* normal, rational, right-minded, all there (*infml*), balanced, stable, sound, sober, level-headed, sensible, judicious (*fml*), reasonable, moderate.
E3 insane, mad, crazy, foolish.

sanitary *adjective* clean, pure, uncontaminated, unpolluted, aseptic, germ-free, disinfected,

hygienic, salubrious (*fml*), healthy, wholesome.

F3 insanitary, unwholesome.

sanity *noun* normality, rationality, reason, sense, common sense, balance of mind, stability, soundness, level-headedness, judiciousness.

F3 insanity, madness.

sap *verb* bleed, drain, exhaust, weaken, undermine, deplete, reduce, diminish, impair.

F3 strengthen, build up, increase.

sarcastic *adjective* ironical, satirical, mocking, taunting, sneering, derisive, scathing, disparaging, cynical, incisive, cutting, biting, caustic.

sardonic *adjective* mocking, jeering, sneering, derisive, scornful, sarcastic, biting, cruel, heartless, malicious, cynical, bitter.

Satanic *adjective* Satanical, diabolical, devilish, demonic, fiendish, hellish, infernal, inhuman, malevolent, wicked, evil.

F3 holy, divine, godly, saintly, benevolent.

satire *noun* ridicule, irony, sarcasm, wit, burlesque, skit, send-up, spoof, take-off, parody, caricature, travesty.

satirical *adjective* ironical, sarcastic, mocking, irreverent, taunting, derisive, sardonic, incisive, cutting, biting, caustic, cynical, bitter.

satisfaction *noun* **1** *felt some satisfaction at her achievements*: gratification, contentment, happiness, pleasure, enjoyment, comfort, ease, well-being, fulfilment, self-satisfaction, pride. **2** *demand satisfaction from the company*: settlement, compensation, reimbursement, indemnification, damages, reparation, amends, redress, recompense, requital, vindication.

F3 **1** dissatisfaction, displeasure.

satisfactory *adjective* acceptable, passable, up to the mark, all right, OK (*infml*), fair, average, competent, adequate, sufficient, suitable, proper.

F3 unsatisfactory, unacceptable, inadequate.

satisfy *verb* **1** *nothing seems to satisfy him/satisfy their hunger*: gratify, indulge, content, please, delight, quench, slake, sate, satiate, surfeit. **2** *satisfy requirements*: meet, fulfil, discharge, settle, answer, fill, suffice, serve, qualify. **3** *satisfy herself that it was true*: assure, convince, persuade.

F3 **1** dissatisfy. **2** fail.

saturate *verb* soak, steep, souse, drench, waterlog, impregnate, permeate, imbue, suffuse, fill.

saunter *verb* stroll, amble, mosey (*infml*), mooch (*infml*), wander, ramble, meander.

▪ *noun* stroll, walk, constitutional, ramble.

savage *adjective* wild, untamed, undomesticated, uncivilized,

primitive, barbaric, barbarous, fierce, ferocious, vicious, beastly, cruel, inhuman, brutal, sadistic, bloodthirsty, bloody, murderous, pitiless, merciless, ruthless, harsh.
≠ tame, civilized, humane, mild.

save *verb* **1** *save money/time*: economize, cut back, conserve, preserve, keep, retain, hold, reserve, store, lay up, set aside, put by, hoard, stash (*infml*), collect, gather. **2** *saving them from a watery grave*: rescue, deliver, liberate, free, salvage, recover, reclaim. **3** *build a wall to save the village from the floods*: protect, guard, screen, shield, safeguard, spare, prevent, hinder.
≠ **1** spend, squander, waste, discard.

savings *noun* capital, investments, nest egg, fund, store, reserves, resources.

saviour *noun* rescuer, deliverer, redeemer, liberator, emancipator, guardian, protector, defender, champion.
≠ destroyer.

savour *verb* relish, enjoy, delight in, revel in, like, appreciate.
≠ shrink from.

savoury *adjective* **1** *makes a very savoury soup*: tasty, appetizing, delicious, mouthwatering, luscious, palatable. **2** *sweet or savoury pancakes*: salty, spicy, aromatic, piquant, tangy.
≠ **1** unappetizing, tasteless, insipid. **2** sweet.

say *verb* **1** *say the words aloud/said his name*: express, phrase, put, render, utter, voice, articulate, enunciate, pronounce, mention, deliver, speak, orate, recite, repeat, read. **2** *she said, 'I haven't seen you for ages!'*: exclaim, comment, remark, observe. **3** *what does it say in the papers/the instruction manual?*: tell, instruct, order, communicate, convey, intimate, report, announce, declare, state. **4** *it's said they are very rich*: assert, affirm, maintain, claim, allege, rumour. **5** *what do these figures say to you?*: suggest, imply, signify, reveal, disclose, divulge. **6** *I'd say it was about two o'clock/can't say yet how much it will be*: guess, estimate, reckon, judge, imagine, suppose, assume, presume, surmise.

saying *noun* adage, proverb, dictum, precept (*fml*), axiom, aphorism, maxim, motto, slogan, phrase, expression, quotation, statement, remark.

scale[1] *noun* ratio, proportion, measure, degree, extent, spread, reach, range, scope, compass, spectrum, gamut, sequence, series, progression, order, hierarchy, ranking, ladder, steps, gradation, graduation, calibration, register.

scale[2] *verb* climb, ascend, mount, clamber, scramble, shin up, conquer, surmount.

scamper *verb* scuttle, scurry, scoot, dart, dash, run, sprint, rush, hurry, hasten, fly, romp, frolic, gambol.

scan *verb* **1** *scan the horizon*: examine, scrutinize, study, search, survey, sweep, investigate, check. **2** *scanning the pages of the book*: skim, glance at, flick through, thumb through.

scandal *noun* outrage, offence, outcry, uproar, furore, gossip, stir, rumours, smear, dirt, discredit, dishonour, disgrace, shame, embarrassment, ignominy.

scandalize *verb* shock, horrify, appal, dismay, disgust, repel, revolt, offend, affront, outrage.

scandalous *adjective* shocking, appalling, atrocious, abominable, monstrous, unspeakable, outrageous, disgraceful, shameful, disreputable, infamous, improper, unseemly, defamatory, scurrilous, slanderous, libellous, untrue.

scanty *adjective* deficient, short, inadequate, insufficient, scant, little, limited, restricted, narrow, poor, meagre, insubstantial, thin, skimpy, sparse, bare.
E3 adequate, sufficient, ample, plentiful, substantial.

scar *noun* mark, lesion, wound, injury, blemish, stigma.
▪ *verb* mark, disfigure, spoil, damage, brand, stigmatize.

scarce *adjective* few, rare, infrequent, uncommon, unusual, sparse, scanty, insufficient, deficient, lacking.
E3 plentiful, common.

scarcely *adverb* hardly, barely, only just.

scarcity *noun* lack, shortage, dearth, deficiency, insufficiency, paucity (*fml*), rareness, rarity, infrequency, uncommonness, sparseness, scantiness.
E3 glut, plenty, abundance, sufficiency, enough.

scare *verb* frighten, startle, alarm, dismay, daunt, intimidate, unnerve, threaten, menace, terrorize, shock, appal, panic, terrify.
E3 reassure, calm.
▪ *noun* fright, start, shock, alarm, panic, hysteria, terror.
E3 reassurance, comfort.

scared *adjective* frightened, fearful, nervous, anxious, worried, startled, shaken, panic-stricken, terrified.
E3 confident, reassured.

scary *adjective* frightening, alarming, daunting, intimidating, disturbing, shocking, horrifying, terrifying, hair-raising, bloodcurdling, spine-chilling, chilling, creepy, eerie, spooky (*infml*).

scathing *adjective* sarcastic, scornful, critical, trenchant (*fml*), cutting, biting, caustic, acid, vitriolic, bitter, harsh, brutal, savage, unsparing.
E3 complimentary.

scatter *verb* disperse, dispel, dissipate, disband, disunite, separate, divide, break up, disintegrate, diffuse, broadcast, disseminate, spread, sprinkle, sow, strew, fling, shower.
E3 gather, collect.

scatterbrained *adjective* forgetful, absent-minded, empty-headed, feather-brained, scatty (*infml*), careless, inattentive, thoughtless, unreliable, irresponsible, frivolous.
≠ sensible, sober, efficient, careful.

scattering *noun* sprinkling, few, handful, smattering.
≠ mass, abundance.

scavenge *verb* forage, rummage, rake, search, scrounge.

scenario *noun* outline, synopsis, summary, résumé, storyline, plot, scheme, plan, programme, projection, sequence, situation, scene.

scene *noun* **1** *the scene of the crime*: place, area, spot, locale, site, situation, position, whereabouts, location, locality, environment, milieu, setting, contact, background, backdrop, set, stage. **2** *rural scene/a battle scene*: landscape, panorama, view, vista, prospect, sight, spectacle, picture, tableau, pageant. **3** *a scene from the film*: episode, incident, part, division, act, clip. **4** *don't make a scene*: fuss, commotion, to-do (*infml*), performance, drama, exhibition, display, show.

scenery *noun* landscape, terrain, panorama, view, vista, outlook, scene, background, setting, surroundings, backdrop, set.

scenic *adjective* panoramic, picturesque, attractive, pretty, beautiful, grand, striking, impressive, spectacular, breathtaking, awe-inspiring.
≠ dull, dreary.

scent *noun* **1** *the scent of roses*: perfume, fragrance, aroma, bouquet, smell, odour. **2** *follow the scent*: track, trail.
≠ 1 stink.
▪ *verb* smell, sniff (out), nose (out), sense, perceive, detect, discern, recognize.

scented *adjective* perfumed, fragrant, sweet-smelling, aromatic.
≠ malodorous, stinking.

sceptic *noun* doubter, unbeliever, disbeliever, agnostic, atheist, rationalist, questioner, scoffer, cynic.
≠ believer.

sceptical *adjective* doubting, doubtful, unconvinced, unbelieving, disbelieving, questioning, distrustful, mistrustful, hesitating, dubious, suspicious, scoffing, cynical, pessimistic.
≠ convinced, confident, trusting.

schedule *noun* timetable, programme, agenda, diary, calendar, itinerary, plan, scheme, list, inventory, catalogue, table, form.
▪ *verb* timetable, time, table, programme, plan, organize, arrange, appoint, assign, book, list.

scheme *noun* **1** *draw up a traffic-calming scheme*: programme,

schedule, plan, project, idea, proposal, proposition, suggestion, draft, outline, blueprint, schema, diagram, chart, layout, pattern, design, shape, configuration, arrangement. **2** *hatch a scheme for defrauding the company*: intrigue, plot, conspiracy, device, stratagem, ruse, ploy, shift, manoeuvre, tactic(s), strategy, procedure, system, method.
▪ *verb* plot, conspire, connive, collude, intrigue, machinate, manoeuvre, manipulate, pull strings, mastermind, plan, project, contrive, devise, frame, work out.

scholar *noun* pupil, student, academic, intellectual, egghead (*infml*), authority, expert.

scholarship *noun* **1** *a work of great scholarship*: erudition, learnedness, learning, knowledge, wisdom, education, schooling. **2** *a scholarship to a public school*: grant, award, bursary, endowment, fellowship, exhibition.

school *noun* college, academy, institute, institution, seminary, faculty, department, discipline, class, group, pupils, students.
▪ *verb* educate, teach, instruct, tutor, coach, train, discipline, drill, verse, prime, prepare, indoctrinate.

schooling *noun* education, book-learning, teaching, instruction, tuition, coaching, training, drill, preparation, grounding, guidance, indoctrination.

science

Sciences include:

acoustics, aerodynamics, aeronautics, agricultural science, anatomy, anthropology, archaeology, astronomy, astrophysics, behavioural science, biochemistry, biology, biophysics, botany, chemistry, climatology, computer science, cybernetics, diagnostics, dietetics, domestic science, dynamics, earth science, ecology, economics, electrodynamics, electronics, engineering, entomology, environmental science, food science, genetics, geochemistry, geographical science, geology, geophysics, hydraulics, information technology, inorganic chemistry, materials science, mathematics, mechanical engineering, mechanics, medical science, metallurgy, meteorology, microbiology, mineralogy, natural science, nuclear physics, organic chemistry, ornithology, pathology, pharmacology, pharmacy, physics, physiology, psychology, radiochemistry, robotics, space technology, telecommunications, thermodynamics, toxicology, ultrasonics, veterinary science, zoology.

---

scientific *adjective* methodical, systematic, controlled, regulated, analytical, mathematical, exact, precise, accurate, scholarly, thorough.

scoff[1] *verb* mock, ridicule, poke fun, taunt, tease, rib (*infml*), jeer, sneer, pooh-pooh, scorn, despise, revile, deride, belittle, disparage (*fml*), knock (*infml*).
praise, compliment, flatter.

scoff[2] *verb* (*infml*) eat, consume, devour, put away (*infml*), gobble, guzzle, wolf (*infml*), bolt, gulp.
fast, abstain.

scold *verb* chide, tell off (*infml*), tick off (*infml*), reprimand, reprove, rebuke, take to task, admonish, upbraid (*fml*), reproach, blame, censure, lecture, nag.
praise, commend.

scoop *verb* gouge, scrape, hollow, empty, excavate, dig, shovel, ladle, spoon, dip, bail.
▪ *noun* **1** *a large metal scoop*: ladle, spoon, dipper, bailer, bucket, shovel. **2** (*infml*) *get a scoop for his newspaper*: exclusive, coup, inside story, revelation, exposé, sensation.

scope *noun* **1** *the scope of the enquiry*: range, compass, field, area, sphere, ambit, terms of reference, confines, reach, extent, span, breadth, coverage. **2** *scope for improvement*: room, space, capacity, elbow-room, latitude, leeway, freedom, liberty, opportunity.

scorch *verb* burn, singe, char, blacken, scald, roast, sear, parch, shrivel, wither.

scorching *adjective* burning, boiling, baking, roasting, sizzling, blistering, sweltering, torrid, tropical, searing, red-hot.

score *noun* **1** *what's the latest score?*: result, total, sum, tally, points, marks. **2** *making deep scores in the rock*: scratch, line, groove, mark, nick, notch.
▪ *verb* **1** *score a goal/point*: record, register, chalk up, notch up, count, total, make, earn, gain, achieve, attain, win, have the advantage, have the edge, be one up. **2** *score a notch on the table top*: scratch, scrape, graze, mark, groove, gouge, cut, incise, engrave, indent, nick, slash.

scorn *noun* contempt, scornfulness, disdain, sneering, derision, mockery, ridicule, sarcasm, disparagement (*fml*), disgust.
admiration, respect.
▪ *verb* mock, disdain, deride, laugh at, hold in contempt, scoff at, slight, sneer at, dismiss.
admire, respect.

scornful *adjective* contemptuous, disdainful, supercilious, haughty, arrogant, sneering, scoffing, derisive, mocking, jeering, sarcastic, scathing, disparaging, insulting, slighting, dismissive.
admiring, respectful.

scour[1] *verb* scrape, abrade, rub, polish, burnish, scrub, clean, wash.

scour[2] *verb* search, hunt, comb, drag, ransack, rummage, forage.

scourge *noun* affliction,

misfortune, torment, terror, bane, evil, curse, plague, penalty, punishment.
F blessing, godsend, boon.

scowl *verb, noun* frown, glower, glare, grimace, pout.
F smile, grin, beam.

scramble *verb* **1** *scrambling up the rocks*: climb, scale, clamber, crawl, shuffle, scrabble, grope. **2** *scrambling to get on the bus*: rush, hurry, hasten, run, push, jostle, struggle, strive, vie, contend.
▪ *noun* rush, hurry, race, dash, hustle, bustle, commotion, confusion, muddle, struggle, free-for-all, mêlée.

scrap[1] *noun* **1** *scraps of paper/ material/food*: bit, piece, fragment, part, fraction, crumb, morsel, bite, mouthful, sliver, shred, snippet. **2** *not a single scrap remained*: atom, iota, grain, particle, mite, trace, vestige, remnant, morsel. **3** *a heap of scrap/sell the old car for scrap*: waste, junk, rubbish, refuse.
▪ *verb* discard, throw away, jettison, shed, abandon, drop, dump, ditch (*infml*), cancel, axe, demolish, break up, write off.
F recover, restore.

scrap[2] *noun* fight, scuffle, brawl, dust-up (*infml*), quarrel, row, argument, squabble, wrangle, dispute, disagreement.
F peace, agreement.

scrape *verb* grate, grind, rasp, file, abrade, scour, rub, clean, remove, erase, scrabble, claw, scratch, graze, skin, bark, scuff.

scrappy *adjective* bitty, disjointed, piecemeal, fragmentary, incomplete, sketchy, superficial, slapdash, slipshod.
F complete, finished.

scratch *verb* claw, gouge, score, mark, cut, incise, etch, engrave, scrape, rub, scuff, graze, gash, lacerate.
▪ *noun* mark, line, scrape, scuff, abrasion, graze, gash, laceration.

scream *verb, noun* shriek, screech, cry, shout, yell, bawl, roar, howl, wail, squeal, yelp.

screen *verb* **1** *screening a film*: show, present, broadcast. **2** *a hedge that screens the garden*: shield, protect, safeguard, defend, guard, cover, mask, veil, cloak, shroud, hide, conceal, shelter, shade. **3** *screen the candidates*: vet, evaluate, sort, grade, sift, sieve, filter, process, gauge, examine, scan.
F **2** uncover, expose.
▪ *noun* partition, divider, shield, guard, cover, mask, veil, cloak, shroud, concealment, shelter, shade, awning, canopy, net, mesh.

screw *verb* fasten, adjust, tighten, contract, compress, squeeze, extract, extort, force, constrain, pressurize, turn, wind, twist, wring, distort, wrinkle.

scribble *verb* write, pen, jot, dash off, scrawl, doodle.

script *noun* **1** *a film script*: text, lines, words, dialogue, screenplay, libretto, book. **2** *old-fashioned* *copperplate script*: writing, handwriting, hand, longhand, calligraphy, letters, manuscript, copy.

scrub *verb* rub, brush, clean, wash, cleanse, scour.

scruffy *adjective* untidy, messy, unkempt, dishevelled, bedraggled, run-down, tattered, shabby, disreputable, worn-out, ragged, seedy, squalid, slovenly.
F3 tidy, well-dressed.

scruples *noun* standards, principles, morals, ethics.

scrupulous *adjective* painstaking, meticulous, conscientious, careful, rigorous, strict, exact, precise, minute, nice (*fml*).
F3 superficial, careless, reckless.

scrutinize *verb* examine, inspect, study, scan, analyse, sift, investigate, probe, search, explore.

scuff *verb* scrape, scratch, graze, abrade, rub, brush, drag.

scuffle *noun* fight, scrap, tussle, brawl, fray, set-to, rumpus, commotion, disturbance, affray.

sculpt *verb* sculpture, carve, chisel, hew, cut, model, mould, cast, form, shape, fashion.

scum *noun* **1** *scum rising to the surface of the water*: froth, foam, film, impurities. **2** *he described them as the scum of the earth*: dross, dregs, rubbish, trash.

scurry *verb* dash, rush, hurry, hasten, bustle, scramble, scuttle, scamper, scoot, dart, run, sprint, trot, race, fly, skim, scud.

sea *noun* **1** *go to sea/sail the seven seas*: ocean, main, deep, briny (*infml*). **2** *a sea of faces*: multitude, abundance, profusion, mass.

seal *verb* **1** *seal a jar*: close, shut, stop, plug, cork, stopper, waterproof, fasten, secure. **2** *seal the bargain*: settle, conclude, finalize, stamp.
F3 **1** unseal.
▪ *noun* stamp, signet, insignia, imprimatur, authentication, assurance, attestation, confirmation, ratification.

seam *noun* **1** *burst along the back seam*: join, joint, weld, closure, line. **2** *coal seam*: layer, stratum, vein, lode.

sear *verb* burn, scorch, brown, fry, sizzle, seal, cauterize, brand, parch, shrivel, wither.

search *verb* seek, look, hunt, rummage, rifle, ransack, scour, comb, sift, probe, explore, frisk (*infml*), examine, scrutinize, inspect, check, investigate, inquire, pry.
▪ *noun* hunt, quest, pursuit, rummage, probe, exploration, examination, scrutiny, inspection, investigation, inquiry, research, survey.

searching *adjective* penetrating, piercing, keen, sharp, close, intent, probing, thorough, minute.
F3 vague, superficial.

season *noun* period, spell, phase, term, time, span, interval.
▪ *verb* flavour, spice, salt.

seasoned *adjective* mature, experienced, practised, well-versed, veteran, old, hardened, toughened, conditioned, acclimatized, weathered.
F3 inexperienced, novice.

seasoning *noun* flavouring, spice, condiment, salt, pepper, relish, sauce, dressing.

seat *noun* **1** *a garden seat*: chair, bench, pew, stool, throne. **2** *the seat of government*: place, site, situation, location, headquarters, centre, heart, hub, axis, source, cause, bottom, base, foundation, footing, ground.

seating *noun* seats, chairs, places, room, accommodation.

secluded *adjective* private, cloistered, sequestered, shut away, cut off, isolated, lonely, solitary, remote, out-of-the-way, sheltered, hidden, concealed.
F3 public, accessible.

second[1] *adjective* **1** *a second helping/a second chance*: duplicate, twin, double, repeated, additional, further, extra, supplementary, alternative, other, alternate, next, following, subsequent, succeeding. **2** *the first and second places*: secondary, subordinate, lower, inferior, lesser, supporting.
▪ *noun* helper, assistant, backer, supporter.
▪ *verb* approve, agree with, endorse, back, support, help, assist, aid, further, advance, forward, promote, encourage.

second[2] *noun* moment, minute, tick (*infml*), instant, flash, jiffy (*infml*).

secondary *adjective* subsidiary, subordinate, lower, inferior, lesser, minor, unimportant, ancillary, auxiliary, supporting, relief, back-up, reserve, spare, extra, second, alternative, indirect, derived, resulting.
F3 primary, main, major.

second-rate *adjective* inferior, substandard, second-class, second-best, poor, low-grade, shoddy, cheap, tawdry, mediocre, undistinguished, uninspired, uninspiring.
F3 first-rate.

secret *adjective* **1** *kept it secret/secret activities*: private, discreet, covert, hidden, concealed, unseen, shrouded, covered, disguised, camouflaged, undercover, furtive, surreptitious, stealthy, sly, underhand, under-the-counter, hole-and-corner, cloak-and-dagger, clandestine, underground. **2** *a secret mission/file marked 'secret'*: classified, restricted, confidential, hush-hush (*infml*), unpublished, undisclosed, unrevealed, unknown. **3** *secret code*: cryptic, mysterious, occult, arcane, recondite (*fml*), deep. **4** *a secret place in his heart*: secretive, close, retired, secluded, out-of-the-way.
F3 **1** public, open. **2** well-known.
▪ *noun* confidence, mystery, enigma, code, key, formula, recipe.

secretary *noun* personal assistant, PA, typist, stenographer, clerk.

secretive *adjective* tight-lipped, close, cagey (*infml*), uncommunicative, unforthcoming, reticent, reserved, withdrawn, quiet, deep, cryptic, enigmatic.
F3 open, communicative, forthcoming.

sectarian *adjective* factional, partisan, cliquish, exclusive, narrow, limited, parochial, insular, narrow-minded, bigoted, fanatical, doctrinaire, dogmatic, rigid.
F3 non-sectarian, cosmopolitan, broad-minded.

section *noun* division, subdivision, chapter, paragraph, passage, instalment, part, component, fraction, fragment, bit, piece, slice, portion, segment, sector, zone, district, area, region, department, branch, wing.
F3 whole.

sector *noun* zone, district, quarter, area, region, section, division, subdivision, part.
F3 whole.

secure *adjective* **1** *keep valuables in a secure place*: safe, protected, sheltered, shielded, immune, impregnable, fortified, fast, tight, fastened, locked, fixed, immovable. **2** *secure foundations/ a secure income*: stable, steady, solid, firm, well-founded, reliable, dependable, steadfast. **3** *secure in the knowledge*: certain, sure, confident, assured, reassured.
F3 **1** insecure, vulnerable. **2** unstable, unreliable. **3** uneasy, ill at ease.
▪ *verb* **1** *secure their agreement*: obtain, acquire, gain, get. **2** *secure the lid/rope/gates*: fasten, attach, fix, make fast, tie, moor, lash, chain, lock (up), padlock, bolt, batten down, nail, rivet.
F3 **1** lose. **2** unfasten.

sedate *adjective* staid, dignified, solemn, grave, serious, sober, decorous, proper, seemly, demure, composed, unruffled, serene, tranquil, calm, quiet, cool, collected, imperturbable, unflappable (*infml*), deliberate, slow-moving.
F3 undignified, lively, agitated.

sediment *noun* deposit, residue, grounds, lees, dregs.

see *verb* **1** *see it in the distance*: perceive, glimpse, discern, spot, make out, distinguish, identify, sight, notice, observe, watch, view, look at, mark, note. **2** *could see it in her mind's eye/could see it coming*: imagine, picture, visualize, envisage, foresee, anticipate. **3** *I see your point*: understand, comprehend, grasp, fathom, follow, realize, recognize, appreciate, regard, consider, deem. **4** *just couldn't see the answer*: discover, find out, learn, ascertain, determine, decide. **5** *see them into the study*: lead, usher, accompany, escort. **6** *seeing* *another woman*: court, go out with, date. **7** *going to see his family*: visit, meet, spend time with. **8** *see her about it*: interview, consult.

seed *noun* pip, stone, kernel, nucleus, grain, germ, sperm, ovum, egg, ovule, spawn, embryo, source, start, beginning.

seek *verb* look for, search for, hunt, pursue, follow, inquire, ask, invite, request, solicit, petition, entreat, want, desire, aim, aspire, try, attempt, endeavour, strive.

seem *verb* appear, look, feel, sound, pretend to be.

seeming *adjective* apparent, ostensible, outward, superficial, surface, quasi-, pseudo, specious.
F3 real.

seep *verb* ooze, leak, exude, well, trickle, dribble, percolate, permeate, soak.

seethe *verb* **1** *ocean seething beneath the tiny yacht/street seething with people*: boil, simmer, bubble, effervesce, fizz, foam, froth, ferment, rise, swell, surge, teem, swarm. **2** *mind seething with powerful emotions*: rage, fume, smoulder, storm.

segment *noun* section, division, compartment, part, bit, piece, slice, portion, wedge.
F3 whole.

segregate *verb* separate, keep apart, cut off, isolate, quarantine, set apart, exclude.
F3 unite, join.

seize *verb* grab, snatch, grasp, clutch, grip, hold, take, confiscate, impound, appropriate, commandeer, hijack, annex, abduct, catch, capture, arrest, apprehend, nab (*infml*), collar (*infml*).
F3 let go, release, hand back.

seizure *noun* fit, attack, convulsion, paroxysm, spasm.

seldom *adverb* rarely, infrequently, occasionally, hardly ever.
F3 often, usually.

select *verb* choose, pick, single out, decide on, appoint, elect, prefer, opt for.
▪ *adjective* selected, choice, top, prime, first-class, first-rate, hand-picked, élite, exclusive, limited, privileged, special, excellent, superior, posh (*infml*).
F3 second-rate, ordinary, general.

selective *adjective* particular, choosy (*infml*), careful, discerning, discriminating.
F3 indiscriminate.

self *noun* ego, personality, identity, person.

self-conscious *adjective* uncomfortable, ill at ease, awkward, embarrassed, shamefaced, sheepish, shy, bashful, coy, retiring, shrinking, self-effacing, nervous, insecure.
F3 natural, unaffected, confident.

self-control *noun* calmness, composure, cool (*infml*), patience, self-restraint, restraint, self-denial, temperance, self-discipline, self-mastery, will-power.

self-indulgent *adjective* hedonistic, dissolute, dissipated, profligate, extravagant, intemperate, immoderate.
F abstemious.

selfish *adjective* self-interested, self-seeking, self-serving, mean, miserly, mercenary, greedy, covetous, self-centred, egocentric, egotistic(al).
F unselfish, selfless, generous, considerate.

selfless *adjective* unselfish, altruistic, self-denying, self-sacrificing, generous, philanthropic.
F selfish, self-centred.

self-respect *noun* pride, dignity, self-esteem, self-assurance, self-confidence.

sell *verb* barter, exchange, trade, auction, vend, retail, stock, handle, deal in, trade in, traffic in, merchandise, hawk, peddle, push, advertise, promote, market.
F buy.

seller *noun* vendor, merchant, trader, dealer, supplier, stockist, retailer, shopkeeper, salesman, saleswoman, agent, representative, rep (*infml*), traveller.
F buyer, purchaser.

send *verb* **1** *send a letter/payment*: post, mail, dispatch, consign, remit, forward, convey, deliver. **2** *message was sent out by radio*: transmit, broadcast, communicate. **3** *sending them flying/sending out smoke and flames*: propel, drive, move, throw, fling, hurl, launch, fire, shoot, discharge, emit, direct.

senile *adjective* old, aged, doddering, decrepit, failing, confused.

senior *adjective* older, elder, higher, superior, high-ranking, major, chief.
F junior.

seniority *noun* priority, precedence, rank, standing, status, age, superiority, importance.

sensation *noun* **1** *a sensation of falling/no sensation in his limbs*: feeling, sense, impression, perception, awareness, consciousness. **2** *the report caused a sensation*: commotion, stir, agitation, excitement, thrill, furore, outrage, scandal.

sensational *adjective* **1** *a sensational success*: exciting, thrilling, electrifying, breathtaking, startling, amazing, astounding, staggering, dramatic, spectacular, impressive, exceptional, excellent, wonderful, marvellous, smashing (*infml*). **2** *sensational headlines*: scandalous, shocking, horrifying, revealing, melodramatic, lurid.
F **1** ordinary, run-of-the-mill.

sense *noun* **1** *the five senses/a sense of longing*: feeling, sensation, impression, perception, awareness, consciousness, appreciation, faculty. **2** *had the sense to realize what was* *happening*: reason, logic, mind, brain(s), wit(s), wisdom, intelligence, cleverness, understanding, discernment, judgement, intuition. **3** *get the sense of what he was saying/in another sense*: meaning, significance, definition, interpretation, implication, point, purpose, substance.

2 foolishness.

▪ *verb* feel, suspect, intuit, perceive, detect, notice, observe, realize, appreciate, understand, comprehend, grasp.

senseless *adjective* **1** *a senseless thing to do*: foolish, stupid, unwise, silly, idiotic, mad, crazy, daft (*infml*), ridiculous, ludicrous, absurd, meaningless, nonsensical, fatuous, irrational, illogical, unreasonable, pointless, purposeless, futile. **2** *knocked senseless*: unconscious, out, stunned, anaesthetized, deadened, numb, unfeeling.

1 sensible, meaningful. **2** conscious.

sensible *adjective* wise, prudent, judicious (*fml*), well-advised, shrewd, far-sighted, intelligent, level-headed, down-to-earth, commonsense, sober, sane, rational, logical, reasonable, realistic, practical, functional, sound.

senseless, foolish, unwise.

sensitive *adjective* **1** *sensitive to heat/sensitive about one's appearance*: susceptible, vulnerable, impressionable, tender, emotional, thin-skinned, temperamental, touchy, irritable, sensitized, responsive, aware, perceptive, discerning, appreciative. **2** *sensitive instruments*: delicate, fine, exact, precise.

1 insensitive, thick-skinned. **2** imprecise, approximate.

sensual *adjective* self-indulgent, voluptuous, worldly, physical, animal, carnal, fleshly, bodily, sexual, erotic.

ascetic.

sentence *noun* judgement, decision, verdict, condemnation, pronouncement, ruling, decree, order.

▪ *verb* judge, pass judgement on, condemn, doom, punish, penalize.

sentiment *noun* **1** *agree with that sentiment*: thought, idea, feeling, opinion, view, judgement, belief, persuasion, attitude. **2** *full of flowery sentiment*: emotion, sensibility, tenderness, soft-heartedness, romanticism, sentimentality, mawkishness.

sentimental *adjective* tender, soft-hearted, emotional, gushing, touching, pathetic, tear-jerking, weepy (*infml*), maudlin, mawkish, nostalgic, romantic, lovey-dovey (*infml*), slushy, mushy, sloppy, schmaltzy, soppy, corny (*infml*).

unsentimental, realistic, cynical.

separate *verb* divide, sever, part,

split (up), divorce, part company, diverge, disconnect, uncouple, disunite, disaffiliate, disentangle, segregate, isolate, cut off, abstract, remove, detach, withdraw, secede.
F3 join, unite, combine.
▪ *adjective* single, individual, particular, independent, alone, solitary, segregated, isolated, apart, divorced, divided, disunited, disconnected, disjointed, detached, unattached, unconnected, unrelated, different, disparate, distinct, discrete, several, sundry.
F3 together, attached.

septic *adjective* infected, poisoned, festering, putrefying, putrid.

sequel *noun* follow-up, continuation, development, result, consequence, outcome, issue, upshot, pay-off, end, conclusion.

sequence *noun* succession, series, run, progression, chain, string, train, line, procession, order, arrangement, course, track, cycle, set.

serene *adjective* calm, tranquil, cool, composed, placid, untroubled, undisturbed, still, quiet, peaceful.
F3 troubled, disturbed.

series *noun* set, cycle, succession, sequence, run, progression, chain, string, line, train, order, arrangement, course.

serious *adjective* **1** *a serious error*: important, significant, weighty, momentous, crucial. **2** *a serious accident/illness*: grave, severe, dangerous, acute. **3** *had a serious effect*: severe, critical, deep, far-reaching. **4** *she wore a serious expression/was not a serious attempt*: unsmiling, long-faced, humourless, grim, solemn, sober, stern, thoughtful, pensive, earnest, sincere.
F3 **1** trivial, slight. **2** minor, slight, trivial. **3** minor, marginal. **4** smiling, facetious, frivolous.

servant *noun* domestic, maid, valet, steward, attendant, retainer, hireling, lackey, menial, skivvy (*infml*), slave, help, helper, assistant, ancillary.
F3 master, mistress.

serve *verb* **1** *serve two masters/serving their own ends*: wait on, attend, minister to, work for, help, aid, assist, benefit, further. **2** *serve a purpose*: fulfil, complete, answer, satisfy, discharge, perform, act, function. **3** *serve the lunch*: distribute, dole out, present, deliver, provide, supply.

service *noun* **1** *in the service of the king/do a service for someone*: employment, work, labour, business, duty, function. **2** *be of service to them*: use, usefulness, utility, advantage, benefit, help, assistance. **3** *church service*: worship, observance, ceremony, rite.
▪ *verb* maintain, overhaul, check, repair, recondition, tune.

servile *adjective* obsequious, sycophantic, toadying, cringing,

fawning, grovelling, bootlicking, slavish, subservient, subject, submissive, humble, abject, low, mean, base, menial.
F assertive, aggressive.

session *noun* sitting, hearing, meeting, assembly, conference, discussion, period, time, term, semester, year.

set *verb* **1** *set it down on the floor*: put, place, locate, situate, position, arrange, prepare, lodge, fix, stick, park, deposit. **2** *set a time/limit*: schedule, appoint, designate, specify, name, prescribe, ordain, assign, allocate, impose, fix, establish, determine, decide, conclude, settle, resolve. **3** *set the clocks*: adjust, regulate, synchronize, co-ordinate. **4** *the sun sets*: go down, sink, dip, subside, disappear, vanish. **5** *when the jam has set*: congeal, thicken, gel, stiffen, solidify, harden, crystallize.
F **4** rise.
▪ *noun* batch, series, sequence, kit, outfit, compendium, assortment, collection, class, category, group, band, gang, crowd, circle, clique, faction.
▪ *adjective* scheduled, appointed, arranged, prepared, prearranged, fixed, established, definite, decided, agreed, settled, firm, strict, rigid, inflexible, prescribed, formal, conventional, traditional, customary, usual, routine, regular, standard, stock, stereotyped, hackneyed.
F movable, free, spontaneous, undecided.

setback *noun* delay, hold-up, problem, snag, hitch, hiccup, reverse, misfortune, upset, disappointment, defeat.
F boost, advance, help, advantage.

setting *noun* mounting, frame, surroundings, milieu, environment, background, context, perspective, period, position, location, locale, site, scene, scenery.

settle *verb* **1** *settled the dispute*: arrange, order, adjust, reconcile, resolve, complete, conclude. **2** *settled on a branch/the bottom of the tank*: sink, subside, drop, fall, descend, land, alight. **3** *I settled for the blue one*: choose, appoint, fix, establish, determine, decide, agree, confirm. **4** *settled in the States*: colonize, occupy, populate, people, inhabit, live, reside. **5** *settle a bill*: pay, clear, discharge.

set-up *noun* system, structure, organization, arrangement, business, conditions, circumstances.

sever *verb* cut, cleave, split, rend, part, separate, divide, cut off, amputate, detach, disconnect, disjoin, disunite, dissociate, estrange, alienate, break off, dissolve, end, terminate.
F join, unite, combine, attach.

several *adjective* some, many, various, assorted, sundry, diverse, different, distinct, separate, particular, individual.

severe *adjective* **1** *severe discipline/a severe expression*: stern, disapproving, sober, strait-laced, strict, rigid, unbending, harsh, tough, hard, difficult, demanding, arduous, punishing, rigorous, grim, forbidding, cruel, biting, cutting, scathing, pitiless, merciless, oppressive, relentless, inexorable, acute, bitter, intense, extreme, fierce, violent, distressing, serious, grave, critical, dangerous. **2** *a severe black dress*: plain, simple, unadorned, unembellished, functional, restrained, austere, ascetic.
OPP 1 kind, compassionate, sympathetic, lenient, mild. **2** decorated, ornate.

sew *verb* stitch, tack, baste, hem, darn, embroider.

shabby *adjective* **1** *shabby clothes*: ragged, tattered, frayed, worn, worn-out, mangy, moth-eaten, scruffy, tatty, disreputable, dilapidated, run-down, seedy, dirty, dingy, poky. **2** *a shabby trick*: contemptible, despicable, rotten, mean, low, cheap, shoddy, shameful, dishonourable.
OPP 1 smart. **2** honourable, fair.

shade *noun* **1** *sit in the shade*: shadiness, shadow, darkness, obscurity, semi-darkness, dimness, gloom, gloominess, twilight, dusk, gloaming. **2** *a shade for his eyes*: awning, canopy, cover, shelter, screen, blind, curtain, shield, visor, umbrella, parasol. **3** *a bright shade of pink*: colour, hue, tint, tone, tinge.
▪ *verb* shield, screen, protect, cover, shroud, veil, hide, conceal, obscure, cloud, dim, darken, shadow, overshadow.

shadow *noun* **1** *room was in shadow*: shade, darkness, obscurity, semi-darkness, dimness, gloom, twilight, dusk, gloaming, cloud, cover, protection. **2** *see his shadow through the mist*: silhouette, shape, image, representation. **3** *not a shadow of doubt*: trace, hint, suggestion, suspicion, vestige, remnant.
▪ *verb* **1** *shadowing the garden*: overshadow, overhang, shade, shield, screen, obscure, darken. **2** *shadowing the man through the town*: follow, tail, dog, stalk, trail, watch.

shady *adjective* **1** *a shady nook*: shaded, shadowy, dim, dark, cool, leafy. **2** (*infml*) *a shady character*: dubious, questionable, suspect, suspicious, fishy (*infml*), dishonest, crooked, unreliable, untrustworthy, disreputable, unscrupulous, unethical, underhand.
OPP 1 sunny, sunlit, bright. **2** honest, trustworthy, honourable.

shaft *noun* handle, shank, stem, upright, pillar, pole, rod, bar, stick, arrow, dart, beam, ray, duct, passage.

shake *verb* **1** *shaking his fist/wind shaking the branches/the earth* *shook under them*: wave, flourish, brandish, wag, waggle, agitate, rattle, joggle, jolt, jerk, twitch, convulse, heave, throb, vibrate, oscillate, fluctuate, waver, wobble, totter, sway, rock, tremble, quiver, quake, shiver, shudder. **2** *the news shook her*: upset, distress, shock, frighten, unnerve, intimidate, disturb, discompose, unsettle, agitate, stir, rouse.

shaky *adjective* **1** *a shaky hand/ start*: trembling, quivering, faltering, tentative, uncertain. **2** *a shaky bridge*: unstable, unsteady, insecure, precarious, wobbly, rocky, tottery, rickety, weak.
F3 **1** steady. **2** firm, strong.

shallow *adjective* superficial, surface, skin-deep, one-dimensional, slight, flimsy, trivial, frivolous, foolish, idle, empty, meaningless, unscholarly, ignorant, simple.
F3 deep, profound.

sham *noun* pretence, fraud, counterfeit, forgery, fake, imitation, simulation, hoax, humbug.

shame *noun* disgrace, dishonour, discredit, stain, stigma, disrepute, infamy, scandal, ignominy, humiliation, degradation, shamefacedness, remorse, guilt, embarrassment, mortification.
F3 honour, credit, distinction, pride.
▪ *verb* embarrass, mortify, abash, confound, humiliate, ridicule, humble, put to shame, show up, disgrace, dishonour, discredit, debase, degrade, sully (*fml*), taint, stain.

shameful *adjective* **1** *a shameful waste of money*: disgraceful, outrageous, scandalous, indecent, abominable, atrocious, wicked, mean, low, vile, reprehensible, contemptible, unworthy, ignoble. **2** *was shameful for the whole family*: embarrassing, mortifying, humiliating, ignominious.
F3 **1** honourable, creditable, worthy.

shameless *adjective* unashamed, unabashed, unrepentant, impenitent, barefaced, flagrant, blatant, brazen, brash, audacious, insolent, defiant, hardened, incorrigible.
F3 ashamed, shamefaced, contrite.

shape *noun* **1** *a square shape/ could see the shape of a ship through the fog*: form, outline, silhouette, profile, model, mould, pattern, cut, lines, contours, figure, physique, build, frame, format, configuration. **2** *adopted the shape of a swan*: appearance, guise, likeness, semblance. **3** *in good shape*: condition, state, form, health, trim, fettle.
▪ *verb* form, fashion, model, mould, cast, forge, sculpt, carve, whittle, make, produce, construct, create, devise, frame, plan, prepare, adapt, adjust, regulate, accommodate, modify, remodel.

Geometrical shapes include:
circle, crescent, ellipse, oval, quadrant, semicircle; triangle, equilateral triangle, isosceles triangle, scalene triangle; oblong, quadrilateral, rectangle, square; decagon, diamond, dodecagon, hexagon, heptagon, kite, nonagon, octagon, parallelogram, pentagon, polygon, rhombus, trapezium; cone, cube, cuboid, cylinder, decahedron, dodecahedron, hemisphere, octahedron, pentahedron, polyhedron, prism, pyramid, sphere, tetrahedron.

shapeless *adjective* formless, amorphous, unformed, nebulous, unstructured, irregular, misshapen, deformed, dumpy.

share *verb* divide, split, go halves, partake, participate, share out, distribute, dole out, give out, deal out, apportion, allot, allocate, assign.
▪ *noun* portion, ration, quota, allowance, allocation, allotment, lot, part, division, proportion, percentage, cut (*infml*), dividend, due, contribution, whack (*infml*).

sharp *adjective* **1** *a sharp needle*: pointed, keen, edged, knife-edged, razor-sharp, cutting, serrated, jagged, barbed, spiky. **2** *a sharp outline*: clear, clear-cut, well-defined, distinct, marked, crisp. **3** *a sharp operator*: quick-witted, alert, shrewd, astute, perceptive, observant, discerning, penetrating, clever, crafty, cunning, artful, sly. **4** *sharp pain*: sudden, abrupt, violent, fierce, intense, extreme, severe, acute, piercing, stabbing. **5** *sharp-tasting*: pungent, piquant, sour, tart, vinegary, bitter, acerbic, acid. **6** *sharp wit*: trenchant (*fml*), incisive, cutting, biting, caustic, sarcastic, sardonic, scathing, vitriolic, acrimonious.
F3 **1** blunt. **2** blurred. **3** slow, stupid. **4** gentle. **5** bland. **6** mild.
▪ *adverb* punctually, promptly, on the dot, exactly, precisely, abruptly, suddenly, unexpectedly.
F3 approximately, roughly.

sharpen *verb* edge, whet, hone, grind, file.
F3 blunt.

shatter *verb* break, smash, splinter, shiver, crack, split, burst, explode, blast, crush, demolish, destroy, devastate, wreck, ruin, overturn, upset.

shed[1] *verb* **1** *snake shed its skin*: cast (off), moult, slough, discard. **2** *lorry shed its load*: drop, spill, pour, shower, scatter. **3** *shedding a pale light*: diffuse, emit, radiate, shine, throw.

shed[2] *noun* outhouse, lean-to, hut, shack.

sheen *noun* lustre, gloss, shine, shimmer, brightness, brilliance, shininess, polish, burnish.
F3 dullness, tarnish.

sheer *adjective* **1** *sheer nonsense*: utter, complete, total, absolute, thorough, mere, pure,

unadulterated, downright, out-and-out, rank, thoroughgoing, unqualified, unmitigated. **2** *a sheer drop*: vertical, perpendicular, precipitous, abrupt, steep. **3** *sheer fabric*: thin, fine, flimsy, gauzy, gossamer, translucent, transparent, see-through.
2 gentle, gradual. **3** thick, heavy.

sheet *noun* cover, blanket, covering, coating, coat, film, layer, stratum, skin, membrane, lamina, veneer, overlay, plate, leaf, page, folio, piece, panel, slab, pane, expanse, surface.

shelf *noun* ledge, mantelpiece, sill, step, bench, counter, bar, bank, sandbank, reef, terrace.

shell *noun* covering, hull, husk, pod, rind, crust, case, casing, body, chassis, frame, framework, structure, skeleton.
▪ *verb* hull, husk, pod.

shelter *verb* cover, shroud, screen, shade, shadow, protect, safeguard, defend, guard, shield, harbour, hide, accommodate, put up.
expose.
▪ *noun* cover, roof, shade, shadow, protection, defence, guard, security, safety, sanctuary, asylum, haven, refuge, retreat, accommodation, lodging.
exposure.

sheltered *adjective* covered, shaded, shielded, protected, cosy, snug, warm, quiet, secluded, isolated, retired, withdrawn, reclusive, cloistered, unworldly.
exposed.

shield *verb* defend, guard, protect, safeguard, screen, shade, shadow, cover, shelter.
expose.

shift *verb* change, vary, fluctuate, alter, adjust, move, budge, remove, dislodge, displace, relocate, reposition, rearrange, transpose, transfer, switch, swerve, veer.

shifty *adjective* untrustworthy, dishonest, deceitful, scheming, contriving, tricky, wily, crafty, cunning, devious, evasive, slippery, furtive, underhand, dubious, shady (*infml*).
dependable, honest, open.

shimmer *verb* glisten, gleam, glimmer, glitter, scintillate, twinkle.

shine *verb* **1** *sun shining on the sea*: beam, radiate, glow, flash, glare, gleam, glint, glitter, sparkle, twinkle, shimmer, glisten, glimmer. **2** *shining their shoes*: polish, burnish, buff, brush, rub. **3** *shine at athletics*: excel, stand out.

shining *adjective* **1** *shining armour*: bright, radiant, glowing, beaming, flashing, gleaming, glittering, glistening, shimmering, twinkling, sparkling, brilliant, resplendent, splendid, glorious. **2** *a shining example*: conspicuous, outstanding, leading, eminent, celebrated, distinguished, illustrious.
1 dark.

shiny *adjective* polished, burnished, sheeny, lustrous, glossy, sleek, bright, gleaming, glistening.
F3 dull, matt.

ship *noun* vessel, craft, liner, steamer, tanker, ferry.

shirk *verb* dodge, evade, avoid, duck (*infml*), shun, slack, skive (*infml*).

shiver *verb* shudder, tremble, quiver, quake, shake, vibrate, palpitate, flutter.
▪ *noun* shudder, quiver, shake, tremor, twitch, start, vibration, flutter.

shock *verb* disgust, revolt, sicken, offend, appal, outrage, scandalize, horrify, astound, stagger, stun, stupefy, numb, paralyse, traumatize, jolt, jar, shake, agitate, unsettle, disquiet, unnerve, confound, dismay.
F3 delight, please, gratify, reassure.
▪ *noun* fright, start, jolt, impact, collision, surprise, bombshell, thunderbolt, blow, trauma, upset, distress, dismay, consternation, disgust, outrage.
F3 delight, pleasure, reassurance.

shocking *adjective* appalling, outrageous, scandalous, horrifying, disgraceful, deplorable, intolerable, unbearable, atrocious, abominable, monstrous, unspeakable, detestable, abhorrent (*fml*), dreadful, awful, terrible, frightful, ghastly, hideous, horrible, disgusting, revolting, repulsive, sickening, nauseating, offensive, distressing.
F3 acceptable, satisfactory, pleasant, delightful.

shoddy *adjective* inferior, second-rate, cheap, tawdry, tatty, trashy, rubbishy, poor, careless, slipshod, slapdash.
F3 superior, well-made.

shoot *verb* **1** *shooting arrows/a gun*: fire, discharge, launch, propel, hurl, fling, project. **2** *shoot forwards*: dart, bolt, dash, tear, rush, race, sprint, speed, charge, hurtle. **3** *shoot rabbits/shot him in the back*: hit, kill, blast, bombard, gun down, snipe at, pick off.
▪ *noun* sprout, bud, offshoot, branch, twig, sprig, slip, scion.

shop

Types of shop include:
bazaar, cash-and-carry, corner shop, department store, e-shop, farmer's market, hypermarket, indoor market, market, mini-market, shopping mall, supermarket, superstore; baker, butcher, candy store (*US*), confectioner, dairy, delicatessen, farm shop, fish and chip shop, fishmonger, greengrocer, grocer, health-food shop, off-licence, sweet shop, take-away, tobacconist, tuck shop; bookshop, boutique, charity shop, chemist, draper, dress shop, drugstore (*US*), florist, haberdasher, hardware shop, ironmonger, jeweller, milliner, newsagent, outfitter, pharmacy, radio and TV shop,

saddler, shoe shop, stationer, tailor, toy shop, video shop; barber, betting shop, bookmaker, bookie (*infml*), hairdresser, launderette, pawnbroker, post office.

---

shore *noun* seashore, beach, sand(s), shingle, strand, waterfront, front, promenade, coast, seaboard, lakeside, bank.

short *adjective* **1** *a short stay/story*: brief, cursory, fleeting, momentary, transitory, ephemeral, concise, succinct, terse, pithy, compact, compressed, shortened, curtailed, abbreviated, abridged, summarized. **2** *was rather short with me*: brusque, curt, gruff, snappy, sharp, abrupt, blunt, direct, rude, impolite, discourteous, uncivil. **3** *a short person*: small, little, low, petite, diminutive, squat, dumpy. **4** *short supply/rations*: inadequate, insufficient, deficient, lacking, wanting, low, poor, meagre, scant, sparse.

F3 **1** long, lasting. **2** polite. **3** tall. **4** adequate, ample.

shortage *noun* inadequacy, insufficiency, deficiency, shortfall, deficit, lack, want, need, scarcity, paucity (*fml*), poverty, dearth, absence.

F3 sufficiency, abundance, surplus.

shortcoming *noun* defect, imperfection, fault, flaw, drawback, failing, weakness, foible.

shorten *verb* cut, trim, prune, crop, dock, curtail, truncate, abbreviate, abridge, reduce, lessen, decrease, diminish, take up.

F3 lengthen, enlarge, amplify.

shortly *adverb* soon, before long, presently, by and by.

short-sighted *adjective* **1** *becoming more short-sighted as she gets older*: myopic, near-sighted. **2** *a short-sighted view/attitude*: improvident (*fml*), imprudent, injudicious, unwise, impolitic, ill-advised, careless, hasty, ill-considered.

F3 **1** long-sighted, far-sighted.

shot *noun* **1** *a shot from a gun*: bullet, missile, projectile, ball, pellet, slug (*infml*), discharge, blast. **2** (*infml*) *have a shot at the answer*: attempt, try, effort, endeavour, go (*infml*), bash (*infml*), crack (*infml*), stab (*infml*), guess.

shout *noun, verb* call, cry, scream, shriek, yell, roar, bellow, bawl, howl, bay, cheer.

shove *verb* push, thrust, drive, propel, force, barge, jostle, elbow, shoulder, press, crowd.

show *noun* **1** *all show/did it for show*: ostentation, parade, display, flamboyance, panache, pizzazz (*infml*), showiness, exhibitionism, affectation, pose, pretence, illusion, semblance, façade, impression, appearance, air. **2** *a show of strength/a West End show*: demonstration, presentation, exhibition, exposition, fair, display, parade, pageant, extravaganza, spectacle, entertainment, performance, production, staging, showing, representation.

▪ *verb* **1** *show how it is done/show good judgement*: reveal, expose, uncover, disclose, divulge, present, offer, exhibit, manifest, display, indicate, register, demonstrate, prove, illustrate, exemplify, explain, instruct, teach, clarify, elucidate. **2** *show him out*: lead, guide, conduct, usher, escort, accompany, attend.

F3 **1** hide, cover.

shower *noun* rain, stream, torrent, deluge, hail, volley, barrage.

▪ *verb* spray, sprinkle, rain, pour, deluge, inundate, overwhelm, load, heap, lavish.

showy *adjective* flashy, flamboyant, ostentatious, gaudy, garish, loud, tawdry, fancy, ornate, pretentious, pompous, swanky (*infml*), flash (*infml*).

F3 quiet, restrained.

shred *noun* ribbon, tatter, rag, scrap, snippet, sliver, bit, piece, fragment, jot, iota, atom, grain, mite, whit, trace.

shrewd *adjective* astute, judicious (*fml*), well-advised, calculated, far-sighted, smart, clever, intelligent, sharp, keen, acute, alert, perceptive, observant, discerning, discriminating, knowing, calculating, cunning, crafty, artful, sly.

F3 unwise, obtuse, naive, unsophisticated.

shriek *verb, noun* scream, screech, squawk, squeal, cry, shout, yell, wail, howl.

shrill *adjective* high, high-pitched, treble, sharp, acute, piercing, penetrating, screaming, screeching, strident, ear-splitting.

F3 deep, low, soft, gentle.

shrink *verb* **1** *shrink in size*: contract, shorten, narrow, decrease, lessen, diminish, dwindle, shrivel, wrinkle, wither. **2** *shrink from the blows/direct confrontation*: recoil, back away, shy away, withdraw, retire, balk, quail, cower, cringe, wince, flinch, shun.

F3 **1** expand, stretch. **2** accept, embrace.

shrivel *verb* wrinkle, pucker, wither, wilt, shrink, dwindle, parch, dehydrate, desiccate, scorch, sear, burn, frizzle.

shudder *verb* shiver, shake, tremble, quiver, quake, heave, convulse.

▪ *noun* shiver, quiver, tremor, spasm, convulsion.

shuffle *verb* **1** *shuffle the cards*: mix (up), intermix, jumble, confuse, disorder, rearrange, reorganize, shift around, switch. **2** *shuffle across the room*: shamble, scuffle, scrape, drag, limp, hobble.

shun *verb* avoid, evade, elude, steer clear of, shy away from, spurn, ignore, cold-shoulder, ostracize.

F3 accept, embrace.

shut *verb* close, slam, seal, fasten, secure, lock, latch, bolt, bar.
F3 open.

shy *adjective* timid, bashful, reticent, reserved, retiring, diffident, coy, self-conscious, inhibited, modest, self-effacing, shrinking, hesitant, cautious, chary, suspicious, nervous.
F3 bold, assertive, confident.

sick *adjective* **1** *a sick child*: ill, unwell, indisposed, laid up, poorly, ailing, sickly, under the weather, weak, feeble. **2** *I feel sick*: vomiting, queasy, nauseous, bilious, seasick, airsick. **3** *sick of waiting*: bored, fed up (*infml*), tired, weary, disgusted, nauseated.
F3 1 well, healthy.

sickening *adjective* nauseating, revolting, disgusting, offensive, distasteful, foul, vile, loathsome, repulsive.
F3 delightful, pleasing, attractive.

sickly *adjective* **1** *a sickly child*: unhealthy, infirm, delicate, weak, feeble, frail, wan, pallid, ailing, indisposed, sick, faint, languid. **2** *a sickly taste*: nauseating, revolting, sweet, syrupy, cloying, mawkish.
F3 1 healthy, robust, sturdy, strong.

sickness *noun* **1** *recovering from a long sickness*: illness, disease, malady, ailment, complaint, affliction, ill-health, indisposition, infirmity. **2** *symptoms are sickness and dizziness*: vomiting, nausea, queasiness, biliousness.
F3 1 health.

side *noun* **1** *the side of the lake/shape has four sides*: edge, margin, fringe, periphery, border, boundary, limit, verge, brink, bank, shore, quarter, region, flank, hand, face, facet, surface. **2** *her side of the story*: standpoint, viewpoint, view, aspect, angle, slant. **3** *working for the same side*: team, party, faction, camp, cause, interest.
▪ *adjective* lateral, flanking, marginal, secondary, subsidiary, subordinate, lesser, minor, incidental, indirect, oblique.

sidetrack *verb* deflect, head off, divert, distract.

sideways *adverb* sidewards, edgeways, laterally, obliquely.
▪ *adjective* sideward, side, lateral, slanted, oblique, indirect, sidelong.

sidle *verb* slink, edge, inch, creep, sneak.

sift *verb* **1** *sift the flour and sugar*: sieve, strain, filter, riddle, screen, winnow, separate, sort. **2** *sifting through a pile of papers*: examine, scrutinize, investigate, analyse, probe, review.

sigh *verb* breathe, exhale, moan, complain, lament, grieve.

sight *noun* **1** *lose his sight*: vision, eyesight, seeing, observation, perception. **2** *out of sight*: view, look, glance, glimpse, range, field of vision, visibility. **3** *what a sight!*: appearance, spectacle, show, display, exhibition, scene, eyesore, monstrosity, fright (*infml*).
▪ *verb* see, observe, spot, glimpse,

perceive, discern, distinguish, make out.

sign *noun* **1** *a sign of peace*: symbol, token, character, figure, representation, emblem, badge, insignia, logo. **2** *gave a sign of annoyance*: indication, mark, signal, gesture, evidence, manifestation, clue, pointer, hint, suggestion, trace. **3** *the sign said 'Keep off the grass'*: notice, poster, board, placard. **4** *a sign of things to come*: portent, omen, forewarning, foreboding, harbinger (*fml*).
▪ *verb* autograph, initial, endorse, write.

signal *noun* sign, indication, mark, gesture, cue, go-ahead, password, light, indicator, beacon, flare, rocket, alarm, alert, warning, tip-off.
▪ *verb* wave, gesticulate, gesture, beckon, motion, nod, sign, indicate, communicate.

signature *noun* autograph, initials, mark, endorsement, inscription.

significant *adjective* **1** *significant improvement*: important, relevant, consequential, momentous, weighty, serious, noteworthy, critical, vital, marked, considerable, appreciable. **2** *significant gesture*: meaningful, symbolic, expressive, suggestive, indicative, symptomatic.
F3 **1** insignificant, unimportant, trivial. **2** meaningless.

signify *verb* **1** *the colour red signifies danger*: mean, denote, symbolize, represent, stand for, indicate, show, express, convey, transmit, communicate, intimate, imply, suggest. **2** *that doesn't signify*: matter, count.

silence *noun* quiet, quietness, hush, peace, stillness, calm, lull, noiselessness, soundlessness, muteness, dumbness, speechlessness, taciturnity, reticence, reserve.
F3 noise, sound, din, uproar.
▪ *verb* quiet, quieten, hush, mute, deaden, muffle, stifle, gag, muzzle, suppress, subdue, quell, still, dumbfound.

silent *adjective* inaudible, noiseless, soundless, quiet, peaceful, still, hushed, muted, mute, dumb, speechless, tongue-tied, taciturn, mum, reticent, reserved, tacit, unspoken, unexpressed, understood, voiceless, wordless.
F3 noisy, loud, talkative.

silhouette *noun* outline, contour, delineation, shape, form, configuration, profile, shadow.

silky *adjective* silken, fine, sleek, lustrous, glossy, satiny, smooth, soft, velvety.

silly *adjective* foolish, stupid, imprudent, senseless, pointless, idiotic, daft (*infml*), ridiculous, ludicrous, preposterous, absurd, meaningless, irrational, illogical, childish, puerile (*fml*), immature, irresponsible, scatterbrained.
F3 wise, sensible, sane, mature, clever, intelligent.

silt *noun* sediment, deposit, alluvium, sludge, mud, ooze.

similar *adjective* like, alike, close, related, akin, corresponding, equivalent, analogous, comparable, uniform, homogeneous.
F3 dissimilar, different.

similarity *noun* likeness, resemblance, similitude, closeness, relation, correspondence, congruence, equivalence, analogy, comparability, compatibility, agreement, affinity, homogeneity, uniformity.
F3 dissimilarity, difference.

simmer *verb* boil, bubble, seethe, stew, burn, smoulder, fume, rage.

simple *adjective* **1** *a simple question*: easy, elementary, straightforward, uncomplicated, uninvolved, clear, lucid, plain, understandable, comprehensible. **2** *a simple peasant*: unsophisticated, natural, innocent, artless, guileless, ingenuous, naive, green. **3** *he's a bit simple*: foolish, stupid, silly, idiotic, half-witted, simple-minded, feeble-minded, backward.
F3 1 difficult, hard, complicated, intricate. **2** sophisticated, worldly.

simplicity *noun* simpleness, ease, straightforwardness, clarity, purity, plainness, restraint, naturalness, innocence, artlessness, candour, openness, sincerity, directness.
F3 difficulty, complexity, intricacy, sophistication.

simplify *verb* disentangle, untangle, decipher, clarify, paraphrase, abridge, reduce, streamline.
F3 complicate, elaborate.

simply *adverb* **1** *he was simply asking*: merely, just, only, solely, purely. **2** *that's simply ridiculous*: utterly, completely, totally, wholly, absolutely, quite, really, undeniably, unquestionably, clearly, plainly, obviously. **3** *simply made/put*: easily, straightforwardly, directly, intelligibly.

simultaneous *adjective* synchronous, synchronic, concurrent, contemporaneous, coinciding, parallel.
F3 asynchronous.

sin *noun* wrong, offence, transgression, trespass (*fml*), misdeed, lapse, fault, error, crime, wrongdoing, sinfulness, wickedness, iniquity (*fml*), evil, impiety, ungodliness, unrighteousness, guilt.
▪ *verb* offend, transgress, trespass (*fml*), lapse, err, misbehave, stray, go astray, fall, fall from grace.

sincere *adjective* honest, truthful, candid, frank, open, direct, straightforward, plain-spoken, serious, earnest, heartfelt, wholehearted, real, true, genuine, pure, unadulterated, unmixed, natural, unaffected, artless, guileless, simple.

F3 insincere, hypocritical, affected.

sing *verb* chant, intone, vocalize, croon, serenade, yodel, trill, warble, chirp, pipe, whistle, hum.

singe *verb* scorch, char, blacken, burn, sear.

single *adjective* one, unique, singular, individual, particular, exclusive, sole, only, lone, solitary, separate, distinct, free, unattached, unmarried, celibate, unshared, undivided, unbroken, simple, one-to-one, man-to-man.
F3 multiple.

single-minded *adjective* determined, resolute, dogged, persevering, tireless, unwavering, fixed, unswerving, undeviating, steadfast, dedicated, devoted.

sinister *adjective* ominous, menacing, threatening, disturbing, disquieting, unlucky, inauspicious, malevolent, evil.
F3 auspicious, harmless, innocent.

sink *verb* **1** *sinking to her knees/ sinking below the waves*: descend, slip, fall, drop, slump, lower, stoop, succumb, lapse, droop, sag, dip, set, disappear, vanish. **2** *hope is sinking fast*: decrease, lessen, subside, abate, dwindle, diminish, ebb, fade, flag, weaken, fail, decline, worsen, degenerate, degrade, decay, collapse. **3** *sink like a stone/sinking it in concrete*: dive, plunge, plummet, submerge, immerse, engulf, drown.
F3 **1** rise. **2** increase. **3** float.

sip *verb* taste, sample, drink, sup.
▪ *noun* taste, drop, spoonful, mouthful.

sit *verb* **1** *sit on a branch*: settle, rest, perch, roost. **2** *when the parliament sits*: meet, assemble, gather, convene, deliberate.

site *noun* location, place, spot, position, situation, station, setting, scene, plot, lot, ground, area.
▪ *verb* locate, place, position, situate, station, set, install.

sitting *noun* session, period, spell, meeting, assembly, hearing, consultation.

situation *noun* **1** *the situation of the house*: site, location, position, place, spot, seat, locality, locale, setting, scenario. **2** *what's the latest situation?*: state of affairs, case, circumstances, predicament, state, condition, status.

size *noun* magnitude, measurement(s), dimensions, proportions, volume, bulk, mass, height, length, extent, range, scale, amount, greatness, largeness, bigness, vastness, immensity.

sizeable *adjective* large, substantial, considerable, respectable, goodly, largish, biggish, decent, generous.
F3 small, tiny.

skeleton *noun* bones, frame, structure, framework, bare bones, outline, draft, sketch.

sketch *verb* draw, depict, portray, represent, pencil, paint, outline, delineate, draft, rough out, block out.

▪ *noun* drawing, vignette, design, plan, diagram, outline, delineation, skeleton, draft.

sketchy *adjective* rough, vague, incomplete, unfinished, scrappy, bitty, imperfect, inadequate, insufficient, slight, superficial, cursory, hasty.
F3 full, complete.

skilful *adjective* able, capable, adept, competent, proficient, deft, adroit, handy, expert, masterly, accomplished, skilled, practised, experienced, professional, clever, tactical, cunning.
F3 inept, clumsy, awkward.

skill *noun* skilfulness, ability, aptitude, facility, handiness, talent, knack, art, technique, training, experience, expertise, expertness, mastery, proficiency, competence, accomplishment, cleverness, intelligence.

skilled *adjective* trained, schooled, qualified, professional, experienced, practised, accomplished, expert, masterly, proficient, able, skilful.
F3 unskilled, inexperienced.

skim *verb* **1** *skimming the surface of the water*: brush, touch, skate, plane, float, sail, glide, fly. **2** *skim through the documents*: scan, look through, skip.

skimp *verb* economize, scrimp, pinch, cut corners, stint, withhold.
F3 squander, waste.

skin *noun* hide, pelt, membrane, film, coating, surface, outside, peel, rind, husk, casing, crust.
▪ *verb* flay, fleece, strip, peel, scrape, graze.

skinny *adjective* thin, lean, scrawny, scraggy, skeletal, skin-and-bone, emaciated, underfed, undernourished.
F3 fat, plump.

skip *verb* **1** *skipped down the street*: hop, jump, leap, dance, gambol, frisk, caper, prance. **2** *skip a page*: miss, omit, leave out, cut.

skirmish *noun* fight, combat, battle, engagement, encounter, conflict, clash, brush, scrap, tussle, set-to, dust-up (*infml*).

skirt *verb* circle, circumnavigate, border, edge, flank, bypass, avoid, evade, circumvent.

skulk *verb* lurk, hide, prowl, sneak, creep, slink.

sky *noun* space, atmosphere, air, heavens, the blue.

slab *noun* piece, block, lump, chunk, hunk, wodge (*infml*), wedge, slice, portion.

slack *adjective* **1** *trousers are too slack*: loose, limp, sagging, baggy. **2** *a slack period*: quiet, idle, inactive, sluggish, slow. **3** *a slack attitude to his studies*: neglectful, negligent, careless, inattentive, remiss, permissive, lax, relaxed, easy-going (*infml*).
F3 **1** tight, taut, stiff, rigid. **2** busy. **3** diligent.
▪ *noun* looseness, give, play, room, leeway, excess.
▪ *verb* idle, shirk, skive (*infml*), neglect.

slacken *verb* loosen, release,

relax, ease, moderate, reduce, lessen, decrease, diminish, abate, slow (down).
F3 tighten, increase, intensify, quicken.

slam *verb* bang, crash, dash, smash, throw, hurl, fling.

slander *noun* defamation (*fml*), calumny (*fml*), misrepresentation, libel, scandal, smear, slur, aspersion (*fml*), backbiting.
▪ *verb* defame (*fml*), vilify (*fml*), malign, denigrate, disparage (*fml*), libel, smear, slur, backbite.
F3 praise, compliment.

slant *verb* tilt, slope, incline, lean, list, skew, angle.
▪ *noun* **1** *a downwards slant*: slope, incline, gradient, ramp, camber, pitch, tilt, angle, diagonal. **2** *give the story a different slant*: bias, emphasis, attitude, viewpoint.

slanting *adjective* sloping, tilted, oblique, diagonal.

slap *noun* smack, spank, cuff, blow, bang, clap.
▪ *verb* **1** *slap someone's face*: smack, spank, hit, strike, cuff, clout, bang, clap. **2** *slap on paint*: daub, plaster, spread, apply.

slash *verb* cut, slit, gash, lacerate, rip, tear, rend.
▪ *noun* cut, incision, slit, gash, laceration, rip, tear, rent.

slaughter *noun* killing, murder, massacre, extermination, butchery, carnage, blood-bath, bloodshed.
▪ *verb* kill, slay (*fml*), murder, massacre, exterminate, liquidate, butcher.

slave *noun* servant, drudge, vassal, serf, villein, captive.
▪ *verb* toil, labour, drudge, sweat, grind, slog.

slavery *noun* servitude, bondage, captivity, enslavement, serfdom, thraldom, subjugation.
F3 freedom, liberty.

sleek *adjective* shiny, glossy, lustrous, smooth, silky, well-groomed.
F3 rough, unkempt.

sleep *verb* doze, snooze, slumber, kip (*infml*), doss (down) (*infml*), hibernate, drop off, nod off, rest, repose.
▪ *noun* doze, snooze, nap, forty winks, shut-eye (*infml*), kip (*infml*), slumber, hibernation, rest, repose, siesta.

sleepless *adjective* unsleeping, awake, wide-awake, alert, vigilant, watchful, wakeful, restless, disturbed, insomniac.

sleepy *adjective* drowsy, somnolent (*fml*), tired, weary, heavy, slow, sluggish, torpid, lethargic, inactive, quiet, dull, soporific (*fml*), hypnotic.
F3 awake, alert, wakeful, restless.

slender *adjective* **1** *tall and slender*: slim, thin, lean, slight, svelte, graceful. **2** *a slender chance*: faint, remote, slight, inconsiderable, tenuous, flimsy, feeble, inadequate, insufficient, meagre, scanty.
F3 **1** fat. **2** appreciable, considerable, ample.

slice *noun* piece, sliver, wafer,

rasher, tranche, slab, wedge, segment, section, share, portion, helping, cut (*infml*), whack (*infml*).
▪ *verb* carve, cut, chop, divide, segment.

slick *adjective* **1** *a slick operator*: glib, plausible, deft, adroit, dexterous, skilful, professional. **2** *slick hair*: smooth, sleek, glossy, shiny, polished.

slide *verb* slip, slither, skid, skate, ski, toboggan, glide, plane, coast, skim.

slight *adjective* **1** *a slight mistake/bump*: minor, unimportant, insignificant, negligible, trivial, paltry, modest, small, little, inconsiderable, insubstantial. **2** *a slight figure*: slender, slim, diminutive, petite, delicate.
1 major, significant, noticeable, considerable. **2** large, muscular.
▪ *noun* insult, affront, slur, snub, rebuff, rudeness, discourtesy, disrespect, contempt, disdain, indifference, disregard, neglect.
respect, praise, compliment, flattery.

slim *adjective* **1** *a slim waist*: slender, thin, lean, svelte, trim. **2** *a slim chance of success*: slight, remote, faint, poor.
1 fat, chubby. **2** strong, considerable.
▪ *verb* lose weight, diet, reduce.

slimy *adjective* **1** *slimy mud*: mucous, viscous, oily, greasy, slippery. **2** *hate the slimy way he talks to the boss*: servile, obsequious, sycophantic, toadying, smarmy, oily, unctuous (*fml*).

sling *verb* **1** *slinging it away*: throw, hurl, fling, catapult, heave, pitch, lob, toss, chuck (*infml*). **2** *slinging his bow over his shoulder*: hang, suspend, dangle, swing.

slink *verb* sneak, steal, creep, sidle, slip, prowl, skulk.

slip[1] *verb* **1** *slipped on the ice*: slide, glide, skate, skid, stumble, trip, fall, slither. **2** *slipped into the room unseen*: slink, sneak, steal, creep.
▪ *noun* mistake, error, slip-up (*infml*), bloomer (*infml*), blunder, fault, indiscretion, omission, oversight, failure.

slip[2] *noun* piece, strip, voucher, chit, coupon, certificate.

slippery *adjective* slippy, icy, greasy, glassy, smooth, dangerous, treacherous, perilous.
rough.

slipshod *adjective* careless, slapdash, sloppy, slovenly, untidy, negligent, lax, casual.
careful, fastidious, neat, tidy.

slit *verb* cut, gash, slash, slice, split, rip, tear.
▪ *noun* opening, aperture, vent, cut, incision, gash, slash, split, tear, rent.

slither *verb* slide, slip, glide, slink, creep, snake, worm.

sliver *noun* flake, shaving, paring, slice, wafer, shred, fragment, chip, splinter, shiver, shard.

slogan *noun* jingle, motto, catch-phrase, catchword, watchword, battle-cry, war cry.

slop *verb* spill, overflow, slosh, splash, splatter, spatter.

slope *verb* slant, lean, tilt, tip, pitch, incline, rise, fall.
▪ *noun* incline, gradient, ramp, hill, ascent, descent, slant, tilt, pitch, inclination.

sloppy *adjective* **1** *a sloppy mixture*: watery, wet, liquid, runny, mushy, slushy. **2** *sloppy work*: careless, hit-or-miss, slapdash, slipshod, slovenly, untidy, messy, clumsy, amateurish. **3** *sloppy song*: soppy, sentimental, schmaltzy, slushy, mushy.
F3 **1** solid. **2** careful, exact, precise.

slot *noun* hole, opening, aperture, slit, vent, groove, channel, gap, space, time, vacancy, place, spot, position, niche.
▪ *verb* insert, fit, place, position, assign, pigeonhole.

slouch *verb* stoop, hunch, droop, slump, lounge, loll, shuffle, shamble.

slow *adjective* **1** *a slow pace*: leisurely, unhurried, lingering, loitering, dawdling, lazy, sluggish, slow-moving, creeping, gradual, deliberate, measured, plodding. **2** *too slow to understand what you meant*: stupid, slow-witted, dim, thick (*infml*). **3** *a slow journey*: prolonged, protracted, long-drawn-out, tedious, boring, dull, uninteresting, uneventful.
F3 **1** quick, fast, swift, rapid, speedy. **2** clever, intelligent. **3** brisk, lively, exciting.
▪ *verb* brake, decelerate, delay, hold up, retard, handicap, check, curb, restrict.
F3 speed, accelerate.

slowly *adverb* leisurely, gradually, lazily, sluggishly, unhurriedly.

sluggish *adjective* lethargic, listless, torpid, heavy, dull, slow, slow-moving, slothful, lazy, idle, inactive, lifeless, unresponsive.
F3 brisk, vigorous, lively, dynamic.

slump *verb* **1** *trade slumped*: collapse, fall, drop, plunge, plummet, sink, decline, deteriorate, worsen, crash, fail. **2** *he slumped against the wall*: droop, sag, bend, stoop, slouch, loll, lounge, flop.
▪ *noun* recession, depression, stagnation, downturn, low, trough, decline, deterioration, worsening, fall, drop, collapse, crash, failure.
F3 boom.

sly *adjective* wily, foxy, crafty, cunning, artful, guileful, clever, canny, shrewd, astute, knowing, subtle, devious, shifty, tricky, furtive, stealthy, surreptitious, underhand, covert, secretive, scheming, conniving, mischievous, roguish.
F3 honest, frank, candid, open.

smack *verb* hit, strike, slap, spank, whack (*infml*), thwack (*infml*), clap, box, cuff, pat, tap.
▪ *noun* blow, slap, spank, whack (*infml*), thwack (*infml*), box, cuff, pat, tap.
▪ *adverb* bang, slap-bang, right,

plumb, straight, directly, exactly, precisely.

small *adjective* **1** *a small man/dog/house/child*: little, tiny, minute, minuscule, short, slight, puny, petite, diminutive, pint-size(d) (*infml*), miniature, mini, pocket, pocket-sized, young. **2** *a small fee/amount*: petty, trifling, trivial, unimportant, insignificant, minor, inconsiderable, negligible. **3** *a person of small means*: inadequate, insufficient, scanty, meagre, paltry, mean, limited.
F3 **1** large, big, huge. **2** great, considerable. **3** ample.

smart *adjective* **1** *smart clothes/appearance*: elegant, stylish, chic, fashionable, modish, neat, tidy, spruce, trim, well-groomed. **2** *a smart fellow/move*: clever, intelligent, bright, sharp, acute, shrewd, astute.
F3 **1** dowdy, unfashionable, untidy, scruffy. **2** stupid, slow.
▪ *verb* sting, hurt, prick, burn, tingle, twinge, throb.

smash *verb* **1** *smash a window*: break, shatter, shiver, ruin, wreck, demolish, destroy, defeat, crush. **2** *smashed his fist down on the table*: crash, collide, strike, bang, bash, thump.

smattering *noun* bit, modicum, dash, sprinkling, basics, rudiments, elements.

smear *verb* daub, plaster, spread, cover, coat, rub, smudge, streak.

smell *noun* odour, whiff, scent, perfume, fragrance, bouquet, aroma, redolence, stench, stink, reek, pong (*infml*).
▪ *verb* sniff, nose, scent, stink, reek, pong (*infml*).

smelly *adjective* malodorous, pongy (*infml*), stinking, reeking, foul, bad, off, fetid, putrid, high, strong.

smile *noun, verb* grin, beam, simper, smirk, leer, laugh.

smoke *noun* fumes, exhaust, gas, vapour, mist, fog, smog.

smooth *adjective* **1** *a nice smooth surface*: level, plane, even, flat, horizontal, flush. **2** *a smooth ride/landing*: steady, unbroken, flowing, regular, uniform, rhythmic, easy, effortless. **3** *smooth water*: shiny, polished, glossy, silky, glassy, calm, undisturbed, serene, tranquil, peaceful. **4** *a smooth operator*: suave, agreeable, smooth-talking, glib, plausible, persuasive, slick, smarmy, unctuous (*fml*), ingratiating.
F3 **1** rough, lumpy. **2** bumpy, irregular, erratic, unsteady. **3** rough, choppy.
▪ *verb* **1** *smooth out any wrinkles/bumps*: iron, press, roll, flatten, level, plane, file, sand, polish. **2** *smooth their feelings*: ease, alleviate, assuage (*fml*), allay, mitigate, calm, mollify.
F3 **1** roughen, wrinkle, crease.

smother *verb* suffocate, asphyxiate, strangle, throttle, choke, stifle, extinguish, snuff, muffle, suppress, repress, hide, conceal, cover, shroud, envelop, wrap.

smoulder *verb* burn, smoke, fume, rage, seethe, simmer.

smudge *verb* blur, smear, daub, mark, spot, stain, dirty, soil.
▪ *noun* blot, stain, spot, blemish, blur, smear, streak.

smug *adjective* complacent, self-satisfied, superior, holier-than-thou, self-righteous, priggish, conceited.
F3 humble, modest.

snack *noun* refreshment(s), bite, nibble, titbit, elevenses (*infml*).

snag *noun* disadvantage, inconvenience, drawback, catch, problem, difficulty, complication, setback, hitch, obstacle, stumbling block.
▪ *verb* catch, rip, tear, hole, ladder.

snap *verb* **1** *the twig snapped*: break, crack, split, separate. **2** *dog snapped at him*: bite, nip, bark, growl, snarl. **3** *snapped it up*: snatch, seize, catch, grasp, grip.
▪ *noun* break, crack, bite, nip, flick, fillip, crackle, pop.

snappy *adjective* cross, irritable, edgy, touchy, brusque, quick-tempered, ill-natured, crabbed, testy.

snare *verb* trap, ensnare, entrap, catch, net.
▪ *noun* trap, wire, net, noose, catch, pitfall.

snarl[1] *verb* growl, grumble, complain.

snarl[2] *verb* tangle, knot, ravel, entangle, enmesh, embroil, confuse, muddle, complicate.

snatch *verb* grab, seize, kidnap, take, nab (*infml*), pluck, pull, wrench, wrest (*fml*), gain, win, clutch, grasp, grip.

sneak *verb* **1** *sneaked away under cover of darkness*: creep, steal, slip, slink, sidle, skulk, lurk, prowl, smuggle, spirit. **2** *promised not to sneak about it to his teacher*: tell tales, split (*infml*), inform on, grass on (*slang*).
▪ *noun* tell-tale, informer, grass (*slang*).

sneaking *adjective* private, secret, furtive, surreptitious, hidden, lurking, suppressed, grudging, nagging, niggling, persistent, worrying, uncomfortable, intuitive.

sneer *verb* scorn, disdain, look down on, deride, scoff, jeer, mock, ridicule, gibe, laugh, snigger.

snide *adjective* derogatory, disparaging, sarcastic, cynical, scornful, sneering, hurtful, unkind, nasty, mean, spiteful, malicious, ill-natured.
F3 complimentary.

sniff *verb* breathe, inhale, snuff, snuffle, smell, nose, scent.

snigger *verb, noun* laugh, giggle, titter, chuckle, sneer.

snippet *noun* piece, scrap, cutting, clipping, fragment, particle, shred, snatch, part, portion, segment, section.

snobbish *adjective* supercilious, disdainful, snooty (*infml*), stuck-up (*infml*), toffee-nosed (*infml*), superior, lofty, high and mighty, arrogant, pretentious, affected, condescending, patronizing.

snoop *verb* spy, sneak, pry, nose, interfere, meddle.

snooze *verb* nap, doze, sleep, kip (*infml*).

▪ *noun* nap, catnap, forty winks, doze, siesta, sleep, kip (*infml*).

snub *verb* rebuff, brush off, cut, cold-shoulder, slight, rebuke, put down, squash, humble, shame, humiliate, mortify.

snug *adjective* cosy, warm, comfortable, homely, friendly, intimate, sheltered, secure, tight, close-fitting.

soak *verb* wet, drench, saturate, penetrate, permeate, infuse, bathe, marinate, souse, steep, submerge, immerse.

soaking *adjective* soaked, drenched, sodden, waterlogged, saturated, sopping, wringing, dripping, streaming.

F3 dry.

soar *verb* fly, wing, glide, plane, tower, rise, ascend, climb, mount, escalate, spiral, rocket.

F3 fall, plummet.

sob *verb* cry, weep, bawl, howl, blubber, snivel.

sober *adjective* **1** *stay sober*: teetotal, temperate, moderate, abstinent, abstemious. **2** *a sober attitude/group of gentlemen*: solemn, dignified, serious, staid, steady, sedate, quiet, serene, calm, composed, unruffled, unexcited, cool, dispassionate, level-headed, practical, realistic, reasonable, rational, clear-headed. **3** *sober dark suit*: sombre, drab, dull, plain, subdued, restrained.

F3 **1** drunk, intemperate. **2** frivolous, excited, unrealistic, irrational. **3** flashy, garish.

so-called *adjective* alleged, supposed, purported, ostensible, nominal, self-styled, professed, would-be, pretended.

sociable *adjective* outgoing, gregarious, friendly, affable, companionable, genial, convivial, cordial, warm, hospitable, neighbourly, approachable, accessible, familiar.

F3 unsociable, withdrawn, unfriendly, hostile.

social *adjective* communal, public, community, common, general, collective, group, organized.

society *noun* **1** *living in a modern society*: community, population, culture, civilization, nation, people, mankind, humanity. **2** *the Royal Society/form a society*: club, circle, group, association, organization, company, corporation, league, union, guild, fellowship, fraternity, brotherhood, sisterhood, sorority. **3** *high society*: upper classes, aristocracy, gentry, nobility, élite.

soft *adjective* **1** *a soft bed*: yielding, pliable, flexible, elastic, plastic, malleable, spongy, squashy, pulpy. **2** *soft colours*: pale, light, pastel, delicate, subdued, muted, quiet, low, dim, faint, diffuse, mild, bland, gentle, soothing, sweet, mellow, melodious, dulcet, pleasant. **3** *soft fur/skin*: furry, downy, velvety, silky, smooth. **4** *you're too soft with that boy*: lenient, lax, permissive, indulgent, tolerant, easy-going (*infml*), kind, generous, gentle, merciful, soft-hearted, tender. **5** *don't go soft on us now!*: sensitive, weak, spineless.

F3 1 hard. **2** harsh. **3** rough. **4** strict, severe. **5** tough.

soften *verb* moderate, temper, mitigate, lessen, diminish, abate, alleviate, ease, soothe, palliate (*fml*), quell, assuage (*fml*), subdue, mollify, appease, calm, still, relax.

soft-hearted *adjective* sympathetic, compassionate, kind, benevolent, charitable, generous, warm-hearted, tender, sentimental.

F3 hard-hearted, callous.

soggy *adjective* wet, damp, moist, soaked, drenched, sodden, waterlogged, saturated, sopping, dripping, heavy, boggy, spongy, pulpy.

soil[1] *noun* earth, clay, loam, humus, dirt, dust, ground, land, region, country.

soil[2] *verb* dirty, stain, spot, smudge, smear, foul, muddy, pollute, defile (*fml*), besmirch (*fml*), sully (*fml*), tarnish.

sole *adjective* only, unique, exclusive, individual, single, singular, one, lone, solitary, alone.

F3 shared, multiple.

solemn *adjective* **1** *a solemn expression/vow*: serious, grave, sober, sedate, sombre, glum, thoughtful, earnest, awed, reverential. **2** *a solemn occasion*: grand, stately, majestic, ceremonial, ritual, formal, ceremonious, pompous, dignified, august, venerable, awe-inspiring, impressive, imposing, momentous.

F3 1 light-hearted. **2** frivolous.

solicit *verb* ask (for), request, seek, crave, beg, beseech, entreat, implore, plead, pray, apply (for), supplicate, sue, petition, canvass, importune.

solid *adjective* **1** *solid rock/ foundation*: hard, firm, dense, compact, strong, sturdy, substantial, sound, unshakable. **2** *a solid wall of people/a solid white line*: unbroken, continuous, uninterrupted. **3** *a solid person*: reliable, dependable, trusty, worthy, decent, upright, sensible, level-headed, stable, serious, sober. **4** *solid gold*: real, genuine, pure, concrete, tangible.

F3 1 liquid, gaseous, hollow. **2** broken, dotted. **3** unreliable, unstable. **4** unreal.

solidarity *noun* unity, agreement, accord, unanimity, consensus, harmony, concord, cohesion, like-mindedness, camaraderie, team spirit, soundness, stability.

F3 discord, division, schism.

solidify *verb* harden, set, jell,

congeal, coagulate, clot, cake, crystallize.
F3 soften, liquefy, dissolve.

solitary *adjective* sole, single, lone, alone, lonely, lonesome, friendless, unsociable, reclusive, withdrawn, retired, sequestered, cloistered, secluded, separate, isolated, remote, out-of-the-way, inaccessible, unfrequented, unvisited, untrodden.
F3 accompanied, gregarious, busy.

solitude *noun* aloneness, loneliness, reclusiveness, retirement, privacy, seclusion, isolation, remoteness.
F3 companionship.

solution *noun* **1** *the solution to the problem*: answer, result, explanation, resolution, key, remedy. **2** *an alkaline solution*: mixture, blend, compound, suspension, emulsion, liquid.

solve *verb* work out, figure out, puzzle out, decipher, crack, disentangle, unravel, answer, resolve, settle, clear up, clarify, explain, interpret.

sombre *adjective* dark, funereal, drab, dull, dim, obscure, shady, shadowy, gloomy, dismal, melancholy, mournful, sad, joyless, sober, serious, grave.
F3 bright, cheerful, happy.

sometimes *adverb* occasionally, now and again, now and then, once in a while, from time to time.
F3 always, never.

song *noun* tune, melody, ballad, chant, refrain, chorus, number, ditty.

Types of song include:
air, anthem, aria, ballad, barcarole, blues, calypso, cantata, canticle, canzone, carol, chanson, chant, chorus, dirge, ditty, elegy, folk-song, hymn, jingle, lay, love-song, lied, lullaby, madrigal, nursery rhyme, ode, plainsong, pop song, psalm, rap, recitative, requiem, roundelay, serenade, shanty, spiritual, threnody, wassail, yodel. *See also* **poem**.

---

soon *adverb* shortly, presently, in a minute, before long, in the near future.

soothe *verb* alleviate, relieve, ease, salve, comfort, allay, calm, compose, tranquillize, settle, still, quiet, hush, lull, pacify, appease, mollify, assuage (*fml*), mitigate, soften.
F3 aggravate, irritate, annoy, vex.

sophisticated *adjective* **1** *a sophisticated lifestyle/appearance*: urbane, cosmopolitan, worldly, worldly-wise, cultured, cultivated, refined, polished. **2** *sophisticated technology*: advanced, highly-developed, complicated, complex, intricate, elaborate, delicate, subtle.
F3 1 unsophisticated, naive. **2** primitive, simple.

soppy *adjective* sentimental, lovey-dovey (*infml*), weepy (*infml*), sloppy, slushy, mushy, corny (*infml*), mawkish, cloying, soft (*infml*), silly, daft (*infml*).

sordid *adjective* dirty, filthy, unclean, foul, vile, squalid, sleazy, seamy, seedy, disreputable, shabby, tawdry, corrupt, degraded, degenerate, debauched, low, base, despicable, shameful, wretched, mean, miserly, niggardly, grasping, mercenary, selfish, self-seeking.
F3 pure, honourable, upright.

sore *adjective* **1** *a sore head*: painful, hurting, aching, smarting, stinging, tender, sensitive, inflamed, red, raw. **2** *sore about his insulting comments*: annoyed, irritated, vexed, angry, upset, hurt, wounded, afflicted, aggrieved, resentful.
F3 2 pleased, happy.
▪ *noun* wound, lesion, swelling, inflammation, boil, abscess, ulcer.

sorrow *noun* sadness, unhappiness, grief, mourning, misery, woe, distress, affliction, anguish, heartache, heartbreak, misfortune, hardship, trouble, worry, trial, tribulation, regret, remorse.
F3 happiness, joy.

sorry *adjective* **1** *said he was sorry for what he'd done*: apologetic, regretful, remorseful, contrite, penitent, repentant, conscience-stricken, guilt-ridden, shamefaced. **2** *in a sorry state*: pathetic, pitiful, poor, wretched, miserable, sad, unhappy, dismal. **3** *sorry to hear the sad news*: sympathetic, compassionate, understanding, pitying, concerned, moved.
F3 1 impenitent, unashamed. **2** happy, cheerful. **3** uncaring.

sort *noun* kind, type, genre, ilk, family, race, breed, species, genus, variety, order, class, category, group, denomination (*fml*), style, make, brand, stamp, quality, nature, character, description.
▪ *verb* class, group, categorize, distribute, divide, separate, segregate, sift, screen, grade, rank, order, classify, catalogue, arrange, organize, systematize.

soul *noun* **1** *touched his soul*: spirit, psyche, mind, reason, intellect, character, inner being, essence, life, vital force. **2** *ship carrying two hundred souls*: individual, person, man, creature.

sound[1] *noun* **1** *the sound of hammering*: noise, din, report, resonance, reverberation, tone, timbre. **2** *by the sound of it, he isn't very optimistic*: tenor, description.
▪ *verb* ring, toll, chime, peal, resound, resonate, reverberate, echo.

sound[2] *adjective* **1** *in sound condition*: fit, well, healthy, vigorous, robust, sturdy, firm, solid, whole, complete, intact, perfect, unbroken, undamaged, unimpaired, unhurt, uninjured. **2** *a sound argument*: valid, well-founded, reasonable, rational, logical, orthodox, right, true, proven, reliable, trustworthy, secure, substantial, thorough, good.

F3 **1** unfit, ill, shaky. **2** unsound, unreliable, poor.

sour *adjective* tart, sharp, acid, pungent, vinegary, bitter, rancid.
F3 sweet, sugary.

source *noun* origin, derivation, beginning, start, commencement, cause, root, rise, spring, fountainhead, wellhead, supply, mine, originator, authority, informant.

souvenir *noun* memento, reminder, remembrance, keepsake, relic, token.

sovereign *noun* ruler, monarch, king, queen, emperor, empress, potentate, chief.
▪ *adjective* ruling, royal, imperial, absolute, unlimited, supreme, paramount, predominant, principal, chief, dominant, independent, autonomous.

sow *verb* plant, seed, scatter, strew, spread, disseminate, lodge, implant.

space *noun* **1** *space to grow/move*: room, place, seat, accommodation, capacity, volume, extent, expansion, scope, range, play, elbow-room, leeway, margin. **2** *an empty space*: blank, omission, gap, opening, lacuna, interval, intermission, chasm.

spacious *adjective* roomy, capacious, ample, big, large, sizable, broad, wide, huge, vast, extensive, open, uncrowded.
F3 small, narrow, cramped, confined.

span *noun* spread, stretch, reach, range, scope, compass, extent, length, distance, duration, term, period, spell.
▪ *verb* arch, vault, bridge, link, cross, traverse, extend, cover.

spare *adjective* reserve, emergency, extra, additional, leftover, remaining, unused, over, surplus, superfluous, supernumerary, unwanted, free, unoccupied.
F3 necessary, vital, used.
▪ *verb* **1** *no one was spared in the attack*: pardon, let off, reprieve, release, free. **2** *can spare £5*: grant, allow, afford, part with.

sparing *adjective* economical, thrifty, careful, prudent, frugal, meagre, miserly.
F3 unsparing, liberal, lavish.

spark *noun* flash, flare, gleam, glint, flicker, hint, trace, vestige, scrap, atom, jot.
▪ *verb* kindle, set off, trigger, start, cause, occasion, prompt, provoke, stimulate, stir, excite, inspire.

sparkle *verb* **1** *diamonds sparkled*: twinkle, glitter, scintillate, flash, gleam, glint, glisten, shimmer, coruscate, shine, beam. **2** *champagne sparkles*: effervesce, fizz, bubble.
▪ *noun* twinkle, glitter, flash, gleam, glint, flicker, spark, radiance, brilliance, dazzle, spirit, vitality, life, animation.

sparse *adjective* scarce, scanty, meagre, scattered, infrequent, sporadic.
F3 plentiful, thick, dense.

spasm *noun* burst, eruption, outburst, frenzy, fit, convulsion, seizure, attack, contraction, jerk, twitch, tic.

spasmodic *adjective* sporadic, occasional, intermittent, erratic, irregular, fitful, jerky.
F3 continuous, uninterrupted.

spate *noun* flood, deluge, torrent, rush, outpouring, flow.

speak *verb* talk, converse, say, state, declare, express, utter, voice, articulate, enunciate, pronounce, tell, communicate, address, lecture, harangue, hold forth, declaim, argue, discuss.

speaker *noun* lecturer, orator, spokesperson, spokesman, spokeswoman.

special *adjective* **1** *a special occasion*: important, significant, momentous, major, noteworthy, distinguished, memorable, remarkable, extraordinary, exceptional. **2** *her own special way of doing things*: different, distinctive, characteristic, peculiar, singular, individual, unique, exclusive, select, choice, particular, specific, unusual, precise, detailed.
F3 **1** normal, ordinary, usual. **2** general, common.

speciality *noun* forte, talent, strength, field, specialty, pièce de résistance.

specific *adjective* precise, exact, fixed, limited, particular, special, definite, unequivocal, clear-cut, explicit, express, unambiguous.
F3 vague, approximate.

specification *noun* requirement, condition, qualification, description, listing, item, particular, detail.

specify *verb* stipulate, spell out, define, particularize, detail, itemize, enumerate, list, mention, cite, name, designate, indicate, describe, delineate.

specimen *noun* sample, example, instance, illustration, model, pattern, paradigm, exemplar, representative, copy, exhibit.

spectacle *noun* show, performance, display, exhibition, parade, pageant, extravaganza, scene, sight, curiosity, wonder, marvel, phenomenon.

spectacular *adjective* grand, splendid, magnificent, sensational, impressive, striking, stunning, staggering, amazing, remarkable, dramatic, daring, breathtaking, dazzling, eye-catching, colourful.
F3 unimpressive, ordinary.

spectator *noun* watcher, viewer, onlooker, looker-on, bystander, passer-by, witness, eye-witness, observer.
F3 player, participant.

speculate *verb* wonder, contemplate, meditate, muse, reflect, consider, deliberate, theorize, suppose, guess, conjecture, surmise, gamble, risk, hazard, venture.

speech *noun* **1** *slurred speech/*

typical speech of a countryman: diction, articulation, enunciation, elocution, delivery, utterance, voice, language, tongue, parlance, dialect, jargon. **2** *make a speech*: oration (*fml*), address, discourse, talk, lecture, harangue, spiel (*infml*), conversation, dialogue, monologue, soliloquy.

speechless *adjective* dumbfounded, thunderstruck, amazed, aghast, tongue-tied, inarticulate, mute, dumb, silent, mum.
talkative.

speed *noun* velocity, rate, pace, tempo, quickness, swiftness, rapidity, celerity, alacrity, haste, hurry, dispatch, rush, acceleration.
slowness, delay.
▪ *verb* race, tear, belt (*infml*), zoom, career, bowl along, sprint, gallop, hurry, rush, hasten, accelerate, quicken, put one's foot down (*infml*), step on it (*infml*).
slow, delay.

spell[1] *noun* period, time, bout, session, term, season, interval, stretch, patch, turn, stint.

spell[2] *noun* charm, incantation, magic, sorcery, witchery, bewitchment, enchantment, fascination, glamour.

spellbound *adjective* transfixed, hypnotized, mesmerized, fascinated, enthralled, gripped, entranced, captivated, bewitched, enchanted, charmed.

spend *verb* **1** *spend money*: disburse (*fml*), pay out, fork out (*infml*), shell out (*infml*), invest, lay out, splash out (*infml*), waste, squander, fritter, expend, consume, use up, exhaust. **2** *spend time/the day*: pass, fill, occupy, use, employ, apply, devote.
1 save, hoard.

sphere *noun* **1** *a golden sphere*: ball, globe, orb. **2** *not within its sphere of influence*: domain, realm, province, department, territory, field, range, scope, compass, rank, function, capacity.

spherical *adjective* round, rotund, ball-shaped, globe-shaped.

spicy *adjective* piquant, hot, pungent, tangy, seasoned, aromatic, fragrant.
bland, insipid.

spike *noun* point, prong, tine, spine, barb, nail, stake.

spill *verb* overturn, upset, slop, overflow, disgorge, pour, tip, discharge, shed, scatter.

spin *noun* **1** *a spin of the wheel*: turn, revolution, twist, gyration, twirl, pirouette, whirl, swirl. **2** *go for a spin*: drive, ride, run.
▪ *verb* turn, revolve, rotate, twist, gyrate, twirl, pirouette, wheel, whirl, swirl, reel.

spine *noun* **1** *curvature of the spine*: backbone, spinal column, vertebral column, vertebrae. **2** *a porcupine's spines*: horn, barb, prickle, bristle, quill.

spineless *adjective* weak, feeble, irresolute, ineffective, cowardly, faint-hearted, lily-livered, yellow

(*infml*), soft (*infml*), wet, submissive, weak-kneed.
F3 strong, brave.

spiral *adjective* winding, coiled, corkscrew, helical, whorled, scrolled, circular.
▪ *noun* coil, helix, corkscrew, screw, whorl, convolution.

spirit *noun* **1** *her troubled spirit*: soul, psyche, mind, breath, life. **2** *haunted by spirits*: ghost, spectre, phantom, apparition, angel, demon, fairy, sprite. **3** *have a lot of spirit*: liveliness, vivacity, animation, sparkle, vigour, energy, zest, fire, ardour, motivation, enthusiasm, zeal, enterprise, resolution, willpower, courage, backbone, mettle. **4** *the spirit of the law*: meaning, sense, substance, essence, gist, tenor, character, quality. **5** *in good spirits*: mood, humour, temper, disposition, temperament, feeling, morale, attitude, outlook.

spirited *adjective* lively, vivacious, animated, sparkling, high-spirited, vigorous, energetic, active, ardent, zealous, bold, courageous, mettlesome, plucky, feisty (*infml*).
F3 spiritless, lethargic, cowardly.

spiritual *adjective* unworldly, incorporeal (*fml*), immaterial, otherworldly, heavenly, divine, holy, sacred, religious, ecclesiastical.
F3 physical, material.

spit *verb* expectorate, eject, discharge, splutter, hiss.

spite *noun* spitefulness, malice, venom, gall, bitterness, rancour, animosity, ill feeling, grudge, malevolence, malignity, ill nature, hate, hatred.
F3 goodwill, compassion, affection.

spiteful *adjective* malicious, venomous, catty, snide, barbed, cruel, vindictive, vengeful, malevolent, malignant, ill-natured, ill-disposed, nasty.
F3 charitable, affectionate.

splash *verb* bathe, wallow, paddle, wade, dabble, plunge, wet, wash, shower, spray, squirt, sprinkle, spatter, splatter, splodge (*infml*), spread, daub, plaster, slop, slosh, plop, surge, break, dash, strike, buffet.
▪ *noun* spot, patch, splatter, splodge, burst, touch, dash.

splendid *adjective* brilliant, dazzling, glittering, lustrous, bright, radiant, glowing, glorious, magnificent, gorgeous, resplendent, sumptuous, luxurious, lavish, rich, fine, grand, stately, imposing, impressive, great, outstanding, remarkable, exceptional, sublime, supreme, superb, excellent, first-class, wonderful, marvellous, admirable.
F3 drab, ordinary, run-of-the-mill.

splendour *noun* brightness, radiance, brilliance, dazzle, lustre, glory, resplendence, magnificence, richness, grandeur, majesty, solemnity, pomp,

ceremony, display, show, spectacle.
F3 drabness, squalor.

splinter *noun* sliver, shiver, chip, shard, fragment, flake, shaving, paring.
▪ *verb* split, fracture, smash, shatter, shiver, fragment, disintegrate.

split *noun* **1** *a split in the rock*: division, separation, partition, break, breach, gap, cleft, crevice, crack, fissure, rupture, tear, rent, rip, rift, slit, slash. **2** *a split in the party/church*: schism, disunion, dissension, discord, difference, divergence, break-up.
▪ *adjective* divided, cleft, cloven, bisected, dual, twofold, broken, fractured, cracked, ruptured.
▪ *verb* divide, separate, partition, part, disunite, disband, open, gape, fork, diverge, break, splinter, shiver, snap, crack, burst, rupture, tear, rend, rip, slit, slash, cleave, halve, slice up, share, distribute, parcel out.

spoil *verb* **1** *spoiled his good looks*: mar, upset, wreck, ruin, destroy, damage, impair, harm, hurt, injure, deface, disfigure, blemish. **2** *spoil the child*: indulge, pamper, cosset, coddle, mollycoddle, baby, spoon-feed. **3** *food will spoil in this heat*: deteriorate, go bad, go off, sour, turn, curdle, decay, decompose.

spongy *adjective* soft, cushioned, yielding, elastic, springy, porous, absorbent, light.

sponsor *noun* patron, backer, angel (*infml*), promoter, underwriter, guarantor, surety.
▪ *verb* finance, fund, bankroll, subsidize, patronize, back, promote, underwrite, guarantee.

spontaneous *adjective* natural, unforced, untaught, instinctive, impulsive, unpremeditated, free, willing, unhesitating, voluntary, unprompted, impromptu, extempore.
F3 forced, studied, planned, deliberate.

sport *noun* exercise, activity, pastime, amusement, entertainment, diversion, recreation, play.

Sports include:
badminton, fives, lacrosse, ping-pong (*infml*), squash, table-tennis, tennis; American football, Australian rules football, baseball, basketball, billiards, boules, bowls, cricket, croquet, football, Gaelic football, golf, handball, hockey, hurling, netball, pétanque, pitch and putt, polo, pool, putting, rounders, rugby, shinty, snooker, soccer, tenpin bowling, volleyball; athletics, cross-country, hurdling, running; angling, canoeing, diving, fishing, rowing, sailing, skin-diving, surfing, swimming, synchronized swimming, water polo, water-skiing, windsurfing, yachting; bobsleigh, curling, ice-hockey, ice-skating, skiing, snowboarding, speed skating, tobogganing, luge; aerobics, aquarobics, fencing, gymnastics,

jogging, keep-fit, roller-skating, trampolining; archery, darts, quoits; boxing, judo, jujitsu, karate, tae kwon do, weightlifting, wrestling; climbing, mountaineering, orienteering, potholing, rock-climbing, walking; cycle racing, drag-racing, go-karting, greyhound racing, motor racing, speedway racing, stock-car racing; clay-pigeon shooting, shooting; horse-racing, hunting, show-jumping; gliding, paragliding, sky-diving.

---

sporting *adjective* sportsmanlike, gentlemanly, decent, considerate, fair.
F3 unsporting, ungentlemanly, unfair.

spot *noun* **1** *spots of blood/colour*: dot, speckle, fleck, mark, speck, blotch, blot, smudge, daub, splash, stain, discoloration. **2** *a spot on her chin*: pimple, blemish, flaw, zit (*slang*). **3** *find a secluded spot*: place, point, position, situation, location, site, scene, locality.
▪ *verb* see, notice, observe, detect, discern, identify, recognize.

spotless *adjective* immaculate, clean, gleaming, spick and span, unmarked, unstained, unblemished, unsullied, pure, chaste, virgin, untouched, innocent, blameless, faultless, irreproachable.
F3 dirty, impure.

spotted *adjective* dotted, speckled, flecked, mottled, dappled, pied.

spotty *adjective* pimply, pimpled, blotchy, spotted.

spout *verb* jet, spurt, squirt, spray, shoot, gush, stream, surge, erupt, emit, discharge.

sprawl *verb* spread, straggle, trail, ramble, flop, slump, slouch, loll, lounge, recline, repose.

spray *verb* shower, spatter, sprinkle, scatter, diffuse, wet, drench.
▪ *noun* **1** *a fine salt spray*: moisture, drizzle, mist, foam, froth. **2** *paint sold in sprays*: aerosol, atomizer, sprinkler.

spread *verb* **1** *spreading outwards*: stretch, extend, sprawl, broaden, widen, dilate, expand, swell, mushroom, proliferate, escalate. **2** *spreading its wings/sails*: open, unroll, unfurl, unfold, fan out, cover, lay out, arrange. **3** *spreading panic/disease/gossip*: scatter, strew, diffuse, radiate, disseminate, broadcast, transmit, communicate, promulgate, propagate, publicize, advertise, publish, circulate, distribute.
F3 **1** contract. **2** fold, furl. **3** suppress.
▪ *noun* **1** *the spread of its wings*: stretch, reach, span, extent, expanse, sweep, compass. **2** *the spread of disease*: advance, development, expansion, increase, proliferation, escalation, diffusion, dissemination, dispersion.

sprightly *adjective* agile, nimble, spry, active, energetic, lively,

spirited, vivacious, hearty, brisk, jaunty, cheerful, blithe, airy.
F3 doddering, inactive, lifeless.
spring[1] *verb* **1** *spring back/spring to his feet*: jump, leap, vault, bound, hop, bounce, rebound, recoil. **2** *springing from the earth*: originate, derive, come, stem, arise, start, proceed, issue, emerge, emanate, appear, sprout, grow, develop.
▪ *noun* **1** *a sudden spring into the air*: jump, leap, vault, bound. **2** *need a bed with more spring in it/ had a spring in his step*: springiness, resilience, give, flexibility, elasticity, bounce, buoyancy.
spring[2] *noun* source, origin, beginning, cause, root, fountainhead, wellhead, wellspring, well, geyser, spa.
springy *adjective* bouncy, resilient, flexible, elastic, stretchy, rubbery, spongy, buoyant.
F3 hard, stiff.
sprinkle *verb* shower, spray, spatter, scatter, strew, dot, pepper, dust, powder.
sprint *verb* run, race, dash, tear, belt (*infml*), dart, shoot.
sprout *verb* shoot, bud, germinate, grow, develop, come up, spring up.
spruce *adjective* smart, elegant, neat, trim, dapper, well-dressed, well-turned-out, well-groomed, sleek.
F3 scruffy, untidy.
spur *verb* goad, prod, poke, prick, stimulate, prompt, incite, drive, propel, impel, urge, encourage, motivate.
F3 curb, discourage.
▪ *noun* incentive, encouragement, inducement, motive, stimulus, incitement, impetus, fillip.
F3 curb, disincentive.
spurt *verb* gush, squirt, jet, shoot, burst, erupt, surge.
spy *noun* secret agent, undercover agent, double agent, mole (*infml*), fifth columnist, scout, snooper.
▪ *verb* spot, glimpse, notice, observe, discover.
squabble *verb* bicker, wrangle, quarrel, row, argue, dispute, clash, brawl, scrap, fight.
squalid *adjective* dirty, filthy, unclean, foul, disgusting, repulsive, sordid, seedy, dingy, untidy, slovenly, unkempt, broken-down, run-down, neglected, uncared-for, low, mean, nasty.
F3 clean, pleasant, attractive.
squander *verb* waste, misspend, misuse, lavish, blow (*infml*), fritter away, throw away, dissipate, scatter, spend, expend, consume.
square *verb* settle, reconcile, tally, agree, accord, harmonize, correspond, match, balance, straighten, level, align, adjust, regulate, adapt, tailor, fit, suit.
▪ *adjective* quadrilateral, rectangular, right-angled, perpendicular, straight, true, even, level.
squash *verb* **1** *squashed the tomatoes*: crush, flatten, press,

squeeze, compress, crowd, trample, stamp, pound, pulp, smash, distort. **2** *squashing any protest/his ego*: suppress, silence, quell, quash, annihilate, put down, snub, humiliate.

F3 **1** stretch, expand.

squat *verb* crouch, stoop, bend, sit.

▪ *adjective* short, stocky, thickset, dumpy, chunky, stubby.

F3 slim, lanky.

squeak *verb, noun* squeal, whine, creak, peep, cheep.

squeal *verb, noun* cry, shout, yell, yelp, wail, scream, screech, shriek, squawk.

squeamish *adjective* queasy, nauseated, sick, delicate, fastidious, particular, prudish.

squeeze *verb* **1** *squeeze a lemon/ squeezing her tight*: press, squash, crush, pinch, nip, compress, grip, clasp, clutch, hug, embrace, enfold, cuddle. **2** *squeeze into a corner*: cram, stuff, pack, crowd, wedge, jam, force, ram, push, thrust, shove, jostle.

▪ *noun* press, squash, crush, crowd, congestion, jam.

squirt *verb* spray, spurt, jet, shoot, spout, gush, discharge, emit, eject, expel.

stab *verb* pierce, puncture, cut, wound, injure, gore, knife, spear, stick, jab, thrust.

▪ *noun* **1** *felt a stab of pain*: ache, pang, twinge, prick, puncture, cut, incision, gash, wound, jab. **2** (*infml*) *have a stab at it*: try, attempt, endeavour, bash (*infml*).

stable *adjective* steady, firm, secure, fast, sound, sure, constant, steadfast, reliable, established, well-founded, deep-rooted, strong, sturdy, durable, lasting, enduring, abiding, permanent, unchangeable, unalterable, invariable, immutable, fixed, static, balanced.

F3 unstable, wobbly, shaky, weak.

stack *noun* heap, pile, mound, mass, load, accumulation, hoard, stockpile.

▪ *verb* heap, pile, load, amass, accumulate, assemble, gather, save, hoard, stockpile.

staff *noun* personnel, workforce, employees, workers, crew, team, teachers, officers.

stage *noun* point, juncture, step, phase, period, division, lap, leg, length, level, floor.

▪ *verb* mount, put on, present, produce, give, do, perform, arrange, organize, stage-manage, orchestrate, engineer.

stagger *verb* **1** *staggering to its feet*: lurch, totter, teeter, wobble, sway, rock, reel, falter, hesitate, waver. **2** *the price staggered me*: surprise, amaze, astound, astonish, stun, stupefy, dumbfound, flabbergast (*infml*), shake, shock, confound, overwhelm.

stagnant *adjective* still, motionless, standing, brackish, stale, sluggish, torpid, lethargic.

F3 fresh, moving.

stagnate *verb* vegetate, idle, languish, decline, deteriorate, degenerate, decay, rot, rust.

staid *adjective* sedate, calm, composed, sober, demure, solemn, serious, grave, quiet, steady.
F3 jaunty, debonair, frivolous, adventurous.

stain *verb* **1** *stained the tablecloth/his reputation*: mark, spot, blemish, blot, smudge, discolour, dirty, soil, taint, contaminate, sully (*fml*), tarnish, blacken, disgrace. **2** *stained her hair/lips/fingernails red*: dye, tint, tinge, colour, paint, varnish.
▪ *noun* mark, spot, blemish, blot, smudge, discoloration, smear, slur, disgrace, shame, dishonour.

stake *noun* **1** *a major stake in the football club*: bet, wager, pledge, interest, concern, involvement, share, investment, claim. **2** *a stake supporting a sapling*: cane, post, pole.
▪ *verb* gamble, bet, wager, pledge, risk, chance, hazard, venture.

stale *adjective* **1** *stale bread*: dry, hard, old, musty, fusty, flat, insipid, tasteless. **2** *the same stale old phrases*: overused, hackneyed, clichéd, stereotyped, jaded, worn-out, unoriginal, trite, banal, commonplace.
F3 **1** crisp. **2** new.

stalemate *noun* draw, tie, deadlock, impasse, standstill, halt.
F3 progress.

stalk[1] *verb* track, trail, hunt, follow, pursue, shadow, tail, haunt.

stalk[2] *noun* stem, twig, branch, trunk.

stall *verb* play for time, delay, hedge, equivocate, obstruct, stonewall, temporize.

stamina *noun* energy, vigour, strength, power, force, grit, resilience, resistance, endurance, indefatigability, staying power.
F3 weakness.

stammer *verb* stutter, stumble, falter, hesitate, splutter.

stamp *verb* **1** *stamp on someone's foot*: trample, crush, beat, pound. **2** *stamping his passport*: imprint, impress, print, inscribe, engrave, emboss, mark. **3** *stamping them as terrorists*: brand, label, categorize, identify, characterize.
▪ *noun* print, imprint, impression, seal, signature, authorization, mark, hallmark, attestation, brand, cast, mould, cut, form, fashion, sort, kind, type, breed, character, description.

stampede *noun* charge, rush, dash, sprint, flight, rout.
▪ *verb* charge, rush, dash, tear, run, sprint, gallop, shoot, fly, flee, scatter.

stance *noun* posture, deportment, carriage, bearing, position, standpoint, angle, viewpoint, point of view, attitude.

stand *verb* **1** *stand it in the corner*: put, place, set, erect, up-end, position, station. **2** *I can't stand it*: bear, tolerate, abide, endure, suffer, experience, undergo, withstand, weather. **3** *stand for the national anthem*: rise, get up, stand up.

▪ *noun* base, pedestal, support, frame, rack, table, stage, platform, place, stall, booth.

standard *noun* **1** *not up to their usual standard*: norm, average, type, model, pattern, example, sample, guideline, benchmark, touchstone, yardstick, rule, measure, gauge, level, criterion, requirement, specification, grade, quality. **2** *the royal standard*: flag, ensign, pennant, pennon, colours, banner.

▪ *adjective* normal, average, typical, stock, classic, basic, staple, usual, customary, popular, prevailing, regular, approved, accepted, recognized, official, orthodox, set, established, definitive.

F3 abnormal, unusual, irregular.

standardize *verb* normalize, equalize, homogenize, stereotype, mass-produce.

F3 differentiate.

standards *noun* principles, ideals, morals, ethics.

standpoint *noun* position, station, vantage point, stance, viewpoint, angle, point of view.

standstill *noun* stop, halt, pause, lull, rest, stoppage, jam, log-jam, hold-up, impasse, deadlock, stalemate.

F3 advance, progress.

staple *adjective* basic, fundamental, primary, key, main, chief, major, principal, essential, necessary, standard.

F3 minor.

star *noun* celebrity, personage, luminary, idol, lead, leading man, leading lady, superstar.

stare *verb* gaze, look, watch, gape, gawp, gawk, goggle, glare.

stark *adjective* bare, barren, bleak, bald, plain, simple, austere, harsh, severe, grim, dreary, gloomy, depressing.

start *verb* **1** *start a business/walking/the singing*: begin, commence, originate, initiate, introduce, pioneer, create, found, establish, set up, institute, inaugurate, launch, open, kick off (*infml*), instigate, activate, trigger, set off, set out, leave, depart, appear, arise, issue. **2** *started at the sudden noise*: jump, jerk, twitch, flinch, recoil.

F3 **1** stop, finish, end.

▪ *noun* **1** *the start of business*: beginning, commencement, outset, inception, dawn, birth, break, outburst, onset, origin, initiation, introduction, foundation, inauguration, launch, opening, kick-off (*infml*). **2** *gave a start*: jump, jerk, twitch, spasm, convulsion.

F3 **1** stop, finish, end.

startle *verb* surprise, amaze, astonish, astound, shock, scare, frighten, alarm, agitate, upset, disturb.

F3 calm.

starving *adjective* hungry,

underfed, undernourished, ravenous, famished.

state *verb* say, declare, announce, report, communicate, assert, aver, affirm, specify, present, express, put, formulate, articulate, voice.
▪ *noun* **1** *his state of health*: condition, shape, situation, position, circumstances, case. **2** *co-operation between states*: nation, country, land, territory, kingdom, republic, government. **3** *lie in state*: pomp, ceremony, dignity, majesty, grandeur, glory, splendour.
▪ *adjective* national, governmental, public, official, formal, ceremonial, pompous, stately.

stately *adjective* grand, imposing, impressive, elegant, majestic, regal, royal, imperial, noble, august, lofty, pompous, dignified, measured, deliberate, solemn, ceremonious.
F3 informal, unimpressive.

statement *noun* account, report, bulletin, communiqué, announcement, declaration, proclamation, communication, utterance, testimony.

static *adjective* stationary, motionless, immobile, unmoving, still, inert, resting, fixed, constant, changeless, unvarying, stable.
F3 dynamic, mobile, varying.

station *noun* place, location, position, post, headquarters, base, depot.
▪ *verb* locate, set, establish, install, garrison, post, send, appoint, assign.

stationary *adjective* motionless, immobile, unmoving, still, static, inert, standing, resting, parked, moored, fixed.
F3 mobile, moving, active.

statue *noun* figure, head, bust, effigy, idol, statuette, carving, bronze.

status *noun* rank, grade, degree, level, class, station, standing, position, state, condition, prestige, eminence, distinction, importance, consequence, weight.
F3 unimportance, insignificance.

staunch *adjective* loyal, faithful, hearty, strong, stout, firm, sound, sure, true, trusty, reliable, dependable, steadfast.
F3 unfaithful, weak, unreliable.

stay *verb* **1** *staying the same*: continue, endure, abide (*fml*), remain, linger, persist. **2** *stay in London*: reside, dwell, live, settle, sojourn (*fml*).
F3 1 go, leave.
▪ *noun* visit, holiday, stopover, sojourn (*fml*).

steady *adjective* stable, balanced, poised, fixed, immovable, firm, settled, still, calm, imperturbable, equable, even, uniform, consistent, unvarying, unchanging, constant, persistent, unremitting, incessant, uninterrupted, unbroken, regular, rhythmic, steadfast, unwavering.
F3 unsteady, unstable, variable, wavering.

■ *verb* balance, stabilize, fix, secure, brace, support.

steal *verb* **1** *steal a car/his ideas*: thieve, pilfer, filch, pinch (*infml*), nick (*infml*), take, appropriate, snatch, swipe, shoplift, poach, embezzle, lift, plagiarize. **2** *steal out of the room*: creep, tiptoe, slip, slink, sneak.

F3 **1** return, give back.

stealthy *adjective* surreptitious, clandestine, covert, secret, unobtrusive, secretive, quiet, furtive, sly, cunning, sneaky, underhand.

F3 open.

steam *noun* vapour, mist, haze, condensation, moisture, dampness.

steep *adjective* **1** *a steep slope*: sheer, precipitous, headlong, abrupt, sudden, sharp. **2** (*infml*) *prices are a little too steep for me*: excessive, extreme, stiff, unreasonable, high, exorbitant, extortionate, overpriced.

F3 **1** gentle, gradual. **2** moderate, low.

steer *verb* pilot, guide, direct, control, govern, conduct.

stem[1] *noun* stalk, shoot, stock, branch, trunk.

stem[2] *verb* stop, halt, arrest, stanch, staunch, block, dam, check, curb, restrain, contain, resist, oppose.

step *noun* **1** *take a step back/heard his step on the stairs*: pace, stride, footstep, tread, footprint, print, trace, track. **2** *what's the next step?*: move, act, action, deed, measure, procedure, process, proceeding, progression, movement, stage, phase, degree. **3** *the first step on the ladder*: rung, stair, level, rank, point.

■ *verb* pace, stride, tread, stamp, walk, move.

stereotype *verb* categorize, pigeonhole, typecast, standardize, formalize, conventionalize.

F3 differentiate.

sterile *adjective* **1** *operate in sterile conditions*: germ-free, aseptic, sterilized, disinfected, antiseptic, uncontaminated. **2** *a sterile plant/ a sterile argument*: infertile, barren, arid, bare, unproductive, fruitless, pointless, useless, abortive.

F3 **1** septic, contaminated. **2** fertile, fruitful.

sterilize *verb* disinfect, fumigate, purify, clean, cleanse.

F3 contaminate, infect.

stern *adjective* strict, severe, authoritarian, rigid, inflexible, unyielding, hard, tough, rigorous, stringent, harsh, cruel, unsparing, relentless, unrelenting, grim, forbidding, stark, austere.

F3 kind, gentle, mild, lenient.

stew *verb* boil, simmer, braise, casserole.

stick[1] *verb* **1** *sticking his head through the window*: thrust, poke, stab, jab, pierce, penetrate, puncture, spear, transfix. **2** *sticking the two edges together*: glue, gum, paste, cement, bond, fuse, weld, solder, adhere, cling, hold. **3** *mud sticking to his clothes*: attach, affix, fasten, secure, fix, pin, join, bind.

stick[2] *noun* branch, twig, wand, baton, staff, sceptre, cane, birch, rod, pole, stake.

sticky *adjective* **1** *a sticky substance*: adhesive, gummed, tacky, gluey, gummy, viscous, glutinous, gooey (*infml*). **2** (*infml*) *a sticky situation*: difficult, tricky, thorny, unpleasant, awkward, embarrassing, delicate.

F∃ 1 dry. **2** easy.

stiff *adjective* **1** *stiff joints*: rigid, inflexible, unbending, unyielding, hard, solid, hardened, solidified, firm, tight, taut, tense. **2** *his manner was very stiff*: formal, ceremonious, pompous, standoffish, cold, prim, priggish, austere, strict, severe, harsh. **3** *a stiff test*: difficult, hard, tough, arduous, laborious, awkward, exacting, rigorous.

F∃ 1 flexible. **2** informal. **3** easy.

stiffen *verb* harden, solidify, tighten, tense, brace, reinforce, starch, thicken, congeal, coagulate, jell, set.

stifle *verb* smother, suffocate, asphyxiate, strangle, choke, extinguish, muffle, dampen, deaden, silence, hush, suppress, quell, check, curb, restrain, repress.

F∃ encourage.

stigma *noun* brand, mark, stain, blot, spot, blemish, disgrace, shame, dishonour.

F∃ credit, honour.

still *adjective* stationary, motionless, lifeless, stagnant, smooth, undisturbed, unruffled, calm, tranquil, serene, restful, peaceful, hushed, quiet, silent, noiseless.

F∃ active, disturbed, agitated, noisy.

▪ *verb* calm, soothe, allay, tranquillize, subdue, restrain, hush, quieten, silence, pacify, settle, smooth.

F∃ agitate, stir up.

▪ *adverb* yet, even so, nevertheless, nonetheless, notwithstanding, however.

stilted *adjective* artificial, unnatural, stiff, wooden, forced, constrained.

F∃ fluent, flowing.

stimulate *verb* rouse, arouse, animate, quicken (*fml*), fire, inflame, inspire, motivate, encourage, induce, urge, impel, spur, prompt, goad, provoke, incite, instigate, trigger off.

F∃ discourage, hinder, prevent.

stimulus *noun* incentive, encouragement, inducement, spur, goad, provocation, incitement.

F∃ discouragement.

sting *verb* **1** *bee stung him on the nose*: bite, prick, hurt, injure, wound. **2** *eyes were stinging with the smoke*: smart, tingle, burn, pain.

▪ *noun* bite, nip, prick, smart, tingle.

stingy *adjective* mean, miserly,

niggardly, tight-fisted (*infml*), parsimonious, penny-pinching.
F3 generous, liberal.

stink *verb* smell, reek, pong (*infml*), hum (*infml*).
▪ *noun* smell, odour, stench, pong (*infml*), niff (*infml*).

stint *noun* spell, stretch, period, time, shift, turn, bit, share, quota.

stir *verb* **1** *breeze stirring the leaves*: move, budge, touch, affect, inspire, excite, thrill, disturb, agitate, shake, tremble, quiver, flutter, rustle. **2** *stir the cake mixture*: mix, blend, beat.

stock *noun* **1** *put new stock on the shelves/a good stock of tinned food*: goods, merchandise, wares, commodities, capital, assets, inventory, repertoire, range, variety, assortment, source, supply, fund, reservoir, store, reserve, stockpile, hoard. **2** *of Welsh and Irish stock*: parentage, ancestry, descent, extraction, family, line, lineage, pedigree, race, breed, species, blood.
▪ *adjective* standard, basic, regular, routine, ordinary, run-of-the-mill, usual, customary, traditional, conventional, set, stereotyped, hackneyed, overused, banal, trite.
F3 original, unusual.
▪ *verb* keep, carry, sell, trade in, deal in, handle, supply, provide.

stocky *adjective* sturdy, solid, thickset, chunky, short, squat, dumpy, stubby.
F3 tall, skinny.

stomach *noun* tummy (*infml*), gut, inside(s), belly, abdomen, paunch, pot.
▪ *verb* tolerate, bear, stand, abide, endure, suffer, submit to, take.

stony *adjective* **1** *a stony expression/silence*: blank, expressionless, hard, cold, frigid, icy, indifferent, unfeeling, heartless, callous, merciless, pitiless, inexorable, hostile. **2** *stony beach*: pebbly, shingly, rocky.
F3 **1** warm, soft-hearted, friendly.

stoop *verb* **1** *he stooped to get under the low fence*: hunch, bow, bend, incline, lean, duck, squat, crouch. **2** *even stooped to blackmail*: descend, sink, lower oneself, resort, go so far as, condescend, deign.

stop *verb* **1** *stop shouting/stop the train*: halt, cease, end, finish, conclude, terminate, discontinue, suspend, interrupt, quit, pause, refrain, desist, pack in (*infml*). **2** *stop him entering*: prevent, bar, frustrate, thwart, intercept, hinder, impede, check, restrain. **3** *stop up the hole in the pipe/stop the bleeding*: seal, close, plug, block, obstruct, arrest, stem, stanch.
F3 **1** start, continue.
▪ *noun* **1** *get off at the next stop*: station, terminus, destination. **2** *a short stop*: rest, break, pause, stage. **3** *come to a stop*: halt, standstill, stoppage, cessation, end, finish, conclusion, termination, discontinuation.

F3 3 start, beginning, continuation.

stoppage *noun* stop, halt, standstill, arrest, blockage, obstruction, check, hindrance, interruption, shutdown, closure, strike, walk-out, sit-in.
F3 start, continuation.

stopper *noun* cork, bung, plug.

store *verb* save, keep, put aside, lay by, reserve, stock, lay in, deposit, lay down, lay up, accumulate, hoard, salt away, stockpile, stash (*infml*).
F3 use.
▪ *noun* **1** *a good store of food for the winter*: stock, supply, provision, fund, reserve, mine, reservoir, hoard, cache, stockpile, accumulation, quantity, abundance, plenty, lot. **2** *keep all the boxes in the store*: storeroom, storehouse, warehouse, repository, depository.
F3 1 scarcity.

storey *noun* floor, level, stage, tier, flight, deck.

storm *noun* **1** *winter storms*: tempest, thunderstorm, squall, blizzard, gale, hurricane, whirlwind, tornado, cyclone. **2** *a storm of protest*: outburst, uproar, furore, outcry, row, rumpus, commotion, tumult, disturbance, turmoil, stir, agitation, rage, outbreak, attack, assault.
F3 2 calm.
▪ *verb* charge, rush, attack, assault, assail, roar, thunder, rage, rant, rave, fume.

Kinds of storm include:
blizzard, buran, cloudburst, cyclone, downpour, dust devil, dust storm, electrical storm, gale, haboob, hailstorm, hurricane, ice storm, monsoon, rainstorm, sand storm, snow storm, squall, tempest, thunderstorm, tornado, typhoon, whirlwind.

stormy *adjective* tempestuous, squally, rough, choppy, turbulent, wild, raging, windy, gusty, blustery, foul.
F3 calm.

story *noun* **1** *tell us a story/write a story*: tale, fairy tale, fable, myth, legend, novel, romance, fiction, yarn, anecdote, episode, plot, narrative, history, chronicle, record, account, relation, recital, report, article, feature. **2** *accused her of telling stories*: lie, falsehood, untruth, fib.

Types of story include:
adventure story, anecdote, bedtime story, blockbuster (*infml*), children's story, comedy, black comedy, crime story, detective story, fable, fairy story, fairy tale, fantasy, folk tale, ghost story, historical novel, horror story, legend, love story, mystery, myth, parable, romance, saga, science fiction, sci-fi (*infml*), short story, spine-chiller, spy story, tall story, thriller, western, whodunnit (*infml*), yarn (*infml*). *See also* **literature**.

stout *adjective* **1** *getting rather stout/stout arms*: fat, plump, fleshy, portly, corpulent, overweight, heavy, bulky, big, brawny, beefy, hulking, burly, muscular, athletic. **2** *stout packaging*: strong, tough, durable, thick, sturdy, robust, hardy, vigorous. **3** *a stout defence*: brave, courageous, valiant, plucky, fearless, bold, intrepid, dauntless, resolute, stalwart.

F3 **1** thin, lean, slim. **2** weak. **3** cowardly, timid.

stow *verb* put away, store, load, pack, cram, stuff, stash (*infml*).

F3 unload.

straight *adjective* **1** *a straight line*: level, even, flat, horizontal, upright, vertical, aligned, direct, undeviating, unswerving, true, right. **2** *keep things straight*: tidy, neat, orderly, shipshape, organized. **3** *he's absolutely straight*: honourable, honest, law-abiding, respectable, upright, trustworthy, reliable, straightforward, fair, just. **4** *a straight answer*: frank, candid, blunt, forthright, direct. **5** *straight whisky*: undiluted, neat, unadulterated, unmixed.

F3 **1** bent, crooked. **2** untidy. **3** bent (*infml*), dishonest. **4** evasive. **5** diluted.

▪ *adverb* directly, point-blank, honestly, frankly, candidly.

straighten *verb* unbend, align, tidy, neaten, order, arrange.

F3 bend, twist.

straightforward *adjective* **1** *first part of the exam was quite straightforward*: easy, simple, uncomplicated, clear, elementary. **2** *a very straightforward person*: honest, truthful, sincere, genuine, open, frank, candid, direct, forthright.

F3 **1** complicated. **2** evasive, devious.

strain[1] *verb* **1** *strain a muscle*: pull, wrench, twist, sprain, tear, stretch, extend, tighten, tauten. **2** *strain the gravy*: sieve, sift, screen, separate, filter, purify, drain, wring, squeeze, compress, express. **3** *don't strain yourself*: weaken, tire, tax, overtax, overwork, labour, try, endeavour, struggle, strive, exert, force, drive.

▪ *noun* stress, anxiety, burden, pressure, tension, tautness, pull, sprain, wrench, injury, exertion, effort, struggle, force.

F3 relaxation.

strain[2] *noun* stock, ancestry, descent, extraction, family, lineage, pedigree, blood, variety, type.

strained *adjective* forced, constrained, laboured, false, artificial, unnatural, stiff, tense, unrelaxed, uneasy, uncomfortable, awkward, embarrassed, self-conscious.

F3 natural, relaxed.

strand *noun* fibre, filament, wire, thread, string, piece, length.

stranded *adjective* marooned, high and dry, abandoned, forsaken, in the lurch, helpless, aground, grounded, beached, shipwrecked, wrecked.

strange *adjective* **1** *strange feeling/behaviour*: odd, peculiar, funny (*infml*), curious, queer, weird, bizarre, eccentric, abnormal, irregular, uncommon, unusual, exceptional, remarkable, extraordinary, mystifying, perplexing, unexplained. **2** *visit strange places*: new, novel, untried, unknown, unheard-of, unfamiliar, unacquainted, foreign, alien, exotic.

E3 **1** ordinary, common. **2** well-known, familiar.

stranger *noun* newcomer, visitor, guest, non-member, outsider, foreigner, alien.

E3 local, native.

strangle *verb* throttle, choke, asphyxiate, suffocate, stifle, smother, suppress, gag, repress, inhibit.

strap *noun* thong, tie, band, belt, leash.

strategic *adjective* important, key, critical, decisive, crucial, vital, tactical, planned, calculated, deliberate, politic, diplomatic.

E3 unimportant.

strategy *noun* tactics, planning, policy, approach, procedure, plan, programme, design, scheme.

stray *verb* wander (off), get lost, err, ramble, roam, rove, range, meander, straggle, drift, diverge, deviate, digress.

▪ *adjective* **1** *stray cats and dogs*: lost, abandoned, homeless, wandering, roaming. **2** *hit by a stray bullet*: random, chance, accidental, freak, odd, erratic.

streak *noun* line, stroke, smear, band, stripe, strip, layer, vein, trace, dash, touch, element, strain.

▪ *verb* **1** *streaked with red and white*: fleck, striate, smear, daub. **2** *streaked past us*: speed, tear, hurtle, sprint, gallop, fly, dart, flash, whistle, zoom, whizz, sweep.

stream *noun* **1** *fishing in the stream*: river, creek, brook, beck, burn, rivulet, tributary. **2** *the Gulf Stream*: current, drift. **3** *a steady stream of letters*: flow, run, gush, flood, deluge, cascade, torrent.

▪ *verb* issue, well, surge, run, flow, course, pour, spout, gush, flood, cascade.

streamlined *adjective* aerodynamic, smooth, sleek, graceful, efficient, well-run, smooth-running, rationalized, time-saving, organized, slick.

E3 clumsy, inefficient.

strength *noun* toughness, robustness, sturdiness, lustiness, brawn, muscle, sinew, power, might, force, vigour, energy, stamina, health, fitness, courage, fortitude, spirit, resolution, firmness, effectiveness, potency, concentration, intensity, vehemence.

E3 weakness, feebleness, impotence.

strengthen *verb* reinforce, brace, steel, fortify, buttress, bolster, support, toughen, harden, stiffen, consolidate, substantiate,

corroborate, confirm, encourage, hearten, refresh, restore, invigorate, nourish, increase, heighten, intensify.
F3 weaken, undermine.

strenuous *adjective* **1** *strenuous work*: hard, tough, demanding, gruelling, taxing, laborious, uphill, arduous, tiring, exhausting. **2** *made a strenuous effort*: active, energetic, vigorous, eager, earnest, determined, resolute, spirited, tireless, indefatigable.
F3 1 easy, effortless.

stress *noun* **1** *suffer from stress*: pressure, strain, tension, worry, anxiety, weight, burden, trauma, hassle (*infml*). **2** *put great stress on being polite*: emphasis, accentuation, force, weight, importance, significance.
F3 1 relaxation.
▪ *verb* emphasize, accentuate, highlight, underline, underscore, repeat.
F3 understate, downplay.

stretch *verb* pull, tighten, tauten, strain, tax, extend, lengthen, elongate, expand, spread, unfold, unroll, inflate, swell, reach.
F3 compress.
▪ *noun* **1** *a stretch of water*: expanse, spread, sweep, reach, extent, distance, space, area, tract. **2** *a short stretch in prison*: period, time, term, spell, stint, run.

strict *adjective* **1** *a strict disciplinarian*: stern, authoritarian, no-nonsense, firm, rigid, inflexible, stringent, rigorous, harsh, severe, austere. **2** *strict examination of their methods*: exact, precise, accurate, literal, faithful, true, absolute, utter, total, complete, thoroughgoing, meticulous, scrupulous, particular, religious.
F3 1 easy-going (*infml*), flexible. **2** loose.

strident *adjective* loud, clamorous, vociferous, harsh, raucous, grating, rasping, shrill, screeching, unmusical, discordant, clashing, jarring, jangling.
F3 quiet, soft.

strife *noun* conflict, discord, dissension, controversy, animosity, friction, rivalry, contention, quarrel, row, wrangling, struggle, fighting, combat, battle, warfare.
F3 peace.

strike *noun* **1** *go on strike*: industrial action, work-to-rule, go-slow, stoppage, sit-in, walk-out, mutiny, revolt. **2** *strikes against enemy targets*: hit, blow, stroke, raid, attack.
▪ *verb* **1** *strike because of poor pay*: stop work, down tools, work to rule, walk out, protest, mutiny, revolt. **2** *striking the gong*: hit, knock, collide with, slap, smack, cuff, clout, thump, wallop (*infml*), beat, pound, hammer (*infml*), buffet. **3** *striking at the enemy*: raid, attack, afflict. **4** *struck me as odd*: impress, affect, touch, register.

striking *adjective* noticeable,

conspicuous, salient, outstanding, remarkable, extraordinary, memorable, impressive, dazzling, arresting, astonishing, stunning (*infml*).
F3 unimpressive.

string *noun* **1** *a piece of string*: twine, cord, rope, cable, line, strand, fibre. **2** *a string of disasters*: series, succession, sequence, chain, line, row, file, queue, procession, train.
▪ *verb* thread, link, connect, tie up, hang, suspend, festoon, loop.

strip[1] *verb* peel, skin, flay, denude, divest, deprive, undress, disrobe, unclothe, uncover, expose, lay bare, bare, empty, clear, gut, ransack, pillage, plunder, loot.
F3 dress, clothe, cover.

strip[2] *noun* ribbon, thong, strap, belt, sash, band, stripe, lath, slat, piece, bit, slip, shred.

stripe *noun* band, line, bar, chevron, flash, streak, fleck, strip, belt.

strive *verb* try, attempt, endeavour, struggle, strain, work, toil, labour, fight, contend, compete.

stroke *verb* caress, fondle, pet, touch, pat, rub, massage.
▪ *noun* **1** *give the cat a gentle stroke*: caress, pat, rub. **2** *a single stroke of the axe*: blow, hit, knock, swipe. **3** *removed with a stroke of the pen*: sweep, flourish, movement, action, move, line.

stroll *verb* saunter, amble, dawdle, ramble, wander.
▪ *noun* saunter, amble, walk, constitutional, turn, ramble.

strong *adjective* **1** *strong shoes/arms*: tough, resilient, durable, hard-wearing, heavy-duty, robust, sturdy, firm, sound, lusty, strapping, stout, burly, well-built, beefy, brawny, muscular, sinewy, athletic, fit, healthy, hardy, powerful, mighty, potent. **2** *strong feelings/colours/support*: intense, deep, vivid, fierce, violent, vehement, keen, eager, zealous, fervent, ardent, dedicated, staunch, stalwart, determined, resolute, tenacious, strong-minded, strong-willed, self-assertive. **3** *strong taste/drink*: highly-flavoured, piquant, hot, spicy, highly-seasoned, sharp, pungent, undiluted, concentrated. **4** *strong argument*: convincing, persuasive, cogent, effective, telling, forceful, weighty, compelling, urgent.
F3 **1** weak, feeble. **2** indecisive. **3** mild, bland. **4** unconvincing.

stronghold *noun* citadel, bastion, fort, fortress, castle, keep, refuge.

structure *noun* construction, erection, building, edifice, fabric, framework, form, shape, design, configuration, conformation, make-up, formation, arrangement, organization, set-up.

struggle *verb* strive, work, toil, labour, strain, agonize, fight, battle, wrestle, grapple,

contend, compete, vie.
≠ yield, give in.
▪ *noun* difficulty, problem, effort, exertion, pains, agony, work, labour, toil, clash, conflict, strife, fight, battle, skirmish, encounter, combat, hostilities, contest.
≠ ease, submission, co-operation.

stub *noun* end, stump, remnant, counterfoil.

stubborn *adjective* obstinate, stiff-necked, mulish, pigheaded, obdurate, intransigent, rigid, inflexible, unbending, unyielding, dogged, persistent, tenacious, headstrong, self-willed, wilful, refractory, difficult, unmanageable.
≠ compliant, flexible, yielding.

stuck *adjective* **1** *door is stuck*: fast, jammed, firm, fixed, fastened, joined, glued, cemented. **2** *stuck for an answer*: beaten, stumped (*infml*), baffled.
≠ **1** loose.

student *noun* undergraduate, postgraduate, scholar, schoolboy, schoolgirl, pupil, disciple, learner, trainee, apprentice.

studious *adjective* scholarly, academic, intellectual, bookish, serious, thoughtful, reflective, diligent, hardworking, industrious, assiduous (*fml*), careful, attentive, earnest, eager.
≠ lazy, idle, negligent.

study *verb* read, learn, revise, cram, swot (*infml*), mug up (*infml*), read up, research, investigate, analyse, survey, scan, examine, scrutinize, peruse, pore over, contemplate, meditate, ponder, consider, deliberate.
▪ *noun* **1** *needs further study*: reading, homework, preparation, learning, revision, cramming, swotting (*infml*), research, investigation, inquiry, analysis, examination, scrutiny, inspection, contemplation, consideration, attention. **2** *my father's study*: office, den (*infml*).

Subjects of study include:
accountancy, agriculture, anatomy, anthropology, archaeology, architecture, art, astrology, astronomy, biology, botany, building studies, business studies, calligraphy, chemistry, citizenship, civil engineering, classics, commerce, computer studies, cosmology, craft, creative writing, dance, design, design and technology, drama, dressmaking, driving, ecology, economics, education, electronics, engineering, environmental studies, ethnology, fashion, fitness, food technology, forensics, gender studies, genetics, geography, geology, heraldry, history, home economics, horticulture, information and communication technology (ICT), information technology (IT), journalism, languages, law, leisure studies, librarianship, linguistics, literature, logistics, management studies, marine studies,

marketing, mathematics, mechanics, media studies, medicine, metallurgy, metaphysics, meteorology, music, mythology, natural history, oceanography, ornithology, pathology, personal and social education (PSE), personal, health and social education (PHSE), pharmacology, pharmacy, philosophy, photography, physics, physiology, politics, pottery, psychology, religious studies, science, shorthand, social sciences, sociology, sport, statistics, surveying, technology, theology, tourism, visual arts, web design, zoology.

---

stuff *verb* **1** *stuff some clothes into a bag*: pack, stow, load, fill, cram, crowd, force, push, shove, ram, wedge, jam, squeeze, compress. **2** (*infml*) *stuff themselves with sweets*: gorge, gourmandize (*fml*), overindulge, guzzle, gobble, sate, satiate.
E **1** unload, empty. **2** nibble.
▪ *noun* **1** *what's this stuff for?*: material, fabric, matter, substance. **2** (*infml*) *don't touch my stuff*: belongings, possessions, things, objects, articles, goods, luggage, paraphernalia, gear (*infml*), clobber (*infml*), kit, tackle, equipment, materials.

stuffy *adjective* **1** *a stuffy room*: musty, stale, airless, unventilated, suffocating, stifling, oppressive, heavy, close, muggy, sultry. **2** *had to visit our stuffy old relatives*: staid, strait-laced, prim, conventional, old-fashioned, pompous, dull, dreary, uninteresting, stodgy.
E **1** airy, well-ventilated. **2** informal, modern, lively.

stumble *verb* **1** *stumble on the uneven ground*: trip, slip, fall, lurch, reel, stagger, flounder, blunder. **2** *stumbled at the difficult words*: stammer, stutter, hesitate, falter.

stump *noun* end, remnant, trunk, stub.
▪ *verb* (*infml*) defeat, outwit, confound, perplex, puzzle, baffle, mystify, confuse, bewilder, flummox (*infml*), bamboozle (*infml*), dumbfound.
E assist.

stun *verb* amaze, astonish, astound, stagger, shock, daze, stupefy, dumbfound, flabbergast (*infml*), overcome, confound, confuse, bewilder.

stunning *adjective* (*infml*) beautiful, lovely, gorgeous, ravishing, dazzling, brilliant, striking, impressive, spectacular, remarkable, wonderful, marvellous, great, sensational.
E ugly, awful.

stunt[1] *noun* feat, exploit, act, deed, enterprise, trick, turn, performance.

stunt[2] *verb* stop, arrest, check, restrict, slow, retard, hinder, impede, dwarf.
E promote, encourage.

stupid *adjective* silly, foolish, irresponsible, ill-advised, indiscreet, foolhardy, rash,

senseless, mad, lunatic, brainless, half-witted, idiotic, imbecilic, moronic, feeble-minded, simple-minded, slow, dim, dull, dense, thick, dumb, dopey, crass, inane, puerile (*fml*), mindless, futile, pointless, meaningless, nonsensical, absurd, ludicrous, ridiculous, laughable.
F3 sensible, wise, clever, intelligent.

sturdy *adjective* strong, robust, durable, well-made, stout, substantial, solid, well-built, powerful, muscular, athletic, hardy, vigorous, flourishing, hearty, staunch, stalwart steadfast, firm, resolute, determined.
F3 weak, flimsy, puny.

stutter *verb* stammer, hesitate, falter, stumble, mumble.

style *noun* **1** *a style of jacket/architecture/painting*: appearance, cut, design, pattern, shape, form, sort, type, kind, genre, variety, category. **2** *have style*: elegance, smartness, chic, flair, panache, stylishness, taste, polish, refinement, sophistication, urbanity, fashion, vogue, trend, mode, dressiness, flamboyance, affluence, luxury, grandeur. **3** *a different style of management*: technique, approach, method, manner, mode, fashion, way, custom.
F3 **2** inelegance, tastelessness.

stylish *adjective* chic, fashionable, à la mode, modish, in vogue, voguish, trendy (*infml*), snappy, natty (*infml*), snazzy (*infml*), dressy, smart, elegant, classy (*infml*), polished, refined, sophisticated, urbane.
F3 old-fashioned, shabby.

suave *adjective* polite, courteous, charming, agreeable, affable, soft-spoken, smooth, unctuous (*fml*), sophisticated, urbane, worldly.
F3 rude, unsophisticated.

subconscious *adjective* subliminal, unconscious, intuitive, inner, innermost, hidden, latent, repressed, suppressed.
F3 conscious.

subdue *verb* overcome, quell, suppress, repress, overpower, crush, defeat, conquer, vanquish (*fml*), overrun, subject, subjugate, humble, break, tame, master, discipline, control, check, moderate, reduce, soften, quieten, damp, mellow.
F3 arouse, awaken.

subdued *adjective* **1** *looking rather subdued*: sad, downcast, dejected, crestfallen, quiet, serious, grave, solemn. **2** *a subdued murmur*: quiet, muted, hushed, soft, dim, shaded, sombre, sober, restrained, unobtrusive, low-key, subtle.
F3 **1** lively, excited. **2** striking, obtrusive.

subject *noun* /**sub**-jekt/ topic, theme, matter, issue, question, point, case, affair, business, discipline, field.
▪ *adjective* **1** *subject to change*: liable, disposed, prone,

susceptible, vulnerable, open, exposed. **2** *a subject nation*: subjugated, captive, bound, obedient, answerable, subordinate, inferior, subservient, submissive. **3** *subject to the weather*: dependent, contingent on (*fml*), conditional.

1 invulnerable. **2** free, superior. **3** unconditional.

▪ *verb* /sub-**jekt**/ expose, lay open, submit, subjugate, subdue.

subjective *adjective* biased, prejudiced, personal, individual, idiosyncratic, emotional, intuitive, instinctive.

objective, unbiased, impartial.

sublime *adjective* exalted, elevated, high, lofty, noble, majestic, great, grand, imposing, magnificent, glorious, transcendent, spiritual.

lowly, base.

submerge *verb* submerse, immerse, plunge, duck, dip, sink, drown, engulf, overwhelm, swamp, flood, inundate, deluge.

surface.

submissive *adjective* yielding, unresisting, resigned, patient, uncomplaining, accommodating, biddable, obedient, deferential, ingratiating, subservient, humble, meek, docile, subdued, passive.

intransigent, intractable.

submit *verb* **1** *submit to pressure/the enemy*: yield, give in, surrender, capitulate, knuckle under, bow, bend, stoop, succumb, agree, comply. **2** *submit an application*: present, tender, offer, put forward, suggest, propose, table, state, claim, argue.

1 resist. **2** withdraw.

subordinate *adjective* secondary, auxiliary, ancillary, subsidiary, dependent, inferior, lower, junior, minor, lesser.

superior, senior.

▪ *noun* inferior, junior, assistant, attendant, second, aide, dependant, underling (*infml*).

superior, boss.

subscribe *verb* **1** *subscribe to a theory*: support, endorse, back, advocate, approve, agree. **2** *subscribe to several charities*: give, donate, contribute.

subscription *noun* membership fee, dues, payment, donation, contribution, offering, gift.

subsequent *adjective* following, later, future, next, succeeding, consequent, resulting, ensuing.

previous, earlier.

subside *verb* sink, collapse, settle, descend, fall, drop, lower, decrease, lessen, diminish, dwindle, decline, wane, ebb, recede, moderate, abate, die down, quieten, slacken, ease.

rise, increase.

subsidize *verb* support, back, underwrite, sponsor, finance, fund, aid, promote.

subsidy *noun* grant, allowance, assistance, help, aid, contribution, sponsorship, finance, support, backing.

subsistence *noun* living,

survival, existence, livelihood, maintenance, support, keep, sustenance, nourishment, food, provisions, rations.

substance *noun* **1** *a slimy substance*: matter, material, stuff, fabric. **2** *a being with no substance*: essence, pith, entity, body, solidity, concreteness, reality, actuality, ground, foundation.

substantial *adjective* large, big, sizable, ample, generous, great, considerable, significant, important, worthwhile, massive, bulky, hefty, well-built, stout, sturdy, strong, sound, durable.
F3 small, insignificant, weak.

substitute *verb* **1** *substitute one thing for another*: change, exchange, swap, switch, interchange, replace. **2** *substituting for the manager*: stand in, fill in (*infml*), cover, deputize, understudy, relieve.
▪ *noun* reserve, stand-by, temp (*infml*), supply, locum, understudy, stand-in, replacement, relief, surrogate, proxy, agent, deputy, makeshift, stopgap.

subtle *adjective* **1** *subtle colours/taste/humour*: delicate, understated, implied, indirect, slight, tenuous, faint, mild, fine, nice (*fml*), refined, sophisticated, deep, profound. **2** *subtle argument*: artful, cunning, crafty, sly, devious, shrewd, astute.
F3 **1** blatant, obvious. **2** artless, open.

subtract *verb* deduct, take away, remove, withdraw, debit, detract, diminish.
F3 add.

subversive *adjective* seditious, treasonous, treacherous, traitorous, inflammatory, incendiary, disruptive, riotous, weakening, undermining, destructive.
F3 loyal.

succeed *verb* **1** *succeed in life/the attempt*: triumph, make it, get on, thrive, flourish, prosper, make good. **2** *winter succeeds autumn*: follow, replace.
F3 **1** fail. **2** precede.

succeeding *adjective* following, next, subsequent, ensuing, coming, to come, later, successive.
F3 previous, earlier.

success *noun* **1** *owed her success to hard work*: triumph, victory, luck, fortune, prosperity, fame, eminence. **2** *he/she/it was a success*: celebrity, star, somebody, winner, bestseller, hit, sensation.
F3 **1** failure, disaster.

successful *adjective* **1** *successful candidate/team/business/businessman*: victorious, winning, lucky, fortunate, prosperous, wealthy, thriving, flourishing, booming, moneymaking, lucrative, profitable, rewarding, satisfying, fruitful, productive. **2** *a successful writer*: famous, well-known, popular, leading, bestselling, top, unbeaten.
F3 **1** unsuccessful, unprofitable, fruitless. **2** unknown.

succession *noun* sequence, series, order, progression, run, chain, string, cycle, continuation, flow, course, line, train, procession.

successive *adjective* consecutive, sequential, following, succeeding.

succulent *adjective* fleshy, juicy, moist, luscious, mouthwatering, lush, rich, mellow.
F3 dry.

succumb *verb* give way, yield, give in, submit, knuckle under, surrender, capitulate, collapse, fall.
F3 overcome, master.

suck *verb* draw in, absorb, soak up, extract, drain.

sudden *adjective* unexpected, unforeseen, surprising, startling, abrupt, sharp, quick, swift, rapid, prompt, hurried, hasty, rash, impetuous, impulsive, snap (*infml*).
F3 expected, predictable, gradual, slow.

sue *verb* prosecute, charge, indict, summon, solicit, appeal.

suffer *verb* **1** *suffer in silence*: hurt, ache, agonize, grieve, sorrow. **2** *suffer humiliation*: bear, support, tolerate, endure, sustain, experience, undergo, go through, feel.

suffering *noun* pain, discomfort, agony, anguish, affliction, distress, misery, hardship, ordeal, torment, torture.
F3 ease, comfort.

sufficient *adjective* enough, adequate, satisfactory, effective.
F3 insufficient, inadequate.

suffocate *verb* asphyxiate, smother, stifle, choke, strangle, throttle.

suggest *verb* **1** *suggest a solution*: propose, put forward, advocate, recommend, advise, counsel. **2** *what are you suggesting?*: imply, insinuate, hint, intimate, evoke, indicate.

suggestion *noun* **1** *make a good suggestion*: proposal, proposition, motion, recommendation, idea, plan. **2** *the suggestion was that she was incompetent*: implication, insinuation, innuendo, hint, intimation, suspicion, trace, indication.

suit *verb* satisfy, gratify, please, answer, match, tally, agree, correspond, harmonize.
F3 displease, clash.
▪ *noun* outfit, costume, dress, clothing.

suitable *adjective* appropriate, fitting, convenient, opportune, suited, due, apt, apposite, relevant, applicable, fit, adequate, satisfactory, acceptable, befitting, becoming, seemly, proper, right.
F3 unsuitable, inappropriate.

sulk *verb* mope, brood, pout.

sulky *adjective* brooding, moody, morose, resentful, grudging, disgruntled, put out, cross, bad-tempered, sullen, aloof, unsociable.
F3 cheerful, good-tempered, sociable.

sullen *adjective* sulky, moody, morose, glum, gloomy, silent, surly, sour, perverse, obstinate, stubborn.
F3 cheerful, happy.

sultry *adjective* hot, sweltering, stifling, stuffy, oppressive, close, humid, muggy, sticky.
F3 cool, cold.

sum *noun* total, sum total, aggregate, whole, entirety, number, quantity, amount, tally, reckoning, score, result.

summarize *verb* outline, précis, condense, abridge, abbreviate, shorten, sum up, encapsulate, review.
F3 expand (on).

summary *noun* synopsis, résumé, outline, abstract, précis, condensation, digest, compendium, abridgement, summing-up, review, recapitulation.
▪ *adjective* short, succinct, brief, cursory, hasty, prompt, direct, unceremonious, arbitrary.
F3 lengthy, careful.

summit *noun* top, peak, pinnacle, apex, point, crown, head, zenith, acme, culmination, height.
F3 bottom, foot, nadir.

summon *verb* call, send for, invite, bid, beckon, gather, assemble, convene, rally, muster, mobilize, rouse, arouse.
F3 dismiss.

sundry *adjective* various, diverse, miscellaneous, assorted, varied, different, several, some, a few.

sunken *adjective* submerged, buried, recessed, lower, depressed, concave, hollow, haggard, drawn.

sunny *adjective* **1** *a sunny day*: fine, cloudless, clear, summery, sunshiny, sunlit, bright, brilliant. **2** *a sunny disposition*: cheerful, happy, joyful, smiling, beaming, radiant, light-hearted, buoyant, optimistic, pleasant.
F3 **1** sunless, dull. **2** gloomy.

sunrise *noun* dawn, crack of dawn, daybreak, daylight.

sunset *noun* sundown, dusk, twilight, gloaming, evening, nightfall.

superb *adjective* excellent, first-rate, first-class, superior, choice, fine, exquisite, gorgeous, magnificent, splendid, grand, wonderful, marvellous, admirable, impressive, breathtaking.
F3 bad, poor, inferior.

superficial *adjective* surface, external, exterior, outward, apparent, seeming, cosmetic, skin-deep, shallow, slight, trivial, lightweight, frivolous, casual, cursory, sketchy, hasty, hurried, passing, one-dimensional.
F3 internal, deep, thorough.

superior *adjective* **1** *superior accommodation*: excellent, first-class, first-rate, top-notch (*infml*), top-flight (*infml*), high-class, exclusive, choice, select, fine, de luxe, admirable, distinguished, exceptional, unrivalled, par

excellence. **2** *superior to mine*: better, preferred, greater, higher, senior. **3** *a superior air*: haughty, lordly, pretentious, snobbish, snooty (*infml*), supercilious, disdainful, condescending, patronizing.
F3 **1** inferior, average. **2** worse, lower. **3** humble.
▪ *noun* senior, elder, better, boss, chief, principal, director, manager, foreman, supervisor.
F3 inferior, junior, assistant.

superiority *noun* advantage, lead, edge, supremacy, ascendancy, pre-eminence, predominance.
F3 inferiority.

superlative *adjective* best, greatest, highest, supreme, transcendent, unbeatable, unrivalled, unparalleled, matchless, peerless, unsurpassed, unbeaten, consummate, excellent, outstanding.
F3 poor, average.

supernatural *adjective* paranormal, unnatural, abnormal, metaphysical, spiritual, psychic, mystic, occult, hidden, mysterious, miraculous, magical, phantom, ghostly.
F3 natural, normal.

superstition *noun* myth, old wives' tale, fallacy, delusion, illusion.

superstitious *adjective* mythical, false, fallacious, irrational, groundless, delusive, illusory.
F3 rational, logical.

supervise *verb* oversee, watch over, look after, superintend, run, manage, administer, direct, conduct, preside over, control, handle.

supervision *noun* surveillance, care, charge, superintendence, oversight, running, management, administration, direction, control, guidance, instruction.

supervisor *noun* overseer, inspector, superintendent, boss, chief, director, administrator, manager, foreman, forewoman.

supple *adjective* flexible, bending, pliant, pliable, plastic, lithe, graceful, loose-limbed, double-jointed, elastic.
F3 stiff, rigid, inflexible.

supplement *noun* addition, extra, insert, pull-out, addendum, appendix, codicil, postscript, sequel.
▪ *verb* add to, augment, boost, reinforce, fill up, top up, complement, extend, eke out.
F3 deplete, use up.

supplementary *adjective* additional, extra, auxiliary, secondary, complementary, accompanying.

supplies *noun* stores, provisions, food, equipment, materials, necessities.

supply *verb* provide, furnish, equip, outfit, stock, fill, replenish, give, donate, grant, endow, contribute, yield, produce, sell.
F3 take, receive.
▪ *noun* source, amount, quantity,

stock, fund, reservoir, store, reserve, stockpile, hoard, cache.
F3 lack.

support *verb* **1** *support one's team/local charities*: back, second, defend, champion, advocate, promote, foster, help, aid, assist, rally round, finance, fund, subsidize, underwrite. **2** *supporting the roof*: hold up, bear, carry, sustain, brace, reinforce, strengthen, prop, buttress, bolster. **3** *support his family*: maintain, keep, provide for, feed, nourish.
F3 1 oppose. **3** live off.
▪ *noun* **1** *have the support of the majority*: backing, allegiance, loyalty, defence, protection, patronage, sponsorship, approval, encouragement, comfort, relief, help, aid, assistance. **2** *a roof support*: prop, stay, post, pillar, brace, crutch, foundation, underpinning.
F3 1 opposition, hostility.

supporter *noun* fan, follower, adherent, advocate, champion, defender, seconder, patron, sponsor, helper, ally, friend.
F3 opponent.

suppose *verb* assume, presume, expect, infer, conclude, guess, conjecture, surmise, believe, think, consider, judge, imagine, conceive, fancy, pretend, postulate, hypothesize.
F3 know.

supposed *adjective* alleged, reported, rumoured, assumed, presumed, reputed, putative (*fml*), imagined, hypothetical.
F3 known, certain.

supposition *noun* assumption, presumption, guess, conjecture, speculation, theory, hypothesis, idea, notion.
F3 knowledge.

suppress *verb* crush, stamp out, quash, quell, subdue, stop, silence, censor, stifle, smother, strangle, conceal, withhold, hold back, contain, restrain, check, repress, inhibit.
F3 encourage, incite.

supreme *adjective* best, greatest, highest, top, crowning, culminating, first, leading, foremost, chief, principal, head, sovereign, pre-eminent, predominant, prevailing, world-beating, unsurpassed, second-to-none, incomparable, matchless, consummate, transcendent, superlative, prime, ultimate, extreme, final.
F3 lowly, poor.

sure *adjective* **1** *a sure sign/sure to know*: certain, convinced, assured, confident, decided, positive, definite, unmistakable, clear, accurate, precise, unquestionable, indisputable, undoubted, undeniable, irrevocable, inevitable, bound. **2** *guided by his sure hand*: safe, secure, fast, solid, firm, steady, stable, guaranteed, reliable, dependable, trustworthy, steadfast, unwavering, unerring, unfailing, infallible, effective.

1 unsure, uncertain, doubtful. 2 unsafe, insecure.

surface *noun* outside, exterior, façade, veneer, covering, skin, top, side, face, plane.
inside, interior.
▪ *verb* rise, arise, come up, emerge, appear, materialize, come to light.
sink, disappear, vanish.

surly *adjective* gruff, brusque, churlish, ungracious, bad-tempered, cross, crabbed, grouchy, crusty, sullen, sulky, morose.
friendly, polite.

surpass *verb* beat, outdo, exceed, outstrip, better, excel, transcend, outshine, eclipse.

surplus *noun* excess, residue, remainder, balance, superfluity, glut, surfeit.
lack, shortage.
▪ *adjective* excess, superfluous, redundant, extra, spare, remaining, unused.

surprise *verb* startle, amaze, astonish, astound, stagger, flabbergast (*infml*), bewilder, confuse, nonplus, disconcert, dismay.
▪ *noun* amazement, astonishment, incredulity, wonder, bewilderment, dismay, shock, start, bombshell, revelation.
composure.

surprised *adjective* startled, amazed, astonished, astounded, staggered, flabbergasted (*infml*), thunderstruck, dumbfounded, speechless, shocked, nonplussed.
unsurprised, composed.

surprising *adjective* amazing, astonishing, astounding, staggering, stunning, incredible, extraordinary, remarkable, startling, unexpected, unforeseen.
unsurprising, expected.

surrender *verb* capitulate, submit, resign, concede, yield, give in, cede, give up, quit, relinquish, abandon, renounce, forgo, waive.

surround *verb* encircle, ring, girdle, encompass, envelop, encase, enclose, hem in, besiege.

surrounding *adjective* encircling, bordering, adjacent, adjoining, neighbouring, nearby.

surroundings *noun* neighbourhood, vicinity, locality, setting, environment, background, milieu, ambience.

survey *verb* view, contemplate, observe, supervise, scan, scrutinize, examine, inspect, study, research, review, consider, estimate, evaluate, assess, measure, plot, plan, map, chart, reconnoitre.
▪ *noun* review, overview, scrutiny, examination, inspection, study, appraisal, assessment, measurement.

survive *verb* outlive, outlast, endure, last, stay, remain, live, exist, withstand, weather.
succumb, die.

susceptible *adjective* liable, prone, inclined, disposed, given, subject, receptive, responsive, impressionable, suggestible, weak, vulnerable, open, sensitive, tender.

F3 resistant, immune.

suspect *verb* **1** *no cause to suspect the truth of what he says*: doubt, distrust, mistrust, call into question. **2** *I suspect he's not happy*: believe, fancy, feel, guess, conjecture, speculate, surmise, suppose, consider, conclude, infer.

▪ *adjective* suspicious, doubtful, dubious, questionable, debatable, unreliable, iffy (*infml*), dodgy (*infml*), fishy (*infml*).

F3 acceptable, reliable.

suspend *verb* **1** *suspended from the ceiling*: hang, dangle, swing. **2** *suspend the hearing*: adjourn, interrupt, discontinue, cease, delay, defer, postpone, put off, shelve. **3** *suspend them from school*: expel, dismiss, exclude, debar.

F3 2 continue. **3** restore, reinstate.

suspense *noun* uncertainty, insecurity, anxiety, tension, apprehension, anticipation, expectation, expectancy, excitement.

F3 certainty, knowledge.

suspicion *noun* **1** *filled with suspicion*: doubt, scepticism, distrust, mistrust, wariness, caution, misgiving, apprehension. **2** *had a suspicion something was wrong*: idea, notion, hunch.

F3 1 trust.

suspicious *adjective* **1** *a suspicious look*: doubtful, sceptical, unbelieving, suspecting, distrustful, mistrustful, wary, chary, apprehensive, uneasy. **2** *a suspicious character*: dubious, questionable, suspect, irregular, shifty, shady (*infml*), dodgy (*infml*), fishy (*infml*).

F3 1 trustful, confident. **2** trustworthy, innocent.

sustain *verb* **1** *sustaining them through the winter*: nourish, provide for, nurture, foster, help, aid, assist, comfort, relieve, support, uphold, endorse, bear, carry. **2** *can't sustain that pace*: maintain, keep going, keep up, continue, prolong, hold.

sustained *adjective* prolonged, protracted, long-drawn-out, steady, continuous, constant, perpetual, unremitting.

F3 broken, interrupted, intermittent, spasmodic.

swagger *verb* bluster, boast, crow, brag, swank (*infml*), parade, strut.

▪ *noun* bluster, show, ostentation, arrogance.

swallow *verb* **1** *swallow the medicine*: consume, devour, eat, gobble up, guzzle, drink, quaff, knock back (*infml*), gulp, down (*infml*). **2** *swallowed up in the fog*: engulf, enfold, envelop, swallow up, absorb, assimilate.

swamp *noun* bog, marsh, fen, slough, quagmire, quicksand, mire, mud.

▪ *verb* flood, inundate, deluge, engulf, submerge, sink, drench, saturate, waterlog, overload, overwhelm, besiege, beset.

swap, **swop** *verb* exchange, transpose, switch, interchange, barter, trade, traffic.

swarm *noun* crowd, throng, mob, mass, multitude, myriad, host, army, horde, herd, flock, drove, shoal.

▪ *verb* **1** *swarmed into the stadium*: flock, flood, stream, mass, congregate, crowd, throng. **2** *swarming with tourists*: teem, crawl, bristle, abound.

sway *verb* **1** *sway from side to side*: rock, roll, lurch, swing, wave, oscillate, fluctuate, bend, incline, lean, divert, veer, swerve. **2** *swaying public opinion*: influence, affect, persuade, induce, convince, convert, overrule, dominate, govern.

swear *verb* **1** *swearing revenge*: vow, promise, pledge, avow, attest (*fml*), asseverate (*fml*), testify, affirm, assert, declare, insist. **2** *swearing at the top of his voice*: curse, blaspheme.

swear-word *noun* expletive, four-letter word, curse, oath, imprecation, obscenity, profanity, blasphemy, swearing, bad language.

sweat *noun* **1** *soaking with sweat*: perspiration, moisture, stickiness. **2** *get into a sweat about it*: anxiety, worry, agitation, panic. **3** *takes a lot of sweat to achieve*: toil, labour, drudgery, chore.

▪ *verb* perspire, swelter, exude.

sweep *verb* **1** *sweep the floor*: brush, dust, clean, clear, remove. **2** *swept through the room*: pass, sail, fly, glide, scud, skim, glance, whisk, tear, hurtle.

▪ *noun* arc, curve, bend, swing, stroke, movement, gesture, compass, scope, range, extent, span, stretch, expanse, vista.

sweeping *adjective* general, global, all-inclusive, all-embracing, blanket, across-the-board, broad, wide-ranging, extensive, far-reaching, comprehensive, thoroughgoing, radical, wholesale, indiscriminate, oversimplified, simplistic.

≠ specific, narrow.

sweet *adjective* **1** *a sweet taste*: sugary, syrupy, sweetened, honeyed, saccharine, luscious, delicious. **2** *a sweet nature*: pleasant, delightful, lovely, attractive, beautiful, pretty, winsome, cute, appealing, lovable, charming, agreeable, amiable, affectionate, tender, kind, treasured, precious, dear, darling. **3** *a sweet smell*: fresh, clean, wholesome, pure, clear, perfumed, fragrant, aromatic, balmy. **4** *sweet music*: melodious, tuneful, harmonious, euphonious, musical, dulcet, soft, mellow.

≠ **1** savoury, salty, sour, bitter. **2** unpleasant, nasty, ugly. **3** foul. **4** discordant.

▪ *noun* dessert, pudding, afters (*infml*).

sweeten *verb* sugar, honey,

mellow, soften, soothe, appease, temper, cushion.
F3 sour, embitter.

swell *verb* expand, dilate, inflate, blow up, puff up, bloat, distend, fatten, bulge, balloon, billow, surge, rise, mount, increase, enlarge, extend, grow, augment, heighten, intensify.
F3 shrink, contract, decrease, dwindle.
▪ *noun* billow, wave, undulation, surge, rise, increase, enlargement.

swelling *noun* lump, tumour, bump, bruise, blister, boil, inflammation, bulge, protuberance (*fml*), puffiness, distension (*fml*), enlargement.

sweltering *adjective* hot, tropical, baking, scorching, stifling, suffocating, airless, oppressive, sultry, steamy, sticky, humid.
F3 cold, cool, fresh, breezy, airy.

swerve *verb* turn, bend, incline, veer, swing, shift, deviate, stray, wander, diverge, deflect, sheer.

swift *adjective* fast, quick, rapid, speedy, express, flying, hurried, hasty, short, brief, sudden, prompt, ready, agile, nimble, nippy (*infml*).
F3 slow, sluggish, unhurried.

swindle *verb* cheat, defraud, diddle, do (*infml*), overcharge, fleece, rip off (*infml*), trick, deceive, dupe, con (*infml*), bamboozle (*infml*).
▪ *noun* fraud, fiddle, racket, sharp practice, double-dealing, trickery, deception, con (*infml*), rip-off (*infml*).

swing *verb* hang, suspend, dangle, wave, brandish, sway, rock, oscillate, vibrate, fluctuate, vary, veer, swerve, turn, whirl, twirl, spin, rotate.
▪ *noun* sway, rock, oscillation, vibration, fluctuation, variation, change, shift, movement, motion, rhythm.

swipe *verb* hit, strike, lunge, lash out, slap, whack (*infml*), wallop (*infml*), sock (*infml*).
▪ *noun* stroke, blow, slap, smack, clout, whack (*infml*), wallop (*infml*).

swirl *verb* churn, agitate, spin, twirl, whirl, wheel, eddy, twist, curl.

switch *verb* change, exchange, swap, trade, interchange, transpose, substitute, replace, shift, rearrange, turn, veer, deviate, divert, deflect.
▪ *noun* change, alteration, shift, exchange, swap, interchange, substitution, replacement.

swivel *verb* pivot, spin, rotate, revolve, turn, twirl, pirouette, gyrate, wheel.

swollen *adjective* bloated, distended, inflated, tumid, puffed up, puffy, inflamed, enlarged, bulbous, bulging.
F3 shrunken, shrivelled.

swoop *verb* dive, plunge, drop, fall, descend, stoop, pounce, lunge, rush.

swop *see* **swap**.

sword *noun* blade, foil, rapier, sabre, scimitar.

swot *verb* (*infml*) study, work,

learn, memorize, revise, cram, mug up (*infml*), bone up (*infml*).

syllabus *noun* curriculum, course, programme, schedule, plan.

symbol *noun* sign, token, representation, mark, emblem, badge, logo, character, ideograph, figure, image.

symbolic *adjective* symbolical, representative, emblematic, token, figurative, metaphorical, allegorical, meaningful, significant.

symbolize *verb* represent, stand for, denote, mean, signify, typify, exemplify, epitomize, personify.

symmetry *noun* balance, evenness, regularity, parallelism, correspondence, proportion, harmony, agreement.

F3 asymmetry, irregularity.

sympathetic *adjective* understanding, appreciative, supportive, comforting, consoling, commiserating, pitying, interested, concerned, solicitous, caring, compassionate, tender, kind, warm-hearted, well-disposed, affectionate, agreeable, friendly, congenial, like-minded, compatible.

F3 unsympathetic, indifferent, callous, antipathetic.

sympathize *verb* understand, comfort, commiserate, pity, feel for, empathize, identify with, respond to.

F3 ignore, disregard.

sympathy *noun* **1** *feel sympathy for them*: understanding, comfort, consolation, condolences, commiseration, pity, compassion, tenderness, kindness, warmth, thoughtfulness, empathy, fellow-feeling, affinity, rapport. **2** *was in sympathy with their aims*: agreement, accord, correspondence, harmony.

F3 **1** indifference, insensitivity, callousness. **2** disagreement.

symptom *noun* sign, indication, evidence, manifestation, expression, feature, characteristic, mark, token, warning.

synthetic *adjective* manufactured, man-made, simulated, artificial, ersatz, imitation, fake, bogus, mock, sham, pseudo.

F3 genuine, real, natural.

system *noun* **1** *a good system of government*: method, mode, technique, procedure, process, routine, practice, usage, rule. **2** *have to have some sort of system*: organization, structure, set-up, systematization, co-ordination, orderliness, methodology, logic, classification, arrangement, order.

systematic *adjective* methodical, logical, ordered, well-ordered, planned, well-planned, organized, well-organized, structured, systematized, standardized, orderly, businesslike, efficient.

F3 unsystematic, arbitrary, disorderly, inefficient.

T*t*

table *noun* **1** *a work table*: board, slab, counter, worktop, desk, bench, stand. **2** *a table of contents*: diagram, chart, graph, timetable, schedule, programme, list, inventory, catalogue, index, register, record.

taboo *adjective* forbidden, prohibited, banned, proscribed, unacceptable, unmentionable, unthinkable.

F⇄ permitted, acceptable.

▪ *noun* ban, interdiction (*fml*), prohibition, restriction, anathema, curse.

tack *noun* **1** *carpet tacks*: nail, pin, drawing pin, staple. **2** *go off on a different tack*: course, path, bearing, heading, direction, line, approach, method, way, technique, procedure, plan, tactic, attack.

▪ *verb* add, append, attach, affix, fasten, fix, nail, pin, staple, stitch, baste.

tackle *noun* **1** *a rugby tackle*: attack, challenge, interception, intervention, block. **2** *all their climbing/fishing tackle*: equipment, tools, implements, apparatus, rig, outfit, gear (*infml*), trappings, paraphernalia.

▪ *verb* **1** *tackle the problem immediately*: begin, embark on, set about, try, attempt, undertake, take on, challenge, confront, encounter, face up to, grapple with, deal with, attend to, handle, grab, seize, grasp. **2** *tackling one of the forwards*: intercept, block, halt, stop.

F⇄ **1** avoid, sidestep.

tactful *adjective* diplomatic, discreet, politic, judicious (*fml*), prudent, careful, delicate, subtle, sensitive, perceptive, discerning, understanding, thoughtful, considerate, polite, skilful, adroit.

F⇄ tactless, indiscreet, thoughtless, rude.

tactic *noun* approach, course, way, means, method, procedure, plan, stratagem, scheme, ruse, ploy, subterfuge, trick, device, shift, move, manoeuvre.

tactical *adjective* strategic, planned, calculated, artful, cunning, shrewd, skilful, clever, smart, prudent, politic, judicious (*fml*).

tactics *noun* strategy, campaign, plan, policy, approach, line of attack, moves, manoeuvres.

tactless *adjective* undiplomatic,

indiscreet, indelicate, inappropriate, impolitic, imprudent, careless, clumsy, blundering, insensitive, unfeeling, hurtful, unkind, thoughtless, inconsiderate, rude, impolite, discourteous.
F3 tactful, diplomatic, discreet.

tag *noun* label, sticker, tab, ticket, mark, identification, note, slip, docket.
▪ *verb* **1** *tag all the boxes that need to be moved*: label, mark, identify, designate. **2** *tagged on at the end*: add, append, annex, adjoin, affix, fasten.

tail *noun* end, extremity, rear, rear end, rump, behind (*infml*), posterior (*infml*), appendage.
▪ *verb* follow, pursue, shadow, dog, stalk, track, trail.

tailor *verb* fit, suit, cut, trim, style, fashion, shape, mould, alter, modify, adapt, adjust, accommodate.

tailor-made *adjective* made-to-measure, custom-built, ideal, perfect, right, suited, fitted.
F3 unsuitable.

taint *verb* contaminate, infect, pollute, adulterate, corrupt, deprave, stain, blemish, blot, smear, tarnish, blacken, dirty, soil, muddy, defile (*fml*), sully (*fml*), harm, damage, blight, spoil, ruin, shame, disgrace, dishonour.

take *verb* **1** *took his hand/a seat/ the next three games/his mother's name*: seize, grab, snatch, grasp, hold, catch, capture, get, obtain, acquire, secure, gain, win, derive, adopt, assume, pick, choose, select, accept, receive. **2** *take five from ten*: remove, eliminate, take away, subtract, deduct. **3** *taking anything that wasn't nailed down*: steal, filch, purloin (*fml*), nick (*infml*), pinch (*infml*), appropriate, abduct, carry off. **4** *takes courage*: need, necessitate, require, demand, call for. **5** *take me home*: convey, carry, bring, transport, ferry, accompany, escort, lead, guide, conduct, usher. **6** *can't take pain*: bear, tolerate, stand, stomach, abide, endure, suffer, undergo, withstand.
F3 **1** leave, refuse. **2** add, put back.

takeover *noun* merger, amalgamation, combination, incorporation, coup.

takings *noun* receipts, gate, proceeds, profits, gain, returns, revenue, yield, income, earnings, pickings.

tale *noun* story, yarn, anecdote, spiel (*infml*), narrative, account, report, rumour, tall story, old wives' tale, superstition, fable, myth, legend, saga, lie, fib, falsehood, untruth, fabrication.

talent *noun* gift, endowment, genius, flair, feel, knack, bent, aptitude, faculty, skill, ability, capacity, power, strength, forte.
F3 inability, weakness.

talented *adjective* gifted, brilliant, well-endowed, versatile, accomplished, able, capable,

proficient, adept, adroit, deft, clever, skilful.
F3 inept.

talk *verb* speak, utter, articulate, say, communicate, converse, chat, gossip, natter (*infml*), chatter, discuss, confer, negotiate.
▪ *noun* **1** *a lot of talk about nothing/ have a long talk*: conversation, dialogue, discussion, conference, meeting, consultation, negotiation, chat, chatter, natter (*infml*), gossip, hearsay, rumour, tittle-tattle. **2** *give a talk*: lecture, seminar, symposium, speech, address, discourse, sermon, spiel (*infml*).

talkative *adjective* garrulous, voluble, vocal, communicative, forthcoming, unreserved, expansive, chatty, gossipy, verbose, wordy.
F3 taciturn, quiet, reserved.

tall *adjective* high, lofty, elevated, soaring, towering, big, great, giant, gigantic.
F3 short, low, small.

tame *adjective* **1** *a tame owl*: domesticated, broken in, trained, disciplined, manageable, tractable, amenable, gentle, docile, meek, submissive, unresisting, obedient, biddable. **2** *party was pretty tame*: dull, boring, tedious, uninteresting, humdrum, flat, bland, insipid, weak, feeble, uninspired, unadventurous, unenterprising, lifeless, spiritless.
F3 1 wild, unmanageable, rebellious. **2** exciting.
▪ *verb* domesticate, house-train, break in, train, discipline, master, subjugate, conquer, bridle, curb, repress, suppress, quell, subdue, temper, soften, mellow, calm, pacify, humble.

tamper *verb* interfere, meddle, mess (*infml*), tinker, fiddle, fix, rig, manipulate, juggle, alter, damage.

tang *noun* sharpness, bite, piquancy, pungency, taste, flavour, savour, smack, smell, aroma, scent, whiff, tinge, touch, trace, hint, suggestion, overtone.

tangible *adjective* touchable, tactile, palpable, solid, concrete, material, substantial, physical, real, actual, perceptible, discernible, evident, manifest, definite, positive.
F3 intangible, abstract, unreal.

tangle *noun* knot, snarl-up, twist, coil, convolution, mesh, web, maze, labyrinth, mess, muddle, jumble, mix-up, confusion, entanglement, embroilment, complication.
▪ *verb* entangle, knot, snarl, ravel, twist, coil, interweave, interlace, intertwine, catch, ensnare, entrap, enmesh, embroil, implicate, involve, muddle, confuse.
F3 disentangle.

tantalize *verb* tease, taunt, torment, torture, provoke, lead on, titillate, tempt, entice, bait, balk, frustrate, thwart.
F3 gratify, satisfy, fulfil.

tantrum *noun* temper, rage, fury, storm, outburst, fit, scene.

tap[1] *verb* hit, strike, knock, rap, beat, drum, pat, touch.
▪ *noun* knock, rap, beat, pat, touch.

tap[2] *noun* stopcock, valve, faucet, spigot, spout.

tape *noun* band, strip, binding, ribbon, video, cassette.
▪ *verb* record, video, bind, secure, stick, seal.

taper *verb* narrow, attenuate (*fml*), thin, slim, decrease, reduce, lessen, dwindle, fade, wane, peter out, tail off, die away.
F3 widen, flare, swell, increase.
▪ *noun* spill, candle, wick.

target *noun* aim, object, end, purpose, intention, ambition, goal, destination, objective, butt, mark, victim, prey, quarry.

tariff *noun* price list, schedule, charges, rate, toll, tax, levy, customs, excise, duty.

tarnish *verb* discolour, corrode, rust, dull, dim, darken, blacken, sully (*fml*), taint, stain, blemish, spot, blot, mar, spoil.
F3 polish, brighten.

tart[1] *noun* pie, flan, pastry, tartlet, patty.

tart[2] *adjective* **1** *if it's too tart, add some sugar*: sharp, acid, sour, bitter, vinegary, tangy, piquant, pungent. **2** *got a tart response to my question*: biting, cutting, trenchant (*fml*), incisive, caustic, astringent, acerbic, scathing, sardonic.
F3 bland, sweet.

task *noun* job, chore, duty, charge, imposition, assignment, exercise, mission, errand, undertaking, enterprise, business, occupation, activity, employment, work, labour, toil, burden.

taste *noun* **1** *a taste of garlic*: flavour, savour, relish, smack, tang. **2** *a taste of things to come*: sample, bit, piece, morsel, titbit, bite, nibble, mouthful, sip, drop, dash, soupçon. **3** *a taste for adventure*: liking, fondness, partiality, preference, inclination, leaning, desire, appetite. **4** *have good taste/shows taste*: discrimination, discernment, judgement, perception, appreciation, sensitivity, refinement, polish, culture, cultivation, breeding, decorum, finesse, style, elegance, tastefulness.
F3 1 blandness. **3** distaste. **4** tastelessness.
▪ *verb* savour, relish, sample, nibble, sip, try, test, differentiate, distinguish, discern, perceive, experience, undergo, feel, know.

Ways of describing taste include:
acid, acrid, appetizing, bitter, bittersweet, citrus, creamy, delicious, flavoursome, fruity, hot, meaty, moreish, mouthwatering (*infml*), peppery, piquant, pungent, salty, savoury, scrumptious (*infml*), sharp, sour, spicy, sugary, sweet, tangy, tart, vinegary, yummy (*infml*).

---

tasteful *adjective* refined, polished, cultured, cultivated,

elegant, smart, stylish, aesthetic, artistic, harmonious, beautiful, exquisite, delicate, graceful, restrained, well-judged, judicious (*fml*), correct, fastidious, discriminating.
F3 tasteless, garish, tawdry.

tasteless *adjective* **1** *this soup is tasteless*: flavourless, insipid, bland, mild, weak, watery, flat, stale, dull, boring, uninteresting, vapid. **2** *tasteless comment/decoration*: inelegant, graceless, unseemly, improper, indiscreet, crass, rude, crude, vulgar, kitsch, tacky (*infml*), naff (*slang*), cheap, tawdry, flashy, gaudy, garish, loud.
F3 1 tasty. **2** tasteful, elegant.

tasty *adjective* luscious, palatable, appetizing, mouthwatering, delicious, flavoursome, succulent, scrumptious (*infml*), yummy (*infml*), tangy, piquant, savoury, sweet.
F3 tasteless, insipid.

tattered *adjective* ragged, frayed, threadbare, ripped, torn, tatty, shabby, scruffy.
F3 smart, neat.

taunt *verb* tease, torment, provoke, bait, goad, jeer, mock, ridicule, gibe, rib (*infml*), deride, sneer, insult, revile, reproach.
▪ *noun* jeer, catcall, gibe, dig, sneer, insult, reproach, taunting, teasing, provocation, ridicule, sarcasm, derision, censure.

taut *adjective* tight, stretched, contracted, strained, tense, unrelaxed, stiff, rigid.
F3 slack, loose, relaxed.

tax *noun* levy, charge, rate, tariff, customs, contribution, imposition, burden, load.
▪ *verb* levy, charge, demand, exact, assess, impose, burden, load, strain, stretch, try, tire, weary, exhaust, drain, sap, weaken.

teach *verb* instruct, train, coach, tutor, lecture, drill, ground, verse, discipline, school, educate, enlighten, edify, inform, impart, inculcate, advise, counsel, guide, direct, show, demonstrate.
F3 learn.

teacher *noun* schoolteacher, schoolmaster, master, schoolmistress, mistress, educator, pedagogue, tutor, lecturer, professor, don, instructor, trainer, coach, adviser, counsellor, mentor, guide, guru.
F3 pupil.

teaching *noun* **1** *the teaching of English/teaching as a profession*: instruction, tuition, training, grounding, schooling, education, pedagogy. **2** *the church's teachings*: dogma, doctrine, tenet, precept (*fml*), principle.

team *noun* side, line-up, squad, shift, crew, gang, band, group, company, stable.

tear *verb* **1** *tearing his sleeve on the wire/tore it into shreds*: rip, rend, divide, rupture, sever, shred, scratch, claw, gash, lacerate, mutilate, mangle. **2** *tore the book out of his hand*: pull, snatch, grab,

seize, wrest (*fml*). **3** *tear down the street*: dash, rush, hurry, speed, race, run, sprint, fly, shoot, dart, bolt, belt (*infml*), career, charge.
▪ *noun* rip, rent, slit, hole, split, rupture, scratch, gash, laceration.

tearful *adjective* crying, weeping, sobbing, whimpering, blubbering, sad, sorrowful, upset, distressed, emotional, weepy (*infml*).
F3 happy, smiling, laughing.

tease *verb* taunt, provoke, bait, annoy, irritate, aggravate (*infml*), needle (*infml*), badger, worry, pester, plague, torment, tantalize, mock, ridicule, gibe, banter, rag (*infml*), rib (*infml*).

technical *adjective* mechanical, technological, scientific, electronic, computerized, specialized, expert, professional.

technique *noun* method, system, procedure, manner, fashion, style, mode, way, means, approach, course, performance, execution, delivery, artistry, craftsmanship, skill, facility, proficiency, expertise, know-how (*infml*), art, craft, knack, touch.

tedious *adjective* boring, monotonous, uninteresting, unexciting, dull, dreary, drab, banal, humdrum, tiresome, wearisome, tiring, laborious, long-winded, long-drawn-out.
F3 lively, interesting, exciting.

teenage *adjective* teenaged, adolescent, young, youthful, juvenile, immature.

telepathy *noun* mind-reading, thought transference, sixth sense, ESP, clairvoyance.

telephone *verb* phone, ring (up), call (up), dial, buzz (*infml*), contact, get in touch.

tell *verb* **1** *tell him the news*: inform, notify, let know, acquaint, impart, communicate, speak, utter, say, state, confess, divulge, disclose, reveal. **2** *tell a story*: narrate, recount, relate, report, announce, describe, portray, mention. **3** *told them to wait*: order, command, direct, instruct, authorize. **4** *tell them apart/tell which is which*: differentiate, distinguish, discriminate, discern, recognize, identify, discover, see, understand, comprehend.

temper *noun* **1** *the temper of the meeting*: mood, humour, nature, temperament, character, disposition. **2** *in a temper*: anger, rage, fury, passion, tantrum, paddy (*infml*), annoyance, irritability, ill-humour. **3** *lose one's temper*: calm, composure, self-control, cool (*infml*).
F3 **2** calmness, self-control. **3** anger, rage.
▪ *verb* **1** *tempering his threats with some encouraging words*: moderate, lessen, reduce, calm, soothe, allay, assuage (*fml*), palliate (*fml*), mitigate, modify, soften. **2** *tempering the steel*: harden, toughen, strengthen.

temperament *noun* nature, character, personality, disposition, tendency, bent, constitution, make-up, soul, spirit, mood, humour, temper, state of mind, attitude, outlook.

temperamental *adjective* moody, emotional, neurotic, highly-strung, sensitive, touchy, irritable, impatient, passionate, fiery, excitable, explosive, volatile, mercurial, capricious, unpredictable, unreliable.
F3 calm, level-headed, steady.

temple *noun* shrine, sanctuary, church, tabernacle, mosque, pagoda, synagogue, chapel.

tempo *noun* time, rhythm, metre, beat, pulse, speed, velocity, rate, pace.

temporary *adjective* impermanent, provisional, interim, makeshift, stopgap, temporal, transient, transitory, passing, ephemeral, evanescent, fleeting, brief, short-lived, momentary.
F3 permanent, everlasting.

tempt *verb* entice, coax, persuade, woo, bait, lure, allure, attract, draw, seduce, invite, tantalize, provoke, incite.
F3 discourage, dissuade, repel.

temptation *noun* enticement, inducement, coaxing, persuasion, bait, lure, allure, appeal, attraction, draw, pull, seduction, invitation.

tenant *noun* renter, lessee, leaseholder, occupier, occupant, resident, inhabitant.

tend[1] *verb* incline, lean, bend, bear, head, aim, lead, go, move, gravitate.

tend[2] *verb* look after, care for, cultivate, keep, maintain, manage, handle, guard, protect, watch, mind, nurture, nurse, minister to, serve, attend.
F3 neglect, ignore.

tendency *noun* trend, drift, movement, course, direction, bearing, heading, bias, partiality, predisposition, propensity, readiness, liability, susceptibility, proneness, inclination, leaning, bent, disposition.

tender[1] *adjective* **1** *a tender caress*: kind, gentle, caring, humane, considerate, compassionate, sympathetic, warm, fond, affectionate, loving, amorous, romantic, sentimental, emotional, sensitive, tender-hearted, soft-hearted. **2** *of tender years*: youthful, immature, green, raw, new, inexperienced, impressionable, vulnerable. **3** *tender meat*: soft, succulent, fleshy, dainty, delicate. **4** *skin is still a bit tender*: sore, painful, aching, smarting, bruised, inflamed, raw.
F3 **1** hard-hearted, callous. **2** mature. **3** tough, hard.

tender[2] *verb* offer, proffer, extend, give, present, submit, propose, suggest, advance, volunteer.
▪ *noun* offer, bid, estimate, quotation, proposal, proposition, suggestion, submission.

tense *adjective* **1** *muscles were tense*: tight, taut, stretched, strained, stiff, rigid. **2** *feel tense*: nervous, anxious, worried, jittery,

uneasy, apprehensive, edgy, fidgety, restless, jumpy, overwrought, keyed up. **3** *a tense moment*: stressful, exciting, worrying, fraught.
F3 **1** loose, slack. **2** calm, relaxed.

tension *noun* **1** *increase the tension on the rope*: tightness, tautness, stiffness, strain, stress, pressure. **2** *suffering from nervous tension*: nervousness, anxiety, worry, uneasiness, apprehension, edginess, restlessness, suspense.
F3 **1** looseness. **2** calm(ness), relaxation.

tentative *adjective* experimental, exploratory, speculative, hesitant, faltering, cautious, unsure, uncertain, doubtful, undecided, provisional, indefinite, unconfirmed.
F3 definite, decisive, conclusive, final.

tepid *adjective* lukewarm, cool, half-hearted, unenthusiastic, apathetic.
F3 cold, hot, passionate.

term *noun* **1** *not familiar with that term*: word, name, designation, appellation (*fml*), title, epithet, phrase, expression. **2** *in his second term at university*: time, period, course, duration, spell, span, stretch, interval, space, semester, session, season.
▪ *verb* call, name, dub, style, designate, label, tag, title, entitle.

terminal *adjective* fatal, deadly, lethal, mortal, incurable.
F3 initial.

terminology *noun* language, jargon, phraseology, vocabulary, words, terms, nomenclature.

terms *noun* **1** *on good terms*: relations, relationship, footing, standing, position. **2** *the terms of the agreement*: conditions, specifications, stipulations, provisos, provisions, qualifications, particulars. **3** *our terms are very reasonable*: rates, charges, fees, prices, tariff.

terrestrial *adjective* earthly, worldly, global, mundane.
F3 extraterrestrial, cosmic, heavenly.

terrible *adjective* bad, awful, frightful, dreadful, shocking, appalling, outrageous, disgusting, revolting, repulsive, offensive, abhorrent (*fml*), hateful, horrid, horrible, unpleasant, obnoxious, foul, vile, hideous, gruesome, horrific, harrowing, distressing, grave, serious, severe, extreme, desperate.
F3 excellent, wonderful, superb.

terrific *adjective* **1** *a terrific show*: excellent, wonderful, marvellous, super, smashing (*infml*), outstanding, brilliant, magnificent, superb, fabulous (*infml*), fantastic (*infml*), cool (*infml*), sensational, amazing, stupendous, breathtaking. **2** *a terrific monster/price*: huge, enormous, gigantic, tremendous, great, intense, extreme, excessive.
F3 **1** awful, terrible, appalling.

terrify *verb* petrify, horrify, appal,

shock, terrorize, intimidate, frighten, scare, alarm, dismay.

territory *noun* country, land, state, dependency, province, domain, preserve, jurisdiction, sector, region, area, district, zone, tract, terrain.

terror *noun* fear, panic, dread, trepidation, horror, shock, fright, alarm, dismay, consternation, terrorism, intimidation.

terrorize *verb* threaten, menace, intimidate, oppress, coerce, bully, browbeat, frighten, scare, alarm, terrify, petrify, horrify, shock.

test *verb* try, experiment, examine, assess, evaluate, check, investigate, analyse, screen, prove, verify.

▪ *noun* trial, try-out, experiment, examination, assessment, evaluation, check, investigation, analysis, proof, probation, ordeal.

testify *verb* give evidence, depose, state, declare, assert, swear, avow, attest (*fml*), vouch, certify, corroborate, affirm, show, bear witness.

testimony *noun* evidence, statement, affidavit, submission, deposition, declaration, profession, attestation, affirmation, support, proof, verification, confirmation, witness, demonstration, manifestation, indication.

text *noun* words, wording, content, matter, body, subject, topic, theme, reading, passage, paragraph, sentence, book, textbook, source.

texture *noun* consistency, feel, surface, grain, weave, tissue, fabric, structure, composition, constitution, character, quality.

thank *verb* say thank you, be grateful, appreciate, acknowledge, recognize, credit.

thankful *adjective* grateful, appreciative, obliged, indebted, pleased, contented, relieved.
F3 ungrateful, unappreciative.

thankless *adjective* unrecognized, unappreciated, unrequited, unrewarding, unprofitable, fruitless.
F3 rewarding, worthwhile.

thanks *noun* gratitude, gratefulness, appreciation, acknowledgement, recognition, credit, thanksgiving, thank-offering.

thaw *verb* melt, defrost, de-ice, soften, liquefy, dissolve, warm, heat up.
F3 freeze.

theatrical *adjective* **1** *theatrical props*: dramatic, thespian. **2** *theatrical behaviour*: melodramatic, histrionic, mannered, affected, artificial, pompous, ostentatious, showy, extravagant, exaggerated, overdone.

Types of theatrical performance include:

ballet, burlesque, cabaret, circus, comedy, black comedy, comedy of humours, comedy of manners, comedy of menace, commedia dell'arte, duologue, farce, fringe theatre, Grand Guignol, kabuki, kitchen-sink, legitimate drama, masque, melodrama, mime, miracle play, monologue, morality play, mummery, music hall, musical, musical comedy, mystery play, Noh, opera, operetta, pageant, pantomime, play, Punch and Judy, puppet theatre, revue, street theatre, tableau, theatre-in-the-round, Theatre of the Absurd, Theatre of Cruelty, tragedy.

theft *noun* robbery, thieving, stealing, pilfering, larceny, shoplifting, kleptomania, fraud, embezzlement.

theme *noun* subject, topic, thread, motif, keynote, idea, gist, essence, burden, argument, thesis, dissertation, composition, essay, text, matter.

theoretical *adjective* hypothetical, conjectural, speculative, abstract, academic, pure, ideal.

F3 practical, applied, concrete.

theory *noun* hypothesis, supposition, assumption, presumption, surmise, guess, conjecture, speculation, idea, notion, abstraction, philosophy, thesis, plan, proposal, scheme, system.

F3 certainty, practice.

therapy *noun* treatment, remedy, cure, healing, tonic.

therefore *adverb* so, then, consequently, as a result, thus (*fml*).

thick *adjective* **1** *thick waist/sweater/forest*: wide, broad, fat, heavy, solid, dense, impenetrable, close, compact. **2** *thick cream/soup*: concentrated, condensed, viscous, coagulated, clotted. **3** *thick with shoppers*: full, packed, crowded, chock-a-block, swarming, teeming, bristling, brimming, bursting, numerous, abundant. **4** (*infml*) *can be a bit thick sometimes*: stupid, foolish, slow, dull, dim-witted, brainless, simple.

F3 **1** thin, slim, slender, slight. **3** sparse. **4** clever, brainy (*infml*).

thicken *verb* condense, stiffen, congeal, coagulate, clot, cake, gel, jell, set.

F3 thin.

thicket *noun* wood, copse, coppice, grove, spinney.

thickness *noun* **1** *wood/paint of the right thickness*: width, breadth, diameter, density, viscosity, bulk, body. **2** *several thicknesses of material*: layer, stratum, ply, sheet, coat.

F3 **1** thinness.

thief *noun* robber, bandit, mugger, pickpocket, shoplifter, burglar, house-breaker, plunderer, poacher, stealer, pilferer, filcher, kleptomaniac, swindler, embezzler.

thin *adjective* **1** *thin arms/a few thin sheep*: lean, slim, slender, narrow, attenuated (*fml*), slight, skinny, bony, skeletal, scraggy, scrawny, lanky, gaunt, spare,

underweight, undernourished, emaciated. **2** *thin fabric*: fine, delicate, light, flimsy, filmy, gossamer, sheer, see-through, transparent, translucent. **3** *thin pickings*: sparse, scarce, scattered, scant, meagre, poor, inadequate, deficient, scanty, skimpy. **4** *thin soup*: weak, feeble, runny, watery, diluted.

F **1** fat, broad. **2** thick, dense, solid. **3** plentiful, abundant. **4** strong.

▪ *verb* **1** *thinning out towards the end/thin out the plants*: narrow, attenuate (*fml*), diminish, reduce, trim, weed out. **2** *thin the paint*: weaken, dilute, water down.

thing *noun* **1** *make things out of wood*: article, object, entity, creature, body, substance. **2** *one of the things we need to discuss*: item, detail, particular, feature, factor, element, point, fact, concept, thought. **3** *the thing that turns the wheels*: device, contrivance, gadget, tool, implement, instrument, apparatus, machine, mechanism. **4** *have things to do*: act, deed, feat, action, task. **5** *a strange thing happened*: circumstance, eventuality, happening, occurrence, event, incident, phenomenon, affair, proceeding.

things *noun* belongings, possessions, effects, paraphernalia, stuff (*infml*), goods, luggage, baggage, equipment, gear (*infml*), clobber (*infml*), odds and ends, bits and pieces.

think *verb* **1** *think it was true*: believe, hold (*fml*), consider, regard, esteem, deem, judge, estimate, reckon, calculate, determine, conclude, reason. **2** *think of the consequences*: conceive, imagine, suppose, presume, surmise, expect, foresee, envisage, anticipate. **3** *think it over*: ponder, mull over, chew over, ruminate, meditate, contemplate, muse, cogitate, reflect, deliberate, weigh up, recall, recollect, remember.

thinking *noun* reasoning, philosophy, thoughts, conclusions, theory, idea, opinion, view, outlook, position, judgement, assessment.

▪ *adjective* reasoning, rational, intellectual, intelligent, cultured, sophisticated, philosophical, analytical, reflective, contemplative, thoughtful.

thirst *noun* **1** *dying of thirst*: thirstiness, dryness, drought. **2** *a thirst for knowledge*: desire, longing, yearning, hankering, craving, hunger, appetite, lust, passion, eagerness, keenness.

thirsty *adjective* **1** *hungry and thirsty*: dry, parched (*infml*), gasping (*infml*), dehydrated, arid. **2** *thirsty for knowledge*: desirous, longing, yearning, hankering, craving, hungry, burning, itching, dying, eager, avid, greedy.

thorn *noun* spike, point, barb

prickle, spine, bristle, needle.

thorough *adjective* full, complete, total, entire, utter, absolute, perfect, pure, sheer, unqualified, unmitigated, out-and-out, downright, sweeping, all-embracing, comprehensive, all-inclusive, exhaustive, thoroughgoing, intensive, in-depth, conscientious, efficient, painstaking, scrupulous, meticulous, careful.

F3 partial, superficial, careless.

though *conjunction* although, even if, notwithstanding, while, allowing, granted.

▪ *adverb* however, nevertheless, nonetheless, yet, still, even so, all the same, for all that.

thought *noun* **1** *give it some thought*: thinking, attention, heed, regard, consideration, study, scrutiny, introspection, meditation, contemplation, cogitation, reflection, deliberation. **2** *had thoughts of being a lawyer/ what are your thoughts on this?*: idea, notion, concept, conception, belief, conviction, opinion, view, judgement, assessment, conclusion, plan, design, intention, purpose, aim, hope, dream, expectation, anticipation. **3** *have some thought for others*: thoughtfulness, consideration, kindness, care, concern, compassion, sympathy, gesture, touch.

thoughtful *adjective* **1** *in thoughtful silence*: pensive, wistful, dreamy, abstracted, reflective, contemplative, introspective, thinking, absorbed, studious, serious, solemn. **2** *a thoughtful act*: considerate, kind, unselfish, helpful, caring, attentive, heedful, mindful, careful, prudent, cautious, wary.

F3 **2** thoughtless, insensitive, selfish.

thoughtless *adjective* **1** *a thoughtless thing to say*: inconsiderate, callous, unthinking, insensitive, unfeeling, tactless, undiplomatic, unkind, selfish, uncaring. **2** *in a thoughtless moment*: absent-minded, inattentive, heedless, mindless, foolish, stupid, silly, rash, reckless, ill-considered, imprudent, careless, negligent, remiss.

F3 **1** thoughtful, considerate. **2** careful.

thrash *verb* **1** *was thrashed severely*: punish, beat, whip, lash, flog, scourge, cane, belt, spank, clobber, wallop (*infml*), lay into. **2** *thrashed the opposition*: defeat, beat, trounce, hammer (*infml*), slaughter (*infml*), crush, overwhelm, rout. **3** *thrashing about in the water*: thresh, flail, toss, jerk.

thread *noun* **1** *sewing thread*: cotton, yarn, strand, fibre, filament, string, line. **2** *lose the thread of the argument*: course, direction, drift, tenor, theme, motif, plot, storyline.

threadbare *adjective* worn,

frayed, ragged, moth-eaten, scruffy, shabby.

F3 new.

threat *noun* menace, warning, omen, portent, presage, foreboding, danger, risk, hazard, peril.

threaten *verb* menace, intimidate, browbeat, pressurize, bully, terrorize, warn, portend, presage, forebode, foreshadow, endanger, jeopardize, imperil.

threatening *adjective* menacing, warning, cautionary, ominous, inauspicious, sinister, grim, looming, impending.

threshold *noun* doorstep, sill, doorway, door, entrance, brink, verge, starting-point, dawn, beginning, start, outset, opening.

thrifty *adjective* economical, saving, frugal, sparing, prudent, careful.

F3 extravagant, profligate, prodigal, wasteful.

thrill *noun* excitement, adventure, pleasure, stimulation, charge, kick (*infml*), buzz (*infml*), sensation, glow, tingle, throb, shudder, quiver, tremor.

▪ *verb* excite, electrify, galvanize, exhilarate, rouse, arouse, move, stir, stimulate, flush, glow, tingle, throb, shudder, tremble, quiver, shake.

F3 bore.

thrive *verb* flourish, prosper, boom, grow, increase, advance, develop, bloom, blossom, gain, profit, succeed.

F3 languish, stagnate, fail, die.

throb *verb* pulse, pulsate, beat, palpitate, vibrate, pound, thump.

throttle *verb* strangle, choke, asphyxiate, suffocate, smother, stifle, gag, silence, suppress, inhibit.

through *preposition* **1** *through the streets*: between, by, via, by way of, by means of, using. **2** *all through the night*: throughout, during, in. **3** *through his efforts*: because of, as a result of, thanks to.

▪ *adjective* direct, express, non-stop.

throw *verb* **1** *throw a stone*: hurl, heave, lob, pitch, chuck (*infml*), sling, cast, fling, toss, launch, propel, send. **2** *throw light on something*: shed, cast, project, direct. **3** *was thrown to the ground*: bring down, floor, upset, overturn, dislodge, unseat, unsaddle, unhorse.

▪ *noun* heave, lob, pitch, sling, fling, toss, cast.

thrust *verb* push, shove, butt, ram, jam, wedge, stick, poke, prod, jab, lunge, pierce, stab, plunge, press, force, impel, drive, propel.

▪ *noun* push, shove, poke, prod, lunge, stab, drive, impetus, momentum.

thud *noun, verb* thump, clump, knock, clunk, smack, wallop (*infml*), crash, bang, thunder.

thump *noun* knock, blow, punch, clout, box, cuff, smack, whack (*infml*), wallop (*infml*), crash, bang, thud, beat, throb.

▪ *verb* hit, strike, knock, punch, clout, box, cuff, smack, thrash, whack (*infml*), wallop (*infml*), crash, bang, thud, batter, pound, hammer, beat, throb.

thunder *noun* boom, reverberation, crash, bang, crack, clap, peal, rumble, roll, roar, blast, explosion.

▪ *verb* boom, resound, reverberate, crash, bang, crack, clap, peal, rumble, roll, roar, blast.

thus *adverb* so, hence, therefore, consequently, then, accordingly, like this, in this way, as follows.

thwart *verb* frustrate, foil, stymie, defeat, hinder, impede, obstruct, block, check, baffle, stop, prevent, oppose.

F3 help, assist, aid.

tick *noun* **1** *the tick of the clock*: click, tap, stroke, tick-tock. **2** (*infml*) *wait a tick*: moment, instant, flash, jiffy (*infml*), second, minute.

▪ *verb* **1** *tick the box*: mark, indicate, choose, select. **2** *clock ticking*: click, tap, beat.

ticket *noun* pass, card, certificate, token, voucher, coupon, docket, slip, label, tag, sticker.

tickle *verb* excite, thrill, delight, please, gratify, amuse, entertain, divert.

tide *noun* current, ebb, flow, stream, flux, movement, course, direction, drift, trend, tendency.

tidy *adjective* **1** *a tidy cupboard/appearance*: neat, orderly, methodical, systematic, organized, clean, spick-and-span, shipshape, smart, spruce, trim, well-kept, ordered, uncluttered. **2** (*infml*) *a tidy sum*: large, substantial, sizable, considerable, good, generous, ample.

F3 **1** untidy, messy, disorganized. **2** small, insignificant.

▪ *verb* neaten, straighten, order, arrange, clean, smarten, spruce up, groom.

tie *verb* knot, fasten, secure, moor, tether, attach, join, connect, link, unite, rope, lash, strap, bind, restrain, restrict, confine, limit, hamper, hinder.

▪ *noun* **1** *breaking all his family ties*: connection, link, liaison, relationship, bond, affiliation, obligation, commitment, duty, restraint, restriction, limitation, hindrance. **2** *ended in a tie*: draw, dead heat, stalemate, deadlock.

tier *noun* floor, storey, level, stage, stratum, layer, belt, zone, band, echelon, rank, row, line.

tight *adjective* **1** *keep the line tight/tight clothes/a tight space*: taut, stretched, tense, rigid, stiff, firm, fixed, fast, secure, close, cramped, constricted, compact, snug, close-fitting. **2** *a tight seal*: hermetic, -proof, impervious, airtight, watertight. **3** *tight security*: strict, severe, stringent, rigorous.

F3 **1** loose, slack. **2** open. **3** lax.

tilt *verb* slope, incline, slant, pitch, list, tip, lean.

▪ *noun* slope, incline, angle, inclination, slant, pitch, list.

timber *noun* wood, trees, forest, beam, lath, plank, board, log.

time *noun* **1** *stay for a short/long time*: spell, stretch, period, term, season, session, span, duration, interval, space, while. **2** *in time with the music*: tempo, beat, rhythm, metre, measure. **3** *at that time in his life*: moment, point, juncture, stage, instance, occasion, date, day, hour. **4** *in Roman times/in the time of Napoleon*: age, era, epoch, life, lifetime, generation, heyday, peak.
▪ *verb* clock, measure, meter, regulate, control, set, schedule, timetable.

Periods of time include:
eternity, era, eon, age, generation, period, epoch, millennium, century, lifetime, quinquennium, year, light-year, yesteryear, quarter, month, fortnight, week, midweek, weekend, long weekend, day, weekday, hour, minute, second, moment, instant, millisecond, microsecond, nanosecond; dawn, sunrise, sun-up, the early hours, wee small hours (*infml*), morning, morn, a.m., daytime, midday, noon, high noon, p.m., afternoon, teatime, evening, twilight, dusk, sunset, nightfall, bedtime, night, night-time; season, spring, summer, midsummer, autumn, fall (*US*), winter, midwinter.

---

timeless *adjective* ageless, immortal, everlasting, eternal, endless, permanent, lasting, enduring, changeless, unchanging, unending, abiding (*fml*).

timely *adjective* well-timed, seasonable, suitable, appropriate, convenient, opportune, propitious, prompt, punctual.
ill-timed, unsuitable, inappropriate.

timetable *noun* schedule, programme, agenda, calendar, diary, rota, roster, list, listing, curriculum.

timid *adjective* shy, bashful, modest, shrinking, retiring, nervous, apprehensive, afraid, timorous, fearful, cowardly, faint-hearted, spineless, irresolute.
brave, bold, audacious.

tinge *noun* tint, dye, colour, shade, touch, trace, suggestion, hint, smack, flavour, pinch, drop, dash, bit, sprinkling, smattering.
▪ *verb* tint, dye, stain, colour, shade, suffuse, imbue.

tingle *verb* sting, prickle, tickle, itch, thrill, throb, quiver, vibrate.

tinker *verb* fiddle, play, toy, trifle, potter, dabble, meddle, tamper.

tint *noun* dye, stain, rinse, wash, colour, hue, shade, tincture, tinge, tone, cast, streak, trace, touch.

tiny *adjective* minute, microscopic, infinitesimal, teeny (*infml*), small, little, slight, negligible, insignificant, diminutive, petite, dwarfish, pint-sized (*infml*), pocket, miniature, mini (*infml*).

F3 huge, enormous, immense.

tip[1] *noun* end, extremity, point, nib, apex, peak, pinnacle, summit, acme, top, cap, crown, head.

tip[2] *verb* lean, incline, slant, list, tilt, topple over, capsize, upset, overturn, spill, pour out, empty, unload, dump.

tip[3] *noun* **1** *gave us a few useful tips*: clue, pointer, hint, suggestion, advice, warning, tip-off, information, inside information, forecast. **2** *gave the waiter a tip*: gratuity, gift, perquisite (*fml*).
▪ *verb* **1** *tipped us off*: advise, suggest, warn, caution, forewarn, tip off, inform, tell. **2** *tip the driver*: reward, remunerate.

tire *verb* weary, fatigue, wear out, exhaust, drain, enervate.
F3 enliven, invigorate, refresh.

tired *adjective* **1** *felt very tired*: weary, drowsy, sleepy, flagging, fatigued, worn out, exhausted, dog-tired, drained, jaded, bushed (*infml*), whacked (*infml*), shattered (*infml*), beat (*infml*), dead-beat (*infml*), all in (*infml*), knackered (*infml*). **2** *tired of waiting*: fed up, bored, sick.
F3 **1** lively, energetic, rested, refreshed.

tireless *adjective* untiring, unwearied, unflagging, indefatigable, energetic, vigorous, diligent, industrious, resolute, determined.
F3 tired, lazy.

tiresome *adjective* troublesome, trying, annoying, irritating, exasperating, wearisome, dull, boring, tedious, monotonous, uninteresting, tiring, fatiguing, laborious.
F3 interesting, stimulating, easy.

tiring *adjective* wearying, fatiguing, exhausting, draining, demanding, exacting, taxing, arduous, strenuous, laborious.

title *noun* **1** *what's her (job) title?*: name, appellation (*fml*), denomination (*fml*), term, designation, label, epithet, nickname, pseudonym, rank, status, office, position. **2** *the title of the play*: heading, headline, caption, legend, inscription.
▪ *verb* entitle, name, call, dub, style, term, designate, label.

toast *verb* grill, brown, roast, heat, warm.
▪ *noun* drink, pledge, tribute, salute, compliment, health.

together *adverb* jointly, in concert, side by side, shoulder to shoulder, in unison, as one, simultaneously, at the same time, all at once, collectively, en masse, closely, continuously, consecutively, successively, in succession, in a row, hand in hand.
F3 separately, individually, alone.

toil *noun* labour, hard work, donkey-work, drudgery, sweat, graft (*infml*), industry, application, effort, exertion, elbow grease.
▪ *verb* labour, work, slave, drudge, sweat, grind, slog, graft (*infml*), plug away (*infml*), persevere, strive, struggle.

token *noun* **1** *a love token*: symbol, emblem, representation, mark, sign, indication, manifestation, demonstration, expression, evidence, proof, clue, warning, reminder, memorial, memento, souvenir, keepsake. **2** *gift token*: voucher, coupon, counter, disc.
▪ *adjective* symbolic, emblematic, nominal, minimal, perfunctory (*fml*), superficial, cosmetic, hollow, insincere.

tolerable *adjective* bearable, endurable, sufferable, acceptable, passable, adequate, reasonable, fair, average, all right, OK (*infml*), not bad, mediocre, indifferent, so-so (*infml*), unexceptional, ordinary, run-of-the-mill.
F3 intolerable, unbearable, insufferable.

tolerant *adjective* patient, forbearing, long-suffering, open-minded, fair, unprejudiced, broad-minded, liberal, charitable, kind-hearted, sympathetic, understanding, forgiving, lenient, indulgent, easy-going (*infml*), permissive, lax, soft.
F3 intolerant, biased, prejudiced, bigoted, unsympathetic.

tolerate *verb* endure, suffer, put up with, bear, stand, abide, stomach, swallow, take, receive, accept, admit, allow, permit, condone, countenance, indulge.

toll[1] *verb* ring, peal, chime, knell, sound, strike, announce, call.

toll[2] *noun* charge, fee, payment, levy, tax, duty, tariff, rate, cost, penalty, demand.

tomb *noun* grave, burial-place, vault, crypt, sepulchre, catacomb, mausoleum, cenotaph.

tone *noun* **1** *tone of voice*: note, timbre, pitch, volume, intonation, modulation, inflection, accent, stress, emphasis, force, strength. **2** *brown tones*: tint, tinge, colour, hue, shade, cast, tonality. **3** *gauge the tone of the meeting*: air, manner, attitude, mood, spirit, humour, temper, character, quality, feel, style, effect, vein, tenor, drift.
▪ *verb* match, co-ordinate, blend, harmonize.

tongue *noun* language, speech, discourse, talk, utterance, articulation, parlance, vernacular, idiom, dialect, patois.

tonic *noun* cordial, pick-me-up, restorative, refresher, bracer, stimulant, shot in the arm (*infml*), boost, fillip.

too *adverb* **1** *like him too*: also, as well, in addition, besides, moreover, likewise. **2** *too expensive*: excessively, inordinately, unduly, over, overly, unreasonably, ridiculously, extremely, very.

tool *noun* implement, instrument, utensil, gadget, device, contrivance, contraption, apparatus, appliance.

top *noun* **1** *top of the class/hill*: head, tip, vertex, apex, crest, crown, peak, pinnacle, summit, acme, zenith, culmination, height.

2 *put the top back on the toothpaste*: lid, cap, cover, cork, stopper.
FA **1** bottom, base, nadir.
▪ *adjective* highest, topmost, upmost, uppermost, upper, superior, head, chief, leading, first, foremost, principal, sovereign, ruling, pre-eminent, dominant, prime, paramount, greatest, maximum, best, finest, supreme, crowning, culminating.
FA bottom, lowest, inferior.
▪ *verb* **1** *ice cream topped with raspberry sauce*: tip, cap, crown, cover, finish (off), decorate, garnish. **2** *that tops everything*: beat, exceed, outstrip, better, excel, best, surpass, eclipse, outshine, outdo, surmount, transcend.

topic *noun* subject, theme, issue, question, matter, point, thesis, text.

topical *adjective* current, contemporary, up-to-date, up-to-the-minute, recent, newsworthy, relevant, popular, familiar.

topple *verb* totter, overbalance, tumble, fall, collapse, upset, overturn, capsize, overthrow, oust.

torment *verb* tease, provoke, annoy, vex, trouble, worry, harass, hound, pester, bother, bedevil, plague, afflict, distress, harrow, pain, torture, persecute.

torrent *noun* stream, volley, outburst, gush, rush, flood, spate, deluge, cascade, downpour.
FA trickle.

torture *verb* pain, agonize, excruciate, crucify, rack, martyr, persecute, torment, afflict, distress.
▪ *noun* pain, agony, suffering, affliction, distress, misery, anguish, torment, martyrdom, persecution.

toss *verb* **1** *toss a coin/toss it away*: flip, cast, fling, throw, chuck (*infml*), sling, hurl, lob. **2** *tossed from side to side*: roll, heave, pitch, lurch, jolt, shake, agitate, rock, thrash, squirm, wriggle.

total *noun* sum, whole, entirety, totality, all, lot, mass, aggregate, amount.
▪ *adjective* full, complete, entire, whole, integral, all-out, utter, absolute, unconditional, unqualified, outright, undisputed, perfect, consummate, thoroughgoing, sheer, downright, thorough.
FA partial, limited, restricted.
▪ *verb* add (up), sum (up), tot (up), count (up), reckon, amount to, come to, reach.

touch *noun* **1** *the touch of her hand*: feel, texture, brush, stroke, caress, pat, tap, contact. **2** *a touch of garlic*: trace, spot, dash, pinch, soupçon, suspicion, hint, suggestion, speck, jot, tinge, smack. **3** *has the right touch*: skill, art, knack, flair, style, method, manner, technique, approach.
▪ *verb* **1** *touched his face*: feel, handle, finger, brush, graze, stroke, caress, fondle, pat, tap, hit, strike. **2** *touching on either side*:

contact, meet, abut, adjoin, border. **3** *touched her heart*: move, stir, upset, disturb, impress, inspire, influence, affect. **4** *her letters touched on the subject more than once*: mention, concern, broach, speak of, remark on, refer to, allude to, cover, deal with. **5** *couldn't touch him for sheer skill*: reach, attain, equal, match, rival, better.

touchy *adjective* irritable, irascible, quick-tempered, bad-tempered, grumpy, grouchy, crabbed, cross, peevish, captious, edgy, over-sensitive.
F3 calm, imperturbable.

tough *adjective* **1** *a tough material*: strong, durable, resilient, resistant, hardy, sturdy, solid, rigid, stiff, inflexible, hard, leathery. **2** *tough character*: rough, violent, vicious, callous, hardened, obstinate. **3** *a tough regime*: harsh, severe, strict, stern. **4** *had to be pretty tough to survive*: firm, resolute, determined, tenacious. **5** *a tough job/problem*: arduous, laborious, exacting, hard, difficult, puzzling, perplexing, baffling, knotty, thorny, troublesome.
F3 1 fragile, delicate, weak, tender. **2** gentle, soft. **3** gentle. **5** easy, simple.

tour *noun* circuit, round, visit, expedition, journey, trip, outing, excursion, drive, ride, course.
▪ *verb* visit, go round, sightsee, explore, travel, journey, drive, ride.

tourist *noun* holidaymaker, visitor, sightseer, tripper, excursionist, traveller, voyager, globetrotter.

tournament *noun* championship, series, competition, contest, match, event, meeting.

tow *verb* pull, tug, draw, trail, drag, lug, haul, transport.

towards *preposition* **1** *towards the end*: to, approaching, nearing, close to, nearly, almost. **2** *his feelings towards her*: regarding, with regard to, with respect to, concerning, about, for.

tower *noun* steeple, spire, belfry, turret, fortification, bastion, citadel, fort, fortress, castle, keep.

toxic *adjective* poisonous, harmful, noxious, unhealthy, dangerous, deadly, lethal.
F3 harmless, safe.

toy *noun* plaything, game, doll, knick-knack.
▪ *verb* play, tinker, fiddle, sport, trifle, dally.

trace *noun* trail, track, spoor, footprint, footmark, mark, token, sign, indication, evidence, record, relic, remains, remnant, vestige, shadow, hint, suggestion, suspicion, soupçon, dash, drop, spot, bit, jot, touch, tinge, smack.
▪ *verb* **1** *trace the picture/trace the outline with his finger*: copy, draw, sketch, outline, delineate, depict, mark, record, map, chart. **2** *trace his missing family*: find, discover, detect, unearth, track (down), trail, stalk, hunt, seek, follow, pursue, shadow.

track *noun* footstep, footprint, footmark, scent, spoor, trail, wake, mark, trace, slot, groove, rail, path, way, route, orbit, line, course, drift, sequence.
▪ *verb* stalk, trail, hunt, trace, follow, pursue, chase, dog, tail, shadow.

trade *noun* **1** *the trade in manufactured goods/trade is brisk*: commerce, traffic, business, dealing, buying, selling, shopkeeping, barter, exchange, transactions, custom. **2** *learning his trade*: occupation, job, business, profession, calling, craft, skill.
▪ *verb* traffic, peddle, do business, deal, transact, buy, sell, barter, exchange, swap, switch, bargain.

trademark *noun* brand, label, name, sign, symbol, logo, insignia, crest, emblem, badge, hallmark.

trader *noun* merchant, tradesman, broker, dealer, buyer, seller, vendor, supplier, wholesaler, retailer, shopkeeper, trafficker, peddler.

traditional *adjective* conventional, customary, habitual, usual, accustomed, established, fixed, long-established, time-honoured, old, historic, folk, oral, unwritten.
F3 unconventional, innovative, new, modern, contemporary.

traffic *noun* vehicles, shipping, transport, transportation, freight.
▪ *verb* peddle, buy, sell, trade, do business, deal, bargain, barter, exchange.

tragedy *noun* adversity, misfortune, unhappiness, affliction, blow, calamity, disaster, catastrophe.

tragic *adjective* sad, sorrowful, miserable, unhappy, unfortunate, unlucky, ill-fated, pitiable, pathetic, heartbreaking, shocking, appalling, dreadful, awful, dire, calamitous, disastrous, catastrophic, deadly, fatal.
F3 happy, comic, successful.

trail *verb* **1** *trailing along behind*: drag, pull, tow, droop, dangle, extend, stream, straggle, dawdle, lag, loiter, linger. **2** *trailing the thieves to their hideout*: track, stalk, hunt, follow, pursue, chase, shadow, tail.
▪ *noun* track, footprints, footmarks, scent, trace, path, footpath, road, route, way.

train *verb* teach, instruct, coach, tutor, educate, improve, school, discipline, prepare, drill, exercise, work out, practise, rehearse.
▪ *noun* **1** *train of events*: sequence, succession, series, progression, order, string, chain, line, file, procession, convoy, cortège, caravan. **2** *the queen and her train of courtiers*: retinue, entourage, attendants, court, household, staff, followers, following.

training *noun* teaching, instruction, coaching, tuition, education, schooling, discipline, preparation, grounding, drill, exercise, working-out, practice, learning, apprenticeship.

trait *noun* feature, attribute, quality, characteristic, idiosyncrasy, peculiarity, quirk.

traitor *noun* betrayer, informer, deceiver, double-crosser, turncoat, renegade, deserter, defector, quisling, collaborator.
E3 loyalist, supporter, defender.

tramp *verb* walk, march, tread, stamp, stomp, stump, plod, trudge, traipse, trail, trek, hike, ramble, roam, rove.
▪ *noun* vagrant, vagabond, hobo, down-and-out, dosser (*infml*).

trample *verb* tread, stamp, crush, squash, flatten.

trance *noun* dream, reverie, daze, stupor, unconsciousness, spell, ecstasy, rapture.

tranquil *adjective* calm, composed, cool, imperturbable, unexcited, placid, sedate, relaxed, laid-back (*infml*), serene, peaceful, restful, still, undisturbed, untroubled, quiet, hushed, silent.
E3 agitated, disturbed, troubled, noisy.

transaction *noun* deal, bargain, agreement, arrangement, negotiation, business, affair, matter, proceeding, enterprise, undertaking, deed, action, execution, discharge.

transfer *verb* change, transpose, move, shift, remove, relocate, transplant, transport, carry, convey, transmit, consign, grant, hand over.
▪ *noun* change, changeover, transposition, move, shift, removal, relocation, displacement, transmission, handover, transference.

transform *verb* change, alter, adapt, convert, remodel, reconstruct, transfigure, revolutionize.
E3 preserve, maintain.

transit *noun* passage, journey, travel, movement, transfer, transportation, conveyance, carriage, haulage, shipment.

transition *noun* passage, passing, progress, progression, development, evolution, flux, change, alteration, conversion, transformation, shift.

transitional *adjective* provisional, temporary, passing, intermediate, developmental, changing, fluid, unsettled.
E3 initial, final.

translate *verb* interpret, render, paraphrase, simplify, decode, decipher, transliterate, transcribe, change, alter, convert, transform, improve.

translation *noun* rendering, version, interpretation, gloss, crib, rewording, rephrasing, paraphrase, simplification, transliteration, transcription, change, alteration, conversion, transformation.

transmission *noun* **1** *transmission of diseases*: broadcasting, diffusion, spread, communication, conveyance, carriage, transport, shipment, sending, dispatch, relaying, transfer. **2** *a live transmission*: broadcast, programme, show, signal.

F3 **1** reception.

transmit *verb* communicate, impart, convey, carry, bear, transport, send, dispatch, forward, relay, transfer, broadcast, radio, disseminate, network, diffuse, spread.

F3 receive.

transparent *adjective* **1** *transparent plastic*: clear, see-through, translucent, sheer. **2** *meaning was transparent*: plain, distinct, clear, lucid, explicit, unambiguous, unequivocal, apparent, visible, obvious, evident, manifest, patent, undisguised, open, candid, straightforward.

F3 **1** opaque. **2** unclear, ambiguous.

transplant *verb* move, shift, displace, remove, uproot, transfer, relocate, resettle, repot.

F3 leave.

transport *verb* convey, carry, bear, take, fetch, bring, move, shift, transfer, ship, haul, remove, deport.

▪ *noun* conveyance, carriage, transfer, transportation, shipment, shipping, haulage, removal.

trap *noun* snare, net, noose, springe, gin, booby-trap, pitfall, danger, hazard, ambush, trick, wile, ruse, stratagem, device, trickery, artifice, deception.

▪ *verb* snare, net, entrap, ensnare, enmesh, catch, take, ambush, corner, trick, deceive, dupe.

trash *noun* rubbish, garbage, refuse, junk, waste, litter, sweepings, scum, dregs.

trauma *noun* injury, wound, hurt, damage, pain, suffering, anguish, agony, torture, ordeal, shock, jolt, upset, disturbance, upheaval, strain, stress.

F3 healing.

traumatic *adjective* painful, hurtful, injurious, shocking, upsetting, distressing, disturbing, unpleasant, frightening, stressful.

F3 healing, relaxing.

travel *verb* journey, voyage, go, wend, move, proceed, progress, wander, ramble, roam, rove, tour, cross, traverse.

F3 stay, remain.

▪ *noun* travelling, touring, tourism, globetrotting.

Methods of travel include:

aviate, bike (*infml*), bus, commute, cruise, cycle, drive, fly, freewheel, hike, hitch-hike, march, motor, orienteer, paddle, pilot, punt, ramble, ride, row, sail, shuttle, skate, ski, steam, swim, trek, walk.

Forms of travel include:

circumnavigation, cruise, drive, excursion, expedition, exploration, flight, hike, holiday, jaunt, journey, march, migration, mission, outing, pilgrimage, ramble, ride, safari, sail, tour, trek, trip, visit, voyage, walk.

---

traveller *noun* **1** *a seasoned traveller*: tourist, explorer, voyager, globetrotter, holidaymaker, tripper (*infml*), excursionist, passenger, commuter, wanderer, rambler, hiker, wayfarer, migrant, nomad. **2** *a commercial traveller*: salesman, saleswoman, representative, rep (*infml*), agent.

travelling *adjective* touring, wandering, roaming, roving, wayfaring, migrating, migrant, migratory, nomadic, itinerant, peripatetic, mobile, moving, vagrant, homeless, unsettled.
F3 fixed.

treacherous *adjective* **1** *a treacherous plot*: traitorous, disloyal, unfaithful, faithless, unreliable, untrustworthy, false, untrue, deceitful, double-crossing. **2** *treacherous roads*: dangerous, hazardous, risky, perilous, precarious, icy, slippery.
F3 **1** loyal, faithful, dependable. **2** safe, stable.

tread *verb* walk, step, pace, stride, march, tramp, trudge, plod, stamp, trample, walk on, press, crush, squash.
▪ *noun* walk, footfall, footstep, step, pace, stride.

treason *noun* treachery, perfidy, disloyalty, duplicity (*fml*), subversion, sedition, mutiny, rebellion.
F3 loyalty.

treasure *noun* fortune, wealth, riches, money, cash, gold, jewels, hoard, cache.
▪ *verb* prize, value, esteem, revere, worship, love, adore, idolize, cherish, preserve, guard.
F3 disparage, belittle.

treat *noun* indulgence, gratification, pleasure, delight, enjoyment, fun, entertainment, excursion, outing, party, celebration, feast, banquet, gift, surprise, thrill.
▪ *verb* **1** *how will you treat this question?*: deal with, manage, handle, use, regard, consider, discuss, cover. **2** *treat the patient*: tend, nurse, minister to, attend to, care for, heal, cure. **3** *treat you to lunch*: pay for, buy, stand, give, provide, entertain, regale, feast.

treatment *noun* **1** *treatment of disease*: healing, cure, remedy, medication, therapy, surgery, care, nursing. **2** *the treatment of waste/the paper's treatment of the story*: management, handling, use, usage, conduct, discussion, coverage.

treaty *noun* pact, convention, agreement, covenant, compact, negotiation, contract, bond, alliance.

tree *noun* bush, shrub, evergreen, conifer.

Trees include:

acacia, acer, alder, almond, apple, ash, aspen, balsa, bay, beech, birch, blackthorn, blue gum, box, cedar, cherry, chestnut, coconut palm, cottonwood, cypress, date palm, dogwood, Dutch elm, ebony, elder, elm, eucalyptus, fig, fir, gum, hawthorn, hazel, hickory, hornbeam, horse chestnut, Japanese maple, larch, laurel, lime, linden, mahogany, maple, monkey puzzle, mountain ash, oak, palm, pear, pine, plane, plum, poplar, prunus, pussy willow, redwood, rowan, rubber tree, sandalwood, sapele, sequoia, silver birch, silver maple, spruce, sycamore, teak, walnut, weeping willow, whitebeam, willow, witch hazel, yew, yucca; bonsai, conifer, deciduous, evergreen, fruit, hardwood, ornamental, palm, softwood. *See also* **wood**.

---

trek *noun* hike, walk, march, tramp, journey, expedition, safari.
▪ *verb* hike, walk, march, tramp, trudge, plod, journey, rove, roam.

tremble *verb* shake, vibrate, quake, shiver, shudder, quiver, wobble, rock.

tremendous *adjective* wonderful, marvellous, stupendous, sensational, spectacular, extraordinary, amazing, incredible, terrific, impressive, huge, immense, vast, colossal, gigantic, towering, formidable.
F3 ordinary, unimpressive.

tremor *noun* shake, quiver, tremble, shiver, quake, quaver, wobble, vibration, agitation, thrill, shock, earthquake.
F3 steadiness.

trend *noun* course, flow, drift, tendency, inclination, leaning, craze, rage (*infml*), fashion, vogue, mode, style, look.

trespass *verb* invade, intrude, encroach, poach, infringe, violate, offend, wrong.
F3 obey, keep to.

trial *noun* **1** *on trial/go to trial*: litigation, lawsuit, hearing, inquiry, tribunal. **2** *medical trials*: experiment, test, examination, check, dry run, dummy run, practice, rehearsal, audition, contest. **3** *the trials of life*: affliction, suffering, grief, misery, distress, adversity, hardship, ordeal, trouble, nuisance, vexation, tribulation.
F3 **3** relief, happiness.
▪ *adjective* experimental, test, pilot, exploratory, provisional, probationary.

tribe *noun* race, nation, people, clan, family, house, dynasty, blood, stock, group, caste, class, division, branch.

tribute *noun* praise, commendation, compliment, accolade, homage, respect, honour, credit, acknowledgement, recognition, gratitude.

trick *noun* fraud, swindle, deception, deceit, artifice, illusion, hoax, practical joke, joke, leg-pull (*infml*), prank, antic, caper, frolic, feat, stunt, ruse, wile, dodge, subterfuge, trap, device, knack, technique, secret.
▪ *verb* deceive, delude, dupe, fool, hoodwink, beguile, mislead, bluff, hoax, pull someone's leg (*infml*), cheat, swindle, diddle, defraud,

con (*infml*), trap, outwit.

trickery *noun* deception, illusion, sleight-of-hand, pretence, artifice, guile, deceit, dishonesty, cheating, swindling, fraud, imposture, double-dealing, monkey business, funny business (*infml*), chicanery, skulduggery, hocus-pocus.
F3 straightforwardness, honesty.

trickle *verb* dribble, run, leak, seep, ooze, exude, drip, drop, filter, percolate.
F3 stream, gush.
▪ *noun* dribble, drip, drop, leak, seepage.
F3 stream, gush.

tricky *adjective* difficult, awkward, problematic, complicated, knotty, thorny, delicate, ticklish.
F3 easy, simple.

trifle *noun* **1** *turn the sound up a trifle*: little, bit, spot, drop, dash, touch, trace. **2** *bought you a little trifle for your jewellery box*: toy, plaything, trinket, bauble, knick-knack, triviality, nothing.
▪ *verb* toy, play, sport, flirt, dally, dabble, fiddle, meddle, fool.

trigger *verb* cause, start, initiate, activate, set off, spark off, provoke, prompt, elicit, generate, produce.
▪ *noun* lever, catch, switch, spur, stimulus.

trim *adjective* **1** *a trim little craft/a trim appearance*: neat, tidy, orderly, shipshape, spick-and-span, spruce, smart, dapper. **2** *a trim waist*: slim, slender, streamlined, compact.
F3 1 untidy, scruffy.
▪ *verb* **1** *trim his hair/beard/the hedge*: cut, clip, crop, dock, prune, pare, shave, neaten, tidy. **2** *trim the dress with lace*: decorate, ornament, embellish, garnish, dress.
▪ *noun* condition, state, order, form, shape, fitness, health.

trimmings *noun* **1** *roast beef with all the trimmings*: garnish, decorations, ornaments, frills, extras, accessories. **2** *fabric trimmings*: cuttings, clippings, parings, ends.

trio *noun* threesome, triad, triumvirate, trinity, triplet, trilogy.

trip *noun* outing, excursion, tour, jaunt, ride, drive, spin, journey, voyage, expedition, foray.
▪ *verb* stumble, slip, fall, tumble, stagger, totter, blunder.

triple *adjective* treble, triplicate, threefold, three-ply, three-way.
▪ *verb* treble, triplicate.

triumph *noun* **1** *fresh from his triumph in the Olympics*: win, victory, conquest, walk-over, success, achievement, accomplishment, feat, coup, masterstroke, hit, sensation. **2** *couldn't disguise the triumph in her voice*: exultation, jubilation, rejoicing, celebration, elation, joy, happiness.
F3 1 failure.
▪ *verb* win, succeed, prosper, conquer, vanquish (*fml*), overcome, overwhelm, prevail, dominate, celebrate, rejoice, glory, gloat.
F3 lose, fail.

triumphant *adjective* winning, victorious, conquering, successful, exultant, jubilant, rejoicing, celebratory, glorious, elated, joyful, proud, boastful, gloating, swaggering.
F3 defeated, humble.

trivial *adjective* unimportant, insignificant, inconsequential, incidental, minor, petty, paltry, trifling, small, little, inconsiderable, negligible, worthless, meaningless, frivolous, banal, trite, commonplace, everyday.
F3 important, significant, profound.

troop *noun* contingent, squadron, unit, division, company, squad, team, crew, gang, band, bunch, group, body, pack, herd, flock, horde, crowd, throng, multitude.
▪ *verb* go, march, parade, stream, flock, swarm, throng.

troops *noun* army, military, soldiers, servicemen, servicewomen.

trophy *noun* cup, prize, award, souvenir, memento.

tropical *adjective* hot, torrid, sultry, sweltering, stifling, steamy, humid.
F3 arctic, cold, cool, temperate.

trot *verb* jog, run, scamper, scuttle, scurry.

trouble *noun* **1** *have a lot of trouble/tell her his troubles*: problem, difficulty, struggle, annoyance, irritation, bother, nuisance, inconvenience, misfortune, adversity, trial, tribulation, pain, suffering, affliction, distress, grief, woe, heartache, concern, uneasiness, worry, anxiety, agitation. **2** *trouble in the streets*: unrest, strife, tumult, commotion, disturbance, disorder, upheaval. **3** *back trouble*: disorder, complaint, ailment, illness, disease, disability, defect. **4** *too much trouble to do it*: effort, exertion, pains, care, attention, thought.
F3 **1** relief, calm. **2** order. **3** health.
▪ *verb* annoy, vex, harass, torment, bother, inconvenience, disturb, upset, distress, sadden, pain, afflict, burden, worry, agitate, disconcert, perplex.
F3 reassure, help.

troublemaker *noun* agitator, rabble-rouser, instigator, ringleader, stirrer, mischief-maker.
F3 peacemaker.

troublesome *adjective* annoying, irritating, vexatious, irksome, bothersome, inconvenient, difficult, hard, tricky, thorny, taxing, demanding, laborious, tiresome, wearisome.
F3 easy, simple.

trough *noun* gutter, conduit, trench, ditch, gully, channel, groove, furrow, hollow, depression.

truant *noun* absentee, deserter, runaway, idler, shirker, skiver (*infml*), dodger.
▪ *adjective* absent, missing, runaway.

truce *noun* ceasefire, peace, armistice, cessation, moratorium, suspension, stay, respite, let-up (*infml*), lull, rest, break, interval, intermission.
F3 war, hostilities.

truck *noun* lorry, van, wagon, juggernaut, float.

trudge *verb* tramp, plod, clump, stump, lumber, traipse, slog, labour, trek, hike, walk, march.

true *adjective* **1** *the true facts*: real, genuine, authentic, actual, veritable (*fml*), exact, precise, accurate, correct, right, factual, truthful, veracious (*fml*), sincere, honest, legitimate, valid, rightful, proper. **2** *a true friend*: faithful, loyal, constant, steadfast, staunch, firm, trustworthy, trusty, honourable, dedicated, devoted.
F3 1 false, wrong, incorrect, inaccurate. **2** unfaithful, faithless.

truly *adverb* very, greatly, extremely, really, genuinely, sincerely, honestly, truthfully, undeniably, indubitably, indeed, in fact, in reality, exactly, precisely, correctly, rightly, properly.
F3 slightly, falsely, incorrectly.

trumpet *noun* bugle, horn, clarion, blare, blast, roar, bellow, cry, call.
▪ *verb* blare, blast, roar, bellow, shout, proclaim, announce, broadcast, advertise.

trunk *noun* **1** *pack a large trunk*: case, suitcase, chest, coffer, box, crate. **2** *trunk of a tree*: shaft, stock, stem, stalk. **3** *spots appear mainly round the waist and on the trunk*: torso, body.

trust *noun* **1** *have trust in God/ betray someone's trust*: faith, belief, credence, credit, hope, expectation, reliance, confidence, assurance, conviction, certainty. **2** *hold the money in trust*: care, charge, custody, safekeeping, guardianship, protection, responsibility, duty.
F3 1 distrust, mistrust, scepticism, doubt.
▪ *verb* **1** *trust in providence*: believe, imagine, assume, presume, suppose, surmise, hope, expect, rely on, depend on, count on, bank on, swear by. **2** *trusted him with a large sum of money*: entrust, commit, consign, confide, give, assign, delegate.
F3 1 distrust, mistrust, doubt, disbelieve.

trusting *adjective* trustful, credulous, gullible, naive, innocent, unquestioning, unsuspecting, unguarded, unwary.
F3 distrustful, suspicious, cautious.

trustworthy *adjective* honest, upright, honourable, principled, dependable, reliable, steadfast, true, responsible, sensible.
F3 untrustworthy, dishonest, unreliable, irresponsible.

truth *noun* **1** *spoke with truth and reason*: truthfulness, veracity, candour, frankness, honesty, sincerity, genuineness,

authenticity, realism, exactness, precision, accuracy, validity, legitimacy, honour, integrity, uprightness, faithfulness, fidelity. **2** *the truth of the matter/discover the truth*: facts, reality, actuality, fact, axiom, maxim, principle, truism.
F **1** deceit, dishonesty, falseness. **2** lie, falsehood.

truthful *adjective* veracious (*fml*), frank, candid, straight, honest, sincere, true, veritable (*fml*), exact, precise, accurate, correct, realistic, faithful, trustworthy, reliable.
F untruthful, deceitful, false, untrue.

try *verb* **1** *try to escape*: attempt, endeavour, venture, undertake, seek, strive. **2** *try the case*: hear, judge. **3** *trying it out*: test, sample, taste, inspect, examine, investigate, evaluate, appraise.
▪ *noun* **1** *have another try*: attempt, endeavour, effort, go (*infml*), bash (*infml*), crack (*infml*), shot (*infml*), stab (*infml*). **2** *give it a try*: test, trial, sample, taste.

trying *adjective* annoying, irritating, aggravating (*infml*), vexatious, exasperating, troublesome, tiresome, wearisome, difficult, hard, tough, arduous, taxing, demanding, testing.
F easy.

tub *noun* bath, basin, vat, tun, butt, cask, barrel, keg.

tube *noun* hose, pipe, cylinder, duct, conduit, spout, channel.

tuck *verb* **1** *tucked it into her pocket*: insert, push, thrust, stuff, cram. **2** *tucked around the waist*: fold, pleat, gather, crease.

tuft *noun* crest, beard, tassel, knot, clump, cluster, bunch.

tug *verb* pull, draw, tow, haul, drag, lug, heave, wrench, jerk, pluck.

tuition *noun* teaching, instruction, coaching, training, lessons, schooling, education.

tumble *verb* fall, stumble, trip, topple, overthrow, drop, flop, collapse, plummet, pitch, roll, toss.

tune *noun* melody, theme, motif, song, air, strain.
▪ *verb* pitch, harmonize, set, regulate, adjust, adapt, temper, attune, synchronize.

tuneful *adjective* melodious, melodic, catchy, musical, euphonious, harmonious, pleasant, mellow, sonorous.
F tuneless, discordant.

tunnel *noun* passage, passageway, gallery, subway, underpass, burrow, hole, mine, shaft, chimney.

turbulent *adjective* rough, choppy, stormy, blustery, tempestuous, raging, furious, violent, wild, tumultuous, unbridled, boisterous, rowdy, disorderly, unruly, undisciplined, obstreperous, rebellious, mutinous, riotous, agitated, unsettled, unstable, confused, disordered.
F calm, composed.

turmoil *noun* confusion, disorder, tumult, commotion, disturbance, trouble, disquiet, agitation, turbulence, stir, ferment, flurry, bustle, chaos, pandemonium, bedlam, noise, din, hubbub, row, uproar.
F3 calm, peace, quiet.

turn *verb* **1** *turn round and round/ turn left*: revolve, circle, spin, twirl, whirl, twist, gyrate, pivot, hinge, swivel, rotate, roll, move, shift, invert, reverse, bend, veer, swerve, divert. **2** *turned into a butterfly*: make, transform, change, alter, modify, convert, adapt, adjust, fit, mould, shape, form, fashion, remodel. **3** *turn cold*: go, become, grow. **4** *turn to them in a crisis*: resort, have recourse, apply, appeal. **5** *milk has turned*: sour, curdle, spoil, go off, go bad.
▪ *noun* **1** *give it a couple of turns/a turn in the road*: revolution, cycle, round, circle, rotation, spin, twirl, twist, gyration, bend, curve, loop, reversal. **2** *a turn for the worse*: change, alteration, shift, deviation. **3** *it's your turn*: go, chance, opportunity, occasion, stint, period, spell.

turning *noun* turn-off, junction, crossroads, fork, bend, curve, turn.

tutor *noun* teacher, instructor, coach, educator, lecturer, supervisor, guide, mentor, guru, guardian.
▪ *verb* teach, instruct, train, drill, coach, educate, school, lecture, supervise, direct, guide.

tweak *verb, noun* twist, pinch, squeeze, nip, pull, tug, jerk, twitch.

twilight *noun* dusk, half-light, gloaming, gloom, dimness, sunset, evening.

twin *noun* double, look-alike, likeness, duplicate, clone, match, counterpart, corollary, fellow, mate.
▪ *adjective* identical, matching, corresponding, symmetrical, parallel, matched, paired, double, dual, duplicate, twofold.

twine *noun* string, cord, thread, yarn.
▪ *verb* wind, coil, spiral, loop, curl, bend, twist, wreathe, wrap, surround, encircle, entwine, plait, braid, knit, weave.

twinge *noun* pain, pang, throb, spasm, throe, stab, stitch, pinch, prick.

twinkle *verb* sparkle, glitter, shimmer, glisten, glimmer, flicker, wink, flash, glint, gleam, shine.
▪ *noun* sparkle, scintillation, glitter, shimmer, glisten, glimmer, flicker, wink, flash, glint, gleam, light.

twirl *verb* spin, whirl, pirouette, wheel, rotate, revolve, swivel, pivot, turn, twist, gyrate, wind, coil.

twist *verb* **1** *twisting from left to right*: turn, screw, wring, spin, swivel, wind, zigzag, bend, coil, spiral, curl, wreathe, twine, entwine, intertwine, weave, entangle, wriggle, squirm, writhe.

2 *twisted his ankle*: wrench, rick, sprain, strain. **3** *twisting my words*: change, alter, garble, misquote, misrepresent, distort, contort, warp, pervert.
▪ *noun* **1** *twists in the road*: turn, screw, spin, roll, bend, curve, arc, curl, loop, zigzag, coil, spiral, convolution, squiggle, tangle. **2** *a twist of fate*: change, variation. **3** *gave the story a fascinating twist*: surprise, quirk, oddity, peculiarity.

twitch *verb* jerk, jump, start, blink, tremble, shake, pull, tug, tweak, snatch, pluck.
▪ *noun* spasm, convulsion, tic, tremor, jerk, jump, start.

twitter *verb* chirp, chirrup, tweet, cheep, sing, warble, whistle, chatter.

two-faced *adjective* hypocritical, insincere, false, lying, deceitful, treacherous, double-dealing, devious, untrustworthy.
F3 honest, candid, frank.

tycoon *noun* industrialist, entrepreneur, captain of industry, magnate, mogul, baron, supremo, capitalist, financier.

type *noun* **1** *types of people/ animals/plants*: sort, kind, form, genre, variety, strain, species, breed, group, class, category, subdivision, classification, description, designation, stamp, mark, order, standard. **2** *conform to type*: archetype, embodiment, prototype, original, model, pattern, specimen, example. **3** *set in type*: print, printing, characters, letters, lettering, face, fount, font.

typical *adjective* standard, normal, usual, average, conventional, orthodox, stock, model, representative, illustrative, indicative, characteristic, distinctive.
F3 atypical, unusual.

typify *verb* embody, epitomize, encapsulate, personify, characterize, exemplify, symbolize, represent, illustrate.

tyrannical *adjective* dictatorial, despotic, autocratic, absolute, arbitrary, authoritarian, domineering, overbearing, high-handed, imperious, magisterial, ruthless, harsh, severe, oppressive, overpowering, unjust, unreasonable.
F3 liberal, tolerant.

tyrant *noun* dictator, despot, autocrat, absolutist, authoritarian, bully, oppressor, slave-driver, taskmaster.

U

ugly *adjective* **1** *an ugly face*: unattractive, unsightly, plain, unprepossessing, ill-favoured, hideous, monstrous, deformed. **2** *an ugly scene*: unpleasant, disagreeable, nasty, horrid, objectionable, offensive, disgusting, revolting, repulsive, vile, frightful, terrible.
1 attractive, beautiful, handsome, pretty. **2** pleasant.

ultimate *adjective* **1** *the ultimate round in the competition*: final, last, closing, concluding, eventual, terminal, furthest, remotest, extreme. **2** *the ultimate adventure*: utmost, greatest, highest, supreme, superlative, perfect. **3** *the ultimate priority*: radical, fundamental, primary.

ultimately *adverb* finally, eventually, at last, in the end, after all.

umpire *noun* referee, linesman, judge, adjudicator, arbiter, arbitrator, mediator, moderator.

umpteen *adjective* a good many, numerous, plenty, millions, countless, innumerable.
few.

unable *adjective* incapable, powerless, impotent, unequipped, unqualified, unfit, incompetent, inadequate.
able, capable.

unacceptable *adjective* intolerable, inadmissible, unsatisfactory, unsuitable, disappointing, undesirable, unwelcome, objectionable, offensive, unpleasant.
acceptable, satisfactory.

unaccompanied *adjective* alone, unescorted, unattended, lone, solo, single-handed.
accompanied.

unanimous *adjective* united, concerted, joint, common, as one, in agreement, in accord, harmonious.
disunited, divided.

unapproachable *adjective* inaccessible, remote, distant, aloof, standoffish, withdrawn, reserved, unsociable, unfriendly, forbidding.
approachable, friendly.

unassuming *adjective* unassertive, self-effacing, retiring, modest, humble, meek, unobtrusive, unpretentious, simple, restrained.
presumptuous, assertive, pretentious.

unattached *adjective* unmarried, single, free, available, footloose, fancy-free, independent, unaffiliated.
F3 engaged, committed.

unauthorized *adjective* unofficial, unlawful, illegal, illicit, illegitimate, irregular, unsanctioned.
F3 authorized, legal.

unavoidable *adjective* inevitable, inescapable, inexorable, certain, sure, fated, destined, obligatory, compulsory, mandatory, necessary.
F3 avoidable.

unaware *adjective* oblivious, unconscious, ignorant, uninformed, unknowing, unsuspecting, unmindful, heedless, blind, deaf.
F3 aware, conscious.

unbalanced *adjective* **1** *mind became unbalanced*: insane, mad, crazy, lunatic, deranged, disturbed, demented, irrational, unsound. **2** *an unbalanced report*: biased, prejudiced, one-sided, partisan, unfair, unjust, unequal, uneven, asymmetrical, lopsided, unsteady, unstable.
F3 **1** sane. **2** unbiased.

unbeatable *adjective* invincible, unconquerable, unstoppable, unsurpassable, matchless, supreme, excellent.

unbelievable *adjective* incredible, inconceivable, unthinkable, unimaginable, astonishing, staggering, extraordinary, impossible, improbable, unlikely, implausible, unconvincing, far-fetched, preposterous.
F3 believable, credible.

unborn *adjective* embryonic, expected, awaited, coming, future.

unbreakable *adjective* indestructible, shatterproof, toughened, resistant, proof, durable, strong, tough, rugged, solid.
F3 breakable, fragile.

uncalled-for *adjective* gratuitous, unprovoked, unjustified, unwarranted, undeserved, unnecessary, needless.
F3 timely.

uncanny *adjective* weird, strange, queer, bizarre, mysterious, unaccountable, incredible, remarkable, extraordinary, fantastic, unnatural, unearthly, supernatural, eerie, creepy, spooky (*infml*).

uncertain *adjective* **1** *uncertain what to do*: unsure, unconvinced, doubtful, dubious, undecided, ambivalent, hesitant, wavering, vacillating. **2** *weather is uncertain*: inconstant, changeable, variable, erratic. **3** *a few uncertain steps*: irregular, shaky, unsteady, unreliable. **4** *outcome is uncertain*: unpredictable, unforeseeable, undetermined, unsettled, unresolved, unconfirmed, indefinite, vague, insecure, risky, iffy (*infml*).

F3 **1** certain, sure. **3** steady. **4** predictable.

uncharitable *adjective* unkind, cruel, hard-hearted, callous, unfeeling, insensitive, unsympathetic, unfriendly, mean, ungenerous.
F3 kind, sensitive, charitable, generous.

uncharted *adjective* unexplored, undiscovered, unplumbed, foreign, alien, strange, unfamiliar, new, virgin.
F3 familiar.

unclear *adjective* indistinct, hazy, dim, obscure, vague, indefinite, ambiguous, equivocal, uncertain, unsure, doubtful, dubious.
F3 clear, evident.

uncomfortable *adjective* **1** *uncomfortable conditions/bed/shoes*: cramped, hard, cold, ill-fitting, irritating, painful, disagreeable. **2** *an uncomfortable silence followed*: awkward, embarrassed, self-conscious, uneasy, troubled, worried, disturbed, distressed, disquieted, conscience-stricken.
F3 **1** comfortable. **2** relaxed.

unconcerned *adjective* indifferent, apathetic, uninterested, nonchalant, carefree, relaxed, complacent, cool, composed, untroubled, unworried, unruffled, unmoved, uncaring, unsympathetic, callous, aloof, remote, distant, detached, dispassionate, uninvolved, oblivious.
F3 concerned, worried, interested.

unconditional *adjective* unqualified, unreserved, unrestricted, unlimited, absolute, utter, full, total, complete, entire, whole-hearted, thoroughgoing, downright, outright, positive, categorical, unequivocal.
F3 conditional, qualified, limited.

unconscious *adjective* **1** *was unconscious for several minutes*: stunned, knocked out, out, out cold (*infml*), out for the count (*infml*), concussed, comatose, senseless, insensible. **2** *unconscious of his surroundings*: unaware, oblivious, blind, deaf, heedless, unmindful, ignorant. **3** *an unconscious reaction*: involuntary, automatic, reflex, instinctive, impulsive, innate, subconscious, subliminal, repressed, suppressed, latent, unwitting, inadvertent, accidental, unintentional.
F3 **1** conscious. **2** aware. **3** intentional.

uncouth *adjective* coarse, crude, vulgar, rude, ill-mannered, unseemly, improper, clumsy, awkward, gauche, graceless, unrefined, uncultivated, uncultured, uncivilized, rough.
F3 polite, refined, urbane.

uncover *verb* unveil, unmask, unwrap, strip, bare, open, expose, reveal, show, disclose, divulge, leak, unearth, exhume, discover, detect.
F3 cover, conceal, suppress.

undaunted *adjective* undeterred, undiscouraged, undismayed, unbowed, resolute, steadfast, brave, courageous, fearless, bold, intrepid, dauntless, indomitable.
F3 discouraged, timorous.

undecided *adjective* uncertain, unsure, in two minds, ambivalent, doubtful, hesitant, wavering, irresolute, uncommitted, indefinite, vague, dubious, debatable, moot, unsettled, open.
F3 decided, certain, definite.

undeniable *adjective* irrefutable, unquestionable, incontrovertible, sure, certain, undoubted, proven, clear, obvious, patent, evident, manifest, unmistakable.
F3 questionable.

under *preposition* below, underneath, beneath, lower than, less than, inferior to, subordinate to.
F3 over, above.

undercover *adjective* secret, hush-hush (*infml*), private, confidential, spy, intelligence, underground, clandestine, surreptitious, furtive, covert, hidden, concealed.
F3 open, unconcealed.

underestimate *verb* underrate, undervalue, misjudge, miscalculate, minimize, belittle, disparage (*fml*), dismiss.
F3 overestimate, exaggerate.

undergo *verb* experience, suffer, sustain, submit to, bear, stand, endure, weather, withstand.

underground *adjective* **1** *an underground passage*: subterranean, buried, sunken, covered, hidden, concealed. **2** *an underground movement*: secret, covert, undercover, revolutionary, subversive, radical, experimental, avant-garde, alternative, unorthodox, unofficial.

undergrowth *noun* brush, scrub, vegetation, ground cover, bracken, bushes, brambles, briars.

underhand *adjective* unscrupulous, unethical, immoral, improper, sly, crafty, sneaky, stealthy, surreptitious, furtive, clandestine, devious, dishonest, deceitful, deceptive, fraudulent, crooked (*infml*), shady (*infml*).
F3 honest, open, above board.

underline *verb* mark, underscore, stress, emphasize, accentuate, italicize, highlight, point up.
F3 play down, soft-pedal.

underlying *adjective* basic, fundamental, essential, primary, elementary, root, intrinsic, latent, hidden, lurking, veiled.

undermine *verb* mine, tunnel, excavate, erode, wear away, weaken, sap, sabotage, subvert, vitiate, mar, impair.
F3 strengthen, fortify.

underprivileged *adjective* disadvantaged, deprived, poor, needy, impoverished, destitute, oppressed.
F3 privileged, fortunate, affluent.

underrate *verb* underestimate, undervalue, belittle, disparage (*fml*), depreciate, dismiss.
F3 overrate, exaggerate.

understand *verb* **1** *understand what you mean*: grasp, comprehend, take in, follow, get (*infml*), cotton on (*infml*), fathom, penetrate, make out, discern, perceive, see, realize, recognize, appreciate, accept. **2** *understand their distress*: sympathize, empathize, commiserate. **3** *I understood everyone was invited*: believe, think, know, hear, learn, gather, assume, presume, suppose, conclude.
F3 1 misunderstand.

understanding *noun* **1** *shows little understanding of the subject*: grasp, comprehension, knowledge, wisdom, intelligence, intellect, sense, judgement, discernment, insight, appreciation, awareness, impression, perception, belief, idea, notion, opinion, interpretation. **2** *come to an understanding*: agreement, arrangement, pact, accord, harmony. **3** *show patience and understanding*: sympathy, empathy.
▪ *adjective* sympathetic, compassionate, kind, considerate, sensitive, tender, loving, patient, tolerant, forbearing, forgiving.
F3 unsympathetic, insensitive, impatient, intolerant.

understood *adjective* accepted, assumed, presumed, implied, implicit, inferred, tacit, unstated, unspoken, unwritten.

understudy *noun* stand-in, double, substitute, replacement, reserve, deputy.

undertake *verb* **1** *undertake to pay the loan*: pledge, promise, guarantee, agree, contract, covenant. **2** *undertaking a new venture*: begin, commence, embark on, tackle, try, attempt, endeavour, take on, accept, assume.

undertaking *noun* **1** *a whole new undertaking*: enterprise, venture, business, affair, task, project, operation, attempt, endeavour, effort. **2** *gave me an undertaking*: pledge, commitment, promise, vow, word, assurance.

undertone *noun* hint, suggestion, whisper, murmur, trace, tinge, touch, flavour, feeling, atmosphere, undercurrent.

underwater *adjective* subaquatic, undersea, submarine, submerged, sunken.

underwrite *verb* endorse, authorize, sanction, approve, back, guarantee, insure, sponsor, fund, finance, subsidize, subscribe, sign, initial, countersign.

undisputed *adjective* uncontested, unchallenged, unquestioned, undoubted, indisputable, incontrovertible, undeniable, irrefutable, accepted, acknowledged, recognized,

sure, certain, conclusive.
debatable, uncertain.

undivided *adjective* solid, unbroken, intact, whole, entire, full, complete, combined, united, unanimous, concentrated, exclusive, whole-hearted.

undo *verb* **1** *undo the fastenings*: untie, unbuckle, unbutton, unzip, unlock, unwrap, unwind, open, loose, loosen, separate. **2** *will undo all our hard work*: annul, nullify, invalidate, cancel, offset, neutralize, reverse, overturn, upset, quash, defeat, undermine, subvert, mar, spoil, ruin, wreck, shatter, destroy.
1 fasten, do up.

undoing *noun* downfall, ruin, ruination, collapse, destruction, defeat, overthrow, reversal, weakness, shame, disgrace.

undone *adjective* **1** *leave tasks undone*: unaccomplished, unfulfilled, unfinished, uncompleted, incomplete, outstanding, left, omitted, neglected, forgotten. **2** *shirt/ button is undone*: unfastened, untied, unlaced, unbuttoned, unlocked, open, loose.
1 done, accomplished, complete. **2** fastened.

undress *verb* strip, peel off (*infml*), disrobe, take off, divest, remove, shed.

undue *adjective* unnecessary, needless, uncalled-for, unwarranted, undeserved, unreasonable, disproportionate, excessive, immoderate, inordinate, extreme, extravagant, improper.
reasonable, moderate, proper.

unduly *adverb* too, over, excessively, immoderately, inordinately, disproportionately, unreasonably, unjustifiably, unnecessarily.
moderately, reasonably.

unearth *verb* dig up, exhume, disinter, excavate, uncover, expose, reveal, find, discover, detect.
bury.

unearthly *adjective* **1** *an unearthly screech*: supernatural, ghostly, eerie, uncanny, weird, strange, spine-chilling. **2** *at an unearthly hour*: unreasonable, outrageous, ungodly.
2 reasonable.

uneasy *adjective* uncomfortable, anxious, worried, apprehensive, tense, strained, nervous, agitated, shaky, jittery, edgy, upset, troubled, disturbed, unsettled, restless, impatient, unsure, insecure.
calm, composed.

unemployed *adjective* jobless, out of work, laid off, redundant, unwaged, on the dole (*infml*), idle, unoccupied.
employed, occupied.

unending *adjective* endless, never-ending, unceasing, ceaseless, incessant, interminable, constant, continual, perpetual, everlasting, eternal, undying.
transient, intermittent.

unequal *adjective* different, varying, dissimilar, unlike, unmatched, uneven, unbalanced, disproportionate, asymmetrical, irregular, unfair, unjust, biased, discriminatory.
F equal.

unequivocal *adjective* unambiguous, explicit, clear, plain, evident, distinct, unmistakable, express, direct, straight, definite, positive, categorical, incontrovertible, absolute, unqualified, unreserved.
F ambiguous, vague, qualified.

uneven *adjective* **1** *uneven ground*: rough, bumpy. **2** *results were uneven*: irregular, intermittent, spasmodic, fitful, jerky, unsteady, variable, changeable, fluctuating, erratic, inconsistent, patchy.
F **1** flat, level. **2** consistent, regular.

uneventful *adjective* uninteresting, unexciting, quiet, unvaried, boring, monotonous, tedious, dull, routine, humdrum, ordinary, commonplace, unremarkable, unexceptional, unmemorable.
F eventful, memorable.

unexpected *adjective* unforeseen, unanticipated, unpredictable, chance, accidental, fortuitous (*fml*), sudden, abrupt, surprising, startling, amazing, astonishing, unusual.
F expected, predictable.

unfair *adjective* unjust, inequitable, partial, biased, prejudiced, bigoted, discriminatory, unbalanced, one-sided, partisan, arbitrary, undeserved, unmerited, unwarranted, uncalled-for, unethical, unscrupulous, unprincipled, wrongful, dishonest.
F fair, just, unbiased, deserved.

unfaithful *adjective* disloyal, treacherous, false, untrue, deceitful, dishonest, untrustworthy, unreliable, fickle, inconstant, adulterous, two-timing, duplicitous, double-dealing.
F faithful, loyal, reliable.

unfamiliar *adjective* strange, unusual, uncommon, curious, alien, foreign, uncharted, unexplored, unknown, different, new, novel, unaccustomed, unacquainted, inexperienced, unpractised, unskilled, unversed.
F familiar, customary, conversant (*fml*).

unfashionable *adjective* outmoded, dated, out-of-date, out, passé, old-fashioned, antiquated, obsolete.
F fashionable.

unfasten *verb* undo, untie, loosen, unlock, open, uncouple, disconnect, separate, detach.
F fasten.

unfavourable *adjective* inauspicious, unpromising, ominous, threatening, discouraging, inopportune,

untimely, unseasonable, ill-suited, unfortunate, unlucky, disadvantageous, bad, poor, adverse, contrary, negative, hostile, unfriendly, uncomplimentary.
⇄ favourable, auspicious, promising.

unfinished *adjective* incomplete, uncompleted, half-done, sketchy, rough, crude, imperfect, lacking, wanting, deficient, undone, unaccomplished, unfulfilled.
⇄ finished, perfect.

unfit *adjective* **1** *unfit for consumption/service*: unsuitable, inappropriate, unsuited, ill-equipped, unqualified, ineligible, untrained, unprepared, unequal, incapable, incompetent, inadequate, ineffective, useless. **2** *too unfit to run for a bus*: unhealthy, out of condition, flabby, feeble, decrepit.
⇄ **1** fit, suitable, competent. **2** healthy.

unfold *verb* **1** *as the plot is unfolded*: reveal, disclose, show, present, describe, explain, clarify, elaborate. **2** *unfold a map*: open, spread, flatten, straighten, stretch out, undo, unfurl, unroll, uncoil, unwrap, uncover.
⇄ **1** withhold, suppress. **2** fold, wrap.

unforeseen *adjective* unpredicted, unexpected, unanticipated, surprising, startling, sudden, unavoidable.
⇄ expected, predictable.

unforgivable *adjective* unpardonable, inexcusable, unjustifiable, indefensible, reprehensible, shameful, disgraceful, deplorable.
⇄ forgivable, venial.

unfortunate *adjective* **1** *the unfortunate family/an unfortunate mistake*: unlucky, luckless, hapless, unsuccessful, poor, wretched, unhappy, doomed, ill-fated, hopeless, calamitous, disastrous, ruinous. **2** *made an unfortunate remark*: regrettable, lamentable, deplorable, adverse, unfavourable, unsuitable, inappropriate, inopportune, untimely, ill-timed.
⇄ **1** fortunate, happy. **2** favourable, appropriate.

unfounded *adjective* baseless, groundless, unsupported, unsubstantiated, unproven, unjustified, idle, false, spurious, trumped-up, fabricated.
⇄ substantiated, justified.

unfriendly *adjective* unsociable, standoffish, aloof, distant, unapproachable, inhospitable, uncongenial, unneighbourly, unwelcoming, cold, chilly, hostile, aggressive, quarrelsome, inimical, antagonistic, ill-disposed, disagreeable, surly, sour.
⇄ friendly, amiable, agreeable.

ungainly *adjective* clumsy, awkward, gauche, inelegant, gawky, unco-ordinated, lumbering, unwieldy.
⇄ graceful, elegant.

ungrateful *adjective* unthankful, unappreciative, ill-mannered, ungracious, selfish, heedless.
F3 grateful, thankful.

unguarded *adjective* **1** *in an unguarded moment*: unwary, careless, incautious, imprudent, impolitic, indiscreet, undiplomatic, thoughtless, unthinking, heedless, foolish, foolhardy, rash, ill-considered. **2** *an unguarded entrance*: undefended, unprotected, exposed, vulnerable, defenceless.
F3 1 guarded, cautious. **2** defended, protected.

unhappy *adjective* **1** *could tell that she was unhappy*: sad, sorrowful, miserable, melancholy, depressed, dispirited, despondent, dejected, downcast, crestfallen, long-faced, gloomy. **2** *an unhappy combination of circumstances*: unfortunate, unlucky, ill-fated, unsuitable, inappropriate, inapt, ill-chosen, tactless, awkward, clumsy.
F3 1 happy. **2** fortunate, suitable.

unharmed *adjective* undamaged, unhurt, uninjured, unscathed, whole, intact, safe, sound.
F3 harmed, damaged.

unhealthy *adjective* **1** *most unhealthy nation in Europe*: unwell, sick, ill, poorly, ailing, sickly, infirm, invalid, weak, feeble, frail, unsound. **2** *an unhealthy climate*: unwholesome, insanitary, unhygienic, harmful, detrimental, morbid, unnatural.
F3 1 healthy, fit. **2** wholesome, hygienic, natural.

unheard-of *adjective* unthinkable, inconceivable, unimaginable, undreamed-of, unprecedented, unacceptable, offensive, shocking, outrageous, preposterous.
F3 normal, acceptable.

unidentified *adjective* unknown, unrecognized, unmarked, unnamed, nameless, anonymous, incognito, unfamiliar, strange, mysterious.
F3 identified, known, named.

uniform *noun* outfit, costume, livery, insignia, regalia, robes, dress, suit.
▪ *adjective* same, identical, like, alike, similar, homogeneous, consistent, regular, equal, smooth, even, flat, monotonous, unvarying, unchanging, constant, unbroken.
F3 different, varied, changing.

unify *verb* unite, join, bind, combine, integrate, merge, amalgamate, consolidate, coalesce, fuse, weld.
F3 separate, divide, split.

unimportant *adjective* insignificant, inconsequential, irrelevant, immaterial, minor, trivial, trifling, petty, slight, negligible, worthless.
F3 important, significant, relevant, vital.

uninhabited *adjective* unoccupied, vacant, empty, deserted, abandoned, unpeopled, unpopulated.

uninhibited *adjective* unconstrained, unreserved, unselfconscious, liberated, free, unrestricted, uncontrolled, unrestrained, abandoned, natural, spontaneous, irrepressible, frank, candid, open, relaxed, informal.
F3 inhibited, repressed, constrained, restrained.

uninterested *adjective* indifferent, unconcerned, uninvolved, bored, listless, apathetic, impassive, unenthusiastic, blasé, unresponsive.
F3 interested, concerned, enthusiastic, responsive.

uninteresting *adjective* boring, tedious, monotonous, humdrum, dull, drab, dreary, dry, flat, tame, uneventful, unexciting, uninspiring, unimpressive.
F3 interesting, exciting.

uninterrupted *adjective* unbroken, continuous, non-stop, unending, constant, continual, steady, sustained, undisturbed, peaceful.
F3 broken, intermittent.

uninvited *adjective* unasked, unsought, unsolicited, unwanted, unwelcome.
F3 invited.

union *noun* alliance, coalition, league, association, federation, confederation, confederacy, merger, combination, amalgamation, blend, mixture, synthesis, fusion, unification, unity.
F3 separation, alienation, estrangement.

unique *adjective* single, one-off, sole, only, lone, solitary, unmatched, matchless, peerless, unequalled, unparalleled, unrivalled, incomparable, inimitable.
F3 common.

unit *noun* item, part, element, constituent, piece, component, module, section, segment, portion, entity, whole, one, system, assembly.

unite *verb* join, link, couple, marry, ally, co-operate, band, associate, federate, confederate, combine, pool, amalgamate, merge, blend, unify, consolidate, coalesce, fuse.
F3 separate, sever.

united *adjective* allied, affiliated, corporate, unified, combined, pooled, collective, concerted, one, unanimous, agreed, in agreement, in accord, like-minded.
F3 disunited.

universal *adjective* worldwide, global, all-embracing, all-inclusive, general, common, across-the-board, total, whole, entire, all-round, unlimited.

unjust *adjective* unfair, inequitable, wrong, partial, biased, prejudiced, one-sided, partisan, unreasonable, unjustified, undeserved.
F3 just, fair, reasonable.

unkempt *adjective* dishevelled, tousled, rumpled, uncombed,

ungroomed, untidy, messy, scruffy, shabby, slovenly.
F3 well-groomed, tidy.

unkind *adjective* cruel, inhuman, inhumane, callous, hard-hearted, unfeeling, insensitive, thoughtless, inconsiderate, uncharitable, nasty, malicious, spiteful, mean, malevolent, unfriendly, uncaring, unsympathetic.
F3 kind, considerate.

unknown *adjective* unfamiliar, unheard-of, strange, alien, foreign, mysterious, dark, obscure, hidden, concealed, undisclosed, secret, untold, new, uncharted, unexplored, undiscovered, unidentified, unnamed, nameless, anonymous, incognito.
F3 known, familiar.

unlawful *adjective* illegal, criminal, illicit, illegitimate, unconstitutional, outlawed, banned, prohibited, forbidden, unauthorized.
F3 lawful, legal.

unlikely *adjective* **1** *an unlikely story*: improbable, implausible, far-fetched, unconvincing, unbelievable, incredible, unimaginable, unexpected, doubtful, dubious, questionable, suspect, suspicious. **2** *an unlikely chance*: slight, faint, remote, distant.
F3 **1** likely, plausible.

unlimited *adjective* limitless, unrestricted, unbounded, boundless, infinite, endless, countless, incalculable, immeasurable, vast, immense, extensive, great, indefinite, absolute, unconditional, unqualified, all-encompassing, total, complete, full, unconstrained, unhampered.
F3 limited.

unlucky *adjective* unfortunate, luckless, unhappy, miserable, wretched, ill-fated, ill-starred, jinxed, doomed, cursed, unfavourable, inauspicious, ominous, unsuccessful, disastrous.
F3 lucky.

unmistakable *adjective* clear, plain, distinct, pronounced, obvious, evident, manifest, patent, glaring, explicit, unambiguous, unequivocal, positive, definite, sure, certain, unquestionable, indisputable, undeniable.
F3 unclear, ambiguous.

unmoved *adjective* unaffected, untouched, unshaken, dry-eyed, unfeeling, cold, dispassionate, indifferent, impassive, unresponsive, unimpressed, firm, adamant, inflexible, unbending, undeviating, unwavering, steady, unchanged, resolute, resolved, determined.
F3 moved, affected, shaken.

unnatural *adjective* abnormal, anomalous, freakish, irregular, unusual, strange, odd, peculiar, queer, bizarre, extraordinary, uncanny, supernatural, inhuman, perverted.
F3 natural, normal.

unnecessary *adjective* unneeded, needless, uncalled-for, unwanted, non-essential, dispensable, expendable, superfluous, redundant, tautological.
F3 necessary, essential, indispensable.

unnoticed *adjective* unobserved, unremarked, unseen, unrecognized, undiscovered, overlooked, ignored, disregarded, neglected, unheeded.
F3 noticed, noted.

unobtrusive *adjective* inconspicuous, unnoticeable, unassertive, self-effacing, humble, modest, unostentatious, unpretentious, restrained, low-key, subdued, quiet, retiring.
F3 obtrusive, ostentatious.

unoccupied *adjective* uninhabited, vacant, empty, free, idle, inactive, workless, jobless, unemployed.
F3 occupied, busy.

unofficial *adjective* unauthorized, illegal, informal, off-the-record, personal, private, confidential, undeclared, unconfirmed.
F3 official.

unorthodox *adjective* unconventional, nonconformist, heterodox, alternative, fringe, irregular, abnormal, unusual.
F3 orthodox, conventional.

unpaid *adjective* **1** *unpaid bills*: outstanding, overdue, unsettled, owing, due, payable. **2** *unpaid work*: voluntary, honorary, unsalaried, unwaged, unremunerative, free.
F3 1 paid.

unpalatable *adjective* **1** *mixed flour and water into an unpalatable goo*: unappetizing, distasteful, insipid, bitter, uneatable, inedible. **2** *found the truth pretty unpalatable*: unpleasant, disagreeable, unattractive, offensive, repugnant.
F3 1 palatable. **2** pleasant.

unparalleled *adjective* unequalled, unmatched, matchless, peerless, incomparable, unrivalled, unsurpassed, supreme, superlative, rare, exceptional, unprecedented.

unpleasant *adjective* disagreeable, ill-natured, nasty, objectionable, offensive, distasteful, unpalatable, unattractive, repulsive, bad, troublesome.
F3 pleasant, agreeable, nice.

unpopular *adjective* disliked, hated, detested, unloved, unsought-after, unfashionable, undesirable, unwelcome, unwanted, rejected, shunned, avoided, neglected.
F3 popular, fashionable.

unprecedented *adjective* new, original, revolutionary, unknown, unheard-of, exceptional, remarkable, extraordinary, abnormal, unusual, freakish, unparalleled, unrivalled.
F3 usual.

unpredictable *adjective* unforeseeable, unexpected, changeable, variable, inconstant, unreliable, fickle, unstable, erratic, random, chance.
F3 predictable, foreseeable, constant.

unprepared *adjective* unready, surprised, unsuspecting, ill-equipped, unfinished, incomplete, half-baked, unplanned, unrehearsed, spontaneous, improvised, ad-lib, off-the-cuff.
F3 prepared, ready.

unprotected *adjective* unguarded, unattended, undefended, unfortified, unarmed, unshielded, unsheltered, uncovered, exposed, open, naked, vulnerable, defenceless, helpless.
F3 protected, safe, immune.

unqualified *adjective* untrained, inexperienced, amateur, ineligible, unfit, incompetent, incapable, unprepared, ill-equipped.
F3 qualified, professional.

unravel *verb* unwind, undo, untangle, disentangle, free, extricate, separate, resolve, sort out, solve, work out, figure out, puzzle out, penetrate, interpret, explain.
F3 tangle, complicate.

unreal *adjective* false, artificial, synthetic, mock, fake, sham, imaginary, visionary, fanciful, make-believe, pretend (*infml*), fictitious, made-up, fairy-tale, legendary, mythical, fantastic, illusory, immaterial, insubstantial, hypothetical.
F3 real, genuine.

unrealistic *adjective* impractical, idealistic, romantic, quixotic, impracticable, unworkable, unreasonable, impossible.
F3 realistic, pragmatic.

unreasonable *adjective* **1** *an unreasonable punishment*: unfair, unjust, biased, unjustifiable, unjustified, unwarranted, undue, uncalled-for. **2** *unreasonable behaviour*: irrational, illogical, inconsistent, arbitrary, absurd, nonsensical, far-fetched, preposterous, mad, senseless, silly, foolish, stupid, headstrong, opinionated, perverse. **3** *unreasonable demands*: excessive, immoderate, extravagant, exorbitant, extortionate.
F3 **1** reasonable, fair. **2** rational, sensible. **3** moderate.

unrecognizable *adjective* unidentifiable, disguised, incognito, changed, altered.

unrelated *adjective* unconnected, unassociated, irrelevant, extraneous, different, dissimilar, unlike, disparate, distinct, separate, independent.
F3 related, similar.

unreliable *adjective* unsound, fallible, deceptive, false, mistaken, erroneous, inaccurate, unconvincing, implausible, uncertain, undependable, untrustworthy, unstable, fickle, irresponsible.

E3 reliable, dependable, trustworthy.

unrest *noun* protest, rebellion, turmoil, agitation, restlessness, dissatisfaction, dissension, disaffection, worry.
E3 peace, calm.

unrivalled *adjective* unequalled, unparalleled, unmatched, matchless, peerless, incomparable, inimitable, unsurpassed, supreme, superlative.

unruly *adjective* uncontrollable, unmanageable, ungovernable, intractable, disorderly, wild, rowdy, riotous, rebellious, mutinous, lawless, insubordinate, disobedient, wayward, wilful, headstrong, obstreperous.
E3 manageable, orderly.

unsatisfactory *adjective* unacceptable, imperfect, defective, faulty, inferior, poor, weak, inadequate, insufficient, deficient, unsuitable, displeasing, dissatisfying, unsatisfying, frustrating, disappointing.
E3 satisfactory, pleasing.

unscathed *adjective* unhurt, uninjured, unharmed, undamaged, untouched, whole, intact, safe, sound.
E3 hurt, injured.

unscrupulous *adjective* unprincipled, ruthless, shameless, dishonourable, dishonest, crooked (*infml*), corrupt, immoral, unethical, improper.
E3 scrupulous, ethical, proper.

unseen *adjective* unnoticed, unobserved, undetected, invisible, hidden, concealed, veiled, obscure.
E3 visible.

unsettled *adjective* **1** *was unsettled by the noise*: disturbed, upset, troubled, agitated, anxious, uneasy, tense, edgy, flustered, shaken, unnerved, disoriented, confused. **2** *unsettled weather*: changeable, variable, unpredictable, inconstant, unstable, insecure, unsteady, shaky. **3** *unsettled bills*: unpaid, outstanding, owing, payable, overdue.
E3 **1** composed. **2** settled. **3** paid.

unshakable *adjective* firm, well-founded, fixed, stable, immovable, unassailable, unwavering, constant, steadfast, staunch, sure, resolute, determined.
E3 insecure.

unsociable *adjective* unfriendly, aloof, distant, standoffish, withdrawn, introverted, reclusive, retiring, reserved, taciturn, unforthcoming, uncommunicative, cold, chilly, uncongenial, unneighbourly, inhospitable, hostile.
E3 sociable, friendly.

unsolicited *adjective* unrequested, unsought, uninvited, unasked, unwanted, unwelcome, uncalled-for, voluntary, spontaneous.
E3 requested, invited.

unsound *adjective* **1** *reasoning is*

unsound: faulty, flawed, defective, ill-founded, fallacious, false, erroneous, invalid, illogical. **2** *of unsound mind*: unhealthy, unwell, ill, diseased, weak, frail, unbalanced, deranged, unhinged.
F3 **1** sound. **2** sound, well.

unspeakable *adjective* unutterable, inexpressible, indescribable, awful, dreadful, frightful, terrible, horrible, shocking, appalling, monstrous, inconceivable, unbelievable.

unspoilt *adjective* preserved, unchanged, untouched, natural, unaffected, unsophisticated, unharmed, undamaged, unimpaired, unblemished, perfect.
F3 spoilt, affected.

unspoken *adjective* unstated, undeclared, unuttered, unexpressed, unsaid, voiceless, wordless, silent, tacit, implicit, implied, inferred, understood, assumed.
F3 stated, explicit.

unsung *adjective* unhonoured, unpraised, unacknowledged, unrecognized, overlooked, disregarded, neglected, forgotten, unknown, anonymous, obscure.
F3 honoured, famous, renowned.

unsure *adjective* uncertain, doubtful, dubious, suspicious, sceptical, unconvinced, unpersuaded, undecided, hesitant, tentative.
F3 sure, certain, confident.

unsuspecting *adjective* unwary, unaware, unconscious, trusting, trustful, unsuspicious, credulous, gullible, ingenuous, naive, innocent.
F3 suspicious, knowing.

unthinkable *adjective* inconceivable, unimaginable, unheard-of, unbelievable, incredible, impossible, improbable, unlikely, implausible, unreasonable, illogical, absurd, preposterous, outrageous, shocking.

untimely *adjective* early, premature, unseasonable, ill-timed, inopportune, inconvenient, awkward, unsuitable, inappropriate, unfortunate, inauspicious.
F3 timely, opportune.

untold *adjective* uncounted, unnumbered, unreckoned, incalculable, innumerable, uncountable, countless, infinite, measureless, boundless, inexhaustible, undreamed-of, unimaginable.

untouched *adjective* unharmed, undamaged, unimpaired, unhurt, uninjured, unscathed, safe, intact, unchanged, unaltered, unaffected.

unused *adjective* leftover, remaining, surplus, extra, spare, available, new, fresh, blank, clean, untouched, unexploited, unemployed, idle.
F3 used.

unusual *adjective* uncommon, rare, unfamiliar, strange, odd,

curious, queer, bizarre, unconventional, irregular, abnormal, extraordinary, remarkable, exceptional, different, surprising, unexpected.
F3 usual, normal, ordinary.

unveil *verb* uncover, expose, bare, reveal, disclose, divulge, discover.
F3 cover, hide.

unwanted *adjective* undesired, unsolicited, uninvited, unwelcome, outcast, rejected, unrequired, unneeded, unnecessary, surplus, extra, superfluous, redundant.
F3 wanted, needed, necessary.

unwarranted *adjective* unjustified, undeserved, unprovoked, uncalled-for, groundless, unreasonable, unjust, wrong.
F3 warranted, justifiable, deserved.

unwelcome *adjective* **1** *unwelcome visitors*: unwanted, undesirable, unpopular, uninvited, excluded, rejected. **2** *unwelcome news*: unpleasant, disagreeable, upsetting, worrying, distasteful, unpalatable, unacceptable.
F3 1 welcome, desirable. **2** pleasant.

unwieldy *adjective* unmanageable, inconvenient, awkward, clumsy, ungainly, bulky, massive, hefty, weighty, ponderous, cumbersome.
F3 handy, dainty.

unwilling *adjective* reluctant, disinclined, indisposed, resistant, opposed, averse, lo(a)th, slow, unenthusiastic, grudging.
F3 willing, enthusiastic.

unwind *verb* **1** *unwind the spool*: unroll, unreel, unwrap, undo, uncoil, untwist, unravel, disentangle. **2** (*infml*) *unwind in front of the TV*: relax, wind down, calm down.
F3 1 wind, roll.

unwitting *adjective* unaware, unknowing, unsuspecting, unthinking, unconscious, involuntary, accidental, chance, inadvertent, unintentional, unintended, unplanned.
F3 knowing, conscious, deliberate.

unwritten *adjective* verbal, oral, word-of-mouth, unrecorded, tacit, implicit, understood, accepted, recognized, traditional, customary, conventional.
F3 written, recorded.

upbringing *noun* bringing-up, raising, rearing, breeding, parenting, care, nurture, cultivation, education, training, instruction, teaching.

update *verb* modernize, revise, amend, correct, renew, renovate, revamp.

upgrade *verb* promote, advance, elevate, raise, improve, enhance.
F3 downgrade, demote.

upheaval *noun* disruption, disturbance, upset, chaos, confusion, disorder, turmoil, shake-up (*infml*), revolution, overthrow.

uphill *adjective* hard, difficult, arduous, tough, taxing, strenuous, laborious, tiring, wearisome, exhausting, gruelling, punishing.
F3 easy.

uphold *verb* support, maintain, hold to, stand by, defend, champion, advocate, promote, back, endorse, sustain, fortify, strengthen, justify, vindicate.
F3 abandon, reject.

upkeep *noun* maintenance, preservation, conservation, care, running, repair, support, sustenance, subsistence, keep.
F3 neglect.

upper *adjective* higher, loftier, superior, senior, top, topmost, uppermost, high, elevated, exalted, eminent, important.
F3 lower, inferior, junior.

uppermost *adjective* highest, loftiest, top, topmost, greatest, supreme, first, primary, foremost, leading, principal, main, chief, dominant, predominant, paramount, pre-eminent.
F3 lowest.

upright *adjective* **1** *an upright post*: vertical, perpendicular, erect, straight. **2** *upright citizens*: righteous, good, virtuous, upstanding, noble, honourable, ethical, principled, incorruptible, honest, trustworthy.
F3 1 horizontal, flat. **2** dishonest.

uprising *noun* rebellion, revolt, mutiny, rising, insurgence, insurrection, revolution.

uproar *noun* noise, din, racket, hubbub, hullabaloo, pandemonium, tumult, turmoil, turbulence, commotion, confusion, disorder, clamour, outcry, furore, riot, rumpus.

uproot *verb* pull up, rip up, root out, weed out, remove, displace, eradicate, destroy, wipe out.

upset *verb* **1** *upsetting his parents*: distress, grieve, dismay, trouble, worry, agitate, disturb, bother, fluster, ruffle, discompose, shake, unnerve, disconcert, confuse, disorganize. **2** *upset the milk jug*: tip, spill, overturn, capsize, topple, overthrow, destabilize, unsteady.
▪ *noun* **1** *a bit of an upset in the government*: trouble, worry, agitation, disturbance, bother, disruption, upheaval, shake-up (*infml*), reverse, surprise, shock. **2** *stomach upset*: disorder, complaint, bug (*infml*), illness, sickness.
▪ *adjective* distressed, grieved, hurt, annoyed, dismayed, troubled, worried, agitated, disturbed, bothered, shaken, disconcerted, confused.

upshot *noun* result, consequence, outcome, issue, end, conclusion, finish, culmination.

upside down *adjective, adverb* inverted, upturned, wrong way up, upset, overturned, disordered, muddled, jumbled, confused, topsy-turvy, chaotic.

up-to-date *adjective* current, contemporary, modern,

fashionable, trendy (*infml*), latest, recent, new, state-of-the-art.
F out-of-date, old-fashioned.

urban *adjective* town, city, inner-city, metropolitan, municipal, civic, built-up.
F country, rural.

urge *verb* **1** *urge caution*: advise, counsel, recommend, advocate, encourage, exhort. **2** *urged him to leave*: implore, beg, beseech, entreat, plead. **3** *urged them on*: push, drive, goad, impel, spur, hasten, induce, incite, instigate, press, constrain, compel, force.
F **1** discourage, dissuade. **3** deter, hinder.
▪ *noun* desire, wish, inclination, fancy, longing, yearning, itch, impulse, compulsion, impetus, drive, eagerness.
F disinclination.

urgent *adjective* immediate, instant, top-priority, important, critical, crucial, imperative, exigent, pressing, compelling, persuasive, earnest, eager, insistent, persistent.
F unimportant.

usage *noun* treatment, handling, management, control, running, operation, employment, application, use.

use *verb* utilize, employ, exercise, practise, operate, work, apply, wield, handle, treat, manipulate, exploit, enjoy, consume, exhaust, expend, spend.
▪ *noun* utility, usefulness, value, worth, profit, advantage, benefit, good, avail, help, service, point, object, end, purpose, reason, cause, occasion, need, necessity, usage, application, employment, operation, exercise.

used *adjective* second-hand, cast-off, hand-me-down, nearly new, worn, dog-eared, soiled.
F unused, new, fresh.

useful *adjective* handy, convenient, all-purpose, practical, effective, productive, fruitful, profitable, valuable, worthwhile, advantageous, beneficial, helpful.
F useless, ineffective, worthless.

useless *adjective* futile, fruitless, unproductive, vain, idle, unavailing, hopeless, pointless, worthless, unusable, broken-down, clapped-out (*infml*), unworkable, impractical, ineffective, inefficient, incompetent, weak.
F useful, helpful, effective.

usual *adjective* normal, typical, stock, standard, regular, routine, habitual, customary, conventional, accepted, recognized, accustomed, familiar, common, everyday, general, ordinary, unexceptional, expected, predictable.
F unusual, strange, rare.

usually *adverb* normally, generally, as a rule, ordinarily, typically, traditionally, regularly, commonly, by and large, on the whole, mainly, chiefly, mostly.
F exceptionally.

utensil *noun* tool, implement,

instrument, device, contrivance, gadget, apparatus, appliance.

utmost *adjective* **1** *with the utmost care*: extreme, maximum, greatest, highest, supreme, paramount. **2** *the utmost limit*: farthest, furthermost, remotest, outermost, ultimate, final, last.

▪ *noun* best, hardest, most, maximum.

utter[1] *adjective* absolute, complete, total, entire, thoroughgoing, out-and-out, downright, sheer, stark, arrant, unmitigated, unqualified, perfect, consummate.

utter[2] *verb* speak, say, voice, vocalize, verbalize, express, articulate, enunciate, sound, pronounce, deliver, state, declare, announce, proclaim, tell, reveal, divulge.

utterly *adverb* absolutely, completely, totally, fully, entirely, wholly, thoroughly, downright, perfectly.

U-turn *noun* about-turn, volte-face, reversal, backtrack.

vacancy *noun* opportunity, opening, position, post, job, place, room, situation.

vacant *adjective* **1** *is this seat vacant?*: empty, unoccupied, unfilled, free, available, void, not in use, unused, uninhabited. **2** *a vacant stare*: blank, expressionless, vacuous, inane, inattentive, absent, absent-minded, unthinking, dreamy.

F3 **1** occupied, engaged.

vacuum *noun* emptiness, void, nothingness, vacuity, space, chasm, gap.

vague *adjective* **1** *a vague outline*: ill-defined, blurred, indistinct, hazy, dim, shadowy, misty, fuzzy, nebulous, obscure. **2** *a vague feeling of nausea*: indefinite, imprecise, unclear, uncertain, undefined, undetermined, unspecific, generalized, inexact, ambiguous, evasive, loose, woolly.

F3 **1** clear. **2** definite.

vain *adjective* **1** *a vain attempt*: useless, worthless, futile, abortive, fruitless, pointless, unproductive, unprofitable, unavailing, hollow, groundless, empty, trivial, unimportant. **2** *a vain little man*: conceited, proud, self-satisfied, arrogant, self-important, egotistical, bigheaded (*infml*), swollen-headed (*infml*), stuck-up (*infml*), affected, pretentious,

ostentatious, swaggering.
F3 **1** fruitful, successful. **2** modest, self-effacing.

valid *adjective* **1** *a valid argument*: logical, well-founded, well-grounded, sound, good, cogent, convincing, telling, conclusive, reliable, substantial, weighty, powerful, just. **2** *a valid passport*: official, legal, lawful, legitimate, authentic, bona fide, genuine, binding, proper.
F3 **1** false, weak. **2** unofficial, invalid.

valley *noun* dale, vale, dell, glen, hollow, cwm, depression, gulch.

valuable *adjective* **1** *necklace is very valuable*: precious, prized, valued, costly, expensive, dear, high-priced, treasured, cherished, estimable. **2** *valuable advice*: helpful, worthwhile, useful, beneficial, invaluable, constructive, fruitful, profitable, important, serviceable, worthy, handy.
F3 **1** worthless. **2** useless.

value *noun* **1** *what's the value of the painting?*: cost, price, rate, worth. **2** *of little value*: worth, use, usefulness, utility, merit, importance, desirability, benefit, advantage, significance, good, profit.
▪ *verb* **1** *value his opinion highly*: prize, appreciate, treasure, esteem, hold dear, respect, cherish. **2** *valuing the house*: evaluate, assess, estimate, price, appraise, survey, rate.
F3 **1** disregard, neglect.

vanish *verb* disappear, fade, dissolve, evaporate, disperse, melt, die out, depart, exit, fizzle out, peter out.
F3 appear, materialize.

vanity *noun* conceit, conceitedness, pride, arrogance, self-conceit, self-love, self-satisfaction, narcissism, egotism, pretension, ostentation, affectation, airs, bigheadedness (*infml*), swollen-headedness (*infml*).
F3 modesty.

vapour *noun* steam, mist, fog, smoke, breath, fumes, haze, damp, dampness, exhalation.

variable *adjective* changeable, inconstant, varying, shifting, mutable, unpredictable, fluctuating, fitful, unstable, unsteady, wavering, vacillating, temperamental, fickle, flexible.
F3 fixed, invariable, stable.

variation *noun* diversity, variety, deviation, discrepancy, diversification, alteration, change, difference, departure, modification, modulation, inflection, novelty, innovation.
F3 monotony, uniformity.

varied *adjective* assorted, diverse, miscellaneous, mixed, various, sundry, heterogeneous (*fml*), different, wide-ranging.
F3 standardized, uniform.

variety *noun* **1** *sell a variety of cold*

meats: assortment, miscellany, mixture, collection, medley, pot-pourri, range. **2** *nature displays endless variety*: difference, diversity, dissimilarity, discrepancy, variation, multiplicity. **3** *a new variety of rose*: sort, kind, class, category, species, type, breed, brand, make, strain.
F3 **2** uniformity, similitude (*fml*).

various *adjective* different, differing, diverse, varied, varying, assorted, miscellaneous, heterogeneous (*fml*), distinct, diversified, mixed, many, several.

varnish *noun* lacquer, glaze, resin, polish, gloss, coating.

vary *verb* **1** *vary the order/his route*: change, alter, modify, modulate, diversify, reorder, transform, alternate, permutate. **2** *opinions vary*: diverge, differ, disagree, depart, fluctuate.

vast *adjective* huge, immense, massive, gigantic, enormous, great, colossal, extensive, tremendous, sweeping, unlimited, fathomless, immeasurable, never-ending, monumental, monstrous, far-flung.

vault[1] *verb* leap, spring, bound, clear, jump, hurdle, leap-frog.

vault[2] *noun* cellar, crypt, strongroom, repository, cavern, depository, wine-cellar, tomb, mausoleum.

veer *verb* swerve, swing, change, shift, diverge, deviate, wheel, turn, sheer, tack.

vegetable

Vegetables include:

artichoke, asparagus, aubergine, bean, bean sprout, beetroot, bok choy, broad bean, broccoli, Brussels sprout, butter bean, cabbage, calabrese, capsicum, carrot, cassava, cauliflower, celeriac, celery, chicory, courgette, cress, cucumber, eggplant (*US*), endive, fennel, French bean, garlic, Jerusalem artichoke, jicama, kale, kohlrabi, leek, lentil, lettuce, mangetout, marrow, mooli, mushroom, okra, onion, parsnip, pea, pepper, petit pois, potato, spud (*infml*), pumpkin, radish, runner bean, shallot, soya bean, spinach, spring onion, squash, swede, sweetcorn, sweet potato, turnip, water chestnut, watercress, yam, zucchini (*US*).

vegetate *verb* stagnate, degenerate, deteriorate, rusticate, go to seed, idle, rust, languish.

vehement *adjective* impassioned, passionate, ardent, fervent, intense, forceful, emphatic, heated, strong, powerful, urgent, enthusiastic, animated, eager, earnest, forcible, fierce, violent, zealous.
F3 apathetic, indifferent.

vehicle

Vehicles include:

barouche, bicycle, bike (*infml*), boat, bobsleigh, boneshaker (*infml*), brougham, bus, cab, camper, car, caravan, caravanette, charabanc, coach, cycle, dog-cart, double-decker, dray, fork-lift truck, four-in-hand, gig, hackney carriage, hansom, juggernaut, landau, litter, lorry, minibus, minivan, monorail, moped, motorcycle, motorbike, omnibus, pantechnicon, penny-farthing, phaeton, plane, post-chaise, Pullman, rickshaw, scooter, sedan chair, ship, sled, sledge, sleeper, sleigh, stagecoach, steam-roller, sulky, surrey, tandem, tank, taxi, toboggan, tractor, trailer, train, tram, trap, tricycle, troika, trolleybus, truck, tube, van, wagon, wagon-lit.

---

veil *verb* screen, cloak, cover, mask, shadow, shield, obscure, conceal, hide, disguise, shade.
F3 expose, uncover.
▪ *noun* cover, cloak, curtain, mask, screen, disguise, film, blind, shade, shroud.

vendetta *noun* feud, blood-feud, enmity, rivalry, quarrel, bad blood, bitterness.

veneer *noun* front, façade, appearance, coating, surface, show, mask, gloss, pretence, guise, finish.

vengeance *noun* retribution, revenge, retaliation, reprisal, requital, tit for tat.
F3 forgiveness.

venom *noun* **1** *snake venom*: poison, toxin. **2** *a voice filled with venom*: rancour, ill-will, malice, malevolence, spite, bitterness, acrimony, hate, virulence.

venomous *adjective* **1** *venomous toad*: poisonous, toxic, virulent, harmful, noxious. **2** *venomous look*: malicious, spiteful, vicious, vindictive, baleful, hostile, malignant, rancorous, baneful.
F3 **1** harmless.

vent *noun* opening, hole, aperture, outlet, passage, orifice, duct.
▪ *verb* air, express, voice, utter, release, discharge, emit.

ventilate *verb* air, aerate, freshen.

venture *verb* **1** *venture to suggest*: dare, advance, make bold, put forward, presume, suggest, volunteer. **2** *venturing a small bet*: risk, hazard, endanger, imperil, jeopardize, speculate, wager, stake.
▪ *noun* risk, chance, hazard, speculation, gamble, undertaking, project, adventure, endeavour, enterprise, operation, fling.

verbal *adjective* spoken, oral, verbatim, unwritten, word-of-mouth.

verdict *noun* decision, judgement, conclusion, finding, adjudication, assessment, opinion, sentence.

verge *noun* border, edge, margin, limit, rim, brim, brink, boundary, threshold, extreme, edging.

verify *verb* confirm, corroborate, substantiate, authenticate, bear out, prove, support, validate, testify, attest (*fml*).
F3 invalidate, discredit.

versatile *adjective* adaptable,

flexible, all-round, multipurpose, multifaceted, adjustable, many-sided, general-purpose, functional, resourceful, handy, variable.
F3 inflexible.

verse *noun* poetry, rhyme, stanza, metre, doggerel, jingle.

versed *adjective* skilled, proficient, practised, experienced, familiar, acquainted, learned, knowledgeable, conversant (*fml*), seasoned, qualified, competent, accomplished.

version *noun* **1** *his version of the events*: rendering, reading, interpretation, account, translation, paraphrase, adaptation, portrayal. **2** *create an updated version*: type, kind, variant, form, model, style, design.

vertical *adjective* upright, perpendicular, upstanding, erect, on end.
F3 horizontal.

very *adverb* extremely, greatly, highly, deeply, truly, terribly (*infml*), remarkably, excessively, exceedingly, acutely, particularly, really, absolutely, noticeably, unusually.
F3 slightly, scarcely.
▪ *adjective* actual, real, same, selfsame, identical, true, genuine, simple, utter, sheer, pure, perfect, plain, mere, bare, exact, appropriate.

vet *verb* investigate, examine, check, scrutinize, scan, inspect, survey, review, appraise, audit.

veteran *noun* master, past master, old hand, old stager, old-timer, pro (*infml*), war-horse.
F3 novice, recruit.
▪ *adjective* experienced, practised, seasoned, long-serving, expert, adept, proficient, old.
F3 inexperienced.

veto *verb* reject, turn down, forbid, disallow, ban, prohibit, rule out, block.
F3 approve, sanction.
▪ *noun* rejection, ban, embargo, prohibition, thumbs-down (*infml*).
F3 approval, assent.

viable *adjective* feasible, practicable, possible, workable, usable, operable, achievable, sustainable.
F3 impossible, unworkable.

vibrant *adjective* animated, vivacious, vivid, bright, brilliant, colourful, lively, responsive, sparkling, spirited, thrilling, dynamic, electrifying, electric.

vibrate *verb* quiver, pulsate, shudder, shiver, resonate, reverberate, throb, oscillate, tremble, undulate, sway, swing, shake.

vice *noun* **1** *stamp out vice*: evil, evil-doing, depravity, immorality, wickedness, sin, corruption, iniquity (*fml*), profligacy (*fml*), degeneracy. **2** *smoking is one of his vices*: fault, failing, defect, shortcoming, weakness, imperfection, blemish, bad habit, besetting sin.
F3 **1** virtue, morality.

vicious *adjective* **1** *a vicious crime*: wicked, bad, wrong, immoral, depraved, unprincipled, diabolical, corrupt, debased, perverted, profligate (*fml*), vile, heinous (*fml*). **2** *a vicious lie*: malicious, spiteful, vindictive, virulent, cruel, mean, nasty, slanderous, venomous, defamatory. **3** *a vicious dog*: savage, wild, violent, barbarous, brutal, dangerous.

F3 **1** virtuous. **2** kind.

victim *noun* sufferer, casualty, prey, scapegoat, martyr, sacrifice, fatality.

F3 offender, attacker.

victimize *verb* oppress, persecute, discriminate against, pick on, prey on, bully, exploit.

victorious *adjective* conquering, champion, triumphant, winning, unbeaten, successful, prize-winning, top, first.

F3 defeated, unsuccessful.

victory *noun* conquest, win, triumph, success, superiority, mastery, vanquishment (*fml*), subjugation, overcoming.

F3 defeat, loss.

view *noun* **1** *hold the opposite view*: opinion, attitude, belief, judgement, estimation, feeling, sentiment, impression, notion. **2** *a view of the sea*: sight, scene, vision, vista, outlook, prospect, perspective, panorama, landscape.

▪ *verb* **1** *viewed it in a different light*: consider, regard, contemplate, judge, think about, speculate. **2** *viewed the scene*: observe, watch, see, examine, inspect, look at, scan, survey, witness, perceive.

viewer *noun* spectator, watcher, observer, onlooker.

viewpoint *noun* attitude, position, perspective, slant, standpoint, stance, opinion, angle, feeling.

vigilant *adjective* watchful, alert, attentive, observant, on one's guard, on the lookout, cautious, wide-awake, sleepless, unsleeping.

F3 careless.

vigorous *adjective* energetic, active, lively, healthy, strong, strenuous, robust, lusty, sound, vital, brisk, dynamic, forceful, forcible, powerful, stout, spirited, full-blooded, effective, efficient, enterprising, flourishing, intense.

F3 weak, feeble.

vigour *noun* energy, vitality, liveliness, health, robustness, stamina, strength, resilience, soundness, spirit, verve, gusto, activity, animation, power, potency, force, forcefulness, might, dash, dynamism.

F3 weakness.

vile *adjective* **1** *a vile person*: base, contemptible, debased, depraved, degenerate, bad, wicked, wretched, worthless, sinful, miserable, mean, evil, impure, corrupt, despicable, disgraceful, degrading, vicious, appalling. **2** *the coffee was vile*: disgusting, foul,

nauseating, sickening, repulsive, repugnant, revolting, noxious, offensive, nasty, loathsome, horrid.
F3 **1** pure, worthy. **2** pleasant, lovely.

villain *noun* evil-doer, miscreant (*fml*), scoundrel, rogue, malefactor (*fml*), criminal, reprobate, rascal.

vindicate *verb* justify, uphold, support, maintain, defend, establish, advocate, assert, verify.

vindictive *adjective* spiteful, unforgiving, implacable, vengeful, relentless, unrelenting, revengeful, resentful, punitive, venomous, malevolent, malicious.
F3 forgiving.

vintage *noun* year, period, era, epoch, generation, origin, harvest, crop.
▪ *adjective* choice, best, fine, prime, select, superior, rare, mature, old, ripe, classic, venerable, veteran.

violence *noun* **1** *the violence of the attack was shocking*: force, strength, power, vehemence, might, intensity, ferocity, fierceness, severity, tumult, turbulence, wildness. **2** *prevent violence*: brutality, destructiveness, cruelty, bloodshed, murderousness, savagery, passion, fighting, frenzy, fury, hostilities.

violent *adjective* **1** *a violent storm*: intense, strong, severe, sharp, acute, extreme, harmful, destructive, devastating, injurious, powerful, painful, agonizing, forceful, forcible, harsh, ruinous, rough, vehement, tumultuous, turbulent. **2** *a violent attack*: cruel, brutal, aggressive, bloodthirsty, impetuous, hot-headed, headstrong, murderous, savage, wild, vicious, unrestrained, uncontrollable, ungovernable, passionate, furious, intemperate, maddened, outrageous, riotous, fiery.
F3 **1** calm, moderate. **2** peaceful, gentle.

virtual *adjective* effective, essential, practical, implied, implicit, potential.

virtually *adverb* practically, in effect, almost, nearly, as good as, in essence.

virtue *noun* **1** *her goodness and virtue*: morality, rectitude, uprightness, worthiness, righteousness, probity (*fml*), integrity, honour, incorruptibility, justice, high-mindedness, excellence. **2** *the plan has many virtues*: quality, worth, merit, advantage, asset, credit, strength.
F3 **1** vice.

virtuoso *noun* expert, master, maestro, prodigy, genius.

virtuous *adjective* good, moral, righteous, upright, worthy, honourable, irreproachable, incorruptible, exemplary, unimpeachable, high-principled, blameless, clean-living, excellent, innocent.
F3 immoral, vicious.

visible *adjective* perceptible, discernible, detectable, apparent, noticeable, observable, distinguishable, discoverable, evident, unconcealed, undisguised, unmistakable, conspicuous, clear, obvious, manifest, open, palpable, plain, patent.
F3 invisible, indiscernible, hidden.

vision *noun* **1** *saw a vision*: apparition, hallucination, illusion, delusion, mirage, phantom, ghost, chimera, spectre, wraith. **2** *had a vision of his perfect house*: idea, ideal, conception, insight, view, picture, image, fantasy, dream, daydream. **3** *have excellent vision*: sight, seeing, eyesight, perception, discernment, far-sightedness, foresight, penetration.

visit *verb* call on, call in, stay with, stay at, drop in on (*infml*), stop by (*infml*), look in, look up, pop in (*infml*), see.
▪ *noun* call, stay, stop, excursion, sojourn (*fml*).

visitor *noun* caller, guest, company, tourist, holidaymaker.

visualize *verb* picture, envisage, imagine, conceive.

vital *adjective* **1** *a vital factor*: critical, crucial, important, imperative, key, significant, basic, fundamental, essential, necessary, requisite, indispensable, urgent, life-or-death, decisive, forceful. **2** *strong and vital*: living, alive, lively, life-giving, invigorating, spirited, vivacious, vibrant, vigorous, dynamic, animated, energetic, quickening (*fml*).
F3 **1** inessential, peripheral. **2** dead.

vitality *noun* life, liveliness, animation, vigour, energy, vivacity, spirit, sparkle, go (*infml*), exuberance, strength, stamina.

vivacious *adjective* lively, animated, spirited, high-spirited, effervescent, ebullient, cheerful, sparkling, bubbly, light-hearted.

vivid *adjective* **1** *a vivid shade of orange*: bright, colourful, intense, strong, rich, vibrant, brilliant, glowing, dazzling, vigorous, dramatic, flamboyant, animated, lively. **2** *have vivid memories*: memorable, powerful, graphic, clear, distinct, striking, sharp, realistic.
F3 **1** colourless, dull. **2** vague.

vocabulary *noun* language, words, glossary, lexicon, dictionary, word-book, thesaurus.

vocal *adjective* **1** *vocal accompaniment*: spoken, said, oral, uttered, voiced. **2** *a very vocal minority*: articulate, eloquent, expressive, noisy, clamorous, shrill, strident, outspoken, frank, forthright, plain-spoken.
F3 **1** unspoken. **2** inarticulate.

vocation *noun* calling, pursuit, career, métier, mission, profession, trade, employment, work, role, post, job, business, office.

vogue *noun* fashion, mode, style, craze, popularity, trend, prevalence, acceptance, custom, fad (*infml*), the latest (*infml*), the rage (*infml*), the thing (*infml*).

voice *noun* **1** *a deep voice/the voice of the people*: speech, utterance, articulation, language, words, sound, tone, intonation, inflection, expression, mouthpiece, medium, instrument, organ (*fml*). **2** *have a voice in what goes on*: say, vote, opinion, view, decision, option, will.
▪ *verb* express, say, utter, air, articulate, speak of, verbalize, assert, convey, disclose, divulge, declare, enunciate.

void *noun* emptiness, vacuity, vacuum, chasm, blank, blankness, space, lack, want, cavity, gap, hollow, opening.
▪ *adjective* annulled, inoperative, invalid, cancelled, ineffective, futile, useless, vain, worthless.
⇄ valid.

volatile *adjective* changeable, inconstant, unstable, variable, erratic, temperamental, unsteady, unsettled, fickle, mercurial, unpredictable, capricious, restless, giddy, flighty, up and down (*infml*), lively.
⇄ constant, steady.

volume *noun* **1** *volume of the tank*: bulk, size, capacity, dimensions, amount, mass, quantity, aggregate, amplitude, body. **2** *in two volumes*: book, tome, publication.

voluntary *adjective* **1** *voluntary work*: free, gratuitous, optional, spontaneous, unforced, willing, unpaid, honorary. **2** *decision was voluntary*: conscious, deliberate, purposeful, intended, intentional, wilful.
⇄ **1** compulsory. **2** involuntary.

volunteer *verb* offer, propose, put forward, present, suggest, step forward, advance.

vomit *verb* be sick, bring up, heave, retch, puke (*infml*), throw up (*infml*).

vote *noun* ballot, poll, election, franchise, referendum.
▪ *verb* elect, ballot, choose, opt, plump for, declare, return.

vouch for *verb* guarantee, support, back, endorse, confirm, certify, affirm, assert, attest to, speak for, swear to, uphold.

vow *verb* promise, pledge, swear, dedicate, devote, profess, consecrate, affirm.
▪ *noun* promise, oath, pledge.

voyage *noun* journey, trip, passage, expedition, crossing.

vulgar *adjective* **1** *thought the decoration looked vulgar*: tasteless, flashy, gaudy, tawdry, cheap and nasty (*infml*). **2** *vulgar manners*: unrefined, uncouth, coarse, common, crude, ill-bred, impolite, indecorous. **3** *a vulgar word*: indecent, suggestive, risqué, rude, indelicate.
⇄ **1** tasteful. **2** correct. **3** decent.

vulnerable *adjective* unprotected, exposed, defenceless, susceptible, weak, sensitive, wide open.
⇄ protected, strong, invulnerable.

waddle *verb* toddle, totter, wobble, sway, rock, shuffle.

waffle *verb* jabber, prattle, blather, rabbit on (*infml*), witter on (*infml*).
▪ *noun* blather, prattle, wordiness, padding, nonsense, gobbledegook (*infml*), hot air (*infml*).

waft *verb* drift, float, blow, transport, transmit.

wag *verb* shake, waggle, wave, sway, swing, bob, nod, wiggle, oscillate, flutter, vibrate, quiver, rock.

wage *noun* pay, fee, earnings, salary, wage-packet, payment, stipend, remuneration, emolument (*fml*), allowance, reward, hire, compensation, recompense.
▪ *verb* carry on, conduct, engage in, undertake, practise, pursue.

wail *verb* moan, cry, howl, lament, weep, complain, yowl (*infml*).

wait *verb* delay, linger, hold back, hesitate, pause, hang around, hang fire, remain, rest, stay.
F3 proceed, go ahead.
▪ *noun* hold-up, hesitation, delay, interval, pause, halt.

waive *verb* renounce, relinquish, forgo, resign, surrender, yield.

wake[1] *verb* rise, get up, arise, rouse, come to, bring round.
F3 sleep.
▪ *noun* funeral, death-watch, vigil, watch.

wake[2] *noun* **1** *in the wake of the election*: trail, track, path, aftermath. **2** *the ship's wake*: backwash, wash, rear, train, waves.

waken *verb* stimulate, stir, activate, arouse, animate, excite, fire, galvanize.

walk *verb* step, stride, pace, proceed, advance, march, plod, tramp, traipse, trek, trudge, saunter, amble, stroll, tread, hike, promenade, move, hoof it (*infml*), accompany, escort.
▪ *noun* **1** *a funny walk*: carriage, gait, step, pace, stride. **2** *go for a walk*: stroll, amble, ramble, saunter, march, hike, tramp, trek, traipse, trudge, trail. **3** *a tree-lined walk*: footpath, path, walkway, avenue, pathway, promenade, alley, esplanade, lane, pavement, sidewalk.

walk-over *noun* pushover (*infml*), doddle (*infml*), child's play, piece of cake (*infml*), cinch (*infml*).

wall *noun* **1** *cell wall/garden wall/*

walls of steel: partition, screen, panel, divider, fence, hedge, enclosure, membrane, bulkhead. **2** *the castle walls*: fortification, barricade, rampart, parapet, stockade, embankment, bulwark, palisade.

wallow *verb* **1** *wallow in mud*: loll, lie, roll, wade, welter, lurch, flounder, splash. **2** *wallow in nostalgia*: indulge, luxuriate, relish, revel, bask, enjoy, glory, delight.

wander *verb* **1** *wander the countryside/wander home*: roam, rove, ramble, meander, saunter, stroll, prowl, drift, range, stray, straggle. **2** *wander from the point*: digress, diverge, deviate, depart, go astray, swerve, veer, err. **3** *wandering in his mind*: ramble, rave, babble, gibber.

▪ *noun* excursion, ramble, stroll, saunter, meander, prowl, cruise.

wanderer *noun* itinerant, traveller, voyager, drifter, rover, rambler, stroller, stray, straggler, ranger, nomad, gypsy, vagrant, vagabond, rolling stone (*infml*).

wane *verb* diminish, decrease, decline, weaken, subside, fade, dwindle, ebb, lessen, abate, sink, drop, taper off, dim, droop, contract, shrink, fail, wither.

F3 increase, wax.

want *verb* **1** *wants something to eat/wanted peace*: desire, wish, crave, covet, fancy, long for, pine for, yearn for, hunger for, thirst for. **2** *wants a lick of paint*: need, require, demand, lack, miss, call for.

▪ *noun* **1** *satisfy their wants*: desire, demand, longing, requirement, wish, need, appetite. **2** *suffer from want*: poverty, privation (*fml*), destitution.

wanton *adjective* malicious, immoral, shameless, arbitrary, unprovoked, unjustifiable, unrestrained, rash, reckless, wild.

war *noun* warfare, hostilities, fighting, battle, combat, conflict, strife, struggle, bloodshed, contest, contention, enmity.

F3 peace, ceasefire.

ward *noun* **1** *a hospital ward*: room, apartment, unit. **2** *an electoral ward*: division, area, district, quarter, precinct, zone. **3** *a ward of court*: charge, dependant, protégé(e), minor.

wares *noun* goods, merchandise, commodities, stock, products, produce, stuff.

warfare *noun* war, fighting, hostilities, battle, arms, combat, strife, struggle, passage of arms, contest, conflict, contention, discord, blows.

F3 peace.

warlike *adjective* belligerent, aggressive, bellicose, pugnacious (*fml*), combative, bloodthirsty, war-mongering, militaristic, hostile, antagonistic, unfriendly.

F3 friendly, peaceable.

warm *adjective* **1** *warm water*: heated, tepid, lukewarm. **2** *warm support*: ardent, passionate,

fervent, vehement, earnest, zealous. **3** *a warm welcome*: friendly, amiable, cordial, affable, kindly, genial, hearty, hospitable, sympathetic, affectionate, tender. **4** *a warm climate*: fine, sunny, balmy, temperate, close.
F3 **1** cool. **2** indifferent. **3** unfriendly. **4** cool.
▪ *verb* **1** *warm the milk*: heat (up), reheat, melt, thaw. **2** *warming her heart*: animate, interest, please, delight, stimulate, stir, rouse, excite.
F3 **1** cool.

warmth *noun* **1** *the warmth of its body*: warmness, heat. **2** *the warmth of the people*: friendliness, affection, cordiality, tenderness. **3** *replied with some warmth*: ardour, enthusiasm, passion, fervour, zeal, eagerness.
F3 **1** coldness. **2** unfriendliness. **3** indifference.

warn *verb* caution, alert, admonish, advise, notify, counsel, put on one's guard, inform, tip off (*infml*).

warning *noun* **1** *give them some warning/sound a warning*: caution, alert, admonition, advice, notification, notice, advance notice, counsel, hint, lesson, alarm, threat, tip-off (*infml*). **2** *dark clouds were the first warning of a storm brewing*: omen, augury, premonition, presage, sign, signal, portent.

warp *verb* twist, bend, contort, deform, distort, kink, misshape, pervert, corrupt, deviate.
F3 straighten.

warrant *noun* authorization, authority, sanction, permit, permission, licence, guarantee, warranty, security, pledge, commission, voucher.

wary *adjective* cautious, guarded, careful, chary, on one's guard, on the lookout, prudent, distrustful, suspicious, heedful, attentive, alert, watchful, vigilant, wide-awake.
F3 unwary, careless, heedless.

wash *verb* **1** *wash clothes/the floors*: clean, cleanse, launder, scrub, swab down, rinse, swill. **2** *wash before dinner*: bathe, bath, shower, douche, shampoo.

waste *verb* **1** *don't waste your money*: squander, misspend, misuse, fritter away, dissipate, lavish, spend, throw away, blow (*infml*). **2** *wasting energy*: consume, erode, exhaust, drain, destroy, spoil.
F3 **1** economize. **2** preserve.
▪ *noun* **1** *a waste of money*: squandering, dissipation (*fml*), prodigality (*fml*), wastefulness, extravagance, loss. **2** *a waste of his talent*: misapplication, misuse, abuse, neglect. **3** *dispose of waste*: rubbish, refuse, trash, garbage, leftovers, debris, dregs, effluent, litter, scrap, slops, dross.
▪ *adjective* **1** *waste materials*: useless, worthless, unwanted, unused, left-over, superfluous, supernumerary, extra. **2** *waste*

land: barren, desolate, empty, uninhabited, bare, devastated, uncultivated, unprofitable, wild, dismal, dreary.

wasted *adjective* **1** *wasted effort*: unnecessary, needless, useless. **2** *thin and wasted faces*: emaciated, withered, shrivelled, shrunken, gaunt, washed-out, spent.

wasteful *adjective* extravagant, spendthrift, prodigal, profligate, uneconomical, thriftless, unthrifty, ruinous, lavish, improvident (*fml*).
F3 economical, thrifty.

wasteland *noun* wilderness, desert, barrenness, waste, wild(s), void.

watch *verb* **1** *watch him closely*: observe, see, look at, regard, note, notice, mark, stare at, peer at, gaze at, view. **2** *watch my bag*: guard, look after, keep an eye on, mind, protect, superintend, take care of, keep. **3** *watch for those holes in the road*: pay attention, be careful, take heed, look out.
▪ *noun* **1** *wearing a watch*: timepiece, wristwatch, clock, chronometer. **2** *keep (a) watch*: vigilance, watchfulness, vigil, observation, surveillance, notice, lookout, attention, heed, alertness, inspection, supervision.

watchful *adjective* vigilant, attentive, heedful, observant, alert, guarded, on one's guard, wide awake, suspicious, wary, chary, cautious.
F3 unobservant, inattentive.

water *noun* rain, sea, ocean, lake, river, stream.
▪ *verb* wet, moisten, dampen, soak, spray, sprinkle, irrigate, drench, flood, hose.
F3 dry out, parch.

waterfall *noun* fall, cascade, chute, cataract, torrent.

watertight *adjective* **1** *hull is watertight*: waterproof, sound, hermetic. **2** *a watertight alibi*: impregnable, unassailable, airtight, flawless, foolproof, firm, incontrovertible.
F3 1 leaky.

watery *adjective* **1** *watery eyes/grave*: liquid, fluid, moist, wet, damp. **2** *a rather watery soup*: weak, watered-down, diluted, insipid, tasteless, thin, runny, soggy, flavourless, washy, wishy-washy (*infml*).
F3 1 dry.

wave *verb* **1** *waved to his parents*: beckon, gesture, gesticulate, indicate, sign, signal, direct. **2** *waving a stick*: brandish, flourish, flap, flutter, shake, sway, swing. **3** *waving in the wind*: waft, quiver, ripple.
▪ *noun* **1** *waves crashing on the shore*: breaker, roller, billow, ripple, tidal wave, wavelet, undulation, white horse (*infml*). **2** *a wave of relief/protest*: surge, sweep, swell, upsurge, groundswell, current, drift, movement, rush, tendency, trend, stream, flood, outbreak, rash.

waver *verb* **1** *wavering between one and the other*: vacillate, falter,

hesitate, dither, fluctuate, vary, seesaw. **2** *wavering on the edge*: oscillate, shake, sway, wobble, tremble, totter, rock.
E3 1 decide.

wavy *adjective* undulating, rippled, curly, curvy, ridged, sinuous, winding, zigzag.

way *noun* **1** *the usual way*: method, approach, manner, technique, procedure, means, mode, system, fashion. **2** *study their ways/it's just his way*: custom, practice, habit, usage, characteristic, idiosyncrasy, trait, style, conduct, nature. **3** *the way home*: direction, course, route, path, road, channel, access, avenue, track, passage, highway, street, thoroughfare, lane.

wayward *adjective* wilful, capricious, perverse, contrary, changeable, fickle, unpredictable, stubborn, self-willed, unmanageable, headstrong, obstinate, disobedient, rebellious, insubordinate, intractable, unruly, incorrigible.
E3 tractable, good-natured.

weak *adjective* **1** *a weak excuse/chest*: feeble, frail, infirm, unhealthy, sickly, delicate, debilitated, exhausted, fragile, flimsy. **2** *a weak spot*: vulnerable, unprotected, unguarded, defenceless, exposed. **3** *a weak government/argument*: powerless, impotent, spineless, cowardly, indecisive, ineffectual, irresolute, poor, lacking, lame, inadequate, defective, deficient, inconclusive, unconvincing, untenable. **4** *a weak signal*: faint, slight, low, soft, muffled, dull, imperceptible. **5** *weak tea*: insipid, tasteless, watery, thin, diluted, runny.
E3 1 strong. **2** secure. **3** powerful. **4** strong. **5** strong.

weaken *verb* **1** *weaken their hold*: enfeeble, exhaust, debilitate, sap, undermine, dilute, diminish, lower, lessen, reduce, moderate, mitigate, temper, soften (up), thin, water down. **2** *storm weakened*: tire, flag, fail, give way, droop, fade, abate, ease up, dwindle.
E3 1 strengthen.

weakness *noun* **1** *weakness of body*: feebleness, debility, infirmity, impotence, frailty, powerlessness, vulnerability. **2** *have many weaknesses*: fault, failing, flaw, shortcoming, blemish, defect, deficiency, foible. **3** *a weakness for chocolate*: liking, inclination, fondness, penchant, passion, soft spot (*infml*).
E3 1 strength. **2** strength. **3** dislike.

wealth *noun* **1** *have considerable wealth*: money, cash, riches, assets, affluence, prosperity, funds, mammon, fortune, capital, opulence, means, substance, resources, goods, possessions, property, estate. **2** *a wealth of reading material*: abundance, plenty, bounty, fullness, profusion, store.
E3 1 poverty.

wealthy *adjective* rich,

prosperous, affluent, well-off, moneyed, opulent, comfortable, well-heeled, well-to-do, flush (*infml*), loaded (*infml*), rolling in it (*infml*).
F3 poor, impoverished.

wear *verb* **1** *wearing green/a hat*: dress in, have on, put on, don, sport, carry, bear, display, show. **2** *wear away/down*: deteriorate, erode, corrode, consume, fray, rub, abrade, waste, grind.
▪ *noun* **1** *men's wear*: clothes, clothing, dress, garments, outfit, costume, attire. **2** *wear and tear*: deterioration, erosion, corrosion, wear and tear, friction, abrasion.

weary *adjective* tired, exhausted, fatigued, sleepy, worn out, drained, drowsy, jaded, all in (*infml*), done in (*infml*), dead beat (*infml*), dog-tired (*infml*), whacked (*infml*).
F3 refreshed.

weather *noun* climate, conditions, temperature.
▪ *verb* **1** *weather the storm*: endure, survive, live through, come through, ride out, rise above, stick out, withstand, surmount, stand, brave, overcome, resist, pull through, suffer. **2** *face weathered by sun, wind, and rain*: expose, toughen, season, harden.
F3 **1** succumb.

Types of weather include:
breeze, cloud, cyclone, deluge, dew, downpour, drizzle, drought, fog, frost, gale, hail, haze, heatwave, hurricane, hoar frost, ice, lightning, mist, monsoon, rain, rainbow, shower, sleet, slush, smog, snow, snowstorm, squall, storm, sunshine, tempest, thaw, thunder, tornado, twister (*infml*), typhoon, whirlwind, wind.

weave *verb* **1** *weaving the strands together*: interlace, lace, plait, braid, intertwine, spin, knit, entwine, intercross, fuse, merge, unite. **2** *weaving a complicated story*: create, compose, construct, contrive, put together, fabricate. **3** *weaving from side to side*: wind, twist, zigzag, criss-cross.

web *noun* network, net, netting, lattice, mesh, webbing, interlacing, weft, snare, tangle, trap.

wedding *noun* marriage, matrimony, nuptials (*fml*), wedlock, bridal.
F3 divorce.

wedge *noun* lump, block, chunk, wodge, chock.
▪ *verb* jam, cram, pack, ram, squeeze, stuff, push, lodge, block, thrust, crowd, force.

weep *verb* cry, sob, moan, lament, wail, mourn, grieve, bawl, blubber, snivel, whimper, blub (*infml*).
F3 rejoice.

weigh *verb* **1** *weighing heavily on them*: bear down, oppress. **2** *weigh the odds*: consider, contemplate, evaluate, meditate on, mull over, ponder, think over, examine, reflect on, deliberate.

weight *noun* **1** *the great weight made his legs buckle*: heaviness,

gravity, burden, load, pressure, mass, force, ballast, tonnage, poundage. **2** *add weight to his statement*: importance, significance, substance, consequence, impact, moment, influence, value, authority, clout (*infml*), power, preponderance, consideration.
F3 **1** lightness.
▪ *verb* bias, unbalance, slant, prejudice.

weighty *adjective* **1** *several weighty volumes*: heavy, burdensome, substantial, bulky. **2** *a weighty decision*: important, significant, consequential, crucial, critical, momentous, serious, grave, solemn. **3** *a weighty problem*: demanding, difficult, exacting, taxing.
F3 **1** light. **2** unimportant.

weird *adjective* strange, uncanny, bizarre, eerie, creepy, supernatural, unnatural, ghostly, freakish, mysterious, queer, grotesque, spooky (*infml*), far-out (*infml*), way-out (*infml*).
F3 normal, usual.

welcome *adjective* acceptable, desirable, pleasing, pleasant, agreeable, gratifying, appreciated, delightful, refreshing.
F3 unwelcome.
▪ *noun* reception, greeting, salutation (*infml*), acceptance, hospitality, red carpet (*infml*).
▪ *verb* greet, hail, receive, salute, meet, accept, approve of, embrace.
F3 reject, snub.

weld *verb* fuse, unite, bond, join, solder, bind, connect, seal, link, cement.
F3 separate.

welfare *noun* wellbeing, health, prosperity, happiness, benefit, good, advantage, interest, profit, success.

well[1] *noun* spring, well-spring, fountain, fount, source, reservoir, wellhead, waterhole.
▪ *verb* flow, spring, surge, gush, stream, brim over, jet, spout, spurt, swell, pour, flood, ooze, run, trickle, rise, seep.

well[2] *adverb* rightly, correctly, properly, skilfully, ably, expertly, successfully, adequately, sufficiently, suitably, easily, satisfactorily, thoroughly, greatly, fully, considerably, completely, agreeably, pleasantly, happily, kindly, favourably, splendidly, substantially, comfortably, readily, carefully, clearly, highly, deeply, justly.
F3 badly, inadequately, incompetently, wrongly.
▪ *adjective* **1** *feel well*: healthy, in good health, fit, able-bodied, sound, robust, strong, thriving, flourishing. **2** *all is well*: satisfactory, right, all right, good, pleasing, proper, agreeable, fine, lucky, fortunate.
F3 **1** ill. **2** bad.

wellbeing *noun* welfare, happiness, comfort, good.

wet *adjective* **1** *wet clothes/ground*: damp, moist, soaked, soaking, sodden, saturated, soggy, sopping, watery, waterlogged, drenched, dripping, spongy, dank, clammy. **2** *a wet day*: raining, rainy, showery, teeming, pouring, drizzling, humid.

F3 1 dry. **2** dry.

▪ *verb* moisten, damp, dampen, soak, saturate, drench, steep, water, irrigate, spray, splash, sprinkle, imbue, dip.

F3 dry.

whack *verb* hit, strike, smack, thrash, slap, beat, bash (*infml*), bang, cuff, thump, box, buffet, rap, wallop (*infml*), belt (*infml*), clobber (*infml*), clout (*infml*), sock (*infml*).

▪ *noun* smack, slap, blow, hit, rap, stroke, thump, cuff, box, bang, clout (*infml*), bash (*infml*), wallop (*infml*).

wheel *verb* turn, rotate, circle, gyrate, orbit, spin, twirl, whirl, swing, roll, revolve, swivel.

wheeze *verb* pant, gasp, cough, hiss, rasp, whistle.

whereabouts *noun* location, position, place, situation, site, vicinity.

whet *verb* **1** *whet the blade*: sharpen, hone, file, grind. **2** *whet their appetite*: stimulate, stir, rouse, arouse, provoke, kindle, quicken (*fml*), incite, awaken, increase.

F3 1 blunt. **2** dampen.

whiff *noun* breath, puff, hint, trace, blast, draught, odour, smell, aroma, sniff, scent, reek, stink, stench.

whim *noun* fancy, caprice, notion, quirk, freak, humour, conceit, fad, vagary, urge.

whimper *verb* cry, sob, weep, snivel, whine, grizzle, mewl, moan, whinge (*infml*).

▪ *noun* sob, snivel, whine, moan.

whimsical *adjective* fanciful, capricious, playful, impulsive, eccentric, funny, droll, curious, queer, unusual, weird, odd, peculiar, quaint, dotty (*infml*).

whine *noun* **1** *dog whining*: cry, whimper, moan, wail. **2** *whining about the cost*: complaint, grumble, grouse, gripe (*infml*), grouch (*infml*).

▪ *verb* **1** *dog gave a pathetic whine*: cry, sob, whimper, grizzle, moan, wail. **2** *always has some whine or other*: complain, carp, grumble, whinge (*infml*), gripe (*infml*), grouch (*infml*).

whip *verb* **1** *whipping the horses*: beat, flog, lash, flagellate, scourge, birch, cane, strap, thrash, punish, chastise, discipline, castigate (*fml*). **2** *whipped it away/whipped past*: pull, jerk, snatch, whisk, dash, dart, rush, tear, flit, flash, fly.

▪ *noun* lash, scourge, switch, birch, cane, horsewhip, riding-crop, cat-o'-nine-tails.

whirl *verb* swirl, spin, turn, twist, twirl, pivot, pirouette, swivel, wheel, rotate, revolve, reel, roll, gyrate, circle.

▪ *noun* **1** *did a whirl*: spin, twirl, twist, gyration, revolution, pirouette, swirl, turn, wheel, rotation, circle, reel, roll. **2** *a whirl* *of excitement*: confusion, daze, flurry, commotion, agitation, bustle, hubbub, hurly-burly, giddiness, tumult, uproar.

whisk *verb* **1** *whisk the eggs*: whip, beat. **2** *whisked down to the shops*: dart, dash, rush, hurry, speed, hasten, race. **3** *whisking the flies away*: brush, sweep, flick, wipe, twitch.

whisper *verb* murmur, mutter, mumble, breathe, hiss, rustle, sigh.
F3 shout.
▪ *noun* murmur, undertone, sigh, hiss, rustle.

whole *adjective* **1** *the whole day/ text*: complete, entire, integral, full, total, unabridged, uncut, undivided, unedited. **2** *a whole dinosaur skeleton*: intact, unharmed, undamaged, unbroken, inviolate, perfect, in one piece, mint, unhurt. **3** *felt whole again*: well, healthy, fit, sound, strong.
F3 1 partial. **2** damaged. **3** ill.
▪ *noun* total, aggregate, sum total, entirety, all, fullness, totality, ensemble, entity, unit, lot, piece, everything.
F3 part.

wholehearted *adjective* unreserved, unstinting, unqualified, passionate, enthusiastic, earnest, committed, dedicated, devoted, heartfelt, emphatic, warm, sincere, unfeigned, genuine, complete, true, real, zealous.
F3 half-hearted.

wholesale *adjective* comprehensive, far-reaching, extensive, sweeping, wide-ranging, mass, broad, outright, total, massive, indiscriminate.
F3 partial.

wholesome *adjective* **1** *wholesome food*: healthy, hygienic, salubrious (*fml*), sanitary, nutritious, nourishing, beneficial, salutary, invigorating, bracing. **2** *wholesome entertainment*: moral, decent, clean, proper, improving, edifying, uplifting, pure, virtuous, righteous, honourable, respectable.
F3 1 unhealthy. **2** unwholesome.

wholly *adverb* completely, entirely, fully, purely, absolutely, totally, utterly, comprehensively, altogether, perfectly, thoroughly, all, exclusively, only.
F3 partly.

wicked *adjective* **1** *a wicked man/ crime*: evil, sinful, immoral, depraved, corrupt, vicious, unprincipled, iniquitous, heinous (*fml*), debased, abominable, ungodly, unrighteous, shameful. **2** *a wicked smell*: bad, unpleasant, harmful, offensive, vile, worthless, difficult, dreadful, distressing, awful, atrocious, severe, intense, nasty, foul, injurious, troublesome, terrible, fierce. **3** *a wicked grin*: naughty, mischievous, roguish.
F3 1 good, upright. **2** harmless.

wide *adjective* **1** *a wide street*: broad, roomy, spacious, vast, immense. **2** *wide eyes*: dilated,

expanded, full. **3** *wide influence*: extensive, wide-ranging, comprehensive, far-reaching, general.
1 narrow. **3** restricted.
▪ *adverb* **1** *shot went wide*: astray, off course, off target, off the mark. **2** *travel far and wide*: fully, completely, all the way.
1 on target.

widen *verb* distend, dilate, expand, extend, spread, stretch, enlarge, broaden.
narrow.

widespread *adjective* extensive, prevalent, rife, general, sweeping, universal, wholesale, far-reaching, unlimited, broad, common, pervasive, far-flung.
limited.

width *noun* breadth, diameter, wideness, compass, thickness, span, scope, range, measure, girth, beam, amplitude, extent, reach.

wield *verb* **1** *wield a weapon*: brandish, flourish, swing, wave, handle, ply, manage, manipulate. **2** *wield power*: have, hold, possess, employ, exert, exercise, use, utilize, maintain, command.

wild *adjective* **1** *a wild horse*: untamed, undomesticated, feral, savage, barbarous, primitive, uncivilized, natural, ferocious, fierce. **2** *wild country*: uncultivated, desolate, waste, uninhabited. **3** *wild behaviour*: unrestrained, unruly, unmanageable, violent, turbulent, rowdy, lawless, disorderly, riotous, boisterous. **4** *a wild night*: stormy, tempestuous, rough, blustery, choppy. **5** *a wild guess*: reckless, rash, imprudent, foolish, foolhardy, impracticable, irrational, outrageous, preposterous, wayward, extravagant. **6** *wild with anxiety*: mad, crazy (*infml*), frenzied, distraught, demented.
1 civilized, tame. **2** cultivated. **3** restrained. **4** calm. **5** sensible. **6** sane.

wilderness *noun* desert, wasteland, waste, wilds, jungle.

wilful *adjective* **1** *wilful damage*: deliberate, conscious, intentional, voluntary, premeditated. **2** *a wilful child*: self-willed, obstinate, stubborn, pigheaded, obdurate, intransigent, inflexible, perverse, wayward, contrary.
1 unintentional. **2** good-natured.

will *noun* **1** *of their own free will*: volition, choice, option, preference, decision, discretion. **2** *the will to live*: wish, desire, inclination, feeling, fancy, disposition, mind. **3** *have a strong will*: purpose, resolve, resolution, determination, will-power, aim, intention, command.
▪ *verb* **1** *willed that it was so*: want, desire, choose, compel, command, decree, order, ordain. **2** *willed his entire estate to his son*: bequeath, leave, hand down, pass on, transfer, confer, dispose of.

willing *adjective* disposed, inclined, agreeable, compliant, ready, prepared, consenting, content, amenable, biddable, pleased, well-disposed, favourable, happy, eager, enthusiastic.
F3 unwilling, disinclined, reluctant.

wilt *verb* droop, sag, wither, shrivel, flop, flag, dwindle, weaken, diminish, fail, fade, languish, ebb, sink, wane.
F3 perk up.

wily *adjective* shrewd, cunning, scheming, artful, crafty, foxy, intriguing, tricky, underhand, shifty, deceitful, deceptive, astute, sly, guileful, designing, crooked, fly (*infml*).
F3 guileless.

win *verb* **1** *win the race*: be victorious, triumph, succeed, prevail, overcome, conquer, come first, carry off, finish first. **2** *win a prize*: gain, acquire, achieve, attain, accomplish, receive, procure, secure, obtain, get, earn, catch, net.
F3 **1** fail, lose.
▪ *noun* victory, triumph, conquest, success, mastery.
F3 defeat.

wind[1] *noun* /wind/ air, breeze, draught, gust, puff, breath, air-current, blast, current, bluster, gale, hurricane, tornado, cyclone.

wind[2] *verb* /waind/ coil, twist, turn, curl, curve, bend, loop, spiral, zigzag, twine, encircle, furl, deviate, meander, ramble, wreathe, roll, reel.

windfall *noun* bonanza, godsend, jackpot, treasure-trove, stroke of luck, find.

window *noun* pane, light, opening, skylight, rose-window, casement, oriel, dormer.

windy *adjective* breezy, blowy, blustery, squally, windswept, stormy, tempestuous, gusty.
F3 calm.

wing *noun* branch, arm, section, faction, group, grouping, flank, circle, coterie, set, segment, side, annexe, adjunct, extension.

wink *verb* blink, flutter, glimmer, glint, twinkle, gleam, sparkle, flicker, flash.
▪ *noun* **1** *the first wink of sunshine*: blink, flutter, sparkle, twinkle, glimmering, gleam, glint. **2** *in the wink of an eye*: instant, second, split second, flash.

winner *noun* champion, victor, prizewinner, world-beater, medallist, title-holder, conqueror.
F3 loser.

winning *adjective* **1** *the winning team*: conquering, triumphant, unbeaten, undefeated, victorious, successful. **2** *winning ways*: winsome, charming, attractive, captivating, engaging, fetching, enchanting, endearing, delightful, amiable, alluring, lovely, pleasing, sweet.
F3 **1** losing. **2** unappealing.

wintry *adjective* cold, chilly, bleak, cheerless, desolate, dismal, harsh, snowy, frosty, freezing, frozen, icy.

wipe *verb* **1** *wiped his mouth/the table*: rub, clean, dry, dust, brush, mop, swab, sponge, clear. **2** *wiped the smile off her face*: remove, erase, take away, take off.

wiry *adjective* muscular, sinewy, lean, tough, strong.
F3 puny.

wisdom *noun* discernment, penetration, sagacity (*fml*), reason, sense, astuteness, comprehension, enlightenment, judgement, judiciousness, understanding, knowledge, learning, intelligence, erudition, foresight, prudence.
F3 folly, stupidity.

wise *adjective* **1** *a wise old man*: discerning, sagacious (*fml*), perceptive, rational, informed, well-informed, understanding, erudite, enlightened, knowing, intelligent, clever, aware, experienced. **2** *a wise decision*: well-advised, judicious (*fml*), prudent, reasonable, sensible, sound, long-sighted, shrewd.
F3 **1** foolish, stupid. **2** ill-advised.

wish *verb* **1** *wishing for success/rain*: desire, want, yearn, long, hanker, covet, crave, aspire, hope, hunger, thirst, prefer, need. **2** *do as she wishes*: ask, bid, require, order, instruct, direct, command.
▪ *noun* **1** *have a wish for a better life*: desire, want, hankering, aspiration, inclination, hunger, thirst, liking, preference, yearning, urge, whim, hope. **2** *carry out his wishes*: request, bidding, order, command, will.

wisp *noun* shred, strand, thread, twist, piece, lock.

wit *noun* **1** *her writing is full of subtle wit*: humour, repartee, facetiousness, drollery, banter, jocularity, levity. **2** *have the wit to realize what was happening*: intelligence, cleverness, brains, sense, reason, common sense, wisdom, understanding, judgement, insight, intellect. **3** *he thinks he is a bit of a wit*: humorist, comedian, comic, satirist, joker, wag.
F3 **1** seriousness. **2** stupidity.

witchcraft *noun* sorcery, magic, wizardry, occultism, the occult, the black art, black magic, enchantment, necromancy, voodoo, spell, incantation, divination, conjuration.

withdraw *verb* **1** *withdrew her hand quickly*: recoil, shrink back, draw back, pull back. **2** *withdrew the accusation*: recant, disclaim, take back, revoke, rescind, retract, cancel, abjure, recall, take away. **3** *withdrew from the world*: depart, go (away), absent oneself, retire, remove, leave, back out, fall back, drop out, retreat, secede. **4** *withdrew the cork*: draw out, extract, pull out.

wither *verb* shrink, shrivel, dry, wilt, droop, decay, disintegrate, wane, perish, fade, languish, decline, waste.
F3 flourish, thrive.

withering *adjective* scornful, contemptuous, scathing, snubbing, humiliating, mortifying, wounding.
F3 encouraging, supportive.

withhold *verb* keep back, retain, hold back, suppress, restrain, repress, control, check, reserve, deduct, refuse, hide, conceal.
F3 give, accord.

withstand *verb* resist, oppose, stand fast, stand one's ground, stand, stand up to, confront, brave, face, cope with, take on, thwart, defy, hold one's ground, hold out, last out, hold off, endure, bear, tolerate, put up with, survive, weather.
F3 give in, yield.

witness *noun* **1** *call the next witness*: testifier, attestant (*fml*), deponent (*fml*). **2** *a witness to the accident*: onlooker, eye-witness, looker-on, observer, spectator, viewer, watcher, bystander.
▪ *verb* **1** *witness the accident*: see, observe, notice, note, view, watch, look on, mark, perceive. **2** *witness his signature*: endorse, sign, countersign.

witty *adjective* humorous, amusing, comic, sharp-witted, droll, whimsical, original, brilliant, clever, ingenious, lively, sparkling, funny, facetious, fanciful, jocular.
F3 dull, unamusing.

wobble *verb* shake, oscillate, tremble, quake, sway, teeter, totter, rock, seesaw, vibrate, waver, dodder, fluctuate, hesitate, dither, vacillate, shilly-shally.

wobbly *adjective* unstable, shaky, rickety, unsteady, wonky (*infml*), teetering, tottering, doddering, doddery, uneven, unbalanced, unsafe.
F3 stable, steady.

woman *noun* female, lady, girl, matriarch, maiden, maid.

wonder *noun* **1** *one of the wonders of the world*: marvel, phenomenon, miracle, prodigy, sight, spectacle, rarity, curiosity. **2** *watch it with wonder*: awe, amazement, astonishment, admiration, wonderment, fascination, surprise, bewilderment.
▪ *verb* **1** *wonder what he's doing*: meditate, speculate, ponder, ask oneself, question, conjecture, puzzle, enquire, query, doubt, think. **2** *wonder at its size*: marvel, gape, be amazed, be surprised.

wonderful *adjective* **1** *had a wonderful time*: marvellous, magnificent, outstanding, excellent, superb, admirable, delightful, phenomenal, sensational, stupendous, tremendous, super (*infml*), terrific (*infml*), brilliant (*infml*), great (*infml*), fabulous (*infml*), fantastic (*infml*). **2** *a wonderful sight*: amazing, astonishing, astounding, startling, surprising, extraordinary, incredible, remarkable, staggering, strange.
F3 **1** appalling, dreadful. **2** ordinary.

wood *noun* **1** *cut the wood*: timber,

lumber, planks. **2** *an oak wood*: forest, woods, woodland, trees, plantation, thicket, grove, coppice, copse, spinney.

Types of wood include:
bitterwood, brushwood, chipboard, cordwood, driftwood, firewood, fruitwood, green wood, hardboard, hardwood, heartwood, kindling, lumber (*US*), matchwood, nutwood, plywood, pulpwood, sapwood, seasoned wood, softwood, timber, whitewood, wood veneer; ash, balsa, beech, cedar, cherry, chestnut, cottonwood, deal, ebony, elm, fir, hazel, mahogany, maple, oak, pine, poplar, redwood, rosewood, sandalwood, sapele, satinwood, sycamore, teak, walnut, willow. *See also* **tree**.

wooded *adjective* forested, timbered, woody, tree-covered, sylvan (*fml*).

wooden *adjective* **1** *wooden planks*: timber, woody. **2** *a wooden expression*: emotionless, expressionless, awkward, clumsy, stilted, lifeless, spiritless, unemotional, stiff, rigid, leaden, deadpan, blank, empty, slow.
F3 **2** lively.

wool *noun* fleece, down, yarn.

woolly *adjective* **1** *a woolly coat*: woollen, fleecy, woolly-haired, downy, shaggy, fuzzy, frizzy. **2** *a bit woolly about yesterday's events*: unclear, ill-defined, hazy, blurred, confused, muddled, vague, indefinite, nebulous.
F3 **2** clear, distinct.
▪ *noun* jumper, sweater, jersey, pullover, cardigan.

word *noun* **1** *what does this word mean?*: name, term, expression, designation, utterance, vocable (*fml*). **2** *have a word with him later*: conversation, chat, talk, discussion, consultation. **3** *get word to his family*: information, news, report, communication, notice, message, bulletin, communiqué, statement, dispatch, declaration, comment, assertion, account, remark, advice, warning. **4** *give you my word*: promise, pledge, oath, assurance, vow, guarantee. **5** *just give the word*: command, order, decree, commandment, go-ahead (*infml*), green light (*infml*).
▪ *verb* phrase, express, couch, put, say, explain, write.

words *noun* **1** *have words with someone*: argument, dispute, quarrel, disagreement, altercation (*fml*), bickering, row, squabble. **2** *write the words of a song*: lyrics, libretto, text, book.

wordy *adjective* verbose, long-winded, loquacious (*fml*), garrulous, prolix, rambling, diffuse, discursive.
F3 concise.

work *noun* **1** *what line of work are you in?*: occupation, job, employment, profession, trade, business, career, calling, vocation, line, line of business, métier,

livelihood, craft, skill. **2** *doing important work for the government*: task, assignment, undertaking, job, chore, responsibility, duty, commission. **3** *takes a lot of hard work*: toil, labour, drudgery, effort, exertion, industry, slog (*infml*), graft (*infml*), elbow grease (*infml*).
▪ *verb* **1** *not working at the moment*: be employed, have a job, earn one's living. **2** *working hard*: labour, toil, drudge, slave. **3** *machine isn't working/working the controls*: function, go, operate, perform, run, handle, manage, use, control. **4** *work a minor miracle*: bring about, accomplish, achieve, create, cause, pull off (*infml*). **5** *working the clay in his hands*: manipulate, knead, mould, shape, form, fashion, make, process.
F3 1 be unemployed. **2** play, rest. **3** fail.

worker *noun* employee, labourer, working man, working woman, artisan, craftsman, tradesman, hand, operative, wage-earner, breadwinner, proletarian.

working *noun* functioning, operation, running, routine, manner, method, action.
▪ *adjective* **1** *working mines*: functioning, operational, running, operative, going. **2** *working man*: employed, active.
F3 1 inoperative. **2** idle.

workmanship *noun* skill, craft, craftsmanship, expertise, art, handicraft, handiwork, technique, execution, manufacture, work, finish.

works *noun* **1** *a textile works*: factory, plant, workshop, mill, foundry, shop. **2** *the devil and all his works*: actions, acts, doings. **3** *the works of Shakespeare*: productions, output, oeuvre, writings, books. **4** *water got into the works*: machinery, mechanism, workings, action, movement, parts, installations.

workshop *noun* works, workroom, atelier, studio, factory, plant, mill, shop.

world *noun* **1** *all over the world*: earth, globe, planet, star, universe, cosmos, creation, nature. **2** *all the world knows*: everybody, everyone, people, human race, humankind, humanity. **3** *in his own little world*: sphere, realm, field, area, domain, division, system, society, province, kingdom.

worn *adjective* **1** *worn carpet/cuffs*: shabby, threadbare, worn-out, tatty, tattered, frayed, ragged. **2** *a worn expression*: exhausted, tired, weary, spent, fatigued, careworn, drawn, haggard, jaded.
F3 1 new, unused. **2** fresh.

worn-out *adjective* **1** *worn-out slippers*: shabby, threadbare, useless, used, tatty, tattered, on its last legs, ragged, moth-eaten, frayed, decrepit. **2** *worn-out by work*: tired out, exhausted, weary, done in (*infml*), all in (*infml*), dog-tired (*infml*).
F3 1 new, unused. **2** fresh.

worried *adjective* anxious, troubled, uneasy, ill at ease, apprehensive, concerned, bothered, upset, fearful, afraid, frightened, on edge, overwrought, tense, strained, nervous, disturbed, distraught, distracted, fretful, distressed, agonized.
F3 calm, unworried, unconcerned.

worry *verb* **1** *worry unnecessarily*: be anxious, be troubled, be distressed, agonize, fret. **2** *stop worrying your father!*: irritate, plague, pester, torment, upset, unsettle, annoy, bother, disturb, vex, tease, nag, harass, harry, perturb, hassle (*infml*).
F3 1 be unconcerned. **2** comfort.
▪ *noun* **1** *have a lot of worries*: problem, trouble, responsibility, burden, concern, care, trial, annoyance, irritation, vexation. **2** *worry showed on her face*: anxiety, apprehension, unease, misgiving, fear, disturbance, agitation, torment, misery, perplexity.
F3 2 comfort, reassurance.

worsen *verb* **1** *worsening the anger they felt*: exacerbate, aggravate, intensify, heighten. **2** *their condition worsened*: get worse, weaken, deteriorate, degenerate, decline, sink, go downhill (*infml*).
F3 improve.

worship *verb* venerate, revere, reverence, adore, exalt, glorify, honour, praise, idolize, adulate, love, respect, pray to, deify.
F3 despise, hate.
▪ *noun* veneration, reverence, adoration, devotion(s), homage, honour, glory, glorification, exaltation, praise, prayer(s), respect, regard, love, adulation, deification, idolatry.

worth *noun* worthiness, merit, value, benefit, advantage, importance, significance, use, usefulness, utility, quality, good, virtue, excellence, credit, desert(s), cost, rate, price, help, assistance, avail.
F3 worthlessness.

worthless *adjective* **1** *a worthless piece of junk*: valueless, useless, pointless, meaningless, futile, unavailing, unimportant, insignificant, trivial, unusable, cheap, poor, rubbishy, trashy, trifling, paltry. **2** *that worthless fellow*: contemptible, despicable, good-for-nothing, vile.
F3 1 valuable. **2** worthy.

worthwhile *adjective* profitable, useful, valuable, worthy, good, helpful, beneficial, constructive, gainful, justifiable, productive.
F3 worthless.

worthy *adjective* praiseworthy, laudable, creditable, commendable, valuable, worthwhile, admirable, fit, deserving, appropriate, respectable, reputable, good, honest, honourable, excellent, decent, upright, righteous.
F3 unworthy, disreputable.

wound *noun* **1** *a head wound*: injury, trauma, hurt, cut, gash,

lesion, laceration, scar. **2** *a wound to the heart*: hurt, distress, trauma, torment, heartbreak, harm, damage, anguish, grief, shock.
▪ *verb* **1** *wounded his leg*: damage, harm, hurt, injure, hit, cut, gash, lacerate, slash, pierce. **2** *a remark that wounded them deeply*: distress, offend, insult, pain, mortify, upset, slight, grieve.

wrap *verb* envelop, fold, enclose, cover, pack, shroud, wind, surround, package, muffle, cocoon, cloak, roll up, bind, bundle up, immerse.
F3 unwrap.

wrapper *noun* wrapping, packaging, envelope, cover, jacket, dust jacket, sheath, sleeve, paper.

wreath *noun* garland, coronet, chaplet, festoon, crown, band, ring.

wreck *verb* destroy, ruin, demolish, devastate, shatter, smash, break, spoil, play havoc with, ravage, write off.
F3 conserve, repair.
▪ *noun* ruin, destruction, devastation, mess, demolition, ruination, write-off, disaster, loss, disruption.

wreckage *noun* debris, remains, rubble, ruin(s), fragments, flotsam, pieces.

wrench *verb* yank, wrest (*fml*), jerk, pull, tug, force, sprain, strain, rick, tear, twist, wring, rip, distort.

wrestle *verb* struggle, strive, fight, scuffle, grapple, tussle, combat, contend, contest, vie, battle.

wretch *noun* scoundrel, rogue, villain, good-for-nothing, ruffian, rascal, vagabond, miscreant (*fml*), outcast.

wretched *adjective* **1** *in a wretched state*: atrocious, awful, deplorable, appalling. **2** *she was wretched for a whole month*: unhappy, sad, miserable, melancholy, depressed, dejected, disconsolate, downcast, forlorn, gloomy, doleful, distressed, broken-hearted, crestfallen. **3** *a wretched attempt*: pathetic, pitiable, pitiful, unfortunate, sorry, hopeless, poor. **4** *where's that wretched dog?*: contemptible, despicable, vile, worthless, shameful, inferior, low, mean, paltry.
F3 **1** excellent. **2** happy. **3** enviable. **4** worthy.

wriggle *verb* squirm, writhe, wiggle, worm, twist, snake, slink, crawl, edge, sidle, manoeuvre, squiggle, dodge, extricate, zigzag, waggle, turn.

wring *verb* **1** *wringing her hands*: squeeze, twist, wrench, wrest (*fml*), extract, mangle, screw. **2** *will get the answer if I have to wring it out of him*: exact, extort, coerce, force.

wrinkle *noun* furrow, crease, corrugation, line, fold, gather, pucker, crumple.
▪ *verb* crease, corrugate, furrow, fold, crinkle, crumple, shrivel, gather, pucker.

write *verb* pen, inscribe, record, jot down, set down, take down, transcribe, scribble, scrawl, correspond, communicate, draft, draw up, copy, compose, create.

writer *noun* author, scribe, wordsmith, novelist, dramatist, essayist, playwright, columnist, diarist, hack, penpusher, scribbler, secretary, copyist, clerk.

Types of writer include:
annalist, author, autobiographer, bard, biographer, blogger, chronicler, clerk, columnist, copyist, copywriter, correspondent, court reporter, diarist, dramatist, editor, essayist, fabler, fiction writer, ghost writer, hack, historian, journalist, leader-writer, lexicographer, librettist, lyricist, novelist, pen-friend, penman, pen-pal, penpusher (*infml*), penwoman, playwright, poet, poet laureate, reporter, rhymer, satirist, scribbler, scribe, scriptwriter, short-story writer, stenographer, storyteller, technical writer, web author.

---

writhe *verb* squirm, wriggle, thresh, thrash, twist, wiggle, toss, coil, contort, struggle.

writing *noun* **1** *can't read the writing*: handwriting, calligraphy, script, penmanship, scrawl, scribble, hand, print. **2** *one of his many writings on the subject*: document, letter, book, composition, letters, literature, work, publication.

wrong *adjective* **1** *the wrong date*: inaccurate, incorrect, mistaken, erroneous, false, fallacious, in error, imprecise. **2** *what you did was wrong*: inappropriate, unsuitable, unseemly, improper, indecorous, unconventional, unfitting, incongruous, inapt. **3** *a wrong act*: unjust, unethical, unfair, unlawful, immoral, illegal, illicit, dishonest, criminal, crooked (*infml*), reprehensible, blameworthy, guilty, to blame, bad, wicked, sinful, iniquitous, evil. **4** *something is wrong*: defective, faulty, out of order, amiss, awry.
F≡ 1 correct, right. **2** suitable, right. **3** good, moral.
▪ *noun* sin, misdeed, offence, crime, immorality, sinfulness, transgression, wickedness, wrongdoing, trespass (*fml*), injury, grievance, abuse, injustice, iniquity (*fml*), inequity (*fml*), infringement, unfairness, error.
F≡ right.
▪ *verb* abuse, ill-treat, mistreat, maltreat, injure, ill-use, hurt, harm, discredit, dishonour, misrepresent, malign, oppress, cheat.

wrongdoer *noun* offender, law-breaker, transgressor, criminal, delinquent, felon, miscreant (*fml*), evil-doer, sinner, trespasser, culprit.

wrongful *adjective* immoral, improper, unfair, unethical, unjust, unlawful, illegal, illegitimate, illicit, dishonest, criminal, blameworthy, dishonourable, wrong, reprehensible, wicked, evil.

F rightful.

wry *adjective* ironic, sardonic, dry, sarcastic, mocking, droll.

yank *verb, noun* jerk, tug, pull, wrench, snatch, haul, heave.

yardstick *noun* measure, gauge, criterion, standard, benchmark, touchstone, comparison.

yarn *noun* **1** *cotton yarn*: thread, fibre, strand. **2** *tells some really good yarns*: story, tale, anecdote, fable, fabrication, tall story, cock-and-bull story (*infml*).

yawning *adjective* gaping, wide, wide-open, huge, vast, cavernous.

yearly *adjective* annual, per year, per annum, perennial.

yearn for *verb* long for, pine for, desire, want, wish for, crave, covet, hunger for, hanker for, ache for, languish for, itch for.

yell *verb* shout, scream, bellow, roar, bawl, shriek, squeal, howl, holler (*infml*), screech, squall, yelp, yowl, whoop.

F whisper.

▪ *noun* shout, scream, cry, roar, bellow, shriek, howl, screech, squall, whoop.

F whisper.

yelp *verb* yap, bark, squeal, cry, yell, yowl, bay.

▪ *noun* yap, bark, yip, squeal, cry, yell, yowl.

yield *verb* **1** *yield to the enemy*: surrender, renounce, abandon, abdicate, cede, part with, relinquish. **2** *yield to temptation*: give way, capitulate, concede, submit, succumb, give (in), admit defeat, bow, cave in, knuckle under, resign oneself, go along with, permit, allow, acquiesce, accede, agree, comply, consent. **3** *yield fruit/an income*: produce, bear, supply, provide, generate, bring in, bring forth, furnish, return, earn, pay.

F **1** hold. **2** resist, withstand.

▪ *noun* return, product, earnings, harvest, crop, produce, output, profit, revenue, takings, proceeds, income.

young *adjective* **1** *young lambs/people*: youthful, juvenile, baby, infant, junior, adolescent. **2** *young shoots*: immature, early, new, recent, green, growing, fledgling, unfledged, inexperienced.

F **1** adult, old. **2** mature, old.

▪ *noun* offspring, babies, issue, litter, progeny (*fml*), brood, children, family.

youngster *noun* child, boy, girl, toddler, youth, teenager, kid (*infml*).

youth *noun* **1** *arrested a youth*: adolescent, youngster, juvenile, teenager, kid (*infml*), boy, young man. **2** *the youth of today*: young people, the young, younger generation. **3** *in her/his youth*: adolescence, childhood, immaturity, boyhood, girlhood.
E3 3 adulthood.

youthful *adjective* young, boyish, girlish, childish, immature, juvenile, inexperienced, fresh, active, lively, well-preserved.
E3 aged.

Zz

zeal *noun* ardour, fervour, passion, warmth, fire, enthusiasm, devotion, spirit, keenness, zest, eagerness, earnestness, dedication, fanaticism, gusto, verve.
E3 apathy, indifference.

zealous *adjective* ardent, fervent, impassioned, passionate, devoted, burning, enthusiastic, intense, fanatical, militant, keen, eager, earnest, spirited.
E3 apathetic, indifferent.

zero *noun* nothing, nought, nil, nadir, bottom, cipher, zilch (*infml*), duck, love.

zest *noun* **1** *zest for life*: gusto, appetite, enthusiasm, enjoyment, keenness, zeal, exuberance, interest. **2** *lemon zest*: flavour, taste, savour, tang, piquancy.
E3 1 apathy.

zigzag *verb* meander, snake, wind, twist, curve.
▪ *adjective* meandering, crooked, serpentine, sinuous, twisting, winding.
E3 straight.

zodiac

The signs of the zodiac (with their symbols) are:
Aries (Ram), Taurus (Bull), Gemini (Twins), Cancer (Crab), Leo (Lion), Virgo (Virgin), Libra (Balance), Scorpio (Scorpion), Sagittarius (Archer), Capricorn (Goat), Aquarius (Water-bearer), Pisces (Fishes).

zone *noun* region, area, district, territory, section, sector, belt, sphere, tract, stratum.

zoom *verb* race, rush, tear, dash, speed, fly, hurtle, streak, flash, shoot, whirl, dive, buzz, zip.

Word workshop

Your writing will have added interest if you avoid using the same words too often. In this word workshop we look at some words that are often overused, and we consider other words that you might use instead of these to add variety to your writing.

It is worth thinking carefully about the following words and taking care not to use them too often, especially if there are more interesting alternatives available:

bad
big
get
good
great
nice
really
say
very

All of these words are discussed in the following pages. However, these are not the only words that are often overused. Other words you should be careful about using too much include *eat*, *go*, *happy*, *lot*, *small*, *thing*, *want* and *walk*. The main part of the thesaurus will help you to find interesting alternatives for all these words.

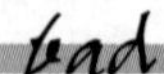

bad

Beware of using **bad** too often in your writing. Try out some of the following instead.

a person's character

disagreeable	unpleasant	wicked
evil	vile	

bad behaviour

disobedient	mischevious	rude
ill-behaved	naughty	

something, eg fruit or milk, that has gone bad

decayed	putrid	sour
mouldy	rancid	
off	rotten	

feeling bad

annoyed	upset	unwell

something that has a harmful effect

adverse	dangerous	unhealthy
damaging	harmful	

something that has been done or made badly

defective	inferior	unsatisfactory
faulty	poor	useless
imperfect	substandard	

The following passage shows ways in which you can use other words to avoid repeating **bad**. Try describing things instead of simply saying they were bad.

'I have had such a ~~bad~~ *terrible* day,' moaned Asif. 'What happened?' asked Innes. 'First of all,' replied Asif, 'the weather was ~~bad~~ *awful* and I got soaked on my way to school. Then I got a ~~bad~~ *poor* mark in French.' 'Don't feel too ~~bad~~ *upset* about that,' said Innes, 'at least you're not in trouble for being ~~bad~~ *disobedient* in class.' 'At lunch-time the milk was ~~bad~~ *off*,' continued Asif, 'and I couldn't drink it because I'm sure it would have been ~~bad~~ *harmful* to drink. Then I went to the cinema with Hilary but the film was ~~bad~~ *useless* and we left before it had ended. Now I feel ~~bad~~ *unwell* and I'm sure I have a cold because of the ~~bad~~ *dreadful* weather this morning. I hope tomorrow isn't as ~~bad~~ *unpleasant*!'

Have you ever had such a terrible day? Describe it, but remember to use as many different substitutes for **bad** as you can.

Beware of using **big** too often in your writing. Try out some of the following instead.

big in size, amount, etc

colossal	great	massive
considerable	huge	sizeable
enormous	humungous *(infml)*	spacious
extensive	immense	vast
gigantic	mammoth	

a big person or creature

bulky	hefty	stocky
burly	large	tall
giant	muscular	well-built

someone or something important

eminent	main	serious
famous	momentous	significant
important	principal	well-known
influential	prominent	

kind, considerate, etc behaviour or acts

generous	gracious	magnaminous

In the following article, there are suggestions for how synonyms might be used to avoid repeating **big**.

The Daily News

Yesterday was a ~~big~~ *momentous* day for the town of Hillgrove. ~~Big~~ *Enormous* crowds turned out for the return of the local boy Darren Songster who is a ~~big~~ *famous* pop star. The ~~big~~ *burly* man, who grew up in the ~~big~~ *sprawling* suburb of Lower Sunnymeadow was delighted by the ~~big~~ *massive* reception. 'It is very ~~big~~ *generous* of people to come out to welcome me,' he announced. 'I have travelled to many ~~big~~ *huge* cities and attended ~~big~~ *important* events but it is always a ~~big~~ *huge* pleasure to come home.'

Try writing a newspaper article about some important event. Use as many different words as you can instead of **big**.

get

Beware of using **get** too often in your writing. Try out some of the following instead.

get something, eg money

acquire	obtain
earn	receive

get something, eg a prize

achieve	gain	win

get someone to do something

coax	influence	urge
convince	persuade	
induce	sway	

get someone or something from somewhere

acquire	fetch	seize
catch	procure	
collect	secure	

get to a destination

arrive	reach

come to be (rich, etc)

become	grow

get to do something

arrange	organize
manage	succeed

understand something

comprehend	realize

get a disease

catch
come down with
contract
develop
pick up

In the following passage, there are some suggestions for how synonyms from the list might be used to avoid repeating **get** (and its forms **getting** and **got**).

From: Emma
To: Pete
cc:
Subject: Paul's visit

received
I just ~~got~~ an email from Paul. He said he
persuade
might be able to ~~get~~ his parents to let him
manage
visit for my birthday. I hope he can ~~get~~ to do
buy
it. I've asked him to ~~get~~ the latest CD by that
understood
new French band. I'm not sure if he ~~got~~
what I was asking for, because my French
arrive
isn't that good. He's supposed to ~~get~~ here
on the 28 June. I must go, my mother has
come down with fetch
~~got~~ the flu and I have to ~~get~~ my brother from
football practice.

Talk soon

Emma

Beware of using **good** too often in your writing. Try out some of the following instead.

a person's ability

accomplished
capable
clever
competent
expert
gifted
proficient
skilled
talented

a person's character

decent
dependable
exemplary
honest
moral
reliable
trustworthy
upright
virtuous
worthy

a person's personality

considerate
friendly
gracious
kind
sympathetic

something that has a positive effect

advantageous
beneficial
profitable
rewarding
valuable
worthwhile

good behaviour

obedient
polite
respectful
well-behaved
well-mannered

an event, eg a holiday

agreeable
enjoyable
excellent
fine
first-class
pleasant
pleasing
pleasurable
superb
wonderful

something large

considerable
sizeable
substantial

The following postcard shows ways in which some of these synonyms can be used instead of repeating **good**.

Dear Hazel,

We're having a really ~~good~~ wonderful time on holiday. The weather is ~~good~~ lovely and the hotel is ~~good~~ superb. Julie has been learning to swim but she's not very ~~good~~ proficient yet. The twins are not being too ~~good~~ well-behaved but the staff are very ~~good~~ friendly. On the whole the holiday has been very ~~good~~ worthwhile for us. Hope you are feeling ~~good~~ fine. See you next week,

Kate

Hazel Black
3 Sunnymeadows
Hopeville
HV3 6ZY

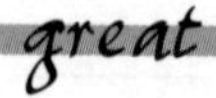

Beware of using **great** too often in your writing. Try out some of the following instead.

large in size

big
colossal
enormous
gigantic
huge
immense
impressive
large
mammoth
massive
vast

important or well-known in a particular field

celebrated
distinguished
eminent
famous
fine
glorious
noteworthy
outstanding
prominent
remarkable
renowned

good at something

able
experienced
expert
practised
professional
skilful
skilled
talented

important

chief
leading
main
major
primary
principal
serious
significant

very good

excellent
fabulous
fantastic
first-rate *(infml)*
marvellous
superb
terrific *(infml)*
tremendous
wonderful

doing something with, eg great care

considerable
excessive
extreme
pronounced

Instead of using **great** in the following passage, you might use some of the synonyms discussed.

The Museum of Film shows classic films on a ~~great~~ *huge* screen. The ~~great~~ *expert* staff make sure that everything runs smoothly. In the exhibitions, all the ~~great~~ *significant* actors in film history are represented, right up to the ~~great~~ *celebrated* stars of the present day. The museum has taken ~~great~~ *considerable* care to make sure that there is something of interest for everyone and it is a ~~great~~ *marvellous* place to visit for the day.

Beware of using **nice** too often in your writing. It is a rather uninteresting word, and you might try out some of the following instead.

a person's appearance

attractive	good-looking	pretty
cute	handsome	

a person's personality

agreeable	good	polite
amiable	good-natured	sweet
charming	helpful	thoughtful
considerable	kind	warm
friendly	likeable	wonderful
generous	pleasant	

for an object, eg a painting, or a place

beautiful	charming	lovely

for a piece of clothing, eg a dress

elegant	glamorous	stylish
fashionable	smart	

for a room, house, etc

comfortable	homely
cosy	snug

for a meal

delicious	scrumptious	yummy *(infml)*
mouth-watering	tasty	

for the weather

fine	pleasant	warm
mild	sunny	

for an event or occasion, eg a holiday

delighted
enjoyable
glorious
lovely
wonderful

Instead of repeating **nice** in the following passage, you might use some of the synonyms discussed.

> Dear Sheena
>
> It was really ~~nice~~ *kind* of you to invite me to your birthday party yesterday. I had a really ~~nice~~ *wonderful* time. You looked ~~nice~~ *pretty* in your new dress. The food was ~~nice~~ *delicious*, especially your birthday cake. We were also lucky that the weather was ~~nice~~ *sunny* and we could play in your ~~nice~~ *beautiful* garden. I would also like to thank your parents for being so ~~nice~~ *generous* to all of us. I hope you enjoyed all the ~~nice~~ *lovely* presents you received.
>
> Thank you again,
>
> Mary

Write a thank-you card to someone thanking them for a present which they have given you or a party or event to which they invited you. Try to think of as many substitutes as you can for the word **nice**.

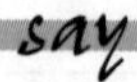

When you are writing down what people have said it can become boring if you repeat the words **say** and **said**. Try out some of the following instead to indicate more about the way in which people speak.

to report

affirm	convey	relate
announce	declare	state
assert	inform	tell
communicate		

to ask

demand	interrogate	question
inquire	query	

to reply

answer	respond	return
counter	retort	

to speak unclearly

babble	murmur	stutter
mumble	mutter	whisper

to speak angrily

nag	snap	yell
shout	snarl	

to speak happily

chortle	giggle	laugh
chuckle	joke	

to complain or speak sadly

cry	grumble	sob
groan	protest	whine

Instead of repeating **say/said** in the following passage, you might use some of the synonyms discussed opposite.

"Where have you been?" ~~said~~ *demanded* Peter.

"It's none of your business!" ~~said~~ *snapped* Chloe.

"We're in trouble now," ~~said~~ *murmured* Sheila.

"You've been gone for hours, I've been worried!" ~~said~~ *cried* Peter.

"You worry too much," Chloe ~~said~~ *grumbled*.

"Of course I do. It's late and I didn't know where you were," ~~said~~ *replied* Peter.

"Stop panicking. You can always reach us on our mobiles!" ~~said~~ *laughed* Sheila.

"I tried them but they were switched off," Peter ~~said~~ *protested*.

"That's because we were in the cinema," ~~said~~ *responded* Chloe.

"Well, let me know the next time if you are going to be late," Peter ~~said~~ *insisted*.

very / really

Try to avoid using **very** and **really** too often in your writing. Here are some words that you could use instead to give emphasis.

absolutely	excessively	noticeably	unbelievably
acutely	extremely	particularly	uncommonly
deeply	greatly	remarkably	unusually
exceedingly	highly	severely	
exceptionally	incredibly	truly	

The passage that follows has some suggestions for synonyms you might choose to avoid using **very** and **really** too often.

Due to ~~very~~ *exceptionally* heavy freezing rain and fog, driving conditions are ~~very~~ *highly* dangerous, especially on ~~very~~ *particularly* isolated or high roads. Police are asking motorists to be ~~really~~ *exceedingly* careful because visibility is ~~very~~ *severely* limited. They also advise avoiding travelling unless journeys are ~~really~~ *absolutely* necessary. There is no end in sight to the ~~very~~ *unusually* bad weather so travelling conditions will remain ~~very~~ *extremely* hazardous for the next few days.”

Word games

Match the Synonyms

Below you will find two lists of words. The words in List B are all SYNONYMS of the words in List A – but they are jumbled up. Can you find the correct pairs?

A	B
ill	sadness
legend	large
grief	irritate
run	conceal
scare	dwell
ready	meadow
big	myth
grab	difficult
confess	prepared
live	frighten
friend	sick
annoy	snatch
hard	sprint
hide	chum
field	admit

The solution is on page 630.

Match the Antonyms

This time the words in List B are all ANTONYMS of the words in List A – but they are jumbled up. Can you find the correct pairs?

A	B
different	artificial
begin	fiction
smooth	punishment
obey	cease
scold	delight
increase	sturdy
genuine	rarely
afraid	rough
reward	thrifty
fact	defy
horrible	reduce
disgust	similar
flimsy	lovely
often	brave
extravagant	praise

The solution is on page 630.

Antonym Word Ladders

On each ladder, remove ONE letter from the first word and replace it with another letter to make the second word; then remove ONE letter from the second word and replace it with another letter to make the third word. Continue until you finally end up with an antonym for the first word. The first one has been done for you.

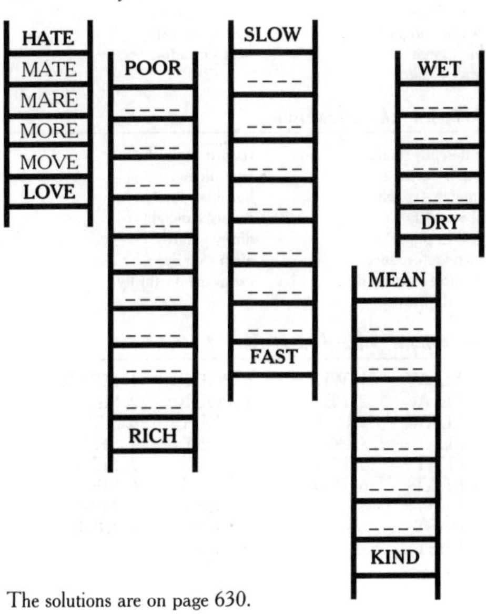

The solutions are on page 630.

Solutions

Match the Synonyms

ill - sick
legend - myth
grief - sadness
run - sprint
scare - frighten
ready - prepared
big - large
grab - snatch
confess - admit
live - dwell
friend - chum
annoy - irritate
hard - difficult
hide - conceal
field - meadow

Match the Antonyms

different - similar
begin - cease
smooth - rough
obey - defy
scold - praise
increase - reduce
genuine - artificial
afraid - brave
reward - punishment
fact - fiction
horrible - lovely
disgust - delight
flimsy - sturdy
often - rarely
extravagant - thrifty

Antonym Word Ladders

1. **SLOW**
2. FLOW
3. FLAW
4. FLAT
5. FEAT
6. PEAT
7. PEST
8. PAST
9. **FAST**

1. **WET**
2. PET
3. PAT
4. PAY
5. PRY
6. **DRY**

1. **POOR**
2. POUR
3. POUT
4. POST
5. MOST
6. MUST
7. RUST
8. RUSE
9. RISE
10. RICE
11. **RICH**

1. **MEAN**
2. MEAT
3. SEAT
4. SENT
5. SEND
6. MEND
7. MIND
8. **KIND**